Visible Learning

W9-CIG-050

This unique and ground-breaking book is the result of 15 years' research and synthesises over 800 meta-analyses relating to the influences on achievement in school-aged students. It builds a story about the power of teachers and of feedback, and constructs a model of learning and understanding.

Visible Learning presents research involving many millions of students and represents the largest ever collection of evidence-based research into what actually works in schools to improve learning. Areas covered include the influences of the student, home, school, curricula, teacher, and teaching strategies. A model of teaching and learning is developed based on the notion of visible teaching and visible learning.

A major message within the book is that what works best for students is similar to what works best for teachers. This includes an attention to setting challenging learning intentions, being clear about what success means, and an attention to learning strategies for developing conceptual understanding about what teachers and students know and understand.

Although the current evidence-based fad has turned into a debate about test scores, this book is about using evidence to build and defend a model of teaching and learning. A major contribution to the field, it is a fascinating benchmark for comparing many innovations in teaching and schools.

John Hattie is Professor of Education and Director of the Visible Learning Labs, University of Auckland, New Zealand.

Visible Learning

A synthesis of over 800 meta-analyses
relating to achievement

John A. C. Hattie

Routledge
Taylor & Francis Group

LONDON AND NEW YORK

First published 2009
by Routledge
2 Park Square, Milton Park, Abingdon, Oxon OX14 4RN

Simultaneously published in the USA and Canada
by Routledge
711 Third Avenue, 8th Floor, New York, NY, 10017
www. routledge.com
Reprinted 2009 (three times), 2010 (three times)

Routledge is an imprint of the Taylor & Francis Group, an informa business

© 2009 John A. C. Hattie

Typeset in Bembo by
Bookcraft Ltd, Stroud, Gloucestershire
Printed and bound in the United States of America
by Edwards Brothers, Lillington, NC

All rights reserved. No part of this book may be reprinted or reproduced or
utilised in any form or by any electronic, mechanical, or other means, now known
or hereafter invented, including photocopying and recording, or in any information
storage or retrieval system, without permission in writing from the publishers.

British Library Cataloguing in Publication Data
A catalogue record for this book is available from the British Library

Library of Congress Cataloging-in-Publication Data
Hattie, John.
Visible learning: a synthesis of meta-analyses relating to achievement/John A. C.
Hattie.
   p. cm.
   Includes bibliographical references.
   1. Learning—Longitudinal studies. 2. Teaching—Longitudinal studies. 3. Effective
teaching—Longitudinal studies. 4. Teacher effectiveness—Longitudinal studies.
   I. Title.
LB1060.H388 2008
370.15'23—dc22   2008021702

ISBN10: 0-415-47617-8 (hbk)
ISBN10: 0-415-47618-6 (pbk)
ISBN10: 0-203-88733-6 (ebk)

ISBN13: 978-0-415-47617-1 (hbk)
ISBN13: 978-0-415-47618-8 (pbk)
ISBN13: 978-0-203-88733-2 (ebk)

Contents

Tables

Figures

Preface

Elliott is my hero. On his fifth birthday he was diagnosed with leukemia, and this past year has been his *annus horribilis*. On the day of the diagnosis, it was impressive to see the medical team immediately begin interventions. While they aimed to make Elliott stable, the diagnosis regime burst into action. They knew which tests were needed to make the correct diagnosis and when they were satisfied with the initial diagnosis they immediately moved to interventions. Thus began a year of constant monitoring and feedback to the medical team about Elliott's progress. All throughout they collected evidence of progress, they knew what success looked like, and kept all informed about this evidence. Elliott went through many ups and downs, lost his hair (as did I when he gave me a No. 1 cut as his Christmas present, although I drew a line when he asked to shave my eyebrows off as well), and had daily injections in the front of his legs, but he never balked, and throughout the treatment maintained his sparkly personality. The family was never in the dark about what was happening, books were provided, sessions offered, and support for treatment was excellent. The messages in this book owe a lot to Elliott.

This book started in Gil Sax's office in 1990 searching and coding meta-analyses. Motivation to continue the search was inspired by Herb Walberg, and continued in Perth in Australia, North Carolina in the US, and finished here in Auckland in New Zealand. It is a journey that has taken 15 years. The messages have been questioned, labelled provocative, liked, and dismissed, among other more positive reactions. The typical comments are: "the results do not mirror my experience", "why have you not highlighted my pet method", "you are talking about averages and I'm not average", and "you are missing the nuances of what happens in classrooms". There are many criticisms and misunderstandings about what I am *and* am not saying.

So let me start with what this book is not.

1   It is *not* a book about classroom life, and does not speak to the nuances and details of what happens within classrooms. Instead it synthesizes research based on what happens in classrooms; as it is more concerned with main effects than interactions. Although I have spent many hundreds of hours in classrooms in many countries, have observed, interviewed, and aimed to dig quite deeply into the nuances of classrooms, this book will not show these details of class living.

2   It is *not* a book about what cannot be influenced in schools—thus critical discussions about class, poverty, resources in families, health in families, and nutrition are not included—but this is NOT because they are unimportant, indeed they may be more

important than many of the influences discussed in this book. It is just that I have not included these topics in my orbit.

3 It is *not* a book that includes qualitative studies. It only includes studies that have used basic statistics (means, variances, sample sizes). Again, this should not mean qualitative studies are not important or powerful but just that I have had to draw some lines around what can be accomplished over a 15-year writing span.

4 It is *not* a book about criticism of research, and I have deliberately not included much about moderators of research findings based on research attributes (quality of study, nature of design) again not because these are unimportant (my expertise is measurement and research design), but because they have been dealt with elsewhere by others (e.g., Lipsey & Wilson, 1993; Sipe & Curlette, 1996a, 1996b).

Rather this is a book about synthesizing many meta-analyses. It is based on over 50,000 studies, and many millions of students—and this is a cut down version of what I could have included as I also collected studies on affective and physical outcomes and on many other outcomes of schooling. I occasionally receive emails expressing disbelief that I have had the time to read so many studies. No, I have not read all primary studies, but as will be seen I have read all meta-analyses, and in some cases many of the primary studies. I am an avid reader, thoroughly enjoy learning the arts of synthesizing and detecting main ideas, and want to create explanations from the myriad of ideas in our discipline. The aim of this book is not to overwhelm with data—indeed my first attempt was discarded after 500 pages of trenchant details; who would care about such details? Instead this book aims to have a message, a story, and a set of supporting accounts of this story.

The message about schools is a positive one. So often when talking about the findings in this book, teachers think I am attacking them as below average, non-thinking, boring drones. In New Zealand, for example, it is clear to me why we rank in the top half-dozen nations in reading, mathematics, and science—we have a nation of excellent teachers. They exist and there are many of them. This book is a story of many real teachers I have met, seen, and some who have taught my own boys. Many teachers already think in the ways I argue in this book; many are seeking to always improve and constantly monitor their performances to make a difference to what they do; and many inspire the love of learning that is one of the major outcomes of any school. This is not a book claiming that teachers are below par, that the profession is terrible, and that we all need to "put in more effort and do better". Nearly all studies in the book are based on real students in front of real teachers in real schools—and that so many of the effects are powerful is a testament that excellence is happening. *The* major message is that we need a barometer of what works best, and such a barometer can also establish guidelines as to what is excellent—too often we shy from using this word thinking that excellence is unattainable in schools. Excellence is attainable: there are many instances of excellence, some of it fleeting, some of it aplenty. We need better evaluation to acknowledge and esteem it when it occurs—as it does.

Acknowledgments

There are so many who have contributed to the data, the book, and the message, and who have provided feedback over these past 15 years: Nola Purdie, Krystoff Krawowski, Richard Fletcher, Thakur Karkee, Earl Irving, Trisha Lundberg, Lorrae Ward, Michael Scriven, Richard Jaeger, Geoff Petty, and Russell Bishop. I am especially indebted to Janet Rivers for her attention to the details and to Debbie Waayer for her remarkable skills in finding articles, referencing, and data skills, and in ensuring that I completed this book. Others have been critics and this is among the more welcome contributions for any author: Lexie Grudnoff, Gavin Brown, Adrienne Alton-Lee, Christine Rubie-Davis, Misty Sato, David Moseley, Heidi Leeson, Brian Marsh, Sandra Frid, Sam Stace, and John Locke. I particular thank Gene Glass for his development of meta-analysis that allowed me and many others to stand on his shoulders to peer into what makes a difference to teaching and learning.

But most of all I thank my family—they have endured this book, shaped the many versions of the message, and provided the feedback that only a loving family can give. Unlike most children who are asked about their day at school each night at the dinner table, my boys have endured the same interrogation every night of their school years: What feedback did you receive about your learning today? Thanks to my boys—Joel, Kyle, Kieran, Billy, Bobby, and Jamie—you are my inspirations for living. And most of all to Janet—the one who has given unconditional positive regard through the ups and downs of moving a family across many countries, putting up with "yet another study", and being the love of my life. The size of your effect on my life exceeds any reported in this book.

Chapter 1

The challenge

In the field of education, one of the most enduring messages is that "everything seems to work". It is hard to find teachers who say they are "below average" teachers, and everyone (parent, politician, school leader) has a reason why their particular view about teaching or school innovation is likely to be successful. Indeed, rhetoric and game-play about teaching and learning seems to justify "everything goes". We acknowledge that teachers teach differently from each other; we respect this difference and even enshrine it in terms like "teaching style" and "professional independence". This often translates as "I'll leave you alone, if you leave me alone to teach my way." While teachers talk to their colleagues about curriculum, assessment, children, and lack of time and resources, they rarely talk about their teaching, preferring to believe that they may teach differently (which is acceptable provided they do not question one another's right to teach in their particular ways). We pass laws that are more about structural concerns than about teaching concerns: such as class size, school choice, and social promotion, as if these are clear winners among the top-ranking influences on student learning. We make school-based decisions about ability grouping, detracking or streaming, and social promotion, again appealing to claims about influences on achievement. For most teachers, however, teaching is a private matter; it occurs behind a closed classroom door, and it is rarely questioned or challenged. We seem to believe that every teacher's stories about success are sufficient justification for leaving them alone. We will see throughout this book that there is a good reason for acknowledging that most teachers can demonstrate such success. Short of unethical behaviors, and gross incompetence, there is much support for the "everything goes" approach. However herein lies a major problem.

It is the case that we reinvent schooling every year. Despite any successes we may have had with this year's cohort of students, teachers have to start again next year with a brand new cohort. The greatest change that most students experience is the level of competence of the teacher, as the school and their peers typically are "similar" to what they would have experienced the previous year. It is surely easy to see how it is tempting for teachers to re-do the successes of the previous year, to judge students in terms of last year's cohort, and to insist on an orderly progression through that which has worked before. It is required of teachers, however, that they re-invent their passion in their teaching; they must identify and accommodate the differences brought with each new cohort of students, react to the learning as it occurs (every moment of learning is different), and treat the current cohort of students as if it is the first time that the teacher has taught a class—as it is for the students with this teacher and this curricula.

As will be argued throughout this book, the act of teaching reaches its epitome of success after the lesson has been structured, after the content has been delivered, and after the classroom has been organized. The art of teaching, and its major successes, relate to "what happens next"—the manner in which the teacher reacts to how the student interprets, accommodates, rejects, and/or reinvents the content and skills, how the student relates and applies the content to other tasks, and how the student reacts in light of success and failure apropos the content and methods that the teacher has taught. Learning is spontaneous, individualistic, and often earned through effort. It is a timeworn, slow and gradual, fits-and-starts kind of process, which can have a flow of its own, but requires passion, patience, and attention to detail (from the teacher and student).

So much evidence

The research literature is rich in recommendations as to what teachers and schools should do. Carpenter (2000), for example, counted 361 "good ideas" published in the previous ten years of *Phi Delta Kappan* (e.g., Hunter method, assertive discipline, Goals 2000, TQM, portfolio assessment, essential schools, block scheduling, detracking, character education). He concluded that these good ideas have produced very limited gains, if any. Similarly, Kozol (2005, p. 193) noted that there have been "galaxies of faded names and optimistic claims," such as "Focus Schools", "Accelerated Schools", "Blue Ribbon Schools", "Exemplary Schools", "Pilot Schools", "Model Schools", "Quality Schools", "Magnet Schools", and "Cluster Schools"—all claiming they are better and different, with little evidence of either. The research evidence relating to "what works" is burgeoning, even groaning, under a weight of such "try me" ideas. Most are justified by great stories about lighthouse schools, inspiring principals and inspiring change agents, and tales of wonderful work produced by happy children with contented parents and doting teachers. According to noted change-theory expert, Michael Fullan, one of the most critical problems our schools face is "not resistance to innovation, but the fragmentation, overload, and incoherence resulting from the uncritical and uncoordinated acceptance of too many different innovations (Fullan & Stiegelbauer, 1991, p. 197). Richard Elmore (1996) has long argued that education suffers not so much from an inadequate *supply* of good programs as from a lack of *demand* for good programs—and instead we so often *supply* yet another program rather than nurture *demand* for good programs.

There is so much known about what makes a difference in the classroom. A glance at the journals on the shelves of most libraries, and on web pages, would indicate that the state of knowledge in the discipline of education is healthy. The worldwide picture certainly is one of plenty; we could have a library solely consisting of handbooks about teaching, most of which cannot be held in the hand. Most countries have been through many waves of reform, including new curricula, new methods of accountability, reviews of teacher education, professional development programs, charter schools, vouchers, and management models. We have blamed the parents, the teachers, the classrooms, the resources, the textbooks, the principals, and even the students. Listing all the problems and all the suggested remedies could fill this book many times over.

There are thousands of studies promulgating claims that this method works or that innovation works. We have a rich educational research base, but rarely is it used by teachers, and rarely does it lead to policy changes that affect the nature of teaching. It may be that the research is written in a non-engaging style for teachers, or maybe when research is presented to teachers it is done in a manner that fails to acknowledge that teachers come to research with strong theories of their own about what works (for them). Further, teachers are often very "context specific", as the art for many of them is to modify programs to fit their particular students and teaching methods—and this translation is rarely acknowledged.

How can there be so many published articles, so many reports providing directions, so many professional development sessions advocating this or that method, so many parents and politicians inventing new and better answers, while classrooms are hardly different from 200 years ago (Tyack & Cuban, 1995)? Why does this bounty of research have such little impact? One possible reason is the past difficulties associated with summarizing and comparing all the diverse types of evidence about what works in classrooms. In the 1970s there was a major change in the manner that we reviewed the research literature. This approach offered a way to tame the massive amount of research evidence so that it could offer useful information for teachers. The predominant method had always been to write a synthesis of many published studies in the form of an integrated literature review. However in 1976 Gene Glass introduced the notion of meta-analysis—whereby the effects in each study, where appropriate, are converted to a common measure (an effect size), such that the overall effects could be quantified, interpreted, and compared, and the various moderators of this overall effect could be uncovered and followed up in more detail. Chapter 2 will outline this method in more detail. This method soon became popular and by the mid 1980s more than 100 meta-analyses in education were available. This book is based on a synthesis (a method referred to by some as meta-meta-analysis) of more than 800 meta-analyses about influences on learning that have now been completed, including many recent ones. It will develop a method such that the various innovations in these meta-analyses can be ranked from very positive to very negative effects on student achievement. It demonstrates that the reason teachers can so readily convince each other that they are having success with their particular approach is because the reference point in their arguments is misplaced. Most importantly, it aims to derive some underlying principles about why some innovations are more successful than others in influencing student achievement.

An explanatory story, not a "what works" recipe

The aim is to provide more than a litany of "what works", as too often such lists provide yet another set of recommendations devoid of underlying theory and messages, they tend to not take into account any moderators or the "busy bustling business" of classrooms, and often they appeal to claims about "common sense". If common sense is the litmus test then everything could be claimed to work, and maybe therein lies the problems with teaching. As Glass (1987) so eloquently argued when the first *What Works: Politics and research* was released, such appeals to common sense can mean that there is no need for more research dollars. Such claims can ignore the realities of classroom life, and they too often mistake correlates for causes. Michael Scriven (1971; 1975; 2002) has long written about mistaking correlates of learning with causes. His claim is that various correlates of school outcomes, say the use of advance organizers, the maintenance of eye contact, or high time on task, should not be confused with good teaching. While these may indeed be correlates of learning, it is still the case that good teaching may include none of these attributes. It may be that increasing these behaviors in some teachers also leads to a decline in other attributes (e.g., caring and respect for students). Correlates, therefore, are not to be confused with the causes.

For example, one of the major results presented in this book relates to increasing the amount of feedback because it is an important correlate of student achievement. However, one should not immediately start providing more feedback and then await the magical increases in achievement. As will be seen below, increasing the amount of feedback in order to have a positive effect on student achievement requires a change in the conception of what it means to be a teacher; it is the feedback to the teacher about what students can and cannot do that is more powerful than feedback to the student, and it necessitates a different way of interacting and respecting students (but more on this later). It would be an incorrect interpretation of the power of feedback if a teacher were to encourage students to provide more feedback. As Nuthall (2007) has shown, 80% of feedback a student receives about his or her work in elementary (primary) school is from other students. But 80% of this student-provided feedback is incorrect! It is important to be concerned about the climate of the classroom before increasing the amount of feedback (to the student or teacher) because it is critical to ensure that "errors" are welcomed, as they are key levers for enhancing learning. It is critical to have appropriately challenging goals as then the amount and directedness of feedback is maximized. Simply applying a recipe (e.g., "providing more feedback") will not work in our busy, multifaceted, culturally invested, and changing classrooms.

The wars as to what counts as evidence for causation are raging as never before. Some have argued that the only legitimate support for causal claims can come from randomized control trials (RCTs, i.e., trials in which subjects are allocated to an experimental or a control group according to a strictly random procedure). There are few such studies among the many outlined in this book, although it could be claimed that there are many "evidence-informed" arguments in this book. While the use of randomized control trials is a powerful method, Scriven (2005) has argued that a higher gold standard relates to studies that are capable of establishing conclusions "beyond reasonable doubt". Throughout this book, many correlates will be presented, as most meta-analyses seek such correlates of enhanced student achievement. A major aim is to weave a story from these data that has some convincing power and some coherence, although there is no claim to make these "beyond reasonable doubt". Providing explanations is sometimes more difficult than identifying causal effects.

Most of these claims about design and RCTs are part of the move towards evidence-based decision making, and the current debate about influences on student learning is dominated by discussion of the need for "evidence". Evidence-based this and that are the buzz words, but while we collect evidence, teachers go on teaching. The history of teaching over the past 200 years has attested the enduring focus of teachers on notions of "what works" despite the number of solutions urging teachers to move in a different direction. Such "what works" notions rarely have high levels of explanatory power. The model I will present in Chapter 3 may well be speculative, but it aims to provide high levels of explanation for the many influences on student achievement as well as offer a platform to compare these influences in a meaningful way. And while I must emphasize that these ideas are clearly speculative, there is both solace and promise in the following quotation from Popper:

> Bold ideas, unjustified anticipations, and speculative thought, are our only means for interpreting nature: our only organon, our only instrument, for grasping her. And we must hazard them to win our prize. Those among us who are unwilling to expose their ideas to the hazard of refutation do not take part in the scientific game.
>
> (Popper, K. R., 1968, p. 280)

While we collect evidence, teachers go on teaching

As already noted, the practice of teaching has changed little over the past century. The "grammar" of schooling, in Tyack and Cuban's (1995) terms, has remained constant: the age-grading of students, division of knowledge into separate subjects, and the self-contained classroom with one teacher. Many innovations have been variously "welcomed, improved, deflected, co-opted, modified, and sabotaged" (p. 7), and schools have developed rules and cultures to control the way people behave when in them. Most of us have been "in school" and thus know what a "real school" is and should be. The grammar of schooling has persisted partly because it enables teachers to discharge their duties in a predictable fashion, cope with the everyday tasks that others expect of them, and provide much predictability to all who encounter schools.

One of the "grammars of schooling" is that students are to be made responsible for their learning. This can easily turn into a conception that some students are deficient in their desire for, and achievements from teaching. As Russell Bishop and his colleagues have demonstrated, such deficit thinking is particularly a problem when teachers are involved with minority students (e.g., Bishop, Berryman, & Richardson, 2002). From their interviews, they illustrated that the influences on Māori students' educational achievement differed for each of parents, students, principals, and teachers (Figure 1.1). Students, parents, and principals see the relationships between teachers and students as having the greatest influence on Māori students' educational achievement. In contrast, teachers identify the main influences on Māori students' educational achievement as being Māori students themselves, their homes and/or the structure of the schools. Teachers engage in the discourse of the child and their home by pathologising Māori students' lived experiences and by explaining their lack of educational

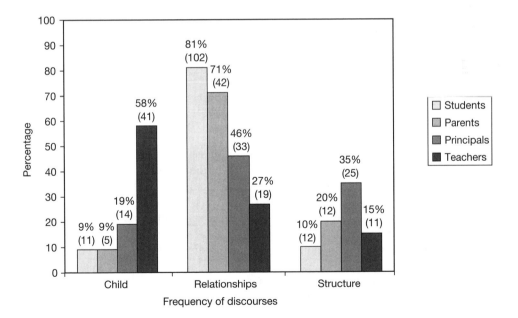

Figure 1.1 Percentage of responses as to the claimed influences on student learning by students, parents, principals, and teachers

achievement in deficit terms. My colleague Alison Jones calls this type of thinking a "discourse of disadvantage" (Jones & Jacka, 1995). They do not see themselves as the agents of influence, see very few solutions, and see very little that they can do to solve the problems.

From their extensive classroom observations, analyses of achievement results, and working with teachers of minority students, Bishop *et al.* have devised a model of teaching Māori students based on caring for all students, and the primacy of the act of teaching. The major features of Bishop's model include the creation of a visible, appropriate context for learning such that the student's culture is involved in a process of co-learning, which involves the negotiation of learning contexts and content. The teacher provides supportive feedback and helps students to learn by acknowledging and using the students' prior knowledge and experiences, and monitoring to check if students know what is being taught, what is to be learnt, or what is to be produced. It involves the teacher teaching the students something, instructing them how to produce something, and giving them instructions as to the processes of learning. This is a high level of teaching activity, indeed.

Concluding comments

This introduction has highlighted the amazing facility of those in the education business to invent solutions and see evidence for their pet theories and for their current actions. Everything seems to work in the improvement of student achievement. There are so many solutions and most have some form of evidence for their continuation. Teachers can thus find some support to justify almost all their actions—even though the variability about what works is enormous. Indeed, we have created a profession based on the principle of "just leave me alone as I have evidence that what I do enhances learning and achievement".

One aim of this book is to develop an explanatory story about the key influences on student learning—it is certainly not to build another "what works" recipe. The major part of this story relates to the power of directed teaching, enhancing what happens next (through feedback and monitoring) to inform the teacher about the success or failure of their teaching, and to provide a method to evaluate the relative efficacy of different influences that teachers use.

It is important from the start to note at least two critical codicils. Of course, there are many outcomes of schooling, such as attitudes, physical outcomes, belongingness, respect, citizenship, and the love of learning. This book focuses on student achievement, and that is a limitation of this review. Second, most of the successful effects come from innovations, and these effects from innovations may *not* be the same as the effects of teachers in regular classrooms—the mere involvement in asking questions about the effectiveness of any innovation may lead to an inflation of the effects. This matter will be discussed in more detail in the concluding chapter, where an attempt is made to identify the effects of "typical" teachers compared to "innovations" in teaching. Indeed, the role of "teaching as intervention" is developed throughout the chapters in this book.

Chapter 2

The nature of the evidence

A synthesis of meta-analyses

> It is the mark of an educated man … that in every subject he looks for only so much precision as its nature permits.
>
> (Aristotle, 350BC)

This chapter outlines the methodology relating to the evidence used in the remainder of this book. The fundamental unit of analysis is 800+ meta-analyses and how the major results from these studies can be placed along a single continuum. The chapter then outlines some of the problems of meta-analyses, discusses some of the previous attempts to synthesize meta-analyses, and then introduces some of the major overall findings from the synthesis of the 800+ meta-analyses.

Would it not be wonderful if we could create a single continuum of achievement effects, and locate all possible influences of achievement on this continuum? Figure 2.1 shows one possible depiction of this continuum.

Influences on the left of this continuum are those that decrease achievement, and those on the right increase achievement. Those near the zero point have no influence on achievement outcomes.

The next task was to adopt an appropriate scale so that as many outcomes as possible from thousands of studies are converted to this single scale. This was accomplished using effect sizes, and this scale has been among the marvelous advances in the analysis of research studies over the past century. An effect size provides a common expression of the magnitude of study outcomes for many types of outcome variables, such as school achievement. An effect size of $d = 1.0$ indicates an increase of one standard deviation on the outcome—in this case the outcome is improving school achievement. A one standard deviation increase is typically associated with advancing children's achievement by two to three years, improving the rate of learning by 50%, or a correlation between some variable (e.g., amount of homework) and achievement of approximately $r = 0.50$. When

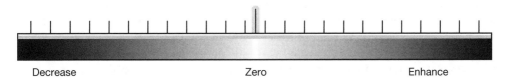

Decrease   Zero   Enhance

Figure 2.1 An achievement continuum

implementing a new program, an effect size of 1.0 would mean that, on average, students receiving that treatment would exceed 84% of students not receiving that treatment.

Cohen (1988) argued that an effect size of $d = 1.0$ should be regarded as a large, blatantly obvious, and grossly perceptible difference, and as an example he referred to the difference between the average IQ of PhD graduates and high school students. Another example is the difference between a person at 5'3" (160 cm) and 6'0" (183 cm)—which would be a difference visible to the naked eye. The use of effect sizes highlights the importance of the magnitude of differences, which is contrary to the usual emphasis in much of our research literature on statistical significance. Cohen (1990) has commented that "under the sway of the Fisherian scheme [or dependence on statistical significance], there has been little consciousness of how big things are ... science is inevitably about magnitudes ... and meta-analysis makes a welcome force toward the accumulation of knowledge" (pp. 1309–1310).

Thus, we have a continuum and a scale (effect size) to ascertain which of the many possible influences affect achievement. Many textbooks detail how effect sizes can be calculated from various summary statistics such as t-tests, ANOVAs, repeated-measures (e.g., Glass, 1977; Glass, McGaw, & Smith, 1981; Hedges & Olkin, 1985). Statistically, an effect size can be calculated in two major ways:

$$\text{Effect size} = [\text{Mean}_{\text{treatment}} - \text{Mean}_{\text{control}}]/\text{SD}$$

or

$$\text{Effect size} = [\text{Mean}_{\text{end of treatment}} - \text{Mean}_{\text{beginning of treatment}}]/\text{SD}$$

where SD is the pooled sample standard deviation. There are many minor modifications to these formulas, and for more detail the interested reader is referred to Glass, McGaw, & Smith (1981); Rosenthal (1991); Hedges & Olkin (1985); Hunter & Schmidt (1990); and Lipsey & Wilson (2001).

As an example of synthesizing meta-analyses, take an examination of five meta-analyses on homework: Cooper (1989; 1994); Cooper, Robinson, & Patall (2006); DeBaz (1994); Paschal, Weinstein, & Walberg (1984). Over these five meta-analyses there were 161 studies involving more than 100,000 students, which investigated the effects of homework on students' achievement. The average of all these effect sizes was $d = 0.29$, which can be used as the best typical effect size of the influence of homework on achievement. Thus, compared to classes without homework, the use of homework was associated with advancing children's achievement by approximately one year, improving the rate of learning by 15%, about 65% of the effects were positive (that is, improved achievement), 35% of the effects were zero or negative, and the average achievement level of students in classes that prescribed homework exceeded 62% of the achievement levels of the students not prescribed homework. However, an effect size of $d = 0.29$ would not, according to Cohen (1988), be perceptible to the naked eye, and would be approximately equivalent to the difference between the height of a 5'11" (180 cm) and a 6'0" (182 cm) person.

Thus it is possible to devise a unidimensional continuum such as shown in Figure 2.1 that can allow the various effects on achievement to be positioned as they relate to each other. The scale is expressed in effect sizes (or standard deviation units) such that 1.0 is an unlikely—although a very obvious—change in achievement, and 0.0 is no change at all.

This continuum provides the measurement basis to address the question of the relative effects of many factors on achievement.

An alternative way of considering the meaning of an effect size was suggested by McGraw and Wong (1992). They introduced a measure called the common language effect size indicator, which is the probability that a score sampled from one distribution will be greater than a score sampled from some other distribution. Consider as an example the difference in height of the average woman (5'4"/162.5 cm) and the average male (5'10"/177.5 cm), which is a d of 2.0. This d translates into a common language effect (CLE) of 92 percent. Thus we can estimate that in any random pairing the probability of the male being taller than the female is $d = 0.92$; or that in 92 out of 100 blind dates the male will be taller than the female. Now, using the example above, consider the $d = 0.29$ from introducing homework (throughout this book effect sizes are abbreviated, following tradition, to d). The CLE is 21 percent, so that in 21 times out of 100, introducing homework into schools will make a positive difference, or 21 percent of students will gain in achievement compared to those not having homework. Or, if you take two classes, the one using homework will be more effective 21 out of a 100 times. In all examples in this book, the CLE is provided to assist in interpreting the effect size.

We do need to be careful about ascribing adjectives such as small, medium, and large to these effect sizes. Cohen (1988), for example, suggested that $d = 0.2$ was small, $d = 0.5$ medium, and $d = 0.8$ large, whereas the results in this book could suggest $d = 0.2$ for small, $d = 0.4$ for medium, and $d = 0.6$ for large when judging educational outcomes. In many cases this would probably be reasonable, but there are situations where this would be just too simple. Consider, for example, the effects of an influence such as behavioral objectives, which has an overall small effect of $d = 0.20$ (see Chapter 9), and reciprocal teaching, which has an overall large effect of $d = 0.74$. It may be that the cost of implementing behavioral objectives is so small that it is worth using them to gain an influence on achievement, albeit small, whereas it might be too expensive to implement reciprocal teaching to gain the larger effect. Instead of considering only the size of an effect, we should be looking for patterns in the various effect sizes and the causal implications across effect sizes, and making policy decisions on an overall investigation of the differences in effect sizes.

Further, there are many examples that show small effects may be important. A vivid example comes from medicine. Rosenthal and DiMatteo (2001) demonstrated that the effect size of taking low dose aspirin in preventing a heart attack was $d = 0.07$, indicating that less than one-eighth of one percent of the variance in heart attacks was accounted for by using aspirin. Although the effect size is small, this translates into the conclusion that 34 out of every 1,000 people would be saved from a heart attack if they used low dose aspirin on a regular basis. This sounds worth it to me.

Meyer *et al.* (2001) list other seemingly small effect sizes with important consequences: the impact of chemotherapy on breast cancer survival ($d = 0.12$), the association between a major league baseball player's batting average and success in obtaining a hit in a particular instance at bat ($r = 0.06$), the value of antihistamines for reducing sneezes and a runny nose ($d = 0.22$), and the link between prominent movie critics' reviews and box office success ($d = 0.34$).

Even more interestingly, it can be possible to identify various moderators that may enhance or detract from the overall average effect. For example, to use the homework case discussed above, it may be that males have greater improvements (i.e., have a higher effect size) than females, younger students' achievement gains may be different from older ones', the effects may be greater in mathematics than reading. And indeed, the effects do decrease with age: primary students gain least from homework ($d = 0.15$) and secondary students have greater gains ($d = 0.64$, see Chapter 10).

Also, the nature of the achievement outcome may turn out to be critical. That is, when one is seeking influences on a very specific, narrow outcome (e.g., improvement in addition, understanding of phonics), then it may be likely that the effect size will be greater than when one is seeking influences on a more generalizable, wider concept (e.g., numeracy or reading achievement). While the synthesis of research on the effects of narrow or wide influences (Hattie, 1992) did not find such differences, it is still important to be aware of the potential of this moderator.

Problems with meta-analysis

Glass (2000) celebrated the 25th anniversary of the invention of the term "meta-analysis" (see also Hunt, 1997) by noting the growth of interest in meta-analysis shifting from an original "preoccupation of a very small group of statisticians" to a current "minor academic industry" (Glass, 2000, p. 1). About 25 percent of all articles in *Psychological Bulletin* have the term "meta-analysis" in the title, and he particularly noted the adoption of the method in medicine. Not surprisingly, given this growth, there remain many criticisms of meta-analysis. A common criticism is that it combines "apples and oranges" and such combining of many seemingly disparate studies is fraught with difficulties. It is the case, however, that in the study of fruit nothing else is sensible. The converse argument is absurd: no two things can be compared unless they are the same! Glass argued that "The question of 'sameness' is not an *a priori* question at all; apart from being a logical impossibility, it is an empirical question" (2000, p. 2). No two studies are the same and the only question of interest is how they vary across the factors we conceive as important.

Another criticism, which Cronbach (1982) referred to as the "flat earth society", is that meta-analysis seeks the *big facts* and often does not explain the complexity nor appropriately seek the moderators. However, meta-analysis indeed can seek moderators, and, as will be seen throughout this book, classrooms are places where complexities abound and all participants constantly try to interpret, engage or disengage, and make meaning out of this variegated landscape. While there are many common themes, sometimes "averages do not do it justice" (Glass, 2000, p. 9). However, the issue (which will be discussed throughout this book) is that the generalizability of the overall effect is an empirical issue, and, as will be seen, there are far fewer moderators than are commonly thought.

A further criticism is that the findings from meta-analysis are based on historical claims—that is, they are based on "past" studies, and the future is not so bound by what worked yesterday. It is critical to always appreciate that the meta-analyses in this book are indeed historical—that is what a research review is: a synthesis of published studies. The degree to which these past studies influence today's or tomorrow's schools is an interpretative issue for the reader.

Eysenck (1984) has been particularly critical of the use of low quality studies in any synthesis, promoting the cliché "garbage in—garbage out". In meta-analysis, it is possible to address this question by ascertaining if the effects are affected by quality, and in general they are not. For example, Lipsey and Wilson (1993) summarized 302 meta-analyses in psychology and education, and used a number of outcomes (besides achievement) in their analyses (the overall effect was $d = 0.50$, $SD = 0.29$). They found no differences between studies that only included random versus non-random design studies ($d = 0.46$ vs. $d = 0.41$), or between high ($d = 0.40$) and low ($d = 0.37$) quality studies. There was a bias upwards from the published ($d = 0.53$) compared to non-published studies ($d = 0.39$), although sample size was unrelated to effect size ($d = -0.03$). Sipe and Curlette (1996) found no relationship between the overall effect size of 97 meta-analyses ($d = 0.34$) and sample size, number of variables coded, type of research design, and a slight increase for published ($d = 0.46$) versus unpublished ($d = 0.36$) meta-analyses. There is one exception that can be predicted from the principles of statistical power: if the effect sizes are close to zero, then the probability of having high confidence in this effect is probably related to the sample size (see Cohen, 1988; 1990).

There is every reason to check the effects of quality, but no reason to throw out studies automatically because of lower quality. An excellent example is the recent synthesis by Torgerson *et al.* (2004), who identified 29 studies from a total of 4,555 potentially relevant papers reporting evaluations of interventions in adult literacy and/or numeracy that were published between 1980 and 2002. Their criterion of acceptance was that only "quality" studies—that is, those studies that used randomized controlled trials— were selected. To decide that it is worthwhile to include only certain types of designs or only studies meeting some criteria of quality presupposes that the studies using only the specified designs or levels of quality are the best representatives of the population estimates. This is speculation, and by using meta-analysis these concerns are subject to verification.

When the studies from Torgerson *et al.* (2004) are examined, it is clear that many of their randomized control studies were of low quality. The median sample size was only 52, and given there were at least two groups (experimental and control) the "typical" study had only 26 people in each group. The average attrition rate was 66 percent, so two-thirds of each sample did not complete the study. It would have been more defensible to include all possible studies, code them for the nature of the experimental design *and* for the quality of the study, and then use meta-analysis techniques to address whether the effects differed as a consequence of design and quality. The aim should be to summarize all possible studies regardless of their design—and then ascertain if quality is a moderator to the final conclusions (see Benseman, Sutton, & Lander, 2005 for a full analysis).

As noted in Chapter 1, Scriven (2005) has argued that a more critical criterion for all scientific conclusions is "beyond reasonable doubt (BRD)", and in some cases randomized studies do not come close to being beyond reasonable doubt. "It seems more appropriate to think of 'gold standard' designs in causal research as those that meet the BRD standard, rather than those that have certain design features … The existence of more threats to internal or external validity in quasi-experimental designs does not entail a reduction of validity for well-done studies below BRD levels" (pp. 45–46). Scriven noted that one of the advocates of random controlled designs, Cook (2004), claimed that "Interpreting [randomized control trial] results depends on many other things—an unbiased assignment process, adequate statistical power, a consent process that does not distort the populations to which results can be generalized, and the absence of treatment-correlated attrition, resentful demoralization, treatment seepage and other unintended products of comparing treatments. Dealing with these matters requires observation, analysis and argumentation." As this last sentence notes, there may be many other research designs that can address critical education questions. Design method and quality of studies are mediators, not prior conditions for choosing studies in a synthesis of studies.

A more statistical concern is that there can be quite a difference depending on whether the author of the meta-analysis used a random or a fixed model to calculate the effect sizes. The fixed effects model can be viewed as a special case of the random model where the variance of the universe effect size is zero; the random model allows generalization to the entire research domain whereas the fixed model allows an estimate of *one* universe effect size underlying all studies available (Kisamore & Brannick, 2008; Schulze, 2004). Typically, but not necessarily, the mean effect size from estimates based on the random model can be appreciably higher than when a fixed model is used. Hence, combining or comparing effects generated from the two models may differ solely because different models are used and not as a function of the topic of interest. Given that the majority of meta-analyses so far published have used the fixed effect model, then this fixed model has been used in this book. Where effects have been based on the random model and this seems to make a difference to the means, this is noted.

Previous attempts at synthesizing meta-analyses

There have been previous attempts to synthesize across meta-analyses. For example, I have published a study based on 134 meta-analyses of studies of educational innovations (Hattie, 1987; 1992). This research concluded that educational innovations can be expected to change average achievement outcomes by 0.4 standard deviations and affective outcomes by 0.2 standard deviations. Some overall findings were drawn about the factors above and below this average benchmark. Innovation, for example, was a theme underlying most of these positive effects. That is, a constant and deliberate attempt to improve the quality of learning on behalf of the system, the principal, and the teacher, typically related to improved achievement. The implementation of innovations probably captures the enthusiasm of the teacher implementing the innovation and the excitement of the students attempting something innovative. Often this has been explained as an experimental artifact in terms of a Hawthorne effect. However, another reason is that when teachers introduce innovation there can be a heightened attention to what is making a difference and what is not, and it is this attention to what is not working that can make the difference—feedback to the teacher about the effects of their actions!

I realized that the most powerful single influence enhancing achievement is feedback. This led me on a long journey to better understand this notion of feedback. After researching and reviewing feedback from a student's perspective (e.g., help-seeking behaviors) and from a teacher to student perspective (e.g., better comments on tests, increasing the amount of feedback in a class), it dawned on me that the most important feature was the creation of situations in classrooms for the teachers to receive more feedback about their teaching—and then the ripple effect back to the student was high (Hattie & Timperley, 2007). Indeed, my team and I have devised a computer-based classroom assessment tool primarily focused on enhancing such feedback (see www.asTTle.org.nz)—but that is another story.

When investigating the continuum of achievement, there is remarkable generality—remarkable because of the preponderance of educational researchers and teachers who argue for treating students individually, and for dealing with curriculum areas as if there were unique teaching methods associated with English, mathematics, and so on. The findings from this synthesis apply, reasonably systematically, to all age groups, all curriculum areas, and to most teachers. It did not seem to matter whether the achievement outcomes were broad or narrow. The average effects of broad constructs and narrow outcomes were slightly lower ($d = 0.23$) compared with those categorized into broad constructs and broad outcomes ($d = 0.43$), narrow constructs and narrow outcomes ($d = 0.37$), and narrow constructs and broad outcomes ($d = 0.35$). Generality is the norm, but, as with many things, there are exceptions.

The majority of the findings of the meta-analyses were derived from studies conducted in English-speaking, highly developed countries (particularly, but not exclusively, the United States). We should not generalize the findings of these meta-analyses to non-English speaking, or non-highly developed countries. Note, for example, the results of a study by Heyneman and Loxley (1983), drawing on 52,252 elementary school-age pupils, 12,085 teachers, and 2,710 classes from 29 developing countries. They concluded that, relative to high-income countries, academic achievement in low-income countries was affected more by pupils' social status and less by teacher quality.

Kulik and Kulik (1989) reviewed more than 100 meta-analyses, including those relating to instructional methods and design. They concluded that "most of the well-known systems devised for improving instruction have acceptable records in evaluation studies" (p. 289). This was an appropriately cautious claim at that early stage of synthesizing across meta-analyses. They concluded that there were promising effects from curricular innovations (especially in science), and suggested that it was important to be cautious about effects from teacher education programs (which were lower than anticipated). They claimed that large effects were not the norm, although there were few negative effects. The major message for teachers was that there were many advantages with providing clear definitions of learning tasks for students, having a requirement of mastery on class activities and quizzes, and providing increased feedback, but policies relating to reorganizing classrooms did not get much support. These messages of learning intentions, success criteria, direct teaching, and the power of feedback—rather than being concerned with structural adaptations—are still powerful two decades later.

Walberg used my earlier synthesis (Hattie, 1987) to defend his nine-factor "Education Productivity" model, which he argued incorporated the three major psychological causes of learning (Reynolds & Walberg, 1998). The first was student aptitude (prior achievement, $d = 0.92$; age or maturation, $d = 0.51$; motivation, self-concept, willingness to persevere on learning tasks $d = 0.18$). The second was instruction (time in learning, $d = 0.47$; quality of teaching, $d = 0.18$). The third was psychological environments (morale or student perceptions of classroom social group, $d = 0.47$; home environment, $d = 0.36$; peer group outside school, $d = 0.20$; minimal leisure-time mass media exposure, particularly television, $d = 0.20$). More recently he argued that "each of the first five factors—prior achievement, development, motivation, and the quantity and quality of instruction—seems necessary for learning in school. Without at least a small amount of each, the student may learn little … (each) appears necessary but insufficient by itself for effective learning" (Walberg, 2006, pp. 103–106). Quality is an important enhancement of study time, and the four psychological environments expand and enhance learning time.

Marzano (1998) was critical of these attempts by me, Walberg, and others, claiming that basing a synthesis on "brand names" could be misleading. For example, he argued that the categories we used in our syntheses were too broad and included too many varied treatments, and that instead the categories used should be specific and functional enough to provide guidance for classroom practice. He used four basic building blocks in his synthesis: knowledge ($d = 0.60$), the cognitive system ($d = 0.75$), the meta-cognitive system ($d = 0.55$), and the self-system ($d = 0.74$). Marzano used 4,057 effect sizes and found an overall effect size of $d = 0.65$. (This overall effect is somewhat larger than reported later in this book, as Marzano did not include many of the school and structural influences.) He reported on eight moderators:

1   whether the technique was designed for use by the teacher ($d = 0.61$) or the student ($d = 0.73$);
2   the degree of specificity of the influence (he argued that the more specific the influence, the higher the effect, although the means were $d = 0.67$, $d = 0.64$, $d = 0.64$ for least to most specific);
3   grade level of students (no differences);
4   student ability (low $d = 0.64$; middle $d = 0.70$; and high $d = 0.91$);
5   duration of treatment (shortened programs < 3 weeks $d = 0.69$ vs. > 4 weeks $d = 0.52$);
6   the specificity of dependent measures in the treatment (very specific $d = 0.97$, appropriate $d = 0.91$, and very general $d = 0.55$);
7   methodological quality (no difference);
8   publication type (published $d = 0.72$ vs. unpublished $d = 0.64$).

From his very systematic review he concluded that the "best way to teach organizing ideas—concepts, generalizations, and principles—appears to be to present those constructs in a rather direct fashion" (Marzano, 1998, p. 106) and then have students apply these concepts to new situations. He regarded the meta-cognitive system as the "engine" or primary vehicle for enhancement of the mental processes within the cognitive system and recommended providing students with clear targets of knowledge and skills, and strategies for the processes involved with what they are learning. Marzano, Gaddy, and Dean (2000) outlined an excellent and extremely fascinating set of implications for teachers and the learning processes deriving from these analyses. In a further re-analysis of these effect sizes, Marzano (2000) argued that 80 percent of the variance in achievement could be accounted for by student effects, 7 percent by school effects, and 13 percent by teacher effects. He then used these estimates to evaluate the effects on student achievement of an ineffective, an average, and an exceptional teacher in an ineffective, an average, and an exceptional school respectively. Average schools and average teachers, although he said they did little harm, also did little to influence students' relative position on the distribution of achievement for all students; ineffective teachers, no matter how effective the school, had a negative impact on the standings of all students, whereas students of exceptional teachers, even in ineffective schools, either maintained or increased achievement, many quite substantially. "Exceptional performance on the part of teachers not only compensates for average performance at the school level, but even ineffective performance at the school level" (Marzano, 2000, p. 81).

Synthesizing the meta-analyses

This book is not another meta-analysis. There are hundreds of those. Instead, this book aims to synthesize over 800 meta-analyses about the influences on achievement to present a more global perspective on what are and what are not key influences on achievement.

The project started by collecting 134 meta-analyses and proposing a set of common themes as to why some influences were more or less influential than others (Hattie, 1992). Since 1992, this collection of meta-analyses has been supplemented with a large number of other meta-analyses; over the past few years these have all been coded—at the study level—and the current database has a line for each meta-analysis that summarizes and categorizes the study and notes the effect sizes and standard errors which are needed for the calculations reported in this book.

It was possible to locate a total of about 800 meta-analyses, which encompassed 52,637 studies, and provided 146,142 effect sizes about the influence of some program, policy, or innovation on academic achievement in school (early childhood, elementary, high, and tertiary). Topics *not* included are those concerning English as a second language, affective or physical outcomes, and meta-analyses where the number of studies was fewer than four. When the same meta-analysis has been published multiple times, (e.g., when dissertations are rewritten as articles), only the most recent or most accessible is included.

As can be imagined, these effects cover most school subjects (although the majority are reading, mathematics, science, and social studies), all ages, and a myriad of comparisons. These effects are based on many millions of students across the main areas of influence—from the student, the home, the effects of schools, teachers, curricula, and teaching methods and strategies. The total number of students identified in the meta-analyses is large. Only 286 of the meta-analyses included total sample size but together these alone totaled 83 million students. Using the average sample size per study, this would multiply out to about 236 million students in total. However, it is likely that many students would have participated in more than one study, and thus this is a gross estimate of sample size. Even so, it would be safe to conclude that these studies are based on many millions of students.

Appendix A lists all the meta-analyses included in this book, provides the number of studies, people, and effect sizes, along with the average effect size, standard error (if provided), and common language effect. The meta-analyses are listed by the chapters they are referred to in this book. Appendix B lists these influences in their rank order.

The distribution of effect sizes

To start, let us see an overall distribution of all the effect sizes (Figure 2.2) from each of the 800+ meta-analyses. The bars that indicate points on the y-axis represent the number of effects in each category, while the x-axis gives the categories of effect sizes.

There are six immediate implications from Figure 2.2 that are critical to the arguments in this book:

1 The effects follow a normal distribution. To those immersed in large-scale statistics, this would not be surprising: normality is often, but not necessarily, present when there are large sample sizes. The normal distribution, however, is a consequence of the data and not imposed on it. Given this normal distribution, there are as many influences above the mean effect size as there are below it, and, most importantly, the mean is a reasonably good indicator of all the influences on achievement.

2 Almost everything works. Ninety percent of all effect sizes in education are positive. Of the ten percent that are negative, about half are "expected" (e.g., effects of disruptive students); thus about 95 percent of all things we do have a positive influence on

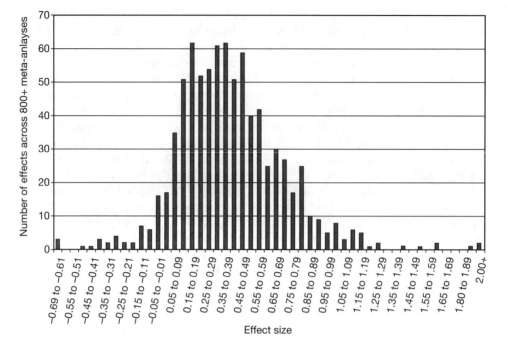

Figure 2.2 Distribution of effect sizes across all meta-analyses

achievement. When teachers claim that they are having a positive effect on achievement or when a policy improves achievement this is almost a trivial claim: virtually everything works. One only needs a pulse and we can improve achievement.

3   Setting the bar at zero is absurd. If we set the bar at zero and then ask that teachers and schools "improve achievement", we have set a very very low bar indeed. No wonder every teacher can claim that they are making a difference; no wonder we can find many answers as to how to enhance achievement; no wonder every child improves. As noted at the outset of this book, it is easy to find programs that make a difference. Raising achievement that is enhancing learning beyond an effect size of $d = 0.0$ is so low a bar as to be dangerous and is most certainly misleading.

4   Set the bar at $d = 0.40$. The average effect size is $d = 0.40$. This average summarizes the typical effect of all possible influences in education and should be used as the benchmark to judge effects in education. Effects lower than $d = 0.40$ can be regarded as in need of more consideration, although (as discussed earlier) it is not as simple as saying that all effects below $d = 0.40$ are not worth having (it depends on costs, interaction effects, and so on). Certainly effects above $d = 0.40$ are worth having and a major focus of this book is trying to understand the common denominators of what makes a difference (i.e., the effect sizes above compared to those below $d = 0.40$). Throughout this book this $d = 0.40$ effect size is referred to as the hinge-point or h-point, as this is the point on the continuum that provides the hinge or fulcrum around which all other effects are interpreted.

5   Innovations are more than teaching: Teachers average an effect of $d = 0.20$ to $d = 0.40$ per year on student achievement. This h-point of $d = 0.40$ does *not* mean that this

is the typical effect of teaching or teachers. It does not mean that merely placing a teacher in front of a class would lead to an improvement of 0.40 standard deviations. In most studies summarized in this book, there is a deliberate attempt to change, improve, plan, modify, and innovate. The best available estimate as to the effects of schooling is based on longitudinal studies. For example, the National Assessment of Educational Progress (NAEP, Johnson and Zwick, 1990) surveyed what students in American schools know and can do in the subject areas of reading, writing, civics, United States history, mathematics, and science. The students were sampled at ages 9, 13, and 17, and the testing has been repeated every two years. The average effect size across the six subject areas was $d = 0.24$ per year. In our own New Zealand studies, we have estimated that the yearly effect in reading, mathematics, and writing from Years 4 to 13 ($N = 83,751$) is $d = 0.35$—although this is not linear: in some years and for some subjects there is more or less growth. The inference for the argument in this book is that teachers typically can attain between $d = 0.20$ to $d = 0.40$ growth per year—and that this is to be considered *average*. They should be seeking greater than $d = 0.40$ for their achievement gains to be considered above average, and greater than $d = 0.60$ to be considered excellent.

6   The variance is important. This typical effect size of $d = 0.40$ may not be uniform across all students or all implementations of any influence. There may be many moderators. For example, the typical effect size of homework is $d = 0.29$, but the effects are greater for high school students and closer to zero for elementary school students. The major point of this "achievement barometer" or "achievement continuum" is to provide a basis to interpret the effects of change, both the overall effects and effects broken down by important moderators.

The typical effect: the hinge-point

The effect size of 0.40 sets a level where the effects of innovation enhance achievement in such a way that we can notice real-world differences, and this should be a benchmark of such real-world change. It is not a magic number that should become like a $p < 0.05$ cut-off point, but a guideline to begin discussions about what we can aim for if we want to see students change. It provides a "standard" from which to judge effects: it is a comparison based on typical, real-world effects rather than based on the strongest cause possible, or with the weakest cause imaginable. It is not unreasonable to claim that at least half of all implementations, at least half of all students, and at least half of all teachers *can and do* attain this h-point of $d = 0.40$ change as a consequence of their actions.

An aim of this book is to position the various influences along this continuum, relative to the typical $d = 0.40$ effect. The fundamental claim is that influences in education are relative: we should judge the success of an innovation relative to $d = 0.40$ (and certainly not $d = 0.0$). To return to the homework example used earlier, the typical influence after introducing homework was just below the typical effect across all possible influences. Thus, when the influence of homework is compared to the more usual zero point, those who argue that homework is effective would say "yes", but when the effects from classes without homework are compared to the typical effect across all other influences, then homework is well below an average effect—there are many more innovations that have greater effects. Maybe it is not so surprising that teachers have found that the effect of prescribing homework is not as dramatic as many advocates and researchers promised. The advocates and researchers compare the outcome to zero, but we should be comparing the effect to alternative innovations. The null hypothesis ($d = 0.0$) is not the question of interest, so it is no wonder that the answer is misleading; introducing nearly any innovation is better than its absence. The null hypothesis is virtually certain to be false before analysis commences and thus it is uninformative (see Novick & Jackson, 1974).

The main contributors

Table 2.1 presents the average effect for each of the major categories of contributors to learning. The averages of all effects are quite similar with the exception that school differences are far less critical to enhancing achievement: take two students of the same ability and it matters less to which school they go than the influences of the teacher, curricula program, or teaching they experience.

Figure 2.3 presents the number of meta-analyses from these 800+ meta-analyses relative to average $d = 0.40$ h-point. There are just as many home, student, curricula, and teaching effects above as below the average, more teaching effects above 0.40, and many more school effects below $d = 0.40$. But averages can hide too much. The remainder of this book works through each of these major categories of influences, chapter by chapter, and aims to more deeply evaluate the underlying causes of what specific innovations and influences are above and below average. Each chapter will work through a number of innovations and influences; sufficient detail is given for each of these innovations to give a sense of the claims, but the primary aim is to draw inferences for the overall model outlined in Chapter 3.

The barometer of influences

We seem to have no barometers of success or failure to show what works and what does not work in education. Yes, we do have tests, lots of them, which we use to evaluate whether students have gained sufficiently. But this is not enough. An influence may "work", but by how much, and how differently from other influences? Some innovations or actions are more influential than others. Instead of asking "What works?" we should be asking "What works best?" as the answers to these two questions are quite different. As has been indicated already, the answer to the first questions is "Almost everything" whereas the answer to the second is more circumscribed—and some things work *better* and some work *worse* relative to the many possible alternatives.

Table 2.1 Average effect for each of the major contributors to learning

Contribution	No.	Studies	People	Effects	d	SE	CLE
Student	139	11,101	7,513,406	38,282	0.40	0.044	29%
Home	36	2,211	11,672,658	5,182	0.31	0.058	22%
School	101	4,150	4,416,898	13,348	0.23	0.072	16%
Teacher	31	2,225	402,325	5,559	0.49	0.049	35%
Curricula	144	7,102	6,899,428	29,220	0.45	0.076	32%
Teaching	365	25,860	52,128,719	55,143	0.42	0.071	30%
Average	816	52,649	83,033,433	146,626	0.40	0.062	28%

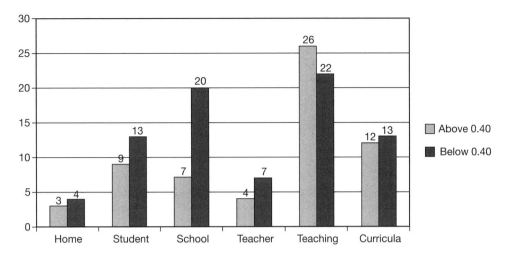

Figure 2.3 Number of meta-analyses above and below the h-point

We need a barometer that addresses whether the various teaching methods, school reforms, and so on are worthwhile relative to possible alternatives. We need clear goalposts of excellence for all in our schools to aspire towards, and most importantly, for them to know when they get there. We need a barometer of success that helps teachers to understand which attributes of schooling assist students in attaining these goalposts.

Figure 2.4 outlines one such barometer that has been developed for use throughout this book. The development of this barometer began not by asking whether this or that innovation was working, but whether this teaching worked better than possible alternatives; not by asking whether this innovation was having positive effects compared to not having the innovation, but whether the effects from this innovation were better for students than what they would achieve if they had received alternative innovations.

For each of the many attributes investigated in the chapters in this book, the average of each influence is indexed by an arrow through one of the zones on the barometer. All influences above the h-point ($d = 0.40$) are labeled in the "Zone of desired effects" as these are the influences that have the greatest impact on student achievement outcomes.

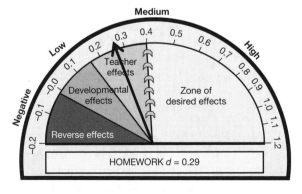

KEY	
Standard error	0.027 (Low)
Rank	88th
Number of meta-analyses	5
Number of studies	161
Number of effects	295
Number of people (4)	105,282

Figure 2.4 A typical barometer of influence

The typical effects from teachers are between $d = 0.15$ and $d = 0.40$, as identified from the longitudinal studies discussed above. Any influences in this zone are similar to what teachers can accomplish in a typical year of schooling. The zone between $d = 0.0$ and $d = 0.15$ is what students could probably achieve if there was no schooling (and is estimated from the findings in countries with no or limited schooling). Maturation alone can account for much of the enhancement of learning (see Cahan & Davis, 1987). Thus, any effects below $d = 0.15$ can be considered potentially harmful and probably should not be implemented. The final category includes the reverse effects—those that decrease achievement—and these are certainly not wanted.

The arrow points to the average effect of the various meta-analyses on the particular topic (in the above it is $d = 0.29$ for the five homework meta-analyses. The variability (or standard error) of the average effect sizes from each meta-analysis is not always easy to determine. Often the information is not provided, and it is well known that the variance is very much related (inversely) to the sample size of studies—the more studies there are, the greater the variance. Across all 800+ meta-analyses the typical standard error of the mean is about $d = 0.07$—and to provide a broad sense of variance, any influence where the average "spread of effects" is less than $d = 0.04$ is deemed low, between $d = 0.041$ and $d = 0.079$ is deemed medium and greater than $d = 0.08$ is deemed large. While these are crude estimates, it is more important to read the discussion about each influence to ascertain whether important sources of variance could be identified to explain differential effects within that influence. In many cases there is insufficient information to estimate the standard error and thus it is not provided in the summary information. The information under the barometer allows an interpretation of how confident we can be about this summary information: the number of meta-analyses on each category (five in the above case), based on 161 studies, and 295 effect sizes. There were 105,282 students in the four meta-analyses that provided information about sample size. The average effect is $d = 0.29$, with a standard error of 0.027 (considered "low" relative to all meta-analyses). The effects of homework, in this example, rank 88th of all 138 meta-analyses (see Appendix B).

Relation between effect size and sample size

A funnel plot is often used to examine whether a meta-analysis is based on a biased sample of studies (Light & Pillemer, 1984). The funnel plot is a scatterplot of effect sizes versus the number of studies (in this case), with each data point representing one study. Because meta-analyses with a larger number of studies are more likely to better estimate the effect size, they tend to lie in a narrow band at the top of the scatterplot, while the smaller meta-analyses (with expected greater variation in results) fan out over a larger area at the bottom—thus creating the visual impression of an inverted funnel. As can be seen in Figure 2.5, the results from this synthesis show a reasonably symmetric funnel, indicating a lack of publication bias.

Concluding comments

This chapter sets the scene for the interpretation of the 800+ meta-analyses, which form the fundamental dataset used throughout this book. An achievement continuum has been developed along which the many effects can be located, and the importance of the h-point of $d = 0.40$ has been emphasized. The barometer of achievement can be used to assist in seeking the explanation of what leads to successful learning that exceeds the $d = 0.40$ hinge-point.

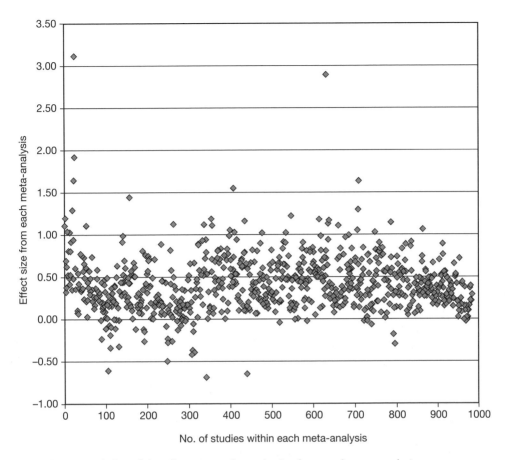

Figure 2.5 Funnel plot of the effect size and sample size from each meta-analysis

Chapter 3

The argument
Visible teaching and visible learning

> We think in generalities, but we live in details.
>
> (Whitehead, 1943, p. 26)

This chapter introduces the major findings that will be elaborated in the following chapters. The aim of this book is not to overwhelm with detail from the more than 50,000 studies and 800+ meta-analyses that form the basis of the discussion. Instead, the aim is to build an explanatory story about the influences on student learning and then to convince the reader of the nature and value of the story by working through the evidence to defend it. It is as much theory generation as it is theory appraisal. The art in any synthesis is the overall message, and the simple adage underlying most of the syntheses in this book is "visible teaching and learning". Visible teaching and learning occurs when learning is the explicit goal, when it is appropriately challenging, when the teacher and the student both (in their various ways) seek to ascertain whether and to what degree the challenging goal is attained, when there is deliberate practice aimed at attaining mastery of the goal, when there is feedback given and sought, and when there are active, passionate, and engaging people (teacher, student, peers, and so on) participating in the act of learning. It is teachers seeing learning through the eyes of students, and students seeing teaching as the key to their ongoing learning. The remarkable feature of the evidence is that the biggest effects on student learning occur when teachers become learners of their own teaching, and when students become their own teachers. When students become their own teachers they exhibit the self-regulatory attributes that seem most desirable for learners (self-monitoring, self-evaluation, self-assessment, self-teaching). Thus, it is visible teaching and learning by teachers and students that makes the difference. The following chapters provide the evidence to defend this overall message.

What teachers *do* matters

The major message is simple—what teachers *do* matters. However, this has become a cliché that masks the fact that the greatest source of variance in our system relates to teachers— they can vary in major ways. The codicil is that what "some" teachers do matters—especially those who teach in a most deliberate and visible manner. When these professionals see learning occurring or not occurring, they intervene in calculated and meaningful ways to alter the direction of learning to attain various shared, specific, and challenging goals. In particular, they provide students with multiple opportunities and alternatives for developing learning strategies based on the surface *and* deep levels of learning some content or domain matter, leading to students building conceptual understanding of this learning which the students and teachers then use in future learning. Learners can be so different, making it difficult for a teacher to achieve such teaching acts—students can be in different learning places at various times using a multiplicity of unique learning strategies, meeting different and appropriately challenging goals. Learning is a very personal journey for the teacher and the student, although there are remarkable commonalities in this journey for both. It requires much skill for teachers to demonstrate to *all* their students that they can see the students' "perspective, communicate it back to them so that they have valuable feedback to self-assess, feel safe, and learn to understand others and the content with the same interest and concern" (Cornelius-White, 2007, p. 23).

The act of teaching requires deliberate interventions to ensure that there is cognitive change in the student: thus the key ingredients are awareness of the learning intentions, knowing when a student is successful in attaining those intentions, having sufficient understanding of the student's understanding as he or she comes to the task, and knowing enough about the content to provide meaningful and challenging experiences in some sort of progressive development. It involves an experienced teacher who knows a range of learning strategies to provide the student when they seem *not* to understand, to provide direction and re-direction in terms of the content being understood and thus maximize the power of feedback, and having the skill to "get out the way" when learning is progressing towards the success criteria.

Of course, it helps if these learning intentions and success criteria are shared with, committed to, and understood by the learner—because in the right caring and idea-rich environment, the learner can then experiment (be right and wrong) with the content and the thinking about the content, and make connections across ideas. A safe environment for the learner (and for the teacher) is an environment where error is welcomed and fostered—because we learn so much from errors and from the feedback that then accrues from going in the wrong direction or not going sufficiently fluently in the right direction. In the same way, teachers themselves need to be in a safe environment to learn about the success or otherwise of their teaching from others.

To facilitate such an environment, to command a range of learning strategies, and to be cognitively aware of the pedagogical means to enable the student to learn requires dedicated, passionate people. Such teachers need to be aware of which of their teaching strategies are working or not, be prepared to understand and adapt to the learner(s) and their situations, contexts, and prior learning, and need to share the experience of learning in this manner in an open, forthright, and enjoyable way with their students and their colleagues.

We rarely talk about passion in education, as if doing so makes the work of teachers seem less serious, more emotional than cognitive, somewhat biased or of lesser import. When we do consider passion, we typically constrain such expressions of joy and involvement to matters unrelated to our teaching (Neumann, 2006). The key components of passion for the teacher and for the learner appear to be the sheer thrill of being a learner or teacher, the absorption that accompanies the process of teaching and learning, the sensations in being involved in the activity of teaching and learning, and the willingness to be involved in deliberate practice to attain understanding. Passion reflects the thrills as well as the frustrations of learning—it can be infectious, it can be taught, it can be modeled, and it can be learnt. It is among the most prized outcomes of schooling and, while rarely studied in any of the studies reviewed in this book, it infuses many of the influences that make the difference to the outcomes. It requires more than content knowledge, acts of skilled teaching, or engaged students to make the difference (although these help). It requires a love of the content, an ethical caring stance to wish to imbue others with a liking or even love of the discipline being taught, and a demonstration that the teacher is not only teaching but learning—typically about the students' processes and outcomes of learning.

Learning is not always pleasurable and easy; it requires over-learning at certain points, spiraling up and down the knowledge continuum, and building a working relationship with others in grappling with challenging tasks. This is the power of deliberative practice. It also requires a commitment to seeking further challenges—and herein lies a major link between challenge and feedback, two of the essential ingredients of learning. The greater the challenge, the higher the probability that one seeks and needs feedback, but the more important it is that there is a teacher to provide feedback and to ensure that the learner is on the right path to successfully meet the challenges.

The key to many of the influences above the $d = 0.40$ h-point is that they are deliberate interventions aimed at enhancing teaching and learning. But the message is to not merely *innovate*—but for us to learn from what makes the difference when teachers innovate. When we innovate we are more aware of what is working and what is not, we are looking for contrary evidence, we are keen to discover any intended and unintended consequences, and we have a heightened awareness of the effects of the innovations on outcomes. In these situations teachers become the learners about their own effects! In any innovation there is deliberate attention to implementation and its effects, there is a degree of challenge, and a valuing of feedback. It is critical that teachers learn about the success or otherwise of their interventions: those teachers who are students of their own effects are the teachers who are the most influential in raising students' achievement. Seeking positive effects on student learning (say, $d > 0.40$) should be a constant theme and challenge for teachers. As this does not accrue by serendipity or accident, then the excellent teacher must be vigilant to what is working and what is *not* working in the classroom.

A concept of excellent teaching

A story serves to illustrate my claims about excellent teaching. Some time ago one of my Master's students completed a meta-analysis on the effects of various programs on self-concept of children and adults (Clinton, 1987). The most successful programs were the Outward Bound or Adventure programs. There are four major features of these programs that led to their positive influence. First, Outward Bound programs have an emphasis on the immediate quality of the experience, as well as aiming to have these immediate experiences have an effect on later experiences. That is, there is a planned and intentional transfer of experiences, knowledge, and decisions during the earlier learning experiences to later experiences (see Hattie, Marsh, Neill, & Richards, 1997 for more details). Second, Outward Bound programs set difficult and specific goals that are known to the learner, and then tasks are structured so that participants can attain these goals. The program provides challenging and specific goals (e.g., successfully negotiating a 60-foot cliff by abseiling or rappelling) and then structures situations (e.g., adequate preparation, social support, etc.) so that participants share a commitment to reaching these goals. Third, the program increases the amount and quality of feedback, which is vital to the learning process. The often dangerous and risky situations demand feedback, and the learning intentions and success criteria are crystal clear. A major function of challenging and specific goals is that they direct attention and effort, and thus the learner is more aware and keen for feedback related to attaining these goals. Fourth, in the Outward Bound program, the instructor is keenly aware of the need to understand and, if necessary, reassess and redirect an individual's coping strategies. Such coping strategies can be cognitive (learning strategies), personal (building of self-efficacy, perseverance in the face of challenge), and social (help seeking, cooperative learning). These four major features are the keys of successful teaching and learning.

As another example, take my involvement in a Bush Search and Rescue Squad which involved teaching the skills and fun of cliff rescues. Consider the following: I am going to take you to the top of a three-storey building and teach you to rappel down the outside of this building. Typically, I would then demonstrate to you how to put on a safety harness, tie the rope in a bowline, and then show you how to lean backwards to commence the descent. In line with the principles of good teaching, I would then ask you, the student, to implement this learning. Typically, such a learning situation leads to much care by the students, an enhanced level of interest in what peers are doing, and high levels of help-seeking behaviors to ensure the knowledge of rope-work is correct and harnesses are correctly positioned. The goals are challenging, specific, and visible, and the learners are committed to them! The learning is actively visible and there are high levels of feedback and monitoring. The learner typically "seeks" the feedback. When a novice first gets to the edge, there is a remarkably high level of peer teaching and learning: it is not natural to fall backwards when descending as it is more typical for the feet to precede the head. When finally the student reaches the bottom there is a surge of excitement appreciating that the challenging goal has been reached (it is abundantly clear what the success criteria are!), the experience was exhilarating, and the learning absorbed in the experience itself. Most want to repeat the experience and continue to enjoy meeting the challenging goals. Moreover, all these acts and most of the "thinking" about the task are visible to the teacher and to the learner. This is the heart of the model of successful teaching and learning advocated in this book.

Visible teaching

It is critical that the teaching and the learning are visible. There is no deep secret called "teaching and learning": teaching and learning are visible in the classrooms of the successful teachers and students, teaching and learning are visible in the passion displayed by the teacher and learner when successful learning and teaching occurs, and teaching and learning requires much skill and knowledge by both teacher and student. The teacher must know when learning is correct or incorrect; learn when to experiment and learn from the experience; learn to monitor, seek and give feedback; and know to try alternative learning strategies when others do not work. What is most important is that teaching is visible to the student, and that the learning is visible to the teacher. The more the student becomes the teacher and the more the teacher becomes the learner, then the more successful are the outcomes.

This explanation of visible teaching relates to teachers as activators, as deliberate change agents, and as directors of learning. This does not mean that they are didactic, spend 80 percent or more of the day talking, and aim to get through the curriculum or lesson come what may. Effective teaching is not the drilling and trilling to the less than willing.

When I reviewed the videotapes of many of the best teachers in the United States (via the National Board for Professional Teaching Standards video assessment task) it was stunning how active and involved the best teachers were in the classrooms—it was clear who was in control in those classrooms. The activity was visible and "in the air"; passive was not a word in the vocabulary of these accomplished teachers—learning was not always loud and heated but it was rarely silent and deadening, and it was often intense, buzzing, and risky.

The model of visible teaching and learning combines, rather than contrasts, teacher-centered teaching and student-centered learning and knowing. Too often these methods are expressed as direct teaching versus constructivist teaching (and then direct teaching is portrayed as bad, while constructivist teaching is considered to be good). Constructivism too often is seen in terms of student-centered inquiry learning, problem-based learning, and task-based learning, and common jargon words include "authentic", "discovery", and "intrinsically motivated learning". The role of the constructivist teacher is claimed to be more of facilitation to provide opportunities for individual students to acquire knowledge and construct meaning through their own activities, and through discussion, reflection and the sharing of ideas with other learners with minimal corrective intervention (Cambourne, 2003; Daniels, 2001; Selley, 1999; von Glasersfeld, 1995). These kinds of statements are almost directly opposite to the successful recipe for teaching and learning as will be developed in the following chapters.

A model of learning

The major point here is that constructivism is *not* a theory of teaching, but a theory of knowing and knowledge, and it is important to understand the role of building constructions of understanding. Bereiter (2002) used Popper's three worlds to make sense of much of what we strive for in school: the physical world, the subjective or mental world, and the world of ideas. These three worlds have major parallels with the three worlds of achievement: surface knowledge of the physical world, the thinking strategies and deeper understanding of the subjective world, and the ways in which students construct knowledge and reality for themselves as a consequence of this surface and deep knowing and understanding. This third world, often forgotten in the passion for teaching facts and thinking skills, is entirely created by humans, is fallible but capable of being improved, and can take on a life of its own. Students often come to lessons with already constructed realities (third worlds), which, if we as teachers do not understand them before we start to teach, can become the stumbling blocks for future learning. If we are successful, then the students' constructed realities (based on their surface and deep knowing) and keenness to explore these worlds are the major legacy of teaching. The contents of this third world are not concrete like books, statues, and teapots (see Bereiter, 2002, pp. 62–63): they are more conceptual. It is certainly the case, as Bereiter documents, that "much of what is meant by the shift from an industrial to a knowledge society is that increasing amounts of work are being done on conceptual objects rather than on the physical objects to which they are related" (Bereiter, 2002, p. 65).

The distinctions are not clean cut, as at all three levels we often learn in a haphazard manner. So much teaching is aimed at the first world—the world of ideas and knowledge, and there is also much discussion about the importance of deep knowledge and thinking skills (the second world). But the task of teaching and learning best comes together when we attend to all three levels: ideas, thinking, and constructing.

> In many situations, it will be impossible to make a clear distinction between knowing or thinking about the conceptual artifact and knowing or thinking about the material world the conceptual artifact applies to [...] What matters is that we recognize conceptual artifacts as real things, recognize creating and improving them as real work, and recognize understanding them as real understanding.
>
> (Bereiter, 2002, p. 67).

The real work of schooling is to create or add value to conceptual artifacts in the same way that builders add value to building artifacts. It is a world of conjectures, explanations, proofs, arguments, and evaluations.

Similarly, there can be many cultural artifacts particular to a culture and an important aspect of education is to teach these artifacts. For example, in New Zealand Māori culture, there is much importance attached to whānau (family), history, and cultural norms. A major focus of schooling is to therefore enable learners to adopt these cultural artifacts as a key part of their own conceptual artifacts—a way to see their world in a similar manner to how the culture has learnt to see its world, and communicate its worldviews and values. The importance is that this three-level view of achievement allows relations between theory and observation, personal and cultural belief and observation, and between personal belief and theory.

> ... there are the relations between different theories, different phenomena, and different people's readings of the same phenomenon. None of these relations are easy. They are all inferential and highly problematic. But they are what people work on when they are building scientific knowledge.
>
> (Bereiter, 2002, p. 91)

Bereiter claimed that there are a number of commitments to knowledge improvement: the third world is not limited to accepted, verified, or important knowledge objects. It can include discredited theories, crank notions, unsolved problems, and new ideas that may or may not gather a following. In this respect, "the third world is more inclusive than the canons of liberal education. This inclusiveness goes a long way toward eliminating the split between established knowledge and students' constructive efforts because it places the ideas created by students in the same world as the ideas handed from authoritative sources" (p. 237). "Knowing one's way around in the world of conceptual artifacts affords a wealth of possibilities not open to people who know that world only from a distance, if at all." (p. 238). Knowledge building is an activity directed toward the third world. It is doing something to a conceptual artifact. Bereiter claimed that knowledge building includes thinking of alternatives, thinking of criticisms, proposing experimental tests, deriving one object from another, proposing a problem, proposing a solution, and criticizing the solution. It is more than knowing, mistakenly believing, or doubting some knowledge object.

Educating is more than teaching people to think—it is also teaching people things that are worth learning. Good teaching involves constructing explanations, criticizing, drawing out inferences, finding applications, and there "should never be a need for the teacher to think of ways to inject more thinking into the curriculum. That would be like trying to inject more aerobic exercise into the lives of Sherpa porters" (Bereiter, 2002, p. 380). If the students are not doing enough thinking, something is seriously wrong with the instruction. "If the only justification for an activity is that it is supposed to encourage or improve thinking, drop it and replace it with an activity that advances students' understanding that increases their mastery of a useful tool" (Bereiter, 2002, p. 381).

Surface, deep, and constructed understanding

There needs to be a major shift, therefore, from an over reliance on surface information (the first world) and a misplaced assumption that the goal of education is deep understanding or development of thinking skills (the second world), towards a balance of surface and deep learning leading to students more successfully constructing defensible theories of knowing and reality (the third world).

For many students, success at school relates to adopting a surface approach to understanding both how and what they should learn, whereas many teachers claim that the goal of their teaching is enhancing deep learning (Biggs & Collis, 1982). Brown (2002), for example, investigated the beliefs about learning of more than 700 15-year-old New Zealand students and 71 of their teachers of English, mathematics, and science. Students argued that learning for them primarily meant exhibiting surface knowledge involving the reproduction of taught material in order to maximize achievement in assessments. In contrast, teachers of these same students claimed that they were teaching towards deep learning outcomes. The students were more governed by the tasks and examinations set by teachers and schools, so, despite claims by teachers, the students were very strategic in concentrating on acquiring sufficient surface and whatever deeper understanding was needed to complete assignments and examinations. (The same phenomenon is especially evident when comparing conceptions of learning by academics and their students; Purdie, 2001.)

Students can be strategic in their approach because most questions and examinations (verbal and written) relate to surface knowledge (Marzano, 1991). For example, Gall (1970) claimed that 60 percent of teachers' questions required factual recall, 20 percent were procedural, and only 20 percent required thought by the students. Other studies have found the proportion of surface thinking questions can be in the order of 80 percent or more (Airasian, 1991; Barnette, Walsh, Orletsky, & Sattes, 1995; Gall, 1984; Kloss, 1988). Teachers' questioning may not elicit deep thinking from students because students understand that questioning is how teachers lead and control classroom activity; in other words, students know that the teacher already knows the answer to the questions (Gipps, 1994; Torrance & Pryor, 1998; Wade & Moje, 2000). So much of daily classroom life is "knowledge telling", and thus surface knowledge is sufficient. Students soon learn that studying or learning with surface strategies or methods (i.e., revision, re-reading, and reviewing of the year's work) leads to success. In contrast, teachers claim to prefer a deep view of learning, usually focused on academic and cognitive development, while at the same time they emphasize surface methods of teaching, usually with the defense that this is what is required in order to prepare students for high-stakes qualification examinations or assessments. This emphasis on surface approaches means that students tend to experience very few opportunities or demands for deep thinking in contemporary classrooms.

To be more specific, *surface* learning involves a knowing or understanding of ideas or facts. In contrast, the two *deep* processes—relational and elaborative—constitute a change in the quality of thinking that is cognitively more challenging than surface questions. Relational responses require integration of at least two separate pieces of given knowledge, information, facts, or ideas. In other words, relational questions require learners to impose an organizing pattern on the given material. Elaborative or extended abstract responses require the learner to go beyond the given information, knowledge, or ideas, and deduce a more general rule or proof that applies to all cases. In such cases, the learner is forced to think beyond the given and bring in related, prior, or new knowledge, ideas, or information in order to create an answer, prediction, or hypothesis that extends to a wider range of situations. From these surface and deep knowing and understandings the learner can construct notions or ideas that then shape the ways they engage in surface and deep learning (the third world of constructed understanding).

These three types of understanding—surface, deep, and constructed or conceptual understanding—are built on the Biggs and Collis (Biggs & Collis, 1982; Collis & Biggs, 1979) SOLO model of student learning that has proven most valuable both in developing models of teaching and learning and also in our understanding of assessment (Hattie & Purdie, 1998; Hattie & Brown, 2004). These forms of building on surface knowledge to develop deep knowledge are becoming common in the research on educational psychology and assessment. It is intriguing to note that the major revision of Bloom's Taxonomy (Anderson, Krathwohl, & Bloom, 2001) introduced four similar levels: factual knowledge (how to be acquainted with a discipline or solve problems in it); conceptual knowledge (interrelationships among elements within a large structure that enable them to function together); procedural knowledge (how to do something, methods of inquiry); and meta-cognitive knowledge (knowledge of cognition in general as well as awareness and knowledge of one's own cognition). This is a major advance on the better-known Bloom's Taxonomy, which confuses levels of knowing with forms of knowledge (see Hattie & Purdie, 1998).

It is critical to note that the claim is not that surface knowledge is necessarily bad and that deep knowledge is essentially good. Instead, the claim is that it is important to have the right balance: you need surface to have deep; and you need to have surface and deep knowledge *and* understanding in a context or set of domain knowledge. The process of learning is a journey from ideas to understanding to constructing and onwards. It is a journey of learning, unlearning, and overlearning. When students can move from idea to ideas and then relate and elaborate on them we have learning—and when they can regulate or monitor this journey then they are teachers of their own learning. Regulation, or meta-cognition, refers to knowledge about one's own cognitive processes (knowledge) and the monitoring of these processes (skillfulness). It is the development of such skillfulness that is an aim of many learning tasks, and developing them so there is a sense of self-regulation.

A reminder about outcomes

As noted in the earlier chapters, the focus of this book is on achievement outcomes. Now this notion has been expanded to achievement outcomes across the three worlds of understanding. It may seem intuitively obvious that the influences on learning that aim for surface learning tend to favor more directed, specific goals, whereas those that aim for deep learning tend to favor more inquiry methods. Not so—this is too simple and can be misleading. Sometimes the deeper concepts need more specific and direct teaching, and sometimes the more surface concepts can be learned via inquiry or problem solving.

A major aim is to develop "over-learning" or fluency of achievement. For example, most of us "over-learnt" learning to walk—we forget the trial and error and pain that was involved when we first learnt to walk; but we can most certainly recognize that struggle to learn to walk when we have a major accident, and must learn this skill anew. We want a sense of fluency and over-learning of worthwhile activities as a major outcome of schooling. There is over-learning when we consider a person fluent in a language or with a musical instrument, or when we consider a student fluent in math, reading, or science. A sufficient level of fluency can lead to other desirable outcomes such as retention, endurance, stability, and application within a domain (Doughty, Chase, & O'Shields, 2004).

When a student attains a high degree of fluency on a topic, then they have more cognitive resources to devote to the next phase in learning. When tasks are very complex for the student, the quality of meta-cognitive skills rather than intellectual ability is the main determinant of learning outcomes (Veenman, Prins, & Elshout, 2002) "because learners have to improvise and use heuristics rather than call upon knowledge and skill components that are associated with intellectual ability" (Prins, Veenman, & Elshout, 2006, p. 377). The novice is more likely to use trial and error strategies, whereas the student with greater knowledge is more likely to search for all possible strategies that might work (Klahr, 2000). The novice aims to produce data, whereas the expert is more interested in data interpretations. The data gathering precedes the data interpretation. These claims are the case for both the learner and for the teacher.

Our cognitive architecture has limitations: we can only remember so many things at once; we can only devote so much cognitive processing power to learning and resolving dilemmas. We build higher order notions or schema to help us retain more in memory at any one time, and we learn various strategies to assist in the learning process. These limitations relate to the notion of cognitive load (e.g., Sweller, 2006). Certainly when first learning new material and ideas we need effective learning strategies and as much cognitive processing power as we can muster. Experts, compared to non-experts, have deeper and more principled problem representations that allow more retrieval and resolution, thus demonstrating how they can effectively use the load on their cognition (e.g., when playing chess, solving equations, reading history). A key difference, however, between experts and novices, is that it is deliberative practice rather than experience that matters—that is, extensive engagement in relevant practice activities for improving performance (as when swimmers swim lap after lap aiming to over learn the key aspects of their strokes, turns, and breathing).

Such deliberative practice activities:

> are at an appropriate, challenging level of difficulty, and enable successive refinement by allowing for repetition, given room to make and correct errors, and providing informative feedback to the learning [...] Given that the deliberate practice requires students to stretch themselves to a higher level of performance, it requires full concentration and is effortful to maintain for extended periods.
>
> (van Gog, Ericsson, Rikers, & Paas, 2005, p. 75)

All this practice leads to higher levels of conscious monitoring and control that leads to more refinement, and more higher order understandings of the surface and deeper level notions (Charness, *et al.* 2005). It is not deliberative practice for the sake of repetitive training, but deliberative practice focused on improving particular aspects of the target performance, to better understand how to monitor, self-regulate and evaluate their performance, and reduce errors.

The six factors

The next seven chapters of this book are structured around six topics—an assessment of the respective contributions to achievement from:

1 the child;
2 the home;
3 the school;
4 the curricula;
5 the teacher;
6 the approaches to teaching (two chapters).

Of course, there are likely to be interactions between these (another topic too rarely subjected to study and meta-analysis) and this will be returned to in the final chapter. There may also be moderators of these influences, although remarkably, such moderators are few and far between. What works best appears to be similar across subject, age, and context.

The child

The contributions the child brings to his or her learning include:

• prior knowledge of learning;
• expectations;
• degree of openness to experiences;
• emerging beliefs about the value and worth to them from investing in learning;
• engagement;
• ability to build a sense of self from engagement in learning, and a reputation as a learner.

The child brings prior knowledge of learning to their classroom—from preschool, from their culture, from television, from home, and from the previous year. Much of this prior knowledge leads to expectations by students and teachers about learning. A child is born into and grows up in a world of expectations. These expectations are powerful enhancers of—or inhibitors to—the opportunities provided in schools. They come from the parents, from the family, from siblings, from peers, from schools, from teachers, from media, and from themselves. Their own expectations can be formed powerfully from experiences in classrooms. By the age of eight, so many students have worked out their place in the rankings of the achievement equation. It is therefore a concern that one of the greatest influences on student achievement identified in this book is that of self-reported grades—students are very adept at knowing how to rate their performance. If these ratings are too low, then such expectations of performance can set limits of what students see as attainable. Hence, there is power in teachers setting more challenging goals, engaging students in the learning towards these goals, and giving students the confidence to set and attain their goals. A student's own predictions of their performance should not be the barriers to exceeding them, as they are for too many students.

A major way these expectations are manifested in the learning situation is via the student's dispositions. The key dispositions are the way the student becomes open to experiences, their emerging beliefs about the value and worth to them from investing in learning, and the manner in which they learn that they can build a sense of self from their engagement in the learning enterprise. While these can be changed within schools, they also can be formed and changed in the home, in the playground, via interactions with non-school activities (books, television), and, powerfully, by peers. There are many opportunities for parents and educators to mould dispositions that aid rather than hinder learning, such as developing the child's willingness to engage in learning, the degree that a child aims to enhance his or her reputation that can be gained from being engaged in learning, helping the child attribute success to factors such as effort rather than ability, and developing in the child a positive attitude towards learning. These positive attitudes of openness to experience, willingness to invest in learning, and intellectual engagement can be fostered in preschools, and then developed to a particularly high level in our schools—providing we can ensure that tasks are appropriately challenging to students, and that success is attributed to their investment in the tasks. This can then lead to a sense of reputation enhancement—students derive a sense of self and reputation among peers that they are "learners" (Carroll, Hattie, Durkin & Houghton, 2001). Therein lies success. Such personal dispositions can have a marked impact on the outcomes of schooling.

As will be shown in Chapter 9, having and sharing challenging goals/learning intentions with students is a major condition of successful learning, but on top of this it helps considerably if students share a commitment and sense of engagement to these goals. Many meta-analyses of the effects of intention on behavior have shown that intentions accounted for 28 percent of the variance of behavior, and is highest when students possess actual control over the behavior (e.g., Armitage & Conner, 2001, $d = 0.24$; Hausenblas, Carron, & Mack, 1997, $d = 0.23$; Milne, Sheeran, & Orbell, 2000, $d = 0.20$; Sheeran, 2002, $d = 0.27$; Webb & Sheeran, 2006, $d = 0.29$ between intentions and behavior change). Working towards appropriately challenging goals requires many attributes, such as commitment, engagement, openness to experience, and a desire to seek a reputation among peers as a learner. Levin (1988) has often argued that one of the most powerful predictors of health, wealth, and happiness in adult life relates more to the number of years in schooling than to achievement. Hence, a major goal of schools should be to *turn us on* to learning (irrespective of where we fall on the achievement ladder) and to assist us to be open to new experiences in learning.

There are many ways to entice engagement in learning. Steinberg, Brown and Dornbusch (1997) have argued that no manner of school reform will be successful until we first face and resolve the engagement problem—and they note that this is not merely an educational problem, but is "a more general barometer of adolescent malaise" (Steinberg, Brown & Dornbusch, 1997, p. 63). Too many students are "physically present but psychologically absent" (p. 67). Part of the problem is that students can be confused (cannot keep up, or classes are too difficult), also so many are bored (too easy, too few consequences of the learning). When one adds Nuthall's (2005) finding that most of the material taught in a class is already known by the students, and Yair's (2000) claim that students spend 85 percent of their time listening (or pretending to listen) to a teacher talking, then we make it difficult to foster engagement (see also Sirotnik, 1985). We need, claims Steinberg, better indicators of success, more challenging material, higher expectations, and more successful ways to orient students to succeed in school rather than merely helping students avoid the negative consequences of failing to graduate.

The home

Influences from the home on student learning include:

- parental expectations and aspirations for their child;
- parental knowledge of the language of schooling.

The home can be a nurturing place for the achievement of students, or it can be a toxic mix of harm and neglect with respect to enhancing learning. Many parents, however, begin with positive expectations for their children, and these expectations can be critical to the success of children when they go to school. A major concern, however, is the extent to which parents know how to "speak the language of schooling" and thus can advantage their children during the school years; some do not know this language and this can be a major barrier to the home contributing to achievement and to the realization of parents' expectations for their children (Clinton, Hattie, & Dixon, 2007). Schools have an important role in helping parents to learn the language of schooling so that the parents can provide every possible assistance to their children in terms of developing the child's learning and love of learning, and in creating the highest possible shared expectations for learning.

The school

School effects include:

- the climate of the classroom, such as welcoming errors, and providing a safe, caring environment;
- peer influences.

The effects of schools too often are overplayed—particularly in developed countries. Take two students of similar ability; in many developed countries it matters not which school they attend. Many of the school effects are structural (e.g., architecture of school, timetabling differences) or working conditions (e.g., class size; tracking, or streaming, of classes; school finances). Of course these are important, but they do not define the differences in student achievement: they are among the least beneficial influences on student achievement. That has not stopped these structural and working conditions becoming the most discussed issues in education.

Indeed, one of the fascinating discoveries throughout my research for this book is discovering that many of the most debated issues are the ones with the least effects. It is a powerful question to ask why such issues as class size, tracking, retention (that is, holding a student back a grade), school choice, summer schools, and school uniforms command such heated discussion and strong claims. Such cosmetic or "coat of paint" reforms are too common. So many structural claims involve the parents (more homework), lead to more rules (and therefore more rule breakers), have hints of cultural imperatives (quietness and conformity is desired), and often include appeals to common sense (reducing class size is obviously a good thing!). However, the most powerful effects of the school relate to features *within* schools, such as the climate of the classroom, peer influences, and the lack of disruptive students in the classroom—all of which allow students and teachers to make errors and develop reputations as learners, and which provide an invitation to learn.

Purkey (Novak, & Purkey, 2001; Purkey, 1992) has built a theory, known as "Invitational Learning", which works from the meaning of invitational as "offering something beneficial for consideration". His claim is that we need to create schools that invite, or cordially summon students to be involved in the learning process. The model is based on four propositions:

1   trust, in that we need to convince not coerce others to engage in what we would like them to consider worthwhile activities;
2   respect, in that we adopt caring and appropriate behaviors when treating others;
3   optimism, in seeking the untapped potential and uniqueness in others;
4   intentionality, in which we create programs by people designed to invite learning.

This is not "niceness" at work, but an approach that places much reliance on the teachers and schools to make learning exciting, engaging, and enduring. Where there are school differences, it is these types of effects that are the most powerful.

The teacher

The teacher contributions to student learning include:

*   the quality of teaching—as perceived by the students;
*   teacher expectations;
*   teachers' conceptions of teaching, learning, assessment, and the students—this relates to teachers' views on whether all students can progress and whether achievement for all is changeable (or fixed), and on whether progress is understood and articulated by teachers;
*   teacher openness—whether teachers are prepared to be surprised;
*   classroom climate—having a warm socio-emotional climate in the classroom where errors are not only tolerated but welcomed;
*   a focus on teacher clarity in articulating success criteria and achievements;
*   the fostering of effort;
*   the engagement of all students.

The current mantra is that *teachers make the difference*. As noted above, this message, like most simple solutions, is not quite right—it is some teachers undertaking certain teaching acts with appropriately challenging curricula and showing students how to *think* or *strategize* about the curricula. Not all teachers are effective, not all teachers are experts, and not all teachers have powerful effects on students. The important consideration is the extent to which they do have an influence on student achievements, and what it is that makes the most difference.

A most critical aspect contributed by the teacher is the quality of their teaching as perceived by the students. Irving (2004) created a student evaluation of high school mathematics teachers based on the National Board for Professional Standards for this domain (www.nbpts.org). After completing a study on the psychometrics of the instrument in New Zealand, he then located a cohort of American teachers who had passed National Board Certification in high school mathematics, and a comparable group who had not passed. He administered student evaluations to both groups. The students were accurate judges of excellence, and could discriminate between teachers who were experienced and expert from those who were experienced and non-expert. The dimensions that contributed most to this discrimination had a focus on cognitive engagement with the content of the mathematics curriculum, and the development of a mathematical way of thinking and reasoning. It is what teachers get the students to do in the class that emerged as the strongest component of the accomplished teachers' repertoire, rather than what the teacher, specifically, does. Students must be actively involved in their learning, with a focus on multiple paths to problem solving. As mathematical thinkers and problem solvers, the students are also encouraged to go beyond the successful solution of the problem to include the interpretation and analysis of the solution. All the while, students are encouraged to greatly value mathematics and the work that they do in mathematics, and always check the quality of their work to strive for the very best standards. As Irving argued, we should not overlook those who are arguably in the best position to evaluate the teachers—the students who share the classroom with the teacher day in and day out. The myths that students are capricious, and that they are likely to award their teachers high grades was not supported by this research (Irving, 2004). High ratings were not awarded lightly (Bendig, 1952; Tagomori & Bishop, 1995).

There is quite a jump down in the size of the effects to the next contributions related to the teacher: their expectations and their conceptions of teaching. As children are born into a world of expectations, similarly they walk into classrooms with their own expectations to confront teachers who also have expectations of them. Teachers also walk into classrooms with conceptions of teaching, learning, assessment, and the students. We need to better understand these conceptions as it seems they are powerful moderators of the success of these teachers. Having low expectations of the students' success is a self-fulfilling prophecy and it appears that expectations are less mediated by between-student attributes (e.g., gender, race) but held for all students in the teacher's class (Rubie-Davies, 2006, 2007; Rubie-Davies, Hattie, & Hamilton, 2006; Weinstein, 2002). What matters are conceptions of teaching, learning, assessment, and teachers having expectations that *all* students can progress, that achievement for *all* is changeable (and not fixed), and that progress for *all* is understood and articulated. It is teachers who are open to experience, learn from errors, seek and learn from feedback from students, and who foster effort, clarity, and engagement in learning.

The curriculum

Aspects relating to the curriculum that have an influence on student learning include:

- developing a curriculum that aims for the best balance of surface and deep understanding;
- ensuring a focus on developing learning strategies to construct meaning;
- having strategies that are planned, deliberate, and having explicit and active programs that teach specific skills and deeper understanding.

It appears from the many studies reviewed in the subsequent chapters that the major influences on achievement cross curriculum boundaries—the more important attribute is the balance of surface or deep understanding within each curriculum subject, which leads to conceptual clarity. The facility to develop a series of learning strategies for assisting students to construct meaning from text, develop understanding from numbers, and learn principles is important. These strategies must be planned, deliberate, and explicit, and there need to be active programs to teach specific skills and deeper understanding in the subject areas. Such strategies can then lead to further engagement in the curriculum, leading to the development of problem solving skills, and to the enjoyment of some control over one's learning. This then leads to further developing learning strategies to master content and understanding. A key feature is that many of these strategies can only be enhanced within a domain of knowledge and there can be little transfer (Hattie, Biggs, & Purdie, 1996). This is particularly the case when learning deeper understanding and developing conceptual understanding.

Teaching approaches

Aspects of teaching approaches that are associated with student learning include:

- paying deliberate attention to learning intentions and success criteria;
- setting challenging tasks;
- providing multiple opportunities for deliberative practice;
- knowing when one (teacher and student) is successful in attaining these goals;
- understanding the critical role of teaching appropriate learning strategies;
- planning and talking about teaching;
- ensuring the teacher constantly seeks feedback information as to the success of his or her teaching on the students.

The model of teaching and learning articulated throughout this chapter is based on having specific learning intentions and success criteria, as these frame the degree of challenge, the purpose, and the goals of the lesson. The common themes in what makes various strategies successful are the stipulation of planning, and in particular teachers talking with other teachers about teaching and planning, deliberate attention to learning intentions and success criteria, and a constant effort to ensure teachers are seeking feedback information as to the success of their teaching on their students. This can be enabled when teachers critically reflect on their own teaching using classroom-based evidence, and it can be maximized when teachers are in a safe and caring environment among colleagues and talking about their teaching.

Concluding comments

Teachers need to be actively engaged in, and passionate about, teaching and learning. They need to be aware of, and update their conceptions and expectations of students, and be directive, influential, and visible to students in their teaching. Teachers need to provide students with *multiple* opportunities and alternatives for developing learning strategies based on the surface and deep levels of learning leading to students building constructions of this learning. What is required are teachers who are aware of what individual students are thinking and knowing, who can construct meaning and meaningful experiences in light of this knowledge, and who have proficient knowledge and understanding of what progression means in their content to provide meaningful and appropriate feedback.

Teachers need to know the learning intentions and success criteria of their lessons, know how well they are attaining these criteria for all students, and know *where to go next* in light of the gap between current students' knowledge and understanding and the success criteria. Teachers are successful to the degree that they can move students from single to multiple ideas then to relate and extend these ideas such that learners construct and reconstruct knowledge and ideas. It is not the knowledge or ideas, but the learner's construction of the knowledge and ideas that is critical. Increases in student learning follow a reconceptualization as well as an acquisition of information.

Enhancing learning also needs school leaders and teachers who can create school, staff-room, and classroom environments where teachers can talk about their teaching, where errors or difficulties are seen as critical learning opportunities, where discarding incorrect knowledge and understandings is welcomed, and where teachers can feel safe to learn, re-learn, and explore their own teaching knowledge and understanding. Teachers must be able to openly discuss the three key feedback questions: "Where are they going?" "How are they going?" and "Where to next?" (The "they" refers to both the teacher and to the student.)

It is also what learners *do* that matters. So often learners become passive recipients of teachers' lessons, but as the meta-analyses throughout this book will demonstrate, the aim is to make students active in the learning process—through actions by teachers and others—until the students reach the stage where they become their own teachers, they can seek out optimal ways to learn new material and ideas, they can seek resources to help them in this learning, and when they can set appropriate and more challenging goals. Students need to be involved in determining success criteria, setting higher expectations, and being open to experiences relating to differing ways of knowing and problem solving. This then leads to their development of beliefs and reputations as a learner, and engaging in self-assessing, self-evaluating, self-monitoring, self-learning, and in learning the surface, deeper, and conceptual domains of worthwhile domains. Kember and Wong (2000) distinguished between active and passive students, and how they perceive good teaching. They found that passive learners preferred teachers who were organized, had clarity of structure, and could specify clear learning objectives, whereas active learners preferred teachers who promoted interaction in class, used a variety of teacher approaches, and displayed high levels of enthusiasm. An aim of schooling should be to maximize the number of active learners, but this requires teachers who can see learning through the eyes of their students and thence know how to engage them in learning that leads to these attributes.

As noted earlier, it is essential to have visible teaching and visible learning. This notion encapsulates directive, activating, and involved sets of actions and content, working with students so that their learning is visible such that it can be monitored, feedback provided, and information given when learning is successful. Fenstermacher and Soltis (2004) imagined the teacher as an executor, using the best learning skills and techniques available to bring about the process of learning. This is similar to the proposal by Salomon and Perkins (1989) that active learning and deep-level processing are central to success and transfer of information; or similar to the claims by Sheerens and Bosker (1997), who concluded that "it seems that highly structured learning or direct teaching, which emphasizes testing and feedback, again emerges as the most effective teaching form" (p. 219). They claimed that for transfer to occur there needs to be deep-level, connected knowledge structures—that is, knowing and understanding needs to be "conceptually deep, cohesive, and connected to other key ideas, relevant prior knowledge, multiple representations, and everyday experi-ence" (Pugh & Bergin, 2006, p. 148). This is particularly powerful when students know what they know and what they do not know (the meta-cognitive awareness) and when they apply cognitive processing and meta-cognitive strategies. Motivational factors influence the success of learning due to the higher levels of engagement that thence promote these learning strategies.

The major argument is that when teaching and learning is visible, there is a greater likelihood of students reaching higher levels of achievement. It involves an accomplished teacher who knows a range of learning strategies to build on the students' surface, deep knowing and understanding, and conceptual understanding. The teacher needs to provide direction and re-direction in terms of the content being understood and thus maximize the power of feedback, and to have the skill to get out of the way when learning is progressing towards the success criteria. It also requires a commitment to seeking further challenges (for the teacher and for the student)—and herein lies a major link between challenge and feedback, two of the essential ingredients of learning. The greater the challenge, the higher the probability that one seeks and needs feedback, and the more important it is that there is a teacher to ensure that the learner is on the right path to successfully meet the challenge.

Chapter 4

The contributions from the student

On each of about 220 days, for around 13 years, children spend five to six hours in school, nine to ten hours at home and in their communities, and about eight to nine hours asleep. When this time is added together with weekend and vacation time, students spend about 15,000 hours in school over a lifetime: or about 30 percent of their waking time is spent in the hands of those legislated to teach them. They also spend twice that amount of time (29,000 hours) at home during these school years, and they also spend 26,000 hours in the care of parents and caregivers *before* they start formal schooling (at about five to six

Table 4.1 Summary information from the meta-analyses on the contributions from the student

Student	No. metas	No. studies	No. people	No. effects	d	SE	CLE	Rank
Background								
Prior achievement	17	3,607	387,690	9,209	0.67	0.098	48%	14
Piagetian programs	1	51	6,000	65	1.28	—	91%	2
Self-report grades	6	209	79,433	305	1.44	0.030	102%	1
Creativity	1	21	45,880	447	0.35	—	25%	78
Attitudes and dispositions								
Personality	4	234	—	1,481	0.19	0.007	14%	109
Self-concept	6	324	305,859	2,113	0.43	0.010	30%	60
Motivation	6	322	110,373	979	0.48	0.047	34%	51
Concentration/ persistence/engagement	5	146	12,968	587	0.48	0.032	34%	49
Reducing anxiety	4	121	83,181	1,097	0.40	—	28%	66
Attitude to mathematics/science	3	288	732,994	664	0.36	—	26%	75
Physical influences								
Pre-term birth weight	2	46	4,489	136	0.54	—	14%	38
Illness	2	13	—	13	0.23	—	16%t	102
Diet	1	23	—	125	0.12	0.037	8%	123
Exercise/relaxation	4	227	1,306	1,971	0.28	0.040	20%	90
Drugs	8	467	13,161	1,839	0.33	0.036	24%	81
Gender	41	2,926	5,594,832	6,051	0.12	0.034	9%	122
Positive view of Ethnicity	1	9	2,661	9	0.32	0.003	23%	84
Preschool experiences								
Early intervention	16	1,704	88,047	9,369	0.47	0.041	33%	52
Preschool programs	11	358	44,532	1,822	0.45	0.065	32%	55
Total	139	11,101	7,513,406	38,174	0.40	0.044	29%	—

years of age). While the influence of schooling is probably substantial, by the time they are in their mid-teens it should also be obvious that what the child brings to the class at the start of his or her schooling, as well as on each and every day, is critical to the outcomes of education. Such out-of-school influences can come from the home, family, culture, and community. This chapter outlines some of these major attributes that the child brings to school, namely (1) background information such as prior achievement and personality dispositions, (2) attitudes and dispositions, (3) physical influences, and (4) preschool experiences.

The fundamental argument in this chapter is that students not only bring to school their prior achievement (from preschool, home, and genetics), but also a set of personal dispositions that can have a marked effect on the outcomes of schooling. While there is no doubt that schools can affect both achievement and learning dispositions, the origins of both are often well in place before the child enters the school yard. For achievement, there are influences from genetics and early development, very early home and social experiences, and opportunities for learning from birth to five years (e.g., preschool and other early interventions). The key dispositional ingredients are the way the child is open to new experiences, children's emerging beliefs about the value and worth of investing in learning, and the manner in which they learn that they can build a sense of self from their engagement in the learning enterprise.

While these personality (and of course achievement) dispositions are brought by the child into the school, they also can be changed by the school—and indeed are often so changed. A major claim in this book is that schools and teachers (and researchers) may need to be more explicit that such dispositions to learning should be key performance indicators of the outcomes of schooling. Many teachers believe that if achievement is enhanced then there is a ripple effect to these dispositions. However, such a belief is not defensible, as such dispositions need planned interventions and may indeed become precursors or barriers to further learning.

As an example of the kind of dispositions that could be fostered in schools, Feist (1998) completed a meta-analysis of the differences in personality between scientists and non-scientists, creative and less creative scientists, and artists and non-artists. Creative people are more autonomous, introverted, open to new experiences, norm-doubting, self-confident, self-accepting, driven, ambitious, dominant, hostile and impulsive—a powerful cocktail. Artists have more emotional instability and are more likely to reject group norms than scientists; and creative scientists are more conscientious, conventional, and open-minded. Of these personality attributes, the attribute of openness to new experiences is critical in the success of these learners. Openness to experiences involves the willingness (and it is an active process) to experience new ideas, to think outside the box, and of not being tied to one way of thinking. It also involves a motivation to explore ideas, and to invest in the process of learning.

Openness and willingness to invest in learning is the major theme of the synthesis of meta-analyses outlined in this chapter, and this willingness to invest can be seen in many children during their first years of schooling. The continuing experience in schools can have a growing influence on this willingness to gain self-confidence and a reputation of being a learner, and such skills can be taught. Such reputation enhancement is particularly powerful during the early adolescent years and it is during these years that the "decision" to continue in education or not is often made (see Carroll, Hattie, Durkin, & Houghton, 2001). Goff and Ackerman (1992); (see also Ackerman & Goff, 1994) have explored this notion under the heading of typical intellectual engagement and they have provided much evidence about the relationship between achievement and engagement derived from the stronger drive that some students have to invest in the development of skills and knowledge than others.

The remaining sections of this chapter refer to the four major contributions from the student: background influences, attitudes and dispositions, physical influences, and preschool effects. Each has a number of sub-categories, and for each sub-category there is a barometer console that shows the average effect size (and related information) for that particular influence; and themes are developed that are then linked together in the summary of the chapter.

Background

Prior achievement

What a child brings to the classroom each year is very much related to their achievement in previous years—brighter children tend to achieve more and not so bright children achieve less. This should not be surprising given that the correlation between ability and achievement is very high. Hattie and Hansford (1982) reported an average correlation of $r = 0.51$ between measures of intelligence and achievement (an effect size, $d = 1.19$). This high relationship accounts for what many researchers call (usually with a sense of surprise) the "Matthew effect", which is based on the biblical notion that the rich get richer and the poorer get poorer or do not gain as much. Prior achievement predicts success from preschool to the first years of schooling (Duncan *et al.*, 2007; La Paro & Pianta, 2000; Schuler, Funke, & Baron-Boldt, 1990), between high school and college or university grades (Kuncel, Hezlett, & Ones, 2001), between college and adult success (Bretz, 1989; Samson, Graue, Weinstein, & Walberg, 1984), and between grades in school and later job performance (Roth, BeVier, Switzer, & Schippmann, 1996).

Right through the education system, prior achievement is a powerful predictor. Schuler, Funke, and Baron-Boldt (1990) found that prior school grades are the best individual predictor for academic success. Fleming and Malone (1983) found that the strongest positive relationships between student characteristics and performance in science were general ability, language ability, and mathematical ability (Lapadat, 1991); and these findings were consistent across grade levels. Similarly, DeBaz (1994) found high correlations

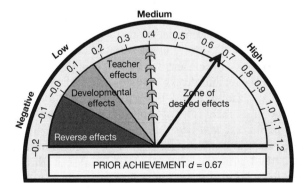

KEY	
Standard error	0.098 (High)
Rank	14th
Number of meta-analyses	17
Number of studies	3,607
Number of effects	9,209
Number of people (8)	387,690

between science outcome measures and ability variables such as prior scholastic ability, science ability, and cognitive reasoning ability (see also Boulanger, 1981; Piburn, 1993). The overall effect size of 0.67 is among the highest effect sizes in this synthesis of meta-analyses, although the common language estimate (CLE, see Chapter 2) should remind us that, on average, prior achievement will lead to gains in achievement on 48 percent of the occasions, although there is much that is unexplained beyond prior achievement (100–48 = 52 percent that is unexplained) and so there is much that schools can influence beyond what the student brings from prior experiences and attainments. It is certainly the case that by the time the child enters school, family, preschool, or genetic factors will have already played a major role in generating subsequent differences in school-based achievement. But one of the most fascinating outcomes of this synthesis of meta-analyses is that there are measures that schools can implement that are more influential than this prior achievement effect.

Duncan *et al.* (2007) found that only preschool mathematics (knowledge of numbers, ordinality), and then to a lesser extent reading (vocabulary; knowing letters, words, and beginning and ending word sounds) predicted subsequent success in school. Behavior (such as externalizing and internalizing problem behaviors) and social skills were not correlated with later academic success. Although he did not conduct a meta-analysis, Feinstein (2003) reviewed the evidence on achievement before entering school using the 1970 Birth Cohort Survey, a longitudinal dataset with over 17,000 United Kingdom children. The focus was on the children's performance at 32 months, 42 months, and at five, ten and 26 years. Their measure of ability at 22 months (i.e., putting on shoes, drawing lines, pointing to facial features) was a good predictor of achievement at age 26. Children in the bottom quartile at 22 months "are significantly less likely to get any qualifications than those in the top quartile", suggesting that "before children have even entered school, very substantial signals about educational progress" are evident (Feinstein, 2003, p. 82). The effects of social class (based on parental occupation) were marked at 22 months, and if anything, the variability increased over time. This dual influence of early achievement and socioeconomic resources contribute much to what a child brings to school.

Lack of academic success

The major difference between students categorized in special education and non-special education relates (as one would expect) to achievement (Kavale & Nye, 1985; McLinden, 1988; Rush, 1992). This is not quite so clear when labels such as "at-risk" and "drop out" are used. Of the many variables that Rush (1992) investigated in his quest to see what distinguished at-risk and drop out students, the only variables where there were differences between at-risk and drop-out students compared with those not so classified were IQ, educational aspirations, and locus of control. There were differences across regions throughout the United States, pointing to the social construction of these labels rather than to some similar notion of what at-risk and drop out students are like. As these students progressed into high school other variables such as lower self-esteem and negative coping strategies become invoked to label them. This is probably because these are consequences of earlier lack of academic success, and this also then leads to attendance problems, retention, and other negative outcomes, and the use of new labels like dyslexia, ADHD, Aspergers Syndrome, and so on (the latter are real phenomena but often over used as convenient labels, Conrad, 2007; Hattie, Biggs, & Purdie, 1996).

Kavale and Nye (1985) looked at parameters of learning disabilities in achievement, linguistic, neuropsychological, and social/behavioral domains. They concluded that learning disability is a complex and multivariate phenomenon involving a number of components each making an important contribution. A comparison of learning disability grouping and normal grouping found that about three-quarters of learning disabled students could be clearly differentiated from normal students displaying deficits that would interfere with their academic ability. Sabornie, Cullinan, Osborne, and Brock (2005) used 58 studies with "high incidence disabilities" and reported large effect size differences between learning disabled children and those with mild intellectual disabilities, but a lack of difference in many school-related behaviors for these same "labeled" students. Approximately 75 percent of those labeled learning disabled and 75 percent of those labeled as having mild intellectual disabilities surpassed the average student with emotional and behavioral disabilities in achievement.

Piagetian programs

Jordan and Brownlee (1981) found that the relationship between the Piagetian stage (logical operations, concrete, formal-operational) and achievement is very high ($r = 0.54$, $d = 1.28$). This is especially the case for mathematics ($d = 0.73$) and it is still high but somewhat less important in reading ($d = 0.40$). In both subjects, seriation ability, or the proficiency to think successively (as is required to decode words on a page, count in order) was the highest correlate. Thus, knowing the ways in which they think, and how this thinking may be constrained by their stages of development may be most important to how teachers choose materials and tasks, how the concept of difficulty and challenge can be realized in different tasks, and the importance of developing successive and simultaneous thinking (Naglieri & Das, 1997; Sweller, 2008).

Self-reported grades

Another form of prior achievement is students' estimates of their own performance—typically formed from past experiences in learning. Students have reasonably accurate understandings of their levels of achievement. Kuncel, Crede, and Thomas (2005) found that high school students had very accurate understandings of their achievement levels across all the subjects ($r = 0.80+$). This was the case for all but minority students who,

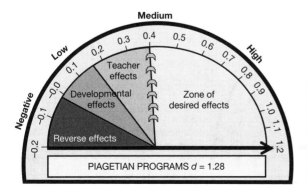

KEY	
Standard error	na
Rank	2nd
Number of meta-analyses	1
Number of studies	51
Number of effects	65
Number of people (1)	6,000

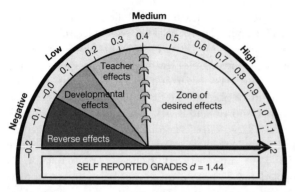

KEY	
Standard error	0.030 (Low)
Rank	1st
Number of meta-analyses	6
Number of studies	209
Number of effects	305
Number of people (4)	79,433

while they received lower grades than non-minority students, were more likely to be less accurate in their self-estimates or self-understanding of their achievement. Overall, however, students were very knowledgeable about their chances of success. On the one hand, this shows a remarkably high level of predictability about achievement in the classroom (and should question the necessity of so many tests when students appear to already have much of the information the tests supposedly provide), but on the other hand, these expectations of success (which are sometimes set lower than students could attain) may become a barrier for some students as they may only perform to whatever expectations they already have of their ability.

Creativity

Creativity is another prior influence on achievement, although achievement almost certainly also has a reciprocal influence on creativity (Hattie & Rogers, 1986; Kim, 2005). Murphy and Alexander (2006) evaluated the influences of knowledge, beliefs, and interests on conceptual change. The overall effects were high ($d = 0.80$), but greatest on domain knowledge ($d = 1.31$), topic beliefs ($d = 0.89$), concept knowledge ($d = 0.69$), and topic knowledge ($d = 0.63$). Programs with more hands-on activities had stronger effects than those relying on more passive methods such as videos or conceptual assignments. Those activities that directly addressed students' initial understandings were much more powerful than those which focused more on the presentation of accurate scientific information with less attention to students' current understandings.

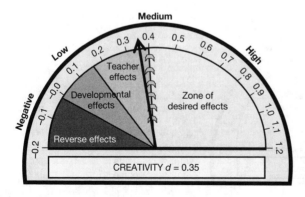

KEY	
Standard error	na
Rank	78th
Number of meta-analyses	1
Number of studies	21
Number of effects	447
Number of people (1)	45,880

Attitudes and dispositions

Personality influences

There were a number of meta-analyses relating to personality influences on achievement, and to the influences on achievement of self-concept, self-estimates of ability, motivation, concentration, and engagement. The overall relationship between achievement and many of the reviewed personality variables (including anxiety, dogmatism, extraversion, locus of control, and neuroticism) is close to zero. The relationships of self-efficacy, self-concept, aspects of motivation, and persistence with achievement, however, are among the larger correlates.

O'Connor and Paunonen (2007) provide three major reasons why personality variables could have an effect on achievement. First, there are behavioral tendencies reflected in personality traits that can affect certain habits that influence academic achievement (e.g., perseverance, conscientiousness, talkativeness). Second, whereas cognitive ability reflects what an individual *can* do, personality traits reflect what an individual *will* do. Third, as students get older, personality as well as cognitive proficiency can combine to better predict subsequent performance (especially motivation-related personality variables). To assess the effects of personality on achievement, O'Connor and Paunonen related the "Big Five" factors to academic achievement. The Big Five personality factors are neuroticism ($d = -0.06$), extraversion $d = -0.10$; Boyd, 2007), openness to experience ($d = 0.10$), agreeableness ($d = 0.12$), and conscientiousness ($d = 0.44$, see McCrae & Costa, 1997). All correlations were small except for conscientiousness, although there was much variance for openness to experience, which suggests that there may be some circumstances when this becomes more critical to enhancing achievement. Conscientious students are thought to be more motivated to perform well academically, are typically more organized, hard-working, diligent, self-disciplined, and achievement-oriented.

Lyubomirsky, King, and Diener (2005) considered the relations between cognitive and happiness outcomes. The average effect ($d = 0.54$) indicated that chronically happy people and those in pleasant moods are more likely to be creative and efficient problem solvers. There is a major moderator, however, as it seems that "people in happy moods can solve complex tasks better and faster thus freeing cognitive capacity for other challenges" (Lyubomirsky, King, & Diener, 2005, p. 839). When in a "good mood we tend to make riskier judgments if nothing is at stake, but make more conservative bets when real losses are possible" (p. 839). Although achievement was not the outcome in this particular

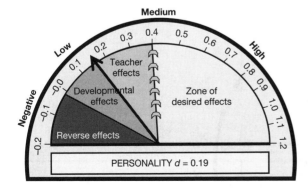

KEY	
Standard error	0.007 (Low)
Rank	109th
Number of meta-analyses	4
Number of studies	234
Number of effects	1,481
Number of people (0)	na

meta-analysis (hence it is also not included in the tables in Appendix A), Witter, Okun, Stock, and Haring (1984) evaluated the effects of education on subjective well-being. From 556 studies, they found a mean of 0.14 for the effects of formal schooling on subjective well-being, with larger effects on life satisfaction and lower effects on happiness (see also Csikszentmihalyi, 1997; 2000; 2002).

Self-concept

I argued that self-concept related to cognitive appraisals, expressed in terms such as prescriptions, expectations, and/or descriptions that we attribute to ourselves (Hattie, 1992). Later I refined the definition in terms of a "rope" analogy. Like a rope, self-concept consists of many fibers or dimensions that intertwine and overlap rather than having any one concept of self-overpowering all (Hattie, 2005). The first premise of the rope model relates to the maxim by Wittgenstein (1958) that the strength in the rope "lies not in one fiber running throughout its length, but in the overlapping of many fibers" (Section 67). The second premise is that there are various "strands" of self-concept that serve as primary motives, that then lead to the invoking of various situation specific orientations of self (or "yarns"), such as self-efficacy, anxiety, performance, or learning orientations. In turn these situation-specific orientations lead us to choose various self-strategies ("fibers") to serve the self-motivations and thus bring meaning and predictability to our sense of self-concept and self-esteem. Hence the rope model works as a series of interweaving threads, to form fibers and thence strands to make the rope—or the sense of continuity we have of ourselves. Primary to this rope model is that self-concept relates more to how we select and interpret the information that we receive and that we present.

Teachers often makes claims about the relationship between self-concept and achievement; the common claim being that students who are high achievers have high self-concept and that it is one of their teaching roles to make students feel good about themselves such that achievement then flows. Such claims presuppose a strong relationship between perceptions of self and achievement. Hansford and Hattie (1982) looked at the relationship between various self-measures and achievement and found there was a low but positive relationship ($r = 0.20$); a finding that has been replicated in the United States by Holden, Moncher, Schinke, and Barker (1990), and in Europe by Muller, Gulling, and Bocci (1988). Although there is generally a stronger relationship between self-concept of ability and achievement, too often this is confounded because the self-concept of ability

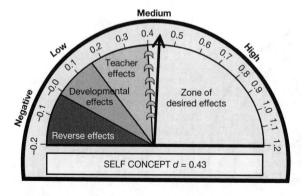

KEY	
Standard error	0.010 (Low)
Rank	60th
Number of meta-analyses	6
Number of studies	324
Number of effects	2,113
Number of people (4)	305,859

measures are more self-*estimates* of ability than self-*concept* of ability (which should also include concepts of pride, worth, and confidence). The relation between self-efficacy and achievement, however, is among the strongest of self-measures (Multon, Brown, & Lent, 1991). In particular, a sense of confidence is a most powerful precursor and outcome of schooling. It is particularly powerful in the face of adversity—when things do not go right, or when errors are made. Having high levels of confidence—"can do", "want to do"—can assist in getting through many roadblocks.

Valentine, Du Bois, and Cooper (2004) conducted a meta-analysis of three causal models that have been proposed to account for the relationship between self-concept and achievement: (a) the skill development model, which suggests that student achievement causes self-concept; (b) the self-enhancement model, which suggests that student self-concept causes achievement; and (c) the reciprocal effects model, which suggests that achievement and self-concept affect each other in a reciprocal fashion. They found that there was more support for the reciprocal effects model of causal relations between self-concept and achievement than for any of the other models examined. Valentine, Du Bois, and Cooper (2004) concluded that "these results lend further support to social cognitive theory, specifically that affective, cognitive, and environmental variables interact in a reciprocal fashion to determine human behavior" (p. 28). This should hardly be surprising given the low covariance between self-concept and achievement.

Further such investigations of causality are unlikely to resolve the directionality. Instead, it is more likely that there are stronger relationships between certain self-strategies and achievement. Achievement is more likely to be increased when students invoke learning rather than performance strategies, accept rather than discount feedback, benchmark to difficult rather than to easy goals, compare themselves to subject criteria rather than to other students, possess high rather than low efficacy to learning, and effect self-regulation and personal control rather than learned helplessness in the academic situation. The willingness to invest in learning, to gain a reputation as a learner, and to show openness to experiences are the key dispositional factors that relate to achievement. Maybe it is the choice of these strategies, not the level of self-concept, that is the precursor to achievement gains, and it is likely that success in achievement also reinforces the choice of these self-strategies. Maybe it is, therefore, not surprising that teachers have more difficulty changing the levels of achievement of those with non-supportive self-strategies; they may have more success if they addressed these strategies *before* attempting to enhance achievement directly.

Motivation

In the 1960s, the British philosopher Richard Peters (1960) challenged the value of the concept of motivation. He argued that the concept of motivation implied a push or pull notion, whereas children make decisions to do this rather than that all the time. Children are moving anyway so discussion about pushing or pulling implies a false assumption of a static being. Indeed, a major mission in education is to ask "Why math rather than billiards?", "Why spend effort on homework and not baseball?", "Why learn more when I know enough to pass?" The minimax principle—minimal effort for maximum gain— can be most strategic but hardly enhancing. Schools, however, tend to always ask for more and the overbearing request for more is often resisted by students who hear such demands from every teacher. A key aspect in the discussion about motivation needs to relate to the

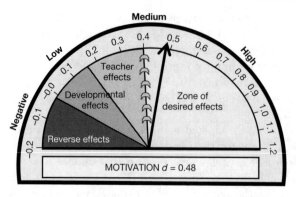

KEY	
Standard error	0.047 (Medium)
Rank	51st
Number of meta-analyses	6
Number of studies	327
Number of effects	979
Number of people (4)	110,373

purposes and goals, the learning intentions and challenges, and the personal strivings of students, as much as it needs to relate to the intrinsic properties of the task and who makes the demands.

There is much value anticipating when student motivation is at its highest. Dörnyei (2001) noted that motivation is highest when students are competent, have sufficient autonomy, set worthwhile goals, get feedback, and are affirmed by others. He also challenged educators to seriously consider student demotivation caused by, for example, public humiliation, devastating test results, or conflicts with teachers or peers. For many, demotivation has more impact than motivation. Such demotivation can directly affect commitment to the goals of learning, turn off the wish for and power of feedback, and decrease involvement. It can take less effort by a teacher to demotivate students compared to the often greater effort required to motivate them—to turn students on to learning.

Having a sense of control over one's learning can be important. Ross (1988) reviewed the evidence on the degree to which students learnt how to control their own learning (when completing science studies) and this was highly related to outcomes. This sense of control over one's learning, or a "person's beliefs about control over life events" (Findley & Cooper, 1983, p. 419) has been often studied. Students who take on personal responsibility for life events such as learning can be labeled *internals*, whereas those who consider learning are out of their hands are *externals*. The typical finding is that more internal beliefs are associated with academic achievement. The influence is greater for males than females, and more so for adolescents than for children or adults (Findley & Cooper, 1983; Kalechstein & Nowicki, 1997), although some have reported no such differences (Sohn, 1982). In their meta-analysis, Frieze, Whitely, Hanusa, and McHugh (1982) found that males make stronger ability attributions regardless of the outcome, whereas females have a slight tendency to attribute failure to luck. The notion that increasing achievement is a function of our efforts and interest is critical to success—there is no point, for example, in investing in study or preparation if we do not believe that our efforts can make a difference. Certainly interest plays a part in choosing subjects and choosing to commit to expending effort, and, as Schiefele, Krapp, and Winteler (1992) discovered, interest is also related to achievement ($d = 0.62$). The effects for interest and achievement were greater for females ($d = 0.70$) than males ($d = 0.50$), for the natural ($d = 0.68$) compared to the social sciences ($d = 0.48$), but similar across grade levels. Twenge, Zhang, and Im (2004) found that there has been an increase over the past two generations in students claiming that learning is more external than internal. They argued that students were becoming more cynical, and using more ineffective stress management strategies, and it could be suggested that the increased emphasis on external accountability testing models has not helped.

Concentration, persistence, and engagement

Engendering a positive attitude to school work may be both a precursor to greater engagement, and a worthwhile outcome in itself. It seems achievement plus effort plus engagement are keys to success in school. We should not make the mistake, however, of thinking that because students look engaged and appear to be putting in effort they are necessarily achieving; this is one of the myths that is held in too many classrooms—busy work alone does not make the difference. The discussion throughout this book about clear learning intentions, transparent success criteria, and making learning visible to the student are the key elements of engaging students.

Engagement in Kumar's (1991) meta-analysis was defined as the effective time within allocated science class that a student actively participated in learning—such as experimenting, attending, participating in discussion, questioning, answering, and taking notes. The overall effects were very high indeed ($d = 1.09$). Similarly, there were high relations between engagement and degree of concentration on tasks (Datta & Narayanan, 1989). Feltz and Landers (1983) showed that one way of enhancing concentration is to mentally visualize the processes and strategies involved in a task: students who mentally visualized various motor tasks were more effective compared to those that did not ($d = 0.48$).

These effects of engagement and concentration seem to be similar across ethnic groups. Cooper and Dorr (1995) found that there were no differences between African American and white students in their need for achievement, personal expectations, feelings of hopelessness, denial of the importance of individual effort, or lack of persistence.

Reducing anxiety

Spielberger (1972, p. 1) described anxiety as the outcome of a "chain reaction consisting of a stressor, a perception of threat, a state reaction, cognitive reappraisal, and coping". The meta-analysis research in education often focuses on two prominent forms of anxiety: test anxiety and mathematics anxiety. The subject of mathematics in particular promotes expressions of anxiety that take such forms as tension and dislike (attitudinal features); worry, helplessness, and mental disorganization (cognitive features); and fear (emotional

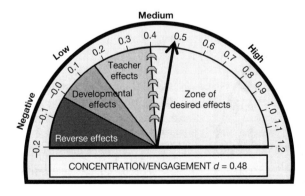

KEY	
Standard error	0.032 (Low)
Rank	49th
Number of meta-analyses	5
Number of studies	146
Number of effects	587
Number of people (3)	12,968

CONCENTRATION/ENGAGEMENT $d = 0.48$

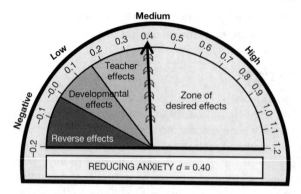

KEY

Standard error	na
Rank	66th
Number of meta-analyses	4
Number of studies	121
Number of effects	1,097
Number of people (3)	83,181

feature). The consequences of anxiety include avoidance of courses and an inability to achieve in the subject (Ma, 1999). The four meta-analyses discussed here were concerned about the effects of anxiety on achievement, although the effects have been reversed to indicate the gain in achievement that can occur if this anxiety is reduced.

Seipp (1991), for example, reported an effect size of -0.43 ($r = -0.21$) between anxiety and performance and noted it was similar for males and females. Worry ($d = -0.44$) was more negatively related to emotionality ($d = -0.30$), and test anxiety ($d = 0.46$) had greater debilitating effects than general anxiety ($d = -0.32$). Hembree (1988) established that test anxiety was significantly related to achievement for students from grade 3 and above. Relationships were stronger for worry than emotionality. Those students with high or low (as opposed to middle) self-concept tended to be more test-anxious, and there were direct relationships to students' fears of negative evaluation, defensiveness, and dislike of tests. Some specific attributes of tests that can invoke higher levels of anxiety include the use of "none of the above" as a multiple choice option, distorted pictures with word problems, and the presence of extraneous information in word problems (Hembree, 1987; Ma, 1999). Teachers need to consider methods to reduce anxiety, as it can be an important barrier to learning.

Attitude to school subjects

Attitude to school involves many dimensions, such as positive or negative feelings, the tendency to engage in or avoid school activities, a belief that one is good at schoolwork

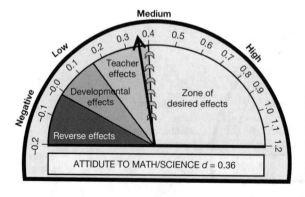

KEY

Standard error	na
Rank	75th
Number of meta-analyses	3
Number of studies	288
Number of effects	664
Number of people (2)	732,994

or not, and a belief that school is useful or not (Aitken, 1969; Ma & Kishor, 1997; Neale, 1969). The effects of attitude to mathematics on mathematics achievement are as substantial as the more generalized personality variables cited above, and potentially more amenable to teacher influences (Ma & Kishor, 1997). There are no major differences relating to sex or grade level (Ma & Kishor, 1997), although girls show slightly more anxiety to mathematics ($d = -0.18$), and less self-confidence in mathematics ($d = -0.12$, Etsey & Snetzler, 1998).

Although developing attitudes towards school and subjects is a desirable outcome of schooling, it clearly is also a correlate of achievement and it is suggested that by enhancing attitudes there could be reciprocal effects on achievement.

Physical attributes

There are a number of background factors that can affect children before they come to school—some are out of the control of the child, for example birth weight or illness, and some are more related to nutrition, exercise, and the use of drugs. Two of the physical attributes are among the most discussed moderators to performance: gender and ethnicity.

Birth weight

Bhutta, Cleves, Casey, Cradock, and Anand (2002) showed that birth weight of pre-term born children was associated with lower cognitive scores at school age compared with the birth weight of full-term-born children. They found that the cognitive scores of pre-term cases and term-born cases were directly proportional to their birth weight. The typical age of measurement of cognitive skills was eight to ten years. They argued that this decrease was not surprising given the developmental vulnerability of the immature brain, and factors such as severity of illness in pre-term neonates, their physiological instability and exposure to early adverse experiences. Of course, there are limitations (as noted in the article) of compounding effects such as socioeconomic, nutritional, and other family factors that could moderate these conclusions.

Corbett and Drewett (2004) investigated those children who failed to thrive in the early days and months, and while the effect size was not as substantial as with the pre-term babies, failure to thrive in infancy was associated with adverse outcomes at a later age. It is

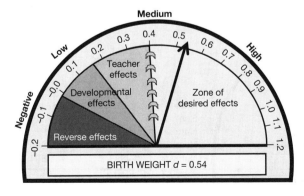

KEY	
Standard error	na
Rank	38th
Number of meta-analyses	2
Number of studies	46
Number of effects	136
Number of people (2)	4,489

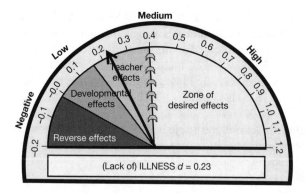

KEY	
Standard error	0.16 (High)
Rank	101st
Number of meta-analyses	2
Number of studies	13
Number of effects	13
Number of people (0)	na

extremely likely, however, that there are many successful interventions to ameliorate these early influences.

Illness

The effects of chronic illness on achievement are negative but small (Sharpe & Rossiter, 2002, $d = -0.20$). When parents were asked to rate the chronicity of the illness, they were much more negative than when children rated the impact of the illness on their achievement, possibly because they are more protective and children may not perceive as many negative effects as being directly related to their illnesses. The negative effects pertained not only to cognitive outcomes ($d = -0.20$) but also to peer activities ($d = -0.29$), psychological functioning ($d = -0.22$), but less so to self-concept ($d = -0.06$). There was not much difference between the chronic illnesses: cancer $d = -0.28$, diabetes $d = -0.23$, anemia $d = -0.26$, bowel disorders $d = -0.32$, and spina bifida $d = -0.26$, but cardiac illness was $d = 0.20$. These differences could also reflect absences from school.

Diet interventions

There have been many arguments that the eating of certain foods or the presence of food additives affects students' achievement. Kavale and Forness (1983), in a meta-analysis looking at hyperactivity and diet treatment, found that the Feingold and Feingold (1979) claim that reduction in artificial food additives (colors and flavors) is not an effective

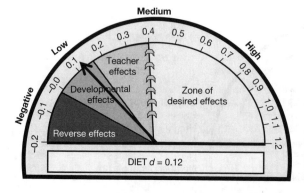

KEY	
Standard error	0.037 (Low)
Rank	123rd
Number of meta-analyses	1
Number of studies	23
Number of effects	125
Number of people (0)	na

intervention for hyperactivity. The negligible treatment effects from such interventions were only just greater than those expected by chance. Similarly Kavale and Dobbins (1993) found that diet interventions have a limited effect in terms of student behavior despite favorable public responses.

Exercise and relaxation

The relation between physical fitness and exercise on cognitive functioning is small but positive (Etnier, Nowell, Landers, & Sibley, 2006; Etnier *et al.*, 1997). The length or intensity of fitness programs did not have a differential effect on cognitive functioning, but relaxation techniques in general, and progressive relaxation techniques in particular, had a small positive effect on cognitive academic variables among elementary school and college level students (Moon, Render, & Pendley, 1985). Dishman and Buckworth (1996) found that intervention programs based on forms of behavior modification were associated with larger effects of physical exercise and achievement. Interventions in community settings and interventions delivered to groups reported larger effects, contrasted with those in schools and other settings or with delivery to individuals and the family. Effects were larger when the physical activity was not supervised compared with a supervised physical activity program. Effects were unrelated to the number of weeks of the intervention or the follow-up period.

Strong *et al.* (2005) identified 850 articles on the effects of physical activity on health and behavior outcomes among school age students. Most interventions used supervised programs of moderate to vigorous physical activity of 30 to 45 minutes for three to five days a week. They found that the addition of physical education to the curriculum resulted in small positive gains in academic performance, and, as important, allocating time away from other subjects to physical education did not detract from achievement in other subjects. The effects came mainly from small positive effects on concentration and memory, and enhanced classroom behavior.

Drug interventions

So often drugs are seen as the answer to reducing behavior problems and for enhancing attention, and there are claims they can increase achievement. The evidence is more equivocal. Purdie, Hattie, and Carroll (2002) investigated the effects of various drugs on

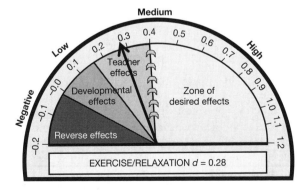

KEY	
Standard error	0.040 (Low)
Rank	90th
Number of meta-analyses	4
Number of studies	227
Number of effects	1,971
Number of people (1)	1,306

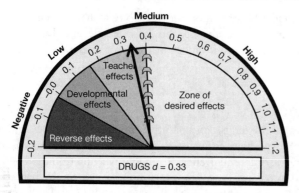

Standard error	0.036 (Low)
Rank	81st
Number of meta-analyses	8
Number of studies	467
Number of effects	1,839
Number of people (7)	13,161

students with attention deficit/hyperactivity disorders (ADHD/ADD) and while there was evidence that the various drugs (both stimulants and depressives) seemed to reduce behavior problems at least when rated by teachers and parents, although not by the students or independent observers (see also Crenshaw, 1997), there were limited effects on achievement. Crenshaw (1997) found an effect of $d = 0.52$ for classroom tests versus $d = 0.25$ for standardized achievement tests. In her meta-analysis, the effects on behavior ($d = 0.68$) were much higher than on achievement ($d = 0.29$). Ottenbacher and Cooper (1983) also found much greater effects on behavior ($d = 0.90$) and increased attention span ($d = 0.84$) compared to academic performance ($d = 0.47$, see also Silva, Munoz, & Alpert, 1996; Thurber & Walker, 1983).

DuPaul and Eckert (1997), however, found that school-based programs had a greater effect on the achievement of ADHD students compared to drug treatments. They investigated in-school treatment programs for ADHD students and their effect on behavior was $d = 0.78$ and achievement $d = 0.58$. Contingency management ($d = 0.94$) and academic interventions ($d = 0.69$) were more effective than cognitive–behavioral procedures ($d = 0.19$) in improving classroom behavior. The latter, they argued, is most effective in enhancing achievement effects.

Kavale (1982) found similar positive effects for stimulants but more so for lower level tasks (memory and copying, $d = 0.41$) than for higher order tasks (reading $d = 0.32$ and mathematics 0.09). In Purdie *et al.* (2002), it is worth noting that the effects of stimulants ($d = 0.35$) was not that different from school-based psychological and educational interventions ($d = 0.39$), social skills training ($d = 0.31$), cognitive and self-regulation programs ($d = 0.58$), and parent training ($d = 0.31$).

It seems that there is a syllogism in play here: drugs reduce behavior problems; when problem behaviors are reduced students are more likely to be attentive; when a student is attentive they may learn. Too often, the conditional "mays" are ignored and the straight causal connection made. While not denying that children with ADHD and other medically derived conditions exist, there does need to be concern about the pathologizing of barriers to learning. The concern for schools is to find teaching and learning processes such that whatever the etiology of non-learning, the aim is to allow students to learn. There are many successful strategies for teaching students to attend, to develop social skills, and to participate in learning, and labels should not be the excuse for why schools are not successful. All students arrive at school unique, and whatever their differences our aim in schooling is to provide optimal conditions for success in learning and not use labels to justify why these students cannot be as successful as any others (Conrad, 2007).

Gender

There is a received wisdom for many in education that there are marked differences in the achievements of males and females. Much of our popular messages are that "men are from Mars, women are from Venus" (Gray, 1993), or "boys are for mathematics and girls are for language"—there are many claims that emphasize the differences between the sexes (single-sex classes or schools, different programs for girls and boys, and so on). The predominant message from the synthesis of meta-analyses, however, is support for Janet Hyde's (2005) argument about gender similarities. This argument proposes that males and females are similar on most, but not all, psychological variables. They are more alike than they are different. The evidence for this claim is overwhelming.

Hyde (2005) collected 124 meta-analyses across many psychological dimensions, and although achievement is the major interest in this book, the message in most other areas is also one of similarity between males and females. Differences in communication (interruptions, talkativeness, self-disclosure, facial expression processing) were small ($d = -0.15$ in favor of females), differences in social and personality variables (aggression, negotiation, helping, leadership, extraversion) were small ($d = 0.18$ in favor of males), and differences in well being were small ($d = -0.06$ in favor of females). Larger differences were noted as exceptions to this similarity message. Males outperformed females in motor performance and physical aggression, and females outperformed males in agreeableness. Hyde also considered nine meta-analyses concerning achievement outcomes (all included in the current synthesis) and reported an effect size of $d = -0.06$ (in favor of females). In the current synthesis, the average across 39 meta-analyses and 2745 effect sizes is $d = 0.12$ (in favor of males). The overall differences are small and the gender similarity hypothesis advocated by Hyde is much supported.

The only question, therefore, is why we are so constantly immersed in debates about gender differences in achievement—they are just not there. The current synthesis shows that where differences are reported, they are minor indeed. For example, while sex differences are virtually zero in verbal ability (Hyde, 1981; Hyde & Linn, 1988) there are very small differences in mathematics (Freeman, 1984; Friedman, 1989; Frost, Hyde, & Fennema, 1994; Hines, 1989; Hyde, Fennema, & Lamon, 1990; Hyde, Fennema, Ryan, Frost, &

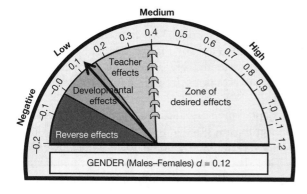

KEY	
Standard error	0.034 (Low)
Rank	122nd
Number of meta-analyses	41
Number of studies	2,926
Number of effects	6,051
Number of people (22)	5,594,832

Hopp, 1990; Linn & Hyde, 1989), and very small differences in science (DeBaz, 1994; Kahl, Fleming, & Malone, 1982; Steinkamp & Maehr, 1984). Girls' motivational orientation was more positive in biological sciences and chemistry, whereas boys outscored girls in physical sciences (Becker & Chang, 1986; Haladyna & Shaughnessy, 1982; Steinkamp & Maehr, 1984; Weinburgh, 1995). Whitley (1997) showed that males see computers as more suited to themselves than do females. Males also see themselves as more competent in computer-related tasks and have higher self-efficacy. Most differences were small.

Cohn (1991), examining sex differences in personality development, found that adolescent girls achieve developmental milestones, including ego development, earlier than boys, but that these differences declined with age. These differences are relatively stable during early and middle adolescence, moderately larger among junior and senior high school students, declining significantly among college-age adults, and disappearing among older men and women. In a meta-analysis of gender differences in temperament, Else-Quest, Hyde, Goldsmith, & Hulle (2006) found that girls have slightly higher scores on attention ($d = 0.23$) and persistence ($d = 0.08$), and very large differences on effortful control ($d = 1.01$) and inhibitory control ($d = 0.41$). Thus girls "display a stronger ability to manage and regulate their attention and inhibit their impulses" (p. 61).

Lytton and Romney (1991) used meta-analysis to investigate whether parents have systematic differences in their patterns of rearing boys and girls. Effect sizes in most socialization areas are small. In North American studies, the only area displaying a significant effect is the encouragement of sex-typed activities such as play and household activities by parents; physical punishment is applied significantly more to boys, and fathers differentiate more than mothers between boys and girls.

A meta-analytic review of gender differences in group performance (Wood, 1987) showed that while all-male groups performed better than all-female ones, the differences once again were small. Female group members' interaction facilitates performance at tasks requiring positive social activities including friendliness and agreement with others, whereas males' styles of interaction facilitate performance on tasks requiring task-oriented behavior such as giving opinions and suggestions.

A related attribute, leadership style, has been studied more in adults (e.g., principals) than school-age students. Pantili, Williams, and Fortune (1991) looked at the effectiveness of assessment by the National Association of Secondary Schools Principals in evaluating desirable criteria for principalship. Criteria such as sensitivity, range of interests, and personal motivation have almost no effect on job performance. Indeed, neither gender nor ethnicity has any significant effect on the assessment centre scores of principals, on any dimension. Eagly, Karau, and Johnson (1992) reviewed 50 studies that compared gender and leadership style in principals of public schools. The most substantial gender difference is the tendency for female principals to lead in a more democratic, less autocratic style and tend to lead in a more task-oriented way than male principals. Men adopt a less collaborative style and are relatively more dominating and directive than women.

Overall, the differences between males and females should not be of major concern to educators. There is more variance within groups of boys and within groups of girls than there are differences between boys and girls. Hyde (2005) noted, for example, that there was no evidence for Gilligan's (1982) claims that women speak in a different moral voice of caring and men in terms of justice, and that there is therefore no reason to believe men or male teachers are not nurturing and girls motivated by a sense of justice. Similarly mathematically talented girls and reading talented boys can be overlooked given the adults' (parents and teachers) beliefs and expectations about sex differences in these areas.

Ethnicity

It was possible to find only one meta-analysis specifically related to ethnic differences and achievement (although the research on desegregation had a focus on ethnicity; see below). The focus of the study by Allen, Bradford, Grimes, Cooper, and Howard (1999) was on racial group orientation and social skills, although they did include achievement as one of their outcomes. Racial group orientation is the degree to which a student has a positive view of his or her own ethnicity. Such students demonstrate enhanced academic success ($d = 0.32$), an increase in positive developmental adjustment ($d = 0.40$), a decline in participation in delinquency ($d = -0.23$), and an improvement in sociability ($d = 0.30$). It certainly seems that maintaining a positive image of our cultural background is most worthwhile.

There has been no meta-analysis, however, exploring differences in ethnicity and achievement. It seems remarkable that one of the more important moderators of influences on achievement has not been the subject to meta-analytic exploration. Within some meta-analyses (but not as many as I would have expected) ethnicity is used as a moderator. There are no differences in effect sizes for the amount of formal schooling (Willig, 1985, African American $d = 0.18$, white $d = 0.16$); the presence of fathers or not (Schneider, 1992, African American $d = 0.25$, white $d = 0.25$; Albanese & Mitchell, 1993, African American $d = 0.24$, white $d = 0.22$), social acceptance (Swanson & Malone, 1992, African American $d = 0.75$, white $d = 0.98$), and no differences in need for achievement (Cooper & Dorr, 1995, white $d = 0.02$ greater than African Americans for studies post-1970). The only difference related to small group learning (Evans & Dion, 1991, white $d = 0.48$, African American and Hispanic $d = 0.97$).

There is no reason, from this limited number of effect sizes, to believe African American and white students are differentially affected by what works best or by the underlying features of the model outlined in Chapter 3. What seems more important is that students have a positive view of their own racial group, and that educators do not engage in the language of deficit theorizing. Accepting that students come to school with different cultural heritages and that they can be allowed and encouraged to have

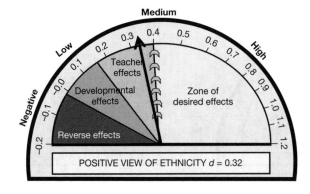

KEY	
Standard error	0.003 (Low)
Rank	84th
Number of meta-analyses	1
Number of studies	9
Number of effects	9
Number of people (1)	2,661

a positive image of their own racial or cultural heritage is an acknowledgment of the importance of culture, and can show the students that they are accepted and welcomed into the learning environment (see Bishop, 2003). Further, so much discussion is about the tail or gaps between white students and students of color—but such language is misleading as there are many gaps in achievement for students of all ethnicities, both above and below the mean of achievement. So often only the gaps below the mean are considered, and worse, generalized as if all students are near the bottom of the distribution (see Hattie, 2008).

Preschool influences

Early interventions

One of the claimed keys to success at school is the amount and nature of preschool experience that a child has before starting school. The overall effect of early intervention (any intervention with preschool age students) is $d = 0.50$, and for preschool programs (a specific program such as kindergarten) is $d = 0.52$. The overall finding is that early intervention programs are more effective if they are structured, intense, include about 15 or more children, and the children are in the program for up to 13 hours a week. This effect accrues similarly for regular students as well as for at-risk, disabled, and special education students. The effects, however, reduce over time and thus there is a need for systematic, sustained, and constant attention to enhancing learning if these early gains are to be maximized.

The benefits of early intervention are evident over a variety of outcome variables (including IQ, motor skills, language, and academic achievement) and across a wide variety of children, conditions, and types of program. The best early predictors of achievement in these meta-analyses are attention distractibility, internalizing behavior problems, language variables, and tests of general cognitive functioning (Horn & Packard, 1985). The more effective programs are more highly structured, and run by well trained staff (Innocenti & White, 1993). There is little support for the widely held belief that involvement of parents leads to more effective early intervention (Casto & Mastropieri, 1986; Casto & White, 1985; K. R. White, 1986), although there is support for the claim, however, that those most in need (disadvantaged students, for example, students from lower socioeconomic areas, or minority students) gained the most (Collins, 1984; Harrell, 1983).

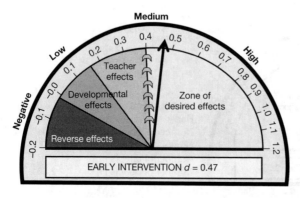

KEY	
Standard error	0.041 (Low)
Rank	52nd
Number of meta-analyses	16
Number of studies	1,704
Number of effects	9,369
Number of people (5)	88,047

EARLY INTERVENTION $d = 0.47$

Preschool programs

Goldring and Presbrey (1986) completed a meta-analysis of preschool intervention programs for disadvantaged children and found that preschool intervention programs do have positive effects regardless of diversities in sites, length of intervention and curriculum models. Children who took part in preschool intervention programs were still showing, in elementary school, a gain of about half a standard deviation more than counterparts who had not taken part in such programs. By high school the gain was negligible. Jones (2002) found that all-day kindergarten had high effects ($d = 0.56$) on achievement in early school—with the greatest effects on reading and language rather than on mathematics ($d = 0.60$ compared with $d = 0.40$). La Paro and Pianta (2000) also reported similar effects of $d = 0.43$ between academic scores in preschool to kindergarten and $d = 0.48$ between kindergarten to first and second grade for academic outcomes (and $d = 0.32$ and $d = 0.29$ respectively for social outcomes).

The type of preschool seems to be an important moderator. Fusaro (1997) found that children attending full-day kindergarten showed significantly greater achievement than those attending half-day. Applegate (1986) reported negative effects for day care compared to home care children on attachment directed towards parent, but they were less frustrated, cried less often, were less tense and showed less attachment towards a non-parent figure, had a greater increase in exploratory behavior, and were less often reprimanded. Day care children showed greater gains on cognitive areas ($d = 0.43$), emotional ($d = 0.56$), and social/behavioral ($d = 0.04$) compared to home care children.

There is little evidence that earlier is better in starting intervention programs, and any effects decline quickly over time (Casto & Mastropieri, 1986; K. R. White, 1986). For example, for disadvantaged populations, the immediate benefits decline rapidly and largely disappear after 60 months (Casto & Mastropieri, 1986; Casto & White, 1984; Kim, Innocenti, & Kim, 1996; White & Casto, 1985; White, 1986). Gilliam and Zigler (2000) synthesized the effects of preschool across 13 American states, and claimed there were sizable effects ($d = 0.2$–0.3) on achievement by the end of preschool, although these effects were not evident by the end of first grade.

Nelson, Westhues, and MacLeod (2003) reported that the effects of these preschool programs were greater if students were in them for at least a year, and were particularly higher for minority students. In mathematics, performance on standardized mathematics ($d = 0.25$) and reading ($d = 0.20$) was higher for participating than for non-participating children. By the upper grades (grades 7–11), a slightly higher percentage of underachieving

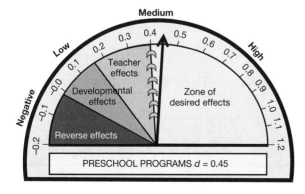

KEY	
Standard error	0.065 (Medium)
Rank	55th
Number of meta-analyses	11
Number of studies	358
Number of effects	1,822
Number of people (4)	44,532

students who had participated in preschool intervention programs did not need special education and were not held back a grade (Goldring & Presbrey, 1986).

Concluding comments

A common theme throughout this chapter is the powerful influences that the child brings into the school—via the effects of their prior achievements, their personality dispositions, and their preschool experiences. Equally noteworthy is the low to non-substantial effects of gender, diet, and exercise. While the very earliest influences of prior achievement (whatever is gained via genetics, early parenting, or preschool intervention) may be least influenced by school education, there are many opportunities throughout school to influence some of the key attributes, such as the willingness to engage in learning, the degree of reputation enhancement that a child can gain from being engaged in learning, the attributions of success to factors such as effort rather than ability, and the raising of positive attitudes towards learning.

Some of the most fascinating and important influences—openness to experience, willingness to invest in learning, and intellectual engagement—can be fostered in preschools, and then developed to a particularly high level in our schools. This can be done by ensuring that tasks are appropriately challenging to students, and that success is attributed to their investment in the tasks. This can then lead to a sense of reputation enhancement, whereby students derive a sense of self and reputation among peers that they are learners. Therein lies success. Such personal dispositions can have a marked effect on the outcomes of schooling. It is also worth noting that while many personality variables increase after students leave compulsory schooling (such as social dominance, agreeableness, conscientiousness, and emotional stability), this is not the case with openness to experience—which is one of the more powerful influences on achievement throughout schooling (Roberts, Walton, & Viechtbauer, 2006).

Many preschool programs can have an effect on these dispositions, as does the early development of successive processing skills, which can give children a head start in the achievement stakes. These successive skills, such as seriation, decoding sequences, and seeing from the parts to the whole appear to be given a major boost by participating in early intervention programs (Naglieri & Das, 2001; Luria, 1976). Students who have begun to master these successive processing skills before they enter formal schooling have an advantage when they begin the more formal learning.

Chapter 5

The contributions from the home

The home can be a nurturing place for the achievement of students, or it can be a place of low expectations and lack of encouragement in learning. Most parents, however, begin with positive aspirations for their children: certainly children are born into a set of expectations and these expectations can be critical to the success of children when they go to school. A major concern is that some parents know how to speak the language of schooling and thus provide an advantage for their children during the school years, and others do not know this language, which can be a major barrier to the home making a contribution to achievement. This chapter investigates the influences of the family resources, the family structure and environment, television, parental involvement, and home visiting. A theme developed in this chapter is that parents can have a major effect in terms of the encouragement and expectations that they transmit to their children. Many parents, however, struggle to comprehend the language of learning and thus are disadvantaged in the methods they use to encourage their children to attain their expectations.

Socioeconomic status

Socioeconomic status (SES) relates to an individual's (or family's, or household's) relative position in the social hierarchy and directly relates to the resources in the home. Such resources refer to parental income, parental education, and parental occupation as three main indicators of SES. The overall effect from the four meta-analyses based on 499 studies (957 effects) is $d = 0.57$, which is thus a notable influence on the student's achievement.

Table 5.1 Summary information from the meta-analyses on the contributions from the home

Home	No. metas	No. studies	No. people	No. effects	d	SE	CLE	Rank
Socioeconomic status	4	499	176,915	957	0.57	0.016	40%	32
Welfare policies	1	8	—	8	−0.12	0.030	−8%	135
Family structure	13	845	10,147,912	1,733	0.17	0.032	12%	113
Home environment	2	35	5,831	109	0.57	—	40%	31
Television	3	37	1,022,000	540	−0.18	—	−12%	137
Parental involvement	11	716	320,000	1,783	0.51	0.178	36%	45
Home visiting	2	71	—	52	0.29	—	20%	89
Total	36	2,211	11,672,658	5,182	0.31	0.058	22%	—

But it is important to consider the influences of these various sub-components of SES before discussing its effects as if it were a unidimensional notion.

In the meta-analysis of 58 studies by Sirin (2005), the effect size between achievement and parental education was $d = 0.60$, parental occupation was $d = 0.56$, and parental income was $d = 0.58$: very similar indeed. Further, there was an effect size of $d = 0.50$ with neighborhood resources, and $d = 0.66$ with free or reduced cost lunches (a common measure of SES in the US). There was little variability in the relation between SES and various types of achievement (verbal $d = 0.64$; mathematics $d = 0.70$; science $d = 0.54$). Sirin made much of a slight increase from pre-school through middle school, but the effects are not that different: pre-school $d = 0.38$, elementary $d = 0.54$, middle $d = 0.62$, and high school $d = 0.52$. The effects were lower for students in rural schools ($d = 0.34$, where there is likely less variability of SES within a school) than in suburban ($d = 0.56$) and urban ($d = 0.48$) schools. Overall, there were not many differences across these effects based on the key components of SES, so the question arises as to how these SES effects influence student achievement.

It is likely that the effects from socioeconomic resources are more influential during the pre-school and early years of schooling. For example, Hart and Risley (1995) showed that when students from lower SES groups start school, they have, on average, spoken about 2.5 million words, whereas those from higher groups have spoken 4.5 million words: this demonstrates a remarkable difference in what students bring to school. The lack of resources, the lower levels of involvement in teaching and schooling, the lesser facilities to realize higher expectations and encouragement, and the lack of knowledge about the language of learning may mean that students from lower SES groups start the schooling process behind others.

We need to be careful, however, about the unit of analysis used in these studies: is it the socioeconomic status of the school or of the student? White's (1982) meta-analysis on the relationship between SES and academic achievement noted the importance of distinguishing between effects based on aggregated units (such as SES of the school) versus effects based on the individual level (such as the SES of the student). The aggregate effect was $d = 0.73$ at the school level, whereas the effect was $d = 0.55$ at the individual student level. Further, Sirin noted that the effect was much lower when the data about SES were provided by the students ($d = 0.38$)—who probably saw less inequity in the difference due to home resources—than when provided by the parents ($d = 0.76$).

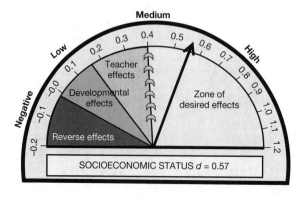

KEY	
Standard error	0.016 (Low)
Rank	32nd
Number of meta-analyses	4
Number of studies	499
Number of effects	957
Number of people (2)	176,915

SES is more important at the school than at the individual level, and for the parents more than for the students. This raises the question of the notion of adequacy of funding at the school level—that is, the sufficiency of resources for optimal academic achievement rather than equity, which usually means smoothing the differential resources at the student or family level but not acknowledging the increased level of problems and issues faced by schools teaching students from poorer backgrounds. A criticism of much of the school effectiveness literature is that the cultures and sub-cultures within schools are often left out (Slee, 1998). Certainly the culture and politics of schools have a major role in explaining why a school is or is not effective. A major premise of this book is that the visibility of teaching and learning is indeed a within-school phenomena, can be encouraged or discouraged by the culture and politics within schools, and probably can only be maximized as a function of within-school cultures and politics.

One of the ways this influence is manifested is that schooling introduces a *language* and set of cultural norms with which many parents, particularly those from lower SES families, are not familiar. In a five-year evaluation of five of the lowest SES schools in New Zealand, we found major consequences when teaching parents the language of schooling (Clinton, Hattie, & Dixon, 2007). This evaluation of what was known as the Flaxmere Project involved a series of innovations related to improving home–school relations within and between these five schools, including giving families computers and employing former teachers as "home-school liaison persons". The home-school liaison persons allowed the parents to learn the language of schooling—that is, the parents learned the language about the nature of learning in today's classrooms, learned how to assist their children to attend and engage in learning, and learned how to speak with teachers and school personnel. Involving parents with the schools via the Flaxmere Project led to enhanced engagement by students in their schooling experiences, improvements in reading achievement, greater skills and better jobs for the parents, greater awareness of the language of schooling, and higher expectations, high satisfaction, and high endorsement of the local schools and the Flaxmere community (the effect sizes ranged from $d = 0.30$–0.60 and occasionally were much higher across many outcomes). The greatest effects were an increased knowledge of the language of schooling and learning by the parents.

Either there can be efforts to reduce the barriers between school and home or the effects of the home on student learning can be compromised as the child is then asked to work in two worlds—the world and language of home, and the world and language of school. For many children this is asking too much. It is also difficult for children in these two worlds to build a reputation as a learner, learn how to seek help in learning, and have a high level of openness to experiences of learning.

Welfare policies

Gennetian, Duncan, Knox, Clark-Kauffman, and London (2004) found in their meta-analysis close to zero effects from students in families who received welfare compared to those not receiving welfare. While they make much of an effect size of $d = -0.10$, by claiming that the effects on adolescents were "significantly worse", it is difficult to imagine the visible effects of findings such as about four percent fewer mothers in the welfare program group reporting that their child performed above average, and only about two percent more of this group of mothers indicating that their child repeated a grade. There are certainly

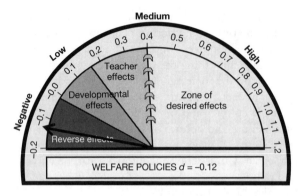

KEY

Standard error	0.030 (Low)
Rank	135th
Number of meta-analyses	1
Number of studies	8
Number of effects	8
Number of people (0)	na

WELFARE POLICIES $d = -0.12$

many other effects of welfare programs for these families that are beneficial, but it seems that there are other more powerful effects on achievement than the welfare status of the family.

Family structure

There are many types of families, and the effects of these different types could be classified as small compared to many other influences.

Single and two-parent families

About 70–80 percent of families have two parents in most Western countries, about 10–20 percent of families are single-parent, and about 2–10 percent are other than these structures. Pong, Dronkers, and Hampden-Thompson (2003) found that single parenthood is associated with lower mathematics and science achievement (although the effects are quite small). They also noted that countries with more generous welfare policies, like Austria, showed the smallest gaps. The greatest gaps were in countries such as the United States and New Zealand, who, they claimed, lagged behind other industrialized countries in providing financial assistance, universal child benefits, tax benefits and maternity leave benefits to single and poorer families. They concluded that "to some extent the investment in national family policies explains why Australia ranks at the top but the United States and New Zealand rank last in the academic resilience of children from single-parent homes" (p. 695).

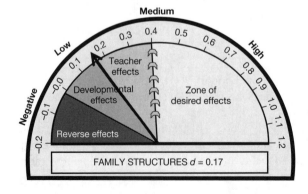

KEY

Standard error	0.032 (Low)
Rank	113th
Number of meta-analyses	13
Number of studies	845
Number of effects	1,733
Number of people (3)	10,147,912

FAMILY STRUCTURES $d = 0.17$

Resident and non-resident fathers

The three meta-analyses on this topic all found small effects on achievement relating to whether a father was present or not in the family. Amato and Gilbreth (1999) found small effects relating to the fathers paying or not paying child support ($d = -0.13$), contact between fathers and children ($d = 0.11$), feeling close ($d = 0.06$), and authoritative parenting ($d = 0.17$). Salzman (1987) found a $d = 0.26$ achievement effect of father-presence compared to father-absence. The effects were slightly higher for achievement ($d = 0.30$) compared to aptitude tests ($d = 0.20$), for elementary and junior high students than for pre-school, but there were no differences for males and females or across socio-economic groups.

Divorce

Compared to children with continuously married parents, children with divorced parents scored lower (but not by much) on measures of academic achievement, psychological adjustment, self-concept and social relations. Amato and Keith (1991) used 92 studies that compared children living in divorced single-parent families with children living in continuously intact families. The overall effect size was $d = 0.16$ lower on school achievement for the children in the former group although this difference was lower for the more recent studies ($d = -0.12$ for more recent studies, compared to $d = -0.23$ for studies 30 or more years ago). Other effects were $d = -0.23$ for conduct, $d = -0.08$ for psychological adjustment, $d = -0.09$ for self-concept, $d = -0.12$ for social adjustment: all small effects. Teachers saw no differences between these two sets of children ($d = -0.04$), and the effects were greater for girls than boys ($d = -0.30$). Amato and Keith also found similar achievement effects ($d = -0.22$) for children who experienced the death of a parent.

Jeynes (2006) compared intact versus parental remarriage and found the effects on achievement of the former over the latter was $d = 0.22$, but there were no differences between children from parental remarriage and those children in divorced or widowed families. He argued it is the increased interactions with two adults that is beneficial, but also suggested it may be difficult for children to make more than one family transition (to single or divorced then to remarriage). Kunz (1995) found a $d = 0.30$ effect, and the effects were slightly lower for school achievement outcomes ($d = 0.25$ for academic achievement, $d = 0.16$ for verbal achievement, but $d = 0.52$ for math achievement). The effects decreased with age, and she related many of the decreases more to the economic differences between one (divorced) and two-parent families. Kunz (2001) was more interested in the effects of divorce on interpersonal influences. From her 53 studies, children who had experienced divorce had less positive interpersonal relationships with their mother and father, but more positive sibling relationships (although the effects are all very small).

Adopted and non-adopted children

Non-adopted children had slightly higher school achievement than their adopted siblings; the adopted children outperformed their non-adopted siblings and peers who were left behind; adopted students did less well in school than non-adopted children—but the effects are small relative to other influences. Most important, age of adoption seems important.

Those who were adopted in their first year showed no differences (d = 0.09), and the effects increased if they were adopted in the second year (d = 0.32), and beyond their second year (d = 0.42). Although there were fewer studies where it was noted whether the children were subject to abuse, neglect, or malnourishment, the effects demonstrated by these studies were much greater (d = 0.46). Overall, van Ijzendoom and Juffer (2005) concluded that it seemed that "adopted children were able to profit from the positive change of environment offered by adoption and subsequent upbringing" (p. 327), but overall the effects are small.

Only and non-only children

A quantitative review of only-born child literature by Falbo and Polit (1986) found that only-born children surpassed all others except firstborns and children from two-child families concerning achievement and intelligence. In addition only-born children surpassed all non-only children, especially those from families with three or more children in positive character attributes and in the positivity of the parent-child relationship. Only-born children are indistinguishable from firstborns and those from small families across all developmental outcomes. Enhanced parental attention and anxiety are seen as facilitating the development of achievement, intellectual ability, and character. Polit and Falbo (1987) conducted a meta-analysis of the affective differences between only-borns and other family structures, and identified achievement motivation as the major discriminator (d = 0.17)—only-borns were more motivated and had better relations with parents (d = 0.13)—otherwise there were no differences across many affective outcomes.

Maternal employment

Since the 1980s, the majority of American mothers have been in employment, although the claim that this was somehow detrimental to their children was still a widely held belief. Goldberg, Prause, Lucas-Thompson, and Himsel (2008) showed that the effects of maternal employment on achievement were indeed trivial (r = 0.032). They could not find differences with respect to SES (middle/upper r = −0.043, lower-middle r = −0.055); ethnicity (white r = −0.028, majority African American and Hispanic r = 0.020), child's age (pre-school r = 0.020, elementary r = 0.061, high school r = 0.019), family structure (one parent r = 0.149, two parent r = −0.009), or whether the work was part time (r = 0.042) or full time (r = −0.005). It does not matter to a child's achievement whether a mother works outside the home or not.

Home environment

The home environment includes measures of the socio-psychological environment and intellectual stimulation in the home. Iverson and Walberg (1982) suggested that achievement is more closely linked to the socio-psychological environment and intellectual stimulation in the home than to parental socioeconomic status indicators such as occupation and education. They were not specific about which of these home indicators were most influential. Gottfried (1984) completed a meta-analysis on studies using the Home Observation for Measurement of the Environment (HOME) scale, which measures

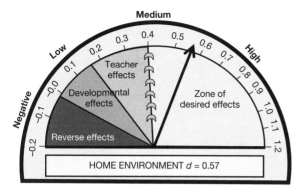

KEY	
Standard error	na
Rank	31st
Number of meta-analyses	2
Number of studies	35
Number of effects	109
Number of people (1)	5,831

responsivity, restriction, punishment, play materials, involvement, and variety. The most consistent and highly correlated factors with achievement were maternal involvement, variety, and play materials (Gottfried, 1984).

Television

The overall effects of television on achievement are small but negative; however, given the changes in technologies available to students (video games, computer and interactive technology), the effects of television on achievement are probably of far less interest and importance than most other influences on achievement.

A meta-analysis examining the effect of leisure-time television on school learning (Williams, Haertel, Haertel, & Walberg, 1982) found a small but negative relationship between hours of viewing and achievement. Effects were consistent across sample size, year, and location of the studies. However, the overall effects across the range of viewing times over a week were not constant. There were slightly positive effects for up to ten hours of viewing a week, while over ten hours viewing was related to negative effects with the strength of effects increasing with viewing up to 35 to 40 hours a week. Additional viewing had little effect. This non-linearity in effects is still found in more recent research (Ennemoser & Schneider, 2007). The adverse effects were greater for females and for those with high IQs.

Razel (2001) used six of the larger national and international data bases that asked about television and achievement. The overall effect was negative and there was this same

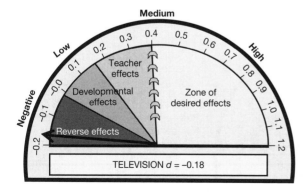

KEY	
Standard error	na
Rank	137th
Number of meta-analyses	3
Number of studies	37
Number of effects	540
Number of people (1)	1,022,000

non-linear effect related to hours of viewing. With up to two hours of television per day, the effects on achievement were small and positive; more than two hours and the achievement to television viewing relationship was negative. As important, the optimal viewing time (that is, when the relationship is at least positively related to achievement) decreases with age—younger children can watch more television with no negative effects, but by age by age seven it is down to one hour, and by 17 it is zero hours.

A similar non-linear effect was reported by Neuman (1988) in a synthesis of findings across eight American states (but not providing an overall effect size). She concluded that there was a curvilinear relation between television viewing and reading skills: children who watched a moderate amount of television (two to three hours daily) scored slightly higher, but those who watched more per day had a slightly lower effect size: But those viewing more than four hours a day had much lower achievement. The variation in effect size between these two groups of viewers, however, was small ($d = 0.15$). Her argument was that these differences were more reflective of parental characteristics. Parents of children who allowed unrestricted and unsupervised viewing tended to have fewer expectations and lower educational aspirations for their children than those who assumed greater control over television viewing. She found no support for the displacement hypothesis as leisure reading, sports activities, and spending time with friends all seemed independent of the time spent watching television. There can also be positive effects of television on pro-social behaviors ($d = 0.63$) and this outweighs the effects of anti-social behaviors ($d = 0.30$, Hearold, 1980).

Parental involvement in learning

There is much variance in the influence of parental involvement. There are negative effects when parents' involvement involves a surveillance approach, lower effects relating to parental involvement in early intervention, and much higher effects relating to parental aspirations and expectations and when parents take a more active approach in learning.

Casto and Lewis (1984) examined studies relating to parental involvement in early intervention programs and found there was little support for the idea that parental involvement leads to more effective intervention programs. They commented that while programs that involved parents could be effective, they were not necessarily more effective than those either not involving parents or involving them in a minor way. Similarly, White, Taylor,

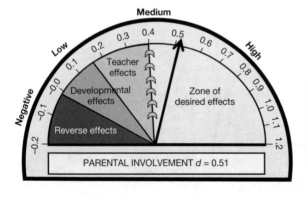

KEY	
Standard error	0.178 (High)
Rank	45th
Number of meta-analyses	11
Number of studies	716
Number of effects	1,783
Number of people (2)	320,000

and Moss (1992) examined the research on parental involvement in early intervention programs and found that claims that parental involvement led to more effective outcomes were without foundation. Often the effect of parental involvement, after the variance due to students and teachers are accounted for, is trivial at best (Innocenti, Huh, & Boyce, 1992).

Hong and Ho (2005) concluded that parent aspirations were the most important influence on their children's achievement, whereas parental supervision in the forms of monitoring students' homework, time watching television, and time going out with friends appeared to have a negative effect on the educational aspirations of adolescent students. Similarly, Rosenzweig (2000) noted that the relationships between student achievement and parental participation ($d = 0.56$) and supportive parenting ($d = 0.43$) were much higher than with homework supervision ($d = 0.19$), participation in school activities ($d = 0.14$), communication with school and teachers ($d = 0.14$), monitoring school progress ($d = 0.12$), providing structure in the home ($d = 0.00$), and controlling and disciplining parental style ($d = -0.09$). These effects were the highest in high SES families, in elementary compared to high schools, and in Asian and Latino compared to white and African American families. Of as much interest are those family variables that negatively relate to achievement. These factors included external rewards, homework surveillance, negative control, and restrictions for unsatisfactory grades. Overall, "the higher the hopes and expectations of parents with respect to the educational attainment of their child, the higher the student's own educational expectations and, ultimately, the greater the student's academic achievement" (Hong & Ho, 2005, p. 40). These high expectations are assisted by greater parent-student communication and the student's control over their own studies (see also Fan and Chen, 2001).

Crimm (1992) reviewed parental involvement and found greatest effects between kindergarten and grade 3 ($d = 0.41$), but these decreased with age (grades 3 to 5 $d = 0.36$, secondary $d = -0.05$). The most successful involvement related to tutoring ($d = 0.49$), and home visits and interactions by teachers ($d = 0.48$), and the lowest were parent training ($d = 0.15$). The highest effects were in reading ($d = 0.40$) while the effects were much lower in mathematics ($d = 0.18$); which is not too surprising given that parents are more likely to read than do mathematics with their children. Jeynes (2005) found that parental involvement was related to school grades ($d = 0.74$) and the best predictor was expectations ($d = 0.58$), which was far greater than parental involvement at the school ($d = 0.21$). In a subsequent study using secondary students, Jeynes (2007) similarly found

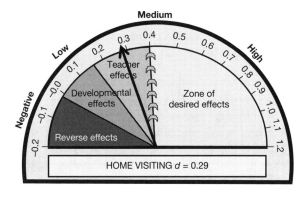

KEY	
Standard error	na
Rank	89th
Number of meta-analyses	2
Number of studies	71
Number of effects	52
Number of people (0)	na

greater effects from parental expectations ($d = 0.88$) than from other parent factors such as checking homework ($d = 0.32$), having household rules ($d = -0.00$), and attendance and participating in school functions ($d = 0.14$).

Senechal (2006) found that a more active involvement by parents was more effective. For example, the effect size from studies where parents taught their children specific literacy skills were twice as effective ($d = 1.15$) as parents listening to their children read ($d = 0.51$), which, in turn, was much more effective than reading to the child ($d = 0.18$). These effects were reasonably consistent from kindergarten to grade 3, for students with ($d = 0.38$) and without reading difficulties ($d = 0.74$), and for families from different socioeconomic status groups.

Home visiting

Sweet and Applebaum (2004) claimed that home visits by school staff not only reduced child abuse but enhanced school achievement. The effect on cognitive outcomes was $d = 0.18$ and on socio-emotional outcomes $d = 0.10$. Black (1991) was more specifically concerned with the effects of home visiting on learning disabled students. Most visits aimed to offer information and to enhance parental coping and child development; on average there were 36 two-hour visits over a year, The overall effect on cognition outcomes was $d = 0.39$, the effect on developmental outcomes (birth weight, developmental gains, health status) was $d = 0.13$, and the effect on social-behavioral outcomes (social functioning, interpersonal, self-esteem) was $d = 1.01$. This seemed to be a consequence of the more powerful effects of parenting ($d = 1.06$) and parent social functioning ($d = 1.52$).

Concluding comments

Parents have major effects in terms of the encouragement and expectations that they transmit to their children. Many parents, however, struggle to comprehend the language of learning and thus are disadvantaged in the methods they use to encourage their children to attain their expectations.

Across all home variables, parental aspirations and expectations for children's educational achievement has the strongest relationship with achievement ($d = 0.80$), while communication (interest in homework and school work, assistance with homework, discussing school progress: $d = 0.38$) have a moderate size effect, and parental home supervision (e.g., home rules for watching television, home surroundings conducive to doing school work: $d = 0.18$) is the weakest. Thus, parents need to hold high aspirations and expectations for their children, and schools need to work in partnership with parents to make their expectations appropriately high and challenging, and then work in partnership with children and the home to realize, and even surpass, these expectations. Too often, the alienation of the home from school reduces the initial expectations. The Flaxmere study, for example, found that, when their children started school, 98 percent of the parents considered that education was very or extremely important to their children's future. Two-thirds of these parents expected their children to attain diplomas and degrees. By the time they left elementary school, these aspirations had been dowsed and the parents mainly wanted their children to "get a job" (Clinton *et al.*, 2007).

Parents should be educated in the language of schooling, so that the home and school can share in the expectations, and the child does not have to live in two worlds—with little understanding between the home and school. Some parents know how to speak the language of schooling and thus provide an advantage for their children during the school years, while others do not know this language, which can be a major barrier to the home contributing to achievement. Parental expectations are far more powerful than many of the structural factors of the home (e.g., single or two-parent families, families with resident or non-resident fathers, divorced parents, adopted or non-adopted children, or only children and non-only children). It is not so much the structure of the family, but rather the beliefs and expectations of the adults in the home that contributes most to achievement.

Chapter 6

The contributions from the school

There have been numerous studies that have attempted to ascertain the amount of variance that can be attributed to the input from the school. Among the most sophisticated are multi-level modeling procedures that can assist in determining this amount of variance relative to other potential influences (Fitz-Gibbon & Kochan, 2000; Teddlie, Reynolds, & Sammons, 2000). This multi-level modeling allows estimation of variability at the student, class, and school levels simultaneously (and assessment of interaction effects across levels). As an example of its use, Konstantopoulos (2005) found that a substantial proportion of the variation in student achievement lies *within* schools and not *between* schools. If the variance is *within*, this means that factors such as teacher variability have a relatively larger effect on student achievement than do school effects. "It appears that the teachers students are assigned to may be more important than the schools they attend" (p. 36).

Alton-Lee (2003) has reviewed many of these studies and ascertained that between zero to 20 percent in student achievement can be attributed to school-level variables and 16 to 60 percent can be attributed to differences between teachers or classes. This spread is critical and seems to be related to specific policies in the various countries from which these data were derived. New Zealand, as an example, has among the lowest percentage of *between*-school variance (about four percent and thus the *within* school variance is much greater.) Using data from the Second International Mathematics Study, Scheerens, Vermeulen, and Pelgrum (1989) found that school effects were undetectable as a source of variance in New Zealand, whereas between-teacher or between-class variance was 42 percent. Harker and Nash (1996; Nash & Harker, 1997) found that the school effect in New Zealand high school performance accounted for between five to ten percent of the variance in mathematics, nine to ten percent of the variance in English, and five to seven percent of the variance in science. The message is that, if you take two students of the same ability, it matters not which school they attend, but it may matter greatly who their teacher is. It is not so much that *teachers matter*, as that the variance *within* schools indicates that some teachers matter more than others!

These messages about the greater relative importance of teachers than schools are commonplace in this literature. Willms (2000) concluded that "the pressure and support for change needs to be directed at particular teachers within schools, not simply at entire schools" (p. 241, italics in original). Muijs and Reynolds (2001, p. vii) asserted that "all the evidence that has been generated in the school effectiveness research community shows that classrooms are far more important than schools in determining how children perform at school." Rowe and Rowe (1993, p. 15) stated that "on the basis of our findings to date it could be argued that effective schools are only effective to the extent that they have effective teachers." Bosker and Witziers' (1996) meta-analysis found that about eight percent can be attributed to school-level variance when achievement is adjusted for initial differences between students and schools; and this variance becomes even smaller when other factors are controlled (such as variance between parallel classes and between grades). Scheerens and Bosker (1997) found that, when adjusting for initial differences between students, schools account for eight percent of the achievement differences.

The situation is quite different in less resourced nations (e.g., throughout Africa) where most variability is *between* schools (Bosker & Witziers, 1996); and in countries where there are high levels of stratification in school types (e.g., academic and vocational). Similarly the teacher variance is lower for achievement in elementary school reading where family and community input is comparably strong whereas teacher variance tends to be higher for mathematics and other curriculum areas that are less directly linked to everyday experiences of students (especially in the home).

One of the sobering conclusions from the above summary is that many of the influences that really make a difference to student learning in developed nations are within schools, from the influence of specific teachers, specific curriculum, and strategies teachers use to teach (Grodsky & Gamoran, 2003). Another important consideration is that there are many more factors *within* schools than teachers—here are also the effects of the culture and ethos of schools, the effects of the principal, and class compositional effects.

This chapter is divided into six major sections:

1 attributes of schools (e.g., finances, types of schools);
2 school compositional effects (e.g., school size, mobility, mainstreaming);
3 leadership;
4 classroom compositional effects (e.g., class size, ability grouping, retention);
5 school curriculum effects (e.g., acceleration, enrichment);
6 classroom influences (e.g., climate, peer influences, disruptive behavior).

Attributes of schools

Finances

Although the meta-analyses seem to indicate that money does not matter, this would be a misleading conclusion. Childs and Shakeshaft (1986) undertook a meta-analysis of studies

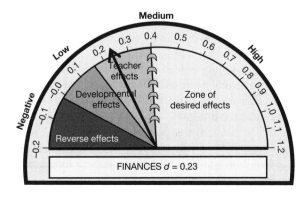

KEY	
Standard error	na
Rank	99th
Number of meta-analyses	4
Number of studies	189
Number of effects	681
Number of people (2)	2,277,017

FINANCES *d* = 0.23

Table 6.1 Summary information from the meta-analyses on the contributions from the school

School	No. metas	No. studies	No. people	No. effects	d	SE	CLE	Rank
Attributes of schools								
School effects	1	168	—	168	0.48	0.019	34%	50
Finances	4	189	2,277,017	681	0.23	—	16%	99
Types of school								
Charter schools	1	18	—	18	0.20	—	14%	107
Religious schools	2	71	54,060	71	0.23	—	16%	101
Summer schools	3	105	28,700	600	0.23	—	16%	98
Desegregation	10	335	6,731	723	0.28	0.060	20%	91
College halls of residence	1	10	11,581	23	0.05	—	3%	130
School composition effects								
School size	1	21	—	120	0.43	—	30%	59
Summer vacation	1	39	—	62	−0.09	—	−6%	134
Mobility	3	181	185,635	540	−0.34	0.005	−24%	138
Out of school experiences	2	52	30,554	50	0.09	—	6%	127
Principals/school leaders	11	491	1,133,657	1,257	0.36	0.03	25%	74
Classroom composition effects								
Class size	3	96	550,339	785	0.21	—	15%	106
Open vs tradiitonal	4	315	—	333	0.01	0.032	0%	133
Ability grouping	14	500	—	1,369	0.12	0.045	9%	121
Multi-grade/age classes	3	94	—	72	0.04	—	3%	131
Within-class grouping	2	129	16,073	181	0.16	—	11%	116
Small group learning	2	78	3,472	155	0.49	—	34%	48
Mainstreaming	5	150	29,532	370	0.28	—	19%	92
Retention	7	207	13,938	2,675	−0.16	—	−11%	136
Curricula for gifted students								
Ability grouping for gifted students	5	125	—	202	0.30	0.064	21%	87
Acceleration	2	37	4,340	24	0.88	0.183	62%	5
Enrichment	3	214	36,336	543	0.39	0.018	28%	68
Classroom influences								
Classroom management	1	100	—	5	0.52	—	37%	42
Classroom cohesion	3	88	26,507	841	0.53	0.016	38%	39
Classroom behavioral	3	160	0	942	0.80	0.290	56%	6
Decreasing disruptive behavior	3	165	8,426	416	0.34	0.037	24%	80
Peer influences	1	12	—	122	0.53	—	37%	41
Total	101	4,150	4,416,898	13,348	0.23	0.072	16%	—

on the relationship between educational expenditure and student achievement and showed that there was a minimal relationship between the two, and the most positive relationship related directly to the costs of instruction; for example for teacher salaries and instructional supplies. Teacher salaries, in turn, were more related to years of teaching experience and not teacher quality. Rolle (2004) also argued that more money was not necessarily needed but that there should be more productive use of existing resources. This is consistent with the claims often made by Hanushek (1989) that there is no consistent statistical relation between educational expenditure and measures of student performance. For example, Hanushek (2003) correlated high school spending per pupil and mathematics scores across 23 countries (from TIMSS, 1998) and found a correlation of $r = 0.06$. So often money is added into the education system with little attention to the efficiency or effectiveness of education outcomes. It is not the amount of money spent that is important, but how it is spent.

Murdock (1987) reported financial aid on college students had a small but positive effect on student persistence, and enabled low-income students to persist at a similar rate to that of students from other socioeconomic groups. While student financial aid is an important tool in helping students to stay in college, other factors such as the type of institution, the length of course, and year in which aid is provided (effects are greater with more senior students than with first-year students) all mediate the effects of financial aid.

In a rebuttal to the claims about the limited effect of increased finances, Hedges, Laine and Greenwald (1994; Greenwald, Hedges, & Laine, 1996) analyzed the effects of differential school inputs on student outcomes. Their analysis showed systematic, positive patterns in the relations between educational resource inputs and student outcomes. An increase in per pupil expenditure of $500 increased the effect on achievement by $d = 0.15$ for per-pupil expenditure, $d = 0.22$ for teacher education, $d = 0.18$ for teacher experience, $d = 0.16$ for teacher salary, and $d = 0.04$ for teacher/student ratio. Thus we can expect "comparable and substantial increases in achievement if resources were targeted to selecting (or retaining) more educated or more experienced teachers" (Greenwald *et al.*, 1996, p. 380). There is little evidence, however, to justify the notion of "substantial", but there is much consistency with other meta-analyses about the importance of the teacher (and costs associated with enhancing teaching).

The seemingly limited effect on finances can be related to the fact that (a) most studies have been conducted in well resourced countries (e.g., the United States, the United Kingdom) where the variance in resources to schools is not so substantial; (b) most finances in schools are tied up not in discretionary but in fixed costs (such as teacher's salaries, busing, and buildings) and these do not vary in proportion of costs across schools within any country; and (c) if the school composition effects are much greater at the within- than between-school level, then costs could make a difference within schools and less of a difference between schools (and most are currently focused on between- and not within- schools). As Hanushek (2002; 2003) has long argued, there are few incentives for a teacher to maximize achievement, as most of the financial incentives are related more directly to school rather than teacher differences.

The emphasis may need to be *not* on the notion of "Does money make a difference?" but on "*How* does money make a difference, particularly above and beyond the fixed costs of running a school (capital, lighting, salaries)?" It is difficult to imagine money does not make a difference at these critical margins. Jonathon Kozol (2005), in his scathing analysis of the restoration of apartheid schooling in America, *The Shame of the Nation,* cites Deborah Meier's comment that "I'll believe money doesn't count the day the rich stop spending so much money on their own children."

Types of schools

Charter schools

Charter schools have been one of the fastest growing sectors in the United States, and are often aimed to provide, so claim the proponents, what the public schools cannot. Charter schools are publicly funded schools that have been freed from some of the regulations and

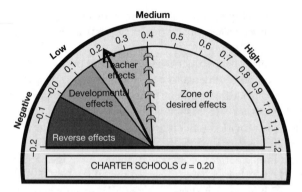

KEY	
Standard error	na
Rank	107th
Number of meta-analyses	1
Number of studies	18
Number of effects	18
Number of people (0)	na

statutes that apply to other public schools. They are often set up as autonomous schools competing with public schools, by non-profit groups or universities, often with a particular flavor, and they usually involve some form of innovative teaching principles. In return, they are expected to have high levels of accountability for student outcomes.

Miron and Nelson (2001) found an effect size of $d = 0.20$ when comparing achievement in charter and regular schools, but when the lower quality studies were excluded, this difference dropped to zero. They concluded that, in spite of the topic's importance to the debate over charter schools and school reform, it is striking how little we currently know about the effect of charter schools on student achievement. They noted that only eight of the 38 states with charter school laws had useable independent evaluations of achievement effects. Not surprisingly, given the close to zero effect, there is a mixture of positive and negative effects, and there is much variation across the states. The hype and promise is much greater than the effects on student achievement.

Religious schools

As was the case with charter schools, much has been written about how different religious schools are from public schools—and indeed they should be. Many have claimed that students in religious schools outperform their public school peers, mainly because of the increased attention to the teacher-student relationship, a greater fostering of parent-school interactions, shared values between families and school, the underlying philosophies of caring and commitment, and a higher work ethic (e.g., Coleman, 1992;

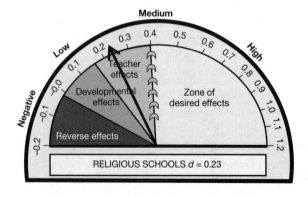

KEY	
Standard error	na
Rank	101st
Number of meta-analyses	2
Number of studies	71
Number of effects	71
Number of people (1)	54,060

Russo & Rogus, 1998). The dividend of attending religious schools is supposedly greater for those from lower socioeconomic backgrounds. Jeynes (2002) found that African American and Hispanic students attending religious schools (mainly Christian schools) had a $d = 0.25$ effect size increase over those who attended a public school. The effects were similar in reading ($d = 0.25$) and mathematics ($d = 0.25$), and also higher on school-related behavior ($d = 0.32$). These effects could not be attributed to differing socioeconomic variables, were remarkably consistent in favor of religious schools, and slightly stronger for high school and middle school than elementary school students.

Summer schools

Does going to summer school make a difference? In general, not much, but it is difficult to ignore even these small gains if they are critical to students who may be already marginal (as that is often the criteria for selection). Cooper, Charlton, Valentine, Muhlenbruck, and Borman (2000) analyzed 93 summer programs and their students scored about $d = 0.23$ greater than those not in summer schools, although the effects were more positive for middle-class than students from disadvantaged backgrounds. Higher effects were found for programs more specifically tailored to the student needs, when parents were involved, for mathematics more than reading, and the effects were the same across all grade levels. Both Cooper *et al.* (2000) and Kim (2002) also found small effects from both remedial and acceleration summer programs.

This pattern was replicated by Kim (2002). He found no significant differences relating to the purposes of the summer school: remediation $d = 0.16$, enrichment $d = 0.16$, bridging to high school $d = 0.25$, assisting grade promotion $d = 0.21$. Nor were there differences as to whether the summer school was related ($d = 0.22$) or not ($d = 0.14$) to the school curriculum, whether it was monitored ($d = 0.16$) or not ($d = 0.16$), whether there was a teacher training component for the summer school ($d = 0.21$) or not ($d = 0.14$), whether it used current teachers at the school ($d = 0.12$) or not ($d = 0.17$) whether food was offered ($d = 0.18$) or not ($d = 0.14$), whether the class sizes were above 25 ($d = 0.18$) or below 25 ($d = 0.15$), or whether the number of hours of instruction were high (< 132 hours $d = 0.11$) or not ($d = 0.16$). High achievers gained more ($d = 0.22$) compared to lower achievers ($d = 0.12$), and middle and higher SES students ($d = 0.21$) gained more than lower SES students ($d = 0.12$).

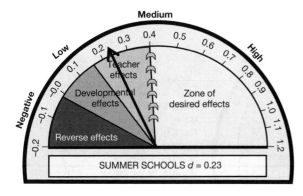

KEY	
Standard error	na
Rank	98th
Number of meta-analyses	3
Number of studies	105
Number of effects	600
Number of people (2)	28,700

SUMMER SCHOOLS $d = 0.23$

Desegregation

Desegregation is a process aimed at ending racial segregation, typically used in reference to the United States, and started in earnest following the Civil Rights legislation in the 1960s. It was argued that by such measures the United States would be more likely to achieve the more ambitious goal of racial integration. McEvoy's (1982) meta-analysis comparing the effect of desegregation on African American students in desegregated and non-desegregated groups concluded that students in desegregated schools performed at higher achievement levels than students in control groups ($d = 0.20$), although he reported no differences on self-esteem. He found that studies with control groups showed greater effect than studies without controls ($d = 0.48$ compared to -0.09); and studies of more than one year demonstrated greater effect than those of less than one year ($d = 0.27$ compared to -0.07). There was not that much difference between mathematics and verbal language skills ($d = 0.28$ and $d = 0.20$), or between elementary and high school students ($d = 0.22$ and $d = 0.18$, respectively).

In contrast to findings on the positive effects of desegregation, both Armor (1983) and Krol (1980) found there to be virtually no effects from desegregation on the achievement of African American students in reading and mathematics. Crain and Mahard (1982) also found that desegregation improved achievement for African American students by about $d = 0.08$, but noted that there were only marked effects in the earliest primary grades ($d = 0.44$). Two methodological factors correlated with the measured effect of desegregation on academic achievement: studies where students received only partial treatment (i.e., began desegregation after completing one or more years of segregated schooling) and the type of control group. Stephan (1983) found that desegregation resulted in improvement in the reading achievement results of African American students but there was no effect on mathematics. Younger students benefited more than older students in reading. In a small number of studies where desegregation was voluntary, reading achievement was significantly better; however the number of studies means this finding is not conclusive. Miller and Carlson (1982) also noted that while they found desegregation to have had a moderate positive effect on the academic achievement of African American students, there was improvement in verbal but not mathematics achievement.

Wortman and Bryant (1985) analyzed much the same data as Stephan (1983) and Krol (1980)—although Wortman and Bryant rejected articles they considered of lower quality, thus removing 79 articles. They then reported a mean effect of $d = 0.45$ but noted that effects "for the better designed quasi-experiments are considerably smaller" (Wortman & Bryant, 1985, p. 304)—reducing the mean effect to $d = 0.20$ for those with no selection

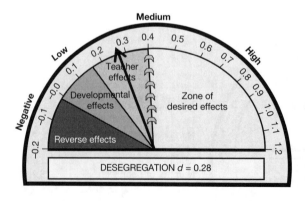

KEY	
Standard error	0.060 (Medium)
Rank	91st
Number of meta-analyses	10
Number of studies	335
Number of effects	723
Number of people (1)	6,731

problems. They found similar effects for elementary ($d = 0.43$) and high school ($d = 0.55$), and reading ($d = 0.57$) was higher than mathematics ($d = 0.33$).

In a different ethnic comparison, Goldring and Addi (1989), examining the ethnic composition of the classroom and in reading comprehension achievement in Israel, found that integrated classrooms, compared to minority segregated classrooms, provided a better learning environment for students of both Asian–African and western origins.

Overall, desegregation is a topic where the meta-analyses show a wide variation in the effect sizes typically relating to the selection process for the inclusion of articles. It is likely that there are many more critical factors than the composition of the classroom that affect achievement—and the success of desegregation may be better assessed to the degree it provides opportunities and diversity than achievement effects.

College halls of residence

Interest in whether residing in residential halls or not has an affect on achievement has been primarily the domain of colleges and universities. Blimling (1999) found that it did not matter whether a student lived in a college, at home, in a fraternity or sorority house, or in off-campus housing or flats. His message was that the zero effect he found should lead to many institutions (such as residential halls) seriously questioning the educational value they were adding to student learning—and clearly they are not adding value at the moment.

School compositional effects

School compositional effects include the size of schools, the effects of summer vacation, mobility, and out-of-school experiences.

School size

Another school level effect is the enrollment size of the school. Stekelenburg (1991) found effects of $d = 0.47$ between size of high school and achievement, which is quite substantial for a structural effect, although he considered these relatively small. He argued that while very small schools can be expensive to operate, the curriculum advantages of larger schools start to reduce in their effectiveness as they grow much beyond 800. He considered the optimal size to be about 800, and argued that the "smaller the high school, the more it

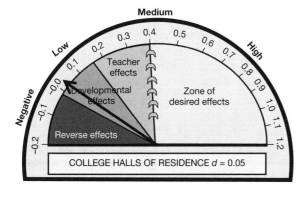

KEY	
Standard error	na
Rank	130th
Number of meta-analyses	1
Number of studies	10
Number of effects	23
Number of people (1)	11,581

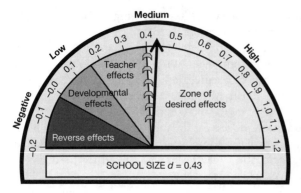

KEY	
Standard error	na
Rank	59th
Number of meta-analyses	1
Number of studies	21
Number of effects	120
Number of people (0)	na

appears that increasing enrollment correlates positively with higher test scores. Consolidating very small (high schools) may be more important than consolidating large ones" (Stekelenburg, 1991, p. 111).

There is thus a message about an "optimal" size, and too small or too large may reduce effectiveness. Ready, Lee, and Welner (2004) explored the effects of school size across more than 800 schools and concluded that achievement gains in mathematics and reading over the course of high school were largest in middle-sized high schools (600–900 students). Similarly, Lee and Smith (1997) found that achievement gains in mathematics and reading over the course of high school were largest in middle-sized high schools (600–800 students). There is an important moderator to this conclusion about optimal school size; the more affluent a school's student cohort then the larger the optimal size, and the higher the proportion of minority students then the smaller the optimal size (Howley & Bickel, 1999; Lee & Smith, 1997). In other organizations there also appears to be a curvilinear relation between size and outcomes: Gooding and Wagner (1985) conducted a meta-analysis of 31 studies of the relationship between organizational size and economic efficacy. After a certain size, they found that increasing the size of a business increased total output but the ratio of output to input typically remained the same, particularly in organizations that depended primarily on human effort, such as schools. A major reason was the increased coordination costs with no return in extra benefits.

Newman *et al.* (2006) reported that teachers and students at smaller schools are more likely to have positive perceptions of their school environment, although costs per student decrease as school size increases. Lee and Smith (1993; 1997) found that in high schools of between 600 to 900 students, there was more teacher collaboration and team teaching, and teachers had more input into decisions affecting their work. Bryk, Easton, Kerbow, Rollow, and Sebring (1993) added other reasons such as better personal social interactions among students and faculty, more leadership experience for students, and a feeling by students that teachers are more interested in them. Perhaps among the more important reasons are that schools with 600 to 900 students typically offer strong core curriculum to all students and there is less likelihood of using electives to stream and dilute the curriculum (cf. Walberg & Walberg, 1994).

Summer vacation

In the early years of formal schooling in America, the school calendar (including the long summer break) was designed to meet the needs of agricultural communities (Cooper, Nye,

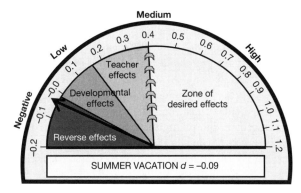

KEY	
Standard error	na
Rank	134th
Number of meta-analyses	1
Number of studies	39
Number of effects	62
Number of people (0)	na

Charlton, Lindsay, & Greathouse, 1996). Today with only about three percent of American's livelihood being linked to agricultural cycles, there have been calls for change to lessen the effect of the long break on learning and on the retention and acquisition of knowledge. Supporters of change consider a three-month break too long as children learn best when learning is continuous, and the break means significant time needs to be spent reviewing previous material in order for learning to commence again (Cooper *et al.*, 1996).

On average, this meta-analysis showed students lost some achievement gains over the summer ($d = -0.09$), and the effects were slightly larger in mathematics ($d = -0.14$) than in reading and language ($d = -0.05$, Cooper *et al.*, 1996). Compared to all other effects, these are minor indeed. Middle class students appeared to gain on grade-level equivalent reading recognition tests over summer ($d = 0.13$) compared to lower class students ($d = -0.14$). There were no moderating effects for gender or race but the negative effect of summer did increase with grade level (see also Burkam, Ready, Lee, & LoGerfo, 2004). It may be that if teachers were more attuned to the proficiencies that students bring into their classrooms, then the first month of the school year could be used to recapture the losses from the summer break reasonably quickly.

Mobility

The effect of student mobility between schools a quite marked. Transience, or mobility across schools, has become a major trend in recent decades. In New Zealand, for example, 40 percent of all students change schools each year (including moving from elementary to

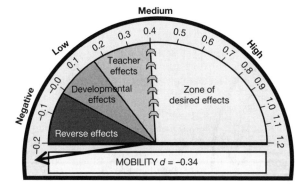

KEY	
Standard error	0.005 (Low)
Rank	138th
Number of meta-analyses	3
Number of studies	181
Number of effects	540
Number of people (1)	185,635

middle, from middle to high and more recently from junior to senior high schools), and in the United States, 20 percent change residence each year. The effects of such mobility on reading and mathematics are negative (Mehana, 1997, $d = -0.27$ vs. $d = -0.22$). Jones (1989), who found similar effects, argued that it was *any* changing of schools that made the negative effect, as mobility was not negatively related to the total number of moves, nor to socioeconomic status or ethnicity.

The reasons for this decline may be many, but a most important cause relates to peer effects. Galton and Willcocks (1983) followed students longitudinally and every change of school caused negative effects. They noted that typically there were adjustment issues, including problems with friendship patterns, particularly friendships to support learning. Whenever there is a major transition in schools, then the key success factor is whether a child makes a friend in the first month (cf., Galton, 1995; Pratt & George, 2005). It is incumbent, therefore, for schools to attend to student friendships and ensure the class makes newcomers welcomed, if this marked decline from mobility is to be reduced.

Out-of-school curriculum experiences

Children have more discretionary time outside school hours than ever before. Some parents worry that out-of-school experiences can involve harm (such as participation in drugs and other non-social activities) or can be non-productive (watching television, playing computer games). Other parents make their children attend private tutor courses, and there has been a remarkable increase in the prevalence of tutor programs over the past decades. It seems surprising that there is not more systematic research on after-school programs, particularly tutoring programs, which are becoming abundant (Bray, 1999). Schools are also offering these out-of-regular class time courses. Lauer *et al.* (2006) found small gains from these out-of-school courses, with similar effects on reading ($d = 0.05$) and mathematics ($d = 0.09$). The more successful programs were shorter rather than longer programs ($d = 0.23$ compared to $d = 0.05$ in reading, and $d = 0.15$ compared to $d = 0.16$ in mathematics), involved one-on-one tutoring ($d = 0.50$ in reading, and $d = 0.22$ in mathematics), were for students from lower elementary (K-2, $d = 0.22$ in reading and $d = 0.22$ in mathematics) and high school ($d = 0.25$ in reading and $d = 0.44$ in mathematics). While it is the case that students at most risk may be in many of these more structured after-school programs, the overall effects are still negligible ($d = 0.09$) compared to what effective teachers can attain in regular classrooms using many other methods of instruction.

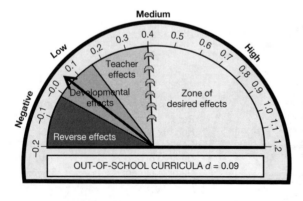

KEY	
Standard error	na
Rank	127th
Number of meta-analyses	2
Number of studies	52
Number of effects	50
Number of people (2)	30,554

OUT-OF-SCHOOL CURRICULA $d = 0.09$

Principals and school leaders

There is so much written about leadership: the seven habits of successful leaders, the personality attributes of leaders, and case studies of inspired leaders of lighthouse schools. But the fundamental issue of interest in this book is the influence of principals on students in their school. In the meta-analyses on the effects of principals, there is an important moderator, relating the type of principal leadership.

There are at least two major forms of leadership: instructional leadership and transformational leadership. Instructional leadership refers to those principals who have their major focus on creating a learning climate free of disruption, a system of clear teaching objectives, and high teacher expectations for teachers and students. Transformational leadership refers to those principals who engage with their teaching staff in ways that inspire them to new levels of energy, commitment, and moral purpose such that they work collaboratively to overcome challenges and reach ambitious goals. The evidence from the meta-analyses supports the power of the former over the latter in terms of the effects on student outcomes. It is school leaders who promote challenging goals, and then establish safe environments for teachers to critique, question, and support other teachers to reach these goals together that have most effect on student outcomes. School leaders who focus on students' achievement and instructional strategies are the most effective (Connell, 1996; Henchey, 2001; Teddlie & Springfield, 1993). It is leaders who place more attention on teaching and focused achievement domains (Hallinger & Murphy, 1986) who have the higher effects.

As an example of this differential effect, Brown (2001) found a mean effect of $d = 0.57$ of leadership influences on student achievement (and $d = 0.54$ on affective outcomes). The effects gained by principals were greater on instructional leadership dimensions (e.g., organization, $d = 0.66$) than from transformational leadership dimensions (consideration $d = 0.36$, inspiration $d = 0.40$). The effects were much higher at the elementary ($d = 0.76$) than for the middle ($d = 0.36$) and high school levels ($d = 0.44$). Similarly, Robinson, Lloyd, and Rowe (in press) reported a similar pattern, in that the effects of instructional leadership on student outcomes ($d = 0.55$) were much greater than the effects of transformational leadership ($d = 0.09$). Specific dimensions of instructional leadership that had greatest effects on student outcomes were promoting and participating in teacher learning and development ($d = 0.91$); planning, coordinating, and evaluating teaching and the curriculum (e.g., direct involvement in the support and evaluation of teaching through regular classroom visits and provision of formative and summative feedback to

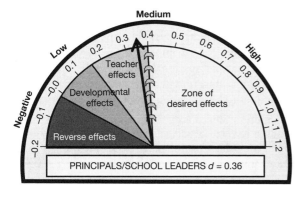

PRINCIPALS/SCHOOL LEADERS $d = 0.36$

KEY	
Standard error	0.031 (Low)
Rank	74th
Number of meta-analyses	11
Number of studies	491
Number of effects	1,257
Number of people (4)	1,133,657

teachers, $d = 0.74$); strategic resourcing (aligning resource selection and allocation to priority teaching goals, $d = 0.60$); establishing goals and expectations ($d = 0.54$); and ensuring an orderly and supportive environment such as protecting time for teaching and learning by reducing external pressures and interruptions and establishing an orderly and supportive environment both inside and outside classrooms ($d = 0.49$). Robinson *et al.* noted that the more generic nature of transformational leadership theory and its focus on leader-follower relations, rather than on the work of improving learning and teaching, may be responsible for its weaker effect on student outcomes. "The more leaders focus their influence, their learning, and their relationships with teachers on the core business of teaching and learning, the greater their likely influence on student outcomes" (Robinson *et al.*, in press, p. 23).

Two meta-analyses specifically investigated the effects of transformational leadership. In Chin's (2007) meta-analysis, it is not clear if instructional leadership studies were therefore excluded. For example, she defined transformational leadership as including shaping and elevating goals and abilities to achieve significant improvements. The effects on teacher job satisfaction are very high ($r = 0.71$), and while lower, the effects on student achievement are also high ($r = 0.48$). Gasper (1992) was more concerned with contrasting transformational and transactional leadership (leaders engaging "in simple exchanges with followers to cause performance contributing to goal attainment", p. 19) and showing the differences on teacher job satisfaction. Clearly, teachers prefer transformational leadership, which is not too surprising given its purpose is to encourage teacher growth and participation through common interests and cooperative actions.

Although Waters, Marzano, and McNulty (2003) did not use the distinction between instructional and transformational leadership in their meta-analysis, the results show a similar pattern. The more important dimensions of leadership that influenced student outcomes related to teachers creating a conversation challenging the status quo of achievement in the school, ensuring that there were current and diverse ways to address these concerns, involving teachers in designing and implementing strategies to enhance achievement, establishing challenging goals of enhanced student achievement, and monitoring use of feedback information to the teachers and school leaders about student progress and effectiveness of teaching. Again, instructional leadership attributes are highlighted.

Another way to evaluate the effects of principals is to review the various leadership competencies derived from the many assessment centers for principals and the resultant effects on student achievement. For the past few decades in the United States, assessment centers have played a key role in assessing thousands of school personnel for selection and placement in principal positions. Pantili, Williams, and Fortune (1991) looked at the effectiveness of assessment by the National Association of Secondary Schools principals (NASSP) in evaluating desirable criteria for the principalship. The strongest correlation with enhanced student outcomes was with organizational ability and leadership ($r = 0.25$) and written communication skills ($r = 0.24$). Transformational criteria such as sensitivity, range of interests, and personal motivation had almost no effect on job performance. Also of interest was that neither gender nor ethnicity has any significant effect on the assessment center scores of principals, on any dimension.

Other correlates with achievement included the extent to which the principals were aware of the goals in the school that needed addressing ($r = 0.66$), the way they ensured that teachers were intellectually stimulated about current theories and practices ($r = 0.64$), whether they were willing to actively challenge the status quo ($r = 0.60$), whether they monitored the effectiveness of school practices and their impact on student learning ($r = 0.56$), the extent to which they communicated and operated from strong ideals and belief about schooling ($r = 0.50$), and whether the principals were knowledgeable about current curriculum, instruction, and assessment practices ($r = 0.48$). The attributes least related to effectiveness were the recognition and rewarding of individual accomplishments ($r = 0.30$), visibility in establishing quality contact and interactions with teachers and students ($r = 0.32$), demonstration of an awareness of the personal aspects of teachers ($r = 0.38$), and adaptation of leadership behavior to the needs of the current situation ($r = 0.44$). Again, a distinction can be drawn between instructional leadership and transformational leadership.

Conclusions from the more general management literature (with some inclusion of effects on students' achievement in school) show similar positive effects on student outcomes for more instructional and purposeful leadership, compared with transformational leadership (where the latter effect is more on the satisfaction and teacher outcomes). For example, Neuman, Edwards, and Raju (1989) investigated the effects of organizational development interventions on satisfaction and other attitudes. Organizational development involves "an effort which is planned, organization wide and managed from the top to increase organization effectiveness and health through planned interventions in the organization's processes, using behavioral science knowledge" (Beckhard, 1969, p. 20). The more successful interventions were goal setting ($d = 0.22$) and team building ($d = 0.30$), and the least successful were what Neuman *et al.* termed "technostructural interventions"; that is those interventions aimed to affect the work content, work method, and relationships among the participants (e.g., job redesign, job enrichment). In one of the few studies on the effects of management methods on student achievement, Miller and Rowan (2006) questioned the value of "organic management" which is a shift from the more hierarchical forms of management to what has "been referred to as a network pattern of control, that is, a pattern of control in which line employees are actively involved in organizational decision making, staff cooperation, and collegiality as a means of coordinating work and resolving technical uncertainties" (p. 220). They found that these organic methods were not especially powerful determinants of student achievement: there was "almost no evidence that organic design features have positive effects on student achievement in general" (p. 242).

Classroom compositional effects

This section includes reviews of class size, open versus traditional classes, ability grouping, multi-age classes, within-class grouping, small group learning, mainstreaming of special education students, single-sex classes, and retention of students (making them repeat a year).

Class size

It is not difficult to find claims for both sides of the argument about whether or not reducing class sizes leads to enhancements in learning outcomes. One side argues that reducing class size leads to more individualized instruction, higher quality instruction, greater scope for innovation and student-centered teaching, increased teacher morale, fewer disruptions, less student misbehavior, and greater ease in engaging students in academic activities. On the

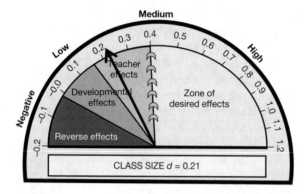

KEY	
Standard error	na
Rank	106th
Number of meta-analyses	3
Number of studies	96
Number of effects	785
Number of people (x)	550,339

other side, there is a voluminous literature that does not support the claim that learning outcomes are enhanced when class sizes are reduced.

Based on a more detailed analysis of the evidence on class size from meta-analyses and other studies, I concluded (Hattie, 2006) that the evidence overall suggests that the results are systematically small; there is much difficulty in reconciling the small effects with the rhetoric about the positive and, for many, obvious profound effects; the effects of those studies supporting lower class sizes are more related to teacher and student work-related conditions, and the effects of those not supporting lower class sizes are more related to the small effects on student learning. It appears that the effects of reducing class size *may* be higher on teacher and student work-related conditions, which then *may* or *may not* translate into effects on student learning.

Table 6.2 summarizes many of the synthesizing studies. Across these meta-analyses, summaries of major initiatives, and newer studies, the average effect size is $d = 0.13$. Thus, the typical effect of reducing class sizes from 25 to 15 is about $d = 0.10$–0.20. Perhaps as interesting as the typical value, is that there is not a lot of variance in these estimates; the mean is a reasonable summary of the effects of reducing class size.

These studies represent a variety of designs including meta-analysis, longitudinal studies, cross-cohort studies; are from many countries (the United States, the United Kingdom, Israel, Bolivia); from across all grades; and use some of the most sophisticated statistical methods available. There is remarkable consistency across the effect sizes from these many diverse studies. This typical effect size of about $d = 0.10$–0.20 could be considered small especially in relation to many other possible interventions—and certainly not worth the billions of dollars that is required to reduce the number of children per classroom. The more important question, therefore, is "Why are the effect sizes from reducing class size so small?"

One reason for these small effect sizes relates to teachers of smaller classes adopting the same teaching methods as they were using in larger classes and thus not optimizing the opportunities presented by having fewer students (Finn, 2002). It is difficult, however, to find studies that investigate or that demonstrate whether the nature of classroom experiences are different in the smaller than in the larger classes. Further, there is a different concept of excellent teaching in larger classes than when teaching smaller classes of 25–30 (see Hattie, 2006 for more details). For classes of 80 or more students, it is probably necessary to assume that individual students are already self-regulated to learn and the major tasks for teachers are to provide content; interpretation of this content; and to assess students on the facility to absorb, and (slightly) transform this content into their words and beliefs (via

Table 6.2 Synthesis of meta-analyses and major studies reducing class size from 25 to 15

Authors	Year	No. of studies	No. of effects	No. of classes	No. of students	d	Outcome
Glass & Smith	1997	77	725	14,358	520,899	0.09	Achievement
Smith & Glass	1980	59	371	—	—	0.24	Non-achievement outcomes
Finn	1988	1	1	79	6,500	0.22	Achievement
	—	1	1	79	6,500	0.12	Achievement (grades 4–6)
	—	1	1	79	6,500	0.02	Self-concept, Motivation
McGiverin et al.	1989	10	24	—	—	0.34	Achievement
Molnar et al.	1999	1	1	411	9,790	0.21	Achievement
Hoxby	2000	1	1	14,593	306,453	0.03	Achievement
Blatchford	2005	1	1	368	9,330	0.23	Achievement
Goldstein et al.	2000	9	36	1,178*	29,440	0.20	Achievement
Dustmann, Rajah, & van Soest	2003	1	1	224	3,811	− 0.04	Achievement
Akerhielm	1995	1	1	1,052*	24,000	0.15	Achievement
Rice	1999	1	1	8,760	24,599	− 0.04	Achievement
Johnson et al.	2003	1	1	168*	3700	0.00	Achievement
Angrist & Lavy	1999	1	1	1,327	46,455*	0.15	Achievement
Urquiola	2000	1	1	608	10,018	0.20	Achievement
Average	—	164	1,165	40,728+	948,540+	0.13	—

* = estimated

structured essays or multiple choice exams). A perusal of student evaluations of teaching of such classes (most evident at the university level) shows the high desirability of organized lectures and lecturers, clear expectations of the examination system, provision of notes and resources, and a well signposted, guided tour through text books, syllabi, and assessments.

When classes move to the 30–80 size, the concept of excellent teaching is the close following of scripts, and chalk or whiteboard lessons, no toleration of deviant behavior in the class, over-learning the rules of classroom behavior, more rigid forms of discipline that allow for little deviance, copying, and high amounts of rote learning, straight rows, all walking through the lessons at the same pace (see Cortazzi & Jin, 2001). In classes of 20–30, grouping becomes possible. There is more opportunity to group students according to ability (or behavior), to encourage peer interactions, to allow for different proficiencies of self-regulation, and some tailoring of curriculum to students (either in topic or pace). There is already a wealth of literature as to the profile of excellent teachers and how they differ from experienced teachers in classes of 20–30 students (e.g., Berliner, 1987, 1988; Borko & Livingston, 1989; Chi, Glaser, & Farr, 1988; Hattie & Clinton, 2008; Housner & Griffey, 1985; Krabbe, 1989; Leinhardt, 1983; Ropo, 1987; Shanteau, 1992; Smith, Baker, Hattie, & Bond, 2008; Sternberg & Horvath, 1995; Strahan, 1989; Swanson, O'Connor, & Cooney, 1990; Tudor, 1992; van der Mars, Vogler, Darst, & Cusimano, 1995; Westerman, 1991; Yekovich, Thompson, & Walker, 1991). It is not convincing, however, to suggest that these attributes necessarily apply to classes of other than this size.

The argument is that moving from one level of class size to another requires a shift in the concept of excellence of teaching—a move from direct (most often transmission) teaching of students (at 80 or more) through attending to teaching and learning (at 20–80), to co-working with a cohort of individual students teaching and learning together (Chan, 2005). The shift required by teachers is not merely to adapt their methods as they move across the levels, but a major re-conceptualization of what it means to be excellent as a teacher at the various levels of class size.

A typical response to this lower than expected effect of reducing class size is to note that many of the more powerful influences identified in this book could be more effective if the class size was lower. With smaller classes, goes the plea, there could be more feedback, more interaction with students and between peers, more diagnosis, and so on. This may indeed be the case, but the evidence so far indicates that when class sizes are smaller, if these influences are implemented, there is still no great difference in student outcomes. Therein is the intriguing question. As noted above, this lack of outcome difference is most likely because teachers do not change their current teaching strategies. The message could be that if teachers were retrained to work with smaller class sizes then indeed many of these optimal strategies may take effect; but merely reducing the number of students in front of teachers appears to change little—in teaching and in outcomes. The reader is reminded that meta-analysis is a method of literature review—the lack of effects from lowering class size summarizes the experiences of past reductions in class size and these experiences indicate that reducing class sizes has not been a powerful moderator on outcomes (although the positive sign of the average effect size suggests that increasing class size is poor policy).

Open vs. traditional

While open education programs are based on underlying philosophical assumptions about the nature, development, and learning of students, they can range widely in type and number of features included in their organization. Some emphasize open space as an essential feature of good practice, others teaching practices (e.g., individual or small-group instruction and a high use of manipulative teaching materials) and the role of the student, and others a combination of features. Although open education had its heyday in the 1970s and 1980s, there are still many of these programs in action (including the one my own boys attended in North Carolina). As was noted in many of these studies, too often classroom architecture may be open but that is no guarantee that the principles of open teaching are present.

Open classrooms make little difference to student learning outcomes. Hetzel, Rasher, Butcher and Walberg (1980) found that while, overall, open education has slightly higher

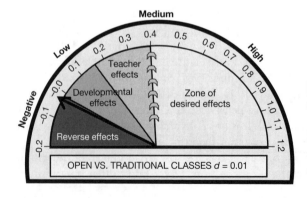

KEY	
Standard error	0.032 (Low)
Rank	133rd
Number of meta-analyses	4
Number of studies	315
Number of effects	333
Number of people (0)	na

outcomes than traditional education, the differences were not great. Peterson (1980) showed that students performed slightly better on achievement tests in traditional compared to open teaching, but did worse on tests of creativity and had slightly less positive attitudes and self-concepts. Madamba (1980) examined the effects of open and traditional schooling structures on aspects of student development and found that open and traditional structures were equally effective in the development of reading comprehension, vocabulary, language, self-concept, and attitude toward school.

Giaconia and Hedges (1982) aimed to identify the features of effective open education. Their findings reinforced Peterson's in that they found that open education programs can aid in producing greater self-concept, creativity, and a positive attitude toward school. Programs effective in producing these non-achievement outcomes were characterized by four features:

1   the emphasis on the role of the child in learning;
2   diagnostic evaluation;
3   use of manipulative materials;
4   individualized instruction.

Multi-age grouping, open space, and team teaching are not factors in distinguishing the more effective from the less effective open education programs. Furthermore, programs that were very effective for non-achievement outcomes produced smaller than average effects on academic achievement.

Ability grouping

In the United States, it is often claimed that about 20 to 40 percent of middle schools assign students to all classes on the basis of ability, and a further 40 percent use some between-class tracking, primarily in reading and mathematics (Epstein & Mac Iver, 1990; Lounsbury & Clark, 1990; Wheelock, 1992). Data from the National Educational Longitudinal Study (NELS) of 25,000 students in nearly 1,000 schools show that about 86 percent of public school students in American middle and high schools are placed in tracked classes.

The fundamental concern relates to whether classes are heterogeneous or homogeneous in ability or achievement. Tracking in the upper high school often involves students

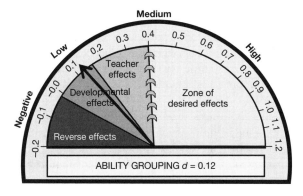

KEY	
Standard error	0.045 (Medium)
Rank	121st
Number of meta-analyses	14
Number of studies	500
Number of effects	1,369
Number of people (0)	na

undertaking different courses, whereas in the earlier grades it typically involves students taking the same subjects but the orientation or pacing of the instruction is intended to differ to match the differing ability levels. At the middle school level, it is more likely that students are tracked in some subjects (e.g., English and/or mathematics) and are in untracked classes for other subjects.

The outcomes can be broadly grouped into achievement effects and equity effects. The latter address the question of whether the gains or losses from tracking are uniformly distributed across various subgroups (e.g., minority versus majority students). Many of the studies also address concerns about whether there are differences in instructional pace and teaching methods moderated by subgroups and whether there is differential access into the tracks on variables other than the avowed tracking variable (e.g., if social class influences access over and above achievement level).

The meta-analysis studies have summarized more than 300 studies of tracking, covering a wide variety of schooling cultures and experiences, in most curriculum subjects, across all age ranges, and across most major educational outcomes. The average effect is a small $d = 0.11$ (see Hattie, 2002; Jaeger & Hattie, 1996; Wilkinson, Parr, Fung, Hattie, & Townsend, 2002 for more detail). The results show that tracking has minimal effects on learning outcomes and profound negative equity effects. The overall effects on mathematics and reading were similarly low (reading $d = 0.00$, mathematics $d = 0.02$), the effects on self-concept were close to zero, and effects on attitudes towards subject matter slightly higher ($d = 0.10$). The overall effects for the three major ability levels across the studies were $d = 0.14$ for high-tracked, $d = -0.03$ for middle-tracked, and $d = 0.09$ for low-tracked students—no one profits.

The effects on equity outcomes are more profound and negative. The most influential in-depth study of teaching and learning in tracked classes is Oakes' (2005) *Keeping track: How schools structure inequality*. Her study was based on an intensive qualitative analysis of 25 junior and senior high schools. The major finding was that many low-track classes are deadening, non-educational environments. Oakes (1992) concluded that "the best evidence suggests that, in most cases, tracking fails to foster the outcomes schools value" (p. 13). Ability grouping fosters friendship networks linked to students' group membership, and these peer groups may contribute to polarized track-related attitudes among high school students, with high-track students becoming more enthusiastic and low-track students more alienated (Oakes, Gamoran, & Page, 1992). In subsequent evaluations, Oakes *et al.* (1993) commented that tracking limits "students' schooling opportunities, achievements, and life chances. Students not in the highest tracks have fewer intellectual challenges, less engaging and supportive classrooms, and fewer well-trained teachers" (p. 20). Shanker (1993), then president of the American Federation of Teachers, in a commentary of Oakes' research, was more earthy: "Kids in these [lower] tracks often get little worthwhile work to do; they spend a lot of time filling in the blanks in workbooks or ditto sheets. And because we expect almost nothing of them, they learn very little" (p. 24). In a similar qualitative design, Page (1991) provided a detailed account of daily activities of eight low-track classes and found that teachers and students came to understandings about how to not push each other too hard so that they could cope, that low tracks were used as "holding tanks" for students with the most severe behavior problems, and that teachers focused on remediation through dull, repetitive seatwork (see also Camarena, 1990; Gamoran, 1993).

Oakes and Wells (1996) claimed that tracking exists to guarantee the unfair distribution of privilege in that white and wealthy students benefit from access to high-status knowledge that low-income students and students of color are denied. Oakes, Ormseth, Bell, and Camp (1990) analyzed 1,200 public and private elementary and high schools in the United States, and found that minority students were seven times more likely to be identified as low-ability than as high-ability students. Those schools that track often explain this ethnic subdivision by reference to past achievement, and thereby argue that tracking can maximize opportunities to alter this. If tracking leads to proportionally more students from lower socioeconomic backgrounds or from particular ethnic groups being placed in lower tracks, then the use of tracking may serve to increase divisions along class, race, and ethnic lines (Haller & Davis, 1980; Rosenbaum, 1980). In his survey of tracking policy in California and Massachusetts, Loveless (1999) concluded that there are massive contradictions in that detracking is taking place in low-achievement schools, in poor schools, and in urban areas; whereas suburban schools, schools in wealthy communities, and high-achieving schools are staying with tracking—indeed, they are embracing it. "This runs counter to the notion of elites imposing a counterproductive policy on society's downtrodden. If tracking is bad policy, society's elites are irrationally reserving it for their own children" (Loveless, 1999, p. 154). Braddock (1990) found that schools with more than 20 percent of their rolls from minority groups were more likely to track than those with fewer minority students.

Oakes, Gamoran and Page (1992) found that Asian students were more likely to be assigned to advanced courses than were Hispanic students with whom their test scores were equivalent. A disproportionate number of low socioeconomic status and disadvantaged minority students occupy the lower tracks and non-college tracks (National Centre for Educational Statistics, 1985; Oakes *et al.*, 1992; Persell, 1979; Vanfossen, Jones, & Spade, 1987). Students of average ability from advantaged families are more likely to be assigned to higher tracks because of actions by their parents, who are often effective managers of their children's schooling (Alexander, Cook, & McDill, 1978; Baker & Stevenson, 1986; Dornbusch, 1994; Lareau, 1987; Useem, 1991, 1992). Further, schools with a larger proportion of minority and lower socioeconomic students are less likely to have sufficient higher-level courses, which effects the probability of students entering higher classes. Moreover, the higher-track programs in these schools are often less rigorous than higher-track classes in schools with fewer minorities and higher socioeconomic students (Oakes *et al.*, 1992).

There is a final conundrum in this research. The empirical evidence leads to a conclusion that there is a close to zero effect from tracking, but the qualitative literature indicates that there may be quite different teaching and interactions in the low versus high tracked classes. The qualitative evidence indicates that low track classes are more fragmented, less engaging, and taught by fewer well-trained teachers. Clearly, if these lower tracked classrooms were more stimulating, challenging, and taught by well-trained teachers there may be gains from tracking for these students: there are not. It seems that the quality of teaching and the nature of the student interactions are the key issues, rather than the compositional structure of the classes.

Multi-grade/multi-age classes

Multi-age classes include students from more than one year level who are taught in the same classroom by the same teacher (also called multi-grade, multi-age, combination, split-grade, vertically grouped, mixed-aged, family group, and non-graded). These are common in very small schools, in many developing nations, and where there are uneven numbers of students at different year levels. Schools also use combination classes because

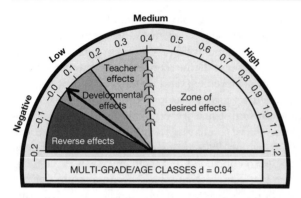

KEY	
Standard error	na
Rank	131st
Number of meta-analyses	3
Number of studies	94
Number of effects	72
Number of people (0)	na

they are believed to have certain pedagogical advantages over single-level classes, as "they allow for more flexible grouping and learning styles, they encourage children to help each other and work together cooperatively and collaboratively, and they present more of a "family" or "community" atmosphere" (Trussell-Cullen, 1994, p. 30).

Kim (1996) used 98 studies of non-graded and graded classes and found low effects ($d = 0.17$) in favor of non-graded classes—and this was consistent across most school subjects: reading $d = 0.16$, language $d = 0.13$, vocabulary $d = 0.17$, mathematics $d = 0.10$. More studies favored non-graded to graded programs. He also compared non-graded with multi-grade and multi-age classes and the overall effect was similarly small. Veenman (1995) conducted a meta-analysis of the cognitive and affective outcomes of multi-grade and multi-age classes in primary schools across a variety of English-speaking and non-English-speaking countries. In reviewing 34 studies comparing multi-grade and single-grade classes and eight studies comparing multi-age and single-age classes, Veenman found no differences in achievement ($d = 0.00$ and $d = -0.03$ for multi-grade and multi-age classes, respectively), and in 13 studies of multi-grade classes and eight studies of multi-age classes, he found small effects on students' attitudes towards school, self-concept, and personal adjustment favoring these classes ($d = 0.10$ and $d = 0.15$, respectively). There was little variation in outcomes by grade or academic area (reading, mathematics, language). As a consequence, Veenman concluded "parents, teachers, and administrators need not worry about the academic progress or social-emotional adjustment of students in multi-grade or multi-age classes. These classes are simply no worse, and simply no better, than single-grade or single-age classes" (Veenman, 1995, p. 367). Veenman also noted that, although few studies provided information on the instructional practices used in the classes, those that did suggested that teachers rarely capitalized on the multi-grade or multi-age arrangement to promote learning from peers (e.g., by using cooperative learning or reciprocal teaching). Nor did teachers group students within the classes across grade or age lines in order to tailor instruction to more homogeneous classes.

Mason and Burns (1996) criticized Veenman's conclusion, arguing that his null finding for multi-grade classes is an artifact of selection bias favoring these classes, combined with lower quality instruction, which counteracts the benefits of selection. They argued that multi-grade classes generally have better students and perhaps better teachers and that these selection factors mask a small negative effect resulting from the increased demands on teachers due to the greater diversity of students (Burns & Mason, 1995; Mason & Burns, 1995, 1996; Mason & Doepner, 1998). Mason and Burns (1996) hypothesized that, when student and teacher selection factors are controlled, comparative studies of achievement in multi-grade and single-grade classes should show a small negative effect in the order of −0.10 of a standard deviation. Mason and Burns also argued that, because of the additional time demands placed on teachers in multi-grade classes, teachers might neglect non-core subjects such as science and social studies.

In a reply to this criticism, Veenman (1995) reported results of a reanalysis, using meta-analytic procedures, on a slightly larger sample of studies. Overall, the results again showed no significant differences in either cognitive or affective outcomes between multi-grade/ multi-age classes and single-grade/single-age classes. The effect sizes were essentially zero for cognitive outcomes and slightly positive, but still close to zero, for affective outcomes. The reanalysis showed a small positive effect of multi-grade classes for students in grades 1 to 3 (mean effect size $d = 0.06$), a near-zero effect for grades 4 to 5 ($d = 0.01$), and a small negative effect for grades 6 to 7 ($d = -0.08$). There was some support for the possibility that student achievement may suffer in subjects such as science (mean effects size $d = -0.19$) and mathematics ($d = -0.25$), but there was no support for the notion that there might be small negative effects in schools where selection factors would not be operative (e.g., in rural schools the mean effect size was $d = 0.10$).

There seems to be some agreement between Veenman and Mason and Burns as both noted that teachers rarely capitalize on multi-grade or multi-age arrangements to promote learning from peers. Instead, teachers tend to teach distinctly different curricula, maintain grade levels, and deliver separate lessons to each grade-level group. In a study of mathematics achievement, Mason and Burns (1996) compared the curriculum, instruction, and organizational formats used by primary school teachers in six multi-grade classes with those used by teachers in 18 single-grade classes—six who used whole-class teaching and 12 who used two within-class ability groups. They coded 153 lessons taught by these teachers according to classroom type, the manner in which the teachers organized students for mathematics, and the nature of teacher-directed and independent-group activities. Teachers of multi-grade classes organized their students into two groups for almost all lessons. Moreover, in independent group activities, students in the multi-grade classes were less productive than were those in the single-grade classes, even compared to those that used a similar two-group structure. Students in the multi-grade classes seldom worked cooperatively to solve problems and seldom helped others who were in need of assistance. Mason and Burns noted that, whereas multi-grade classes might provide opportunities for teachers to use more innovative, developmental approaches, these data provide little support for this notion. There was no evidence of increased opportunities for social growth, peer tutoring, and independent learning for students in the multi-grade classes.

Overall, the effects from multi-grade classes compared to single-age classes are not compelling enough to argue for the effectiveness of one over the other. It is likely that teachers teach in a similar way regardless of the distribution of age range in the class, and the multi-grade classes are often split by age for grouping. There is a deeply embedded grammar of teaching that appears to remain the same regardless of these structural changes in classes. Hence, it is not surprising that there are close to zero findings.

Within-class grouping

Within-class grouping can be defined as "a teacher's practice of forming groups of students of similar ability within an individual class" (Hollifield, 1987, p. 1). This is a very common

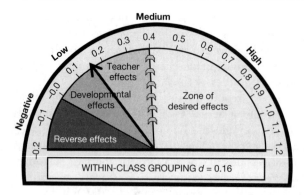

KEY	
Standard error	na
Rank	116th
Number of meta-analyses	2
Number of studies	129
Number of effects	181
Number of people (1)	16,073

practice in New Zealand, for example in reading, 94 percent and in mathematics almost all teachers of Year 5 students in New Zealand reported dividing their classes into groups for instruction (Wagemaker, 1993). There are two major forms of this within-class grouping—ability/achievement grouping and small group learning, with the former being groups formed on a somewhat semi-permanent basis over weeks of instruction and the latter being more spontaneous and usually for specific tasks over a shorter time period.

Kulik and Kulik (1992) conducted a meta-analysis of 19 studies of within-class grouping in the United States. Overall, the mean effect size in favor of within-class grouping (excluding the classes specifically for gifted) was $d = 0.17$. The effect sizes were similar with respect to the abilities of the students in the groups: $d = 0.29$ for high-ability students, $d = 0.17$ for medium-ability students, and $d = 0.21$ for low-ability students. Kulik and Kulik (1992) followed up this review by conducting a further meta-analysis that included 11 studies of within-class grouping, using different criteria for study inclusion. The mean effect size in favor of within-class grouping was $d = 0.25$, but there were slightly higher effects for higher ability ($d = 0.30$) than medium ($d = 0.18$) and lower ability students ($d = 0.16$).

Results from one meta-analysis of ability/achievement grouping (Lou et al., 1996) show a slight advantage of within-class grouping compared to no grouping in promoting student learning (mean effect size $d = 0.17$). Moreover, this analysis shows that the effect of grouping depends on class size. In large classes (more than 35 students) the mean effect of grouping is $d = 0.35$, whereas in small classes (less than 26) the mean effect is $d = 0.22$, and in medium-sized classes (26–35) it is $d = 0.06$. Small-group instruction is also more beneficial when it is compared to traditional whole-class teaching (mean effect size $d = 0.24$) than when it is compared to individualized mastery learning (mean effect size $d = 0.15$), and small groups using cooperative learning perform better (mean effect size $d = 0.28$) than other small groups (mean effect size $d = 0.15$). Low-, medium-, and high-ability students all seem to benefit from being taught in small groups (mean effects size $d = 0.37$, $d = 0.19$, and $d = 0.28$, respectively).

Small-group learning

Small-group learning differs from within-class grouping in that it typically involves assigning a task to a small group and then expecting them to complete this task—and the only meta-analyses on this topic have been conducted at the tertiary level. Lou, Abrami, and d'Apollonia (2001) found that small-group learning had significantly more positive

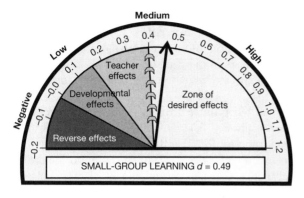

KEY	
Standard error	na
Rank	48th
Number of meta-analyses	2
Number of studies	78
Number of effects	155
Number of people (1)	3,472

effects than individual learning with computer technology on student achievement, group task performance, and several process and affective outcomes. The effects of small group learning were significantly enhanced when students had group work experience or instruction, where specific cooperative learning strategies were employed, and when group size was small. Springer, Stanne, and Donovan (1999) also found there was a similar 0.5 effect on achievement, attitude, and persistence for college students. Small-group learning also led to greater self-esteem among undergraduate students.

A consistent message from studies of the effectiveness of grouping and mixing students within classes by ability or for small groups is that instructional materials and the nature of instruction must be adapted for these specific groups. Simply placing students in small or more homogenous groups is not enough. For grouping to be maximally effective materials and teaching must be varied and made appropriately challenging to accommodate the needs of students at their different levels of ability.

Mainstreaming

The notion of the least restrictive environment for special students has often lead to these students being mainstreamed—that is, placed in regular school classes. Mainstreaming is the concept that students with disabilities should be integrated with their non-disabled peers to the maximum extent possible, and certainly placed in the least restrictive environment. Mainstreaming is often argued more on equity and social justice reasons than in terms of optimal effects on the learning for these students. In specific terms, least restrictive

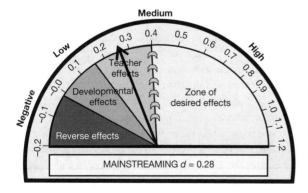

KEY	
Standard error	na
Rank	92nd
Number of meta-analyses	5
Number of studies	150
Number of effects	370
Number of people (2)	29,532

environment does not mean mainstreaming (or as some have termed it, maindumping: Chapman, 1988), but refers to modification of content, materials, classroom management, instructional techniques, and strategies. Full inclusion means that special needs students can and should be educated, with appropriate support, in the same settings as their other peers. This, claim the advocates, leads to increased expectations by teachers, more peer interaction, more learning, and greater self-esteem.

Carlberg and Kavale (1980) found small but positive advantages for mainstream over special classes ($d = 0.12$), and more specifically, $d = 0.15$ for achievement, and $d = 0.11$ for social/personality outcomes. It is important to note that these effect sizes are between students in these special classes and similar students in mainstreamed classes, so the differences are not a measure of non-equivalence between groups. Baker (1994) reported similar effects ($d = 0.08$) in favor of mainstreamed students, with more positive outcomes for mathematics ($d = 0.22$) than for reading ($d = 0.12$). He also found similar effects for those classified mentally retarded ($d = 0.47$) than learning disabled ($d = 0.13$). Wang and Baker (1985) found similar effects across various grades.

Single-sex classes

There is from time to time a resurgence of interest in tracking students by sex within coeducational schools. Much of the interest comes from writers exhorting the advantages that would accrue from these classes for girls (Milligan & Thomson, 1992; Parker, 1985; Willis & Kenway, 1986) citing the differential nature of teacher interactions, intimidation of girls by boys, marking and assessment bias, and the content and presentation of subjects. Gillibrand, Robinson, Brawn, and Osborn (1999) investigated the reasons why 47 of a class of 58 girls chose to enter a single-sex class for physics (taught entirely by males). The major reasons were expectations of better results, avoidance of disruption from boys, wish to be with friends, and desire to experience the novelty. The major reasons for girls choosing mixed-sex classes, on the other hand, were that all-girl classes were demeaning and that in all-girl classes boys could not help them with their work. Kruse, in an extensive series of studies in Denmark (Kruse, 1987, 1989, 1990, 1992, 1994, 1996a, 1996b), reported that solidarity can be strengthened within girls' classes, while the competitive element which often worked in favor of boys was diminished. Parker and Rennie (1997) found that teachers perceived that single-sex classes benefited those girls who were experiencing a great deal of harassment from boys in mixed-sex classes, although there was least benefit for the higher-achieving girls and boys. Their overall conclusion was that any effects were more dependent on the teacher and teacher expectations than whether the class was mixed- or single-sex.

One of the major difficulties in addressing the effect on student learning from comparing students in single-sex compared with coeducational classes has been the problem associated with the non-equivalent group comparisons. Single-sex classes tend to be more selective both in students and teachers, and it is not clear whether it is these selection factors rather than the gender of the student that accounts for any differences (Steedman, 1983). Rowe (Marsh & Rowe, 1996; Rowe, 1988) has conducted the most powerful study of single-compared with mixed-sex classes, as he was able randomize the students and teachers to six single-sex or two mixed-sex classes for mathematics. Across all measures, there were no instances of gains for girls in girls-only classes (or boys in boy-only classes) being significantly more positive than gains for girls (or boys) in mixed-sex classes. Hence, there was "no support for the advantages of single-sex mathematics classes for either boys or girls" (Marsh & Rowe, 1996, p. 153), nor were there effects from the choice of class on subsequent mathematics choices. Similarly, Signorella, Frieze, and Hershey (1996) completed a 10-year longitudinal study of single- and mixed-sex classes within one private school, and concluded that there was "no consistent tendency for students in single-sex classrooms to display less gender stereotyping … [and there was] no consistent advantage to girls in single-sex as compared to mixed-sex classes" (p. 606). Marsh and Rowe did find that brighter students benefited more from being in mixed-sex classes.

Overall, there is very little compelling evidence of a compositional effect related to whether a class is single- or mixed-sex. It needs to be noted that most studies have been conducted on high school students and there is minimal research on these classes at the elementary school level; although there is little reason to suspect that there would be meaningful differences at this level. There are more powerful effects due to the quality of teaching and teacher expectations than to whether a class is all one sex or mixed.

Retention

Retention is the practice of not promoting students up a grade level in school (that is, the student repeats the level) and it is based on the belief that children learn more academically by repeating a grade (Fait, 1982). This is one of the few areas in education where it is difficult to find any studies with a positive ($d > 0.0$) effect, and the few that do exist still hover close to a zero effect. Overall, there are negative effects for students who are retained, and there are more positive effects in the long term for promoted students than for retained students— even when matched for achievement at the time of decision to retain or promote.

Retention has been found to have a negative effect on academic achievement in language arts, reading, mathematics, work-study skills, social studies, and grade point average. Promoted students score better than retained students on social and emotional adjustment, and behavior, self concept, and attitude towards school. Jimerson (2001), in the most recent study on retention, based on 169 achievement effects, found a mean effect of $d = -0.39$, and this negative effect was mirrored across many subjects: language arts ($d = -0.36$), reading ($d = -0.54$), and mathematics ($d = -0.49$). A further 246 effect sizes related to socio-emotional and behavioral outcomes and these also were systematically negative ($d = -0.22$); as was attendance, which was lower for the retained students ($d = -0.65$).

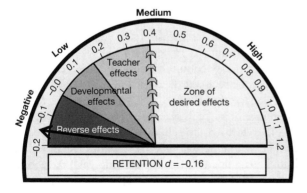

KEY	
Standard error	na
Rank	136th
Number of meta-analyses	7
Number of studies	207
Number of effects	2,675
Number of people (2)	13,938

Holmes (1983; 1989) synthesized the results from 63 studies on the effects of retention and reported an overall effect of $d = -0.15$. Thus the groups of non-promoted or retained students scored $d = 0.15$ standard deviation units lower than the promoted comparison groups on the various outcome measures, over most academic and personal educational outcomes and at every age level. This negative effect increases over time, such that after one year the retained groups were scoring 0.45 standard deviation units lower than the comparison groups who had gone on to the next grade and in many cases were being tested on more advanced material. This difference became larger each subsequent year, with the difference reaching 0.83 standard deviation units for measures taken four or more years after the time of retention. Moreover, being retained one year almost doubled a student's likelihood of dropping out, while failing twice almost guaranteed it. These negative effects are partly caused by schools and teachers not providing special interventions for the retained students, and thereby the students are retained in programs that were not beneficial to them in the previous year. Another possible effect is the negative influence of peer groups on the beliefs of the retained student, and the effects of being forced to interact with students of different ages. Holmes (1989) concluded that it would be difficult to find another educational practice on which the evidence is so unequivocally negative (see also Byrnes, 1989; Cosden, Zimmer, & Tuss, 1993; Dauber, Alexander, & Entwisle, 1993; Foster, 1993; Grissom & Shepard, 1989; House, 1989; Kaczala, 1991; Mantzicopoulos & Morrison, 1992; Meisels & Liaw, 1993; Morris, 1993; Peterson, DeGracie, & Ayabe, 1987; Shepard, 1989; Shepard & Smith, 1989; Tomchin & Impara, 1992).

The effects are bad enough for achievement, but when the negative equity effects are added, the situation is dire for retention. Consider two students of the same achievement, and it is four times more likely that the student of color (African American, Hispanic) will be retained and the other (white) student promoted (Cosden *et al.*, 1993; Meisels & Liaw, 1993). The only question of interest relating to retention is why it persists in the face of this damning evidence.

To cite some typical conclusions: long-term follow-up studies, especially, found no difference in achievement between retained and promoted participants. On teacher ratings of reading and mathematics achievement, there were no differences between the groups. The extra year had produced no benefit for retained children over controls on teacher ratings of social maturity, learner self-concept, or attention at the end of first grade (Shepard & Smith, 1989).

The research indicates that the threat of non-promotion is not a motivating force for students; grade retention does not generally improve achievement or adjustment for developmentally immature students; economically, grade retention is a poor use of the education dollar, because it increases the cost of education (the retained child spends an additional year in the public school system) without any benefits for the vast majority of retained children; characteristics such as low socioeconomic status and peer classroom conduct affect the likelihood that a child will be retained (Byrnes, 1989).

Perhaps one of the most frightening and costly effects of retention is the increased risk of dropping out of school. Although one of its goals is to provide children with the opportunity to be more successful, and therefore stay in school longer, retention clearly has the opposite effect. Being retained one year almost doubled a student's likelihood of dropping out, while failing twice almost guaranteed it. In fact, retention is the second greatest predictor of school drop-out (Foster, 1993).

Students are retained in rather arbitrary and inconsistent ways, and those flunked are more likely to be poor, male and from a minority, although holding students back is practiced to some degree in rich and poor schools alike. The effects of flunking are immediately traumatic to the children and the retained children do worse academically in the future, with many of them dropping out of school altogether. Incredibly, being retained has as much to do with children dropping out as does their academic achievement. It would be difficult to find another educational practice on which the evidence is so unequivocally negative (House, 1989).

School curricula effects for gifted students

The school curricula effects discussed in this section relate to structuring differential curricula experiences for gifted and talented students within schools, such as ability grouping for gifted students, acceleration, and enrichment. Each of these is considered in turn below. In comparing results for the three methods overall, the most effective for influencing the outcomes of gifted students was acceleration ($d = 0.84$). This compares to $d = 0.39$ or enrichment and $d = 0.30$ for ability grouping—which leads to the question of why acceleration is the least implemented of the three.

Ability grouping for gifted students

It is important to separate gifted programs from high-ability tracks. The latter typically receive a faster pace of instruction and more challenging tasks within the same curriculum frameworks as medium- and low-ability students, whereas the former often have different curricula. Herein lies a key distinction. Where there are specific curricula aimed at challenging students at the appropriate level then there is more likelihood of success in engagement and learning. For example, Kulik and Kulik (1984) found that ability grouping had a positive effect on the achievement of gifted and talented elementary school students ($d = 0.49$). Goldring (1990) found that gifted students, when placed in special, homogeneous classes with challenging curricula, achieved more than gifted counterparts in regular classes. For students in special classes, the greatest advantages were in science and social science tests and the smallest were in reading and writing. There was no evidence of negative or differential social effects: there were no differences in general self-concept or creativity for students in special classes and those in regular classes. Vaughn,

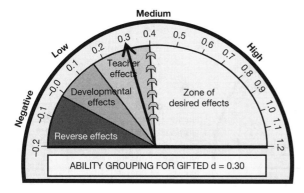

ABILITY GROUPING FOR GIFTED d = 0.30

KEY	
Standard error	0.064 (Medium)
Rank	87th
Number of meta-analyses	5
Number of studies	125
Number of effects	202
Number of people (0)	na

Feldhusen, and Asher (1991) found positive effects from various creativity programs on self-concept ($d = 0.11$), achievement (reading and vocabulary; $d = 0.65$), and creative thinking ($d = 0.44$).

Acceleration

An alternative to special classes for gifted children is to accelerate students through the curricula: "Accelerated instruction enables bright students to work with their mental peers on learning tasks that match their abilities" (Kulik & Kulik, 1984b, p. 84). It typi-cally involves progress through an educational program at rates faster or ages younger than is conventional (Pressey, 1949), although there are many options, such as curriculum compacting or telescoping, and advanced placement. Kulik and Kulik in their meta-anal-yses on the effects of accelerated instruction on students (Kulik & Kulik, 1984a, 1984b) found that accelerated students surpassed the performance of non-accelerated students of an equivalent age and intelligence by nearly one grade level ($d = 0.88$). Kulik (2004) revisited those studies that had some form of controlled design. Those that compared accelerated students with same-age controls had much greater effects ($d = 0.80$) than those that compared accelerated students with older control groups ($d = -0.04$). Again, he concluded that accelerated students did just as well as the bright students in the grades into which they moved. He also noted that accelerated students had higher educational ambitions, and were no different in rates of participation in school activities.

George, Cohn, and Stanley (1979) reviewed the acceleration and enrichment research and concluded that there were no studies which have shown enrichment to provide superior results over accelerative methods; at best, enrichment may only defer boredom. The major question is why there is so much resistance to acceleration, and their claim is that it is usually preconceived and irrational claims about social and emotional acceptability of accelerated students, or some timetabling barriers. Kulik and Kulik (1984a) found that students' attitudes towards schools seemed largely unaffected by instruction in accelerated programs.

If acceleration is so successful then why is it one of least used methods for gifted students? The typical claim is that acceleration is not beneficial from social and interper-sonal perspectives. In a meta-analysis directed at this question of the social effects, Kent (1992) found an average effect of only $d = 0.13$, in favor of gifted students in accelerated programs—if anything, there were positive social effects of acceleration and negative

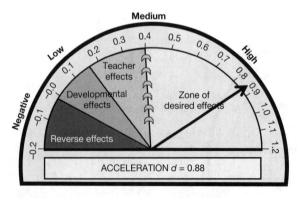

KEY	
Standard error	0.183 (High)
Rank	5th
Number of meta-analyses	2
Number of studies	37
Number of effects	24
Number of people (1)	4,340

effects if *not* accelerated. There were few differences between methods of acceleration (telescoping was the highest effect, $d = 0.15$), or by sex (boys $d = 0.21$, girls $d = 0.15$). Instead, we may need to question the negative social impact on gifted students if they are not accelerated!

Levin (1988) asked, if acceleration is so beneficial for gifted students, why could it not also be used with non-gifted students? Hence, his Accelerated Learning program aims to accelerate the learning of at-risk students so that they are able to perform at grade level by the end of elementary school. These programs involve high expectations, specified deadlines for meeting educational requirements, stimulating instructional programs, planning by all staff, and using all available community resources. The evidence, however, is limited from a meta-analysis standpoint: Borman and D'Agostino (1995) claimed Accelerated Learning had "highly promising evidence of effectiveness" although the overall effect size was only $d = 0.09$.

Enrichment

Enrichment involves activities meant to broaden the educational lives of some group of students (George *et al.*, 1979). Wallace (1989) reported that enrichment was stronger in mathematics ($d = 1.10$) and science ($d = 1.23$) than in reading ($d = 0.59$) or social studies ($d = 0.23$). Programs in which students mastered more mature ideas had higher effects than those with a broader investigation of the regular curriculum. Teachers with more years of teaching gifted students had greater ($d = 0.88$) effects than those with no or limited experience ($d = -0.06$).

There are many forms of enrichment and one of the more common is Feuerstein's Instrumental Enrichment program (Feuerstein, 1980). These programs aim to teach critical thinking skills via a series of 13 to 15 instruments to be completed in one-hour lessons three to five times a week for two to three years. Each instrument concerns a specific cognitive deficiency such as blurred and sweeping perceptions, unplanned impulsive exploratory behavior, lack of receptive verbal tools, lack or impaired conservation of constancy such as size, shape or quantity, deficient need for precision and accuracy, impaired capacity for considering two or more sources of information at once, inadequacy in experiencing the existence of an actual problem and then defining it, inability to select relevant as opposed to irrelevant cues, lack of or impaired need for pursuing logical evidence, and so on. Shiell (2002) reviewed the effects of Feuerstein's

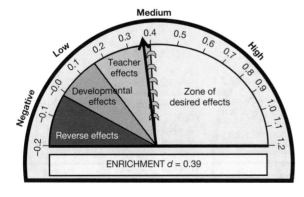

KEY	
Standard error	0.018 (Low)
Rank	68th
Number of meta-analyses	3
Number of studies	214
Number of effects	543
Number of people (2)	36,336

programs and the overall effect on achievement was $d = 0.26$. Romney and Samuels' (2001) meta-analysis found a $d = 0.35$ effect on achievement.

Classroom influences

The final section in this chapter concerns various influences within the class, such as climate of the class, the presence of disruptive students and decreasing this disruptive effect on all students, and peer influences.

Climate of the classroom: classroom management

Marzano (2000) investigated the effects of various classroom management processes on a number of outcomes, including achievement. The effect on achievement from well-managed classrooms was $d = 0.52$ and on heightened engagement was $d = 0.62$. The attributes of teachers that had the greatest influence on ensuring well-managed classrooms and reducing disruption came from having an appropriate mental set ($d = 1.29$) or "with-it-ness" ($d = 1.42$) by the teacher; that is, the teacher had the ability to identify and quickly act on potential behavioral problems, and retained an emotional objectivity ($d = 0.71$). These factors are related to what Langer (1989) called situational aware-ness or mindfulness. The next most effective methods were disciplinary interventions ($d = 0.91$), which included verbal and physical behaviors of teachers that indicated to students that their behavior was appropriate or inappropriate ($d = 1.00$); group contin-gency strategies, which required a specific set of students to reach a certain criterion level of appropriate behavior ($d = 0.98$); tangible recognition, which included those strategies in which students were provided with some symbol or token for appropriate behavior ($d = 0.82$); and interventions that involved a direct and concrete consequence for misbehavior ($d = 0.57$).

Teacher–student relationships were powerful moderators of classroom management ($d = 0.87$, see also Cornelius-White, 2007). The major factors included what Marzano (2000) termed 'high dominance' (clarity of purpose and strong guidance) and 'high cooperation' (concern for the needs and opinions of others and a desire to function as a member of a team). Rules and procedures ($d = 0.76$) involved stated expectations regarding behavior and well articulated rules and procedures that were negotiated with students.

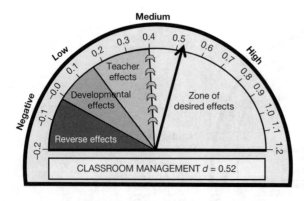

KEY	
Standard error	Na
Rank	42nd
Number of meta-analyses	1
Number of studies	100
Number of effects	5
Number of people (0)	na

Climate of the classroom: group cohesion

Classroom behavior is any behavior taking place in a classroom that either supports or interferes with the capability and capacity of students to learn the tasks and skills required to achieve educationally. The major effect identified by the meta-analyses and a key factor in positive classroom climate is classroom cohesion—the sense that all (teachers and students) are working towards positive learning gains.

Over all the studies in these meta-analyses of classroom climate, there are common attributes that optimize student learning—goal directedness, positive interpersonal relations, and social support. For example, Haertel and Walberg (1980) found that learning outcomes were positively associated with cohesiveness, satisfaction, task difficulty, formality, goal direction, and the material environment. They were negatively associated with friction, cliquishness, apathy, and disorganization. Johnson and Johnson (1987) found that cooperation among adults promoted achievement, positive interpersonal relationships, social support, and self esteem. These findings were consistent across decades with no differences for individual or group rewards, in laboratory or field settings, by study duration, types of tasks involved, or quality of the study.

Evans and Dion (1991) concluded that the relationship between cohesion and performance was both stable and positive. Mullen and Copper (1994) argued that this important relationship—group cohesion—was stronger in smaller rather than larger classroom groups; and they attributed it to commitment to task rather than interpersonal attraction or group pride. In situations with greater cohesiveness it is more likely that there is co-peer learning, tolerance and welcoming of error and thus increased feedback, and more discussion of goals, success criteria, and positive teacher-student and student-student relationships.

Decreasing disruptive behavior

The presence of disruptive students can have negative effects on their own and all other students' achievement outcomes. Thus, reducing disruptive behaviors needs to be a core competency of any successful teacher. The argument here is *not* that these students should be removed, as often the same students in a different class are less disruptive. Rather, it is that teachers need skills to ensure that no student unnecessarily disrupts their own or the learning of any other students in the class. There have been many meta-analyses of the effects of various programs to decrease disruptive behaviors (although these are

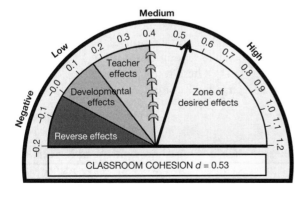

KEY	
Standard error	0.016 (Low)
Rank	39th
Number of meta-analyses	3
Number of studies	88
Number of effects	841
Number of people (2)	26,507

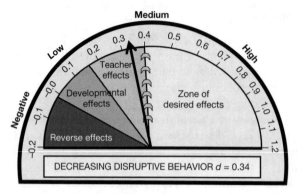

KEY	
Standard error	0.037 (Low)
Rank	80th
Number of meta-analyses	3
Number of studies	165
Number of effects	416
Number of people (3)	8,426

not included in Appendix A as they do not report on achievement effects). For example, Weisz, Weiss, Alicke, and Klotz (1987) found an average effect of $d = 0.79$ from psycho-therapy studies conducted with school age children, Kazdin, Bass, Ayers, and Rodgers (1990) in a larger set of studies found $d = 0.77$, and in particular that behavioral interventions ($d = 0.76$) were much more effective than non-behavioral interventions ($d = 0.35$). The effects were highest for self-control ($d = 0.87$), then treatment of delinquent behaviors ($d = 0.42$), noncompliant behaviors ($d = 0.42$), and aggressive behaviors ($d = 0.34$) (see also Prout & DeMartino, 1986).

Stage and Quiroz (1997) examined interventions aimed at decreasing disruptive behavior in public education classrooms and found they were successful for 78 percent of students treated. Results indicate that these interventions yield comparable results to other meta-analytic studies investigating the effectiveness of psychotherapy for children and adolescents. Studies using teacher rating scales were less likely to show evidence of reductions in disruptive classroom behavior than those using behavioral observation methods. In addition, students treated in classrooms specifically established for disruptive students were more likely to show less disruptive behavior than students treated in regular classrooms. Similarly, Reid, Gonzalez, Nordness, Trout, and Epstein (2004) found a $d = 0.69$ effect from programs to provide treatments for emotionally disturbed students. Ghafoori (2000) synthesized 20 studies on the success of cognitive-behavioral therapy in reducing disruptive behaviors in school settings. The overall effect size was $d = 0.29$; the effects were greater for the lowest socioeconomic students, but similar whether administered by a teacher or not, across ethnicities, and for ADHD and conduct disorder students.

Skiba and Casey (1985) found an effect of 0.91 for interventions for disruptive students. Programs targeting academic outcomes had the greatest effect, then those targeting classroom behavior and social interactions. The most successful programs included social or token reinforcement ($d = 1.38$), cooperation ($d = 1.05$), behavioral consultation ($d = 1.09$), and cognitive behavior modification ($d = 1.0$); the least successful involved social skills training ($d = 0.44$). These results indicate that targeting classroom disruptions via a behavioral approach is the most efficacious.

Peer influences

The effects of peers can be considerable, although it is noted how infrequently peers are involved in the teaching and learning process. In our own work we have identified a

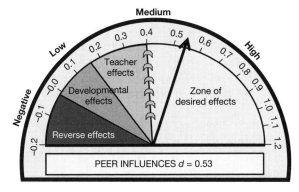

KEY	
Standard error	na
Rank	41st
Number of meta-analyses	1
Number of studies	12
Number of effects	122
Number of people (0)	na

myriad of ways in which peers can influence learning, such as helping, tutoring, providing friendship, giving feedback, and making class/school a place students want to come each day (Wilkinson & Fung, 2002). Peers can assist in providing social comparisons, emotional support, social facilitation, cognitive restructuring, and rehearsal or deliberative practice.

Friendships can play an important part in the classroom environment, as they often involve higher levels of caring, support and help, can ease conflict resolution, and thus lead to more learning opportunities, thence enhancing academic achievement (Anderman & Anderman, 1999). This is particularly the case from early adolescence, where social relationships become particularly important. Levy-Tossman, Kaplan, and Assor (2007) also demonstrated that for many performance-oriented students (i.e., those who focus more on the product or outcome of learning and proving their achievement relative to others), friendship is not often characterized by intimacy, and thus the concerns with social comparison and impression management may lead to them taking on less challenging tasks to ensure demonstrations of competence; whereas many achievement-oriented students (i.e., those who focus more on learning as something valuable and meaningful in itself, aiming to master the learning) had more concern for their personal academic development and growth. The higher the quality of the friendships, the greater the magnification of the influence of the friend—and among adolescents this can lead to gaining a reputation as a learner, a social misfit, an athlete, and so on; some of these reputations can be beneficial or harmful to an individual's academic achievement (Berndt, 2004).

Buhs, Ladd, and Herald (2006) showed how low classroom peer acceptance can be consistently linked with student disengagement (Ladd, 1990; Ladd, Kochenderfer, & Coleman, 1997) and academic achievement (Buhs & Ladd, 2001). These students receive negative behavioral treatment, and become marginalized from classroom peer activities. Exclusion is a process that restricts access to the social and instrumental resources that may be found in class peer activities.

Concluding comments

We all like to think that our school is different; that somehow the culture, people, neighborhood, or special status of our school are unique. Any such differences however, relate to concerns that have little effect on achievement. In most western countries, take two students of the same ability, and it matters not which school they attend. That does not seem to stop the search for the point of difference for schools, and a lot of time spent debating school structural issues: the size of school, the class sizes, the tracking, and the finances—which are among the least influences on student achievement. Many of these matters concern teachers' working conditions, and while I am not suggesting that we should cease to strive for excellent working conditions, focusing our concerns on these matters can be to the detriment of debating more critical matters that affect student achievement outcomes.

Take a common debate in schools: whether there should be a school uniform or not. Since the United States' President Clinton announced that "our public schools should be able to require students to wear school uniforms", many schools (about a quarter of American public schools) have adopted this policy—usually in the name of increased attendance, greater safety, enhanced self-esteem, and improved achievement. Such panaceas abound in our business. It is an easy solution that appeals to the hearts of parents—"Don't they look nice in those uniforms; they must be so proud". Brunsma (2004) completed a synthesis of data using two large American databases to assess the effects of those United States public schools that had or had not implemented school uniform policies. He concluded that "school uniform policies do not significantly alter eighth-grade students' perceptions of their schools' safety climate" (p. 109), and indeed had a negative effect on principals' perceptions of the safety climate of the school. At middle school, both students and principals had stronger negative views about school safety after the introduction of school uniforms.

More importantly, school uniform policies had no effect on academic achievement in elementary school but a significant negative effect in high school. Brunsma concluded that "uniform policies negatively affect all aspects of academic achievement when analysed at the school level" and when such policies are implemented in largely minority high schools, then they are "likely to further exacerbate the academic achievement problems witnessed in these schools" (Brunsma, 2004, p. 132). Further, they had no effect on pro-school or pro-peer attitudes, on attendance, on self-esteem, locus of control, coping skills, level of drug use, or behavior incidents.

Policies on uniforms typically stipulate what a student must wear, whereas dress codes typically say what they cannot wear. The same conclusions as were drawn for school uniform policies seem to be the case for dress codes—no effects.

> There is no evidence from this set of analyses that dress codes or uniforms positively affect the school or its students in discernible ways, nor do they influence the very processes that do affect schools and students (i.e., climate, pro-school attitudes, etc.).
>
> (Brunsma, 2004, p. 142)

And "in some cases, they be more harmful than previously thought" (Brunsma, 2004, p. 154).

One of the fascinating outcomes of this research on school effects is the number of such issues in education where the achievement evidence is close to zero but the heat is as high as it would be if the policy were obviously effective. Why do such issues as class size, tracking, retention, summer schools, and school uniforms command such heat and strong claims? The discourse of schooling is often more in terms of such notions, which, while highly visible, can often have zero effect or the opposite effect to the one intended on achievement. Such cosmetic or "coat of paint" reforms are too common.

These structural claims involve the parents, lead to more rules (and therefore more rule breakers), have hints of cultural imperatives, include appeals to common sense, and aim to reduce diversity.

The most powerful effects of the school relate to features within schools, such as the climate of the classroom, peer influences, and the lack of disruptive students in the classroom. Other powerful effects include adapting curricula to be more appropriately challenging (e.g., through acceleration or differential curricula for gifted students), and having principals who see themselves as instructional leaders at the helm of schools. The influences that are close to zero include mainstreaming, ability grouping, class size, open versus traditional classrooms, multi-grade or age classes, and summer vacation courses. Among the more negative influences are retention, and student mobility across schools.

Chapter 7

The contributions from the teacher

As noted in Chapter 3, the current mantra, that *teachers make the difference,* is misleading. Not all teachers are effective, not all teachers are experts, and not all teachers have powerful effects on students (this is what is meant when it is claimed that the "variance due to teachers" makes the difference! It is teachers' variability in effect and impact that is critical). But there is no doubt that nearly all teachers are effective (that is, if we mean having positive achievement effects, $d > 0.00$) and many can have an effect above the hinge-point in the "zone of desired effects" ($d > 0.40$). The important consideration is the ways that teachers differ in their influence on student achievement—what it is that makes the most difference?

As a mind experiment, recall the teachers who truly made a difference to you when you were at school. I have posed this question to large groups on many occasions and the modal answer is always two to three teachers. During your elementary, middle, and high schools you would have experienced between 40 and 60 teachers. Hence, four to six percent of teachers have left their mark. The research on the reasons we choose these teachers identifies teachers who turn students on to the love and challenge of their subject. When students were asked about their *best* teachers, the common attributes were teachers who built relationships with students (Batten & Girling-Butcher, 1981), teachers who helped students to have different and better strategies or processes to learn the subject (Pehkonen, 1992), and teachers who demonstrated a willingness to explain material and help students with their work (Sizemore, 1981).

As noted at the start of the previous chapter, *within*-school factors, in particular teacher quality, account for a much larger proportion of variance than *between*-school factors. On the basis of 18 studies investigating the magnitude of teacher effects, Nye, Konstantopoulos, and Hedges (2004) reported that somewhere between seven and 21 percent of the variance in achievement gains was associated with variations in teacher effectiveness. This corresponds to an average effect of $d = 0.32$, which means that a one standard deviation increase in teacher effectiveness should increase student achievement gains by about one-third of a standard deviation. The variation in teacher effectiveness is much greater for mathematics than reading outcomes (11 percent on average for mathematics compared to seven percent for reading). Neither teacher experience nor teacher education explained much variance in the teacher effects (never more than five percent). The teacher effects are much larger in low socioeconomic schools, which suggests that the distribution of teacher effectiveness is much more uneven in low socioeconomic schools than in high socioeconomic schools, or as they commented "in low-SES schools, it matters more *which* teacher a child receives than it does in high-SES schools" (Nye *et al.*, 2004, p. 254).

To begin the story about the effects of teachers, let's start with a brief review of who our teachers are. The typical American teacher is a white, Anglo-Saxon or middle class female who has grown up in a suburban or rural area. She is monolingual in English, has traveled very little beyond a 100-mile radius of her home, and hopes to teach in a school similar to those where she grew up. She enters teacher education thinking teaching is a craft, knowing how to teach (but seeking a few strategies to get started and some advice about class management), and aims to become more skilful at defending the perspective she already possesses (Wideen, Mayer-Smith, & Moon, 1998). Cochran-Smith and Zeichner (2005) reported that new teachers were predominantly female, white, monolingual, and taught in hard-to-staff, lower performing, rural, and/or central city schools. They were much older on average than in previous decades (e.g., see Brookhart & Freeman, 1992). Across all teachers, about a fifth were not qualified to teach in their subject area: 23 percent of English, 27 percent of mathematics, 18 percent of science, 61 percent of primary chemistry, 45 percent of biology, 63 percent of physics, and 24 percent of social studies high school teachers were not certified in their field (Ingersoll, 2003; Seastrom, Gruber, Hanke, McGrath, & Cohen, 2002).

This chapter reviews the contributions of the teacher education programs, teacher subject matter knowledge, the importance of the quality of teaching, the quality of the teacher-student relationships, professional development, and teacher expectations.

Teacher training programs

Arthur Levine (2006, p. 109) described teacher education as "the Dodge City of the education world. Like the fabled Wild West town, it is unruly and disordered." There is no standard approach to where and how teachers should be prepared". Walsh (2006, p. 1) also claimed that "the nation's leading teacher educators … concede that there is presently very little empirical evidence to support the methods used to prepare the nation's teachers". For those working in many teacher education institutions, there is the strong claim that there is a "standard' approach, there is order, and there is core knowledge and understandings that all future teachers should have. I have sat through many meetings where colleagues have decided on the essential core knowledge and experiences that should be taught to

Table 7.1 Summary information from the meta-analyses on the contributions from the teacher

School	No. metas	No. studies	No. people	No. effects	d	SE	CLE	Rank
Teacher effects	1	18	—	18	0.32	0.020	23%	85
Teacher training	3	53	—	286	0.11	0.044	8%	124
Microteaching	4	402	—	439	0.88	—	62%	4
Teacher subject matter knowledge	2	92	—	424	0.09	0.016	6%	125
Quality of teaching	5	141	—	195	0.44	0.060	31%	56
Teacher-student relationships	1	229	355,325	1,450	0.72	0.011	51%	11
Professional development	5	537	47,000	1,884	0.62	0.034	44%	19
Expectations	8	674	—	784	0.43	0.081	31%	58
Not labeling students	1	79	—	79	0.61	—	43%	21
Teacher clarity	1	na	—	na	0.75	—	53%	8
Total	31	2,225	402,325	5,559	0.49	0.049	35%	—

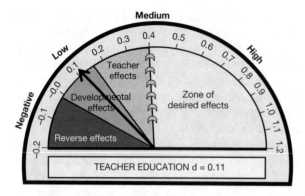

KEY	
Standard error	0.044 (Low)
Rank	124th
Number of meta-analyses	3
Number of studies	53
Number of effects	286
Number of people (0)	na

teacher education students. In every place this has been a long and often vexed discussion, and every time the 'core' knowledge decided on by the group has been different. There is no set of essential experiences that must be taught, let alone a "correct" order for teaching students to become teachers. Moreover, it seems surprising that the education of new teachers seems so data-free; maybe this is where future teachers learn how to ignore evidence, emphasize craft, and look for positive evidence that they are making a difference (somewhere, somehow, with someone!). Spending three to four years in training seems to lead to teachers who are reproducers, teachers who teach like the teacher they liked most when they were at school, and teachers who too often see little value in other than practice-based learning on the job. The common refrain that "the best part of college was practice teaching" or that the real learning occurs *in situ* points to the lack of effect of the college experience (a refrain often advocated by teacher educators who do not seem to realize how ineffectual it makes them sound).

Many of our students come straight from school themselves, and they need to be de-educated from seeing classrooms through their eyes as students and begin to see classrooms through their eyes as a teacher—which means seeing learning through the eyes of the students in front of them. Mary Kennedy (1997) claimed that:

> [The] unusual nature of teacher learning is such that students entering teacher education already 'know' a great deal about their chosen field. Moreover, they will use what they already know to interpret any new skills or new theories they acquire during the formal study of teaching. This fact means that the simple acquisition of new skills or theories is not adequate to alter teaching practices. Therefore, the central task of teacher learning must be to change these conceptions.
>
> (Kennedy, 1997, p. 13)

They need to be persuaded that school subjects consist of more than the facts and rules they themselves learned as students, that there is much to be learned about the complexities and ambiguities in teaching, that teaching is more than snippets of personal craft techniques and common sense, that there are multiple conceptions of teaching which they may never have experienced, and that developing a strong desire to control student behavior can be inconsistent with implementing many conceptual approaches to teaching. Understanding the lens through which teachers view their criteria of success, and their role in learning as well as teaching, is critical to then asking about their effects.

Teachers enter classrooms with these conceptions of teaching, learning, assessment, and curriculum, and these influence how they see classrooms working, students' progression, and themselves as teaching. Teacher education programs can do much to build lenses and conceptions that can lead to teachers being prepared for the rigors of the classroom, with classes of 25 or more students and detailed and busy curricula, and being prepared to question their own expectations, appreciating the need to talk with other teachers about teaching, and, most importantly, seeing learning through students' eyes. Such "Apprenticeship of Observation", as Dan Lortie (2002) refers to this issue, is a significant challenge for student teachers as they move from seeing classrooms as students to seeing classrooms as teachers of students.

The task should be to ask about evidence of what works best in teacher education and subject it to the same scrutiny found in other research studies about teachers and schools. In accreditation exercises, it could be worthwhile to ask about the evidence that teacher education institutions can provide showing they are having an effect on their student teachers; such that these student teachers will have an effect on their own students. Indeed, in my days as psychometric advisor to the National Council for Accreditation of Teacher Education (NCATE), this was the criterion that was uppermost. It was clear that the model of accreditation based on horses and courses—does the college have the right staff and right time on tasks—was a bankrupt model. Instead, the new NCATE model (National Council on the Accreditation of Teacher Education, 2000) was based on asking colleges to articulate their graduating standards and then provide evidence that all graduates were reaching these standards; this was a major shift. No longer could rooms of paper work, bound folders of brilliance, and counting the time spent in class suffice. Instead, colleges needed to change and be transparent about their learning and assessment methods; they had to provide evidence that demonstrated their concept of their standards of graduation; and any or all students could be evaluated as to how well they met these standards.

The meta-analyses relating to teacher education show that the effect size of teacher education on subsequent student outcomes is negligible (about 0.10), although the effect on specific skills is quite high. Qu and Becker (2003) reported a very small effect from only 24 studies—not a lot of studies considering how important this topic should be (and they acknowledged the difficulties in finding even these studies). The effects of four-year college training compared with the effects of alternative certification is $d = -0.01$, and, compared with emergency licenses, $d = 0.14$. The effect for those training in one subject but teaching out of field is $d = 0.09$, but when compared to teachers with full certification who have several years of teaching experience as opposed to emergency teachers, the effect rises to $d = 0.39$—probably reflecting the influences of teaching experience (pedagogical subject matter) and not subject matter knowledge *per se*. Similarly Sparks (2004) commented about how little is known about such an important and well discussed and advocated topic. She reported that fully certified teachers had slightly more effect on student achievement than those with probationary or emergency licenses (across mathematics, science, and reading; $d = 0.12$); and that teachers trained in the field they are teaching in were more effective than those not so trained ($d = 0.38$). While not a meta-analysis, one of the rare random controlled studies involved assigning students to 44 teachers with emergency licenses and 56 trained teachers (Glazerman, Mayer, & Decker, 2006). They found no differences in reading and $d = 0.15$ in mathematics. They concluded that "Teach for America" teachers were "an appealing pool of candidates" (p. 95) particularly as they serve low-income and often difficult-to-staff schools. At best, it was concluded that teacher education programs appear to make some difference compared to emergency licenses. So much more is needed on this topic.

Microteaching

There are larger effects for more specific aspects of the teacher education preparation. Metcalf (1995), for example, carried out a meta-analytic review of studies of on-campus clinical experience for teacher education and found that laboratory experiences produced moderate to strongly positive results for teacher effect, knowledge, and instructional behavior ($d = 0.70$). Such experiences included microteaching, with analysis, reflective teaching, and videotaped role play with debriefing. Microteaching typically involves student-teachers conducting (mini-) lessons to a small group of students (often in a laboratory setting) and then engaging in post-discussions about the lessons. They are usually videotaped for this later analysis, and allow an often intense under-the-microscope view of their teaching. In contrast to conclusions drawn by earlier reviews, Metcalf (1995) argued that laboratory experiences appeared to have a strong effect on teacher behavior and this effect did not significantly decrease over time. Laboratory experiences are effective for in-service teachers. But these methods are far less frequent today.

Bennett (1987) reviewed the effects of various teaching methods within teacher education programs, and reported higher effects for demonstration ($d = 1.65$) and information ($d = 0.63$) than for theory ($d = 0.15$) on trainee teachers' knowledge. He found a similar pattern for attitude outcomes ($d = 0.48, 0.15, -0.08$, respectively), but the reverse for effects on skills: theory ($d = 0.97$), information ($d = 0.35$), and then demonstration ($d = 0.26$). The conclusion was that all components should be included: theory, demonstration, and practice, as well as feedback and coaching, preferably in a distributed rather than condensed manner across many sessions. It was noted, however, that most teacher programs focused on training of low-level skills, reinforcing the skills that were already part of the training teacher's repertoire. It seems that there is too little exposure or teaching of new conceptions of teaching and new ways of teaching.

Overall, the evidence in support of teacher education in general is wanting—both in terms of the number of studies and in the limited evidence of effectiveness from those few studies that do exist. It may be that the effects of teacher education are less on the students of these prospective teachers and greater on the conceptions of what teaching

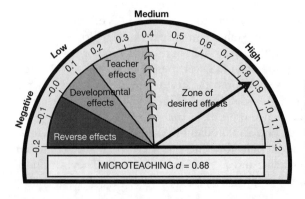

KEY	
Standard error	na
Rank	4th
Number of meta-analyses	4
Number of studies	402
Number of effects	439
Number of people (0)	na

MICROTEACHING $d = 0.88$

involves. Brookhart and Freeman (1992) reported that beginning teachers' conceptions of teaching, while positive, emphasize the value of interpersonal aspects and minimize the importance of academic goals of schooling. Their conception is that teaching is more about telling, and the role of the teacher is to construct lesson sequences to help students work through complex ideas. This is concerning if the model promoted in this book is worth pursuing. The conception of teaching needs to be more related to choosing appropriately challenging learning intentions and success criteria, then *enabling* the students to attain these goals by monitoring and evaluating the effectiveness of their teaching, while constantly aiming to see learning through the eyes of the students, and creating a safe and cooperative climate to make and learn from errors, from each other (teacher, student and peers), and optimize the feedback to the student about what they are learning. The current model seems more related to an extended view of parenting than becoming a behavior change agent!

What may be needed is more study of the best programs. Darling-Hammond (2006) studied exemplary teacher education programs and identified seven features of these programs:

1   coherence based on a common, clear vision of good teaching that permeates all coursework and clinical experiences;
2   well-defined standards of practice and performance that guide and evaluate coursework and clinical work;
3   curriculum grounded in knowledge of child and adolescent development, learning, social contexts, and subject matter pedagogy;
4   extended clinical experiences carefully developed to support the ideas and practices presented in simultaneous closely interwoven coursework;
5   explicit strategies to help student teachers to confront their own deep-seated beliefs and assumptions about learning;
6   strong relationships, common knowledge, and shared beliefs that link all who are teaching these prospective teachers;
7   assessment based on professional standards that evaluates teaching through demonstrations of critical skills and abilities using performance assessments and portfolios.

Teacher subject matter knowledge

There has been a long debate about the importance of teacher subject matter knowledge, with the seemingly obvious claim that teachers need to know their subject to teach it! Shulman (1987) clearly articulated the importance of "pedagogical content knowledge that is the basis of effective teaching". Teaching, according to Shulman, "begins with a teacher's understanding of what is to be learned and how it is to be taught" (p. 7). Despite the plausibility of this claim, there is not a large corpus of evidence to defend it. If there were a large and consistent set of studies showing the power of teacher subject matter knowledge/pedagogical knowledge on subsequent student outcomes, it would seem that it should be well-cited and not elusive to find. The only meta-analysis on the topic, by Ahn and Choi (2004), found a very low effect size of $d = 0.12$ between knowing mathematics and student outcomes. Further, these effects were similarly small at both the elementary and high school level. Darling-Hammond (2006) has argued that it is likely that subject

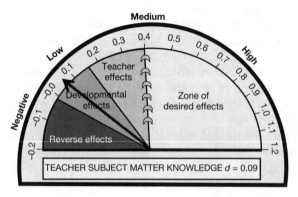

KEY	
Standard error	0.016 (Low)
Rank	125th
Number of meta-analyses	2
Number of studies	92
Number of effects	424
Number of people (0)	na

matter knowledge influences teaching effectiveness up to some level of basic competence but less so thereafter (see also Monk, 1994).

Druva and Anderson (1983), in their meta-analysis on the characteristics of science teachers that affected student outcomes, did find a relation between teaching effectiveness and the number of education courses taken ($d = 0.37$), student teaching grade ($d = 0.34$), and the number of years of teaching experience ($d = 0.33$). Other correlates to student outcomes were teachers with a more intellectual orientation and this suggests that there may be a more underlying general ability that is more critical. For example, Greenwald, Hedges and Laine (1996) found that teachers' academic skills have a positive relationship to student achievement in 50 percent of the studies they analyzed; and thus they suggested that intellectual ability may be more powerful than teacher training. Ferguson and Ladd (1996) found more positive relationships between aggregate teacher scores on the American College test and literacy examinations than on states' teacher licensure examinations and aggregate student performance on standardized tests. Ehrenberg and Brewer (1995) re-examined the Coleman (1966) data and found a significant positive association between teachers' verbal ability and student outcomes. As Hanushek (1989) wrote "Perhaps the closest thing to a consistent conclusion across studies is the finding that teachers who perform well on verbal ability tests do better in the classroom" (p. 48). There is a need for care here, as it could be that verbal ability is a correlate of many important attributes (usually not measured in these studies) such as flexibility, empathy and content knowledge, and such correlates should not be confused with causes. The suggestion, however, is that more generalized verbal proficiency is a key determinant in the later success; when combined with subject knowledge and the teaching skills identified in this book (visible teaching), this may make for excellent effects on achievement.

The importance of teachers having skills in developing interpersonal relationships with students is also important. Colosimo (1984) examined attitude changes with initial teaching experience and found that increases in positive attitudes and self-concepts of new teachers could be expected where teachers were involved in pre-service programs which included interpersonal skills training. The effect on attitudes of the teachers was quite substantial ($d = 0.30$), compared to the effects on achievement. Positive self-attitudes, however, decreased after teachers left colleges and began teaching, particularly for those teaching in inner city rather than suburban schools, possibly because they were less prepared for the inner-city schools. Colosimo suggested that the inclusion of interpersonal skill development and psychological preparation training in traditional teacher education programs was necessary to increase positive attitudes and self-concepts of new teachers. It seems that knowledge, empathy and verbal ability all need to be present. They are greater than the sum of the parts and if one is missing the effectiveness is reduced by more than a third.

Quality of teaching

All the meta-analyses on the relation of the quality of teaching to learning come from student ratings of teachers by college and university students. It appears that student rating of the quality of teachers and teaching is related to learning outcomes, although the feedback that is provided to teachers rarely leads to improvements in their teaching or the effectiveness of the courses. This is despite Irving (2004) finding a high relation between his student evaluation of secondary National Board Certified and non-certified mathematics teachers. The student evaluations could correctly categorize the National Board Certified teachers (NBCTs) over 70 percent of the time, and the non-National Board Certified teachers (non-NBCTs) approximately 60 percent of the time. The effect size between these two groups of teachers on his five student evaluation factors was $d = 0.41$ for student evaluation of the quality of the mathematics teaching, $d = 0.32$ for perceived teachers' commitment to student learning, $d = 0.31$ for engagement with the curriculum, and lower ($d = 0.14$) for relating mathematics to the real world, and for involvement with family and community ($d = 0.07$). The highest correlations involved items relating to:

1   teachers challenging students (encouraging them to think through and solve problems, either by themselves or together as a group $r = 0.64$);
2   high expectations (encouraging students to place a high value on math $r = 0.53$);
3   monitoring and evaluation (getting students to think about the nature and quality of their work $r = 0.46$; encouraging them to test mathematical ideas and discover mathematical principles $r = 0.40$);
4   teaching the language, love, and details of mathematics (helping students construct an understanding of the language and processes of mathematics $r = 0.47$; developing their ability to think and reason mathematically, and have a mathematical point of view $r = 0.41$).

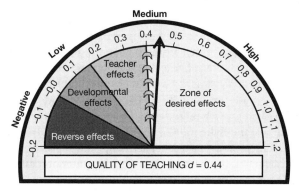

KEY	
Standard error	0.060 (Medium)
Rank	56th
Number of meta-analyses	5
Number of studies	141
Number of effects	195
Number of people (0)	na

QUALITY OF TEACHING $d = 0.44$

Quality teachers, as rated by students, are those who challenge, who have high expectations, who encourage the study of their subject, and who value surface and deep aspects of their subject.

The use of student rating has been hotly contested, although the majority of studies show that they are reliable, trustworthy, and valid (Marsh, 2007). Some have argued that they are merely popularity contests. Abrami, Leventhal, and Perry (1982) conducted a meta-analysis of studies on the influence of an instructor's personality on student ratings of instruction. They found that instructor expressiveness had a substantial effect on student ratings but a small effect on student achievement. In contrast, lecture content had a substantial effect on student achievement but a small effect on student ratings.

Cohen (1981) found an average correlation of $r = 0.43$ between overall teacher rating and student achievement. The relations were highest for perceived teaching skill and knowledge of the subject ($r = 0.50$), planning and organizing the course ($r = 0.47$), rapport with students ($r = 0.31$), and feedback ($r = 0.31$), but the rating was not correlated to the difficulty of the course ($r = -0.02$). As noted earlier, students were reasonable accurate in evaluating their own progress in the course ($r = 0.47$), which also attests to the accuracy of student evaluations of their own learning and probably of the influences of the teacher. Given the value of student evaluations as an index of teaching and their own learning, it is therefore discouraging to note that teachers do not seem to learn much from this important source of information. Cohen (1980; 1981) found that feedback from student ratings has a medium contribution to the improvement of teaching at college level ($d = 0.38$). The effects were amplified when feedback was extended through such processes as consultation (see also Hampton & Reiser, 2004; Lang & Kersting, 2007).

The lack of use of student evaluations in elementary and high schools should be a major concern. The stakes are too high to depend on beliefs that quality is high, or that the students are too immature to have meaningful judgments about the effects of teachers on their learning. A key is not whether teachers are excellent, or even seen to be excellent by colleagues, but whether they are excellent as seen by students—the students sit in the classes, they know whether the teacher sees learning through their eyes, and they know the quality of the relationship. The visibility of learning from the students' perspective needs to be known by teachers so that they can have a better understanding of what learning looks and feels like for the students. Of course, the quality of student evaluation instruments is critical, although the meta-analysis shows little difference in the findings, regardless of the student evaluation questionnaire used.

Another set of studies that have a bearing on the quality of teaching are those investigating the National Board for Professional Teaching Standards (www.nbpts.org). This model involves teachers opting to sit a series of assessments (over six months or more) and then being adjudged certified as an accomplished teacher (in a particular teaching domain such as early childhood, middle grade generalist, early adolescent English language arts, secondary mathematics, and so on (Ingvarson & Hattie, 2008). There are conflicting accounts of the impact of NBCTs on student achievement. Goldhaber and Anthony (2004) compared the growth increases of NBCTs and non-NBCTs on over 600,000 students in North Carolina. They found that NBCTs had growth increases of $d = 0.04$ for reading and $d = 0.05$ for mathematics outcomes. Lustick and Sykes (2006) were more interested in the effects of the National Board Certification process on teacher learning, and reported an effect of $d = 0.47$ in the promotion of learning in teachers, and in particular quite substantial effects in advancing student learning ($d = 0.48$), supporting teaching and student learning

(d = 0.52), and establishing favorable contexts for student learning (d = 0.44).Vandevoort, Amrein-Beardsley and Berliner (2004) compared 35 NBCTs performance to Arizona state averages on achievement over four years.The effect sizes on the gains in achievement were d = 0.12 overall, and specifically d = 0.14 in reading, d = 0.43 in mathematics, and d = 0.09 in language. Sanders, Ashton, and Wright (2005) reported effect sizes of d = 0.09 and d = 0.04 for mathematics and reading from NBCTs compared to non-NBCTs (see also Cavalluzzo, 2004; Goldhaber & Anthony, 2004).

In our own work on NBPTS, we compared NBC teachers who had passed (i.e., were above the cut score) with those just below the cut score (Hattie & Clinton, 2008; Smith, Baker, Hattie, & Bond, 2008).We spent many hours in these teachers' classes and collected a large array of information from the teachers and students (including lesson transcripts, observations, teacher and student interviews, surveys, assignments, and student work).This evidence was independently evaluated and there were differences across all 13 indicators of teaching quality, but the most powerful related to the degree the teachers set appropriately challenging goals for the students: the NBC teachers compared to the non-NBC teachers were more likely, in a systematic and consistent way, to challenge students to think; they regularly promoted varied and appropriate assignments that were demanding and engaging (d = 1.37). Other discriminators included:

1   teachers tested hypotheses about the effects of their teaching (d = 1.09);
2   had a deeper understanding of their teaching and its effects on student learning (d = 1.02);
3   had a sense of control (d = 0.90);
4   had high levels of passion for teaching and learning (d = 0.90);
5   had deep understanding of their subject d = 0.87);
6   were adept at improvisation (d = 0.84);
7   had a problem solving disposition to teaching (d = 0.82);
8   had a positive classroom climate that fostered learning (d = 0.67);
9   had respect for their students (d = 0.61).

While the effects on the writing achievement of their students was far less substantial (d = 0.13), the key difference in the outcomes was that 74 percent of the student work samples in the classes of NBC teachers were judged to reflect a level of deeper understanding (i.e., relational or extended abstract), and 26 percent reflected a more surface understanding.This compares with 29 percent of the work samples of non-NBC teachers so classified as deep and 71 percent as surface. It appears that the quality of teachers (at least as measured by the National Board methods) has important effects on the nature of what teachers do and think, but lower effect on the actual achievement on state tests.They do emphasize and enhance the deeper outcomes to a far greater extent that do non-NBC teachers—and it may be that many state tests are more focused on the surface features of the curricula domains.

On the other side of this equation, having poor teachers can be devastating. Sanders and Rivers (1996) found that the least effective teachers elicited average student gains of roughly 14 percentile points a year, whereas the most effective teachers elicited an average gain of 52 percentile points a year. But more importantly, "the residual effects of relatively ineffectual teachers from prior years can be measured in subsequent student achievement scores" (p. 4). Ineffective teachers were so for all students in that teacher's class, and there was "little evidence of compensatory effect of more effective teachers in later grades" (p. 6). The effects of poor teacher quality tend to persist for years after a student has had such a teacher (Sanders & Rivers, 1996). "If anyone is serious about improving the academic achievement levels for all students, then this improvement will be obtained only by reducing the likelihood that students will be assigned to relatively ineffective teachers." (Sanders, 2000, p. 335).

The final meta-analysis under quality of teacher relates to the effects of the sameness of ethnicity of teacher and students. Clotfelter, Ladd, and Vigdor (2007) found that when a student and a teacher are the same race, the effects on student achievement are no different than when the teachers are from a different background—about $d = 0.02$ for reading and $d = 0.03$ for mathematics. They also found that teachers with more experience are more effective than those with less experience ($d = 0.12$ after 21 to 29 years' experience) with more than half this gain occurring during the first few years of teaching.

Teacher–student relationships

In the first chapter, the work of Russell Bishop and colleagues with Māori students in New Zealand mainstream classes was noted. When students, parents, principals, and teachers were asked about what influences students' achievement, all but the teachers emphasized the relationships between the teachers and the students. The teachers saw the major influence on achievement as a function of the child's attitudes and dispositions, their home, or the working conditions of the school—it is the students who are not learning who are somehow deficient. Building relations with students implies agency, efficacy, respect by the teacher for what the child brings to the class (from home, culture, peers), and allowing the experiences of the child to be recognized in the classroom. Further, developing relationships requires skill by the teacher—such as the skills of listening, empathy, caring, and having positive regard for others.

Cornelius-White (2007) located 119 studies and 1,450 effects, based on 355,325 students, 14,851 teachers, and 2,439 schools. He found a correlation of 0.34 ($d = 0.72$) across all person-centered teacher variables and all student outcomes (achievement and attitudes). The highest relations between person-centered teacher variables and achievement outcomes were for critical/creative thinking ($r = 0.45$), math ($r = 0.36$), verbal ($r = 0.34$), grades ($r = 0.25$). The effect sizes between the eight affective outcomes are depicted in Figure 7.6.

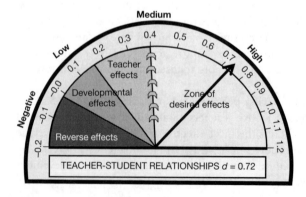

KEY	
Standard error	0.011 (Low)
Rank	11th
Number of meta-analyses	1
Number of studies	229
Number of effects	1,450
Number of people (1)	355,325

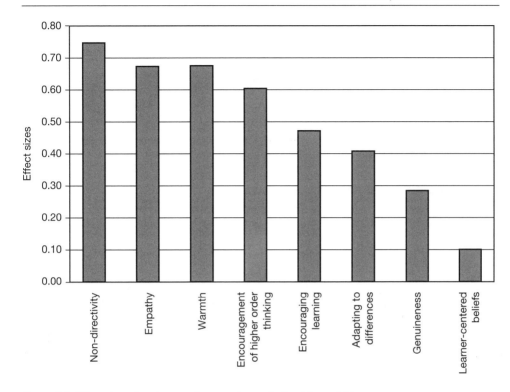

Figure 7.6 Effect sizes for nine teacher–student relationship variables

In classes with person-centered teachers, there is more engagement, more respect of self and others, there are fewer resistant behaviors, there is greater non-directivity (student-initiated and student-regulated activities), and there are higher achievement outcomes. Cornelius-White notes that most students who do not wish to come to school or who dislike school do so primarily because they dislike their teacher. His claim is that to "improve teacher-student relationships and reap their benefits, teachers should learn to facilitate students' development" by demonstrating that they care for the learning of each student as a person (which sends a powerful message about purpose and priority), and empathizing with students—"see their perspective, communicate it back to them so that they have valuable feedback to self-assess, feel safe, and learn to understand others and the content with the same interest and concern." (p. 23).

Professional development

One of the difficulties with reviews of professional development is that the outcomes seem to be more about changes in the teachers, and not the impact of professional development on student outcomes. Wade (1985) for example, divided the outcomes into four groups:

1   reaction—how the teachers felt about the professional development;
2   learning—the amount of learning the teachers accrued;

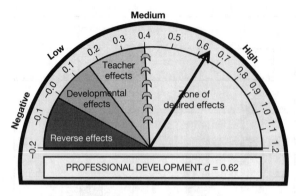

KEY	
Standard error	0.034 (Low)
Rank	19th
Number of meta-analyses	5
Number of studies	537
Number of effects	1,884
Number of people (1)	47,000

3   behavior—whether teachers changed their behavior as a result of the professional development;
4   student outcomes—impact on students.

Professional development is more likely to change teacher learning ($d = 0.90$), but these learnings have less effect on teachers' actual behavior ($d = 0.60$) and teachers' reactions to the professional development ($d = 0.42$), and even less influence on student learning ($d = 0.37$). The four types of instruction found to be most effective on teacher knowledge and behavior were: observation of actual classroom methods; microteaching; video/audio feedback; and practice. Lowest effects were from discussion, lectures, games/simulations, and guided field trips. Coaching, modeling, and production of printed or instructional materials also had lower effects. Higher effect sizes were found in studies where: training groups involved both high school and elementary school teachers rather than only high or only elementary teachers; training programs were initiated, funded or developed by federal, state, government or university rather than by schools or teachers; participants were selected for training; and where training was practical rather than theoretical (Wade, 1985).

Joslin (1980) found that in-service programs were effective in changing teacher achievement, skills, and attitudes, although it was questionable as to whether professional development was effective in attempts to change students through teacher participation in these programs. Harrison (1980) also found that professional development was an effective way in which to improve job performance and satisfaction. The effects were highest for increasing the teacher's knowledge ($d = 1.11$) and affective feelings and satisfaction ($d = 0.85$), and lower but still positive for the effects on student outcomes ($d = 0.47$).

Timperley, Wilson, Barrar, and Fung (2007) found 72 studies that assessed the effects of professional development on student outcomes. The overall effect on academic outcomes was $d = 0.66$, and the effects were highest for science ($d = 0.94$), writing ($d = 0.88$), mathematics ($d = 0.50$), and then reading ($d = 0.34$). The effects did not relate to the size of the cohort in the professional development (<100 $d = 0.84$; 100–999 $d = 0.69$; > 1000 $d = 0.69$), but the effects were greater on low-achieving or special education students ($d = 0.43$) and gifted ($d = 0.31$) than on regular students ($d = 0.18$). More important, Timperley and colleagues used the effect sizes to ascertain seven themes about what works best in professional development. First, the learning opportunities for teachers occurred over an extended period of time—except when powerful ideas formed the basis of new practice and had a high impact on student outcomes (e.g., teaching how to screen students for auditory processing problems). Second, the involvement of external experts was more related to success than within-schools initiatives. Third, it was important to engage the teachers sufficiently during the learning process to deepen their knowledge and extend their skills in ways that improved student outcomes. Fourth, and most critical, effects on student learning were very much a function of professional development that challenged the teachers' prevailing discourse and conceptions about learning (when this discourse was problematic, it was usually based on the assumption that some groups of students could not or would not learn as well as others), or challenging teachers how to teach particular curricula more effectively. Fifth, teachers talking to teachers about teaching (involvement in a professional community of practice) was necessary but not sufficient by itself. This was because teachers were more listened to when challenging problematic beliefs and testing the efficacy of competing ideas, and when discussions were grounded in artifacts representing student learning. Sixth, professional development was more effective when the school leadership supported opportunities to learn, where there was access to relevant expertise, and when opportunities were provided to meet to process new information. Seventh, funding, release time, and whether the involvement was voluntary or compulsory were unrelated to influences on student outcomes.

Expectations

In the education system, it is now widely accepted that teachers do form expectations about student ability and skills and that expectations affect student achievement (Dusek and Joseph, 1985). The question is not "Do teachers have expectations?" but "Do they have false and misleading expectations that lead to decrements in learning or learning gains—and for which students?"

Perhaps the most famous (or infamous) book in education in the past 50 years has been *Pygmalion in the Classroom*. In this book, Rosenthal and Jacobsen (1968) argued that teachers' expectations were powerful influences on the success of student learning. The students they randomly labeled as "bloomers" ("they will show a more significant inflection or spurt in their learning within the next year than will the remaining 80 percent of the children"; p. 66) did indeed increase in achievement by the end of the year. The book, and its reviews, created its share of those inspired, insulted, and infuriated. There were many failures to replicate the results, and there was much attention paid to the methodological problems of this study (Spitz, 1999), but there was the constant

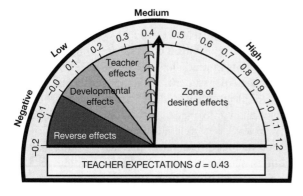

KEY	
Standard error	0.081 (High)
Rank	58th
Number of meta-analyses	8
Number of sudies	674
Number of effects	784
Number of people (0)	na

niggle that expectations were powerful. Some sought to find expectations that led to the disempowerment of various groups (girls, minorities, students sitting at the back of the room), while others noted the power of feedback to correct false expectations. Rauden-bush (1984), in his meta-analysis, argued that the less teachers knew their students prior to receiving the false information, then the stronger the effect on learning. The research on expectations is not now as prevalent as it was in the 1970s and 1980s, but there has been a recent resurgence due to the work of Weinstein (2002) and colleagues.

The first set of meta-analyses discussed in this section relate to the more general issue of interpersonal expectancies (which is that the experimenter tends to obtain the results she or he expects). Rosenthal and Rubin (1978) summarized the results of 345 experiments looking at interpersonal expectancy effects, and found a mean size of $d = 0.70$ over eight different areas of research. This is a large effect. Depending on the type of study examined, the mean size of the effect varied from small for studies of reaction time and laboratory interviews to very large for studies of psychophysical judgments and animal learning. They found that the effect of interpersonal expectations or self-fulfilling prophecies was as great, on average, in everyday life situations as it was in laboratory experiments. The implication for teachers is that teachers (as human beings) are more likely to have their students reach their "expected" outcomes, regardless of the veracity of the expectations.

Harris and Rosenthal (1985) examined 135 studies on the effects of expectations on various behaviors. They claimed that input factors (student sex, age, ethnicity) are the most important mediators in the transmission of expectancies ($d = 0.26$), followed by output (asks questions, frequency of interaction: $d = 0.19$), climate ($d = 0.20$), and feedback (which they considered as praise and criticism: $d = 0.13$). All four combined factors are of higher importance than any individual factor. They did note the low effects of praise, and noted that it may be more important to study the content of the feedback than its frequency, timing, or simple positive versus negative nature.

> In most situations, praise and criticism may refer to routine, almost mechanized, pronouncements of 'Good' or 'No, you're wrong.' This kind of feedback is not informative to the student; consequently, it may have no impact on the child beyond the realization that he or she got the answer right or wrong.
>
> (Harris & Rosenthal, 1985, p. 377)

Smith (1980) found that when labeling information on pupil ability is given to teachers, they reliably rate student ability, achievement, and behavior according to the information provided. Teacher expectations affected their behavior to a modest degree; in particular, more teaching opportunities were given to students for whom there was a favorable expectation. Raudenbush (1984) reported that prior teacher–student contact (of at least two weeks) reduced any negative outcomes, and expectation effects were larger for young students in grade levels 1 and 2, than for students in grade levels 3 and 4.

There has been a long search for which particular students are differentially affected by teacher expectations. Dusek and Joseph (1983) found that student attractiveness ($d = 0.30$), student prior conduct in class, cumulative folder information ($d = 0.85$), and social class ($d = 0.47$ for high and middle compared to low) were related significantly and positively to teacher expectancies. Factors not related included number of parents at home, student gender ($d = 0.20$), previously-taught siblings, name stereotypes, and student ethnicity. But when teachers were given more pertinent information (such as academic information) then factors such as attractiveness became less important. It was also noted that too many of the studies that led to these effects asked teachers to make judgments about unfamiliar students. Jackson, Hunter, and Hodge (1995) derived various reasons why physical attractiveness would be related to achievement. Their meta-analysis supported the notion that attractive people are *perceived* as more intellectually competent than their less attractive peers. These effects were stronger for males than females, and markedly reduced, but not absent, when explicit evidence about competence was present. There were no relations between attractiveness and achievement for adults ($d = 0.02$) but there were for children ($d = 0.41$). It seems that there is an attractiveness bias that benefits these students.

Dusek and Joseph (1983) also cautioned that the effects of expectancies on social versus achievement effects can be quite different and these two should not be confused. It may be the case, for example, that attractive children tend to have better relations than unattractive children with peers—so that the teachers' expectations about these social outcomes is not a bias but a reflection of teachers' experiences. Ritts, Patterson and Tubbs (1992) found that physically attractive students are judged more favorably by teachers on social skills ($d = 0.48$) than on intelligence or academic grades ($d = 0.36$). But it was also the case that more attractive students do receive higher grades on standardized tests and parents also show biases in many actions to attractive children; the key question raised in the study is when and where do attractiveness effects begin and how do they change over time?

The label *learning difficulties* can also have negative effects. Fuchs, Fuchs, Mathes, Lipsey, and Roberts (2002) found 79 studies that compared students with lower reading achievement with those labeled as having learning difficulties. The effect of $d = 0.61$ indicated that the reading scores of 73 percent of low achievers without the label were above the average reading score of low achievers with the label—clearly, labeling leads to differential performance and it is difficult to understand why this is so when there was no evidence that these labeled students have a qualitatively different set of learner characteristics than those not so labeled. At what point does low achievement become so extreme that it represents a real disorder, requiring a different educational response?

It was noted above that Dusek and Joseph (1985) found small effects of race on teacher expectations ($d = 0.11$). Wherever the race advantage is found, however, it favors white and Asian students. Tenenbaum and Ruck (2007) reported that teachers had more positive expectations for European Americans than for minority students ($d = 0.23$; Hispanic $d = 0.46$, African American $d = 0.25$, Asian $d = -0.17$), the effects were greatest in elementary ($d = 0.28$) and high school ($d = 0.26$) and less so for college students ($d = 0.12$). Further, teachers were more likely to make negative assignments (e.g., special education, disciplinary action) for ethnic minorities ($d = 0.31$) and direct more positive or neutral speech to whites ($d = 0.21$), but there was no evidence of more negative speech ($d = 0.02$) to white compared to African Americans or Hispanics. Cooper and Allen (1997) investigated the interactive effects of race on the classroom experiences of white and minority students. The average effect was $d = -0.18$ thus indicating that minority students have different types of interactions with teachers. In particular, there were more negative statements by teachers to non-white students ($d = -0.15$), white students received more positive praise ($d = 0.09$), and overall minority students had fewer interactions with teachers than white students ($d = 0.15$).

So how to make sense of these moderating effects of teacher expectations on student achievement? Two recent sets of research bring some meaning to this domain. First, Weinstein (2002) has provided a new direction for expectancy effects. She has shown that students *know* they are treated differentially in the classroom due to expectations held by teachers, and are quite accurate in informing on how teachers differ in the degree to which they favor some children over others with higher expectations. There are differences in classrooms where teachers aim to select talent for different educational pathways (such as schools with tracking) compared with those where achievement cultures aim to develop talent in each child. There are differences in classes where teachers believe that achievement is difficult to change because it is fixed and innate compared to teachers who believe achievement is changeable (Dweck, 2006). Weinstein also demonstrated that many institutional practices (such as tracking) can lead to beliefs that preclude many opportunities to learn: "Expectancy processes do not reside solely 'in the minds of teachers' but instead are built into the very fabric of our institutions and our society" (Weinstein, 2002, p. 290).

Second, Rubie-Davis and her colleagues (Rubie, 2003, 2006, 2007; Rubie-Davies, Hattie, & Hamilton, 2006) added another concerning dimension to this expectation research with the finding that when teachers hold lower expectations, they do so for *all* the students in the class—it is certainly a teacher effect. Based on this evidence, teachers must stop over-emphasizing ability and start emphasizing progress (steep learning curves are the right of all students regardless of where they start), stop seeking evidence to confirm prior expectations but seek evidence to surprise themselves, find ways to raise the achievement of all, stop creating schools that attempt to lock in prior achievement and experiences, and be evidence-informed about the talents and growth of *all* students by welcoming diversity and being accountable for all (regardless of the teachers' and schools' expectations). "Be prepared to be surprised" seems to be the mantra to avoid negative expectation effects. If teachers and schools are going to have expectations, make them challenging, appropriate, and checkable such that all students are achieving what is deemed valuable. To this we can add the potentially negative effects of students setting their own low expectations (recall the power of self-reported grades) and not being provided with high levels of confidence that they can exceed these expectations and not only attain but enjoy challenging learning intentions.

Labeling students

Many of the meta-analyses reviewed in this section do not have achievement as an outcome, but do relate to how teachers (and parents) differentiate between special and regular students (and many other labels). The controversy in distinguishing between mentally disabled and non-disabled children is often couched between the developmental

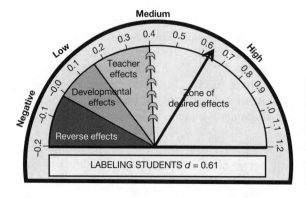

KEY	
Standard error	na
Rank	21st
Number of meta-analyses	1
Number of studies	79
Number of effects	79
Number of people (0)	na

LABELING STUDENTS $d = 0.61$

and cognitive processing claims. The developmental position is that disabled children pass through cognitive developmental stages in an identical manner but differ in rate and the upper limit of development (Inhelder & Piaget, 1964; Piaget, 1970). The information-processing claim is that they differ in the cognitive processes they use in reasoning. Weiss, Weisz, and Bromfield (1986) examined information-processing studies based on the hypotheses that "retarded" and non-"retarded" people pass through Piagetian cognitive developmental stages in an identical order but at a different rate. They noted, however, that differences were not found across all learning areas, with differences in some areas such as discrimination learning (verbal, picture, and three-dimensional object discrimination), but not in others such as conservation and incidental learning. For "retarded" students, there was found to be a strong deficit specific to certain aspects of memory: serial and non-serial auditory; short-term memory; visual-iconic memory; visual short-term memory; cross-modal short-term memory; and visual paired-associate learning. Swanson and Jerman (2006) reviewed the differences between students categorized with mathematics disabilities with age-matched average-achieving peers. From their 28 studies, the mathematics disability students performed much lower on verbal problem solving ($d = -0.58$), naming speed ($d = -0.70$), and verbal word memory ($d = -0.70$), indicating the power of verbal skills in learning mathematics. Swanson and Jerman concluded that their results were "consistent with previous syntheses of the literature that have attributed math disability to working memory deficits" (Swanson & Jerman, 2006, p. 265), particularly verbal working memory.

In reading, Hoskyn and Swanson (2000) found no differences between low achievers and reading disabled students in automaticity (rapid naming, $d = -0.06$) or real-world reading words ($d = 0.02$), but major differences in lexical knowledge ($d = 0.55$), syntactical knowledge ($d = 0.87$), visual-spatial processing ($d = 0.36$) and in phonological processing ($d = 0.25$). The results from their regression of many of these variables led them to conclude that both low achievers and reading-disabled students shared a common problem in phonological processing (although reading difficulty students exhibited an advantage in cognitive processing for other reading measures). It is thus not surprising that Swanson, Carson, and Sachse-Lee (1996) concluded that phonics training has a direct influence on reading achievement (especially spelling and word recognition performance) for these students.

The differences across many *labels*, however, are not always so marked. Kavale and Nye (1985) compared learning-disabled and normal students and found that about 75 percent of learning-disabled students could be clearly differentiated from normal students across all dimensions, displaying deficits that would interfere with their academic ability. Kavale and Forness (1983) reviewed the difference in achievements related to those students classified as brain injured and those with difficulties more related to familial-cultural factors. The 26 studies yielded 241 effect sizes and an average of $d = 0.10$ between the two groups—with differences related to perceptual-motor ($d = 0.11$), cognition ($d = 0.14$), language ($d = 0.10$), behavior ($d = 0.09$), and intelligence $d = 0.05$—so little difference was established. Very often the labels help "classify" these students and can lead to extra funding, but rarely does it make a difference to what works best—regardless of these labels.

Teacher clarity

One of the themes in this book is how important it is for the teacher to communicate the intentions of the lessons and the notions of what success means for these intentions.

KEY	
Standard error	na
Rank	8th
Number of meta-analyses	1
Number of studies	na
Number of effects	na
Number of people (0)	na

TEACHER CLARITY $d = 0.75$

Fendick (1990) investigated teacher clarity, which he defined as organization, explanation, examples and guided practice, and assessment of student learning – such that clarity of speech was a prerequisite of teacher clarity. The correlation was 0.35 ($d = 0.75$) and the effects were larger when students, rather than observers, rated the teachers; for college rather than elementary school teachers; and class size and subject taught made no difference.

Concluding comments

The most critical aspects contributed by the teacher are the quality of the teacher, and the nature of the teacher–student relationships. Medium effects relate to teacher expectations particularly when lower expectations are held for *all* their students, and to teacher professional development effects on achievement. Low effects come from teacher education programs. From the graph of all effects (Appendix A), it appears that few teachers are harmful to students in that they decrease their achievement—although Rubie-Davies (2007) has demonstrated the power of low expectations on systematically decreasing achievement. While the message from this chapter is about the power of teachers, it is teachers *using particular teaching methods*, teachers *with high expectations for all students*, and teachers *who have created positive student-teacher relationships* that are more likely to have the above average effects on student achievement. There appear to be as many teachers who have effects below this $d = 0.4$ hinge-point as there are above, and every year a student faces a huge gamble as to who is at the front of their class—will it be a teacher who has a major positive influence or a teacher who has a less-than-average although positive influence? It is any teacher who does not achieve an average of $d > 0.40$ per year that I do not want my children to experience!

We need to talk about quality teachers in terms of what they do and the effects they have on students. Too often our discussion on what constitutes quality in teachers emphasizes the personal and professional attributes. Maybe we should constrain our discussion from talking about qualities of teachers to the quality of *the effects of teachers on learning*—so the discussion about teaching is more critical than the discussion about teachers (see Chapters 8 and 9).

Teachers' initial teacher training programs have little impact on how well those teachers influence the achievement of their students. Maybe subsequent effects wash out this earlier training, limited as it is in effectiveness, although the low quantity and quality of evidence of teacher training should be a major embarrassment for these institutions who constantly ask for more—more years, more resources, more influence. There is little substantive evidence of the effects of initial teacher training—and the little there is would not suggest that here is a place that could make a difference. Teacher education might be more successful if it placed more emphasis on learning and teaching strategies; on developing teachers' conceptions of teaching as an evidence-based profession (learning from errors as much as from successes); creating an appraisal system that involves a high level of trust and dependence on observed or videotaped reflection/evaluation of practice; and providing beginning teachers with a range of different teaching methods to use when current ones do not work. It might be more successful if it re-introduced micro-skills teaching methods that have demonstrably positive effects on new teachers; developed teachers' understanding of different ways to teach surface, deep, and conceptual knowledge; demonstrated how teachers can build positive relationships with *all* students; and showed how evaluation and assessment of students provides powerful feedback to teachers about how well they are teaching, who they have not taught so well, and where they need to re-teach. A major overhaul of teacher education is well overdue (see Darling-Hammond, 2006) and one way forward is to ask each teacher education program to articulate a set of graduating standards, and then evaluate how appropriate these standards are, and evaluate the nature and quality of evidence provided that all students meet these standards. If employers and independent educationalists sit along with the education program academics in making these decisions, there is a higher likelihood that these programs will then change to concentrate on training new teachers to have an effect on students' learning.

It is difficult to find evidence that subject matter knowledge is important. This is a conundrum. It may be that teachers all have an acceptable amount of subject matter knowledge and thus there is little variance to then associate with student outcomes. But teachers often teach in areas in which they have little training in the content, which suggests an interaction between teaching competence and need for high levels of knowledge in the subject. It would seem that those who have high levels of subject matter knowledge are better placed to understand the content and the optimal progressions of surface and deep learning in that content. Also teachers more knowledgeable about the content should be better placed to provide feedback as students struggle, and help move them from their current understanding to deeper and more richly constructed views of the content. It would be expected that students are more likely to become passionate about and enjoy the subject as they master the content; as opposed to those students who learn in a minimax fashion to pass the test, complete the assignment, and move on to whatever is next prescribed for them. But the evidence is lacking for these claims, and we may need to ask: "what is the minimum subject matter knowledge needed to be an accomplished teacher and how can we optimize the teaching strategies of those teachers with greater subject matter knowledge?" It may also be intriguing to investigate *how* teachers with lesser subject matter knowledge have such positive effects on their students.

Teachers walk into classrooms with conceptions of teaching, learning, curricula, assessment, and their students (Brown, 2004). We need to better understand these conceptions, as it seems they are powerful moderators on the success of these teachers. Having low expectations of the students' success is a self-fulfilling prophecy, and it appears that expectations are less mediated by between-student attributes (gender, race, and so on) than by whether they are held (high or low) for all students. How to invoke high expectations seems critical, and this may require more in-school discussion of appropriate benchmarks across grades, and seeing evidence of performance before starting the year (Nuthall, 2005, shows half of all material taught in any class is already known by the students); so much of the early part of the year involves trial and error as teachers find out proficiencies of students—information which could have more readily been garnered by reviewing student records, and having discussion with previous teachers. As I have argued in the New Zealand context from analyzing achievement performance from 100,000 students, the greatest single issue facing the further enhancement of students is the need for teachers to have a common conception of progress. When a student moves from one teacher to another, there is no guarantee that he or she will experience increasingly challenging tasks, have a teacher with similar (hopefully high) expectations of how to progress up the curricula, or work with a teacher who will grow the student from where he or she is, as opposed to where the teacher believes he or she should be at the start of the year.

To have high expectations and to share a common conception of progress requires teachers to be concerned about the nature of their relationships with their students. My colleague Russell Bishop moves around classes asking students "Does your teacher like you?" and so many ethnic minority students (in New Zealand) say no, but the white students say yes! When teachers are shown the results of surveys (including this question), they are often astonished—primarily because they assumed that the relations were positive, looked for cues that all was well, and rarely saw the classroom through the eyes of the students. The powerful effect of Bishop's work is that, after seeing these results, the teachers are quick to change their practices. The power of positive teacher–student relationships is critical for learning to occur. This relationship involves showing students that the teacher cares for their learning as a student, can "see their perspective, communicate it back to them so that they have valuable feedback to self-assess, feel safe, and learn to understand others and the content with the same interest and concern." (Cornelius-White, 2007, p. 123). Then the powers of developing a warmer socio-emotional climate in the classroom and fostering effort and thus engagement for *all* students are invoked. This requires teachers to enter the classroom with certain conceptions about progress, relationships, and students. It requires them to believe that their role is that of a change agent—that all students *can* learn and progress, that achievement for all is changeable and not fixed, and that demonstrating to all students that they care about their learning is both powerful and effective.

Chapter 8

The contributions from the curricula

This chapter reviews various curricula and special types of programs. Given the attention to literacy and numeracy, it is not surprising that these dominate the literature as outcomes, but there are also meta-analyses relating to writing, drama/arts, science, values, and integrated curricula programs. The chapter also reviews specific programs such as creativity programs, bilingual programs, career interventions, outdoor programs, moral education programs, perceptual motor programs, tactile stimulation programs, and play. Table 8.1 summarizes the data examined.

Curricula programs: reading

Reading is one of the most contested curricula areas, as so many educationalists have made strong claims as to the best way to teach reading. Whatever the best method, if students do not develop sufficient reading acumen by the middle of elementary school, they are handicapped from learning in other curricula – as it does not take long in schooling to move from learning to read to reading to learn. The recent furore over the release of the National Reading Panel's summary of research (Langenberg, Correro, Ferguson, Kamil, & Shaywitz, 2000) or the Australian Literacy Report (Rowe, 2005) demonstrates the often entrenched positions that various researchers and teachers have to the teaching of reading. It is common to polarize the difference as phonics versus whole language, and the proponents of each are well heard. Even the mere act of defining reading can demonstrate the polarized claims. Anderson *et al.* (1985, p. 7) claimed that "reading is the process of constructing meaning from written texts" whereas Wixson, Peters, Weber, and Roeber (1987) preferred a more whole language definition, claiming that reading involves constructing meaning through the "dynamic interaction" among:

1   existing knowledge;
2   information suggested by the text;
3   the context of the reading situation.

This section summarizes 50 meta-analyses on reading research based on over 2,000 studies and about five million students, with an average effect of 0.51, and demonstrates the importance of gaining a *set of learning strategies* to construct meaning from text. This summary of the meta-analyses shows the importance and value of *actively* teaching the skills and strategies of reading across all years of schooling. There need to be planned, deliberate, explicit, and active programs to teach specific skills. Successful reading requires the development

Table 8.1 Summary information from the meta-analyses on the contributions from the curricula

School	No. metas	No. studies	No. people	No. effects	d	SE	CLE	Rank
Reading								
Visual-perception	6	683	379,400	5035	0.55	0.033	39%	35
Vocabulary programs	7	301	—	800	0.67	0.108	47%	15
Phonics instruction	14	425	12,124	5,968	0.60	0.221	43%	22
Sentence combining	2	35	—	40	0.15	0.087	10%	119
Repeated reading	2	54	—	156	0.67	0.080	47%	16
Comprehension programs	9	415	11,585	2,653	0.58	0.056	41%	28
Whole language	4	64	630	197	0.06	0.056	4%	129
Exposure to reading	6	114	118,593	293	0.36	0.090	25%	76
Second/third chance	2	52	5,685	1,395	0.50	—	35%	47
Writing programs	5	262	31,189	341	0.44	0.042	31%	57
Drama/arts programs	10	715	5,807,883	728	0.35	0.090	25%	77
Mathematics and science								
Mathematics	13	677	8,565	2,370	0.45	0.071	32%	54
Use of calculators	5	222	—	1,083	0.27	0.092	19%	93
Science	13	884	243,505	2,592	0.40	0.018	29%	64
Other curricula programs								
Values/moral education programs	2	84	27,064	97	0.24	—	17%	94
Social skills programs	8	540	7,180	2,278	0.40	0.031	27%	65
Career interventions	3	143	159,243	243	0.38	0.050	27%	69
Integrated curricula programs	2	61	7,894	80	0.39	0.050	28%	67
Perceptual-motor programs	1	180	13,000	637	0.08	0.011	6%	128
Tactile stimulation programs	1	19	505	103	0.58	0.145	41%	27
Play programs	2	70	5,056	70	0.50	—	35%	46
Creativity programs	12	685	23,299	837	0.65	0.097	47%	17
Outdoor/adventure programs	3	187	26,845	429	0.52	0.035	37%	43
Extra-curricular programs	5	102	—	68	0.17	0.072	12%	114
Bilingual programs	7	128	10,183	727	0.37	0.140	26%	73
Total	144	7,102	6,899,428	29,220	0.45	0.071	32%	—

of decoding skills, the development of vocabulary and comprehension, and the learning of specific strategies and processes. It is clear that some programs, particularly those based on skills and strategies, are successful, whereas others without such emphases have very minimal effects. Continuing to develop one's proficiency in reading depends on acquiring these skills as well as learning to derive meaning and often enjoyment from the skills of reading.

Reading: visual perception programs

Visual perception refers to the process of organizing and interpreting letters on a page, and is often considered an important aspect of early reading. Kavale and Forness (2000) found that both auditory and visual perception were important predictors of reading for both average students ($d = 0.36$) and students with learning or reading disabilities ($d = 0.38$). There was little difference in accuracy in predicting reading proficiency for many of the auditory perceptual skills (auditory comprehension $d = 0.40$, memory $d = 0.38$, blending $d = 0.38$, discrimination $d = 0.37$), or visual perceptual skills (memory $d = 0.47$, closure $d = 0.43$, discrimination $d = 0.39$, association $d = 0.38$, motor integration $d = 0.36$, spatial

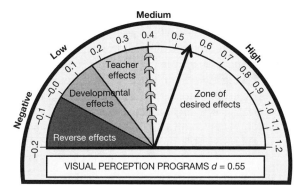

KEY

Standard error	0.033 (Low)
Rank	35th
Number of meta-analyses	6
Number of studies	683
Number of effects	5,035
Number of people (6)	379,400

relation $d = 0.33$), but it was lower for figure-ground discrimination ($d = 0.25$). Further, the ability to *integrate* perceptual stimuli appears no more associated with reading ability than individual auditory or visual skills. More importantly, the effects of the various auditory and visual perceptual skills were similarly related to word recognition and reading comprehension.

There were variations, however, according to the tests used to detect visual perception (Kavale, 1982a). The widely used Frostig development test of visual perception and accompanying training program were significantly less successful predictors of reading achievement than many other measures of visual-motor ability and visual-spatial relationships (e.g., the Bender and Illinois Psycholinguistic Abilities visual subtests). The conclusion was that the Frostig test or program was not particularly useful for either identifying preparing young students to read or for remediating visual perceptual deficits.

Reading: vocabulary programs

Stahl and Fairbanks (1986) found that vocabulary instruction and knowledge of word meanings generally help growth in reading comprehension. A mean effect size of 0.97 indicated that students who experienced vocabulary instruction had major improvements in reading comprehension of passages containing taught words; there was also an effect size of $d = 0.30$ for global measures of comprehension. The most effective vocabulary teaching methods included providing both definitional and contextual information,

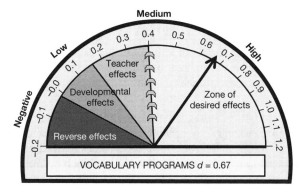

KEY

Standard error	0.108 (High)
Rank	15th
Number of meta-analyses	7
Number of studies	301
Number of effects	800
Number of people (0)	na

involved students in deeper processing, and gave students more than one or two exposures to the words they were to learn. The mnemonic keyword method also had positive effects on recall of definitions and sentence comprehension (see also Mastropieri & Scruggs, 1989). This method involves students first learning a concrete word than sounds like the target word, and then creating an image linking the target word to its definition. For example, for *angler*, a keyword could be *angel* and the interactive image could be an *angel catching a fish*. Klesius and Searls (1990) found similar high effect sizes for this keyword method, but also reported very quick fading effects, with the highest delayed post-test effect of only $d = 0.19$. Fukkink and de Glopper (1998) also examined the effects of instruction in deriving word meaning from context and claimed that the derivation of word meaning was indeed amenable to instruction with even relatively short instruction having positive effects.

Arnold, Myette, and Casto (1986) found that language intervention programs had immediate and positive gains for intellectually handicapped preschool children across many subject characteristics such as demographic, pretreatment language level, type of handicap, and medical history. Where there was significant neurological impairment, intervention effects were reduced. Nye, Foster, and Seaman (1987) found that language intervention in clinical settings was effective with language-disordered children, with experimental subjects moving from the 50th to the 85th percentile as a result of intervention. Treatment was more beneficial for language-disordered children than for those who were learning or reading disabled. Syntax showed the greatest degree of improvement but there was little effect on pragmatic language functioning. There was a greater degree of language improvement with the modeling approach than other methods (e.g., focused stimulation, comprehension). Kavale (1982b) found that psycholinguistic training programs were more affected by the Peabody Language Development Kit (PLDK), a highly structured sequence of lessons designed to increase general verbal ability, than either the Illinois Test of Psycholinguistic Abilities or other types of training activities (e.g., perceptual motor approaches). The structured and sequential nature of PLDK was considered the key element in the greater effectiveness.

These meta-analyses show that vocabulary programs are beneficial in developing reading skills and comprehension.

Reading: phonics instruction

> Phonics instruction teaches beginning readers the alphabetic code and how to use this knowledge to read words. In systematic phonics programs, a planned set of phonics elements is taught sequentially. The set includes the major correspondences between consonant letters and sounds, short and long vowel letters and sounds, and vowel and consonant digraphs ... It also may include blends of letter-sounds that form larger sub-units in words.
>
> (Ehri, Nunes, Stahl, & Willows, 2001, p. 394)

The meta-analysis published by the National Reading Panel (Langenberg *et al.*, 2000) made great play of the power of phonemic awareness in learning to read. They concluded that there are many tasks commonly used to assess and improve phonemic awareness, such as phoneme isolation (what is the first sound in *paste?*); identification (which sound is the same in *bike, boy, bell?*); categorization (recognizing sounds in sequence: *bus, bun, rug*);

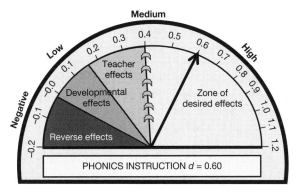

KEY	
Standard error	0.221 (High)
Rank	22nd
Number of meta-analyses	14
Number of studies	425
Number of effects	5,968
Number of people (5)	12,124

blending (which word is s/k/u/l?); segmentation (how many phonemes in *ship*?); and deletion (what word remains when s is removed from *smile*?). The panel argued that an essential part in learning to read involves:

> learning the alphabetic systems, that is, letter-sound correspondences and spelling patterns, and learning how to apply this knowledge in their reading. Systematic phonics instruction is a way of teaching reading that stresses the acquisition of letter-sound correspondents and their use to read and spell words (Harris & Hodges, 1995). Phonics instruction is designed for beginners in the elementary grades and for children having difficulty learning to read.
>
> (Langenberg *et al.*, 2000, p. 2–89)

The National Reading Panel found an overall effect size on phonological outcomes of $d = 0.86$, on reading outcomes of $d = 0.53$, and on spelling of $d = 0.59$. Teaching that focused on one or two types of phonemic awareness led to larger effects than teaching many more; teaching to manipulate phonemes using letters led to greater effects than teaching without letters; as did synthetic phonics programs that emphasized teaching students to convert letters into sounds and then blend the sounds to form recognizable words, and then analyze and blend larger subparts of words and phonemes. These phonemic awareness effects were present whether classroom teachers or computer formats were used, were higher for preschool than for higher grade levels (that is, more powerful in learning to read), and were effective when delivered through tutoring, in small groups, or through teaching classes of students.

These National Reading Panel findings were hotly contested, in part because there were so few studies used from the myriad of reading studies that were available. The findings from other meta-analyses on the teaching of reading, however, are not dissimilar in their conclusions from those of the National Reading Panel. For example, Bus and van Ijzendoorn (1999) conducted a meta-analysis of phonological awareness training programs and early reading. They determined that phonological awareness training should be seen as a causal factor in learning to read. The combined effect sizes for phonological awareness and reading were $d = 0.73$ and $d = 0.70$ for randomized and matched designs respectively. They noted that the effects for long-term studies were smaller than for short-term studies for both awareness and reading skills. At the same time, the effect of phonemic training was still discernable after, on average, 18.5 months.

Other findings included: training in groups for phonological awareness had more effect than individual training; programs combining phonological and letter training were more effective than phonological training alone; training effects were stronger with post-tests assessing simple decoding skills than with real-word identification tests; and preschoolers seemed to benefit from phonological training more than elementary school children, with effects decreasing as age increases. Stuebing, Barth, Cirino, Francis, and Fletcher (2008) reanalyzed the NRP data and concluded that phonics with additional language and literacy activities were the most effective. The core ingredients were phonics, fluency and comprehension.

Ehri, Nunes, Willows, Schuster, Yaghoub-Zadeh and Shanahan, (2001) only considered controlled experiments that included phonics instruction on learning to read. They concluded that:

> [The] benefits of phonemic awareness instruction were replicated multiple times across experiments and thus provided solid support for the claim that PA instruction is more effective than alternative forms of instruction or no instruction in teaching PA and in helping children acquire reading and spelling skills.
>
> (Ehri, *et al.*, 2001, p. 274)

The effects of phonemic awareness were as great with low as with middle and high socioeconomic status students (contrary to claims made by Dressman, 1999). Further, phonemic awareness did increase reading comprehension ($d = 0.34$). Thomas (2000) used kindergarten students (which probably accounts for his higher overall effect size), and concluded that the most successful phonemic awareness program was word recognition skills, implemented for more than 1.5 hours for more than 8 weeks ($d = 1.02$).

Direct instruction methods have been most powerful in teaching phonics skills. Swanson (1999) synthesized empirical evidence from research on reading intervention for students with learning disabilities and found that models that used both direct instruction and taught students strategies for recognizing words improved their reading comprehension performance. Swanson and colleagues (Swanson, Trainin, Necoechea, & Hammill, 2003) also found that measures such as rapid naming and letter identification were highly related to reading—especially reading comprehension. The greatest predictors of reading comprehension were real-word reading and spelling ability followed by word attack skills.

Overall, phonics instruction is powerful in the process of learning to read—both for reading skills and for reading comprehension.

Reading: sentence combining programs

Sentence combining is an instructional strategy that requires students to combine one or more sentences into one compound, complex, or compound-complex sentence (see Fusaro, 1993, p. 228). The effects are small. Neville and Searls (1991) found that sentence-combining as an instructional technique was much more effective at elementary than at high school levels, whereas Fusaro (1993) found that the effects of sentence-combining on reading comprehension were ambiguous across all levels. Overall the various reading meta-analyses, sentence-combining methods do not seem to have high value in the tool kit of reading instruction.

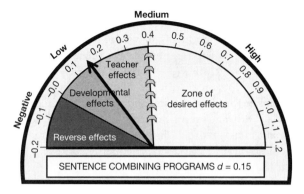

KEY

Standard error	0.087 (High)
Rank	119th
Number of meta-analyses	2
Number of studies	35
Number of effects	40
Number of people (0)	na

Reading: repeated reading programs

Repeated reading consists of re-reading a short and meaningful passage until a satisfactory level of fluency is reached. In their meta-analysis of repeated reading programs Chard, Vaughn, and Tyler (2002) identified a number of variables that they claimed explained the variation in learning to read. The greatest source of variance was the test format—effects from timed tests were larger than from untimed tests, and they argued that this was because timed tests were more likely to assess a student's capacity to automatically apply word recognition and decoding skills. Such automaticity usually develops naturally between second and third grade, but for learning disabled students it is a separate set of skills that need to be taught. Indeed tasks that require high levels of automaticity, such as rapid-naming tasks, are typically the major discriminating tasks between learning disabled and learning enabled children. Their message is clear— the skills of automaticity in word recognition and decoding (the move from accurate to automatic word reading) need to be specifically assessed and taught, especially to learning disabled students. It is perhaps not surprising that such automaticity, or over learning, is a major feature in many second- and third-chance reading programs (see below). Therrien (2004) found that the effects of repeated reading had marked positive effects on reading comprehension as well as reading fluency—although the effect on near transfer (immediate influence and comprehension) was greater ($d = 0.76$) than on far transfer (ability to fluently read or comprehend new passages), although the latter effect ($d = 0.50$) is still substantial.

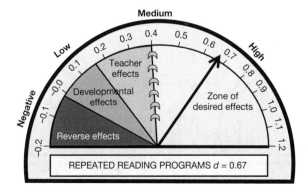

KEY

Standard error	0.080 (High)
Rank	16th
Number of meta-analyses	2
Number of studies	54
Number of effects	156
Number of people (0)	na

Reading: comprehension programs

Rowe (1985) undertook one of the earliest and largest meta-analyses of reading comprehension research. She found that the effects of these programs on vocabulary ($d = 1.77$) were greater that on reading comprehension outcomes ($d = 0.70$), and measures using words as the unit of analysis ($d = 1.28$) were greater than when whole texts were used ($d = 0.82$). In general, the effects were higher for more specific and structured outcomes. The effects were similar for poor ($d = 0.80$) and good readers ($d = 0.74$). Reading comprehension programs with a dominant focus on processing strategies (e.g., inferential reasoning, rules for summarizing, and chunking texts) produced a higher effect ($d = 1.04$) than did the text programs (e.g., repetition of concepts, explicitness, $d = 0.77$), and task programs ($d = 0.69$).

Sencibaugh (2005) reviewed two major programs: those using visually dependent strategies and those that depended on auditory or language strategies. Visually dependent strategies involved the use of pictures that improved reading comprehension, whereas auditory/language-dependent strategies involved language used in either pre-reading or post-reading activities to assist in comprehension. The former had an average effect of $d = 0.94$ and the latter $d = 1.18$, but the key was that these effects accrued only because the teacher had taught these specific strategies to augment reading comprehension. Pflaum, Walberg, Karegianes, and Rasher (1980) examined the viewpoint that different methods for teaching reading cause few differences in achievement. They found that this was largely true except for the superiority of the sound-symbol blending methods (single sounds or letters are taught separately and blended together). They concluded that the support from this form of systematic phonics appeared to be strong: that is, the synthesis of separate sounds associated with letters appears to be superior to many other methods.

Guthrie, McRae, and Klauda (2007) reviewed a specific program to enhance reading comprehension—the concept-oriented reading program. This program is based on the premise that the engaged reader is internally motivated to read, hence the aim is to engage students and attend to motivational as well as reading instruction strategies. The engaged reader is cognitively active in using strategies and seeking to link old to new information; behaviorally active in task participation, effort, and persistence in the face of difficulty; and reading frequently for pleasure and learning. The concept-oriented reading program is a 12-week intervention and each lesson has various segments: oral reading, a mini-lesson on comprehension strategies (inference, asking questions during reading, summarizing, and comprehension monitoring), independent writing and reading, and teacher-guided

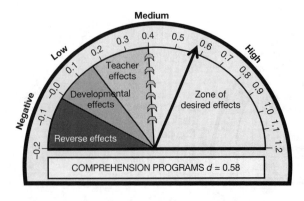

COMPREHENSION PROGRAMS $d = 0.58$

KEY	
Standard error	0.056 (Medium)
Rank	28th
Number of meta-analyses	9
Number of studies	415
Number of effects	2,653
Number of people (6)	11,585

reading in small groups (for modeling, scaffolding, and guided practice). The effects are positive on multiple text comprehension ($d = 0.93$), fluency ($d = 0.73$), and story comprehension ($d = 0.65$), as well as on motivation outcomes (curiosity $d = 0.47$, willingness to engage in challenge, $d = 0.31$, task orientation $d = 0.28$, self-efficacy $d = 0.49$).

Many have argued that words are learned incidentally during reading, and this is a major premise of those who argue that reading is best facilitated by a high frequency of reading experiences. A meta-analysis of studies on incidental word learning during normal reading showed that students learn only about 15 percent of the unknown words they encounter during normal reading (Swanborn & de Glopper, 2002). A low density of unknown words in a text produces a higher word learning change than a high density of unknown words. Students can learn words incidentally while reading; the effects are not only small, but also there is a confound with reading ability—older and more able students learn more word meanings during reading and thus if a student is a poor reader, it is unlikely that they will improve their learning of words just by being asked to read.

Reading: whole language

The whole language approach to reading instruction is based on the idea that the "acquisition of reading skills depends on the context in which these skills are presented. Individual words are learned more easily and fluently when presented within a particular context. The words gather meaning from other words around them and from the structure of the story" (Gee, 1995, p. 5). Gee found that such whole language approaches in reading instruction had positive influences on reading achievement. He did qualify this finding by noting that studies with larger sample sizes produced smaller effects, and interventions shorter than one year did not provide the depth of instruction to produce measurable outcomes.

At first look there is remarkable divergence in the overall effects from the four meta-analyses on whole language approaches. The average effect from the Gee study has an overall positive effect compared to the average from Jeynes and Littell (2000), which has an overall negative effect. There was much overlap in the articles used in these two meta-analyses and the difference is a function of how the authors classified some key studies, and the coding of what constituted whole language. On the latter, Gee included programs with systematic phonics and word study as whole language programs, and thus had what he considered a more "balanced" program of both sets of skills. For example, the study by Tunmer and Nesdale (1985) is classified as whole language, which is opposite

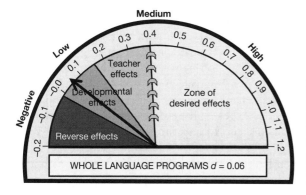

WHOLE LANGUAGE PROGRAMS $d = 0.06$

KEY	
Standard error	0.056 (Medium)
Rank	129th
Number of meta-analyses	4
Number of studies	64
Number of effects	197
Number of people (1)	630

from what Tunmer and Nesdale claimed for their program. Tunmer and Nesdale's three whole language classes, according to Gee, included a "heavy emphasis on the teaching of phonological recoding skills" (p. 421). Trachtenburg and Ferruggia's (1989) study, also classified by Gee as whole language, used various strategies including word lists, letter-sound naming, and decoding techniques. Similarly Gee classified Uhry and Shepherd's (1993) study as whole language, and they used segmentation and spelling instruction, a 10–20 minute phonics lesson, and copying words. If these three studies were reclassified so that they were not included as whole language studies, then the Gee average would shift from $d = +0.65$ to zero—and the average across all whole language meta-analyses to $d = 0.06$ and its rank to 129 out of 138.

Stahl and Miller (1989) also had zero effects ($d = 0.17$ for word recognition and $d = 0.09$ for reading comprehension) from whole language programs. Whole language approaches may be more effective in kindergarten than in first grade, they may produce higher (but still close to zero) effects on measures of word recognition than reading comprehension measures, and they are more effective when used instead of a reading readiness program. They compared the effects to basal readers, and there was a trend towards higher effects for basal reading programs. Stahl, McKenna, and Pagnucco (1994) carried out an update of Stahl and Miller's (1989) meta-analysis on whole language instruction and again reported small effect sizes. They did add that whole language approaches were effective in improving children's attitudes towards reading, and they concluded that there was a slight advantage for traditional approaches on measures of decoding.

The most recent study found a substantial negative relationship between whole language interventions compared to basal readers and learning to read programs. Jeynes and Littell (2000) investigated the effect of whole language instruction on the literacy of low-socio-economic status students from kindergarten through to grade level 3 and found that low socioeconomic status children receiving basal readers did consistently better than their counterparts receiving whole language instruction.

In summary, whole language programs have negligible effects on learning to read—be it on word recognition or on comprehension. Such methods may be of value to later reading, but certainly not for the processes of learning to read; it appears that strategies of reading need to be deliberately taught, especially to students struggling to read.

Reading: exposure to reading

What effect does exposing young children to reading have? The answer seems to be that it depends on who is doing the reading—the parent to engage in the excitement of reading, the teacher who uses reading aloud as a teaching tool, or a volunteer who seems to have little or any effect. Blok (1999) noted the pervasive push by many that teachers read to their young students almost every day. This typically involves "talking with and to the child" as reading fosters a great deal of interaction between the reader, the child, and the text. The overall effect was $d = 0.63$ on oral language and $d = 0.41$ on reading. The effects were higher with younger students, when the groups were small (as this fostered more interactions). It is not, however, merely exposure to reading but also the teaching of reading that makes the difference. Sustained silent reading, time on task alone, and having parents reading have much lower effects.

Having parents read to their children has positive effects on reading, and in particular on vocabulary acquisition. A meta-analysis on intergenerational transmission of literacy

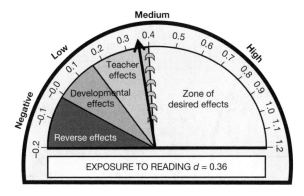

KEY	
Standard error	0.090 (High)
Rank	76th
Number of meta-analyses	6
Number of studies	114
Number of effects	293
Number of people (3)	118,593

affirmed the positive effect of parent–child interactions in supporting children's literacy orientation (Bus, van Ijzendoorn, & Pellegrini, 1995). Parent–preschooler joint book reading experiences were shown to be related to positive outcomes in language growth ($d = 0.67$), emergent literacy ($d = 0.58$) and reading achievement ($d = 0.55$). This was so across all socioeconomic groups. The effects were not restricted to preschoolers but did diminish as children became more able to read on their own.

Reading to children, however, is not sufficient to lead to competent readers—instruction is also needed. Torgerson, King, and Sowden (2002) investigated the effects of unpaid classroom volunteers to provide extra support to children learning to read. Almost half the studies showed negative effects, and the overall relationship was small indeed. Their conclusion was that the "there is little good evidence that the policy of encouraging volunteers to help teach children to read is effective" (p. 443). Exposure and practice in listening to reading is insufficient. Lewis and Samuels (2003) found that more practice at reading was minimally associated with reading gains ($d = 0.10$). The effects were slightly larger for grade 1 to 3 students, second language students, learning disabled students, and students reading below grade level: practice helps minimally but is not enough. Similarly, Yoon (2002) found that sustained silent reading had little effect on reading attitude, and the effects drop to zero above grade 3—students who struggle or do not enjoy reading gain little reading instruction when silent reading; it is another opportunity to engage in an activity confirming that reading is not enjoyable.

Reading: second- and third-chance programs

The Reading Recovery program was invented by Dame Marie Clay, who was also a professor at the University of Auckland in New Zealand. Reading Recovery is a second-chance program undertaken over a 12 to 20-week specified period. Children are discontinued from the program when it is agreed that they are ready to return to regular classroom instruction. D'Agostino and Murphy (2004) found that Reading Recovery students outperformed control students especially on scales in the observation schedule (a key part of the program). They concluded that Reading Recovery "was reaching its fundamental goal of increasing the lowest performing first graders' reading and writing skills to levels comparable with their classroom peers" (p. 35), and there was a "lasting effect, at least by the end of second grade, on broad reading skills".

Students at risk for reading failure who complete the Reading Recovery program have

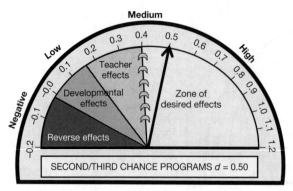

KEY	
Standard error	na
Rank	47th
Number of meta-analyses	2
Number of studies	52
Number of effects	1,395
Number of people (1)	5,685

been found to perform better than those at risk not receiving this intervention (Elbaum, Vaughn, Hughes, & Moody, 2000). Large effect sizes were found for Reading Recovery ($d = 0.96$), and it was highest when Reading Recovery was a supplement to, not a substitute for, classroom teaching. The effects were high for reading comprehension ($d = 0.67$), decoding ($d = 0.56$), and oral reading of words ($d = 0.69$). Elbaum *et al.* concluded that "well-designed, reliably implemented, one-to-one interventions can make a significant contribution to improved reading outcomes for many students whose poor reading skills place them at risk of academic failure" (p. 617).

Overall comments on reading meta-analyses

There is much support for the five pillars of good reading instruction: phonemic awareness, phonics, fluency, vocabulary, and comprehension—and attending to all is far more critical than whether the program teaches one of the five as opposed to another. The most effective programs for teaching reading are, first, to attend to the visual and auditory perceptual skills. Then a combination of vocabulary, comprehension, and phonics instruction with repeated reading opportunities is the most powerful set of instructional methods. The least effective methods are whole language, sentence combining, and assuming that students will learn vocabulary incidentally when reading. If reading is not successful the first time, then second-chance programs such as Reading Recovery are most effective. Another way of summarizing the typical debate is that a teacher using the whole language method needs to be at least ten times more effective in his or her teaching than a teacher using the phonics methods to attain the same outcomes in developing reading vocabulary, skills, and comprehension. A teacher using a combination of vocabulary, phonics, and comprehension methods will be much more effective than either a phonics or a whole language teacher.

It is noted that most of the research, not surprisingly, concentrates on the early years of reading, and there are no meta-analyses and only limited research evidence about teaching to read beyond the first years. In our study of New Zealand classrooms from grades 3 to 12 ($N = 40,000$) we found that there was a flattening of reading in the upper years of elementary school, which then accelerated as the students moved through their high school years (Hattie, 2007). More than 80 percent of students in year 5 are at or *above* expectation, but by year 8 close to half are *below* expectation, returning to about 80 percent *above* by year 11 (see Figure 8.10).

Chall (1983, 1996) has argued that reading is not a process that is the same from the beginning

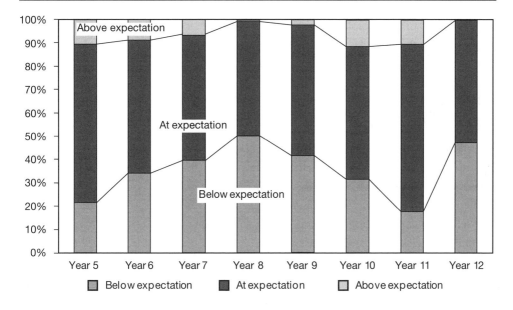

Figure 8.10 The percentage of students performing below, at, and above expectation in each year level

stages through to mature, skilled reading, but one that changes as the reader becomes more able and proficient. We did not find, however, a "4th grade reading slump" as did Chall—there was no slump; just no growth or increase during the upper elementary years. Several potential reasons for this plateau effect were suggested (Hattie, 2007). These reasons include that teachers do not have a common conception of progress in learning to read during these years; most curricula do not attend to reading progressions; and there is so much emphasis placed on early learning to read that we have not built a perceived need to then continue to develop excellent programs to build on this early start. Other factors in the plateau effect could be that an early lack of word meaning would mean readers could fail to capitalize on a sufficient depth and breadth of words to thus sustain growth in reading; a lack of fluency and automaticity (that is, quick and accurate recognition of words and phrases) may hamper growth beyond first learning to read; and that schooling in these upper years has less emphasis on decoding and inference and more on reading of expository tests. Also, previously "unimportant" reading difficulties may appear for the first time in Grade 5 when children encounter informational materials and multiple text types that require more inference, comprehension, vocabulary of less frequent words, connections, and understanding (Snow, Burns, & Griffin, 1998). Finally, we need to learn from what high school teachers do as the flattening turns to an incline when students enter high schools (e.g., they demand that students use their skills in finding information, connections, inference, and understanding—the higher level skills in reading—in the content area literacy and comprehension domains).

Writing programs

Graham and Perin (2007) completed the largest study of writing programs. They recommended that it is powerful to teach strategies for planning, revising, and editing compositions

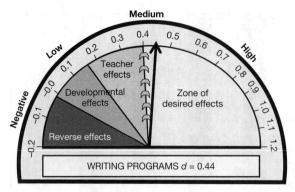

KEY

Standard error	0.042 (Medium)
Rank	57th
Number of meta-analyses	5
Number of studies	262
Number of effects	341
Number of people (3)	31,189

($d = 0.82$), particularly if the students are struggling writers. Effect sizes for various strategies were: strategies for summarizing reading material ($d = 0.82$), working together to plan, draft, revise, and edit ($d = 0.75$), setting clear and specific goals for what students are to accomplish with their writing product ($d = 0.70$), using word processing ($d = 0.55$), and teaching students strategies to write increasingly complex sentences ($d = 0.50$). The results show the power of teaching students the processes and strategies involved in writing, structuring the teaching of writing by having students work together in an organized fashion, and of setting clear and specific goals, especially as to the *purpose* of each piece of writing.

Bangert-Drowns, Hurley, and Wilkinson (2004) also found support for developing writing programs that were more informational, personal, imaginative, or attended to the meta-cognitive reflections of the writing task. Gersten and Baker (2001) found similar effects for strategy teaching with students with learning disabilities. They reported a $d = 0.81$ effect from expressive writing programs with students involved in collaborative practice with teachers ($d = 0.76$), with peers ($d = 0.70$), for teacher modeling of strategy use ($d = 0.68$), for use of procedural prompts ($d = 0.86$), and for use of computers ($d = 0.64$). The emphasis is on explicit teaching of the critical steps of the writing process, the conventions of a writing genre, and guided feedback. They noted that:

> teachers or peers provided frequent feedback to students on the overall quality of writing, missing elements, and strengths. When feedback was combined with instruction on the writing process or text structure, a common vocabulary was created that gave teachers and students a meaningful way to engage in dialogue, which results in improved written products. The prompts helped give teachers or peers concrete suggestions for providing appropriate feedback.
>
> (Gersten & Baker, 2001, p. 266)

Atkinson (1993) reported an effect size of $d = 0.52$ from workshop instructional treatments of writing, $d = 0.32$ from computer support, $d = 0.45$ from teaching of inquiry skills. The common elements of what was successful in workshops were the use of teams, peer-feedback, and collaborative authorship. The effect from the inquiry skills method was similar to that reported by Hillocks (1984, $d = 0.56$) and this typically included exploration of and systematic approaches to learning various strategies in writing. Atkinson also argued that these treatments may be the result of the relationship with an "audience" "either because of the presence of a real and immediate audience as in writing workshops, or because of a need to collaborate with others to complete a task" (p. 105). The importance of including the purpose of writing in the lesson is thus emphasized.

Drama/Arts programs

Kardash and Wright (1987) found that creative drama activities have positive effects on children's achievement at elementary grade levels in oral language skills, self-esteem, moral reasoning, role-taking abilities, and drama skills. Conard's (1992) meta-analysis of experimental studies examined the effect of creative drama on the acquisition of cognitive skills and found an effect size of 0.48 for studies in which creative drama was used as an instructional tool. Creative drama tended to be more effective at the preschool and elementary school levels than for older children, and both regular and remedial students appeared to benefit from and enjoy participating in creative drama. Butzlaff (2000) argued that practice in reading music notation makes the reading of linguistic notation an easier task; this is because the skill in listening to music requires a sensitivity to tonal distinctions that can assist in acquiring a sensitivity to phonological distinctions; reading the repetitive and hence predictable lyrics of songs helps train reading skills; and working together in music groups instils a sense of personal responsibility, which in turns leads to heightened academic responsibility and performance. He was more cautious, however, about the effect size between participating in music programs and achievement in reading, claiming that causality could not be determined from his meta-analysis.

Hetland (2000) related the listening to music by college students and improvement in spatial-temporal reasoning ($d = 0.49$), but she was hard-pressed to find any importance of this finding to education, noted it was remarkably variable, and at best was temporary. It is likely that the two skills—listening to music and spatial reasoning—may be related because they depend on some similar underlying skills. Moga, Burger, Hetland, and Winner (2000) conducted three studies on the relation between studying the arts and creative thinking. There was a medium association for figural but zero for verbal/conceptual creativity outcomes.

> we find some transfer when the bridge is narrow: from experience in the arts, which includes the visual arts, to performance on tests requiring drawing. We find no transfer when the bridge is wide: from experience in the arts to performance on tests requiring one to generate ideas, concepts, or words.
>
> (Moga *et al.*, 2000, p. 102)

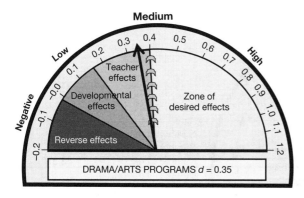

DRAMA/ARTS PROGRAMS *d* = 0.35

KEY	
Standard error	0.090 (High)
Rank	77th
Number of meta-analyses	10
Number of studies	715
Number of effects	728
Number of people (4)	5,807,883

Standley (1996) reviewed 98 studies with 208 effects and found that providing music when students had successfully completed an activity had dramatic effects ($d = 2.90$) in promoting education and therapy objectives. The problem of this meta-analysis is that many of the more extreme effects were from therapy rather than from education—although the effects on education were still very large. Specifically, using music (mainly as a reward) increased behavior across various ability groups (e.g., physically or medically impaired $d = 2.25$; emotionally impaired $d = 2.38$, normal $d = 2.99$, mentally impaired $d = 3.16$). The effects on achievement outcomes was still a very large $d = 2.18$ ($N = 24$). They concluded that "music is highly effective as a contingency for either increasing desirable behavior or reducing undesirable behavior, with slightly better results in increasing behavior. Music interruption is more effective than music initiative as the procedure for establishing the contingency" (p. 124).

Vaughn (2000) found a medium relation between the voluntary study of music and mathematic achievement, but the effects of training in instrumental or vocal music performance were much lower. Playing music in the background while students are taking mathematics tests has only a small positive effect, perhaps an arousal effect, at best. Winner and Cooper (2000) found a very small relation between studying arts and achievement ($d = 0.10$); the relation to verbal was higher ($d = 0.39$) than mathematics ($d = 0.20$). They were careful not to assume causality, and suggested that studying the arts may lead to greater engagement in schooling, which in turn leads to greater academic achievement.

Mathematics programs

The major interests in the mathematics meta-analyses have related to the use of aids such as calculators, manipulative materials, and graphing aids. There are three major themes in these studies. The effects of many of these innovatives are greatest: with the lower compared to higher ability students; when aids are provided to reduce cognitive load (such as using calculators to reduce the load of calculation in problem solving); and with feedback from teachers to students and students to teachers.

The power of feedback to students learning mathematics was highlighted by Baker, Gersten, and Lee (2002). They found that the highest effects accrued when teachers provided feedback data or recommendations to students ($d = 0.71$), then for peer-assisted learning ($d = 0.62$), explicit teacher-led instruction ($d = 0.65$), direct instruction ($d = 0.65$), and concrete feedback to parents ($d = 0.43$). The lowest effects occurred when teachers

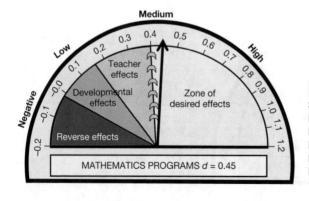

KEY	
Standard error	0.071 (Medium)
Rank	54th
Number of meta-analyses	13
Number of studies	677
Number of effects	2,370
Number of people (4)	8,565

emphasized real-world applications of mathematics ($d = -0.04$). As they noted, one consistent finding was that providing teachers and students with specific information on how each student was performing seemed to enhance mathematics achievement consistently.

Like most curricula domains, there are many packages or ideas about how a subject should be taught. "Modern" or new mathematics was heralded as a major breakthrough as it involved making mathematics more relevant to real-world problems, and involved a high level of use of manipulative materials. The overall effects ($d = 0.24$) are reasonably similar across all levels of schooling, but lower in kindergarten and post-high school (Athappilly, Smidchens, & Kofel, 1983). Lower ability students gain more ($d = 0.35$) than middle ($d = 0.25$) or high ability students ($d = 0.21$). Effects are higher for teaching concepts ($d = 0.36$) and computation ($d = 0.31$), but not application ($d = 0.06$); and higher in algebra ($d = 0.43$) than in arithmetic ($d = 0.21$) and geometry ($d = 0.14$). Overall, the use of manipulative materials does not detract but does little to support the learning of mathematics (Mitchell, 1987). However, there are more effective methods than manipulables. In a study investigating differing methods for teaching high school algebra (Haas, 2005), the greatest effects were from direct instruction ($d = 0.55$) and problem solving ($d = 0.52$), and the lowest effects were from technology-aided ($d = 0.07$) and communication and study skills methods ($d = 0.07$). There were medium effects from cooperative learning ($d = 0.34$) and manipulative, models, and multiple representations ($d = 0.38$). Haas concluded that the higher effects from direct instruction were because of its focus on desired learning outcomes, decisions about pacing and curriculum emphasis, and the emphasis of seeking enhanced learning for all students.

Similarly powerful effects of feedback and strategy teaching are found in studies of teaching mathematics to lower ability students. Lee (2000) investigated the influences on mathematics competencies for learning disabled and lower achieving students. The programs with greatest effect were strategy-based methods ($d = 0.85$), guided practice ($d = 0.86$), peer tutoring ($d = 0.76$), teacher modeling ($d = 0.73$), using specific forms of feedback ($d = 0.62$), using mastery criteria ($d = 0.63$), sequencing examples ($d = 0.58$), and changing instruction on the basis of feedback ($d = 0.42$). The least effective were using the strategy of working within a peer group ($d = 0.15$), using technology for independent practice ($d = 0.16$), using alternative representation modes ($d = 0.26$), and identifying and teaching relevant preskills ($d = 0.28$). Similarly, Sowell (1989) and Parham (Parham, 1983) found that the use of manipulative materials in mathematics had highest effects on the concrete, rather than the more abstract, instructional components.

Use of calculators

One major form of "manipulable" aids is calculators and this has been subject to much debate. With one exception, the meta-analyses show a low but positive (about $d = 0.20$) effect from the presence of calculators in mathematics. The key findings supporting the use of calculators seem to be: a) when they are used for computation, drill and practice work, and for checking work; (b) when they reduce the cognitive 'load' on students so they can attend to other, more mathematical, concepts; and (c) when used for a pedagogical purpose in which they are to be an important element in the teaching and learning process.

Ellington (2000) found that the effects of calculators were greatest for lower ability students ($d = 0.30$), most variable for average ability students ($d = 0.20$), and negative for

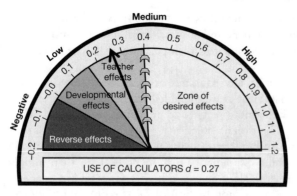

KEY	
Standard error	0.092 (High)
Rank	93rd
Number of meta-analyses	5
Number of studies	22
Number of effects	1,083
Number of people (0)	na

high ability students ($d = -0.23$). The argument was that calculators can assist in reducing the cognitive load for the lower ability students whereas the higher ability students are less constrained by the additional requirements of knowing the computational aspects when learning mathematics. Further, Ellington found that the effects were much higher when calculators were involved in the teaching process; for example, when used for composition problem solving, the effects were $d = 0.72$: "When compared with students who did not use calculators, students in treatment groups were able to solve more problems and make better decisions with regard to selecting methods for generating solutions" (Ellington, 2003, p. 169). Ellington (2006) specifically investigated graphing calculators, and the overall effects were quite low, although the effects were larger for conceptual ($d = 0.72$) compared with procedural ($d = 0.52$) skills. When students were allowed to use these calculators as part of instruction but tested without them, the effects were negative ($d = -0.21$). The conclusion was that the calculator is neither a help nor a hindrance to students' overall mathematics achievement, and at minimum their use helps reduce cognitive load and enhance students' attitudes towards the study of mathematics. Smith (1996) also reported a positive effect of calculators on attitude ($d = 0.37$), but lower effects on computational skills ($d = 0.21$), concept development ($d = 0.19$), problem solving ($d = 0.15$) and graphing skills ($d = -0.05$). He found greater effects for calculators for high school compared to elementary school students—except for the use of graphing calculators in high schools. Nikolaou (2001) found a higher effect on problem solving skills ($d = 0.49$, particularly in pre-algebra classes). He found no differences in the effects relating to socioeconomic status, gender, grade level, student ability level, student ethnicity, or student calculator expertise.

Hembree and Dessart (1986) found that the pedagogical use of calculators improved students' basic skills both in completing exercises and problem solving. Across all grades (and particularly above grade 5, when calculators become more prevalent) and across all ability levels, students using calculators led to greater effects in students' basic skills in operations and particularly in problem solving. The effects on problem solving seem to relate to improved computation and lower cognitive workload demands. They also found that there was a better attitude toward mathematics and an especially higher self-concept in mathematics for those using calculators compared to those not using calculators. Their suggestion was that this enhancement in attitude was probably because the use of calculators helped relieve students' traditional dislike of problems expressed in words (by reducing the cognitive load of having to compute as well as problem solve).

Overall, the presence of feedback, direct instruction, strategy-based methods, high levels of challenge and mastery has much effect on the learning of mathematics. That is, directive teaching makes the difference when teaching mathematics. Using manipulative materials and calculators helps to reduce students' cognitive load and allows them to devote their attention to problem solving

Science programs

Many of the meta-analyses in science investigated competing science curricula. Shymansky (1984) looked at new science programs, most of which were developed in the 1960s and early 1970s. The programs typically emphasized analytic and process skills, integrated laboratory activities as an integral part of the class routine, and higher cognitive skills and appreciation of science. This is in contrast to traditional curricula, which emphasized knowledge of scientific facts, laws, theories, and applications. In general, students on the skills-based programs outperformed students in traditional classes on attitudes, process skills, analytic skills, and achievement (Kyle, 1982). Shymansky, Kyle, and Alport (1983) found positive effects on all outcomes but self-concept. In particular there were higher effects on areas involving higher cognitive skills (critical thinking, problem solving, creativity, logical thinking), and on reading, mathematics, and communication skills. The effects were positive in life sciences, general science, physics, and biology but not in chemistry or earth science. Kyle (1982) also noted that new science curricula in biology produced the most positive scores and also that chemistry and earth science had the least positive effect.

The use of laboratory and more hands–on activities has produced mixed results. Rubin (1996) distinguished between two forms of laboratory experiences. The first form aims to question, explain, and encourage thinking at higher levels, and use a variety of sources to discover answers to questions. The second form uses "the laboratory" to verify what has been previously presented. When these two methods were compared, Rubin found major differences ($d = 0.57$) between these two uses, in favor of the first use. Kyle (1982) reported that students in science classes with a low rather than high emphasis on laboratory activities had higher outcomes. Rubin partly explained these lower effects by introducing an important moderator—laboratory experiences increased outcomes relating to manipulation skills ($d = 1.26$) rather than reasoning skills ($d = 0.06$) or concepts and subject learning ($d = 0.33$).

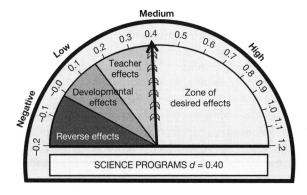

KEY	
Standard error	0.018 (Low)
Rank	64th
Number of meta-analyses	13
Number of studies	844
Number of effects	2,592
Number of people (5)	243,505

Many of these newer curricula emphasized strategies and processing and this required teachers to thus use these methods rather than a more didactic form of teaching. Yeany and Padilla (1983) carried out a research synthesis comparing the effectiveness of various procedures for training science teachers to use better teaching strategies. All procedures were found to have a positive effect on the behavior of science teachers, as did all strategy analysis training methods. This study suggests that the more formalized the training becomes, the greater the effect (replicated by Shymansky *et al.*, 1983). Analysis with feedback was the most effective training technique; observing or analyzing models had an intermediate effect; and just studying an analysis system and self-analysis were least effective. The greatest changes were more on conceptual understanding. Effects were greatest on both innovative and neutral tests, and much lower on tests favoring traditional science content (Weinstein, Boulanger, & Walberg, 1982). Bredderman (1983) cautioned, however, that the advantages of these activity-based curricula for elementary school students may be lost when they later enroll in classrooms where more traditional methods prevail.

Wise and Okey (1983) looked at the effects of various science teaching strategies on achievement. Experimental science teaching techniques, on average, resulted in one third of a standard deviation improvement over traditional techniques. Their results suggest that an effective classroom is one in which students are kept aware of instructional objectives and receive feedback on their progress towards these goals. Students also need to have opportunities to physically interact with instructional materials and engage in a range of activities. Verbal interactions focused on a plan, such as the cognitive level of positioning of questions asked during lessons, were effective. Overall, the effective science classroom reflected considerable teacher planning, with students taking some responsibility for task definition.

Schroeder, Scott, Tolson, Huang, and Lee (2007) also investigated the effects of various science teaching strategies on achievement. The highest effects came from enhanced content strategies (e.g., relating topics to previous experience or learning and engaging students' interest; $d = 1.48$), collaborative learning strategies ($d = 0.67$), inquiry strategies ($d = 0.65$), manipulation strategies ($d = 0.57$), assessment strategies ($d = 0.51$), and instructional technology strategies ($d = 0.48$). They concluded that "if students are placed in an environment in which they can actively connect the instruction to their interests and present understandings and have an opportunity to experience collaborative scientific inquiry under the guidance of an effective teacher, achievement will be accelerated" (p. 1452).

There are many successful methods for engendering conceptual change in science. Guzzetti, Snyder, Glass, and Gamas (1993) found that learning charts ($d = 0.43$), discussion webs ($d = 0.51$), and augmented activation ($d = 0.43$) were more effective than activation of prior knowledge ($d = 0.10$) and question–answer–explanation ($d = 0.02$) in reducing misconceptions from reading science texts. Texts are the most effective way to eliminate misconceptions, either when text is refutational or when text is used in combination with other strategies that cause cognitive conflict. These refutational texts created a form of cognitive dissonance in students' thinking and thus students could be taught to explain why the misconception was incorrect: "Augmented activation activities facilitated cognitive conflict by directing the reader's attention to contradictory information in the text or by providing illustrative demonstrations that caused incongruity with extant beliefs" (Guzzetti *et al.*, 1993, p. 134). Horak (1985) also found positive effects ($d = 0.57$) from students reading science texts that helped them to select important aspects of the written material, and from students reading those texts that aided in building internal connections within the textual materials.

Wise (1996) examined a number of teaching strategies, and found the following effects: teacher questioning ($d = 0.58$), focusing strategies ($d = 0.57$), manipulation strategies (work or practice with physical objects, $d = 0.58$), enhanced materials (teacher modification of instructional materials, $d = 0.52$), use of immediate or explanatory feedback ($d = 0.32$), inquiry strategies ($d = 0.28$), enhanced context strategies (e.g., field trips, games, self-paced learning, $d = 0.26$), and instructional media ($d = 0.18$). He concluded that active construction of meaning is most often likely to occur "when science teachers use strategies that require students to be both physically and mentally engaged" (Wise, 1996, p. 338).

Values and moral education programs

Character education is an umbrella term for many programs: citizenship training, health education, conflict resolution training, life skills, service learning, moral reasoning, moral education, values verification, ethics, and religious education. Berg (2003) investigated 29 values-based character education programs. These programs typically related to character education, citizenship training, life skills, values clarification, moral reasoning, ethics and religious education: "almost anything schools might try to provide outside of academics, especially when the purpose is to help children grow into good people" (Kohn, 1997, p. xx). Most effects related to behavior and attitude ($d = 0.24$) but there were some relating to the effects of these programs on achievement ($d = 0.20$).

The major outcome from moral education programs is the facilitation of moral judgment, that is, the way in which people define decisions or actions as morally right or wrong (Schlaefli, Rest, & Thoma, 1985), and as this is not strictly achievement as typically defined, these are not included in the tables. The overall effect of 0.28 from the moral education programs that emphasized moral dilemma discussions had slightly higher effects ($d = 0.41$) compared to those based on personality development ($d = 0.36$). The effects were greater for adults ($d = 0.61$) than for college students ($d = 0.28$), senior high school students ($d = 0.23$) and junior high school students ($d = 0.22$).

Social skills programs

Social skills or social competence programs are usually provided for learners whose behavior is either highly internalized or highly externalized (e.g., socially isolated and withdrawn, or exhibitionist). The aim is higher levels of social appropriateness, social problem solving

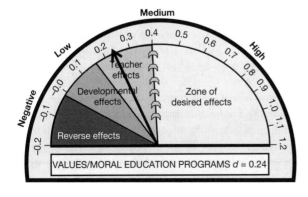

KEY	
Standard error	na
Rank	94th
Number of meta-analyses	2
Number of studies	84
Number of effects	97
Number of people (1)	27,064

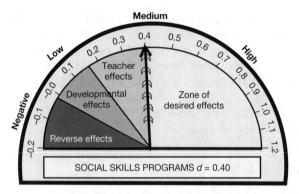

KEY	
Standard error	0.031 (Low)
Rank	65th
Number of meta-analyses	8
Number of studies	540
Number of effects	2,278
Number of people (3)	7,180

skills, self-control, or social perspective training. Over all these meta-analyses involving social skills programs, the effects are stronger on enhancing peer relations (d = 0.80 to d = 0.90) and social outcomes (about d = 0.5 to d = 0.6); lower when the students are initially identified as social problems (d = 0.20); and lowest when academic achievement is the outcome of the social-skill programs (d = 0.10 to d = 0.20). Students with learning disabilities have lower social skills than their non-disabled peers (d = 0.60 to d = 0.70). In all these programs there were mostly short-term gains, indicating a need to provide social skills training on a regular and sustained basis.

Three meta-analyses are more concerned with the effects of social skills training on social outcomes. Beelmann, Pfingsten, and Loesel (1994) found that social competence training was an effective intervention in children's (three to 15 years) social outcomes in the short term (d = 0.61). The effects were greatest on social-cognitive skills (d = 0.77), compared to social interaction skills (d = 0.34), social adjustment (d = 0.18), and self-related cognitions (e.g., self-concept, control beliefs). The greatest effects were for at-risk children and younger children, and larger effect sizes were only found when direct goal criteria such as social-cognitive skills were evaluated. There were few effects on broader constructs such as social adjustment. Furthermore, long-term effects were weak. Social skills programs can make a positive difference to social outcomes, particularly social problem solving programs. Denham and Almeida (1987) were particularly interested in the effects on interpersonal social cognitive problem solving (ICPS) and found similar effects (d = 0.62) (see also Beelmann *et al.*, 1994). An increase in ICPS skills is related to improvement in behavioral adjustment, particularly for elementary-aged children. The more effective programs were behavioral programs, dialogue between teacher and student on social problem solving, and when interventions lasted for 40 lessons or more. Hanson's (1988) review of social skills training literature found that the average participant in a social skills training program was more socially skilful than 74 percent of those who had not been given training (d = 0.65). There were greater effects from measures based on behavioral observation, followed by self-report and role-play, and then teacher ratings.

The domain with the highest effects from social skills training related to peer relations among all students (Schneider, 1992, d = 0.98). He found that there was overall short-term moderate effectiveness in social skills training. The more effective programs were the use of coaching and modeling, particularly when focused on individual peer relation issues. They suggested that students receiving social skills training may benefit in reduced social anxiety, increased comfort in social situations, or enhanced motivation as they are made to feel that meaningful improvements in social behaviors are within reach. The effects on academic achievement were very low ($d = 0.19$).

Two meta-analyses were more concerned with the effects of social training on students with specific issues (emotional or behavioral disorders). Quinn, Kavale, Mathur, Rutherford, and Forness (1999) were particularly concerned with students with emotional or behavioral disorders and not surprisingly found lower overall effects ($d = 0.20$). This effect was similar when rated by teachers, self, peer, experimenter, or parent; and for pro-social behavior (social relations, behavior, problem solving, competence), problem behaviors (family relations, school social behavior, social communication, and disruptive behavior) and for specific social outcomes (anxiety, adjustment, cooperation, self-concept, and aggression). There were no differences related to duration of the intervention, or whether the program was established or published, or created for the particular group. Forness and Kavale (1996) found similar low effects when social skills programs were implemented with children with learning disabilities and social skill deficits ($d = 0.21$). Again, there were no differences in length of treatment, whether peer, teacher, or self assessed, and across social outcomes—with one exception: students in social skills programs believed that their social status was enhanced. Forness and Kavale found that the most effective social skills training included a combination of modeling, coaching, and reinforcement programs particularly when the social skills training related directly to the student's social skills deficit—although the persistence of the effects over time was problematic.

The last two meta-analyses were more concerned with the differences in social skills between learning disabled and non-disabled comparison groups. Kavale and Forness (1996) found high degrees of differences in social skills between learning disabled and non-disabled comparison groups. The differences in social skills were quite marked ($d = 0.65$). Kavale and Forness claimed that students with learning disabilities were generally assessed as having social skills deficits irrespective of who assessed them—teachers, peers, or self (although self-assessments were somewhat harsher). Teachers indicated that they considered students as having "learning difficulties" if they had lower academic competence, particularly if they also had social skill deficits. The dimensions of social skills rated highest by teachers were interaction, adjustment, hyperactivity, and distractibility. The lowest were aggression, conduct disorder, dependency, and personality problems. Peers were more likely to reject, and have limited acceptance of, disabled students, particularly those with lower social competencies. Learning disabled students were less popular, less often selected as friends, and viewed as less cooperative. Swanson and Malone (1992) found that in social situations, disabled students were more likely than non-disabled students to be rejected by peers, less well liked, more likely to be rated as aggressive and immature, perceived as suffering from personality problems, and perceived as having difficulty staying on-task. Children with learning disabilities have an accurate perception of their status within the classroom!

Career education programs

Career education involves activities and experiences designed to increase knowledge of occupations, training paths, job-search skills and decision-making strategies that include the integration of work, family, leisure, and community roles (see www.career-symposium. org/act_Defs.html on 14 April 2005). Career education programs do seem to have positive effects on student outcomes (Baker & Popowicz, 1983). Oliver and Spokane (1988) found

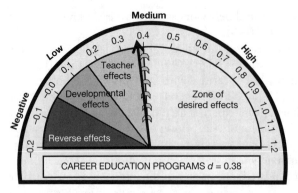

KEY	
Standard error	0.050 (Medium)
Rank	69th
Number of meta-analyses	3
Number of studies	143
Number of effects	243
Number of people (1)	159,243

that career counseling has generally positive effects, with class interventions the most effective but requiring the greatest number of hours. Individual counseling was shown to produce more client gain per hour than other intervention models. Intensity of treatment was the only significant contributor to more positive outcomes. Evans and Burck (1992) found that career education interventions did contribute to academic achievement, but the interventions only improved student academic standards an average of $d = 0.16$ over alternative or control conditions. Elementary school students of average ability benefited most academically, particularly if: they were randomly assigned to groups; the intervention was coupled with mathematics and language arts subject matter; and the program averaged 151 to 200 hours per school year.

Integrated curricula programs

Hartzler (2000) investigated 30 studies using integrated curricula and found different effects by subject: science ($d = 0.61$), language arts ($d = 0.42$), social studies ($d = 0.38$), and mathematics ($d = 0.42$). The most important elements in integrated programs were thematic instruction ($d = 0.46$), and an emphasis on process skills ($d = 0.36$). Integrated programs were more successful in elementary ($d = 0.56$) and middle school ($d = 0.57$) compared to high school ($d = 0.27$); for lower compared to middle and higher achieving students; for ethnically diverse students; and when more experienced teachers implemented the programs.

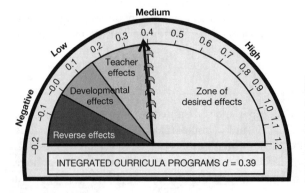

KEY	
Standard error	0.050 (Medium)
Rank	67th
Number of meta-analyses	2
Number of studies	61
Number of effects	80
Number of people (1)	7,894

Hurley (2001) investigated integrated mathematic and science programs. The effects were higher on mathematics ($d = 0.37$) than science ($d = 0.27$). The conclusion was that integrating mathematics into science might be good for science, but the effects for mathematics were greater when taught in sequence with science, particularly when science was taught prior to mathematics—as the effects were the greatest on the subject taught last (probably because of the greater level of integration from the first to the last taught).

Perceptual motor programs

Perceptual motor training is an intervention more often used with learning difficulty students. It was extremely popular in the 1950 to 1970s and is still evident in some schools today. Programs typically include teaching in visual and figure and ground discrimination, visual motor abilities, visual spatial perception, and balance and body awareness. Using 180 studies that examined the effect of perceptual motor training on learning disabled children, Kavale and Mattson (1983) found that overall perceptual motor interventions were not effective in improving academic or cognitive learning. There were no major improvements associated with perceptual/sensory motor outcomes. They did note that the quality of perceptual motor training studies was low and these lower rated studies produced the largest effect sizes. There were relatively higher effects on perceptual sensory motor outcomes (gross motor skills $d = 0.21$, fine motor $d = 0.18$, and visual perception $d = 0.15$) but lower on academic outcomes (reading $d = -0.04$, mathematics $d = 0.10$, language $d = 0.03$, spelling $d = 0.02$, handwriting $d = 0.05$). Such programs, therefore, may have value to enhance perceptual motor outcomes but the effects on achievement are close to zero. Indeed, Kavale and Mattson concluded that "a child receiving perceptual motor training is likely to gain little, if anything, or possibly lose status when compared with a child not receiving such intervention" (p. 171).

Tactile stimulation programs

Tactile stimulation is a type of sensory enrichment or stimulation used with infants, often those at risk of developmental delay, to encourage their development. The evidence of the effectiveness of tactile stimulation used with infants and young children as a form of early intervention to stimulate the senses points to its effectiveness. Those receiving some form

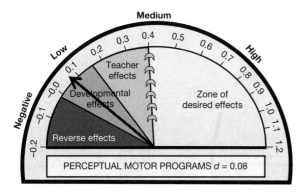

KEY	
Standard error	0.011 (Low)
Rank	128th
Number of meta-analyses	1
Number of studies	180
Number of effects	637
Number of people (1)	13,000

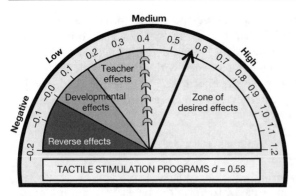

KEY

Standard error	0.145 (High)
Rank	27th
Number of meta-analyses	1
Number of studies	19
Number of effects	103
Number of people (1)	505

of controlled tactile stimulation performed better on a variety of outcome measures than those not receiving the intervention (Ottenbacher *et al.*, 1987). The effects were greatest on social and personal outcomes ($d = 0.61$), physiological ($d = 0.54$), motor/reflex ($d = 0.53$), cognitive/language ($d = 0.36$), and lowest on visual/auditory ($d = 0.18$). Designs associated with weak experimental controls were associated with the largest treatment effects, while designs with more rigorous controls over internal validity produced smaller mean effects.

Play programs

The place of play in enhancing achievement has been long cited and even today it seems it is very powerful. Spies (1987) examined play, problem solving, and creativity in young children and found that there was a small relationship between play and originality for familiar objects, but not for unfamiliar objects, and no effect of play on problem solving. Fisher (1992) in an investigation on the effects of play on development found stronger evidence to suggest play promotes improved performance outcomes both in cognitive-linguistic and affective-social domains. He found somewhat larger effect sizes for ideation fluency (originality or flexibility of association and the kind of divergent thinking characteristic of creative imagination), and for perspective-taking (empathetic role assumption related to greater co-operative behavior, sociability and heightened peer-group popularity). Fisher found some differences in effects between different types of play, with socio-dramatic play having the most striking effect and the smallest effect in imaginative play. Adult-directed

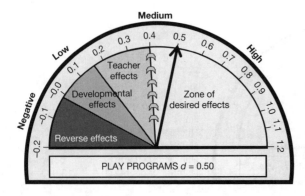

KEY

Standard error	na
Rank	46th
Number of meta-analyses	2
Number of studies	70
Number of effects	70
Number of people (2)	5,056

play showed no more gains that for other play conditions. So, for younger children, play makes a difference. The difference is likely to be related to learning about peer relations and learning how to learn from peers, facing and meeting challenges, the consequence of deliberative practice in play, and the satisfaction from deciding or becoming aware of both the learning intentions and success criteria from being involved in play.

Specific curricula programs

Creativity programs

Since the 1950s, a range of techniques and instructional materials has been developed to facilitate creative thinking. Creativity programs are grounded in a common idea that training, practice, and encouragement in using creative thinking skills can improve an individual's ability to use creative thinking techniques such as thinking with fluency, flexibility, and with an element of the unusual in responses to questions or problems (Cohn, 1986; Rose & Lin, 1984). Overall, creativity programs have a large positive effect on outcomes.

Like most other programs, an emphasis on instructional strategies and direct instruction makes a major difference in the effectiveness of creativity programs. Scope (1998), for example, investigated the effects of instructional variables on creativity, and reported that creativity programs that had a high level of structuring ($d = 0.80$), questioning ($d = 0.73$), and responding to student questioning ($d = 0.70$). These effects were constant across all subject areas. Higgins, Hall, Baumfield, and Moseley (2005) undertook one of the more complete reviews of programs to enhance thinking and creative processing. Across all outcomes the effect size was $d = 0.74$, for cognitive outcomes $d = 0.62$, for curricula achievement $d = 0.62$, and for affective outcomes $d = 1.44$. The greatest effects came from meta-cognitive strategies ($d = 0.96$), cognitive acceleration ($d = 0.61$), and instrumental enrichment ($d = 0.58$). Across curriculum domain, the effects were greatest in mathematics ($d = 0.89$), science ($d = 0.78$), then reading ($d = 0.48$). This team completed an extensive review of various strategies and developed a four-part thinking model (Figure 8.24). Thinking consists of information gathering, building understanding, productive thinking, and strategic and reflective thinking. They argued that the development of strategic and reflective thinking is a major goal of schooling, and the other three are cognitive skills that can develop in unplanned and unreflective ways (Higgins *et al.*, 2005).

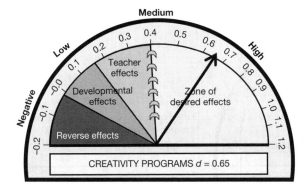

KEY	
Standard error	0.097 (High)
Rank	17th
Number of meta-analyses	12
Number of studies	685
Number of effects	837
Number of people (2)	23,299

Strategic and reflective thinking
Engagement with and management of thinking/learning,
supported by value-grounded thinking (including critically reflective thinking)

Information gathering	**Building understanding**	**Productive thinking**
Experiencing, recognizing and recalling messages & recorded information	Development of meaning Working with patterns & rules Concept formation Organizing ideas	Reasoning understanding causal systematic enquiry Problem solving Creative thinking

Figure 8.24 Higgins *et al.* four-part thinking model

Creativity programs that include explicit instruction are among the most successful (Bangert-Drowns & Bankert, 1990). Cohn (1986) demonstrated that the most successful programs were those based on developing thinking strategies; and that it was easier to improve fluency than originality. He suggested that creativity training was enhanced when activities aimed at setting and meeting high expectations are provided. This may, Cohn suggests, indicate that direct training does not affect ability but merely changes our motivation to do well (see also Kardash & Wright, 1987). Rose and Lin (1984) investigated the long-term effects of creativity training programs and also showed that most of these programs improved verbal creativity, particularly the creative problem solving programs. Bertrand (2005) also found higher effects on verbal than figural achievement. Berkowitz (2006) found that various communication strategies enhanced critical thinking outcomes; for example, participation in public speaking courses ($d = 0.29$), in argumentation-type classes ($d = 0.26$), various types of competitive forensics methods of creatively working through problems ($d - 0.41$).

Outdoor education

One of my students completed a meta-analysis of programs that enhanced self-esteem (Clinton, 1987). Programs run by teachers were the least successful and programs that were more cognitively based than emotionally or affective based were more successful. Over all programs, most systematically successful were Outward Bound or Adventure programs.

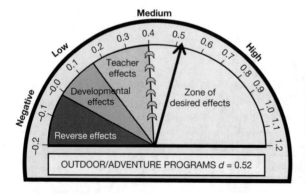

KEY	
Standard error	0.035 (Low)
Rank	43rd
Number of meta-analyses	3
Number of studies	187
Number of effects	429
Number of people (3)	26,845

Hattie, Marsh, Neill, and Richards (1997) reviewed 96 studies and found an average 0.34 increase across outcomes. Perhaps most exciting is that this is one of the few areas in education where the follow-up effects ($d = 0.17$) were positive and were in addition to the effects at the end of the program (so $0.34 + 0.17 = 0.51$). It is rare to find such increasing after-effects from an education intervention, as too many have a diminishing return. Specifically the effects of adventure programs on academic outcomes were $d = 0.46$, leadership $d = 0.38$, self-concept $d = 0.28$, personality $d = 0.37$, and interpersonal outcomes $d = 0.32$. There was, however, much variance between programs, with the Australian far exceeding the American programs—which we suggested was because the former were more oriented to "teaching" (e.g., only those with social science degrees could be employed as instructors) whereas the latter were more oriented to the outdoor experience. There are some adventure programs specifically designed to produce gains in achievement domains and as such have an integrated program of teaching, normal schoolwork, and adventure experiences. These experiences help problem solving skills and peer and cooperative learning, and there is an enhanced level of immediate feedback. A major reason for the success is the way activities are structured to emphasise very challenging learning intentions, the success criteria are clear, the peer support optimized, and not only is feedback given throughout the program but it is actively sought by the participants. Many of the coping strategies that students had when they entered the program were found deficient and needed to be replaced with other more cognitive and peer supportive strategies to ensure that the team overcame the many challenges.

Cason and Gillis (1994) found that longer programs were more effective and younger participants gained more from outdoor programs than older participants. The effect on grades was $d = 0.61$ and on school attendance was $d = 0.47$, which is above the overall average effect of $d = 0.31$. Laidlaw (2000) found an effect of $d = 0.49$ from wilderness and $d = 0.39$ from school camping programs, but longer programs were more effective. We also found that programs longer than 20 days were much more successful than shorter programs (Hattie, Brown, & Keegan, 2005). Learning about facing challenge, seeking feedback, adapting to peer cooperative learning, and enhanced self-regulation about one's skills and strengths seems to last beyond the experience in the outdoors.

Extra-curricular activities

Students do not learn only via the curricula offered in schools, as many partake in extra-curricular activities. Lewis (2004) found 41 studies that investigated the effects of these activities, and the finding of most direct relevance is the $d = 0.47$ effect on academic achievement (even though this is one of the few meta-analyses in this book that used a random effects model, so the effect is possibly inflated compared to most of the others in this book). He also reported an effect of $d = 0.33$ on engagement, $d = 0.29$ on reducing risk behaviors, and $d = 0.23$ on identity formation. Similarly, he found an effect from participating in sports of $d = 0.10$ on achievement, $d = 0.16$ on engagement, $d = -0.16$ on reducing risk behaviors, and $d = 0.15$ on identity formation. Participation in work had a zero ($d = -0.01$) effect on achievement, $d = 0.07$ on engagement, $d = 0.29$ on increasing risk behaviors, and $d = 0.35$ in identity formation. It seems that if we wish students to enhance achievement then extra-curricular activities relating to academic types of activities is optimal, and sport has least effect on most outcomes; a finding replicated by Lewis (2004). It must be considered that many students participate in sport and work not

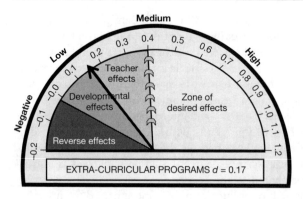

KEY	
Standard error	0.072 (Medium)
Rank	114th
Number of meta-analyses	5
Number of studies	102
Number of effects	68
Number of people (0)	na

EXTRA-CURRICULAR PROGRAMS d = 0.17

expecting any effects on achievement, but because they enjoy it, it engages them, and for many children (like for my boys) keeps them at school—where they gain the dividend of instruction in more academic subjects.

The greatest effects on achievement came from participation in school-based extracurricular activities, then pro-social activities (such as scouting, volunteering, and church activities); participation in the performing arts had the least effect on all outcomes. "The influence of community acts on attendance, interest in school and achievement, and level of investment in activities is just as potent as those of general school activities" (Lewis, 2004, p. 79). Lewis claimed that the effects from work and sport related more to identity formation and peer self-esteem—which are indeed critical attributes of particular importance during adolescence. Lewis concluded that the most effective extra-curricula programs had high levels of organization and structure, were regular, emphasized increasingly complex skill building and goal setting abilities, and involved leadership by one or more competent adults. Such programs provided the development of a sense of belonging, opportunities to develop a social network, provided positive reinforcement and an achievement orientation, allowed participants to have leadership roles, and presented age-appropriate expectations and goals for students.

Bilingual programs

Bilingual education programs are programs where two languages are used as a medium of instruction, in contrast to structured immersion programs where students are instructed

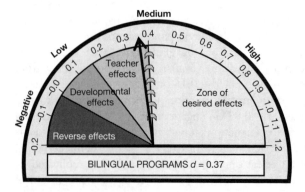

KEY	
Standard error	0.140 (High)
Rank	73rd
Number of meta-analyses	7
Number of studies	128
Number of effects	727
Number of people (3)	10,183

BILINGUAL PROGRAMS d = 0.37

solely in one language. In bilingual education there can be wide variation in the allocation and organization of language use across the timetable and curriculum. There is a high level of variability in these studies, and this reflects the variability in programs (Willig, 1985)—some are remediation programs for immigrants (Oh, 1987), some are programs to teach a second language, and some are related to the preservation of cultural principles (e.g., Māori immersion in Kura Kaupapa schools in New Zealand). The variation in the effect sizes for these programs seems to relate to the quality of teaching competence and the explicit attention to teaching strategies of learning.

Willig (1985) found that participation in bilingual education programs compared to submersion in English showed small to moderate difference favoring bilingual education for tests administered in both English and Spanish. Outcomes were positive for bilingual education for tests of reading, language skills, mathematics, and total achievement administered in English. The results were also in favor of bilingual education when tests were in other languages for reading, language, mathematics, writing, social studies, listening comprehension, and attitudes towards self and school.

A meta-analysis of the Santa Fe Bilingual Education Program results found that the initial impact of the program was greater in the early grades. The bilingual instructional approach had a significant effect on mathematics achievement, but while there were gains in reading, they were small. Overall, the findings support the benefits of bilingual education on student academic performance (Powers & Rossman, 1984). When the language of the residential neighborhood was the same for experimental and comparison groups, effect sizes were positive for bilingual group programs. When the neighborhood language of comparison groups was English and that of experimental groups Spanish there was little difference between groups.

Concluding comments

It is less the content of curricula that is important than the strategies teachers use to implement the curriculum so that students progress upwards through the curricula content. The sharing by teachers of their conceptions about what constitutes progress through the curricula is critical (and this assists in reducing the negative effects of mobility and changing classrooms), as well as ensuring appropriately challenging surface, deep, and conceptual knowledge and understanding. So often changes to curricula are more cosmetic than transformational. Changes are made to the way specific objectives are grouped into higher order concepts, but so often the fundamental objectives do not change, and when teaching methods are cited they usually refer to more passive or to constructivist teaching methods—the very ones that are least successful (no matter how palatable they may seem). Too often there is little attention paid to how to build a common conception of progress across the years studying the curriculum (Hattie, 2006). This makes it harder for teachers, as they then invent their own conceptions of progress, which can be quite different from those of other teachers, even when they are teachers of the same grade within one school. A systematic change to some aspects of the curricula, however, does seem to have a reasonable and substantial effect on student learning. This change typically relates to the inclusion and emphasis on various instructional strategies underlying the curricula, and to the highlighting of learning strategies and skill development in the content area.

Teachers need to help students to develop a series of learning strategies that enables them to construct meaning from text, develop understanding from numbers, and learn principles in science. The teaching of these strategies needs to be planned, deliberate, and explicit, and part of active programs to teach specific skills and deeper understanding. Such strategies can then lead to a student's further engagement in the curricula, lead to the development of problem solving skills, and lead to the enjoyment of some control over one's learning. There are at least two levels of understanding involved: surface knowledge (such as vocabulary programs in reading, phonics instruction), and deep understanding (such as creativity programs). It is necessary to have both levels, and most often there is a simple order in applying them—one needs to *know* something before one can *think about* it. Hence, phonics often precedes comprehension, and placing too much emphasis on the latter before the former is learnt (as is typical of many whole language programs) is not effective. For a student to learn, there must be, at a minimum, time on task, exposure to teaching, collaborative practice between teacher and student, and opportunities to practice. If a student misses the first time, then second and third chance programs need to be available, as they are effective in remediating the deficiencies from the first time around. Innovative techniques that reduce the cognitive load for these lower achieving students are effective (e.g., use of aids such as calculators). For all students, there is a need to identify and then eliminate misconceptions (in reading, mathematics, and science), and this highlights the importance of the teacher looking for the negative—identifying what the child does not know, and determining what instructional strategies the child has or does not have.

The importance of social skills and social competence programs most likely relates to the subsequent enhanced opportunities that accrue from peer co-learning, working together in classes, and minimizing disruption. The highest effects of social skills training related to peer-relations among all students. Similarly, social problem solving skills, self-control, reduction of social anxiety, and social skills in general are important outcomes of schooling. It should not be assumed that all students have these skills or that they could not benefit from systematic social skills interventions, and more research on the progression of learning social skills would be of much benefit to the outcomes of schooling. While most students learn problem solving skills in social and academic contexts, it is clear that they can also be developed in out-of-school activities (e.g., outdoor adventure programs). In such contexts, there is often a high perceived risk, high levels of cooperation needed to survive or perform, and opportunities to develop alternative coping strategies (particularly cognitive rather than emotional strategies). These can then be generalized and used in other contexts. Such programs also demonstrate the power of clear learning intentions, success criteria, and an enhanced frequency and appropriateness of feedback.

Chapter 9

The contributions from teaching approaches—part I

To keep the discussion on the various teaching approaches to a reasonable size, the contributions are divided, somewhat arbitrarily, into two chapters. The first chapter looks at goals, success criteria, and fostering student involvement, and the second other teaching approaches such as direct instruction, school-wide programs, using technology, and out-of school learning. This first of these two chapters follows a model of teaching and learning based on Clarke (2001; Clarke, Timperley, & Hattie, 2003), where the learning intentions and success criteria frame the challenge and purpose of the lesson. If such goal-directed lessons are to be successful, they must also use appropriate feedback, take account of students' views of the process of learning, and ensure students are actively involved in monitoring their own learning and developing their own meta-cognitive skills.

In a portrait of an exemplary school serving students who had been struggling to achieve and not enjoying schooling, Pressley, Gaskins, Solic, and Collins (2006) showed the power of teaching various learning strategies to these students. They claimed that when teachers critically reflected on conceptions of competent thinking and then taught various learning strategies to students, this was more likely to lead to engaging students in acquiring procedural and declarative knowledge and then to the students actually using this knowledge. The exemplary school emphasized the *engagement* of students in the learning process, teachers *articulating strategies of instruction* and paying attention to learning theories, and the school building as an infrastructure to support such instruction. The teachers provided constant scaffolding and modeling, attended to the day-to-day monitoring of students, and *sought feedback about their teaching* while also being concerned with making decisions about *optimal challenging tasks* to assign, and seeking insights from other professionals (e.g., counselors and mentors) about engaging students. There is much more, but the key ingredients of what it means to be strategic in teaching and learning relates to teachers finding ways to engage and motivate students, teach appropriate strategies in the context of various curricula domains, and constantly seeking feedback about how effective their teaching is being with all the students. The portrait by Pressley *et al.* sets the scene for this and the next chapter, which emphasizes the importance of setting challenging tasks, knowing when one (the teacher and the student) is successful in attaining these goals, the power of feedback, and the critical role of teaching appropriate learning strategies.

Table 9.1 Summary information from the meta-analyses on the contributions from teaching approaches

	No. metas	No. studies	No. people	No. effects	d	SE	CLE	Rank
Strategies emphasizing learning intentions								
Goals	11	604	41,342	820	0.56	0.057	40%	34
Behavioral organizers/advance organizers	11	577	3,905	1,933	0.41	0.040	29%	61
Concept mapping	6	287	8,471	332	0.57	0.051	40%	33
Learning hierarchies	1	24	—	24	0.19	—	13%	110
Strategies emphasizing success criteria								
Mastery learning	9	377	9,323	296	0.58	0.055	41%	29
Keller's PIS	3	263	—	162	0.53	—	37%	40
Worked examples	1	62	3,324	151	0.57	0.042	40%	30
Strategies emphasizing feedback								
Feedback	23	1,287	67,931	2,050	0.73	0.061	52%	10
Frequency or effects of testing	8	569	135,925	1,749	0.34	0.044	24%	79
Teaching test taking and coaching	10	267	15,772	364	0.22	0.024	16%	103
Providing formative evaluation	2	30	3,835	78	0.90	0.079	64%	3
Questioning	7	211	—	271	0.46	0.068	32%	53
Teacher immediacy	1	16	5,437	16	0.16	—	8%	115
Strategies emphasizing student perspectives in learning								
Time on task	4	100	—	136	0.38	0.101	27%	70
Spaced vs. massed practice	2	63	—	112	0.71	—	—	12
Peer tutoring	14	767	2,676	1,200	0.55	0.103	39%	36
Mentoring	2	74	10,250	74	0.15	0.047	11%	120
Strategies emphasizing student meta-cognitive/self-regulated learning								
Meta-cognitive strategies	2	63	5,028	143	0.69	0.181	49%	13
Study skills	14	668	29,311	2,217	0.59	0.090	41%	25
Self-verbalization/self-questioning	3	113	3,098	1,150	0.64	0.060	45%	18
Student control over learning	2	65	—	38	0.04	0.176	5%	132
Aptitude-treatment interactions	2	61	1,434	340	0.19	0.070	14%	108
Matching style of learning	8	411	29,911	1,218	0.41	0.016	29%	62
Individualized instruction	9	600	9,380	1,146	0.23	0.056	16%	100
Total	155	7,559	386,353	16,020	0.45	0.071	31%	—

Strategies emphasizing learning intentions

This section on learning intentions covers the teaching strategies of:

1 goals;
2 behavioral objectives;
3 organizers and adjunct questions;
4 concept mapping;
5 learning hierarchies.

Learning intentions describe what it is we want students to learn in terms of the skills, knowledge, attitudes, and values within any particular unit or lesson. Learning intentions should be clear, and provide guidance to the teacher about what to teach, help learners be aware of what they should learn from the lesson, and form the basis for assessing what the students have learnt and for assessing what the teachers have taught well to each student. The activities planned for the lesson need to be focused on these intentions and move away from the all-too-often "busy" work that students might enjoy but which has little relationship to the learning intention.

Clarke, Timperley and Hattie (2003) have noted some important points about learning intentions and planning.

- Not all students in the class will be working at the same level, so it is important to adapt the learning intentions to make them appropriate to all students.
- The amount of time allocated should not be the same for all learning intentions, but should vary depending on whether they are developing concepts, skills or knowledge—*concepts or deeper learning* are likely to need more time than, say, the acquisition of *knowledge* or *surface information*.
- Learning intentions and activities can be grouped, because one activity can contribute to more than one learning intention, or one learning intention may need several activities or several exposures to the activities for the students to understand it fully.
- While learning intentions are what we intend students to learn, the students may also learn other things not planned for, and we need to be aware of these unintended consequences.

A more specific type of learning intention is the "mastery goal". Ames (1992) explained that, with a mastery goal, individuals are oriented toward developing new skills, trying to understand their work, improving their level of competence, or achieving a sense of mastery based on self-referenced standards. Elliott and Dweck (1988) further distinguished between mastery and learning goals. They defined learning goals as about more than the mastery of new things, and claimed that students encouraged to use learning goals were less worried about their intellect, remained focused on-task, and maintained their effective problem-solving strategies. Compatible with this goal construct is Brophy's (1983) description of "motivation to learn" whereby individuals focus on mastering and understanding content and demonstrate a willingness to engage in the process of learning.

Another important aspect of learning intentions is knowing *how* they will be implemented. Learning intentions take the form "I intend to reach x" and by articulating *how* they intend to reach "x", teachers and students are expressing an "implementation intention". Gollwitzer and Sheeran (2006) completed a meta-analysis testing the notion that implementation intentions help teachers and students attain goals. "Implementation intentions should enhance people's ability to initiate, maintain, disengage from, and undertake further goal pursuit and thereby increase the likelihood that strong goal intentions are realized successfully" (p. 20). They used 63 studies and the effect size was $d = 0.65$. It is not just the presence of a learning intention and having commitment that helps, but most importantly it is having a sense of "if-then" that helps the implementation of goal intentions. Thus, the art is setting appropriately challenging goals, developing commitment to attaining them, and developing intentions to implement strategies to attain them.

Goals

Locke and Latham (1990) have provided a compelling set of evidence, including many meta-analyses (but few with school achievement as the outcome) that indicate how critical goals are for enhancing performance. They argued that goals serve a variety of functions that are essential in the teaching process: goals regulate action and they explain the nature of the link between the past and the future; and goals assume that human action is directed by conscious goals and intentions, although they do not assume that all human action is under fully conscious control (as we shall see later). A major finding of their book is that achievement is enhanced to the degree that students and teachers set challenging rather than "do your best" goals, relative to the students' present competencies.

A major reason difficult goals are more effective is that they lead to a clearer notion of success and direct the student's attention to relevant behaviors or outcomes, whereas "doing your best" can fit with a very wide range of goals. It is not the specificity of the goals but the difficulty that is crucial to success. There is a direct linear relationship between the degree of goal difficulty and performance. There are five meta-analyses relative to this contention (Table 9.2) and the overall effect size is a large $d = 0.67$ (these are not all achievement outcomes and so are not included in the Appendices of this book). The performances of the students who have the most challenging goals are over 250 percent higher than the performances of the subjects with the easiest goals (Wood & Locke, 1997).

Also, difficult goals are much better than "do your best" or no assigned goals. Any school with the motto "do your best" should immediately change it to "face your challenges" or "strive to the highest". The following five meta-analyses relate to this contention (Table 9.3). This is because "do your best" goals are easily attained—in one sense, anything you do can be defined as your best. Instead, teachers and learners should be setting challenging goals.

Goals have a self-energizing effect if they are appropriately challenging for the student, as they can motivate students to exert effort in line with the difficulty or demands of the goal. Commitment to the goals helps, but is not necessary for goal attainment—except for special education students, where commitment makes a major difference. Klein, Wesson, Hollenbeck, and Alge (1999) found a high relationship ($d = 0.47$) between goal commitment and subsequent performance, and the effect between commitment and outcome increased as a function of goal difficulty. Donovan and Radosevich (1998) found lower effects of commitment to goals than they expected, but these were still quite high ($d = 0.36$).

Thus, goals inform individuals:

> as to what type or level of performance is to be attained so that they can direct and evaluate their actions and efforts accordingly. Feedback allows them to set reasonable

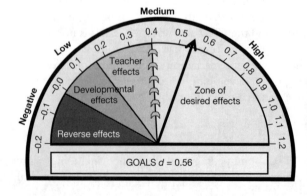

KEY	
Standard error	0.057 (Medium)
Rank	34th
Number of meta-analyses	11
Number of studies	604
Number of effects	820
Number of people (7)	41,342

GOALS $d = 0.56$

Table 9.2 Relation between goal difficulty and performance

Authors	Year	No. studies	No. effects	d
Chidester & Grisgby	1984	12	1,770	0.52
Mento, Steel, & Karren	1987	70	7,407	0.55
Tubbs	1986	56	4,732	0.82
Wofford, Goodwin, & Premack	1992	3	207	0.90
Wood, Mento, & Locke	1987	72	7,548	0.58
Total	—	213	21,664	0.67

goals and to track their performance in relation to their goals so that adjustments in effort, direction, and even strategy can be made as needed.

(Locke & Latham, 1990, p. 23)

The scenario is that effective teachers set appropriately challenging goals and then structure situations so that students can reach these goals. If teachers can encourage students to share commitment to these challenging goals, and if they provide feedback on how to be successful in learning as one is working to achieve the goals, then goals are more likely to be attained.

Because assigned goals provide an individual with normative information on the expected level of performance, such goals have major effects on the development of self-efficacy and confidence, which in turn affects the choice of difficulty of goals. Table 9.4 provides a summary of meta-analyses as to the relationship between higher levels of self-efficacy and goal attainment (average $d = 0.92$).

A basis of many claims about the value of student self-assessment, self-evaluation, self-monitoring, and self-learning is that students have a reasonable understanding of where they are at, where they are going, what it will look like when they get there, and where they will go to next: that is, they have clear goals, learning intentions, and success criteria. Martin (2006) argued that one method to assist students to set task-specific and situation-specific goals was to use the notion of "personal bests". Task-specific goals provide students with clear information about what they are trying to achieve in the immediate future (both in terms of specificity and degree of challenge), and situation-specific goals provide students with the reason they want to achieve a particular outcome (to beat one's previous level of achievement on that goal). He found that setting personal bests had high positive relationships to educational aspirations, enjoyment of school, participation in

Table 9.3 Difficulty compared to "do your best" goals

Authors	Year	No. studies	No. students	d
Chidester & Grigsby	1984	17	2400	0.51
Guzzo, Jette, & Katzell	1985	na	na	0.65
Hunter & Schmidt	1983	17	1278	0.80
Mento, Steel, & Karren	1987	49	5844	0.42
Tubbs	1986	48	4960	0.50
Wood, Mento, & Locke	1987	53	6635	0.43
Total	—	184	21117	0.66

Table 9.4 Relation of self-efficacy to goal attainment

Study	Year	No. studies	d
Ajzen & Madden	1986	169	0.57
Ajzen & Madden	1986	90	0.44
Bandura & Cervone	1986	88	0.43
Garland	1985	127	0.39
Hollenbeck & Brief	1987	47	0.49
Locke, Frederick, Lee, & Bobko	1984	181	0.54
Meyer	1988	90	0.69
Meyer & Gellatly	1988	56	0.62
Meyer & Gellatly	1988	60	0.48
Silver & Greenhaiis	1983	56	0.29
Taylor	1984	223	0.20
Weiss & Rakestraw	1988	80	0.60
Wofford, Goodwin, & Premack	1992	6	1.06
Wood & Locke	1987	517	0.32
Total	—	1784	0.46

class, and persistence on the task. The most salient features of the personal bests were the specificity and degree of challenge of the goals, and that the goals were seen to relate to self-improvement. Personal bests combined the best features of mastery and performance goals, as personal bests "primarily reflect a mastery orientation because it is self-referenced and self-improvement based and yet holds a slice of performance orientation because the student competes with his or her own previous performance" (Martin, 2006, p. 816).

Challenging goals are also effective when teaching special education students. Fuchs and Fuchs (1986) reported an effect of $d = 0.63$ for long-term and $d = 0.67$ for short-term goals. More importantly, there was an interaction effect with the outcome measure. For more probe-like outcomes the effect of challenge was largest for short-term goals ($d = 0.85$ compared to $d = 0.41$), whereas the reverse was the case for global outcomes ($d = 0.45$ for short-term and $d = 0.92$ for long-term goals). This indicates a need, therefore, to set appropriately challenging short-term goals for surface learning outcomes and set appropriately challenging long-term goals for deep learning outcomes.

It has been noted that "challenge" is a relative term—relative to a student's current performance and understanding, and to the success criteria deriving from the learning intention. The challenge should not be so difficult that the goal is seen as unattainable, given the student's level of self-efficacy or confidence; rather, teachers and students must be able to see a pathway to attaining the challenging goal—a pathway which can include strategies for understanding the goal or intention, implementation plans to attain it, and, preferably, a commitment to attaining the goal. Burns (2002) was specific: He used meta-analysis to ascertain the optimal ratio of known to unknown tasks for drill tasks (which is but one specific set of tasks that teachers can engage students with). He found that the ratios differed depending on whether the student was in the acquisition or proficiency stage (the former relates to acquiring the knowledge and information, the latter relates to increasing accuracy and fluency). He also acknowledged that there was a maintenance, generalization, or application stage but there were no studies investigating the appropriate ratios at this stage. Drill ratios were more applicable to the acquisition ($d = 1.09$), than to the proficiency ($d = 0.39$) stage; and the optimal rate seems to be to include at least 90 percent known to unknown items in the tasks ($d = 1.19$) and certainly not less than 50 percent known to unknown ($d = 0.49$). Gickling (1984) showed that the ratios for learning to read needed to be more like ninety-five percent known to five percent unknown words in a text. It is also important for the teacher to choose the tasks with these ratios, as the effects are much greater than when students choose the ratios. While not explored, there are suggestions that the ratios may need to be higher when deeper learning is desired rather than surface knowledge.

Behavioral objectives and advance organizers

Advance organizers can be:

> broadly defined as bridges from the reader's previous knowledge to whatever is to be learned; they are supposed to be more abstract and inclusive than the more specific material to be learned, and to provide a means for organizing the new material.
>
> (Stone, 1983, p. 194)

They are aimed to bridge and link old with new information, and as they are meant to be presented prior to learning, then advance organizers can assist in helping the learner organize and interpret new upcoming instruction. Similarly, behavioral objectives are statements of what students ought to be able to do as a consequence of instruction (Popham, Eisner, Sullivan, & Tyler, 1969), but they tend to be more often used for surface rather than deeper knowledge. The overall effects show much variance but the effects are highest when the learning intentions of the lessons are articulated, when notions of success included, and when these are shared with the students. When they are primarily for the teacher, usually in lesson plans, or aimed primarily at surface learning and not including any deep learning, then the effects are lower. Kozlow (1978) found that behavioral objectives were more effective when they involved comparisons to some standards of performance rather than being expository in nature.

Luiten, Ames, and Ackerman (1980) found that advance organizers have a small but facilitative effect on both learning and retention, with the effect increasing over time ($d = 0.21$). Similarly, Stone (1983) found that advance organizers were associated with increased learning and retention of teaching material. Using advance organizers to introduce new material, by providing a bridge from previous knowledge, did facilitate long-term learning,

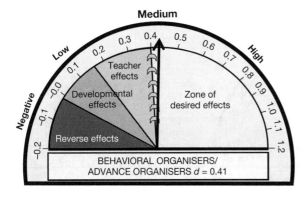

KEY	
Standard error	0.040 (Low)
Rank	61st
Number of meta-analyses	11
Number of studies	577
Number of effects	1,933
Number of people (2)	3,905

BEHAVIORAL ORGANISERS/
ADVANCE ORGANISERS $d = 0.41$

but the effects were lower for written advance organizers compared to non-written ones, and had no effect when used for teaching low-ability or low-knowledge learners. Too often, advance organizers and behavioral objectives tended to be specific, ignore challenge, and have no notions of what would be deemed as success in attaining the objective.

Concept mapping

Concept mapping involves the development of graphical representations of the conceptual structure of the content to be learnt. Thus, it can be considered as a form of learning intention, if for no other reason than it identifies the material to be learnt, oftentimes with indicators of priorities and higher-order concepts. As with behavioral objectives and learning hierarchies, concept mapping derives from Ausubel's (1968) claims that concepts can be organized in hierarchical form in the cognitive structure, and it helps learning if concepts related to what is to be learned can be linked to the concept maps a student already has (see also Novak, 1977). The difference between concept mapping and other organizing methods (e.g., behavioral objectives, learning hierarchies) is that it involves the students in the development of the organizational tool.

The importance of concept mapping relates to its emphasis on summarizing the main ideas in what is to be learnt—although only if the students have some familiarity with the surface knowledge of the (often deeper) concept to be mapped. Concept mapping can assist in synthesizing and identifying the major ideas, themes, and interrelationships—particularly for the learners who do not have these organizing and synthesizing skills. Kim, Vaughn, Wanzek, and Wei (2004) argued that the visual displays of information such as those provided by concept mapping enhance the reading comprehension of students with learning difficulties, possibly by helping these students organize the verbal information and thereby improving their recall.

Moore and Readance (1984) reported greater effects when concept mapping occurred after initial exposure to the material to be mapped (and not before or during this learning; see also Kang, 2002). Nesbit and Adesope (2006) found greater effects when the emphasis was on understanding the central rather than the detailed ideas of the topic being mapped. Nesbit and Adesope also found that there was little difference between concept mapping and asking students to construct an outline of the topic ($d = 0.19$), but the effects were larger for concept mapping when compared to lectures or discussions on the topic ($d = 0.74$). It is the heuristic process of organizing and synthesizing that is the important feature, and

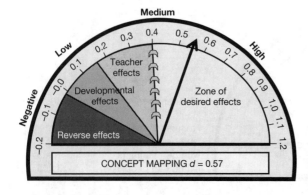

KEY	
Standard error	0.051 (Medium)
Rank	33rd
Number of meta-analyses	6
Number of studies	287
Number of effects	332
Number of people (3)	8,471

concept mapping is but one of many of these methods—but an effective method. It does not seem to matter who does the mapping (student alone, in groups, or teacher, Horton *et al.*, 1993) but the strongest effects are when students provided the terms for the maps, regardless of who then devised the maps. Kim *et al.* (2004), however, found higher effects for teacher- than student-generated maps, whereas Nesbit and Adesope (2006) found higher effects when students were made to construct ($d = 0.81$), rather than just study, concept maps ($d = 0.37$).

Various authors have found that the effects were highest with those students least likely to know the relationship between lower and higher-order notions; that is, with lower rather than higher ability or highly verbal students (Horton *et al.*, 1993; Nesbit & Adesope, 2006; Vásquez & Caraballo, 1993). As Nesbit and Adesope (2006) concluded, many of these gains may be "due to greater learner engagement occasioned by concept mapping … rather than the properties of the concept map as an information medium" (p. 434), although it is noted that the effects from concept mapping were higher than for studying text passages, lists, and outlines. Thus they argue that it is not just the "summarizing/integrating" nature of concept maps, but also there may be a lower cognitive load "by arranging nodes in two-dimensional space to represent relatedness, consolidating all references to a concept in a single symbol, and explicitly labeling links to identify relationships" (p. 434).

Learning hierarchies

A different form of learning intention is to structure the learning in some form of hierarchy, such that it is more effective to acquire first a series of skills that will support later learning. Horon and Lynn (1980) found that learning hierarchies can facilitate learning ($d = 0.19$) and shorten learning time to a small extent ($d = 0.09$). Hierarchical instruction is more effective in promoting learning at the elementary level ($d = 0.44$) than at the high school level ($d = 0.07$). The overall effects are very low.

Strategies emphasizing success criteria

The purpose of the success criteria, or "What are we looking for?" is to make students understand what the teacher is using as the criteria for judging their work, and, of course, to ensure that the teacher is clear about the criteria that will determine if the learning intentions have been successfully achieved. Too often students may know the learning

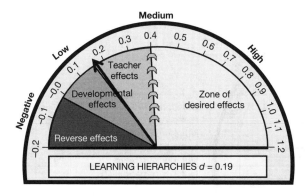

KEY	
Standard error	na
Rank	110th
Number of meta-analyses	1
Number of studies	24
Number of effects	24
Number of people (0)	na

intention, but not how the teacher is going to judge their performance, or when or whether they have been successful. A learning intention of "to learn to use effective adjectives", for instance, does not give the students the marking criteria or how they will be judged. The success criteria, or "How will we know?", need to state as exactly as possible what the students and teacher will want to see. In this case, two alternatives might be: "What you're looking for is that you have used at least five effective adjectives", or "What you're looking for is that you have used an adjective just before a noun on at least four occasions that will help to paint a detailed picture so the reader can understand the feel of the jungle and the light of the jungle". It is important that the success criteria are as clear and specific as possible (at surface or at deep levels, or both) because the teacher (and learner) needs to monitor the students' progress throughout the lesson to make sure they understand the intended meaning. There are three sets of related notions that emphasize success criteria: mastery learning, Keller's personalized system of instruction, and the provision of worked examples.

Mastery learning

The claim underlying mastery learning is that all children can learn when provided with clear explanations of what it means to "master" the material being taught. Other features involved include: appropriate learning conditions in the classroom, such as high levels of cooperation between classmates; high levels of teacher feedback that is both frequent and specific by using diagnostic formative tests; and the regular correction of mistakes students make as they travel along their learning path. Mastery learning requires numerous feedback loops, based on small units of well-defined, appropriately sequenced outcomes. Bloom (1968) defined mastery in terms of behavioral objectives, with class instruction supplemented by feedback or correction mechanisms. Willett, Yamashita, and Anderson (1983, p. 408) added that "tests on unit objectives are followed by supplementary instruction on objectives not attained, and the specific levels of attainment are specified". The important variable in mastery learning is the time required to reach the levels of attainment. The notion is that learning should be held constant and time should be allowed to vary, rather than the opposite, which is the norm in traditional instruction. The teacher determines the pace of the instruction and directs the accompanying feedback and corrective procedures (Guskey & Pigott, 1988). The material is divided into relatively small learning units, each with their own objectives and assessment. Each unit is preceded by brief diagnostic tests,

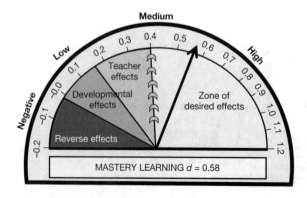

KEY	
Standard error	0.055 (Medium)
Rank	29th
Number of meta-analyses	9
Number of studies	377
Number of effects	296
Number of people (2)	9,323

MASTERY LEARNING *d* = 0.58

which provide information to identify gaps and strengths. No student proceeds to new material until prior or more basic prerequisite material is mastered.

Willett *et al.* (1983) reviewed a dozen different innovations in teaching strategies, and mastery learning had the highest effects. They argued that mastery learning was the most successful innovative system, closely followed my Keller's PSI (see next section). Guskey and Gates (1986) found similar high effects for mastery learning in each of elementary school ($d = 0.94$), high school ($d = 0.72$), and college ($d = 0.65$). In a follow-up study, Guskey and Piggott (1988), using group-based applications of mastery strategies, showed consistently positive effects on both cognitive and affective student learning outcomes. Kulik and Kulik (1986) determined that testing for mastery had positive effects on student achievement both at college and pre-college levels ($d = 0.52$). The effects of mastery testing were particularly strong on lower ability students ($d = 0.96$). Mastery testing, they argued, increased the amount of instructional time required by, on average, 25 percent. Their evidence, however, did not support Bloom's prediction that variation in performance will be reduced to near zero with mastery testing procedures.

Kulik, Kulik, and Bangert-Drowns (1990) found mastery learning programs had a positive effect on examination performance of students in colleges, high schools, and the upper grades of elementary schools, raising examination performance by about half a standard deviation, especially for low-aptitude students. Mastery programs had positive effects on student attitudes towards course content and instruction, but increased student time spent on instructional tasks. Self-paced mastery programs often reduced completion rates in college classes.

The only exception to the positive findings on mastery learning programs is the meta-analysis by Slavin (1987), who found no evidence to support the effectiveness of group-based mastery learning on standardized achievement measures. One of the features of Slavin's argument is that studies that do not meet his criteria should be excluded, which leaves only seven articles—a very small representation of a large set of potential studies. His criteria included: students had to have been tested on their mastery at least once every four weeks, only studies where students were taught as a total group were included, studies could not use a feedback-corrective cycle, interventions had to last a minimum of four weeks, and there had to be at least two experimental and two control groups used.

Keller's Personalized System of Instruction

A specific implementation of mastery learning is the Personalized System of Instruction, developed by Keller and Sherman during the 1960s as a form of programmed instruction that employs a highly structured, student-centered approach to course design that emphasizes self-pacing and mastery (Keller, 1968; Keller & Sherman, 1974). The key features include: students proceed through the course at their own pace; students demonstrate mastery of each component of the course before proceeding to the next; teaching materials and other communications between teachers and students are largely text-based; and teachers are involved more in tutorial support and in providing motivation for students to complete the work and attain the goals. The effects are very similar to the other mastery learning programs. The meta-analyses show that students using PSI had higher grades and higher satisfaction rates than students in conventional classes, but that study time was similar in both types of classes (Kulik, Kulik, & Cohen, 1980).

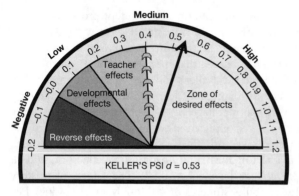

KELLER'S PSI *d* = 0.53

KEY	
Standard error	Na
Rank	40th
Number of meta-analyses	3
Number of studies	263
Number of effects	162
Number of people (0)	na

Worked examples

Another form for demonstrating to students what "success" looks like and thus what the goal could be for their own learning, is by providing them with worked examples (Crissman, 2006). Worked examples typically consist of a problem statement and the appropriate steps to the solution. The defense for providing such worked examples is that they reduce the cognitive load for students such that they concentrate on the processes that lead to the correct answer and not just providing an answer (which may or may not be correct). A typical example of worked examples consists of three parts: an introductory phase (exposure to the example), an acquisition or training phase, and a test phase (assessing the learning). Most studies follow this pattern, although there may be slight deviations, such as the inclusion of a pretest or the introduction of a delayed acquisition or delayed test phase, or both. The studies used for this meta-analysis involved the use of worked examples to alleviate cognitive load in the learner. The overall effect was $d = 0.52$, and most programs were close to this average: intra-example features (such as multiple examples, story variation, example/problem pairs) had an effect size of $d = 0.52$; the effect size for conventional worked examples was $d = 0.49$; integration of sources of information (e.g., diagrams, text) was $d = 0.52$; fading (omitting some of the steps in the example) was $d = 0.60$; inclusion of subgoals was $d = 0.52$; and self-explanations of the steps as they used the worked example was $d = 0.57$. All these various types of instruction using worked examples generally help to reduce cognitive load.

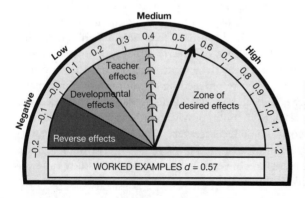

WORKED EXAMPLES *d* = 0.57

KEY	
Standard error	0.042 (Medium)
Rank	30th
Number of meta-analyses	1
Number of studies	62
Number of effects	151
Number of people (1)	3,324

There do seem to be worthwhile effects from providing worked examples to students, but it is more difficult to find evidence of the effects from providing worked examples to teachers (often called exemplars). Peddie, Hattie and Vaughan (1999) completed an exhaustive search of evidence for research on the effects of exemplars and could find much rhetoric and many claims about their importance. When 50-plus organizations that had developed exemplars were asked to send their research, all sent boxes of exemplars, but none were able to send evidence of their effects.

Implementations that emphasize feedback

This section outlines the meanings of feedback, the effects of different types of feedback, feedback via frequent testing, teaching test-taking skills, providing formative evaluation to teachers, questioning to provide teachers and students with feedback, and the immediacy of feedback.

Feedback

When I completed the first synthesis of 134 meta-analyses of all possible influences on achievement (Hattie, 1992) it soon became clear that feedback was among the most powerful influences on achievement. Most programs and methods that worked best were based on heavy dollops of feedback. When I was presenting these early results in Hong Kong, a questioner asked what was meant by feedback, and I have struggled to understand the concept of feedback ever since. I have spent many hours in classrooms (noting its absence, despite the claims of the best of teachers that they are constantly engaged in providing feedback), worked with students to increase self-helping (with little success), and have tried different methods of providing feedback. The mistake I was making was seeing feedback as something *teachers provided to students*—they typically did not, although they made claims that they did it all the time, and most of the feedback they did provide was social and behavioral. It was only when I discovered that feedback was most powerful when it is from the *student to the teacher* that I started to understand it better. When teachers seek, or at least are open to, feedback from students as to what students know, what they understand, where they make errors, when they have misconceptions, when they are not engaged—then teaching and learning can be synchronized and powerful. Feedback to teachers helps make learning visible.

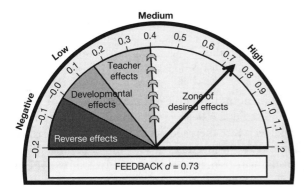

KEY	
Standard error	0.061 (Medium)
Rank	10th
Number of meta-analyses	23
Number of studies	1,287
Number of effects	2,050
Number of people (10)	67,931

Recently a colleague and I published a paper devoted to the power of feedback, which provides a deeper explanation than can be presented in this book (Hattie & Timperley, 2007). But, in summary, feedback is information provided by an agent (e.g., teacher, peer, book, parent, or one's own experience) about aspects of one's performance or understanding. For example, a teacher or parent can provide corrective information, a peer can provide an alternative strategy, a book can provide information to clarify ideas, a parent can provide encouragement, and a learner can look up the answer to evaluate the correctness of a response. *Feedback is a "consequence" of performance.*

To assist in understanding the purpose, effects, and types of feedback, it is useful to consider a continuum of instruction and feedback. At one end of the continuum is a clear distinction between providing instruction and providing feedback. However, when feedback is combined with a correctional review, feedback and instruction become intertwined until "the process itself takes on the forms of new instruction, rather than informing the student solely about correctness" (Kulhavy, 1977, p. 212). To take on this instructional purpose, feedback needs to provide information specifically relating to the task or process of learning that fills a gap between what is understood and what is aimed to be understood (Sadler, 1989), and it can do this in a number of different ways. For example, this may be through affective processes, such as increased effort, motivation, or engagement. Alternatively, the gap may be reduced through a number of different cognitive processes, including helping students to come to a different viewpoint, confirming to the student that they are correct or incorrect, indicating that more information is available or needed, pointing to directions that the student could pursue, and indicating alternative strategies to understand particular information. Winne and Butler (1994) provided an excellent summary in their claim that "feedback is information with which a learner can confirm, add to, overwrite, tune, or restructure information in memory, whether that information is domain knowledge, meta-cognitive knowledge, beliefs about self and tasks, or cognitive tactics and strategies" (p. 5740).

The effect sizes reported in the feedback meta-analyses show considerable variability, which indicates that some types of feedback are more powerful than others. The most effective forms of feedback provide cues or reinforcement to the learner, are in the form of video, audio or computer-assisted instruction feedback, or relate feedback to learning goals. It is also worth noting that the key is feedback that is received and acted upon by students—many teachers claim they provide ample amounts of feedback but the issue is whether students receive and interpret the information in the feedback. At best, each student receives moments of feedback in a single day (Nuthall, 2005; Sirotnik, 1983). Carless (2006) asked students and teachers whether teachers provided detailed feedback that helped students improve their next assignments. About 70 percent of the teachers claimed they provided such detailed feedback often or always, but only 45 percent of students agreed with their teachers' claims. Further, Nuthall (2005) found that most feedback that students obtained in any day in classrooms was from other students, and most of this feedback was incorrect.

Programmed instruction, praise, punishment, and extrinsic rewards were the least effective forms of feedback for enhancing achievement. Indeed, it is doubtful whether rewards should be thought of as feedback at all. Deci, Koestner, and Ryan (1999) have described tangible rewards (stickers, awards, and so on) as contingencies to activities rather than feedback because they contain so little task information. In their meta-analysis of the effects of feedback on motivation, these authors found a negative correlation between extrinsic rewards and task performance ($d = -0.34$). Tangible rewards significantly undermined intrinsic motivation, particularly for interesting tasks ($d = -0.68$) compared to uninteresting tasks ($d = 0.18$). In addition, when the feedback was administered in a controlling manner (e.g., saying that the student performed as they "should" have performed), the effects were even worse ($d = -0.78$). Thus, Deci *et al.* concluded that extrinsic rewards are typically negative because they "undermine people's taking responsibility for motivating or regulating themselves" (Deci *et al.*, 1999, p. 659). Rather, extrinsic rewards are a controlling strategy that often leads to greater surveillance, evaluation, and competition, all of which have been found to undermine enhanced engagement and regulation (Deci & Ryan, 1985).

Providing feedback is not about giving rewards, but rather providing information about the task. Cameron and Pierce (1994) asked about the causal effects of extrinsic rewards and reinforcement on intrinsic motivation (hence this meta-analysis is not included in the Appendices because achievement is not the outcome). The results show that rewards did not significantly affect intrinsic motivation: the effects of rewards were $d = -0.06$ for free time on task, $d = 0.21$ for attitude, $d = 0.08$ for performance during free-time period, and $d = 0.05$ for willingness to volunteer. When intrinsic motivation was measured by attitude toward a task, rewarded subjects reported higher intrinsic motivation than non-rewarded subjects. Verbal rewards appeared to produce a positive effect and tangible rewards suggested a negative effect. Those rewarded with verbal praise or positive feedback showed greater intrinsic motivation and spent more time on a task once the reward was withdrawn than non-rewarded subjects. It is critical, however, to note how small these effects are and thus to conclude that rewards and praise are or are not critical seems moot.

The most systematic study addressing the effects of various types of feedback was published by Kluger and DeNisi (1996). Their meta-analysis included studies of feedback interventions that were not confounded with other manipulations, included at least a control group, measured performance, and included at least ten participants. Although many of their studies were not classroom or achievement based, their messages are of much interest. From the 131 studies, they estimated 470 effect sizes, based on 12,652 participants, and the average effect size was $d = 0.38$, and 32 percent of the effects were negative. Specifically, feedback is more effective when it provides information on correct rather than incorrect responses and when it builds on changes from previous trails. The impact of feedback was also influenced by the difficulty of goals and tasks. There is highest impact when goals are specific and challenging but when task complexity is low. Giving praise for completing a task appears to be ineffective, which is hardly surprising because it contains such little learning-related information. Feedback is more effective when there are perceived low rather than high levels of threat to self-esteem, presumably because low threat conditions allow attention to be paid to the feedback.

Figure 9.9 presents a framework in which feedback can be considered. The claim is made that the main purpose of feedback is to reduce discrepancies between current understandings and performance and a learning intention or goal. The strategies that students and teachers use to reduce this discrepancy depend partly on the level at which the feedback operates. These levels include the level of task performance, the level of process of understanding how to do a task, the regulatory or meta-cognitive process level, and the self or person (unrelated to the specifics of the task). Feedback has differing effects across these levels.

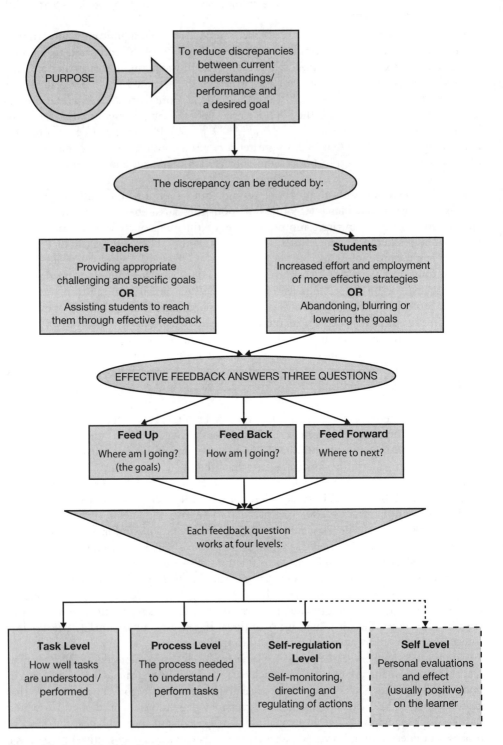

Figure 9.9 A model of feedback

The major feedback questions are "Where am I going?" (learning intentions/goals/ success criteria), "How am I going?" (self-assessment and self-evaluation), and "Where to next?" (progression, new goals). An ideal learning environment or experience is when both teachers and students seek answers to each of these questions. These three questions do not work in isolation at each of the four levels, but typically work together. Feedback relating to "How am I going?" has the power to lead to doing further tasks or "Where to next?" and "Where am I going?". As Sadler (1989) has convincingly argued, it is closing the gap between where the student is and where they are aiming to be that leads to the power of feedback.

So far so good, but the difficulty arises from the way in which feedback works at the four levels noted above. First, feedback can be about the task or product, such as the work is correct or incorrect. This level of feedback may include directions to acquire more, different, or correct information, such as "You need to include more about the Treaty of Versailles". Second, feedback can be aimed at the process used to create the product or complete the task. This kind of feedback is more directly aimed at the processing of information, or learning processes required for understanding or completing the task. For example, a teacher or peer may say to a learner, "You need to edit this piece of writing by attending to the descriptors you have used, so the reader is able to understand the nuances of your meaning", or "This page may make more sense if you use the comprehension strategies we talked about earlier". Third, feedback to the student can be focused at the self-regulation level, including greater skill in self-evaluation, or confidence to engage further on the task. For example, "You already know the key features of the opening of an argument. Check to see whether you have incorporated them in your first paragraph." Such feedback can have major influences on self-efficacy, self-regulatory proficiencies, and self-beliefs about the student as a learner, such that the student is encouraged or informed how to better and more effortlessly continue on the task. Fourth, feedback can be personal in the sense that it is directed to the "self" which, it will be argued below, is too often unrelated to performance on the task. Examples of such feedback include, "You are a great student", "Well done!".

The art is to provide the right form of feedback at, or just above, the level where the student is working—with one exception. Feedback at the self or personal level (usually praise) is rarely effective. Praise is rarely directed at addressing the three feedback questions and so is ineffective in enhancing learning. When feedback draws attention to the self, students try to avoid the risks involved in tackling a challenging assignment, they minimize effort, and they have a high fear of failure (Black & Wiliam, 1998) in order to minimize the risk to the self. Thus, ideally, teaching and learning move from the task to the processes and understandings necessary to learn the task, and then to continuing beyond it to more challenging tasks and goals. This process results in higher confidence and greater investment of effort. This flow typically occurs as the student gains greater fluency and mastery.

We need to be somewhat cautious, however. Feedback is not "the answer" to effective teaching and learning; rather it is but one powerful answer. With inefficient learners or learners at the acquisition (not proficiency) phase, it is better for a teacher to provide elaborations through instruction than to provide feedback on poorly understood concepts. If feedback is directed at the right level it can assist students to comprehend, engage, or develop effective strategies to process the information intended to the learnt. To be effective, feedback needs to be clear, purposeful, meaningful and compatible with students' prior knowledge, and to provide logical connections. It also needs to prompt active information processing on the part of the learner, have low task complexity, relate to specific and clear goals, and provide little threat to the person at the self level. The major discriminator is whether feedback is clearly directed to the various levels of task, processes, or regulation, and not directed to the level of "self". These conditions highlight the importance of classroom climates that foster peer and self-assessment, and allow for learning from mistakes. We need classes that develop the courage to err.

Thus, when feedback is combined with effective instruction in classrooms, it can be very powerful in enhancing learning. As Kluger and DeNisi (1996) noted, a feedback intervention provided for a familiar task that contains cues that support learning, attracts attention to feedback-standard discrepancies at the task level, and is void of cues that direct attention to the self, is likely to yield impressive gains in students' performance. It is important to note, however, that under particular circumstances, instruction is more effective than feedback. Feedback can only build on something; it is of little use when there is no initial learning or surface information. In summary, feedback is what happens second, is one of the most powerful influences on learning, occurs too rarely, and needs to be more fully researched by qualitatively and quantitatively investigating how feedback works in the classroom and learning process.

Frequent testing/Effects of testing

Another form of feedback is repeated testing, but this is only effective if there is feedback from the tests to teachers such that they modify their instruction to attend to the strengths and gaps in student performance. Although performance is increased with more frequent testing, the amount of improvement in achievement diminishes as the number of tests increase (Bangert-Drowns, Kulik, Kulik, & Morgan, 1991). Students taking at least one test during a 15-week term scored about half a standard deviation higher in criterion examinations than students taking no tests. When two groups answered identical test items, superior performance was obtained from students who answered the questions on a large number of short tests rather than on a small number of long tests. The caution is that it may not be the frequency of test taking but that frequent test taking made the learning intentions and success criteria more specific and transparent. Clariana and Koul (2006) found that multiple-try feedback was less effective for surface outcomes ($d = -0.22$) but more effective for higher-order outcomes ($d = 0.10$). "Multiple try

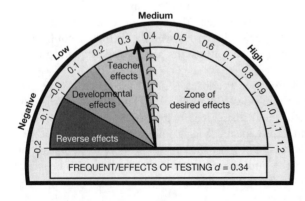

FREQUENT/EFFECTS OF TESTING $d = 0.34$

KEY	
Standard error	0.044 (Medium)
Rank	79th
Number of meta-analyses	8
Number of studies	569
Number of effects	1,749
Number of people (2)	135,925

feedback on error requires the learner to think more about the lesson question, unless the learner just guesses randomly due to frustration or impatience" (p. 261). Similarly, Kim (2005) found that performance assessment was more effective the longer the period it had been implemented—as then students and teachers become more adept at completing this form of assessment.

The effect is not merely from testing and testing, it is from learning from testing. Gocmen (2003), for example, found an effect size of $d = 0.41$ from frequent testing, but this was higher when the testing was accompanied by feedback ($d = 0.62$) compared to no feedback ($d = 0.30$). Lee (2006) investigated the effects of statewide high-stakes testing and test-driven accountability policies on reading and mathematics achievement in the United States (since 1990). He found a $d = 0.36$ effect ($d = 0.29$ for reading and $d = 0.38$ for mathematics), but the effects only occurred in elementary ($d = 0.44$) and middle schools ($d = 0.35$) and not in high schools ($d = 0.03$). States with the strongest accountability programs made greater gains over the years than those with weaker accountability measures, but Lee noted that these gains mapped to similar trajectories from the years before these accountability policies were brought into law! He concluded that "to argue that states adopting strong accountability policies significantly improved student achievement is not convincing until substantial improvements in schooling conditions and practices occur" (p. 26).

Many states in the United States have high-stakes testing and there is also much testing embedded in the No Child Left Behind imperatives. There have been arguments that such frequent testing is akin to a coaching effect, whereas others consider that any gains are because of narrowing the curriculum, teaching to the test, and because too many students are excluded who may not perform so well. Amrein and Berliner (2002) raised much debate with their analysis of the performance of 18 states with high-stakes testing systems and found little effect of these systems on student achievement. This conclusion was contested (e.g., Braun, 2004; Raymond & Hanushek, 2003; Rosenshine, 2003). Lee (2006) used meta-analysis to compare different state policies on the National Assessment of Educational Progress examination. He found six studies favored high-stakes testing states, five were mixed, and one favored low-stakes testing states. The effects were extremely varied ($d = -0.67$ to $d = 1.24$), although it made no difference as to the focus of the accountability—that is, whether the focus is a combination of schools and students $d = 0.38$, for schools alone $d = 0.39$, or for students alone $d = 0.31$. The effects on mathematics ($d = 0.38$) are slightly higher than on reading ($d = 0.29$), and higher for elementary ($d = 0.44$) and middle schools ($d = 0.35$) than for high schools ($d = 0.03$).

Teaching test taking and coaching

The term "coaching" is used to refer to a wide range of test preparation activities carried out in order to improve test scores. Typically, coaching is instruction given or practice undertaken in preparation for taking a test (Cole, 1982). DerSimonian and Laird (1983) evaluated the effect of coaching on Scholastic Aptitude test scores and found that while the results did support the positive effect of coaching on SAT scores, the size of the coaching effect from the matched or randomized studies appeared too small to be practically important. Uncontrolled studies showed more variation in the effects attributed to coaching than matched or randomized studies and higher levels overall.

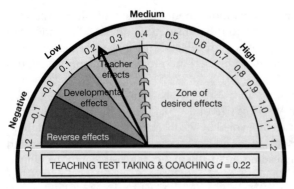

KEY	
Standard error	0.024 (Low)
Rank	103rd
Number of meta-analyses	10
Number of studies	267
Number of effects	364
Number of people (1)	15,772

Bangert-Drowns, Kulik, and Kulik, (1983) found the effects of coaching raised achievement test scores by $d = 0.25$. The level of intervention influenced effect sizes, with effect sizes smaller for short test-taking sessions, larger for more extensive programs, and greatest in single length programs designed to influence broader cognitive skills. An examination of 14 studies on the effectiveness of coaching for aptitude tests (Kulik, Bangert-Drowns, & Kulik, 1984) found that coaching raised scores on SAT as well as intelligence and other aptitude tests. SAT scores were raised $d = 0.15$ standard deviations with scores for aptitude and intelligence tests raised $d = 0.43$ standard deviation. The length of the training program also seems important. Samson (1985) reported that programs continuing for five weeks or more produced greater effects than those of a shorter duration. Samson also noted that the effects were higher with students in upper grades rather than in lower grade levels, and for students from lower socioeconomic backgrounds.

Hausknecht, Halpert, Di Paolo, and Gerrard, 2007 found an overall effect of $d = 0.22$ when test were re-administered, but much less for a third administration of the test. More specifically they found that the magnitude of practice was positively related to the amount of student contact time with coaching ($d = 0.26$), was greater for identical test ($d = 0.46$) than for alternate forms ($d = 0.24$), was similar for tests of analytical ($d = 0.32$) and quantitative measures ($d = 0.30$), and, most importantly, the effects were much greater ($d = 0.70$) when there was some form of test coaching than when there was no such coaching ($d = 0.24$).

Coaching students for SAT tests has moderate effects on SAT performance, although the effects were greater on SAT mathematics than on verbal tests (Becker, 1990). Becker argued that the considerable variability in results of the examination of studies on coaching was because not all coaching is effective. Studies in which the coaching intervention included practice and instruction on answering particular items showed significant advantages over practice in taking complete examinations or instructions in general test-taking skills. The effects of coaching are greater when pre-tests are given in conjunction with the coaching program (Witt, 1993), and when the items in the test follow a format that is more complex and is not usually used (Powers, 1993).

Another form of coaching is to become familiar with the examination process and examiner, particularly in one-to-one testing situations. In these situations, reducing anxiety about the testing context can make a difference. Fuchs and Fuchs (1985) found that examiner familiarity raised test performance by $d = 0.35$ standard deviations. Differential performance favoring the familiar examiner condition was stronger when students were of low socioeconomic status, when students were tested on comparatively difficult tests, and when the examiner had been known to students for a longer duration. A further meta-analysis of the effects of examiner familiarity on student test performance (Fuchs & Fuchs, 1986) supported their 1985 findings. This meta-analysis also showed that students taking examinations scored higher when tested by familiar rather than unfamiliar examiners. The duration of the activity inducing familiarity had a strong positive influence on effect size. Again, low socioeconomic status students performed much better with a familiar examiner, while high socioeconomic status students performed similarly across examiner conditions.

Providing formative evaluation of programs

A major argument throughout this book is the power of feedback to teachers on what is happening in their classroom so that they can ascertain "How am I going?" in achieving the learning intentions they have set for their students, such that they can then decide "Where to next?" for the students. Formative evaluation provides one such form of feedback. Fuchs and Fuchs (1986) examined the effects of systematic formative evaluation by the teachers and found that this technique increased achievement for students with a mild learning disability ($d = 0.70$). The formative evaluations were effective across student age, treatment duration, frequency of measurement, and special needs status. When teachers were required to use data and evidence based models, effect sizes were higher than when data were evaluated by teacher judgment. In addition, when the data was graphed, effect sizes were higher than when data were simply recorded.

It is this feedback to teachers that assists in explaining why most of the more powerful effects are higher than what has been termed the "typical teacher effects" of $d = 0.25$ to $d = 0.40$. It is the attention to the purposes of innovations, the willingness to seek negative evidence (i.e., seeking evidence on where students are not doing well) to improve the teaching innovation, the keenness to see the effects on all students, and the openness to new experiences that make the difference. Interventions are not "change for change's sake" as not all interventions are successful. The major message is for teachers to pay attention to the formative effects of their teaching, as it is these attributes of seeking formative evaluation of the effects (intended and unintended) of their programs that makes for excellence in teaching.

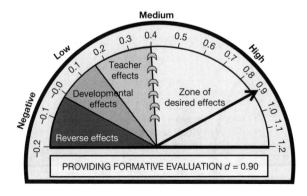

PROVIDING FORMATIVE EVALUATION $d = 0.90$

KEY	
Standard error	0.079 (Medium)
Rank	3rd
Number of meta-analyses	2
Number of studies	30
Number of effects	78
Number of people (1)	3,835

Questioning

Feedback can also come via teachers asking questions of their students, although it is an adage that teachers already know the answer to most of the questions they ask. The use of questions, especially higher-order questions, is often promulgated as a worthwhile teaching strategy: "Questioning opens up possibilities of meaning" (Gadamer, 1993, p. 375); "Questioning is a powerful strategy for building comprehension" (Mantione & Smead, 2003, p. 55); "Good questions lead to improved comprehension, learning, and memory of the materials among school children as well" (Craig *et al.*, 2006, p. 567). The study of the frequency, classification, and training of teacher questioning behaviors is based on the notion that skilled questioning by teachers can guide students to thoughtful and reflective answers and so facilitate higher levels of academic achievement (Samson, Strykowski, Weinstein, & Walberg, 1987).

So much of classroom time is spent with teachers questioning the students. Cotton (1989), for example, reviewed the evidence and found questioning was the second most dominant teaching method (after teacher talk), with teachers spending between 35–50 percent of teaching time posing questioning (e.g., Long & Sato, 1983; van Lier, 1998)— that is about 100 questions per hour (Mohr, 1998)—and the responses from the teacher to the students' answers to these questions was some form of judgment or correction, primarily reinforcing in nature, affirming, restating, and consolidating student responses. Brualdi (1998) claimed that teachers asked 300 to 400 questions per day, and the majority of these were low-level cognitive questions—60 percent recall facts and 20 percent are procedural in nature (Wilen, 1991) These are not open, inquiry questions, as students understand that the teacher already knows the answer (they are "display" questions; 82 percent are of this nature: Cotton, 1989). The reason for so much questioning relates to the conceptions of teaching and learning held by many teachers—that is, their role is to impart knowledge and information about a subject, and student learning is the acquisition of this information through processes of repetition, memorization, and recall: hence the need for much questioning to check that they have recalled this information.

The overall effects of questioning vary, and the major moderator is the type of question asked—surface questions can enhance surface knowing and higher-order questions can enhance deeper understanding. Samson, Strykowski, Weinstein, and Walberg (1987) used 14 studies to contrast the effects of predominantly higher cognitive questions and predominantly factual questions. Higher cognitive questioning strategies were found to have a small positive effect on learning measures. Factual pre-questions can facilitate learning

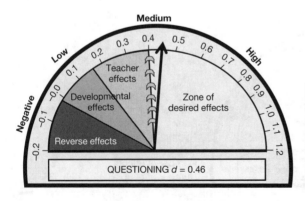

KEY	
Standard error	0.068 (Medium)
Rank	53rd
Number of meta-analyses	7
Number of studies	211
Number of effects	271
Number of people (0)	na

QUESTIONING *d* = 0.46

provided they are directly related to the texts or materials to be learnt (and have a negative effect when the questions asked are unrelated to the text material to be learnt, Hamaker, 1986). Higher-order questions are more effective on both direct and unrelated materials— "these results indicate that higher-order questions may have a somewhat broader general facilitative effect than factual adjunct questions" (Hamaker, 1986, p. 237).

Training in questioning matters. Gliessman, Pugh, Dowden, and Hutchins (1988) found that the questioning skills examined in the studies were very open to change through training. The general effect of training, academic level of trainees within training method, consistency of trainee certification level and pupils taught in practice, as well as consistency across practice and criterion teaching settings were all variables that had significant effects in the acquisition of questioning skills. Redfield and Rousseau (1981) also found that gains in achievement may be expected when teachers are trained in questioning skills. They found that lower level questions are more effective when aiming at surface level information, and a mixture of lower and higher level questions are more effective when aiming at deeper information and understanding. Studies designed to provide monitoring of program implementation show positive effects of 0.66 while those without monitoring showed negative effects (−0.10). Such attention by teachers to monitoring their own actions is powerful (and also reported in Gliessman et al., 1988).

Perhaps of more importance than teacher questioning is analyzing the questions that students ask. As the work of my colleagues and I on the Socratic questioning in the Paideia project has demonstrated, structuring class sessions to entice, teach, and listen to students questioning of students is powerful (Hattie, et al., 1998; Roberts & Billings, 1999).

Teacher immediacy

The immediacy and closeness of responses to the students shows them that teachers are listening and responding. "The applications of immediacy to educational settings introduced the idea that a teacher, through the use of certain cues, could reduce the perceived distance between instructor and learners and thereby influence certain classroom outcomes, especially student learning" (Allen, Witt, & Wheeless, 2006, p. 22). This immediacy is perceived by students as an acknowledgement of their engagement; it reduces the perceived distance between instructor and learners, is seen as rewarding to the student, and increases their level of enthusiasm or commitment to the learning task (Christophel & Gorham, 1995). The effects of teacher immediacy were much stronger on affective learning such

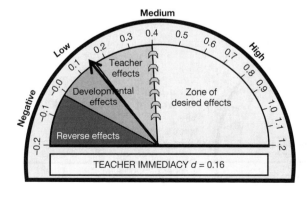

TEACHER IMMEDIACY d = 0.16

KEY	
Standard error	0.042 (Medium)
Rank	115th
Number of meta-analyses	1
Number of studies	16
Number of effects	16
Number of people (1)	5,437

as attitudes to the teacher, course or engaging in the learning experience ($d = 1.15$) than on achievement ($d = 0.16$). From these results, and the correlation between affective and achievement learning, Allen *et al.* (2006) concluded that "teacher immediacy behaviors predict or cause a level of affective learning. In turn, the level of affective learning predicts or causes the level of cognitive thinking. ... (the) teacher creates a motivational affective outcome that subsequently contributes to the generation of a cognitive outcome" (p. 26). They suggested that the teacher's immediacy also provided a source of feedback by the teacher about their interest, caring, and involvement in the student's learning.

Implementations that emphasize student perspectives in learning

The next set of topics relates to seeing learning from the student's perspective. Time on task, self-questioning, self-verbalization, peer tutoring, concept mapping, and the aptitude-treatment interaction.

Time on task

The typical claim is that practice makes perfect. I decided this was the case when I decided to play golf most mornings for a year. While my score dropped dramatically, there came a time when I realized that practice was not enough. Either professional coaching or a change to some physical predispositions would be needed. Further, we certainly do not want more time on task if the learning is not positive—it is like asking an unhealthy obese person to just eat more! Time on learning can involve: longer school days, longer school years, procedural time, time off-task, on-task time, and so on. There are various claims about how much actual time is spent in "engaged" learning time; Berliner (1984), for example, claims that about 40 percent of class time is spent on engaged time—and less of this engaged time is spent on productive time (which is that time that individual students find productive in their learning). So what happens in classes? Yair (2000) put wristwatches on 865 students (from 33 schools) that were programmed to emit signals (beeps) eight times a day for a week. When beeped, the students were asked to record what activity they were engaged in, and their thoughts and mood (which led to 28,193 daily experiences). The students were engaged with their lessons about half the total class time: engaged time was similar for boys and girls, but decreased over school grade. It was higher in mathematics than in English and social sciences, and was lowest when teachers were lecturing

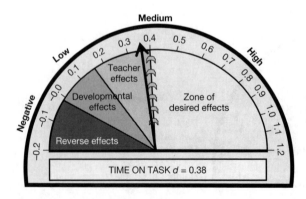

KEY	
Standard error	0.101 (High)
Rank	70th
Number of meta-analyses	4
Number of studies	100
Number of effects	136
Number of people (0)	na

TIME ON TASK $d = 0.38$

or when students were asked to watch television, and highest when students were working in groups or laboratories. The more students felt "challenged, and the greater the academic demand on students—the more the students are engaged with instruction—the less prone they are to external preoccupations" (Yair, 2000, p. 256).

So at best half of student time in class involves engagement in the class activity—perhaps not surprising given so much time is spent listening (or pretending to listen) to teachers talking! Many have thus argued that making the available school time more productive should be the key to enhancing learning—and not merely extending the school day or year (Karweit, 1984; 1985): "Increasing allocated time, without increasing productive time, is unlikely to improve educational performance" (Walberg, Niemiec, & Frederick, 1994, pp. 98–99).

Fredrick (1980) explored the relationship between "engaged" instructional time and instructional outcome from 35 studies, and reported an effect size of $d = 0.34$. Lewis and Samuels (2003) found that more practice at reading was positively associated with reading ability, but the effect was only $d = 0.10$. The effects were slightly larger for grade 1–3 students, second language students, learning disabled students, and students reading below grade level: practice helps but it is not enough.

More important is that practice needs to be deliberate; particularly when first learning new material. Van Gog, Ericsson, Rikers, and Paas (2005) argued that it was not the amount of experience or practice in a domain that is relevant, but rather the amount of deliberate effort to improve performance. Deliberate practice refers to the relevant practice activities aimed to improve performance; it needs to be at "an appropriate, challenging level of difficulty, and enable successive refinement by allowing for repetition, giving room to make and correct errors, and providing informative feedback to the learner" (p. 75). Van Gog *et al.* further noted that such practice requires students to stretch themselves to higher levels of performance, and requires much concentration and effort over extended periods, usually of fixed times over many days. Feltz and Landers (1983) examined the effects of mental practice on motor-skill learning and performance and concluded that mental practice effects are found in both the initial and later stages of learning. Large effect sizes for cognitive tasks were more often achieved in a relatively short practice session and with only a few trials compared to motor and strength tasks.

Spaced and massed practice

It is the frequency of different opportunities rather than merely spending "more" time on task that makes the difference to learning. So teachers need to consider increasing the rate of correct academic responses to deliberative practice opportunities until minimal levels of mastery (defined by success criteria) are met (Walker, Greenwood, Hart, & Carta, 1994). This finding helps us to understand a common denominator to many of the effective practices in this book, such as direct instruction, peer-tutoring, mastery learning, and feedback. It is not over learning for the sake of it. Deliberative practice increases opportunities to not only enhance mastery but also fluency (the core of precision teaching). This is not "drill and practice", which so often can be: dull and repetitive; involve minimal feedback; not extend or provide multiple different experiences; not provide sufficient contextual variability to facilitate transfer of learning; and not be embedded in the context of the deeper and conceptual understandings that are part of the more total learning experience, and which so often aims at the surface knowledge. Deliberative practice can involve

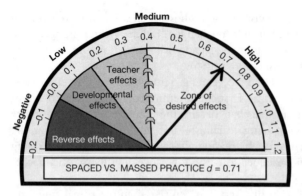

KEY

Standard error	na
Rank	12th
Number of meta-analyses	2
Number of studies	63
Number of effects	112
Number of people (0)	na

SPACED VS. MASSED PRACTICE *d* = 0.71

specific skills and complex performances, and the attainment of success criteria can be motivating and certainly lead to longer retention of sometimes over-learned surface and deep knowing (Péladeau, Forget, & Gagné, 2003).

Nuthall (2005) claimed that students often needed three to four exposures to the learning—usually over several days—before there was a reasonable probability they would learn. This is consistent with the power of spaced rather than massed practice. Donovan and Radosevich (1998) concluded that students in spaced practice conditions performed higher than those in massed practice conditions ($d = 0.46$). Both acquisition ($d = 0.45$) and retention ($d = 0.51$) were enhanced by spaced rather than massed practice. The effectiveness of length of spacing was related to the complexity and challenge of the tasks—stronger effects were found for simple tasks with relatively brief rest periods, and longer rest periods were needed for more complex tasks (at least 24 hours or more).

Peer tutoring

The overall effects of the use of peers as co-teachers (of themselves and of others) in classes is, overall, quite powerful. If the aim is to teach students self-regulation and control over their own learning then they must move from being students to being teachers of themselves. One way to achieve this aim is to use peer tutoring—which too many consider a tool for older students to teach struggling younger children. While it is used for this purpose, the major influence is that it is an excellent method to teach students to become their own teachers. Reviews of tutoring literature have shown that peer tutoring has

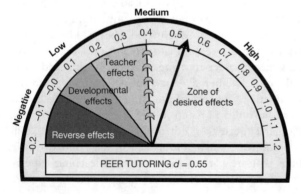

KEY

Standard error	0.103 (High)
Rank	36th
Number of meta-analyses	14
Number of studies	767
Number of effects	1,200
Number of people (3)	2,676

PEER TUTORING *d* = 0.55

many academic and social benefits for both those tutoring *and* those being tutored (Cook, Scruggs, Mastropieri, & Casto, 1985). The overall effects from most of the meta-analyses on this topic are typically above the $d = 0.40$ average.

Hartley's (1977) meta-analysis of the effects on mathematics achievement of different instructional modes found that peer tutoring was the most effective of the various conditions she compared ($d = 0.60$). Peer tutoring was most effective when used as a supplement to, rather than a substitute for, the teacher roles. Cross-age tutors ($d = 0.79$) were more effective than same-age peers ($d = 0.52$) and adult tutors ($d = 0.54$). She also found a commonly reported conclusion: the effects on the tutors ($d = 0.58$) were not that different from the effects on those being tutored ($d = 0.63$) (see also Cook *et al.*, 1985, where supplemental was $d = 0.96$ and substitution was $d = 0.63$).

Peer tutoring has often been used with students with disabilities. Elbaum, Vaughn, Hughes, and Moody (2000) found that the magnitude of peer-tutoring effects did not differ according to whether disabled or non-disabled students acted as tutors or were doing the teaching. Cook, Scruggs, Mastropieri, and Casto (1985) reviewed studies where students with special needs were used as tutors of other students with special needs and found that those being tutored ($d = 0.53$) gained as much as those undertaking the tutoring ($d = 0.58$). Mathes and Fuchs (1991) found that peer tutoring was more effective than the instruction these students typically experienced. Kunsch, Jitendra, and Sood (2007) reported that these peer-mediated interventions were higher with disabled students in general ($d = 0.56$) than when they were in special classes ($d = 0.32$). Phillips (1983) found tutor methods were most effective with students in the acquisition rather than the proficiency phase of learning and when there were clear criterion measures (success criteria) used as targets.

Rohrbeck, Ginsberg-Block, Fantuzzo, and Miller (2003) found that peer interventions that were more student controlled (when peers are involved in setting goals, monitoring performance, evaluating performance, and selecting rewards), the effects were greater than when these were primarily controlled by teachers. When students were self-managers of their learning or the learning of others (in the peer-tutoring situation), then this autonomy led to greater achievement effects.

Thus, when students become teachers of others, they learn as much as those they are teaching. When they have some control or autonomy over this teaching, the effects are higher. It is likely that these effects are more critical when new surface level information is being taught, although it is likely that the tutors may need to understand the material at a deeper level to be effective teachers. This conjecture is not well explored in this literature and could well be subjected to further research. How often do we hear from teachers that "we learnt more when we were asked to teach it" but then see this maxim ignored as teachers enter classrooms and see students as recipients rather than producers of teaching and learning?

Mentoring

Mentoring is a form of peer tutoring, although it is normally involves older persons (often adults) providing academic or social assistance, or both, to younger people—but it also occurs throughout adult work situations to facilitate career development. Such mentoring assumes that supportive relationships with older people are important for personal, emotional, cognitive, and psychological growth. Mentoring usually involves little,

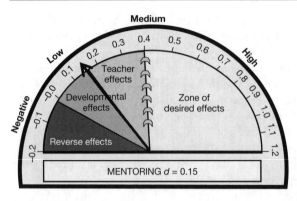

KEY	
Standard error	0.047 (Medium)
Rank	120th
Number of meta-analyses	2
Number of studies	74
Number of effects	74
Number of people (1)	10,250

if any, teaching and is more an "apprentice" model based on social and role model experiences. Mentoring had a close to zero effect on performance outcomes ($d = 0.08$), although there were higher effects on attitudes (satisfaction $d = 0.6$, school attitudes $d = 0.19$), and on motivation and involvement ($d = 0.11$) (Eby, Allen, Evans, Ng, & DuBois, 2008). That is, there is more change on attitudes than achievements, probably because "attitudes are more amenable to change than are outcomes that are more contextually-dependent" (p. 16). It was the case that effects were higher for academic mentoring than for youth (at risk, family-related mentoring) and workplace mentoring.

DuBois, Holloway, Valentine, and Cooper (2002) investigated many outcomes from mentoring. Across their 575 effect sizes, the average was $d = 0.18$ on achievement, and these low effects occurred when the program was one-on-one or in groups; the effects were lower in schools than in workplaces and higher for trained compared with non-trained mentors, but there was no relation with the frequency of contact nor the length of relationship between mentors and youth. The effects were similarly low for emotional or psychological outcomes ($d = 0.20$), problem and high risk behaviors ($d = 0.19$), social competence ($d = 0.16$), and career and employment outcomes ($d = 0.19$).

Implementations using student meta-cognitive and self-regulation learning

Meta-cognition relates to thinking about thinking. This section outlines a series of programs based on teaching various meta-cognitive strategies, including study skills, self-verbalization, self-questioning, aptitude-treatment interactions, matching learning styles, and individualized instruction.

Meta-cognitive strategies

Newell (1990) noted that there are two layers of problem solving: applying a strategy to the problem, and selecting and monitoring that strategy. Such "thinking about thinking" involved in this second layer of problem-solving has recently been referred to by the term "meta-cognition"; this refers to higher-order thinking which involves active control over the cognitive processes engaged in learning. Meta-cognitive activities can include planning how to approach a given learning task, evaluating progress, and monitoring comprehension. A synthesis of effective meta-cognitive training programs (Chiu, 1998),

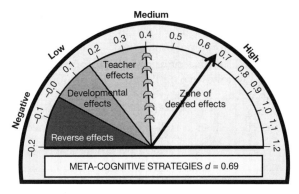

found that such training is more effectively implemented using small-group instruction, with students in higher grades, with remedial students, and in less intensive programs. Haller, Child, and Walberg (1988) assessed the effects of meta-cognitive instruction on reading comprehension, and reported an effect size of $d = 0.71$ (see also Chiu, 1998). The most effective meta-cognitive strategies were awareness of textual inconsistency and the use of self-questioning. The more varied the instructional strategies throughout a lesson, the more students were influenced.

Study skills

Study skills interventions are programs that work on improving student learning using interventions outside what the teacher or teachers involved would normally undertake in the course of teaching. Interventions can be classified as *cognitive, meta-cognitive,* and *affective.* Cognitive interventions focus on the development of task-related skills, such as note taking and summarizing. Meta-cognitive interventions work on self-management learning skills such as planning; monitoring; and where, when, and how to use tactics and strategies. Affective interventions focus on non-cognitive features of learning such as motivation and self-concept (Hattie, Biggs, & Purdie, 1996). The argument in this section is that courses in study skills *alone* can have an effect on the surface level information, but it is necessary to combine the study skills *with the content* to have an effect on the deeper levels of understanding.

Lavery (2008) found a $d = 0.46$ effect on achievement from meta-cognitive study skills

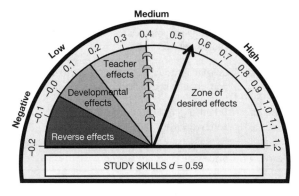

interventions. She found the highest effects from strategies that aimed at the "forethought" phase of learning; such as goal–setting and planning, self-instruction, and self-evaluation (Table 9.5). This strategy is "a major part of the forethought phase of this model (which occurs before the learner engages in the task) and has previously been shown to be a crucial aspect of interventions" (Greiner and Karoly, 1976, p. 497). Self-instruction occurs during the performance phase of the model and is an invaluable tool for guiding the learner through the focusing of attention and use of appropriate strategies. Self-evaluation concludes the cyclical model by allowing the learner to self-reflect on performance in

Table 9.5 Various meta-cognitive strategies and the effect sizes (Lavery, 2008)

Strategy	Definition	Description	No. effects	ES	se
Organizing and transforming	Overt or covert rearrangement of instructional materials to improve learning	Making an outline before writing a paper	89	0.85	0.04
Self-consequences	Student arrangement or imagination of rewards or punishment for success or failure	Putting off pleasurable events until work is completed	75	0.70	0.05
Self-instruction	Self-verbalizing the steps to complete a given task	Verbalizing steps in solving a mathematics problem	124	0.62	0.03
Self-evaluation	Setting standards and using them for self-judgment	Checking work before handing in to teacher	156	0.62	0.03
Help-seeking	Efforts to seek help from either a peer, teacher, or other adult	Using a study partner	62	0.60	0.05
Keeping records	Recording of information related to study tasks	Taking class notes	46	0.59	0.06
Rehearsing and memorizing	Memorization of material by overt or covert strategies	Writing a mathematics formula down until it is remembered	99	0.57	0.04
Goal-setting/ planning	Setting of educational goals or planning subgoals and planning for sequencing, timing, and completing activities related to those goals	Making lists to accomplish during studying	130	0.49	0.03
Reviewing records	Efforts to reread notes, tests, or textbooks to prepare for class or further testing	Reviewing class textbook before going to lecture	131	0.49	0.03
Self-monitoring	Observing and tracking one's own performance and outcomes, often recording them	Keeping records of study output	154	0.45	0.02
Task strategies	Analyzing tasks and identifying specific, advantageous methods for learning	Creating mnemonics to remember facts	154	0.45	0.03
Imagery	Creating or recalling vivid mental images to assist learning	Imagining the consequences of failing to study	6	0.44	0.09
Time management	Estimating and budgeting use of time	Scheduling daily studying and homework time	8	0.44	0.08
Environmental restructuring	Efforts to select or arrange the physical setting to make learning easier	Studying in a secluded place	4	0.22	0.09

relation to the previously set goals. While self-monitoring is very effective, it was not as high as that of self-evaluation, suggesting that self-monitoring in itself (such as ticking off completed tasks) can be much improved if taken a step further, where the learner actually evaluates what they have monitored.

The highest ranked strategy, that of organizing and transforming, has also been found to be a valuable component of many interventions (Hattie *et al.*, 1996). It is likely that the types of strategies included in this category (such as summarizing and paraphrasing) promote a more *active* approach to learning tasks. While several strategies such as record keeping, imagery, time management, and restructuring the learning environment were ranked lowest, it is likely that this is because they are more passive and involve non-active involvement with the content.

With regard to tertiary students, a closer examination of the effect sizes for these students shows that the smaller effects (and in one case a negative effect) generally came from the studies of shorter duration (i.e., those of a few days). Considering that the students in the tertiary studies were often identified as having difficulties with studying or were considered to be "at risk" by their institution, it seems that longer interventions may be required with these students. It is also likely that, as has been previously suggested, study habits are somewhat more "ingrained" with older students, thus making them more resistant to change (Hattie *et al.*, 1996). This was also indicated by one of the studies included in the meta-analysis, that of Nist and Simpson (1989), whereby achievement scores suffered an initial decrease after the implementation of the intervention, suggesting that a longer time frame is necessary, at least with tertiary-age students. There needs to be some un-learning of prior study skills before new learning can occur.

For students struggling to begin to understand, for lower achieving students, and for those wanting higher achievement, then teaching study skills can have advantages. Shrager and Mayer (1989), for example, claimed that note taking may facilitate better test performance for less skilled learners, but not for highly skilled learners. Mastropieri and Scruggs (1989) found the highest effect sizes of all for training special needs students with mnemonic methods of studying (see also Crismore, 1985; Kobayashi, 2005; Rolheiser-Bennett, 1986; Runyan, 1987)—although the effects of study skills programs for those struggling at the college level is quite low (Burley, 1994; Kulik, Kulik, & Shwalb, 1983). The mnemonic keyword strategies involve relating unfamiliar verbal stimuli into acoustically similar representations that become the keywords for remembering (e.g., Roy G. Biv for the colors of the rainbow). They did note that to maximize the chances of this knowledge being transferred and sustaining the learning, it was most effective when students were first able to *read* the text and determine what was important to remember, determine the optimal mnemonic strategy, correctly recall and implement the appropriate steps of strategy adaptation, and self-test, monitor, and correctly apply the learned information in the appropriate situation.

Kobayashi (2005) found that note taking effects were higher when students were given instructor's notes to work from ($d = 0.82$), as these provided exemplars for their own note taking and a rubric to work from when learning from the notes. The effects were higher when notes were provided ($d = 0.41$, compared to not provided ($d = 0.19$), and it was the reviewing of the notes ($d = 0.45$) that was more effective than the taking of the notes. He found no moderation effect relating to the length of the review, the presentation length that led to the taking of notes, or the format of the presentation (video, audio, or live).

Hattie, Biggs, and Purdie (1996) divided study skills programs into those aiming for near- and far-transfer in terms of degree of transfer between training task and outcome measure, and whether they were more out of, or in–context of the discipline, They found greater effects of study skills programs on the lower order thinking tasks (e.g., memory, $d = 1.09$), than on reproductive performance in general ($d = 0.69$), and lower (but still high) on transformational performance ($d = 0.53$). As noted above, programs involving direct teaching of mostly mnemonic devices are highly effective with most students, and also conventional study skills training is effective for near transfer on low-cognitive-level tasks. Programs that were provided outside of the context of the subject matter (the more general study skills programs) were only effective when surface knowledge was the outcome, whereas programs run in-context (associated highly with the subject matter to be learnt) were most effective at surface and deeper knowing and understanding. We concluded that "the best results came when strategy training was used meta-cognitively, with appropriate motivational and contextual support" (Hattie *et al.*, 1996, p. 129) and questioned whether "learning-to-learn" programs that are not embedded in the context of the subject to be learnt are of much value. Three recommendations from the meta-analysis are that training should be (1) in context, (2) use tasks within the same domain as the target content, and (3) promote a high degree of learner activity and meta-cognitive awareness. "Strategy training should be seen as a balanced system in which the individual's abilities, insights, and sense of responsibility are brought into use, so that the strategies that are appropriate to the task at hand can be used" (Hattie *et al.*, 1996, p. 131). The student needs to know various strategies that are appropriate to the task at hand: the how, when, where, and why of their use. Strategy training needs to be embedded in the teaching context itself.

Study skills can also assist students to gain confidence that they are "learners" of the subject. Robbins, Lauver, Le, Davis, Langley, and Carlstrom (2004) found that the best study skills predictors of grade point average (GPA) were academic self-efficacy ($d = 0.38$), and that this confidence was as influential as high school GPA ($d = 0.41$), achievement motivation ($d = 0.26$), social involvement ($d = 0.12$), and academic goals ($d = 0.16$). Similarly, Ley and Young (2001) found self-efficacy to be among the best predictors of GPA ($d = 0.50$) and achievement motivation ($d = 0.30$), and that it had an incremental contribution over and above socioeconomic status, academic achievement, and high school GPA in predicting college outcomes. They argued that there were four principles to embed study regulation support in instruction:

1   guide learners to prepare and structure an effective learning environment;
2   organize instruction and activities to facilitate cognitive and meta-cognitive processes;
3   use instructional goals and feedback to present student monitoring opportunities;
4   provide learners with continuous evaluation information and occasions to self-evaluate.

These four principles can guide embedding study skills support in a wide variety of instructional media and contexts.

Self-verbalization and self-questioning

Self-questioning is one form of self-regulation, and given the comments in the previous section, are probably of more use to those in the early to intermediate phase of skill acquisition and for those of lower to middle ability (cf., de Bruin, Rikers, & Schmidt, 2007).

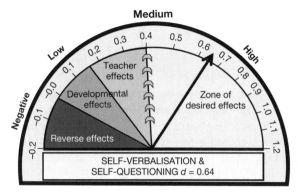

KEY	
Standard error	0.060 (Medium)
Rank	18th
Number of meta-analyses	3
Number of studies	113
Number of effects	1,150
Number of people (2)	3,098

Duzinski (1987) reviewed many procedures that taught a learning strategy or cognitive mediation strategy to students. Self-verbalization was among the most effective of the strategies, and it worked better for task oriented skills (e.g., writing or mathematics). In Huang's (1991) study of student self-questioning, the effects were higher with lower ability students. Similarly, Rock (1985) found that self-instructional training was effective for many students in special education programs.

Huang also noted that the use of self-questioning provided assistance in searching for the information needed, and thus increased student understanding of the messages of the material to be learned. Higher ability students were probably using a variety of self-regulation strategies already and self-questioning may not be as effective for them. The effects were higher for pre-lesson questioning ($d = 0.94$) and post-lesson questioning ($d = 0.86$), compared to questions interspersed during the lesson ($d = 0.52$); when the questionings were delayed ($d = 0.72$) compared to immediate ($d = 0.54$); and where there was teacher modeling ($d = 0.69$) compared to none ($d = 0.47$).

Student control over learning

The effect of student choice and control over learning is somewhat higher on motivation outcomes ($d = 0.30$) than on subsequent student learning ($d = 0.04$; Niemiec, Sikorski, & Walberg, 1996; Patall, Cooper, & Robinson, 2008). Indeed the more instructionally irrelevant choices had higher outcomes (e.g., color of pen to use, what music to listen to when

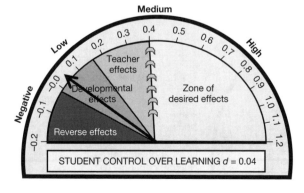

KEY	
Standard error	0.176 (High)
Rank	132nd
Number of meta-analyses	2
Number of studies	65
Number of effects	38
Number of people (0)	na

learning). Such irrelevant choices are less effortful and do not have major consequences on the learning, and too many choices may be overwhelming.

Aptitude-treatment interactions

There are many claims that instruction must be altered for different types of students. This very rich source of literature has commonly been identified by the term "aptitude-treatment interactions." There has been a long search for these aptitude-treatment interactions, and many researchers lost must interest after Cronbach and Snow (1977) produced a magnum opus on the subject. While they were optimistic that such interactions were critical and could be found, they still concluded that "well-substantiated findings regarding ATI [aptitude-treatment interactions] are scarce" (p. 6), and Glass (1970) claimed he did not "know of another statement that has been confirmed so many times by so many people" (p. 210). Since that time the search has continued, and many new aptitude-treatment interactions have emerged under headings such as learning styles (see next section), or differential treatments. All are premised on the search for instruction to accommodate individual differences.

There are few meta-analyses that provide evidence about aptitude-treatment interactions in general, possibly because most meta-analyses have been concerned with main effects. It is rare for meta-analyses to include information about interactions. Many include moderators (e.g., sex, age) but few include mediators, which are at the core of aptitude-treatment interactions (Cronbach & Snow, 1977). Whitener (1989) used the standardized interaction terms from 11 studies to find a weighted average regression coefficient—which is the best measure of the presence of an aptitude-treatment interaction. The average slope difference was about $d = 0.11$, and from her various careful analyses, she found support for the claim that students who have higher prior achievement benefit more than students with lower prior achievement from an increase in instructional support. That is, "higher achieving subjects capitalize on higher support, increasing the difference in performance between high and low achievers" (p. 78). It is important to appreciate that this effect of $d = 0.11$ is the effect after the main effects for prior achievement and treatment have been removed from the variance in learning—and this is worth considering (and as it is an aptitude-treatment interaction effect, it cannot to be compared to the other effects throughout this book). Pintrich, Cross, Kozma, and McKeachie (1986) claimed that aptitude-treatment interaction studies cannot be used with any confidence to construct general principles of

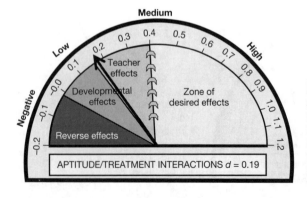

APTITUDE/TREATMENT INTERACTIONS $d = 0.19$

KEY	
Standard error	0.070 (Medium)
Rank	108th
Number of meta-analyses	2
Number of studies	61
Number of effects	340
Number of people (1)	1,434

instructional design, thus echoing Cronbach and Snow's (1977) earlier conclusion (based on a very comprehensive review of all possible research at that time) that "no Aptitude x Treatment interactions are so well confirmed that they can be used directly as guides to instruction" (p. 492).

Matching style of learning

Learning styles are one specific type of aptitude-treatment interaction and presume that different students have differing preferences for particular ways of learning. Often the claim is that when teaching is aligned with the preferred or dominant learning style then achievement is enhanced. For example, Dunn and colleagues (Dunn, Griggs, Olson, Beasley, & Gorman, 1995) claimed that students with strong learning styles, such as auditory, visual, tactile, or kinesthetic styles, showed greater academic gains as a result of congruent instructional interventions than those students who had mixed preferences or moderate preferences. Their model has five dimensions: biological (preference for warm vs. cool temperatures when learning), emotional (persistence vs. needing breaks when learning), sociological (working in groups or alone), physiological (intake while learning, mobility needs) and psychological (global versus analytic processing style differences). The claim is that teaching is more effective when these learning preferences are taken into account—although others have claimed the opposite: that we should be teaching students the learning styles they do not have (Apter, 2001).

It is hard to discern the meaning of some of these meta-analyses. One conclusion, given the average effect size of $d = 0.41$, is that learning style is somewhat important. But when we delve deeper, the model includes a mixture of attributes, especially the confusion of learning styles with learning strategies. Further, many of the meta-analyses correlate the learning style scores with achievement and thus are neither aptitude-treatment interactions nor learning style interventions. Many studies say no more than what students learn is correlated with achievement. Kavale and Forness (1987), for example, were interested in students with learning difficulties and found little support for the claim that there were higher outcomes when teaching students based on some supposed strength in auditory ($d = 0.18$), visual ($d = 0.09$), or kinesthetic $d = 0.18$) preference. Indeed they commented that "the groups seemingly differentiated on the basis of modality preferences actually revealed considerable overlap and it was doubtful whether any of the presumed preferences could really be deemed preferences" and "little (or no) gain in achievement was

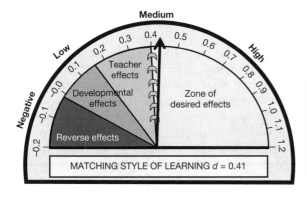

MATCHING STYLE OF LEARNING $d = 0.41$

KEY	
Standard error	0.016 (Low)
Rank	62nd
Number of meta-analyses	8
Number of studies	411
Number of effects	1,218
Number of people (6)	29,911

found when instructional methods were matched to preferred learning modality" (p. 237). Iliff (1994) found that no one style predicted achievement outcomes better than any other: $d = 0.28$ for diverger, $d = 0.29$ for assimilator, $d = 0.28$ for converger, and $d = 0.29$ for accommodator. He concluded that "since this study found the LSI [learning styles inventory] not to be a predictor of learner outcome and career fields of study, researchers will be advised to stop trying to fit square pegs into round holes" (p. 76).

Two meta-analyses seem so different from the others, and include so many errors that they should be excluded. Dunn, Griggs, Olson, Beasley, and Gorman's (1995) meta-analysis was mainly based on doctoral dissertations, many supervised by the authors, with mostly attitudinal outcomes, and many were based on adult samples. There are some unusual aspects in this meta-analysis. Some of the effects are large; Rowan (1988), for example, assigned teachers to in-service courses based on matched and mismatched learning style and preferences for time of day for instruction. The effect size reported is $d = 22.29!$ This translates into a correlation between learning styles and achievement of $d = 0.996$—which is beyond the imaginable. The next largest correlation was $d = 0.887$ from Lashell (1986). She assigned 48 students to a control and 42 to a treatment group. Students' reading styles were evaluated and educational strategies recommended for each student (e.g., preferences were related to phonics-linguistics, whole-word, individualized, or language experience). Using a measure of reading as the outcome, Lashell used a regression analysis including grade, treatment or control group, gender, pre-reading score, teacher's years of education, and others. The Multiple R $= 0.887$ and Dunn *et al.* mistakenly used this R as the effect size—the pre-reading beta-weight, not surprisingly, is the largest predictor, and the treatment over control effect is relatively very small.

In many of the other studies in this meta-analysis there were similar problems; and some of the sample sizes were tiny. Zippert (1985) assigned nine adults to courses to match their (unspecified) learning styles and eight to a control course—both taught by the same instructor; the effect size was $d = 2.5$. Hutto (1982) asked four teachers to teach three classes where they were asked to match instruction to the students' learning preference and three where they were not so matched. Although a number of statistical tests were provided, only one was chosen to be interpreted—in third grade, the matched group exceeded the control group (and this is reported in the meta-analysis). Ingham (1989) gave 314 employees (route sales representatives, mechanics, and management) two lessons—one an auditory strategy with visuals, and one a tactual/kinesthetic strategy with visuals. When matched for preferences, there were differences in their attitudes towards the company training programs.

Overall in the Dunn *et al.* meta-analysis, the correlations were $r = 0.26$ for emotional, $r = 0.23$ for sociological, $r = 0.24$ for environmental, and $r = 0.46$ for physiological and outcomes. Given the studies in this latter group, it seems that matching learning to the students' preferred time of day for learning, intake preferences (food, snacking), mobile versus passive environments, and auditory preferences—but it is just not believable that the correlations of these effects exceed, in most cases, $r = 0.60$. For the same reasons, the meta-analysis by Sullivan (1993) should be disregarded. A student of Dunn, she synthesized 42 studies, but nearly all were the same as in the Dunn *et al.*, paper and included the same analysis flaws. Kavale, Hirshoren, and Forness (1998) also reviewed the Dunn *et al.* meta-analysis and concluded that the "weak rationale, curious procedures, significant omissions, and circumscribed interpretation should all serve as cautions" and that the study has "all the hallmarks of a desperate attempt to rescue a failed model of learning style" (p. 79).

It is difficult to contemplate that some of these single influences (such as whether you prefer to snack, or to sit up straight) explain more of the variance of achievement that so many of the other influences in this book. Mangino (2004), for example, noted that students enrolled in remedial courses had the highest achievement correlations with kinesthetic learning (doing, touching, interaction, $r = 0.64$), need for consistency in learning strategies and not learning in several ways ($r = 0.44$), a strong preference for intake (eating and drinking while learning, $r = 0.41$), and having an authority figure present when learning ($r = 0.34$). Higher achieving students had preferences for learning in several ways ($r = 0.31$), an authority-figure present ($r = 0.28$), the need for structure ($r = 0.38$), no sound ($r = 0.40$), a formal design (a preference to learn sitting up straight; back at a 90 degree angle, $r = 0.47$), and tended to be more motivated ($r = 0.25$). The message is that learners need teachers (authority figures), low cognitive load if in remedial classes, and multiple means of learning if in typical classes. The claims about need for snacking and sitting up straight defy my powers to make sense of them.

An alternative explanation is that when students enjoy learning then achievement is higher. The conditions under which they most enjoy learning are thus correlated, but it is the enjoyment of learning rather than the conditions that are critical. This would explain the correlations between various environmental influences and achievement. Lovelace (2005), for example, included a potpourri of studies relating achievement to modifying classroom environment, structured compared to unstructured situations, working alone or in pairs, effects of time of day of instruction, individual compared to other teaching methods. She argued that achievement is enhanced particularly when there is matching of preferences for mobility, light, auditory, tactual, or intake compared to matching on sound, temperature, design, or kinesthetic.

Slemmer (2002) was particularly interested in how technology-enhanced learning environments accommodate the learning styles of students. While she found small effects relating learning styles to outcomes, the highest effect was when the same treatment was provided for all students and not varying the instruction depending on learning preferences. Tamir (1985) related three cognitive preferences and learning and reported an effect size of $d = -0.28$ with recall (acceptance of information without consideration of implementations, applications, or limitations), $d = 0.32$ with principles (acceptance of information because it exemplifies or illuminates a fundamental principal, concept, or relation), $d = 0.24$ with critical questioning of information regarding its completeness, generalizability, or limitations, and $d = -0.06$ with application and emphasis on the usefulness and applicability of information in a general, social, or scientific context. Lower achievers prefer recall, whereas higher achievement is related to a preference for principles, critical questioning and application.

It is hard not to be skeptical about these learning preference claims. Holt, Denny, Capps, and de Vore (2005) asked whether teachers are able to perceive their students' learning preferences more accurately than random guessing. They found that the percentage correctly assessed was 30 percent whereas by chance the estimate was 25 percent—not a great show of confidence in teachers' ability to ascertain preferences. Coffield, Ecclestone, Moseley, and Hall (2004) completed an extensive analysis of various learning style models. There were few studies that met their minimum acceptability criteria, and they provided many criticisms of the field such as: too much overstatement; poor items and assessments; low validity and negligible impact on practice; and much of the advocacy in this is aimed at commercial ends. Learning strategies, yes; enjoying learning, yes; learning styles, no.

Individual instruction

Individualized instruction is based on the idea that each student has unique interests and past learning experiences, hence an individualized instructional program for each student allows for flexibility in teaching methods and motivational strategies to consider these individual differences. The evidence supporting individualized instruction, however, is not so supportive. Students are typically taught in classes of 20 or more; thus one of the major skills of teachers is to manage such classes, optimize peer co-teaching (even though this is not so common), and capitalize on the similarities and differences among the students.

Hartley's (1977) meta-analysis of the effects on mathematics achievement of different instructional modes found that individualized learning and programmed instruction were only slightly better than regular classroom instruction. In contrast, peer tutoring and computer-assisted instruction were more effective ($d = 0.60$) in increasing achievement. Similarly, Bangert, Kulik, and Kulik (1983) found that use of an individualized teaching system had only a small effect on student achievement in high school courses. There was limited contribution to student self-esteem, critical thinking ability, or attitude towards the subject matter taught when taught through individualized programs.

Waxman, Wang, Anderson, and Walberg (1985a, 1985b) claimed higher effects, but noted the importance of not just teaching the students by means of many individualized programs, but the importance of adapting instruction to the needs of students; ensuring these needs are based on the assessed capabilities of each student; using materials and procedures that allow students to make progress at their own pace; having periodic evaluations used to inform students about mastery; including aspects of self-responsibility for evaluating mastery; having student choice in educational goals; and aiming to have students assist each other in pursuing individual goals. There is no reason, however, why these attributes could not also occur in small or even larger groups.

Individualized instruction has been researched often in mathematics and science programs. Horak (1981) examined the effects of individualized instruction on mathematics achievement at elementary and high school level and found no significant difference to larger groupings. Similarly, Atash and Dawson (1986) examined the effects of the Intermediate Science Curriculum Study (ISCS), a semi-programmed, individualized course, and found that students on this program barely outperformed students taking a traditional junior high science curriculum ($d = 0.09$). Aiello and Wolfle's (1980) meta-analysis of individualized instruction in science in high school through college found individualized instruction to be similarly barely more effective than the traditional lecture approach ($d = 0.08$).

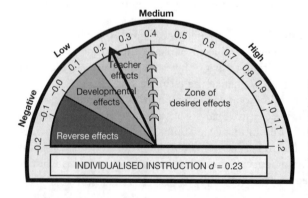

KEY	
Standard error	0.056 (Medium)
Rank	100th
Number of meta-analyses	9
Number of studies	600
Number of effects	1,146
Number of people (2)	9,380

INDIVIDUALISED INSTRUCTION $d = 0.23$

Concluding comments

The argument defended in this chapter is that successful learning is a function of the worthwhileness and clarity of the learning intentions, the specifications, and the success criteria; the power of using multiple and appropriate teaching strategies with a particular emphasis on the presence of feedback focused at the right level of instruction (acquisition or proficiency); seeing learning and teaching from the students' perceptive; and placing reliance on teaching study skills and strategies of learning. Emphasizing learning styles, coaching for tests, mentoring, and individualized instruction are noted for their lack of impact.

The emphasis should be on what students can do, and then on students knowing what they are aiming to do, having multiple strategies for learning to do, and knowing when they have done it. It is teachers having teaching strategies aimed at enhancing the learning that was identified as the outcomes for the lesson, and who provide appropriate feedback to reduce the gap between where the student is and where they need to be. Both student and teacher need to set challenging goals, as this then sets the bar for the standards to be completed (at least, aiming for the h-point of 0.40 or higher effects), and to reach that bar challenging learning intentions, clear success criteria, and feedback will be needed. Setting challenging goals is a powerful part in the overall equation of what makes the difference in learning. Setting learning intentions invokes a "discrepancy–creative process", such that there is often a gap between present performance and where you wish to be (and which involves both teachers and students knowing where they are, where they are going, how they are going, what they need to do next, and how they can reduce this gap). Latham and Locke (2006), however, noted various pitfalls in goal setting, which highlight many of the factors of value noted in this chapter. When students *lack* the knowledge and skills to attain a goal, giving them a challenging goal sometimes leads to poorer performance than telling them to do their best. Goals may have an adverse effect on risk taking, if failure to attain a specific challenging goal is punished. Failures and false starts often are precursors to success. "Positive self-talk regarding an error ('I have made an error, great. I have learned something.') helps to keep our attention on the task rather than on ourselves ('How can I be so stupid?')" (p. 335).

The major messages in this chapter are the importance of learning intentions, success criteria, a classroom environment that not only tolerates but welcomes errors, attention to the challenge of the task, the presence of feedback to reduce the gaps, and a sense of satisfaction and further engagement and perseverance to succeed in the tasks of learning. This outline of successful teaching and learning is for all students—as another of my heroes, Sir Edmund Hillary, claimed with reference to himself, he was a man of modest abilities, and he combined these with a good deal of determination, and rather liked to succeed.

Chapter 10

The contributions from teaching approaches—part II

This chapter investigates a range of teaching strategies, school-wide programs, implementations using technologies, and out-of-school learning. As noted in the previous chapter, there are the same common themes in what makes some of these successful—pre-planning, deliberate attention to learning intentions and success criteria, and a constant effort to ensure teachers are seeking feedback on how successfully they are teaching their students.

Implementations that emphasize teaching strategies

There are many teaching strategies. This section highlights some of the better known, beginning with studies that specifically aim to provide teachers with different teaching strategies or increase their repertoire of different strategies. Then there are discussions of reciprocal teaching, direct instruction, adjunct aids, inductive teaching, inquiry based teaching, problem solving teaching, and cooperative versus competitive versus individualistic teaching.

Teaching strategies

The teaching of strategies covers a wide ambit of methods and has among the higher effect sizes, although most of these meta-analyses relate to special education or students with learning difficulties. As an example of the multiplicity of methods, Swanson and Hoskyn (1998) included instructional components such as: explanation, elaboration, and plans to direct task performance; modeling from teachers including verbal modeling, questioning, and demonstration; reminders to use certain strategies or procedures; step-by-step

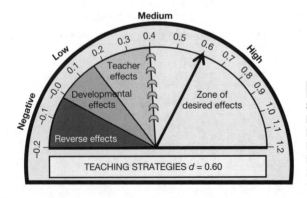

KEY	
Standard error	0.058 (Medium)
Rank	23rd
Number of meta-analyses	14
Number of studies	5,667
Number of effects	13,572
Number of people (7)	1,491,369

TEACHING STRATEGIES *d* = 0.60

Table 10.1 Summary information from the meta-analyses on the contributions from teaching approaches

Strategies	No. metas	No. studies	No. people	No. effects	d	SE	CLE	Rank
Implementations emphasizing teaching strategies								
Teaching strategies	14	5,667	1,491,369	13,572	0.60	0.058	42%	23
Reciprocal teaching	2	38	677	53	0.74	—	52%	9
Direct Instruction	4	304	42,618	597	0.59	0.096	41%	26
Adjunct aids	4	73	9,409	258	0.37	0.043	26%	72
Inductive teaching	2	97	3,595	103	0.33	0.035	23%	83
Inquiry-based teaching	4	205	7,437	420	0.31	0.092	22%	86
Problem-solving teaching	6	221	15,235	719	0.61	0.076	43%	20
Problem-based learning	8	285	38,090	546	0.15	0.085	11%	118
Cooperative learning	10	306	24,025	829	0.41	0.060	29%	63
Cooperative vs. competitive learning	7	1,024	17,000	933	0.54	0.112	39%	37
Cooperative vs. individualistic learning	4	774	—	284	0.59	0.088	42%	24
Competitive vs. individualistic learning	4	831	—	203	0.24	0.232	17%	97
Implementations that emphasize school-wide teaching strategies								
Comprehensive teaching reforms	3	282	41,929,152	1,818	0.22	—	15%	105
Comprehensive interventions for learning disabled students	3	343	56,638	2,654	0.77	0.030	54%	7
Special college programs	2	108	—	108	0.24	0.040	17%	96
Co-teaching/team teaching	2	136	1,617	47	0.19	0.057	13%	111
Implementations using technologies								
Computer-assisted instruction	81	4,875	3,990,028	8,886	0.37	0.059	27%	71
Web-based learning	3	45	22,554	136	0.18	0.124	12%	112
Interactive video methods	6	441	4,800	3,930	0.52	0.076	36%	44
Visual/audio-visual methods	6	359	2,760	231	0.22	0.070	16%	104
Simulations	9	361	6,416	482	0.33	0.092	23%	82
Programmed instruction	7	464	—	362	0.24	0.089	17%	95
Implementations using out of school learning								
Distance education	13	839	4,024,638	1,643	0.09	0.050	6%	126
Home-school programs	1	14	—	14	0.16	—	11%	117
Homework	5	161	105,282	295	0.29	0.027	21%	88
Total	210	17,253	51,742,366	39,123	0.37	0.077	26%	—
Total for all from teaching	365	25,860	52,128,719	55,143	0.42	0.071	30%	—

prompts or multi-process instructions; dialogue between teacher and student; questions from teachers; and provision by the teacher of necessary assistance only. Their meta-analyses only included experimental intervention research on students with learning disabilities. They found higher effect sizes for models of instruction that included direct and strategy instruction. The most successful were sequencing, drill repetition, and strategy cues, and these were particularly high in reading comprehension ($d = 0.82$), vocabulary ($d = 0.79$), and creativity ($d = 0.84$).

Seidel and Shavelson (2007) completed a meta-analysis based on various teaching strategies and included a high proportion of European research literature. They noted that most of the current syntheses of teaching research were framed by a product–process model of learning. These models refers to the various teaching and school processes that interact with student characteristics such as their prior knowledge, and context variables such as home and parents. Together, these processes interact to lead to the products (achievement outcomes). Over the earlier decades, however, the emphasis has been more on holistic patterns, analyzing teaching patterns or regimes instead of single teaching acts. This has drawn more attention to specific processes, usually within different curricula and knowledge domains, and lead to an increase in more sophisticated multi-level analyses of larger data sets (although it is my impression that the literature is more dominated by qualitative studies, often using very few students and one or two teachers. The need for syntheses (akin to meta-analyses) of these qualitative studies is much needed). So, Seidel and Shavelson used a more cognitive processing and learning components model to aggregate their results.

They located 112 studies and used a model developed by Bolhuis (2003) to present the various attributes of teaching (Table 10.2). Their results are appreciably lower than those of most other meta-analyses on these topics (such as the others presented in this book), which they explain by noting differences in the studies included (e.g., using European studies, which are rarely included in meta-analyses due to translation costs, and using only studies with controls for student prerequisites) and the method of categorizing by these attributes based on this new model of teaching.

The most critical dimension was domain-specific processing, which refers to "learning activities that are necessary and most adaptive for knowledge building in a domain" (Seidel & Shavelson, 2007, pp. 460–461). Seidel and Shavelson concluded that such domain-specific activities "consistently represented the most important influence of teaching on student

Table 10.2 Effect sizes for various teaching strategies (from Seidel & Shavelson, 2007)

	Studies	All outcomes		Learning processes		Motivational affective		Cognitive	
		No.	d	No.	d	No.	d	No.	d
Time for learning	34	178	0.08	8	0.29	13	0.24	157	0.06
Organization for learning	17	121	0.02	9	0.02	26	0.12	86	0.00
Social context	20	113	0.08	6	–0.06	35	0.02	72	0.10
Goal setting and orientation	33	133	0.06	38	0.18	19	0.14	98	0.04
Execution of learning activities									
Social/direct experiences	33	202	0.02	21	0.22	24	0.26	157	0.00
Basic processing	29	213	0.04	21	0.10	41	0.16	151	0.02
Domain-specific processing	18	112	0.43	19	0.32	15	0.42	78	0.45
Evaluation of learning	10	87	0.02	—	—	15	0.00	72	0.04
Regulation/monitoring	32	171	0.03	17	0.10	40	0.16	114	0.02

learning and stood out from other components" (2007, p. 483)—regardless of domain (reading, mathematics, science), stage of schooling, or type of learning outcome. This is consistent with the findings of my colleagues and I on the implementation of study skills—surface level study strategies can be learnt across domains, but with deeper strategies the best results are obtained when the strategies are taught directly within the domain (Hattie, Biggs, & Purdie, 1996; see also Baenninger & Newcombe, 1989).

Marzano (1998) started with the 134 studies from my 1987 synthesis of meta-analyses and added more articles to include 4,000 effect sizes of various instructional teaching methods. The overall effect was $d = 0.65$, and this was typical across his four major outcomes: knowledge ($d = 0.60$), cognitive systems ($d = 0.75$), meta-cognitive systems ($d = 0.55$), and self-system ($d = 0.74$). When the instructional technique was designed for the student, the effect was higher ($d = 0.73$) than when the technique was designed for the teacher ($d = 0.61$).

Marzano (1998) concluded that "the effective teacher is one who has clear instructional goals. These goals are communicated both to students and to parents. Ideally, the instructional goals address elements of the knowledge domains as well as the cognitive, meta-cognitive and self-system" (p. 135) and it is most important for the teacher to understand the interrelationships among the various domains.

Reciprocal teaching

Reciprocal teaching was devised as an instructional process to teach students cognitive strategies that might lead to improved learning outcomes (initially in reading

Table 10.3 Effect sizes for various teaching strategies from Marzano (1998)

	No. of studies	d	se
Storage and retrieval processes			
Cues	7	1.13	0.43
Questions	45	0.93	0.14
Direct scheme activation	83	0.75	0.08
Information processing functions			
Matching	51	1.32	0.18
Idea representation	708	0.69	0.03
Information generalization	237	0.11	0.01
Information specification	242	0.38	0.02
Idea representation			
Advanced organizers	358	0.48	0.03
Note taking	36	0.99	0.17
Manipulative	236	0.89	0.06
Knowledge utilization			
Problem solving	343	0.54	0.03
Experimental inquiry	6	1.14	0.47
Meta-cognitive systems			
Goal specification	53	0.97	0.13
Process specification and monitoring	15	0.30	0.08
Dispositional monitoring	15	0.30	0.08
Self systems			
Self attributes	15	0.74	0.19
Efficacy	10	0.80	0.20

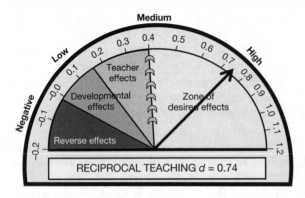

KEY	
Standard error	na
Rank	9th
Number of meta-analyses	2
Number of studies	38
Number of effects	53
Number of people (1)	677

comprehension). The emphasis is on teachers enabling their students to learn and use cognitive strategies such as summarizing, questioning, clarifying, and predicting, and these are "supported through dialogue between teacher and students as they attempt to gain meaning from text" (Rosenshine & Meister, 1994, p. 479). Each student takes a turn at being the "teacher", and often the teacher and students take turns leading a dialogue concerning sections of a text. Students check their own understanding of the material they have encountered by generating questions and summarizing. Expert scaffolding is essential for cognitive development as students move from spectator to performer after repeated modeling by adults. The aim, therefore, is to help students actively bring meaning to the written word, and assist them to learn to monitor their own learning and thinking.

The effect size from both meta-analyses is a very high $d = 0.74$, and both studies found that this high effect was evident regardless of who delivered the intervention, with classroom teachers being able to implement reciprocal teaching with the same level of effect as produced by study authors. Rosenshine and Meister (1994) reported no differences in results by grade level, number of sessions, size of instructional group, number of cognitive strategies taught, or whether the investigator or the teacher did the training. The effects were greater when the comprehension assessments was experimenter-developed ($d = 0.88$) than when using standardized tests ($d = 0.32$), although both short answer tests and tests asking students to summarize passages gave similar results. The effects were highest when there was explicit teaching of cognitive strategies before beginning reciprocal teaching dialogue, showing the importance of modeling and practice as well as giving instruction in the use of the strategies close to the time students used them. The explicit teaching of cognitive strategies and deliberative practice with content when using these strategies makes a major difference.

Direct Instruction

Every year I present lectures to teacher education students and find that they are already indoctrinated with the mantra "constructivism good, direct instruction bad". When I show them the results of these meta-analyses, they are stunned, and they often become angry at having been given an agreed set of truths and commandments against direct instruction. Too often, what the critics mean by direct instruction is didactic teacher-led talking from the front; this should *not* be confused with the very successful "Direct

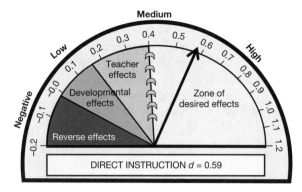

KEY	
Standard error	0.096 (High)
Rank	26th
Number of meta-analyses	4
Number of studies	304
Number of effects	597
Number of people (1)	42,618

Instruction" method as first outlined by Adams and Engelmann (1996). Direct Instruction has a bad name for the wrong reasons, especially when it is confused with didactic teaching, as the underlying principles of Direct Instruction place it among the most successful outcomes.

Direct Instruction involves seven major steps:

1   Before the lesson is prepared, the teacher should have a clear idea of what the *learning intentions* are. What, specifically, should the student be able to do, understand, care about as a result of the teaching?
2   The teacher needs to know what *success criteria* of performance are to be expected and when and what students will be held accountable for from the lesson/activity. The students need to be informed about the standards of performance.
3   There is a need to *build commitment and engagement* in the learning task. In the terminology of Direct Instruction, this is sometimes called a "hook" to grab the student's attention. The aim is to put students into a receptive frame of mind; to focus student attention on the lesson; to share the learning intentions.
4   There are guides to *how the teacher should present the lesson*—including notions such as input, modeling, and checking for understanding. Input refers to providing information needed for students to gain the knowledge or skill through lecture, film, tape, video, pictures, and so on. Modeling is where the teacher shows students examples of what is expected as an end product of their work. The critical aspects are explained through labeling, categorizing, and comparing to exemplars of what is desired. Checking for understanding involves monitoring whether students have "got it" before proceeding. It is essential that students practice *doing it right,* so the teacher must know that students understand before they start to practice. If there is any doubt that the class has not understood, the concept or skill should be re-taught before practice begins.
5   There is the notion of *guided practice*. This involves an opportunity for each student to demonstrate his or her grasp of new learning by working through an activity or exercise under the teacher's direct supervision. The teacher moves around the room to determine the level of mastery and to provide feedback and individual remediation as needed.
6   There is the *closure* part of the lesson. Closure involves those actions or statements by a teacher that are designed to bring a lesson presentation to an appropriate

conclusion: the part wherein students are helped to bring things together in their own minds, to make sense out of what has just been taught. "Any questions? No. OK, let's move on" is not closure. Closure is used to cue students to the fact that they have arrived at an important point in the lesson or the end of a lesson, to help organize student learning, to help form a coherent picture, to consolidate, eliminate confusion and frustration, and so on, and to reinforce the major points to be learned. Thus closure involves reviewing and clarifying the key points of a lesson, tying them together into a coherent whole, and ensuring they will be applied by the student by ensuring they have become part of the student's conceptual network.

7   There is *independent practice*. Once students have mastered the content or skill, it is time to provide for reinforcement practice. It is provided on a repeating schedule so that the learning is not forgotten. It may be homework or group or individual work in class. It is important to note that this practice can provide for decontextualization: enough different contexts so that the skill or concept may be applied to any relevant situation and not only the context in which it was originally learned. For example, if the lesson is about inference from reading a passage about dinosaurs, the practice should be about inference from reading about another topic such as whales. The advocates of Direct Instruction argue that the failure to do this seventh step is responsible for most student failure to be able to apply something learned.

In a nutshell: The teacher decides the learning intentions and success criteria, makes them transparent to the students, demonstrates them by modeling, evaluates if they understand what they have been told by checking for understanding, and re-telling them what they have told by tying it all together with closure (see Cooper, 2006). Carnine (2000, p. 12) summarized the Follow Through findings this way:

> In only one approach, the Direct Instruction (DI) model, were participating students near or at national norms in math and language and close to national norms in reading. Students in … the other Follow Through 8 approaches— discovery learning, language experience, developmentally appropriate practices, and open education—often performed worse than the control group. This poor performance came in spite of tens of thousands of additional dollars provided for each classroom each year.
>
> (Carnine, 2000, p. 12)

Adams and Englemann (1996) made a useful connection between direct instruction and acceleration, as the principal objective of direct instruction is to provide instruction to accelerate the performance of the students; that is, teach more in less clock time, aim at teaching generalizations beyond rote learning, sequence learning and constantly monitor the performance of students as they move to achieve their challenging goals.

One of the common criticisms is that Direct Instruction works with very low-level or specific skills, and with lower ability and the youngest students. These are the not the findings from the meta-analyses. The effects of Direct Instruction are similar for regular ($d = 0.99$), and special education and lower ability students ($d = 0.86$), higher for reading

(d = 0.89) than mathematics (d = 0.50), similar for the more low-level word-attack (d = 0.64) and also for high-level comprehension (d = 0.54), and similar for elementary and high school students (Adams & Engelmann, 1996). Similarly, a 1997 integrative analysis of intervention programs for special education students found direct instruction to be the only one of seven interventions showing strong evidence of effectiveness (Forness, Kavale, Blum, & Lloyd, 1997). To demonstrate that the effects from direct instruction are not specifically teacher effects, Fischer and Tarver (Fischer & Tarver, 1997) delivered mathematics lessons via videodisc; the effects were close to d = 1.00.

The messages of these meta-analyses on Direct Instruction underline the power of stating the learning intentions and success criteria, and then engaging students in moving towards these. The teacher needs to invite the students to learn, provide much deliberative practice and modeling, and provide appropriate feedback and multiple opportunities to learn. Students need opportunities for independent practice, and then there need to be opportunities to learn the skill or knowledge implicit in the learning intention in contexts other than those directly taught.

Adjunct aids

It seems that it is not so much the presence of adjunct aids that enhances achievement, but how and where they are used in the texts, and the level of sophistication of the student when using adjunct aids. Hoeffler and Leutner (2007) found that animations were superior to static pictures (d = 0.46) but it made a difference whether the animation was for decorative purposes (d = 0.29) or for representational purposes (d = 0.89)—that is the notion should be central to the concept being learnt. There were no differences related to the level of realism, although animations acted as significant cues to the students about what was needed to be learnt. Levie and Lentz (1982) compared outcomes from students reading texts with and without illustrations and concluded that:

> when the test of learning is something other than a test of only illustrated text information or only non-illustrated text information, the addition of pictures should not be expected to hinder learning; nor should pictures always be expected to facilitate leaning. Even so, learning is better with pictures in most cases.
>
> (Levie & Lentz, 1982, p. 206)

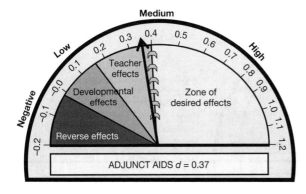

KEY	
Standard error	0.043 (Medium)
Rank	72th
Number of meta-analyses	4
Number of studies	73
Number of effects	258
Number of people (2)	9,409

The more interesting question is how illustrations facilitate learning.

Although not above the h–point of $d = 0.40$, it does seem that adjunct aids can assist learning when they function to attract and direct attention, and highlight main ideas and comprehension, and when the text assists readers to see details in the pictures.

Inductive teaching

Induction is usually described as moving from the specific to the general, while deduction begins with the general and ends with the specific. Lott's (1983) meta-analysis included a comparison of inductive versus deductive teaching approaches in science education. He argued that inductive teaching occurs when educational experiences (such as examples or observations) are provided to students prior to formalizing generalizations; whereas when generalizations are formulated prior to any illustrative examples they are characterized as deductive. As can be seen from the overall effect, it makes no difference which order is used, and this was across many outcomes such as knowledge, application, process, transfer, comprehension, and problem solving.

Klauer and Phye (2008) were more interested in inductive reasoning across all subject areas. Their meta-analysis was related to programs that aimed to teach detecting generalizations, rules or regularities. They developed a series of non-verbal training materials and then analyzed 74 studies that used these methods. The overall effect ($d = 0.59$) is quite high, showing the positive effects of teaching these skills, and supporting the claim that teaching of "making comparisons and contrasts" can be enhanced when taught across context, but they noted that there comes a point after students have acquired inductive reasoning when there needs to be greater knowledge and understanding to more fully capitalize on these methods.

Inquiry-based teaching

Inquiry-based teaching is the art of developing challenging situations in which students are asked to observe and question phenomena; pose explanations of what they observe; devise and conduct experiments in which data are collected to support or contradict their theories; analyze data; draw conclusions from experimental data; design and build models; or any combination of these. Such learning situations are meant to be open-ended in that they do not aim to achieve a single "right" answer for a particular question being

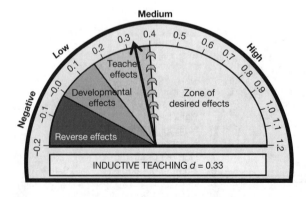

KEY	
Standard error	0.035 (Low)
Rank	83rd
Number of meta-analyses	2
Number of studies	97
Number of effects	103
Number of people (1)	3,595

INDUCTIVE TEACHING $d = 0.33$

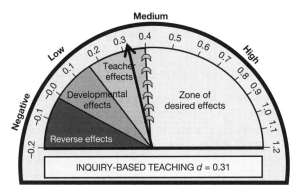

Medium

Low   0.2   0.3   0.4   0.5   0.6   0.7   High

Teacher
effects

Developmental
effects

Zone of
desired effects

Reverse effects

Negative   −0.0 −0.1 −0.2

0.8   0.9   1.0   1.1   1.2

INQUIRY-BASED TEACHING *d* = 0.31

KEY	
Standard error	0.092 (High)
Rank	86th
Number of meta-analyses	4
Number of studies	205
Number of effects	420
Number of people (1)	7,437

addressed, but rather involve students more in the process of observing, posing questions, engaging in experimentation or exploration, and learning to analyze and reason.

Inquiry methods have often been studied in the context of science education. Bredderman (1983), for example, reported a *d* = 0.35 average effect size when teaching science using inquiry/activity based methods. These activities included direct experience, experimentation, and observation as the major sources of information; although he reported large variations across classrooms. The effect on science process (*d* = 0.52) was much greater than the effect on science content (*d* = 0.16). Bredderman (1985) examined the effects of laboratory programs on learning for elementary school students. These programs differed from the traditional science programs in that they did not use textbooks and focused on use of laboratory activities. Bredderman commented that these programs resulted in improved student performance in a number of curricular areas. In addition the use of inquiry programs increased the amount of student laboratory activity and decreased teacher-led discussion in classrooms.

Shymansky, Hedges, and Woodworth (1990) also reported greater effects of inquiry teaching on process (*d* = 0.40) than on content (*d* = 0.26)—and the effects were higher in biology (*d* = 0.30) and physics (*d* = 0.27) compared to chemistry (*d* = 0.10). Effects were greatest at elementary level and decreased as students progressed through their school years. Where science teachers received in-service training in inquiry methods, students significantly outperformed students in traditional programs. Smith (1996) found larger effects from inquiry methods in critical thinking skills (*d* = 1.02) than in achievement (*d* = 0.40), and less in laboratory skills (*d* = 0.24) and process skills (*d* = 0.18). Sweitzer and Anderson (1983) were more interested in effects of inquiry teaching on science teacher education knowledge and practices. They found that a wide variety of teacher education programs, both preservice and in-service, across a range of settings (university and school settings) resulted in changes in teachers' knowledge, classroom behaviors, and attitudes. Again, the effects were twice as large on processes as on content.

Bangert-Drowns and Bankert (1990) found that inquiry-based instruction can foster critical thinking. Two factors were found to be related to critical thinking effect size: cultural factors and teachers. It appeared that some cultural factors may account for the fact that the four largest effect sizes came from studies with atypical populations where students' thinking may not previously have been valued. It would seem that inquiry-based instruction might have powerful effects where students have the cognitive capacity to think critically but have not previously been encouraged to think in this way. Overall, inquiry-based instruction was shown to produce transferable critical thinking skills as well as significant domain benefits, improved achievement, and improved attitude towards the subject.

Problem-solving teaching

Problem solving involves the act of defining or determining the cause of the problem; identifying, prioritizing and selecting alternatives for a solution; or using multiple perspectives to uncover the issues related to a particular problem, designing an intervention plan, and then evaluating the outcome. Mellinger (1991) examined studies on the development of cognitive flexibility in problem solving. The outcome measures used in all the studies were the verbal and figural flexibility scales of the Torrance tests of Creative Thinking. Overall the effects were high—and the influence on verbal flexibility ($d = 0.81$) was much larger than for figural flexibility ($d = 0.40$). Hembree (1992) also found significant direct links between problem solving and various measures of basic performance, in particular skills in basic mathematics. A format consisting of full problem statements supported by diagrams, figures, or sketches directly related to better performance. The teacher characteristic with the most positive effect on students' performance was specialist training in heuristic methods ($d = 0.71$). These methods include, for example, Pólya's (1945) four phases of: (1) understand the problem, (2) obtain a plan of the solution, (3) carry out the plan, and (4) examine the solution obtained.

Marcucci's (1980) meta-analysis of research on methods of teaching mathematical problem solving also supported the power of teaching the heuristic method of problem solving. Curbelo (1984) found similar effects of problem solving in mathematics, but these effects were twice as high as they were in science. Problem solving methods can also have a positive influence on interpersonal outcomes. Almeida and Denham (1984) reported positive effects of interpersonal cognitive problem solving skills on behavioral adjustment and social behaviors (see also Denham & Almeida, 1987).

Problem-based learning

Gijbels (2005) outlined six core characteristics of problem-based learning:

1   Learning is student-centered.
2   Learning occurs in small groups.

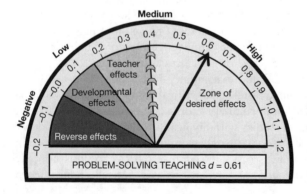

KEY	
Standard error	0.076 (Medium)
Rank	20th
Number of meta-analyses	6
Number of studies	221
Number of effects	719
Number of people (3)	15,235

PROBLEM-SOLVING TEACHING *d* = 0.61

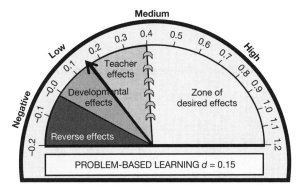

KEY	
Standard error	0.085 (High)
Rank	118th
Number of meta-analyses	8
Number of studies	285
Number of effects	546
Number of people (4)	38,090

3 A tutor is present as facilitator or guide.
4 Authentic problems are presented at the beginning of the learning sequence.
5 The problems encountered are used as tools to achieve the required knowledge and the problem solving skills necessary to eventually solve the problem.
6 New information is acquired through self-directed learning.

As will be seen, this is a topic where it is important to separate the effects on surface and deep knowledge and understanding. For surface knowledge, problem-based learning can have limited and even negative effects, whereas for deeper learning, when students already have the surface level knowledge, problem-based learning can have positive effects. This should not be surprising, as problem-based learning places more emphasis on meaning and understanding than on reproduction, acquisition, or surface level knowledge.

Vernon and Blake (1993), for example, found that the more traditional instructional methods were more effective in raising achievement than problem-based learning ($d= -0.18$)—the outcomes in these studies were predominantly basic science factual knowledge. Dochy, Segers, Van den Bossche, and Gijbels (2003) found an overall negative effect for problem-based learning compared to a conventional learning environment on knowledge ($d = -0.78$) but noted that problem-based learning had a positive effect on skills ($d = 0.66$). It was the case that students taught using problem-based learning had less knowledge but had better recall of the knowledge they had. This is probably because in problem-based learning, knowledge is more often elaborated and, consequentially, the students had a better recall of their knowledge. Similarly, Gijbels, Dochy, Van den Bossche, and Segers (2005) found zero effects from problem-based learning on the learning of concepts ($d = -0.04$), but positive effects on application ($d = 0.40$), and principles ($d = 0.75$). They concluded that "PBL had the most positive effects when the focal constructs being assessed were at the level of understanding the principles that link concepts, the second level of the knowledge structure" (Gijbels *et al.*, 2005, p. 45) It is the application and principles underlying the knowledge, rather than the concepts or knowledge, that are most influenced by problem-based learning. The application of knowledge, not development of knowledge, is the heart of the success of problem-based learning. Smith (2003) also found that effects from problem-based learning were higher in self-directed learning ($d = 0.54$) and attitude toward learning ($d = 0.52$), compared to those for problem solving ($d = 0.30$). Newman (2004) found negative effects for problem-based learning on the "accumulation of facts"—which appeared to be the major outcome from most studies used for this teaching method.

Cooperative, competitive, individualistic and heterogeneous class environments

There are four groups of meta-analyses that involve cooperative learning:

1 those that compare cooperative learning versus heterogeneous classes ($d = 0.41$);
2 those that compare cooperative versus individualistic learning ($d = 0.59$);
3 those that compare cooperative versus competitive learning ($d = 0.54$);
4 those that compare competitive versus individualistic learning ($d = 0.24$).

Both cooperative and competitive learning are more effective than individualistic methods—pointing again to the power of peers in the learning equation.

There seems a universal agreement that cooperative learning is effective, especially when contrasted with competitive and individualistic learning. One of the features I particularly like about the New Zealand education system is that on the international comparisons, New Zealand comes out top on cooperativeness in schools, and also is top in competitiveness. This notion that both could be beneficial seems too often forgotten, as most of the research contrasts one with the other. Further, cooperative learning has a prime effect on enhancing interest and problem solving provided it is set up with high levels of peer involvement. Of course, not all students succeed or even prefer cooperative learning situations, although what is important is less whether some students may enjoy these situations but whether these situations produce greater outcomes, deeper comprehension, and understanding.

All of the many meta-analyses by the Johnsons and their colleagues show high effect sizes, whereas the others hover around the small to medium effects. Johnson, Maruyama, Johnson, Nelson, and Skon (1981) claimed that cooperation was superior to competition in promoting achievement across all subject areas (language arts, reading, mathematics, science, social studies, psychology, and physical education), for all age groups (although it seems that the results are stronger for elementary and high school students than for college students), and for tasks involving concept attainment, verbal problem solving, categorizing, spatial problem solving, retention and memory, motor performance, and guessing-judging-predicting. Further, cooperation with intergroup competition is superior to interpersonal

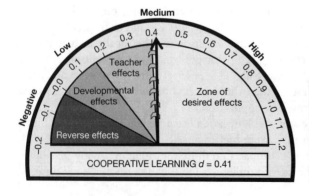

KEY	
Standard error	0.060 (Medium)
Rank	63rd
Number of meta-analyses	10
Number of studies	306
Number of effects	829
Number of people (5)	24,025

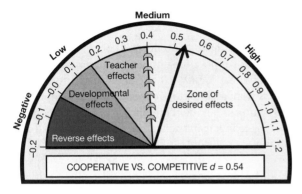

KEY

Standard error	0.112 (High)
Rank	37th
Number of meta-analyses	7
Number of studies	1,024
Number of effects	933
Number of people (1)	17,000

competition and individualistic efforts, and particularly effective in studies using tangible rewards and maximizing tasks.

Johnson and Johnson (1987) argued also that cooperation was most effective among adults as it promoted achievement, positive interpersonal relationships, social support, and self-esteem. The effects were similar across decades, and there were no differences for individual or group rewards, laboratory or field settings, studies lasting one hour or several months, or different types of tasks, and this was independent of the quality of the study. Qin (1992; Qin, Johnson, & Johnson, 1995) found that students who engaged in cooperative learning were more successful in four types of problem solving—linguistic, non-linguistic, well-defined problem, and ill-defined problem—than those in competitive learning ($d = 0.55$). Johnson, Johnson, and Maruyama (1983) found that cooperative experiences promoted more positive relationships among individuals from different ethnic backgrounds, and between handicapped and non-handicapped individuals.

It seems that surface and deeper learning is affected by cooperative or competitive learning. Howard (1996) claimed that scripting, defined as formal directions to implement a cooperative learning session, is effective particularly when new material is organized and elaborated on (deep versus surface processing). Cooperative learning is more effective in reading (Hall, 1988, $d = 0.44$) than in mathematics ($d = 0.01$), and Johnson *et al.* (1981) found that for rote decoding and correcting tasks, cooperation does not seem to be superior. Moreover the effects increase with age: Hall (1988) reported that the effects increased as students moved through elementary ($d = 0.28$), junior high ($d = 0.33$), and

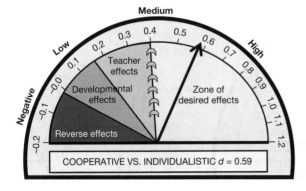

KEY

Standard error	0.088 (High)
Rank	24th
Number of meta-analyses	4
Number of studies	774
Number of effects	284
Number of people (0)	na

high school (d = 0.43). Stevens and Slavin (1991) found high effects when there was individual accountability and group rewards.

Roseth, Fang, Johnson, and Johnson (2006) investigated the effects of cooperative learning on middle school students. They found more support for cooperative than competitive conditions (d = 0.46), cooperative than individualistic (d = 0.55), and competitive versus individualist (d = 0.20). Similarly, the effects were greatest for cooperative over competitive over individualistic for interpersonal attraction. They concluded that under cooperative conditions, interpersonal relations have the strongest influence on achievement, and this clearly points to the value of friendship in the achievement equation. As they concluded, "if you want to increase student academic achievement, give each student a friend" (p. 7). Friendship in schools is not only powerful for the student's sense of well-being but it also facilitates a student's sense of school belonging, provides a sense of worth, and is an important source of positive feelings toward school (Hamm & Fairclough, 2007)—although for too many adolescents friendships can have the opposite effect if they convey the message that "learning is not cool".

Peer learning can be powerful—whether cooperatively or competitively. As Nuthall (2007) has shown, most feedback that students receive is from other students (although most of it is incorrect), and the peer tutoring literature has reinforced the power of peers as teachers and facilitators. When there is some structure to this peer learning (as in most instances of cooperative and competitive learning) then the power of peers can be unleashed. Students are more able to collectively make and learn from errors, and their conversations can assist in having the goals, learning intentions and success criteria from a lesson spelt out for all.

Competitive learning

A competitive situation is one where the students compete to reach a goal—although this competition can be with other students or when students aim to compete with their own previous performance. Competitiveness can be towards "beating" a standard—either a personal best standard, or a standard of the curriculum (competing to reach a goal). In contrast, in an individualistic situation, the outcome for others is ignored as irrelevant to the attainment of personal outcomes (Johnson *et al.*, 1983). As noted above, cooperative learning leads to higher effects than competitive learning, and both are superior to individualistic learning.

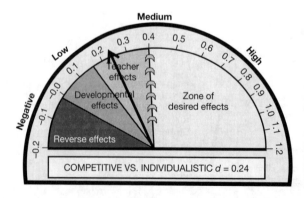

KEY	
Standard error	0.232 (High)
Rank	96th
Number of meta-analyses	4
Number of studies	831
Number of effects	203
Number of people (0)	na

Implementations that emphasize school-wide teaching reform

In one of the more ambitious meta-analyses, Borman, Hewes, Overman, and Brown (2003) reviewed the achievement effects of comprehensive school reform programs. They noted that many comprehensive programs were being "scaled up" at an unprecedented rate, and that these programs were serving millions of students and being implemented in many school districts. Such comprehensive reform appeals to many superintendents and school officials as a systematic answer to the issue of improving teaching. My own experience of these forced reforms to many schools came from being required to evaluate a program that was being forcibly introduced into 91 schools in a North Carolina school district. To me the new method seemed doomed to failure as I never underestimate teachers' skill in continuing to do what they consider works for them and resisting that with which they do not wish to engage. However, resources were poured in, training days scheduled, and there was a major push to make every school a school that used the Paideia method (Roberts, 1998; Roberts & Billings, 1999) The surprise to me was how successful the method was—even teachers whom I knew were "below average" improved, and there was the desired increase in state achievement scores. But when the Superintendent left the district, back the schools went to their previous methods.

The most critical effect was on my own teaching; if this method was so good, why not try it myself? Paideia involves three methods. The first is didactic teaching, so I taught my three-hour class on Messick's (1990) concept of validity, was able to elicit some excellent answers to my questions, and left the class with a sense of confidence that my teaching was at a high level. The second method is the "Paideia seminar", which involves getting the students to ask questions of each other and engage in a dialogue about what they do and do not understand (I as the teacher must not be involved in the questions and answers, but instead my purpose is to facilitate these interactions *between* the students). The quality of the questions and the assertiveness of some answers scared me, as they clearly did not understand what I had so beautifully taught. I realized I had built the skill of asking questions about what I had just said and looking for the students (there are always some) who were keen to retell the story and to nod at the right times (to ensure I continued); they all knew the game we played. Of course, learning occurs when the students learn, not when the teacher has satisfactorily taught. (The third method is coached products.)

Borman *et al.* (2003) noted that effect sizes from studies undertaken by the developers

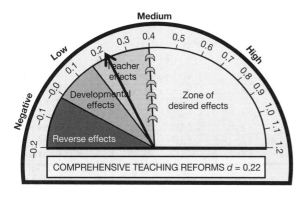

KEY	
Standard error	na
Rank	105th
Number of meta-analyses	3
Number of studies	282
Number of effects	1,818
Number of people (2)	41,929,152

of the programs were systematically higher, there were no differences in effects relating to socioeconomic resources, very little difference by subject, and the effects became most apparent after the fifth year of implementation. They considered the programs with the strongest systematic evidence of effectiveness to be Direct Instruction ($d = 0.21$), Comer's School Development program ($d = 0.18$), and Success for All ($d = 0.18$). Other programs (with more than ten effects) are listed in Table 10.4.

Borman *et al.* (2003) noted that about half of these programs were still evaluated only by their developers, they could be cost-effective (especially for poorer schools) as the costs for developing the program was already invested, but there were still highly variable outcomes. The key components of these programs were the presence of ongoing professional development, measureable goals and benchmarks for student learning, a faculty vote to increase the likelihood of the model's acceptance and buy-in, the use of specific and innovative curricular materials, and instructional practices designed to improve teaching and student learning.

A common aim for introducing these comprehensive reforms is to reduce the achievement gap. Borman and D'Agostino (1996) provided evidence on the effectiveness of "Title I" programs—which are programs funded to assist local boards to improve the achievement of children from low-income families in the United States. They reported an overall increasing achievement for students who participated in Title I programs ($d = 0.12$), and more so in mathematics than reading. Programs aimed at early remediation were more effective than programs aimed at later years, and negative effects were more pronounced over the summer vacation than for students not in Title I programs. The subsequent annual gains for these students during the regular school year alone "may not sustain their relatively large fall/spring achievement improvements" (p. 323). These low effects certainly provide little confidence that these programs *alone* will reduce the achievement gap between

Table 10.4 Summary of effects from comprehensive teaching reforms (Borman *et al.*, 2003)

Program	No. studies	No. effects	d	SE	Age	Focus
Roots and Wings	6	14	0.38	0.04	K–6	students
High Schools That Work	45	64	0.30	0.01	9–12	curriculum
Microsociety	3	32	0.29	0.03	K–8	students
Modern Red Schoolhouse	6	23	0.26	0.03	K–12	curriculum
Onward to Excellence II	4	13	0.25	0.03	K–12	curriculum
American's Choice	2	27	0.22	0.02	K–12	standards
The Learning Network	3	38	0.22	0.02	K–8	teaching
Direct Instruction	49	182	0.21	0.02	K–8	students
Expeditionary Learning Outward Bound Students	6	40	0.19	0.03	K–12	
Success For All	42	173	0.18	0.01	K–8	students
School Development Program	10	25	0.15	0.03	K–12	community
Centre for Effective Schools	1	26	0.13	0.01	K–12	students
Accelerated Schools	6	50	0.09	0.02	K–8	students
Edison	5	209	0.06	0.01	K–12	school
Co-nect	5	42	0.04	0.02	K–12	curriculum
Community Learning Centers	5	17	0.03	0.03	K–8	curriculum
Core Knowledge	6	58	0.03	0.02	K–8	curriculum
High/Scope	4	23	−0.02	0.04	K–3	curriculum

at-risk students and their more advantaged peers. But solace should be found in the final comments: "without the program, children served over the last 30 years would have fallen farther behind academically" (p. 324).

Comprehension interventions for learning disabled students

It would be possible to have a whole book on the effects of the various interventions for students with learning difficulties, and indeed Swanson, Hoskyn, and Lee (1999) have provided such a book. They summarized the research based on group and single-subject designs. For the group design studies, they located 180 studies with a mean effect size of $d = 0.56$. The more successful interventions included meta-cognitive ($d = 0.98$), attribution ($d = 0.79$), and programs in word recognition ($d = 0.71$), reading comprehension ($d = 0.82$), spelling ($d = 0.54$), memory/recall ($d = 0.81$), mathematics ($d = 0.58$), writing ($d = 0.84$), vocabulary ($d = 0.79$), attitude/self-concept ($d = 0.68$), general reading ($d = 0.60$), phonics ($d = 0.70$), creativity ($d = 0.84$), social skills ($d = 0.46$), and language ($d = 0.54$). For the 85 single-subject designs (a rare meta-analysis of these types of studies), the effects were high ($d = 0.90$), with high effects in most areas. Swanson *et al.* concluded from their extensive comparative analyses that a combined direct instruction and strategy instruction model was an "effective procedure for remediating learning disabilities" (Swanson *et al.*, 1999, p. 218). These two approaches are somewhat independent, hence the importance of using both to maximize the effect on achievement. The important instructional components included "attention to sequencing, drill-repetition-practice, segmenting information into parts or units for later synthesis, controlling task difficulty through prompts and cues, making use of technology, systematically modeling problem solving steps, and making use of small interactive groups" (p. 218). They also noted the much higher effects from the "bottom-up" approach to teaching reading that emphasizes accurate word recognition, decoding, and letter awareness, compared to the "top down" approach where reading is viewed as dependent on the reader's cognitive and language abilities (including familiarity with the topic of discourse). More importantly, the direct instruction and strategy training models were superior to both the bottom up and top down models.

A major review of instructional methods to enhance various learning strategies among learning disabled students was also published by Swanson (2000). He found that teaching the 20-plus identified strategies by themselves ($d = 0.72$) or by direct instruction without an emphasis on strategies ($d = 0.72$) was very effective, but even more so when strategy

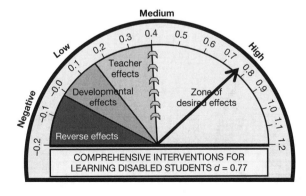

COMPREHENSIVE INTERVENTIONS FOR LEARNING DISABLED STUDENTS $d = 0.77$

KEY	
Standard error	0.058 (Medium)
Rank	7th
Number of meta-analyses	3
Number of studies	343
Number of effects	2,654
Number of people (2)	5,664

training was combined with methods of direct instruction ($d = 0.84$). The strategies with the greatest impact on the achievement outcomes included controlling for difficulty or processing demands of the tasks (scaffolding), directed response and questioning (Socratic teaching, directing students to ask questions), sequencing (breaking down the task, step-by-step prompts), drill-repetition-practice-review, segmentation, and strategy cueing. These effects were stronger in reading ($d = 0.82$) than in mathematics ($d = 0.58$). Swanson (2001) investigated programs to enhance higher-order processing for adolescents with learning disabilities. Programs that included extended deliberative practice yielded larger outcomes, with the strongest instructional components relating to extended practice. The highest effects were in areas of meta-cognition (e.g., planning, self-questioning, interviews of strategy behaviors) and understanding text (e.g., inferential comprehension, thematic understanding, content knowledge). The hardest area to change was related to learned attributions (e.g., self-efficacy and effort). Similar high gains were shown by O'Neal (1985) using cerebral palsy students.

Forness and Kavale (1993) completed a meta-analysis of studies on strategy training addressing memory and learning deficits in learning disabled students. They found that strategy training, especially verbal elaboration, mediation, imagery, and verbal rehearsal, were beneficial for children with mild intellectual disabilities. All children benefited from strategy training; both those with and those without intellectual disabilities. Xin and Jitendra (1999) in their examination of the effects of instruction in solving mathematical word problems for students with learning problems found that strategy training ($d = 0.77$) was effective in facilitating the acquisition of problem solving skills. The results of this study also supported the use of direct instruction, cognitive strategies, and goal-directed strategies to promote student learning. Word-problem solving instruction seemed to have a positive effect on skills maintenance and generalization.

Even when meta-analyses were completed with students across all ranges of ability, the effects were still high for the lower ability students. Fan (1993) investigated the effects of strategy training for all abilities of student, specifically in reading. The effects were greater in high school ($d = 0.85$) and college ($d = 0.62$) than in elementary school ($d = 0.55$), and with lower ($d = 0.89$) and middle ability ($d = 0.71$) compared to higher ability students ($d = 0.28$). Reciprocal teaching ($d = 0.82$) and direct instruction ($d = 0.55$) were among the higher effects, and the effects of these programs were evident across curricula domains. The conclusion was that "in order to facilitate reading across the curriculum, meta-cognitive strategies should be an integral part of the reading curriculum ... [and]

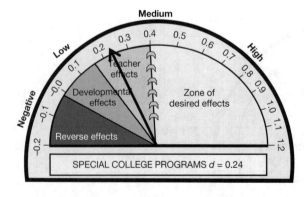

KEY	
Standard error	0.040 (Low)
Rank	96th
Number of meta-analyses	2
Number of studies	108
Number of effects	108
Number of people (0)	na

reading teachers and subject teachers should also work together to design a meta-cognitive reading program which will foster reading and learning (Fan, 1993, pp. 117–118).

Special college programs

There have been many remediation programs for college students. Kulik, Kulik, and Shwalb (1983) claimed that special college programs for high-risk students led to them staying in college longer (62 percent versus 52 percent for control students, although, as noted by the authors, this is a very small effect). The more successful programs related to academic skills ($d = 0.28$), guidance sessions ($d = 0.41$) but the effects of remedial programs have been limited to zero effects ($d = 0.05$). The effects were stronger in new programs and weaker in institutionalized programs, and thus colleges seem more proficient at setting up programs for high-risk students than they are at keeping these programs going.

Co-teaching/Team teaching

Co-teaching involves two teachers working together in a single physical space to deliver instruction, and there are many variants: one teaching, one assisting; station teaching; parallel teaching; alternate teaching; team teaching. The typical claims in favor of team teaching include that it takes into account the strength of both teachers, it spurs creativity as teachers are forced to plan together and can spark off each other, and it allows for more individual attention to students (Armstrong, 1977). However, there is a dearth of literature on the effects of team teaching, which probably reflects its absence in our schools.

Murawski and Swanson (2001) investigated co-teaching with regular and special education teachers of mainstreamed students. They only found six articles, but all reported effects close to the average of $d = 0.31$. Willett, Yamashita, and Anderson (1983) included team teaching in their meta-analysis of effects in science, but did not find much support ($d = 0.06$). We concur with Armstrong's (1977) conclusion that "one is struck by the very basic nature of the questions for which research has failed ... to supply at least tentative answers. Team teaching, it is evident, represents one of those educational practices that have not been subjected to truly intensive and systematic investigation ... At this juncture, little in the research literature provides solace either for team teaching's critics or its most ardent supporters" (p. 83).

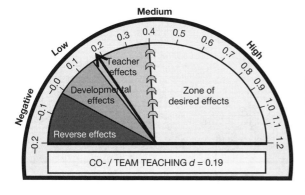

KEY	
Standard error	0.057 (Medium)
Rank	111th
Number of meta-analyses	2
Number of studies	136
Number of effects	47
Number of people (1)	1,617

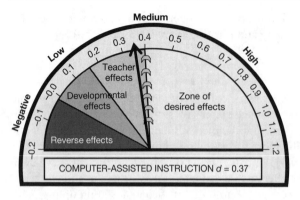

KEY	
Standard error	0.059 (Medium)
Rank	71st
Number of meta-analyses	81
Number of studies	4,875
Number of effects	8,886
Number of people (18)	3,990,028

Implementations using technologies

Computer-assisted instruction

As indicated by the number of studies and meta-analyses, computers are among the hottest topics for research—and the term "computer" now covers a multitude of meanings and implementations from mainframes, desktops, and hand-held devices to the internet. Some of the major uses involve tutoring, managing, simulation, enrichment, programming, and problem solving (Kulik, 1994). Across the 76 meta-analyses on computer-assisted instruction, there were 4,498 studies, 8,096 effects, and about 4 million students—but in this area, more than most, there is much overlap of articles (and hence students) across the meta-analyses. The average effect size across all studies is $d = 0.37$ ($se = 0.02$) and the Common Language Effect (CLE) average is 25 percent; that is, 25 times out of a hundred when computer-aided instruction is used, it will make a positive difference. As can be seen in Figure 10.18, there is a reasonable degree of variability across these meta-analyses.

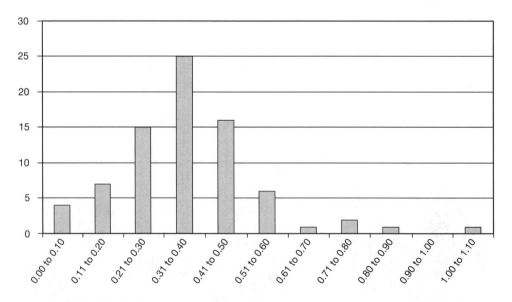

Figure 10.18 The number of computer-based meta-analyses and their overall effect size

There is no correlation of the effect sizes with the year of study, which counters the typical claim that the effect from computers is increasing with the sophistication of the technology (Figure 10.19, $r = 0.05$).

Across the various meta-analyses there were no differences across grades (Table 10.5), or ability levels of the students. There are some differences across subjects but not in any meaningful manner, and there are no differences relating to the duration of the computer intervention. The use of computers can assist in engagement and positive attitudes to learning and school.

The myriad different potential uses of computers have led many to wax lyrical about their future. Some claim that computer-aided instruction will revolutionize how we teach and learn, and some say that computers have come and just sit there mostly unused (Cuban, 2001). My own view is that, like many structural innovations in education, computers can increase the probability of learning, but there is no necessary relation between having computers, using computers, and learning outcomes.

There is no question, however, that the range of uses of computers in classes is wide, although the majority of studies are about teachers using computers in instruction and there are fewer studies about students using them in learning. That is, often the studies compare teaching in classes with and without computers (of some variant) rather than comparing students learning in different ways when using computers. Most of the effects range between $d = 0.20$ and $d = 0.60$; there are some common themes, and these have been used to organize this section.

An analysis of the meta-analyses of computers in schools indicates that computers are used effectively (a) when there is a diversity of teaching strategies; (b) when there is a pre-training in the use of computers as a teaching and learning tool; (c) when there are multiple opportunities for learning (e.g., deliberative practice, increasing time on task); (d) when the student, not teacher, is in "control" of learning; (e) when peer learning is optimized; and (f) when feedback is optimized. This list should be no surprise given the rest of the claims in this book, as they also emphasize the "visible teaching—visible learning" messages.

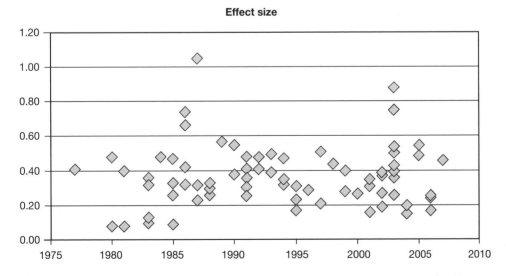

Effect size

Figure 10.19 Relation between effect sizes for computer-based instruction and year of publication

Table 10.5 Summary of effects from computer-based instruction

Grade	No. meta-analyses	No. effects	d
Kindergarten	5	128	0.46
Elementary	25	2710	0.42
Junior high	26	592	0.33
Senior high	9	342	0.46
Post-secondary	12	745	0.38

Gender	No. meta-analyses	No. effects	d
Males	7	139	0.33
Females	7	121	0.25

Ability Level	No. meta-analyses	No. effects	d
Low	12	818	0.35
Average	11	258	0.38
High	10	223	0.33

Subject	No. meta-analyses	No. effects	d
Vocabulary	2	33	0.48
Language arts	3	36	0.38
Reading	8	200	0.35
Comprehension	2	46	0.35
Spelling	2	24	0.73
Writing	4	74	0.35
Math	11	1250	0.21
Science	5	52	0.32
Problem solving	4	68	0.57

Duration	No. meta-analyses	No. effects	d
< 4 weeks	12	315	0.45
4–8 weeks	12	715	0.41
9–12 weeks	13	588	0.39
13–26 weeks	11	620	0.35
> 26 weeks	4	487	0.36

Attitudes	No. meta-analyses	No. effects	d
... towards computers	4	55	0.18
... towards learning/subject	11	391	0.28

The use of computers is more effective when there is a diversity of teaching strategies

An advantage of the computer is that the method of teaching is most likely to be different from that experienced when the teacher instructs the students—at minimum, students get to experience two different teaching strategies and are offered "deliberative practice" in learning knowledge and concepts. Over the many meta-analyses, there was an advantage for computer work to be a supplement ($d = 0.45$, $N = 162$) rather than a substitute or replacement for teacher instruction ($d = 0.30$, $N = 100$;

Table 10.6). There are no differences, however, as to whether it is the same ($d = 0.36$, $N = 522$) or a different teacher ($d = 0.41$, $N = 344$) teaching the students across the two treatments (computer and traditional; Table 10.7).

The use of computers is more effective when there is teacher pre-training in the use of computers as a teaching and learning tool

One of the fascinating findings is that teachers are frequent users of computers—but more for their personal and administrative use; they find it more difficult to see how computers can be related to their particular conceptions of teaching (Cuban, 2001). When many of today's teachers were students in schools, computers were not as common, and many were then taught in teachers' colleges by lecturers who were even more distanced from the use of computers in their teaching and learning. For too many teachers, teaching using computer resources is not part of their "grammar of schooling". Abrami *et al.* (2006) noted that many teachers "are still on the threshold of understanding how to design courses to maximize the potentials of technology" (p. 32). Hence, there needs to be some pre-training in the use of computers as a teaching and learning tool for that use to be effective.

Jones (1991) looked at pre-training variables of the effectiveness of teachers using computers. Across all reports he found a $d = 0.31$ effect, and more than ten hours of pre-training resulting in the greatest effects ($d = 0.53$). More importantly, he claimed that

Table 10.6 Summary of effects from computers as substitute and as supplement to the teacher

Author	Year	Substitute		Supplement	
		No. effects	d	No. effects	d
Bayraktar	2000	27	0.18	81	0.29
Cohen & Dacanay	1992	28	0.36	9	0.56
Hsu	2003	9	0.35	22	0.44
Kuchler	1998	17	0.28	42	0.51
Lee	2004	na	0.29	na	0.41
Yaakub & Finch	2001	19	0.32	8	0.49

Table 10.7 Summary of effects from using computers with the same or a different teacher

Author	Year	Same		Different	
		No. effects	d	No. effects	d
Gordon	1991	43	0.22	79	0.32
Kulik and Kulik	1986b	68	0.23	31	0.32
Kulik, Kulik & Bangert-Drowns	1985	7	0.44	21	0.48
Liao	2005	20	0.59	17	0.71
Kuchler	1998	13	0.62	48	0.40
Fletcher-Flynn & Gravatt	1995	33	0.23	36	0.30
Banger-Drowns	1993	8	0.16	7	0.28
Bayraktar	2000	33	0.22	37	0.21
Cohen & Dacanay	1994	28	0.35	8	0.60
Chen	1994	269	0.58	60	0.51

"less than 10 hours of training is not only unproductive, but it is counterproductive. Those teachers who received such short-term training seem to have classes that achieve substantially less than average computer-using classes, whereas teachers receiving more than 10 hours of training achieve up to 72 percent additional gain beyond the average computer using class". It is noted, however, that this time is better concentrated in a few weeks or less, as there was a decrease in the effect sizes if the course was spread out too long (< 4 weeks $d = 0.67$; 4 to 8 weeks $d = 0.52$; 8 to 14 weeks $d = 0.57$; > 14 weeks $d = 0.32$). Similarly, Ryan (1991) reported effects of $d = 0.53$ from more than ten hours of training, but only $d = 0.19$ from five to ten hours, and $d = 0.14$ from less than five hours of training (see also Lou, Abrami, & d'Apollonia, 2001).

The use of computers is more effective when there are multiple opportunities for learning (e.g., deliberative practice, increasing time on task)

There are many ways whereby the use of computers can assist with multiple learning opportunities. Table 10.8 summarizes some of the major uses, and these range from high effects when using computers in tutorial mode to low effects when using computers for problem solving and simulations.

Tutorials involve structured learning experiences and these have the greatest effect compared to other computer-administered methods. It does seem that many computer packages may be of better instructional quality compared to many teachers' instructional methods and this, as Fletcher-Flynn and Gravatt (1995) claimed, was because of the attention given in these computer packages to making them versatile enough to be used effectively over a range of subjects and educational settings.

Of particular interest is the effects of drill and practice—and despite the moans by many adults, students need much drill and practice. However, it does not need to be dull and boring, but can be, and indeed should be, engaging and informative. Drill is a euphemism for practice: repeated learning of the material under it is mastered—this is the key ingredient in mastery learning, many of the more effective methods outlined in this book, and of deliberative practice. It does not have to be deadly, and a key skill for many teachers is to make deliberative practice engaging and worthwhile. Luik (2007) classified 145 attributes of drills using computers into six categories: motivating the learner, learner control, presentation of information, characteristics of questions, characteristics of replying, and feedback. The key attributes that led to the highest effects included learner control, not losing sight of the learning goal, and the immediate announcement of correctness or otherwise of the answer to the drill.

Many computer games are basically invested with high levels of drill and practice and

Table 10.8 Summary of major uses of computers in classrooms

Method	No. metas	No. effect sizes	d
Tutorials	8	78	0.71
Programming	2	43	0.50
Word processing	2	47	0.42
Drill & practice	9	506	0.34
Simulations	5	94	0.34
Problem solving	7	197	0.26

many students can be thrilled and motivated to engage in these often repetitive tasks to attain higher levels of skill and thus make more progress through the game. Computer games include much engaging drill and practice with increasing levels of challenge that usually is mastered by over learning or undertaking high degrees of drill and practice. So often, the evidence has shown positive effects from using computers to engage in deliberative practice, particularly for those students struggling to first learn a concept. Meta-analyses have also frequently demonstrated that drill and practice routines via computer are more effective than traditional teaching (Burns & Bozeman, 1981). Perhaps teachers should pause and wonder why their traditional teaching is less effective than many computer drill and practice programs.

The use of computers is more effective when the student, not the teacher, is in "control" of learning

One of the key findings from reading the many meta-analyses on computer-aided instruction was that when the student is in "control" over his or her learning (pacing, time allocations for mastery, sequencing and pacing of instructional materials, choice of practice items, reviewing) then the effects were greater than when the teacher was in "control" over these dimensions of learning (Niemiec, Sikorski, & Walberg, 1996). Abrami *et al.* (2006) concluded that it is more important for the student than the teacher to be regulating the technology. Similarly the effects are higher when the learner rather than the system had control. When the software was mostly learner- ($d = 0.41$) rather than system-controlled ($d = -0.02$), the effects were positive provided students were learning in groups (Lou, Abrami, & d'Apolloni, 2001). Cohen and Dacanay (1994) reported an effect of $d = 0.49$ when the package was paced by the student and $d = 0.34$ when paced by the instructor; and $d = 0.60$ when the student was in control and $d = 0.20$ when the student was not in control over pacing.

A good example of the student being in control of his or her learning relates to the use of word processors. When using these packages, students tend to write much more than when asked to write on paper, and the quality of writing is enhanced, especially for the weaker writers (Bangert-Drowns, 1993). This "more" is not more of low quality, as quality of writing and length was highly positively related. Students are more likely to make revisions, write more, and make fewer errors (Goldberg, Russell, & Cook, 2003; Schramm, 1991). Torgerson and Elbourne (2002) completed a meta-analysis of studies conducted between 1992 and 2002 on computers and student writing, and found that, on average, students who used computers when learning to write were not only more engaged and motivated in their writing but produced work that was of greater length and higher quality than students learning to write on paper ($d = 0.40$).

The use of computers is more effective when peer learning is optimized

Using computers in pairs is much more effective than when computers are used alone or in larger groups. Peers can be involved in problem solving, suggesting and trying new strategies, and working through possible next steps. As is noted in the sections on group learning above (cooperation or competition), students can learn most effectively when working together, as it exposes them to multiple perspectives, revision on their thinking, varied explanations for resolving dilemmas, more sources of feedback and correction of errors, and alternative ways to construct knowing. When the group gets too large, there can be reduced opportunity for individual students to explore their beliefs and hypotheses about what is to be learnt, leading to lower levels of learning and (re-)building constructs of knowing. There can be less opportunity to try out ideas and explore alternatives, and in larger groups there can be dominant and more submissive members, which detracts from effective learning in such groups.

Lou, Abrami, and d'Apollonia (2001) reported higher effects for pairs than individuals or more than two in a group. Liao (2007) also found greater effects for small groups ($d = 0.96$) than individuals ($d = 0.56$) or larger groups ($d = 0.39$). Gordon (1991) found effects were larger for learning in pairs ($d = 0.54$) compared to alone ($d = 0.25$); and Kuchler (1998) reported $d = 0.69$ for pairs and $d = 0.29$ for individuals. Lou, Abrami, and d'Apollonia (2001) reported that students learning in pairs had a higher frequency of positive peer interactions ($d = 0.33$), higher frequency of using appropriate learning or task strategies ($d = 0.50$), persevered more on tasks ($d = 0.48$), and more students succeeded ($d = 0.28$) than those learning individually when using computers. Students learning individually requested more help from the teacher ($d = 0.67$) and accomplished tasks faster than those working in groups ($d = 0.16$). There were, however, no differences between learning alone or in groups in attitudes towards computers, or attitudes to learning. The effects of small group learning were significantly enhanced when students had group work experience or instruction, and when specific cooperative learning strategies were employed. From 198 effects from 71 studies, Lou (2004) found that students learning with computers in small groups attempted a greater amount of tasks ($d = 0.15$), used more learning strategies ($d = 0.36$), and had a more positive attitude toward small group learning $d = 0.54$), but there was little difference in attitude towards instruction ($d = 0.07$) and they needed more task completion time in groups than when alone ($d = -0.21$). These results show that when learning using computers, it is important to emphasize discussion and for each student to work with a peer to articulate, explain, and understand a variety of possible hypotheses and solutions.

Such findings led Lou, Abrami, and d'Apollonia (2001) to recommend the following:

- When having students learn with tutorial or practice programs on tasks that are mostly system-controlled and close-ended, it is more effective cognitively and affectively to have students learn in pairs than individually.
- When having students learn with exploratory programs such as simulations and hypermedia resources for discovery learning or with general purpose tools (e.g., Word) for writing, it is important to emphasize discussions and have opportunities for each member to use learning strategies and to articulate, explain, and understand a variety of possible hypotheses and solutions.
- When students work with computers in small groups, it is important to provide them with specific cooperative learning structures and to encourage them to work together and to use appropriate and varied learning strategies.
- Students should be trained to develop group work experience.
- When forming groups it is advantageous to have heterogeneous groups ($d = 1.15$) rather than homogenous groups ($d = 0.51$)—but both types of groups are more effective than working alone.

The use of computers is more effective when feedback is optimized

A further advantage of computers is that they respond to the student despite who they are—male or female, black or white, slow or fast. Teachers claim expertise in their flexibility in anticipating students' reactions and deciding when and to whom to provide feedback, but given the low levels of feedback in most classrooms it is clear that this flexibility means many students miss out. Computer feedback is potentially less threatening to students and can occur in a more programmed manner (Blok, Oostdam, Otter, & Overmaat, 2002).

As noted above, there are many types of feedback, and feedback is optimized when there are appropriate challenging tasks. Timmerman and Kruepke (2006) found that explanations ($d = 0.66$) and remediation ($d = 0.73$) are much more effective than just providing the correct answer ($d = -0.11$, see also Cohen & Dacanay, 1994). Lou, Abrami, and d'Apolloni (2001) found that effects were more positive when tasks were challenging ($d = 0.13$), than when moderately challenging ($d = -0.34$) or not challenging ($d = -0.57$). There is no point asking students to engage in computer-assisted instruction activities unless there is some challenge.

The meta-analysis by Gillingham and Guthrie (1987) provided the highest average of all computer-assisted instruction studies, but it was based on only 13 studies. They established three critical principles included: the teacher needs to use computer-assisted instruction to manage the attention and motivation of the learner, the teacher needs to use computer-assisted instruction to present new subject matter content and learning strategies to the learner, and the teacher needs to use computer-assisted instruction to guide the practice and active involvement of learners.

Mukawa (2006) completed a meta-analysis evaluating Chickering and Ehrmann's (1996) seven principles of good practice for online learning. Their effects were very much lower than those found by Gillingham and Guthrie (1987), but the messages were similar. They found that the highest effects related to computer-assisted instruction encouraging greater student–faculty contact ($d = 0.14$), cooperation among students ($d = 0.10$), active learning ($d = 0.10$), respecting different ways of learning ($d = 0.09$), and emphasizing time on task ($d = 0.07$).

Web-based learning

The use of the world wide web is a fairly recent phenomenon in our classrooms. Over the past decade, the web has become a more important part of the lives of many students,

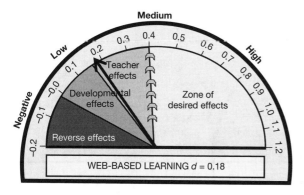

KEY	
Standard error	0.124 (High)
Rank	112th
Number of meta-analyses	3
Number of studies	45
Number of effects	136
Number of people (2)	22,554

WEB-BASED LEARNING *d* = 0.18

but many teachers are not as familiar with some parts of this world as their students are. Students can live in a world of their making and control, and knowledge is but a click away. The older notion of teaching students how to look up encyclopedias, reference books, and over learn details seems far less relevant than teaching them how to conduct Boolean searches, evaluate the credibility of knowledge, and synthesize the plethora of information now available to them.

Olson and Wisher (2002) noted that some have argued that the use of the web often ignores the fundamentals of instructional design—such as interaction and timely feedback. The average effect was small ($d = 0.24$) but the variability was huge across the 15 studies. They noted that these effects are, in general, much lower than effects from other computer-based interventions. They cautioned that the field is new, and that the average effect may become more stable when many more studies are completed. They noted that many of the early adopters were faculty from a diversity of fields not necessarily trained in instructional design. The hope is that "the potential of web-based instruction will increase as pedagogical practices improve, advances in standards for structure learning content programs, and improvements in bandwidth are made" (p. 13).

Interactive video methods

Interactive video, a combination of computer-assisted instruction and video technology, is used as an instructional media for teaching and training (Herschbach, 1984). A study by McNeil and Nelson (1990) found that effect sizes from studies on interactive video were not homogeneous, indicating that cognitive achievement from interactive video instruction is influenced by a wide range of variables such as the nature of instructional content, environmental factors, instructional methods and the learning materials. Program-controlled interactive video appears to be more effective than learner-controlled. McNeil and Nelson also noted that differences in program effectiveness favoring group instruction were possibly explained by factors such as decisions made by the teacher relative to the amount of practice, the extent and kind of feedback, and the nature of remediation procedures. Blanchard, Stock, and Marshall (1999) used meta-analysis over ten implementations of a multimedia curriculum based on video games. They found a very low overall effect, both in mathematics ($d = 0.13$) and language arts ($d = 0.18$), in high ($d = 0.23$) and low ($d = 0.16$) quality implementations of the multimedia method.

Baker and Dwyer (2000) explored the instructional effects of visualization compared to

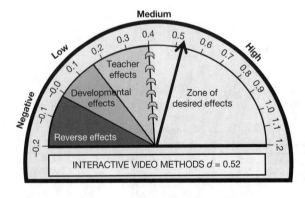

KEY	
Standard error	0.076 (Medium)
Rank	44th
Number of meta-analyses	6
Number of studies	441
Number of effects	3,930
Number of people (1)	4,800

no visualization in interactive video ($d = 0.71$), and argued that the visual presentations can convey the essence of the message to be learned (see also Fletcher, 1989). Clark and Angert (1980) carried out a meta-analytic study on pictorial effectiveness, which focused on the use of static iconic visuals in instructional materials. Four major variables were investigated: illustrations, pacing, grade level, and achievement; and five physical attributes of illustrations: production, shading, context, embellishment, and chroma. Illustrated materials were more effective than verbal descriptions (particularly with high school students); and color illustrations were more effective than black and white.

Mayer (1989) was more concerned with searching for principles of multimedia design that enhanced science outcomes. When multimedia messages were designed in ways that overload visual or verbal working memory then the influences were markedly reduced and it was much more important for the teacher (or text) to help students connect verbal explanations to visual ones. It was more effective for students to receive both visual and verbal materials, as "when only verbal material is presented, the learner may construct an impoverished visual mental model that is insufficient to integrate with the verbal mental model." Having both allows more appropriate visual and verbal models to be built and retained.

Hypermedia incorporates two fundamental concepts: multiple representations of information and interactivities between users and this information. Typically this involves multimedia and computer-assisted instruction. Liao's examination of hypermedia encompasses interactive multimedia, multimedia computer simulations, and interactive videodiscs. Liao (1998) looked at the effects of hypermedia versus traditional instruction on students' achievement and found that there were positive effects for hypermedia over traditional instruction. The effects were greater when regular class teachers rather than specialist teachers were used, in elementary school compared to high school, and when used to supplement rather than substitute regular instruction. Liao noted that hypermedia may be more effective when used as a supplement to traditional learning.

Audio/Visual methods

Visual-based instruction involves the use of a wide range of visual media such as television, film, video, and slides. Willet, Yamashita, and Anderson (1983) found very small effects from these methods: television $d = 0.05$, film $d = -0.07$, slides $d = -0.47$, and tapes $d = -0.27$. Blanchard, Stock, and Marshall (1999) found similar low effects ($d = 0.15$) from their multimedia applications. Further, providing audio-tapes of lessons had a small overall effect on

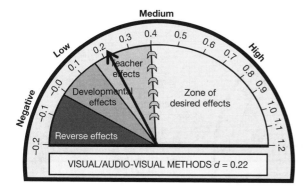

KEY	
Standard error	0.070 (Medium)
Rank	104th
Number of meta-analyses	6
Number of studies	359
Number of effects	231
Number of people (1)	2,760

student achievement in college courses and no major effect on student course evaluations or on course completions (Kulik, Kulik, & Cohen (1980). Shwalb, Shwalb, and Azuma's (1986) study was completed in Japan; they found a lower effect from providing audio-tapes, and this method had the lowest effects of all methods they compared.

Simulations

Simulations and games typically involve the use of a model or game (such as role playing, decision making) with an aim to engage students in learning (although some games are not engaging or fun). Szczurek (1982) defined simulation as:

> an instructional method based on a simplified model or representation of a physical or social reality in which students compete for certain outcomes according to an established set of rules or constraints. The competition can be (1) among themselves as individuals or as groups, or (2) against some specified standard working as individuals or cooperating as a group.
>
> (Szczurek, 1982, p. 27)

Many simulations are not competitive but do aim to mimic real-world problems.

VanSickle (1986) found small effects ($d = 0.12$) for recall of knowledge of facts, concepts, and generalizations, and $d = 0.18$ for retention over time. He concluded that these findings show that simulating and gaming has a small positive effect over alternative instructional techniques, although somewhat larger when compared with lectures only ($d = 0.32$). Dekkers and Donatti (1981) found slightly higher effects for achievement ($d = 0.33$) and similar effects for retention ($d = 0.15$), but much higher attitude effects ($d = 0.64$). McKenna (1991) found a similar effect ($d = 0.38$) and also reported that there were no differences over age groups, but simulations were more effective with lower than higher ability students. Lee (1990), however, found simulation and gaming had higher effect sizes in achievement when used with students in higher grade levels. McKenna found, as did Dekkers and Donatti, that shorter (up to one-week) interventions were more effective than longer interactions. Remmer and Jernsted (1982) examined the effectiveness of simulation games in high school and college level instruction. The effects on achievement were small, leading them to conclude that the use of simulation games on achievement and retention was not more effective than conventional instruction. Armstrong (1991) found an overall

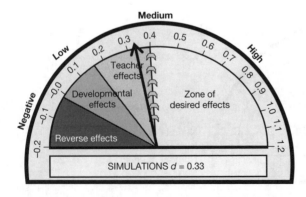

KEY	
Standard error	0.092 (High)
Rank	82nd
Number of meta-analyses	9
Number of studies	361
Number of effects	482
Number of people (0)	na

SIMULATIONS $d = 0.33$

effect (d = 0.29) between computer-based simulations and traditional instruction, and the effects were similar for low-level thinking, high-level thinking, and retention outcomes.

LeJeune (2002) used interactive videodisc-based simulations and computer-simulated experiments in science. These are computer programs that model real world phenomena or duplicate traditional laboratory activities. He divided achievement outcomes into surface (d = 0.34) and deeper outcomes (d = 0.38), and found no effects on attitudes (d = –0.03), or on retention at least two weeks later (d = 0.19). The effects in colleges (d = 0.49) were much greater than in K–12 (d = 0.14). The surface outcomes were greater when taught to confirm what had been taught (d = 0.44) compared to allowing the students to explore during their learning (d = 0.27), but there were no differences when the outcomes were deeper thinking (d = 0.35 versus d = 0.41). His conclusion was that these simulations improved low-level achievement such as the ability to learn scientific facts, comprehend scientific processes, and apply that knowledge to everyday phenomena; and to deeper outcomes such as problem solving ability and other high-level thinking skills.

Programmed instruction

Programmed instruction is a teaching method of presenting new subject matter to students in graded sequence of controlled steps. A book version, for example, presents a problem or issue, then, depending on the student's answer to a question about the material, the student chooses from optional answers which refers them to particular pages of the book to find out why they were correct or incorrect—and then proceed to the next part of the problem or issue. In many ways, programmed instruction was the precursor to many computer-controlled branching and pacing programs. When comparisons are made between many methods, programmed instruction often comes near the bottom. Hartley's (1977) meta-analysis of the effects on mathematics achievement of different instructional modes found that tutoring was the most effective, then computer-assisted instruction, and both were much higher than individual learning packets and programmed instruction. Similarly, Aiello and Wolfle (1980) found programmed instruction the least effective compared to computer-assisted instruction, Keller's personalized system of instruction, audio–tutorials, and finally programmed instruction. Willett, Yamashita and Anderson (Willett *et al.*, 1983) looked at various instructional systems in science education—again, programmed instruction was among the lowest effects.

Kulik, Schwalb, and Kulik (1993) found very low effects from programmed instruction,

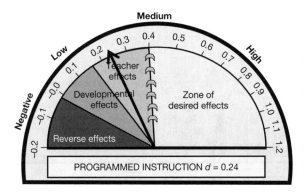

PROGRAMMED INSTRUCTION d = 0.24

KEY	
Standard error	0.089 (High)
Rank	95th
Number of meta-analyses	7
Number of studies	464
Number of effects	362
Number of people (0)	na

especially in mathematics and science. Kulik, Cohen, and Ebeling (1980) found similar small effects with students in higher education, and also noted that there was no support for students enjoying this method of instruction. Boden, Archwamety, and McFarland (2000) found a higher effect of $d = 0.40$, which they attributed to using only older students who were more self-regulating of their learning.

Implementations using out-of-school learning

Three programs are reviewed that involve some aspect of out-of-school learning: distance education, home-school programs, and homework.

Distance education

My first decade as an academic was in a university that specialized in distance learning. It was a great experience in learning to be very well prepared with all courses (as they had to be printed and sent many months before the classes started), with supervising students writing theses (then all was via written letters, and being forced to write a letter helped most students work out what their problem was—and thus supervision was so much easier, as most of the time the student wants the supervisor to listen and work out their problem for them; it also revealed if they could "write" or not). The meta-analyses discussed here show there are no differences in outcomes according to whether a student is a distance student or not—and certainly the message is not that "distance education does not work". The medium is not the message. This is also the case with the newer technologies, which have increased the accessibility of educational opportunities for learners through distance learning. Integral to distance education are instructional features that include a range of media types, such as televised instruction and video conferencing (Allen, Bourhis, Burrell, & Mabry, 2002; Machtmes & Asher, 2000). A meta-analysis by Machtmes and Asher (2000) of the effectiveness of telecourses in distance education found no difference between a traditional classroom with no studio equipment and a distance course with studio equipment.

Cavanaugh's (2001) meta-analysis included only web-delivered K–12 distance programs and she concluded that such programs had a similar effect to traditional face-to-face classroom programs ($d = 0.15$). There were no moderation effects relating to academic content, grade level, type of school, frequency of the distance learning experience, pacing of instruction, timing of instruction, instructor preparation and experience in distance

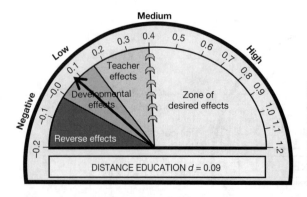

KEY	
Standard error	0.050 (Medium)
Rank	126th
Number of meta-analyses	13
Number of studies	839
Number of effects	1,643
Number of people (7)	4,024,638

DISTANCE EDUCATION $d = 0.09$

education, or the setting of the students. The conclusion was that students can experience similar levels of academic success when they learn using telecommunications and when they learn in classroom settings.

A comparison of student satisfaction with distance education and traditional classrooms in higher education found a slight student *preference* for a live course setting and little difference in *satisfaction* levels (Allen *et al.*, 2002). There is also no difference in levels of satisfaction with distance education methods that include interactive links and those that do not. There is some support for videotaped instruction as a preferred option of instruction over written.

Bernard *et al.* (2004) argued that there were two distinctively different patterns of distance education: synchronous distance education derived from earlier applications of closed circuit television, and that which occurs when two or more classrooms in different locations are joined in real time and run, synchronously, usually from the originating site. We evaluated one of these programs for the North Carolina School of Mathematics and Science (Hattie, *et al.*, 1998). They had linked various schools through closed circuit to the school where the top teachers in the state taught courses in science. The net effect was that once the technology issues had been solved and paid for, the difference was attributable to the quality of the teaching.

Various forms of synchronous distance education include audio and video interactive teleconferencing, and this has become the fastest growing form of distance education in American universities (Mottet, 1998; Ostendorf, 1997). This is contrasted with asynchronous distance education, a derivative of correspondence education, where students work independently and their work is supported with an instructor or tutor. Typically there is some delay (post office, email) between completing the work and any feedback. Bernard *et al.* found zero effects for both synchronous ($d = -0.10$) and asynchronous ($d = 0.05$) on achievement, and negative to zero effects on attitude ($d = -0.19, -0.00$), and retention ($d = 0.00, -0.09$). Lou, Bernard, and Abrami (2006) specifically looked at synchronous ($d = -0.02$) and asynchronous ($d = 0.06$) and concluded that the medium of instruction does not matter; it is how it is used to support instruction and facilitate learning that affects outcomes.

> When media are used to deliver the same instruction simultaneously by the same instructor and with the same course activities and materials, there is little reason to expect undergraduate students to learn differently in the remote sites than at the host site. ... [there is no] difference between the live classroom and the remote site.
>
> (Lou *et al.*, 2006, p. 162)

Zhao, Lei, Yan, Lai, and Tan (2005) argued that the reason they found a major difference between pre- and post-1998 was because of the facility now in many technologies to include interactions between the student and the teacher, and between students. "Whether and how much students interact with peers and instructors seems to be a differentiating quality of distance programs" (p. 1861).

Home-school programs

Penuel *et al.* (2002) were interested in using technology to develop home–school connections in student learning. In particular, they looked at the use of laptops, programs

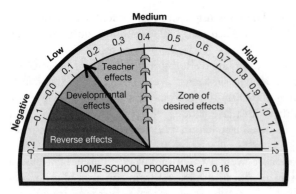

KEY	
Standard error	na
Rank	116th
Number of meta-analyses	1
Number of studies	14
Number of effects	14
Number of people (0)	na

using discrete educational software for use at home and at school, and desktop programs. The effects of these programs on reading were small ($d = 0.10$), slightly higher for mathematics ($d = 0.18$). and highest for writing ($d = 0.34$); there was not a lot of evidence showing enhanced home–school communication or increased parental involvement that affected students' learning.

Homework

Homework involves "tasks assigned to students by school teachers that are meant to be carried out during non-school hours" (Cooper, 1989, p. 7). It is a hotly contested area, and my experience is that many parents judge the effectiveness of schools by the presence or amount of homework—although they expect to not be involved in this learning other than by providing a quiet and secluded space, as they believe that these are the right conditions for deep and meaningful learning. The overall effects are positive, but there are some important moderators.

Cooper (1989) has written many studies and conducted a series of meta-analyses on homework. He argued that the effects of homework are twice as large for high as for junior high, and twice as large again for junior high as for elementary students. The smallest effects were in mathematics, whereas the effects in science and social studies were the largest, with English in the middle. The positive effects of homework were negatively related to the duration of the homework treatment (see also Trautwein, Köller, Schmitz, & Baumert, 2002). Shorter is better, but, for elementary students, Cooper, Lindsay, Nye,

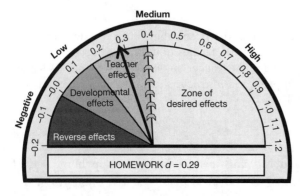

KEY	
Standard error	0.027 (Low)
Rank	88th
Number of meta-analyses	5
Number of studies	161
Number of effects	295
Number of people (4)	105,282

and Greathouse (1998) estimated a correlation of near zero ($d = -0.04$) between time spent on homework and achievement. Student attitude to homework was not related to completion or grade, and nor did parent facilitation relate to student attitude to homework: "Parent support for autonomous student behavior showed a positive relationship to achievement, whereas direct instructional involvement showed a negative relationship" (Cooper, Jackson, Nye, and Lindsay, 2001, p. 197). My reading of Cooper's results suggests that more task-oriented homework had higher effects than did deep learning and problem solving homework. It is likely that this interaction is because of the importance of the teaching cycle to ensure appropriate learning, feedback, and monitoring (especially for deeper learning), whereas rehearsal of basic skills (surface knowledge) can be undertaken with minimal teacher supervision.

The nature of the homework also makes a difference. The effects were highest in mathematics, and lowest in science and social studies. The effects were higher when the material was not complex or if it was novel. Homework involving higher level conceptual thinking, and project based was the least effective. Trautwein, Köller, Schmitz, and Baumert (2002) aimed to identify the key components of homework that made the difference, with a particular emphasis on untangling the interactions between homework and student characteristics. They found that a lot of homework and a lack of monitoring seem to indicate an ineffective teaching method. They warned against homework that undermined a student's motivation and that led to the student internalizing incorrect routines, and they favored short, frequent homework that was closely monitored by the teachers. It would probably be more effective to construct these opportunities under the gaze of a teacher, in the school. Teaching does matter when it comes to students' learning. The manner in which parents become involved may or may not make a difference.

The effects are greater for higher than for lower ability students and for older rather than younger students. For too many students, homework reinforces that they cannot learn by themselves, and that they cannot do the schoolwork. For these students, homework can undermine motivation, internalize incorrect routines and strategies, and reinforce less effective study habits, especially for elementary students. The novelist Richard Russo summed up the views of many students:

> She tried shit like doing her homework for a while, but it was counterproductive since she always did it wrong. Doing homework wrong, to her, was worse than not doing it at all, because doing it required time and effort and yielded the same results as not doing it, which required neither. Besides, our teachers had it all figured out in advance, she said, like who was going to get good grades and who'd flunk.
>
> (Russo, 2007, p. 157)

There are marked differences in effect sizes between elementary ($d = 0.15$) and high school students ($d = 0.64$), which probably reflects the more advanced skills of studying involved in high school. It is important to note, however, that prescribing homework does not help students develop time management skills—there is no evidence this occurs. High school teachers are more likely to assign homework related to learning subject matter, and the effects are highest, whatever the subject, when homework involves rote learning, practice, or rehearsal of the subject matter. Perhaps one set of reasons why the effects of homework are lower in elementary levels is that younger children are less able than older children to ignore irrelevant information or stimulation in their environment, have less effective study habits, and receive little support (from teachers or parents) (Muhlenbruck, Cooper, Nye, & Lindsay, 1999).

Concluding comments

There are many teaching strategies that have an important effect on student learning. Such teaching strategies include explanation, elaboration, plans to direct task performance, sequencing, drill repetition, providing strategy cues, domain-specific processing, and clear instructional goals. These can be achieved using methods such as reciprocal teaching, direct instruction, and problem solving methods. As noted above, effective teaching occurs when the teacher decides the learning intentions and success criteria, makes them transparent to the students, demonstrates them by modeling, evaluates if they understand what they have been told by checking for understanding, and re-telling them what they have told by tying it all together with closure. These effective teaching strategies involve much cooperative pre-planning and discussion between teachers, optimizing peer learning, and require explicit learning intentions and success criteria.

Peers play a powerful role, as is demonstrated in the strategies involving reciprocal teaching, learning in pairs on computers, and both cooperative and competitive learning (as opposed to individualistic learning). Many of the strategies also help reduce cognitive load and this allows students to focus on the critical aspects of learning, which is particularly useful when they are given multiple opportunities for deliberative practice.

The use of resources, such as adjunct aids and computers, can add value to learning. They add a diversity of teaching strategies, provide alternative opportunities to practice and learn, and increase the nature and amount of feedback to the learner and teachers. They do, however, require learning how to optimize their uses.

It is also clear that, yet again, it is the differences in the teachers that make the difference in student learning. Homework in which there is no active involvement by the teacher does not contribute to student learning, and likewise the use, or not, of technologies (such as distance learning) does not show major effects on learning if there is no teacher involvement. Related to these teacher influences are the lower effects of many of the interventions when they are part of comprehensive teaching reforms. Many of these reforms are "top down" innovations, which can mean teachers do not evaluate whether the reforms are working for them or not. Commitment to the teaching strategy, and re-learning how to use many of these methods (through professional development, see Chapter 7) seems important.

Chapter 11

Bringing it all together

Where is the wisdom we have lost in knowledge?
Where is the knowledge we have lost in information?

(Eliot, 1934)

Any book synthesizing meta-analyses is fundamentally a literature review, and thus it builds on the scholarship and research of those who have come before. A major purpose of this book is to generate a model of successful teaching and learning based on the many thousands of studies in 800 and more meta-analyses. The aim is not to merely average the studies and present screeds of data. This is not uncommon; so often meta-analyses have been criticized as mere number crunching exercises, and a book based on more than 800 meta-analyses could certainly have been just that. That was not my intent. Instead, I aimed to build a model based on the theme of "visible teaching, visible learning" that not only synthesized existing literature but also permitted a new perspective on that literature.

What seems needed is not another recipe for success, another quest for certainty, another unmasking of truth—if for no other reason that these are aplenty and no one should be asked to listen to yet another. A recipe would lead to little change, and there would little interest developing policy to build on another recipe. Certainly it could be claimed that more than 800 meta-analyses based on many millions of students is the epitome of "evidence based" decision making. But the current obsession with evidence-based too often ignores the lens that researchers use to make decisions about what to include (as evidence), what to exclude, and how they marshal the evidence to tell their story. It is the *story* that is meant to be the compelling contribution—it is my lens on this evidence.

Michael Scriven claimed that one of the more difficult tasks in research is providing explanation rather than determining causality. Often I may have slipped and made or inferred causality—and in some cases reasonably so. Certainly, the fundamental word in meta-analysis, *effect size*, implies causation (What is the *effect* of *a* on *b*?) and this claim is often not defensible. The claims in this book are more oriented to developing an explanation—a plausible set of claims based on evidence. It is more an abductive than an inductive or deductive exercise (Haig, 2005)—the explanation or story offers a plausible theory, a set of inferences to the best explanation in light of my experience of reviewing and interpreting the many studies, and it is hoped the story is bold enough to be potentially disprovable. My task is to present a series of claims that have high explanatory value, with many (refutable) conjectures.

In the present case, the story is about the visibility of teaching and learning; it is the power of passionate, accomplished teachers who focus on students' cognitive engagement with the content of what it is they are teaching. It is about teachers who focus their skills in developing a way of thinking, reasoning, and emphasizing problem solving and strategies in their teaching about the content they wish students to learn. It is about teachers enabling students to do more than what teachers do unto them; it is the focus on imparting new knowledge and understanding and then considering and monitoring how students gain fluency and appreciation in this new knowledge and build conceptions of this knowing and understanding. It is how teachers and students strategize, think about, play with, and build conceptions about worthwhile knowledge and understanding. Monitoring, assessing, and evaluating the progress in this task is what then leads to the power of feedback—which comes second in the learning equation. Feedback to students involves providing informa-tion and understanding about the tasks that make the difference in light of what the *student* already understands, misunderstands, and constructs. Feedback from students to teachers involves information and understanding about the tasks that make the difference in light of what the *teacher* already understands, misunderstands, and constructs about the learning of his or her students. It matters when teachers see learning through the lens of the student grappling to construct beliefs and knowledge about whatever is the goal of the lesson. This is never linear, not always easy, requires learning and over learning, needs dollops of feed-back, involves much deliberative practice, leads to lots of errors and mis-directions, requires both accommodating and assimilating prior knowledge and conceptions, and demands a sense of excitement and mission to know, understand, and make a difference.

The conclusions are recast here as six signposts towards excellence in education:

1   Teachers are among the most powerful influences in learning.
2   Teachers need to be directive, influential, caring, and actively engaged in the passion of teaching and learning.
3   Teachers need to be aware of what each and every student is thinking and knowing, to construct meaning and meaningful experiences in light of this knowledge, and have proficient knowledge and understanding of their content to provide meaningful and appropriate feedback such that each student moves progressively through the curriculum levels.

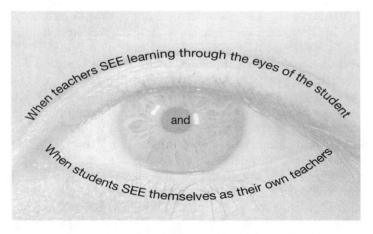

Figure 11.1 A model of Visible teaching – Visible learning

4   Teachers need to *know the learning intentions* and success criteria of their lessons, know *how well they are attaining* these criteria for all students, and know *where to go next* in light of the gap between students' current knowledge and understanding and the success criteria of: "Where are you going?", "How are you going?", and "Where to next?".

5   Teachers need to move from the single idea to multiple ideas, and to relate and then extend these ideas such that learners construct and reconstruct knowledge and ideas. It is not the knowledge or ideas, but the learner's construction of this knowledge and these ideas that is critical.

6   School leaders and teachers need to create school, staffroom, and classroom environments where error is welcomed as a learning opportunity, where discarding incorrect knowledge and understandings is welcomed, and where participants can feel safe to learn, re-learn, and explore knowledge and understanding.

In these six signposts, the word "teachers" is deliberate, as a major theme is when teachers meet to discuss, evaluate, and plan their teaching in light of the feedback evidence about the success or otherwise of their teaching strategies and conceptions about progress and appropriate challenge. This is not critical reflection, but *critical reflection in light of evidence* about their teaching.

Note what is *not* said. There are no claims about additional structural resources, although to achieve the above it helps not to have the hindrance of a lack of resources. There is nothing about class size, about which particular students are present in the school or class, or about which subject is being taught—effective teaching can occur similarly for all students, all ethnicities, and all subjects. There is nothing about between-school differences, which are not a major effect in developed countries. There is little about working conditions of teachers or students—although their effects, though small, are positive, and positive means we should not make these working conditions worse.

Sure, it helps to have students who are committed learners, who are quiet and receptive, who have high levels of self-regulation, and who have financially gifted parents. Such desires are often the basis for claims about school choice. The usual argument is that if only parents had the power (e.g., vouchers) to choose the best schools, then the quality of education would be driven up. Such choice claims imply that lower performing schools would close or change, and that parents who do not make the choice to send their children away from the neighborhood school do not "want" to. New Zealand experienced a voucher-type system for more than a decade, and the disparity between the top and bottom schools increased dramatically. Parents moved their children from the schools in lower socioeconomic areas to those in higher socioeconomic areas; there was "white flight" to the higher socioeconomic areas that left increasingly concentrated ethnic minorities in lower socioeconomic schools. The reasons were not that they were moving to schools where student outcomes were higher (such information was not available in New Zealand) but because they were "fleeing from schools with high proportions of minorities" (Fiske & Ladd, 2000, p. 201). Certainly, children from the more advantaged families were the major beneficiaries of the voucher system (and loudest advocates). With few exceptions, we have to teach *all* in front of us.

Will evidence make a difference?

The theme throughout this book is that the beliefs and conceptions held by teachers need to be questioned—not because they are wrong (or right) but because the essence of good teaching is that teachers' expectations and conceptions must be subjected to debate, refutation, and investigation. Only then can there be major improvements in student achievement. We need to ask about the conceptions of teaching that have led to teachers making decisions about:

- what is best to teach next, without attending closely to what these students already know;
- what materials to choose, with no regard to any evidence (other than prior use) that these are the optimal materials (and so often these materials are made by the cottage industry in teachers' homes);
- how to keep students engaged and busy, but not ensuring that they actually learn;
- what activities provoke the most interest, instead of asking what leads to students putting in effort (it is the effort, not the interest level, of the activity that is important);
- how to maximize the challenge of the learning goals and create structures for students to learn via the challenge, rather than structuring the material so that it is easy to learn.

We can set benchmarks of what progress looks like (preferably $d = 0.40$ for *every* student, at least $d = 0.30$, and certainly not less than $d = 0.20$) per implementation or year. We can agree to learning intentions and success criteria, and we can set the goalpost of accomplished teachers at the level of those who systematically make these differences to students: that is, those who engage them, turn them on to the subject, who inspire them, and who communicate a passion for learning. We also need to recognize that sometimes learning is dull and repetitive, but turning students on to this part of learning requires the same passions. As I learn to make bread, or coach cricket, there are many tasks I have to repeat seemingly endlessly to over learn some skills to thus allow cognitive resources to be freed for other tasks—especially anticipation and a sense of understanding about the bread or state of the cricket game. My cricket coaching requires monitoring process and not just performance—my aim is to be a coach, not a score keeper.

Teachers and principals need to collect the effect sizes within their schools and then ask "What is working best?", "Why is it working best?", and "Who is it not working for?" (e.g., see Petty, 2006; Schagen & Elliot, 2004). This will create a discussion among teachers about teaching. This would require a caring, supportive staffroom, a tolerance of errors, and for learning from other teachers, a peer culture among teachers of engagement, trust, shared passion, and so on. It is the same attributes that work for student learning that also work for teachers' learning. Bryk and Schneider (2002) found that higher levels of trust were reported in schools that eventually could be categorized as academically improving than in those in the non–improving group ($d = 0.61$ for increases in reading and $d = 0.64$ in mathematics). Their message was that trust does not directly affect student learning, but it fosters a set of organizational conditions. Trust reduces the sense of vulnerability that teachers experience as they take on new and uncertain tasks associated with reform; it facilitates teachers' efforts to innovate in their classroom in order to develop more effective instruction, facilitates public problem solving within a school, and creates a moral resource that leads to commitments and greater effort to implement successful innovations (Bryk & Schneider, 2002, p. 117). Trust also maximizes the occurrence of error and thus allows feedback to be powerful in use and effectiveness. To engender reform that will make the difference requires incentives primarily in terms of teachers learning about their teaching, about what is working and for whom, and from sharing *evidence* of the effectiveness of their methods. The current penchant for "reflective teaching" too often ignores that such reflection needs to be based on evidence and not on post-hoc justification. We can go further, as my colleagues and I are doing in a trial of our work, which involves providing a computerized system for teachers to set targets for their students based on the students' prior progress, then creating a dialogue among principal and teachers about the desirability of these targets, and then closely monitoring the success of achieving the targets (Hattie, *et al.*, 2007). Hence the theme of visible teaching and visible learning.

The personal nature of learning

Olson (2003) states it simply—it is students themselves, in the end, not teachers, who decide what students will learn. Thus we must attend to what students are thinking, what their goals are, and why they would want to engage in learning what is offered in schools. Learning is very personal to the teacher *and* to each student. While we assemble students in groups (classes, and within-class groups), the meaning of the implications of education is personal for each of us. This does not mean we need to attend to individualized instruction but that we need to be aware of the progression of knowledge and understanding for each student—and how they learn by themselves, learn with others, and learn with adults, along with an awareness of what they bring from their home and their culture. There are at least three worlds in the classroom (Nuthall, 2005): the public world, which includes teacher-led discussion and work tasks; the private-social word of informal peer interactions, whispers, and note-passing; and the private-individual world of self-talk and thinking. Each world has its own characteristic patterns of behavior, interaction structures, customs, rules, roles, expectations, and discourse.

Nuthall (2005) spent many years putting microphones on every student in the class and monitoring and evaluating their dialogue. This is a robust method of understanding teaching and learning through the eyes of the students—even observations were not sufficient, argued Nuthall, as up to 40 percent of what occurred among students was missed by the observation recordings and observers. No wonder that critical reflection by teachers is barely adequate. His major conclusion related to "how little teachers knew about what was going on in their classrooms" (p. 902). It is, therefore, no surprise that "Teachers often feel that learning outcomes are unpredictable, mysterious, and uncontrollable" (Kennedy, 1999, p. 528). Nuthall found that students lived in a personal and social world of their own in the classroom, they already knew at least 40 percent of what the teachers intended them to learn, a third of what each student learned was not learned by any other student in the class, students learned how and when the teacher would notice them and how to give the appearance of active involvement, and a quarter of the specific concepts and principles that students learned were critically dependent on private peer talk or on self-designed activities or use of resources (Nuthall, 2005). The world of learning and classrooms from the student's personal viewpoint is so often unknown to the teacher—hence reinforcing the major claim in this book about how teachers need to spend more time and energy understanding learning through the eyes of students.

Nuthall found that teachers, rather than seeing learning through the eyes of students, knew their teaching was going well from signs that their students were actively engaged with learning activities. "They monitor the look in their students' eyes, their enthusiasm, their puzzlement, and the questions they ask. In most teachers' minds, the criteria for successful learning are the same as the criteria for successful classroom management" (Nuthall, 2005, p. 916). The focus of teachers' thinking when they were planning and carrying out their role in the classroom was keeping students busily engaged in activities that produced some tangible product. Further, although the learning activity was supposed to produce learning, neither the teachers nor the students talked about learning. Instead, teachers talked about resources, about how long an activity should take, and what would happen if it was not finished on time.

> The teacher is largely cut off from information about what individual students are learning. Teachers are forced to rely on secondary indicators such as the visible signs that students are motivated and interested. They are sustained, however, by the commonly held belief that if students are engaged most of the time in appropriate activities, some kind of learning will be taking place ... Teachers depend on the responses of a small number of key students as indicators and remain ignorant of what most of the class knows and understands.
>
> (Nuthall, 2005, pp. 919–920)

Students' on-task talk was about the same things. When students were asked what they were thinking, "their most common response was that they were thinking about how to get finished quickly or how to the answer with the least possible effort" (Nuthall, 2005, p. 918).

Nuthall (2007) found that the experiences from the less able and more able students were similar. Less able students appeared to learn from their experiences in exactly the same way as the more able students. For both groups of students, a significant proportion of their learning experiences was either self-selected or self-generated, even in traditional classrooms. Those students, regardless of prior ability, who used the classroom and its activities to further their own interests and purposes learned more than those who dutifully did what they were told but did not want or know how to create their own opportunities. It takes "three or four experiences involving interaction with relevant information for a new knowledge construct to be created in working memory and then transferred to long-term memory" (Nuthall, 2000, p. 93). This is not simple repetitions but opportunities to come at the material to be learned in different ways. Students need much deliberative practice distributed over the learning time. Such distributed, rather than spaced, teaching has been noted in Chapter 9, and well studied in psychology. Cepeda, Pashler, Vul, Wixted, and Rohrer (2006) completed a meta-analysis of the effects of distributed practice and concluded that "Distributing practice across different days (instead of grouping learning episodes within a single day) greatly improves the amount of material retained for sizeable periods of time; the literature clearly suggests that distributing practice in this way is likely to markedly improve students' retention of course material" (p. 371). Students who, for reasons of cultural and ethnic differences, may have difficulty participating in a learning activity, not only fail to acquire the knowledge they need to understand and acquire further knowledge; they "learn" that their ability to acquire knowledge is inferior. Such deficit thinking can be reinforced by teachers sharing the same beliefs (Bishop, 2003).

Nuthall argued that teachers should focus on direct observation of the realities of student experience and the processes that students experience in developing knowledge and skill. This involves developing a precise, accurate, and replicable account of both the subjective and objective realities of student experience. This is personalized teaching and personalized learning by the teacher, as only this kind of understanding maximizes the personal learning by the student.

The empirical quest for explanations

The aim in this book has been to provide an explanatory story about active and passionate teachers as contrasted with facilitative and inquiry methods. Teachers who are passionate about making a difference are more likely to make a difference. Consider a contrast between the teacher as an "activator" and the teacher as a "facilitator". In the activist mode, teachers are key agents in all the interventions on the left of Table 11.1, and more facilitative in the interventions on the right hand side. The contrast in effects is marked—from an average of $d = 0.60$ to $d = 0.17$.

These results show that active and guided instruction is much more effective than unguided, facilitative instruction. Kirschner, Sweller, and Clark (2006) provided an extensive review on why providing only minimal guidance during instruction does not work. They contrasted guided models, such as direct instruction, with minimally guided methods such as discovery learning, problem-based learning, inquiry learning, experiential learning, and constructivist learning. These latter methods, they argued, are based on two main assumptions. First, they challenge students to solve "authentic" problems on the assumption that learners construct their own solutions, and second, knowledge is best acquired through experience based on the procedures of the discipline (e.g., developing processes for understanding mathematics rather than learning the skills of mathematics). They noted that each new set of advocates for these approaches seem either unaware of or uninterested in previous evidence that unguided approaches have not been validated. No matter if students preferred less guided methods, they learned less from them (Clark, 1989). Students profit from the facility, active use, and flexibility of various learning strategies (Samuelstuen & Bråten, 2007), and the use of various strategies is a major attribute of expertise in many domains (Lundeberg, 1987; Pressley & Afflerbach, 1995). Constructivism is a form of knowing and not a form of teaching, and it is important not to confuse constructing conceptual knowledge with the current fad of constructivism (Bereiter, 2002; Small, 2003). Constructing conceptual knowledge involves considering learning from the learner's viewpoint; starting from the premise that all learners are active, appreciating that what they learn is socially constructed, and understanding that learners need to create or recreate knowledge of themselves (Phillips, 1995). If this is the

Table 11.1 Effect sizes for teacher as activator and teacher as facilitator

Teacher as activator	d	Teacher as facilitator	d
Reciprocal teaching	0.74	Simulations and gaming	0.32
Feedback	0.72	Inquiry-based teaching	0.31
Teaching students self-verbalization	0.67	Smaller class sizes	0.21
Meta-cognition strategies	0.67	Individualized instruction	0.20
Direct Instruction	0.59	Problem-based learning	0.15
Mastery learning	0.57	Different teaching for boys and girls	0.12
Goals – challenging	0.56	Web-based learning	0.09
Frequent/effects of testing	0.46	Whole language – reading	0.06
Behavioral organizers	0.41	Inductive teaching	0.06
Average activator	0.60	Average facilitator	0.17

meaning of constructivism from a learner perspective, then the more direct and active methods of teaching appear to be optimal for achieving this type of learning. The only way constructive thinking applies to teaching is to the teachers themselves, as they "construct" conceptions, beliefs, and models about how they teach and how students learn. The methods that work best, as identified from the synthesis of meta-analyses, lead to a very active, direct involvement, and high sense of agency, in the learning and teaching process. Such teaching leads to higher levels of learning, autonomy, and self-regulation on behalf of the learner (whether student or teacher).

Another contrast is between active and quality teaching strategies on the one hand, working conditions on the other; and the averages are $d = 0.68$ compared to $d = 0.08$ (Table 11.2). Educational *structures* and *working conditions* have mainly indirect or probabilistic effects on student learning (Barr & Dreeben, 1983). That is, the effects of these structures (e.g., tracking, class size, school mix, finances) are mediated by an array of instructional and peer processes. The presence or otherwise of these kinds of structures can change the *probability* that these processes occur (which then influences student learning). So, for example, reducing class size does not *directly* influence student learning. Rather, reducing class size merely increases the *probability* that the environment can be structured to capitalize on various teaching and peer influences (such as changing self-efficacy, enhancing academic reputations, and altering expectancies for success). Reducing class size rarely has a direct effect on outcomes. I noted in Chapter 6 the many instances when changing these class structures led to no change in the manner in which teachers configured interactions, no change in the nature of the curricula and instructional strategies used by teachers, and no change in the interactions among students (Hattie, 2007). Hence, the claim is that the school and class compositional effects, at best, change probabilities that successful learning conditions can be constructed. Any inspection of the policies of state or federal government, however, would show that there are few policies that directly affect teaching. Most policies are about structural issues such as resources, smaller class sizes, choice (or whom you want to send your children to school with), curriculum, and tests and high stakes assessment. It is rare to find a policy that relates to teaching.

Teaching and learning strategies

The messages in this book relate to the six signposts noted above rather than to endorsing particular methods. It may be very possible to use these signposts and other messages about

Table 11.2 Effect sizes from teaching or working conditions

Teaching	d	Working Conditions	d
Quality of teaching	0.77	Within-class grouping	0.28
Reciprocal teaching	0.74	Adding more finances	0.23
Teacher-student relationships	0.72	Reducing class size	0.21
Providing feedback	0.72	Ability grouping	0.11
Teaching student self-verbalization	0.67	Multi-grade/age classes	0.04
Meta-cognition strategies	0.67	Open vs. traditional classes	0.01
Direct Instruction	0.59	Summer vacation classes	−0.09
Mastery learning	0.57	Retention	−0.16
Average	0.68		0.08

what makes the best difference to teaching and learning to improve many of the methods that may not, on average, be above the $d = 0.40$ hinge–point. For example, team teaching has an overall very low effect ($d = 0.19$), but if team teaching is undertaken with more attention to the feedback from students to the teachers, from each teacher to the other(s), and using appropriately challenging goals and so on, then the effects may be much greater. It is less the "methods" per se, than the principles of effective teaching and learning that matter. Fullan, Hill, and Crévola (2006) have warned against what they term the "prescription trap". Such prescription prescribes "specificity to instruction with the promise of and in some cases the evidence of, increased student performance" (Fullan *et al.*, 2006, p. 9). They claim that prescriptions, like Direct Instruction, more often work in schools where teachers are poorly prepared, where there is a long history of failure, and where there is chaos and disorder. But the method is difficult to maintain, particularly as the students do not become independent learners when they are confronted with new tasks. This is not my reading of this literature, but the point made by Fullan *et al.* about "prescriptions" of a particular teaching package is well worth heeding. It is not a particular method, nor a particular script, that makes the difference; it is attending to personalizing the learning, getting greater precision about how students are progressing in this learning, and ensuring professional learning of the teachers about how and when to provide different or more effective strategies for teaching and learning.

These principles should not be confused with transmission teaching, or what Ben-Ari and Eliassy (2003) called the traditional frontal instructional strategy. This transmission strategy involves primarily teacher directed instruction of tasks to all the class, suggesting uniform ways of performing them. The level of instruction is adjusted to meet the needs of middle to high achieving students, and the pacing of instruction based on feedback from lower achieving students. "As a result, the entire student body suffers, so that fast-paced achievers are not sufficiently stimulated, whereas low achievers may feel frustrated; decreased motivation and off-task behaviors are likely to follow" (Ben-Ari & Eliassy, 2003, p. 145). This then leads to teachers conceiving their role to finding more engaging rather than more challenging tasks, more frontal talking, and asking questions they already know the answers to, lower self-regulation by students, and students learning that progress depends on the teacher-directed methods and tasks.

Instead, active teaching involves more backward design. Rather than starting from the text-books, favored lesson, and time honored activities, start backwards—from the desired results (success criteria related to learning intentions) (van Gog, Ericsson, Rikers, & Paas, 2005; Wiggins & McTighe, 2005). The aim is to help students to develop explicit cognitive schemas to thence self-regulate and teach themselves the knowledge and understanding, to realize why they need to invest deliberative practice, and then for teachers to evaluate the success of their chosen textbooks, favored lessons, methods, and activities to achieve these goals. The aim is to get students to learn the skills of teaching themselves—to self-regulate their learning.

Learning strategies clearly make a difference. Learning strategies enable progress through the three "worlds" of surface, deep, and constructed knowing and understanding. Such strategies assist in reducing cognitive load (e.g., over learning of surface information to assist in developing learning strategies and developing heuristics, Shah & Oppenheimer, 2008) and can assist in deliberative practice, which depends on and can lead to expectations of "can do", a thriving on challenge, deliberative practice, and an appreciation of feedback. For such deliberative practice to be effective there need to be various pre-conditions, of which the most important is that the practice must be embedded into a higher-order set of learnings—practice by itself without relating to more challenging goals is dull, repetitive, and counter to engaging students in learning. Other pre-conditions could include being aware of the learning intentions, goals, advance organizers, showing worked examples, and pre-practice briefs and orientation. Associated conditions can include the effectiveness of deliberative practice (including feedback), alternative learning strategies, and peer tutoring and assistance (see Cannon-Bowers, Rhodenizer, Salas, & Bowers, 1998).

A recent major review by Bransford, Brown, and Cocking (Bransford, Brown, & Cocking, 2000) of how people learn identified three major principles, which are consistent with the findings in these meta-analyses. The first was that students come into classes with preconceptions about how the world works, and teachers need to engage with this initial understanding otherwise the students may fail to grasp the new concepts and information. Second, for teachers to develop student competence, their students must have a deep foundation of factual knowledge, understand the ideas in the context of a conceptual framework, and organize knowledge in ways that facilitate retrieval and application. Third, a meta-cognitive approach to instruction can help students learn to take control of their own learning by defining learning goals and monitoring their progress in achieving them. The key questions are: "Where are we going?", "How are we going?", and "Where to next?".

There is also much consistency with the principles for "how children learn" outlined by Vosniadou (2001): learning requires the active involvement of the learner; learning is primarily a social activity; new knowledge is constructed on the basis of what is already understood and believed; we learn by employing effective and flexible strategies that help us to understand, reason, memorize, and solve problems; learners must know how to plan and monitor their learning, how to set their own learning goals, and how to correct errors; sometimes prior knowledge can stand in the way of learning something new, and students must learn how to solve internal inconsistencies and restructure existing conceptions when necessary; and learning takes considerable time and periods of practice to start building expertise in that area.

This means that teachers need to be "adaptive learning experts" (Bransford *et al.*, 2000; Hatano & Inagaki, 1986), who not only use many of the effective strategies outlined in these chapters but also have high levels of flexibility that allow them to innovate when routines are not enough. They can ascertain when students are not learning, know where to go next, can adapt resources and strategies to assist students meet worthwhile learning intentions, and can recreate or alter the classroom climate to attain these learning goals. "Adaptive experts also know how to continuously expand their expertise, restructuring their knowledge and competencies to meet new challenges" (Darling-Hammond, 2006, p. 11). They have the empathy required "to express concern and take the perspective of a student and it involves cognitive and affective domains of empathy" (Tettegah & Anderson, 2007, p. 50). This involves hearing "the intent and emotions behind what another says and reflecting them back by paraphrasing" (Woolfolk Hoy, 1998, p. 466). Further, teachers need to pay special attention to the way children define, describe, and interpret phenomena and problem-solving situations and begin to understand these experience from the unique perspectives of students (Gage & Berliner, 1998).

The presence of challenging learning intentions has multiple consequences. Students can be induced to invest greater effort, and invest more of their total capacity than under low demand conditions. Such intellectual engagement involves a desire to engage and understand the world, have an interest in a wide variety of things, and not be put off by complex and challenging problems (Goff & Ackerman, 1992). The rate of learning is a direct function of goal difficulty, as is the level of persistence over time to attain difficult goals. It certainly assists if the students are also committed to the goals (and of course they need to know them before committing to them), and doing "one for the Gipper" or "do your best" may help in a few situations but is rarely enough to sustain interest in learning.

Challenging goals increase the effectiveness and need for feedback. If the goal is easy, then feedback is not necessary, but if difficult, there is a greater need for feedback. As Locke and Latham wrote:

> Feedback tells people what is; goals tell them what is desirable. Feedback involves information; goals involve evaluation. Goals inform individuals as to what type or level of performance is to be attained so that they can direct and evaluate their actions and efforts accordingly. Feedback allows them to set reasonable goals and to track their performance in relating to their goals, so that adjustments in effort, direction, and even strategy can be made as needed. Goals and feedback can be considered a paradigm case of the joint effect of motivation and cognition controlling action.
>
> (Locke & Latham, 1990, p. 197)

Classroom contexts are diverse

None of the above should imply that classroom cultures are not critical. Throughout the chapters of this book, the importance of relationships, trust, caring, and safety have been emphasized, as has the importance of teachers choosing worthwhile and appropriately challenging tasks. This highlights the classroom climate and the ethics of making decisions about what is appropriately worthwhile. Evidence does not provide us with rules for action but only with hypotheses for intelligent problem solving, and for making inquiries about our ends of education (Dewey, 1938). Key questions that need to be explored include "What works best?", "Compared to what alternatives?", "When?", "For whom?", and "To what ends?". By itself, "What works?" can be barren (Glass, 1987). It is hoped that the messages in this book highlight the enormous power of the teacher, the amazing power of some of the methods they use, the critical nature of teachers' proficiencies in decision making and making judgments, the vital need to develop a caring relationship with and among students, and the constant need to ask what the desirable outcomes of any "teaching" are—all of which point to the moral dimensions of teaching.

Any recommendations about "what works best" invoke claims about cultural matters that influence and drive classroom interaction and discourse patterns. Consider, for example, the place of "talk" in classrooms. In Alexander's (2003) study of classrooms in many countries, he found that teachers in France, Russia, Britain, and America articulated and enacted three versions of values:

- Individualism (a view that knowledge and expression is personal and unique).
- Community (a view that learning and doing is collaborative in a climate of sharing and caring).
- Collectivism (learning together rather than in small groups, with common ideals and knowledge).

New Zealand classrooms, it would appear, align with Alexander's data on British and American classrooms where one-to-one monitoring, with private and often whispered exchanges, are prominent; in his terms, these classrooms share individualistic and community values. In British classrooms "mistakes" were "embarrassing" and teachers strove to minimize public "mistakes" to avoid the child "losing face". The emphasis tended to be on needing to express "correct" answers and on teacher approval. In contrast, in Russian classrooms problems and "mistakes" were in the public domain to be engaged with alongside "correct" or preferred responses. Collective and public discourse engagement dominated. Where Russian teachers highlighted their role in creating and sustaining dialogue and conversation, British and American teachers aimed to run their classrooms such that conversations were "shared" and seen as "democratic", where there were many teacher-managed sequences of "unchained two-part exchanges", where voices were allowed to be heard rather than creating a strategic expansion of meaning-making. Video studies from the PISA mathematics comparisons across seven countries showed much consistency in lessons, whereby students were asked to solve problems, usually alone or in whole-class groups (rarely in small peer groups), an extensive use of textbooks or work sheets, and teachers talking eight times more than students (Hiebert *et al.*, 2003).

My colleague, Alison Jones, remarked how fascinating it was that I could understand classrooms to the second decimal point. Her comment was a sobering reminder of the importance of the cultural context of the classroom, and what the students and teachers bring to the class from cultural and sociological perspectives. Reducing classrooms to an index number (effect size) could be considered akin to reducing society to unemployment indices, intelligence quotients, or currency rates. This debate about "index numbers" was plentiful in the 1950s and it is well worth remembering the cautions about their use (Guilford, 1954). The variability around the typical value of the effect size can be as informative (as the homework example showed), the unexplained variance is worth knowing as it limits the importance of the wanted variance (and thus highlights the importance of quality measures and research designs), the reference point is critical (as in the argument that the h-point of $d = 0.40$ is a more critical reference point than the usual $d = 0.00$), and the interactions with other variables can dramatically alter the conclusions (as in the learning styles example). Most important to any discussion on indices are "rival plausible hypotheses." The "story" told in this book about visible teaching and visible learning is one set of plausible hypotheses to fit a model to these data and the data to the model—there are certainly many more. Alternative plausible hypotheses are welcomed.

The concept of levels of understanding

As noted at the outset of this book, the focus has been on achievement—but there are many other worthwhile outcomes of schooling. It was surprising to find that, while achievement can be construed across a number of content areas, there was a struggle to find differential effects within the many meta-analyses related to subject. The subject chauvinism of so many high schools may be justified on the basis of the nature of the achievement desired, but good teaching and the most powerful influences on student outcomes seem to be similar across domains. Somewhat surprisingly there was no preponderance of evidence supporting the importance of subject or pedagogical content knowledge. The latter includes not only the content matter (the production view so often studied), and the pedagogical content knowledge (knowing how to teach), but also the teacher knowing when a learner does not comprehend, make mistakes, and so on (see Deng, 2007 for a most worthwhile debate on these issues). One type of content knowledge rarely explored may be more critical—teachers' conception of progress in the subject, knowledge of when to intervene, knowledge of learning theory, and openness to the experience of alternative ways to teach the content. These may be well worth deeper investigation.

In Chapter 3, it was proposed that achievement can be discussed at three levels: surface, deep, and conceptual or constructed understandings. There are also other critical achievement outcomes such as fluency, retention, application, endurance, and problem solving strategies. As well, there are various types of "thinking" and understanding that are critical to developing conceptual understanding: information gathering, building understanding, productive thinking, reflective thinking, strategic management of thinking, and evaluating thinking (Moseley *et al.*, 2004). The model used throughout this book was based on Biggs and Collis's SOLO (Biggs & Collis, 1982) model, and akin to the claims by Bereiter (2002) who used Popper's distinction between three worlds— the physical, the subjective, and the world of ideas. Thus there are multiple meanings of achievement, such as surface, deep, and construction of knowing. It is the case that most tests used in the studies in these meta-analyses are particularly effective at measuring surface features, somewhat effective at measuring deep learning, but rarely effective at measuring the construct representations that students build from their classroom experiences. Knowing is an activity, not a thing, in this third sense, and it is reciprocally constructed in the individual-environment-teacher interaction and not easily objectively defined by a one-off test (Barab & Roth, 2006). Many researchers are aiming to gain a better sense of how measurement would work at this Third World, and this is exciting (Gierl, Zheng, & Cui, 2008; Luecht, 2006; Luecht, Gierl, Tan, & Huff, 2006; Mislevy, 2007). A limitation of many of the results in this book is that they are more related to the surface and deep knowing and less to conceptual understanding.

The zero and hinge point

Even if the story developed to explain the findings is not convincing, the use of the "h-point" ($d = 0.40$) to demarcate the expected value of any innovations in schools is critical. Rather than using the zero point, which is hardly worthwhile, the standards for minimal success in schools should be more like $d = 0.40$. Any innovation, any teaching program, and all teachers should be aiming to demonstrate that the effects on student achievement should exceed $d = 0.40$. This h-point is not only attainable by many innovations but is the average, not the maximum, effect. Many students experience gains of $d = 0.40$, primarily because of excellent teaching; why cannot all?!

So often progress is cast in terms of activities and events and not in terms of increasingly more challenging demands from the underlying concepts in the curricula. Too often, progress is defined in terms of test scores, rather than in terms of proficiencies and competencies of what these test scores supposedly measure. So often in schools, students' achievement is compared to their achievement last year (or before a treatment) with the usual claims that "It worked", "I was happy with it", "I have passed on all the students to the next teacher who has never criticized my teaching of these students", "Yes, some students are not so able but that is more a function of what they brought to the class and not a consequence of my teaching". It turns out that these claims are among the weakest of all.

A fascinating question to ask teachers is: "What percentage of the students in your class go backwards in one year with you?". The concept of going backwards does not just mean those who genuinely fall behind compared with where they started (and they do exist), but also those who do not make the appropriately expected yearly gain for that year, and those who start falling behind or going backwards, compared to what they could achieve, because their teachers have low expectations. In our experience in a large city in the United States, we found 80 percent of students went backwards in some schools—in mathematics in grade 9, where they first encountered algebra, the students struggled to the point that they become disengaged from mathematics, developed beliefs about their lowered performance in mathematics, and often dropped out of mathematics (Hattie, *et al.* 2007). For many, this question of "going backwards" is rarely considered, and this reduces the chance of teachers looking for these students, and thus being in front of rather than behind the problems these students then encounter.

I would go further and claim those students who do not achieve at least a 0.40 improvement in a year are going backwards—they are with respect to those students who do exceed this average. The current standard, however, is more referenced to the zero point, and this is probably why it is difficult to find a below average teacher; why every teacher is considered effective; and why all can find evidence that they have "added value" (i.e., > $d = 0.0$). In addition, too often the claim is that the quality of teachers has little if any variance—one of the greatest myths of teaching is that all teachers are equal. There is an appreciable amount of variability in the effectiveness of teachers (this is demonstrated by, for example, there being so little between-school variance). We may indeed proclaim that all teachers are performing well; but not all students would agree.

If the criterion of success is achieving effect sizes greater than 0 then nearly all teachers could be considered effective. But this is a false comparison and assumes that any achievement is better than none! Students are more discriminating about teachers and, as noted in Chapter 7, Irving (2004) demonstrated that they are often accurate in their discrimination. Perhaps it is no wonder there is an increasing set of problems relating to student engagement. As Steinberg, Brown, and Dornbusch (1997) claimed, so many students "are physically present but psychologically absent" (p. 67). They also cited that about 40 percent of students are "going through the motions" and say they neither try hard nor pay attention. So many cut class and are truant, so many admit to cheating to get through, so many lose interest because they cannot keep up, and so many are bored by the lack of appropriate challenge. So many do not learn that ability is not enough, and that effort is critical. About half who drop out of school claim that classes were not interesting or inviting, and two-thirds claim that not one teacher was interested in their success in learning at school (Bridgeland, Dilulio, & Morison, 2006) All is not rosy with teachers, teaching, and schooling.

It is sobering to realize that we have a teaching cohort that is average, at best, in the eyes of most students. It is sobering to realize that each child will meet only a few teachers who they will consider to have a lasting and positive effect on them. It is sobering to realize that these teachers will be remembered not because they taught social studies or mathematics but because they cared about teaching the students their passion for their subject, gave students confidence in themselves as learners and as people, treated the student as a person, and instilled a love of learning of their subject(s).

But—teachers claim they are doing the best job they can. Principals attend to implementing the best programs they can. Systems aim to devise policies with the greatest effects they can. A major theme in this book is that these intentions—to introduce the best we know—often fall short because the decisions are inappropriately compared, they are inadequately evaluated relative to alternatives, they tend to be related to structural and working conditions and not to teaching strategies and conceptions, and they are evaluated using models that seek success (anything greater than 0 is too often considered successful) and ignore failures. To readdress this problem, a more effective barometer model of relative success has been suggested, such that educators can use this barometer to more effectively ask whether their influences of choice are successful.

What is special about "innovations"?

The typical teacher's effects are about $d = 0.15$ to $d = 0.35$. It is when there is an *intervention* or *innovation* that the effects can increase markedly beyond this. This does not mean that change for the sake of change is needed, as the question is "What are the attributes of innovations that lead to above average effects?". Innovation does not occur merely because it is something new or different. Innovation occurs when a teacher makes a deliberate action to introduce a different (not necessarily new) method of teaching, curriculum, or strategy that is different from what he or she is currently using. The aim is to encourage teachers to construe their teaching in terms of a series of related experimental designs, as then the benefits of the increased attention to outcomes can be accrued. Many of the innovations that appear near the top of the barometer of influence could be conceived as clinical treatments—for example, direct instruction, reciprocal teaching, reading recovery. It is fascinating to compare a meta-analysis of 150 articles concerning the critical change agents in therapy (Holly, 2002). The critical change agents (in order) are knowledge and skills; a plan of action; strategies to overcome setbacks; a high sense of confidence; monitoring progress; a commitment to achieve; social and environment support; and, finally, freedom, control, or choice.

There are various stages to innovation such as initiation, implementation, and evaluation—and most often the "innovation" changes during the implementation. The most critical attribute, however, is that when undertaking an innovation there is a heightened attention to its effects, to feedback to the teacher about the effects of the innovation, and to a focus on the learning intentions and success criteria from any innovation. Innovations carry the risk of failure; innovations help us free ourselves from the structured life and schemes that are created around us. It is this searching for that which is not working, and those students for whom you are not being successful; it is the heightened sense of seeking feedback, the increased attention to the principles of evaluation (discerning that of merit and worth), and the focus on how to seek the evidence of disconfirmation of the teaching so as to improve it that are important. In the search for how science progresses, Karl Popper (1963) claimed that a key was the search for disconfirmation (as so often we see evidence of our success everywhere). When teachers seek evidence that their teaching may *not* have been successful, then the desirable lens of success is in place. The teaching may not be successful for all students, for all parts of the learning intentions, towards all aspects of the success criteria; and even our goals, level of challenge, and processes of both effortful and conduct engagement may need to be constantly questioned.

Why can't they change?

"They" are teachers, policy makers, teacher educators, and oftentimes parents. I started this book by noting that there are many hundreds of solutions as to how to make learning as effective as possible. Teachers are willing to change, although they are probably sick of change. Most changes they experience are to structural and working conditions. But what if the changes were to their own conceptions of teaching and learning in the directions suggested in the book? This requires an openness to the idea, and a willingness to be wrong. That is, a willingness to seek a better alternative to what the teacher is currently doing by evaluating the effects of the change on student learning. Adopting any innovation means discontinuing the use of familiar practice.

The key issue is less how to change, but why we do not. In a fascinating study, Shermer (1997) researched why we tend (often passionately) to believe in ideas even when they do not work. He attributed this to an over reliance on anecdotes, dressing up one's beliefs in the trappings of science or pedagogical language and jargon, making bold claims, relying on one's past experiences rather than others' experiences, claiming that one's own experience is sufficient evidence, and circular reasoning (I am doing it so it must be ok). He also cited various psychological processes that lead to our accepting what we have done as the "best": the need for certainty, control, and simplicity; the seeking of examples to confirm our current methods; the lack of seeking evidence to demonstrate what is *not* working; the attributions of cause to the student when he or she is not learning but to the teacher when the student is learning; and a build up of an immunity to new or different ideas or ways of doing things (and some of these new ideas are indeed wacky). New and revolutionary ideas in teaching will tend to be "resisted rather than welcomed with open arms, because every successful teacher has a vested intellectual, social, and even financial interest in maintaining the status quo. If every revolutionary new idea were welcomed with open arms, utter chaos would be the result" (Cohen, 1985, p. 35). We have an uphill task.

In an analysis of teachers' accounts of classroom experience, Little (2007) noted that teaching was carried out largely out of sight and hearing of other teachers, and thus there was a tendency to rely on narrative accounts to construct a shared understanding. So often teachers depended on "war stories", personal experiences, and a reliance on their own experience to justify their personal preferences. If this swapping of war stories is the closest teachers come to professional conversations, the picture is bleak for the messages in this book about teachers needing to share evidence about their teaching with their colleagues. Little proceeds to show how these conversations could be more productive. The key is to develop teachers' accounts of classroom experience (and I would add "outcomes for the student and for the teachers") as a "useful resource in making sense of more aggregate patterns of student behavior and achievement, [as] … they constitute a resource for learning and instructional decision making anchored in the particularities of classes and curricula" (Little, 2007, p. 237). By questioning one another, eliciting replays and rehearsals, using evidence in these narratives, and offering and revising interpretations and explanations, teachers can build "general principles of practice anchored both in the conceptual frames they had acquired and in the particularities of their experience" (p. 231). But it takes instructional leadership and the creation of a safe and trusting environment to engage in such criticism, a commitment to share evidence about the effects of teaching, and an openness to new experiences. The message about "what works best" for students also applies to "what works best" for teachers.

The theme throughout the findings is that the lens the teacher uses is critical to success, and it needs to be subject to close scrutiny, considered from an "others" viewpoint, and checked for evidence as to whether all students are learning desirable curricular outcomes at a sufficient rate. If the teacher's lens can be changed to seeing learning through the eyes of students, this would be an excellent beginning. This involves teachers seeking countering evidence as to the effectiveness of their teaching, looking for errors in their thinking and knowledge, seeing how students build on prior knowledge and conceptions of learning, asking whether there is sufficient challenge and engagement in the learning, and understanding the strategies students are using when learning and confronting difficulties.

Another reason for the lack of change is the over reliance on teacher judgments rather than evidence. There has been a long history in many areas of placing more reliance on "professional judgments" than on evidence. This debate has percolated in the literature since Meehl's (1954) book *Clinical versus statistical prediction*, in which he found that in all but one of 20 studies, statistical methods were more accurate than or equally as accurate as the clinical methods. Clinical prediction refers to any judgment using informal or intuitive processes to make decisions. Aegisdottir *et al.* (2006) used 173 effect sizes from 69 studies published over the past 56 years, and concluded that there was a somewhat greater accuracy for statistical rather than clinical judgment methods. Similarly, Martin, Quinn, Ruger, and Kim (2004) found that statistical models could predict the outcomes of United States Supreme Court decisions more effectively than a set of independent predictions by 83 legal experts. The most fascinating aspect of this domain of research, which has been replicated many times, is that these findings have had little influence on clinical practice. Practitioners often lack familiarity with evaluation and statistical methods, are often incredulous about the evidence, more highly value interpersonal cues, believe that statistical methods dehumanize, believe that there is more individual variation than group consensus, and are subject to confirmatory biases such that they recall instances in which their predictions were correct but fail to recall those instances in which independent evidence was more accurate.

A further reason is that the contingencies in schools do not attend to student outcomes as much as the working and structural conditions of teaching and learning. Hanushek (1997) has argued that little rides on success or failure, and teachers measure success more in terms of satisfaction they receive from doing a "good job", and the potential approval or disapproval of parents and principals. There are few direct incentives related to student performance and so often, claimed Hanushek, teachers are "simply reacting to the incentive structure that does not emphasize student performance" (p. 305).

Many years ago, Alessi (1988) reviewed more than 5,000 children referred to school psychologists because they were failing at school. Not one located the problem as due to a poor instructional program, poor school practices, a poor teacher, or something to do with school. The problems were claimed, by the teachers, to be related to the home and located within the student. As Engelmann (1991) claimed "An arrogant system would conclude that all the problems were caused by defects in the children, none caused by defects in the system" (p. 298). Instead, Engelmann challenged teachers and schools to ask:

- Precisely where have you seen this practice installed so that it produces effective results?
- Precisely where have you trained teachers so they can uniformly perform within the guidelines of this new system?
- Where is the data that show you have achieved performance that is superior to that achieved by successful programs (not simply the administration's last unsuccessful attempt)?
- Where are your endorsements from historically successful teachers (those whose students outperform demographic predictions)?

The depressing news is that "the closer an innovation gets to the core of schooling, the less likely it is that it will influence teaching and learning on a large scale" (Elmore, 1996, p. 4) and reciprocally those further away from teaching and learning are more likely to become national policies. The problem is not general resistance or failure of schools to change, claimed Elmore, as schools are constantly changing. He located the resistance, as do I, with the conceptions of teaching and learning shared by teachers. "Just leave me alone to teach my way" is the common mantra. We see the increasing numbers of disengaged students as the problems of students or their families, or of society, not of teachers or schools. It is nigh on impossible to legislate changes to conceptions of teaching and learning—and this is where professional development becomes critical. So often the policy changes have little or no effect. The effect of a storm on the ocean is that the "surface is agitated and turbulent, while the ocean floor is calm and serene (if a bit murky). Policy churns dramatically, creating the appearance of major changes ... while deep below the surface, life goes on largely uninterrupted" (Cuban, 1984, p. 234).

A major area in educational research should be why we continue to believe many claims about "what works best" when there is no evidence for these claims (Yates, 2008). The most obvious is class size, as most seem to believe that reducing class size has a major influence on student outcomes. It does not, but listeners to recitations of the evidence so often suspend belief in such claims, and argue from the probabilistic claim—surely reduced class size would lead to many desirable benefits (more feedback, more individualization, better listening to students). Such probability may indeed be the case, but the fascinating question is why the benefits do not accrue when we reduce class sizes (Hattie, 2006). There are so many instances of teachers and parents believing claims when there is an enormous amount of contrary evidence.

If teachers have barely changed teaching methods over the past 200 years, if the predominant mode of classroom "action" is questioning, recall, and the acquisition of large chunks of surface knowledge, where engagement and busyness are sought, then recommendations about the nature of teaching outlined in this book to change this transmission model are unlikely to make a dent. It is so much easier to discuss and seek funds for working conditions—reduced class size, salary, buildings, lengthening school periods or days—or at appeasements to parents (computers, school choice, charter schools, more examinations). We have in education a long history of innovation but it rarely touches but a chosen few. The likelihood of the claims in this book having a major effect will depend more on whether schools can turn, as did much of medicine, to evidence-based claims. The request is for teachers and schools to enhance learning by at least $d = 0.30$ more than last year, and preferably more than $d = 0.40$ before any intervention is considered worthy of retaining or implementing. Putting this challenge squarely on the table of schools and government departments is the most likely mechanism for change.

The nature of evidence

"Evidence" is not neutral. Biesta (2007), for example, has criticized the evidence-based approach such as used in this book on a variety of grounds. First, she claimed that what counts as "effective" crucially depends on judgments about what is educationally desirable. Agreed, but achievement is among what is crucially desirable. Agreed also, there are other critical outcomes such as affective outcomes, persistence and engagement, physical outcomes, and social normative behaviors and skills.

Second, evidence-based methods appear to offer a *neutral* framework that can be applied across areas (such as education, or medicine) and central to the method is the idea of effective intervention. Education, however, is never neutral, and its fundamental purpose is intervention or behavior change. This is what makes teaching a moral profession, with such fundamental issues as: "Why teach this rather than that?", "How does one teach in defensible and ethical ways?". Snook (2003) has argued that teaching involves close personal relationships: between teachers and students, between one student and another, and between one teacher and another. Teaching involves a mission to change people in certain ways. This teaching occurs in schools in which there are hierarchies of control and rules to be obeyed. The "power" in these interactions and contests is very real. Hence, claimed Snook, teaching involves ethics in its aims, its methods and its relationships. He argued that the role of the teacher involved a respect for autonomy, and a respect for reason. He cautioned that "when we hear too much of the technicist teacher, the competent teacher, the skilled teacher, we should remind ourselves that education is essentially a moral enterprise and in that enterprise the ethical teacher has a central role to play" (p. 8).

It is the case that in this book only meta-analyses have been given the privilege of being considered. A review of non-meta-analytic studies could lead to a richer and more nuanced statement of the evidence. I leave this to others to review in this manner, although I have tried to incorporate aspects of these other views in my own summaries of each area. The emerging methodology of qualitative synthesis promises to add a richness to our literature (Au, 2007; Thorne, Jensen, Kearney, Noblit, & Sandelowski, 2004).

The costs as well as the benefits of innovations

It needs to be noted that evidence based on effect sizes alone could lead to poor decisions. For any set of choices, there are costs as well as benefits. The financial costs of the various interventions may need to be taken into account when making decisions about what works best. It may be that we can use some of the cheaper interventions if their effects are positive, and this may be preferable to using some of the more expensive interventions. The problem is that there are many kinds of costs in education: cost-minimization, where the intervention that is least costly is preferred; cost-benefit, where there is a trade-off of the costs and the benefits (in terms of effect size, ease of implementation, consistency with prior teacher practice, alignment with aims of the program); there is also average versus incremental cost-effectiveness, whereby the averages in this book can be considered relative to the average $d = 0.40$, or the incremental or marginal cost-effectiveness ratio, which is the cost of switching from what you are doing now to another treatment. Perhaps more critically, there are also the costs associated with lost opportunities for students to learn or engage in educational activities that truly make a difference—and which many of their fellow students are benefiting from! There are the "suffering costs" of being exposed to interventions with least effectiveness—no matter that the teacher has used the intervention before, how much the teacher enjoys it, or finds evidence to support it from anecdotal and rose-tinted perspectives (e.g., looking for the positives). As Hanushek (2005) and others have demonstrated repeatedly, we spend millions, if not trillions, of dollars investing in innovations, changes, and policies in education without a lot of evidence that this investment is making a difference to student outcomes. They may make a major difference to teachers' and students' working conditions, but not to the achievement outcomes.

The education dollar in the United States has risen a steady 3.5 percent annually over the past 100 years, and the majority (60 percent) is spent on instruction. Odden (2007) argued that increasing the portion spent on instruction will be unlikely to have an effect on student learning, Instead, the schools that doubled performance followed a set of similar strategies such as setting high goals (e.g., 90–95 percent of students to proficiency), analyzed student data to become deeply knowledgeable about the status of student performance in the schools, made use of formative assessments, collectively reviewed evidence on good instruction, used time more productively, and were led by leaders providing instructional leadership.

The cost-benefits of innovations are certainly relatively unexplored. At best, production functions have been used to estimate the relationships between the costs of varying school inputs and the educational outcomes (usually attempting to control for various background features). Such models rarely include the influence of nonpurchased and nonmonetary inputs, (such as peer effects, Hanushek, 1998; Subotnik & Walberg, 2006). In one of the more interesting models, Walberg (1980) proposed using the Cobb-Douglas (1928) production function as it includes many valuable properties. The marginal products of capital and labor are both positive, which means that adding more teaching leads to greater gains (to a point). There are, however, diminishing marginal returns, such that doubling learning time does not mean doubling learning outcomes, or adding more influences and methods may lead to fewer outcomes. Adding more into the teaching situation may not necessarily be as powerful in return as choosing the optimal smaller set of what leads more directly to learning outcomes. This model also highlights the importance of interaction effects or, more importantly, ensuring that the right combination of interventions exists in the right proportions to ensure an interaction effect.

It is unlikely that many of the effects reported in this book are additive—simply coupling together some of the effects does not mean that we can merely "add" the effects together and then expect these changes. There may be some cases where there could be additive effects (e.g., home plus school effects), and there were additive effects from the Adventure programs, but as was noted, this was unusual.

Comparisons of costs can also be most informative. For example, reducing class sizes from 30 to 15 produces an effect size between $d = 0.10$ to $d = 0.20$. Buckingham (2003) estimated that the effects of reducing the overall average ratio of New Zealand elementary and high school students by one student (to 18.4 and 14.5, respectively) was around NZ$113 million per year (it was acknowledged that this ratio is not the same as reducing class size). This cost only provides for one less student per class on average, it would be an ongoing commitment, and is not a one-off investment as it would account only for extra staffing costs. Other additional costs include building more and smaller classrooms, providing additional classroom resources and ongoing professional development, and finding the extra qualified teachers (see also Greenwald, Hedges, & Laine, 1996). Brewer, Krop, Gill, and Reichardt (1999) estimated the costs of reducing class sizes to 18 students in grades 1 to 3 in the United States would require hiring an additional 100,000 teachers at a cost of $US5–6 billion per year, and an additional 55 percent more classrooms. To reduce again from 18 to 15 students would cost a further $US5–6 billion per year. They estimate that this investment could, instead, be used to raise teachers' salaries by $20,000 per year (see also Blatchford, Goldstein, Martin, & Browne, 2002). The right question is to ask "What is the best use of this resource?" or "What could be accomplished if this amount is spent on other innovations with higher effects on student outcomes?".

In a study comparing the relative magnitude of achievement effects resulting from the introduction of textbooks, establishment of radio instruction, and lowering of mean class size, Jamison (1982; see also Heyneman, Jamison, & Montenegro, 1983) estimated that to obtain the achievement benefit gained from increasing the availability of textbooks at a constant increment of cost, schools must lower average class size from 40 to 10 students per teacher. Fuller concluded "in most situations, lowering class size with the intent of raising achievement is not an efficient strategy" (1987, p. 276). Similarly, Levin (1988) compared the cost-effectiveness of four reforms for raising student achievement at the elementary level in reading and mathematics: a longer school day, computer-assisted instruction, cross-age tutoring, and reduced class size. Cross-age tutoring was the most cost-effective. The longer school day and reducing class size by five students showed the smallest returns. Computer-assisted instruction was associated with gains in the middle of the range of results.

The aim of these analyses is not to suggest that the costs of improvement are cheap. As Pressley *et al.* (2006, also see Chapter 7) have noted, the costs of implementing the reforms that seem to have most power in influencing student learning are expensive. These costs are mostly in effort costs of the teachers and school leaders, and in the effort costs of the students. So often these are assumed to be free, or taken from the social and home life of teachers. Changing teachers' conceptions is not easy or cheap. Rogers (1962), for example, proposed an "S-shaped curve of learning" to explain such changes to teachers and teaching. His diffusion model of innovation suggests that initially only a few teachers (typically those open to change, more educated, who have a greater store of knowledge, are self confident, and are not so concerned with the norms of others) begin trying an innovation. Then when there is sufficient critical mix, many more begin to innovate, but it is hard to get acceptance from the final 20 percent plus. Teachers will not just move from not doing a new behavior to doing it; they go through decision phases. Rogers (2003) called these phases: awareness, knowledge, persuasion, decision, implementation, and confirmation. The boundaries between these are not precise, and not all occur, but his argument is that adoption is a process, not a discrete event. There are many ways to make teachers aware of new ideas, but to close the deal and to accelerate the process of innovation adoption there is often a need for interpersonal outreach. The social networks are powerful but often these are the biggest barrier to innovation. Rogers' claims echo the comments in Chapter 1 about Cuban and Tyack's (1995) study of teaching over the past 200 years: 85 percent are resistant to change what they claim works for them; ten percent are willing to change to be more efficient, and five percent are willing to try new innovations. Hence the moves to use accountability, government pressure, compulsion, and the stick rarely change the conceptions or lens of teachers. The costs to make the implementations recommended in this book are among the more expensive, but the claim is that they are the right ones on which to spend our resources.

Implications for policy

In many classrooms and schools, there is evidence of low effect sizes, reliance on poor methods and strategies, a dependence on "war stories" and anecdotes, and an agreement to tolerate different and sometimes poor teaching. We beseech these teachers to be evidence-based but so many government agencies and departments, teacher educators, and others are not evidence-based, and seem reluctant to accept evidence if it is contrary to current policies. There is a preference instead to make changes to structural and working conditions. The clients of schools include government ministers and parents (voters), and it is common to find parents who want schooling for their children better than they experienced. There is a preference for the teaching method that fits the latest ideology, and rarely are these methods assessed by evidence. As the evidence in this book shows, we can do damage in schools—and by this I do not just mean those teachers that have 0 or negative gains over the year: I mean those teachers and schools who do not aim and achieve the h-point ($+d$ = 0.40) effects that so many of our children *do* receive. The others are condemned to mediocrity and lesser opportunities. These high effects can be obtained—they *are* obtained by many teachers in our schools. This is no dream; it is a reality for many students. But for just as many students, the reality is the ordinary—the devil in this story is not the negative, criminal, and incompetent teacher, but the average, let's get through the curricula, behave, be busy, we are "all friends in here" teacher who has no idea of the damage he or she is doing.

Perhaps the most famous example of policy makers not using or being convinced by evidence was Project Follow Through, which started in the late 1960s. It was conducted over 10 years, involved over 72,000 students, and had more than 22 sponsors who worked in more than 180 sites to find the most effective education innovations to break the cycle of poverty through enhancing student learning. The innovations included Direct Instruction, whole language, open education, and developmentally appropriate practices (see Carnine, 2000; House, Glass, McLean, & Walker, 1978 for a history). The students in these programs were compared to control students (Stebbins, 1976; Stebbins, St. Pierre, Proper, Anderson, & Cerva, 1977). All but one program had close to zero effects (some had negative effects). Only Direct Instruction had positive effects on basic skills, on deeper comprehension measures, on social measures, and on affective measures. Meyer (1984) followed these students through to the end of their schooling, and those in the Direct Instruction compared to peers not in this program were twice as likely to graduate from high school, had higher scores on reading (d = 0.43) and mathematics (d = 0.28)—significant long-term differences in the Direct Instruction program effects. The outcome of this study, however, was not to support more implementation of Direct Instruction but to spend more resources on the methods that did not work but were preferred by educators. As Carnine (2000) commented, the romantic view of students discovering learning was more powerful than a method invented by a teacher that actually made a difference; a method that required an attention to detail, to deliberately changing behavior, and to teaching specific skills. The rejection of Direct Instruction in favor of Rousseian inspired methods "is a classic case of an immature profession, one that lacks a solid scientific base and has less respect for evidence than for opinion and ideology" (p. 12).

Consider the following quotation:

> It is hard to conceive of a less scientific enterprise among human endeavors. Virtually anything that could be thought up for treatment was tried out at one time or another, and, once tried, lasted decades or even centuries before being given up. It was, in retrospect, the most frivolous and irresponsible kind of human experimentation, based on nothing but trial and error, and usually resulting in precisely that sequence.
>
> (Thomas 1979, p. 159)

Thomas was referring to the study of medicine and noted how evidence-based medicine was the mechanism for driving out dogma, as dogma does not destroy itself. The evidence-based revolution came through repugnance and pressure from groups that were adversely affected by the poor quality of service in the medical profession. Maybe legal cases about equity in outcomes across various ethnic groups, poor service by teachers, clinical trials of new educational treatments, and a set of international standards and expectations for outcomes from schooling may be the catalyst for change and improvement in education.

More of the same is certainly not the answer. The key question is whether teaching can shift from an immature to a mature profession, from opinions to evidence, from subjective judgments and personal contact to critique of judgments.

Can all this be done?

Two studies make the case that the claims in this book can be attained. First, a recent set of studies provided a portrait of schools that produced high achievement even though they had previously failed. Pressley, Mohan, Raphael, and Fingeret (2007) used grounded theory to build a picture based on interviews, analyses of test scores, and an in-depth study of the school. They concluded

> effective elementary teachers, especially those effective in promoting reading and writing, tend to do the following: They devote much of their class time to academic activity, engaging most students consistently in activities that require them to think as they read, write, and discuss. Effective teachers do explicit teaching (and reteaching as needed) of skills, and this teaching included modeling and explaining skills, followed by guided student practice. That is, effective teachers show a strong balancing of skills instruction and holistic reading and writing activities. Teacher scaffolding and reteaching are salient, accounting for a large proportion of such teachers' effort. Effective teachers connect content learning (i.e., social studies, science, math) to reading and writing instruction. Effective teachers have high expectations and increase the academic demands on their students (i.e., consistently encouraging students to attempt slightly more advanced books and write slightly longer and more complex stories). From the first day of school, effective teachers communicate high expectations for students to self-regulate and take charge of their behavior and academic engagement.
> (Pressley, Mohan, Raphael, & Fingeret, 2007, p. 222)

Second, I was involved in an in-depth investigation of the classrooms of a large cohort of teachers who had passed or not passed National Board Certification (see Chapter 7). Our interest was to evaluate the differences between experienced experts and experienced non-experts. We visited many teachers' classrooms to observe and to collect many artifacts, transcripts of lessons, interviews, questionnaires, and student work (Smith, Baker, Hattie, & Bond, 2008). We choose two groups: half the teachers had passed (just above the cut-score) the rigorous assessment to become National Board Certified teachers and the others had applied but not passed (just below the cut-score; see NBPTS, 2003; http://www.nbpts.org /about/index.cfm). Each set of evidence was independently coded across 13 dimensions identified from a literature review of experienced experts and experienced non-experts. There were marked differences between the two groups, and a stepwise discriminant function analysis indicated that three of the dimensions (challenge, deep representation, and monitoring and feedback) were sufficient to distinguish between the two groups (Figure 11.2).

We coded all student work along the SOLO scale: 74 percent of student work samples in the classes of certified teachers were judged to reflect a level of deeper understanding and 26 percent reflected a more surface understanding. This compares with 29 percent of the work samples of non-certified teachers so classified as deep and 71 percent as surface. The effects of expertise are greatest on deep understanding (Figure 11.3).

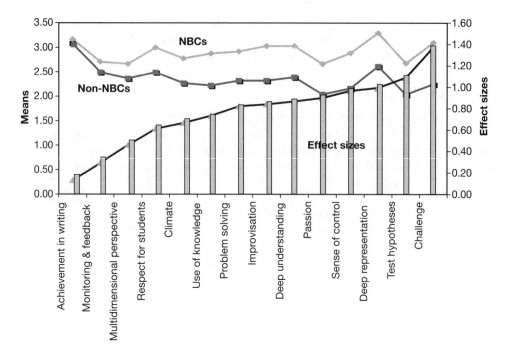

Figure 11.2 The means for the National Board certified teachers (NBCTs) and non-National Board certified teachers (non-NBCTs), and the effect size of the difference between these two groups

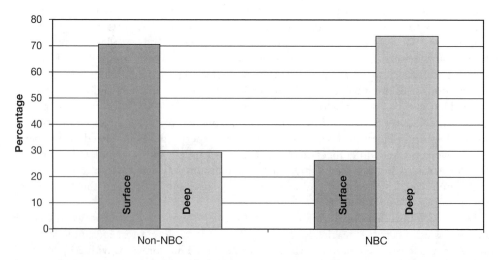

Figure 11.3 Percentage of student work from NBCTs and non-NBCTs classified as surface or deep learning

The conclusion seems clear: experienced experts possess pedagogical content knowledge that is more flexibly and innovatively employed in instruction; they are more able to improvise and to alter instruction in response to contextual features of the classroom situation; they understand at a deeper level the reasons for individual student success and failure on any given academic task; their understanding of students is such that they are more able to provide developmentally appropriate learning tasks that engage, challenge, and even intrigue students, without boring or overwhelming them; they are more able to anticipate and plan for difficulties students are likely to encounter with new concepts; they can more easily improvise when things do not run smoothly; they are more able to generate accurate hypotheses about the causes of student success and failure; and they bring a distinct passion to their work.

Over the years, working with the National Board teachers, as a teacher educator, as a parent, and as a student, I have seen teachers who are stunning, who live the principles outlined in this book, and demonstrably make a difference. They play the game according to the principles outlined here. They question themselves, they worry about which students are not making appropriate progress, they seek evidence of successes and gaps, and they seek help when they need it in their teaching. The future is one of hope as many of these teachers exist in our schools. They are often head-down in the school, not always picked by parents as the better teachers, but the students know and welcome being in their classes. The message in this book is one of hope for an excellent future for teachers and teaching, and based on not just my explanation for 146,000+ effect sizes but on the comfort that there are already many excellent teachers in our profession.

I leave the last words to my friend and colleague Paul Brock:

> Therefore, not just as a professional educator, but as a Dad, I want all future teachers of my Sophie and Millie to abide by three fundamental principles that I believe should underpin teaching and learning in every public school.
>
> First, to nurture and challenge my daughters' intellectual and imaginative capacities way out to horizons unsullied by self-fulfilling minimalist expectations. Don't patronize them with lowest-common-denominator blancmange masquerading as knowledge and learning; nor crush their love for learning through boring pedagogy. Don't bludgeon them with mindless 'busy work' and limit the exploration of the world of evolving knowledge merely to the tyranny of repetitively churned-out recycled worksheets. Ensure that there is legitimate progression of learning from one day, week, month, term and year to the next.
>
> Second, to care for Sophie and Millie with humanity and sensitivity, as developing human beings worthy of being taught with genuine respect, enlightened discipline and imaginative flair.
>
> And third, please strive to maximize their potential for later schooling, post-school education, training and employment and for the quality of life itself so that they can contribute to and enjoy the fruits of living within an Australian society that is fair, just, tolerant, honorable, knowledgeable, prosperous and happy.
>
> When all is said and done, surely this is what every parent and every student should be able to expect of school education: not only as delivered within every public school in NSW, but within every school not only in Australia but throughout the entire world.
>
> (Brock, P., 2004, pp. 250–251)

Appendix A
The meta-analyses by topic

No.	Domain	Author	Year	No. studies	Total no.	No. effects	Mean	se	CLE	Variable
Student										
		Prior achievement								
1	Student	Boulanger	1981	34	—	62	1.09	0.039	77%	Ability related to science learning
2	Student	Hattie & Hansford	1983	72	—	503	1.19	—	84%	Intelligence and achievement
3	Student	Samson, Graue, Weinstein, & Walberg	1984	35	—	209	0.31	—	22%	Academic and occupational performance
4	Student	Kavale & Nye	1985	1077	—	268	0.68	—	48%	Ability component in predicting special ed students
5	Student	Cohen	1984	108	—	108	0.37	0.015	26%	College grades and adult achievement
6	Student	McLinden	1988c	47	2,220	47	0.61	—	43%	Blind vs. sighted on spatial tasks
7	Student	Bretz	1989	39	26,816	39	0.39	—	28%	College to adult success
8	Student	Schuler, Funke, & Baron-Boldt	1990	63	29,422	63	1.02	—	72%	High school grades to university grades
9	Student	Lapadat	1991	33	825	275	0.52	0.060	37%	Language ability of special ed students on achievement
10	Student	Rush	1992	100	236,772	404	0.48	—	34%	Differences in at-risk students
11	Student	Piburn	1993	44	—	186	0.80	—	57%	Prior ability on science achievement
12	Student	La Paro & Pianta	2000	70	7,243	63	1.02	0.370	72%	Preschool to first years of schooling
13	Student	Ernst	2001	23	1,733	32	0.41	—	29%	Early cognition and school achievement
14	Student	Kuncel, Hezlett & Ones	2001	1753	82,659	6589	0.52	0.005	37%	High school grades to university grades
15	Student	Murphy & Alexander	2006	20	—	50	0.80	—	57%	Knowledge, beliefs and interests on conceptual change
16	Student	Trapmann, Hell, Weigand, & Schuler	2007	83	—	83	0.90	—	64%	High school grades to university grades
17	Student	Duncan et al.	2007	6	—	228	0.35	—	24%	Preschool to first years of schooling
		Piagetian programs								
18	Student	Jordan & Brownlee	1981	51	6,000	65	1.28	—	91%	Piagetian tasks and reading and math
		Self-reported grades								
19	Student	Mabe & West	1982	35	13,565	35	0.93	—	65%	Self-evaluation of achievement
20	Student	Falchikov & Boud	1989	57	5,332	96	0.47	—	33%	Self-assessment in college
21	Student	Ross	1998	11	—	60	1.63	—	115%	Self-assessment in second language

Appendix A continues

Appendix A continued

No.	Domain	Author	Year	No. studies	Total no.	No. effects	Mean	se	CLE	Variable
22	Student	Falchikov & Goldfinch	2000	48	4,271	56	1.91	—	135%	Self-assessment in college
23	Student	Kuncel, Crede, & Thomas	2005	29	56,265	29	3.10	0.026	219%	Self-assessment of college GPA
24	Student	Kuncel, Crede, & Thomas	2005	29	—	29	0.60	0.034	42%	Differences between self and recorded grades

Creativity

| 25 | Student | Kim | 2005 | 21 | 45,880 | 447 | 0.35 | — | 25% | Relationship between creativity and achievement |

Attitudes and dispositions

Personality

26	Student	Hattie & Hansford	1983	115	—	1197	0.07	0.007	5%	Personality on achievement
27	Student	O'Connor & Paunonen	2007	23	—	108	0.10	—	7%	Big five and achievement
28	Student	Boyd	2007	50	—	130	0.06	—	4%	Extraversion on achievement
29	Student	Lyubomirsky, King, & Diener	2005	46	—	46	0.54	—	38%	Happiness on achievement

Self-concept

30	Student	Hansford & Hattie	1982	128	202,823	1136	0.41	—	29%	Self-concept
31	Student	Muller, Gullung, & Bocci	1988	38		838	0.36	—	25%	Self-concept
32	Student	Holden, Moncher, Schinke, & Barker	1990	25	—	26	0.37	—	26%	Self-efficacy
33	Student	Multon, Brown, & Lent	1991	36	4,998	38	0.76	—	54%	Self-efficacy
34	Student	Wickline	2003	41	48,038	41	0.35	—	24%	Self-concept
35	Student	Valentine, DuBois, & Cooper	2004	56	50,000	34	0.32	0.010	23%	Self-concept

Motivation

36	Student	Uguroglu & Walberg	1979	40	36,946	232	0.34	0.070	24%	Motivation
37	Student	Findley & Cooper	1983	98	15,285	275	0.36	0.039	25%	Internal locus of control
38	Student	Whitley & Frieze	1985	25	—	25	0.56	—	40%	Success vs. failure attributions
39	Student	Ross	1988	65	—	65	0.73	0.093	52%	Controlling one's study
40	Student	Schiefee, Krapp, & Schreyer	1993	21	—	121	0.65	0.02	46%	Interest and achievement
41	Student	Kalechstein & Nowicki	1997	78	58,142	261	0.23	0.010	16%	Internal locus of control

Concentration/persistence/engagement

42	Student	Feltz & Landers	1983	60	1,766	146	0.48	—	34%	Mental practice on motor skill learning
43	Student	Datta & Narayanan	1989	23	—	45	0.61	—	43%	Concentration on achievement
44	Student	Kumar	1991	16	4,518	102	1.09	0.035	77%	Engagement in science
45	Student	Cooper & Dorr	1995	19	6,684	26	0.21	0.030	15%	Race on need for achievement
46	Student	Mikolashek	2004	28	—	268	0.03	—	2%	Resilience for at risk students

No.	Domain	Author	Year	No. studies	Total no.	No. effects	Mean	se	CLE	Variable
Reducing anxiety										
47	Student	Hembree	1988	46	28,276	176	0.22	—	16%	Reduced test anxiety
48	Student	Seipp	1991	26	36,626	156	0.43	—	30%	Reduction of anxiety on achievement
49	Student	Bourhis & Allen	1992	23	—	728	0.37	—	26%	Lack of communication apprehension
50	Student	Ma	1999	26	18,279	37	0.56	—	40%	Reducing anxiety towards math and achievement
Attitude to mathematics/science										
51	Student	Willson	1983	43	638,333	280	0.32	—	23%	Attitudes to science
52	Student	Bradford	1990	102	—	241	0.29	—	20%	Attitude to mathematics
53	Student	Ma & Kishor	1997	143	94,661	143	0.47	—	33%	Attitude to mathematics
Physical influences										
Pre-term birth weight										
54	Student	Bhutta, Cleves, Casey, Cradock, & Anand	2002	15	3,276	15	0.73	—	52%	Full vs. pre-term birth weight
55	Student	Corbett & Drewett	2004	31	1,213	121	0.34	—	24%	Thriving and failure to thrive in infancy
Illness										
56	Student	Sharpe & Rossiter	2002	7	—	7	0.20	—	14%	Chronic illness (lack of) on achievement
57	Student	Schatz	2003	6	—	6	0.25	—	18%	Non vs. sickle cell disease on achievement
Diet										
58	Student	Kavale & Forness	1983	23	—	125	0.12	0.037	8%	Reduction of artificial food colors
Exercise/relaxation										
59	Student	Moon, Render, & Pendley	1985	20	—	36	0.16	0.088	11%	Relaxation and achievement
60	Student	Etnier, Salazar, Landers, Petruzzelo, Han, & Nowell	1997	134	—	1260	0.25	0.019	18%	Physical fitness and exercise
61	Student	Sibley & Etnier	2002	36	—	104	0.36	—	25%	Physical activity on achievement
62	Student	Etnier, Nowell, Landers, & Sibley	2006	37	1,306	571	0.34	0.013	24%	Aerobic fitness and cognitive performance
Drugs										
63	Student	Ottenbacher & Cooper	1983	61	1,972	61	0.47	0.038	33%	Stimulant medication on achievement
64	Student	Kavale	1982	135	5,300	984	0.58	0.019	41%	Stimulant drug treatment for hyperactivity
65	Student	Thurber & Walker	1983	20	1,219	20	0.23	0.038	16%	Stimulant medication on achievement
66	Student	Kavale & Nye	1984	70	—	401	0.30	0.038	21%	Drug treatment
67	Student	Crenshaw	1997	36	1,030	36	0.29	0.042	21%	Drugs treatment (ADHD) on cognitive outcomes

Appendix A continues

Appendix A continued

No.	Domain	Author	Year	No. studies	Total no.	No. effects	Mean	se	CLE	Variable
68	Student	DuPaul & Ekert	1997	63	637	63	0.31	0.038	22%	School based interventions on ADHD
69	Student	Purdie, Hattie & Carroll	2002	74	2,188	266	0.28	0.038	20%	Drugs treatment (ADHD) on cognitive outcomes
70	Student	Snead	2005	8	815	8	0.20	—	14%	Beh intervention, medication on achievement
Gender – achievement (Male – Female)										
71	Student	Hattie & Hansford	1980	72	—	503	-0.02	—	-1%	Gender and achievement
72	Student	Hyde	1981	16	65,193	16	0.43	—	30%	Gender and cognitive achievement
73	Student	Hyde	1981	27	68,899	27	-0.24	—	-17%	Reading and gender
74	Student	Kahl, Fleming & Malone	1982	169	—	31	0.12	—	8%	Pre-college science and achievement
75	Student	Steinkamp & Maehr	1983	83	—	107	0.19	—	13%	Gender differences in science
76	Student	Freeman	1984	35	—	35	0.09	0.050	6%	Gender differences in mathematics
77	Student	Meehan	1984	53	—	160	0.14	—	10%	Formal operations and gender
78	Student	Johnson, E	1984	9	—	9	0.45	—	32%	Gender in problem solving
79	Student	Linn & Peterson	1985	172	—	263	0.40	—	28%	Spatial achievement and gender
80	Student	Becker & Chang	1986	42	—	42	0.16	—	11%	Science and gender
81	Student	Tohidi, Steinkamp & Maehr	1986	70	—	70	0.32	—	23%	Cognitive functioning and gender
82	Student	Born, Bleichrodt & Van der Flier	1987	17	—	772	0.08	—	6%	Gender in intelligence
83	Student	Hyde & Linn	1988	165	1,418,899	165	-0.11	—	-8%	Gender differences on verbal achievement
84	Student	Friedman	1989	98	227,879	98	0.02	0.016	1%	Math and gender
85	Student	Hines	1989	30	—	260	0.01	—	1%	Math and gender
86	Student	Becker	1989	29	17,603	67	0.16	0.020	11%	Gender differences in science
87	Student	Stumpf & Klieme	1989	18	171,824	18	0.48	—	34%	Spatial achievement and gender
88	Student	Hyde, Fennema & Lamon	1990	100	3,217,489	259	0.20	—	14%	Gender and cognitive achievement
89	Student	Cohn	1991	65	9,000	113	-0.61	—	-43%	Gender on ego enhancement
90	Student	Frost, Hyde & Fennema	1994	100	—	254	0.15	—	11%	Math and gender
91	Student	DeBaz	1994	67	7,026	9	0.26	—	18%	Gender and achievement
92	Student	Schram	1996	13	4,134	18	-0.08	—	-6%	Applied statistics and gender
93	Student	Yang	1997	25	—	25	-0.34	0.054	-24%	Math and gender
94	Student	Lietz	2006	139	—	139	-0.19	—	-13%	Reading and gender
Gender – Attitudes										
95	Student	Cooper, Burger & Good	1980	10	219	10	-0.10	—	-7%	Control beliefs and gender
96	Student	Haladyna & Shaughnessy	1982	49	—	17	0.36	—	25%	Science and gender
97	Student	Hyde, Fenemma, Ryan, Frost & Hopp	1990	70	63,229	126	0.15	—	11%	Math and gender

No.	Domain	Author	Year	No. studies	Total no.	No. effects	Mean	se	CLE	Variable
98	Student	DeBaz	1994	67	89,740	25	0.30	0.027	21%	Science and gender
99	Student	Weinburgh	1995	18	6,753	18	0.20	—	14%	Science and gender
100	Student	Whitley	1997	82	40,491	104	0.23	—	16%	Computers and gender
101	Student	Etsey & Snetzler	1998	96	30,490	304	-0.01	—	-1%	Math and gender

Gender – Leadership

No.	Domain	Author	Year	No. studies	Total no.	No. effects	Mean	se	CLE	Variable
102	Student	Wood	1987	52	3,099	19	0.38	—	27%	Group performance and gender
103	Student	Wood	1987	52	3,099	45	0.39	—	28%	Group performance and gender
104	Student	Eagly & Johnson	1990	370	32,560	370	-0.11	—	-8%	Leadership and gender
105	Student	Pantili, Williams & Fortune	1991	10	—	47	0.18	—	13%	Assessment centers and gender
106	Student	Eagly, Karau & Johnson	1992	50	8,375	125	-0.01	—	-1%	Principal leadership and gender

Gender – Motor outcomes

No.	Domain	Author	Year	No. studies	Total no.	No. effects	Mean	se	CLE	Variable
107	Student	Eaton & Enns	1986	90	8,636	127	0.49	0.040	35%	Motor activity and gender
108	Student	Thomas & French	1985	64	100,195	445	0.62	—	44%	Motor activity and gender

Gender – Behavior outcomes

No.	Domain	Author	Year	No. studies	Total no.	No. effects	Mean	se	CLE	Variable
109	Student	Gaub & Carlson	1997	18	—	17	0.13	—	9%	ADHD and gender
110	Student	Hall	1980	42	—	75	-0.32	—	-23%	Emotional cues and gender
111	Student	Lytton & Romney	1991	172	—	717	-0.02	—	-1%	Socialization and gender

Ethnicity

No.	Domain	Author	Year	No. studies	Total no.	No. effects	Mean	se	CLE	Variable
112	Student	Allen, Bradford, Grimes, Cooper, & Howard	1999	9	2661	9	0.32	0.003	23%	Positive view of own ethnicity

Pre-school interventions

Early intervention

No.	Domain	Author	Year	No. studies	Total no.	No. effects	Mean	se	CLE	Variable
113	Student	Exceptional Child Center	1983	156	—	1436	0.43	0.023	30%	Handicapped and disadvantaged students
114	Student	Harrell	1983	71	—	449	0.42	—	30%	Head start programs
115	Student	Collins	1984	67	—	271	0.27	—	19%	Head start programs
116	Student	Horn & Packard	1985	58	59,998	138	0.90	—	64%	Early prediction of learning problems
117	Student	Casto & White	1985	126	—	663	0.43	0.040	30%	At risk children
118	Student	Ottenbacher & Petersen	1985	38	1,544	118	0.97	0.083	69%	Early intervention for disabled students
119	Student	White & Casto	1985	326	—	2266	0.52	—	37%	Handicapped – long term
120	Student	White & Casto	1985	162	—	1665	0.44	0.026	31%	Handicapped and disadvantaged
121	Student	McKey, Condelli, Ganson, Barrett, McConkey, & Plantz	1985	72	—	17	0.31	—	22%	Head start programs

Appendix A continues

Appendix A continued

No.	Domain	Author	Year	No. studies	Total no.	No. effects	Mean	se	CLE	Variable
122	Student	Casto & Mastropieri	1986	74	—	215	0.68	0.050	48%	Handicapped
123	Student	Murphy	1991	150	—	104	0.46	—	33%	Sesame Street
124	Student	Innocenti & White	1993	155	—	797	0.60	—	42%	Early intervention
125	Student	Kim, Innocenti, & Kim	1996	80	—	659	0.25	0.024	18%	Early intervention
126	Student	Mentore	1999	77	16,888	319	0.48	0.040	34%	Early interventions
127	Student	Crosby	2004	44	2,267	196	0.14	—	10%	Early intervention with disabled or delayed children
128	Student	Bakermans-Kranenburg, van Ijzendoorn, & Bradley	2005	48	7,350	56	0.20	—	14%	Early intervention in the home
	Pre school programs									
129	Student	Snyder & Sheehan	1983	8	—	182	0.48	—	34%	Preschool programs
130	Student	Goldring & Presbrey	1986	11	1,267	11	0.25	—	18%	Preschool programs
131	Student	Applegate	1986	13	—	114	0.42	0.094	30%	Day care
132	Student	Lewis & Vosburgh	1988	65	3,194	444	0.43	—	31%	Kindergarten based
133	Student	Nelson	1994	21	—	135	0.42	0.037	30%	Parent ed programs
134	Student	Fusaro	1997	23	—	23	1.43	—	101%	Full vs. half day kindergarten
135	Student	Gilliam & Zigler	2000	13	—	22	0.17	—	12%	Preschool across 13 states
136	Student	Violato & Russell	2000	101	32,271	101	0.14	—	10%	Day vs. home care
137	Student	Jones	2002	22	—	22	0.56	—	40%	All day kindergarten
138	Student	Nelson, Westhues, & Macleod	2003	34	—	721	0.53	—	37%	Preschool prevention programs
139	Student	Timmerman	2006	47	7,800	47	0.10	—	7%	Family vs. day care
Home										
	Socioeconomic status									
140	Home	White	1982	101	—	620	0.66	—	47%	Socioeconomic status and achievement
141	Home	Fleming & Malone	1983	273	—	21	0.50	—	35%	Student characteristics and science achievement
142	Home	DeBaz	1994	67	47,001	9	0.50	—	35%	Availability of resources in the home
143	Home	Sirin	2005	58	129,914	307	0.61	0.016	43%	Relation between SES and achievement
	Welfare policies									
144	Home	Gennetian, Duncan, Knox, Clark-Kauffman, & London	2004	8	—	8	-0.12	0.030	-8%	Families receiving welfare on school achievement
	Family structure									
145	Home	Falbo & Polit	1986	115	—	115	0.17	0.023	12%	Only vs. non-only children
146	Home	Salzman	1987	137	9,955,118	273	0.26	—	18%	Father present vs. father absent

No.	Domain	Author	Year	No. studies	Total no.	No. effects	Mean	se	CLE	Variable
147	Home	Amato & Keith	1991	39	—	39	0.16	—	11%	Both parents vs. divorced families
148	Home	Wierzbicki	1993	66	—	31	0.13	0.041	9%	Adoptee vs. nonadoptive achievement
149	Home	Kunz	1995	65	—	65	0.30	—	21%	Both parents vs. divorced families
150	Home	Amato & Gilbreth	1999	63	14,471	52	0.12	—	9%	Resident vs. non resident fathers
151	Home	Amato	2001	67	—	177	0.29	—	21%	Resident vs. non resident fathers
152	Home	Reifman, Villa, Amans, Rethinam, & Telesca	2001	35	—	7	0.16	—	11%	Children of intact vs. divorced parents
153	Home	Pong, Dronkers, Hampden-Thompsom	2003	22	—	22	0.13	—	9%	Single vs. two-parent family on math and science
154	Home	vanIjzendoorn, Juffer, Poelhuis	2005	55	—	52	0.19	—	13%	Nonadopted vs. adopted children
155	Home	Goldberg, Prause, Lucas-Thompson, & Himsel	2008	68	178,323	770	0.06	—	5%	Maternal employment on achievement
156	Home	Jeynes	2007	61	—	78	0.22	—	16%	Intact vs. parental re-marriage on achievement

Home environment

No.	Domain	Author	Year	No. studies	Total no.	No. effects	Mean	se	CLE	Variable
157	Home	Iverson & Walberg	1982	18	5,831	92	0.80	—	56%	Home environment and school learning
158	Home	Gottfried	1984	17	—	17	0.34	—	24%	Home environment and early achievement

Television

No.	Domain	Author	Year	No. studies	Total no.	No. effects	Mean	se	CLE	Variable
159	Home	Williams, Haertel, Haertel, & Walberg	1982	23	—	227	-0.12	—	-8%	Leisure time television
160	Home	Neuman	1986	8	—	8	-0.15	—	-11%	TV on reading
161	Home	Razel	2001	6	1,022,000	305	-0.26	—	-18%	TV on achievement

Parental involvement

No.	Domain	Author	Year	No. studies	Total no.	No. effects	Mean	se	CLE	Variable
162	Home	Graue, Weinstein, & Walberg	1983	29	—	29	0.75	0.178	53%	Effects of home instruction
163	Home	Casto & Lewis	1984	76	—	754	0.41	—	29%	Parent involvement in infant and preschool programs
164	Home	Crimm	1992	57	—	57	0.39	—	28%	Parent involvement and achievement
165	Home	White, Taylor, & Moss	1992	205	—	205	0.13	—	9%	Moderate to extensive parent involvement
166	Home	Rosenzweig	2000	34	—	474	0.31	—	22%	Parent involvement and achievement
167	Home	Fan & Chen	2001	92	—	92	0.52	—	37%	Parent involvement and achievement
168	Home	Comfort	2004	94	—	43	0.56	—	40%	Parent training on cognitive/language
169	Home	Jeynes	2005	41	20,000	41	0.74	—	52%	Parental involvement in urban areas – primary
170	Home	Senechal	2006	14	—	14	0.68	—	48%	Family involvement in reading
171	Home	Earhart, Ramirez, Carlson, & Beretvas	2006	22	—	22	0.70	—	49%	Parent involvement and achievement
172	Home	Jeynes	2007	52	300,000	52	0.38	—	27%	Parental involvement in urban areas – high

Appendix A continues

Appendix A continued

No.	Domain	Author	Year	No. studies	Total no.	No. effects	Mean	se	CLE	Variable
Home visiting										
173	Home	Black	1996	11	—	11	0.39	—	28%	Home visiting of learning disabled
174	Home	Sweet & Applebaum	2004	60	—	41	0.18	—	13%	Home visiting
School										
	School effects									
175	School	Scheerens & Bosker	1997	168	—	168	0.48	0.019	34%	School effects
	Finances									
176	School	Childs & Shakeshaft	1986	45	2,205,319	417	0.00	—	0%	Educational expenditure
177	School	Murdock	1987	46	71,698	46	0.06	—	4%	Financial aid on persistence at college
178	School	Hedges, Laine, & Greenwald	1994	38	—	38	0.70	—	49%	Effect of $500 per student on achievement
179	School	Greenwald, Hedges, & Laine	1996	60	—	180	0.14	—	10%	Effect of $500 per student on achievement
Types of schools										
	Charter schools									
180	School	Miron & Nelson	2001	18	—	18	0.20	—	14%	Charter schools
	Religious Schools									
181	School	Jeynes	2002	15	54,060	15	0.25	—	18%	Religious vs. public schooling on achievement
182	School	Jeynes	2004	56	—	56	0.20	—	14%	Religious commitment on achievement
	Summer school									
183	School	Cooper, Charlton, Valentine, Muhlenbruck, & Borman	2000	41	26,500	385	0.28	—	20%	Remedial summer programs
184	School	Cooper, Charlton, Valentine, Muhlenbruck, & Borman	2000	7	2,200	60	0.23	—	16%	Acceleration summer programs
185	School	Kim	2002	57	—	155	0.17	—	12%	Academic summer programs
	Desegregation									
186	School	Krol	1980	71	—	71	0.16	0.049	11%	Desegregated vs. segregated classes in US
187	School	McEvoy	1982	29	—	29	0.20	—	14%	Desegregated vs. segregated classes in US
188	School	Miller & Carlson	1982	19	—	34	0.19	0.028	14%	Desegregated vs. segregated classes in US
189	School	Walberg	1982	19	—	19	0.88	—	62%	Desegregated vs. segregated classes in US
190	School	Armor	1983	19	—	51	0.05	—	4%	Desegregated vs. segregated classes in US
191	School	Bryant	1983	31	—	31	0.45	0.122	32%	Desegregated vs. segregated classes in US
192	School	Crain & Mahard	1983	93	—	323	0.08	0.013	6%	Desegregated vs. segregated classes in US

No.	Domain	Author	Year	No. studies	Total no.	No. effects	Mean	se	CLE	Variable
193	School	Wortman	1983	31	—	98	0.45	0.089	32%	Desegregated vs. segregated classes in US
194	School	Stephan	1983	19	—	63	0.15	—	11%	Desegregated vs. segregated classes in US
195	School	Goldring & Addi	1989	4	6,731	4	0.15	—	11%	Desegregated vs. segregated classes in Israel
College halls of residence										
196	School	Blimling	1999	10	11,581	23	0.05	—	3%	College halls of residence
School compositional effects										
School size										
197	School	Stekelenburg	1991	21	—	120	0.43	—	30%	High school size on achievement
Summer vacation										
198	School	Cooper, Nye, Charlton, Lindsay, & Greathouse	1996	39	—	62	-0.09	—	-6%	Summer vacation on achievement
Mobility										
199	School	Jones	1989	93	51,057	141	-0.50	—	-35%	Mobility and achievement
200	School	Mehana	1997	26	2,889	45	-0.24	0.005	-17%	Mobility and achievement
201	School	Diaz	1992	62	131,689	354	-0.28	—	-20%	Moving from community college to 4-yr institutions
Out of school experiences										
202	School	Lauer, Akiba, Wilkerson, Apthorp, Snow, & Martin-Glenn	2006	30	15,277	24	0.10	—	7%	After school programs on reading and math
203	School	Lauer, Akiba, Wilkerson, Apthorp, Snow, & Martin-Glenn	2006	22	15,277	26	0.07	—	5%	Summer school programs on reading and math
Principals/school leaders										
204	School	Neuman, Edwards, & Raju	1989	126	—	238	0.159	0.034	2%	Organizational development interventions
205	School	Pantili, Williams, & Fortune	1991	32	10,773	32	0.41	—	29%	Assessment ratings of principals and job performance
206	School	Gasper	1992	22	—	25	0.81	—	57%	Transformational leadership
207	School	Bosker & Witziers	1995	21	—	65	0.04	—	3%	Principals on student achievement
208	School	Brown	2001	38	—	339	0.57	0.028	40%	Leadership on student achievement
209	School	Wiseman	2002	59	16,326	59	-0.26	—	-18%	Instructional management on achievement
210	School	Witziers, Bosker, & Kruger	2003	61	—	377	0.02	—	1%	Principals on student achievement
211	School	Waters, Marzano, & McNulty	2003	70	1,100,000	70	0.25	—	18%	Principals on student achievement
212	School	Waters & Marzano	2006	27	—	27	0.49	—	35%	District superintendents on achievement

Appendix A continues

Appendix A continued

No.	Domain	Author	Year	No. studies	Total no.	No. effects	Mean	se	CLE	Variable
213	School	Chin	2007	21	6,558	11	1.12	—	79%	Transformational leadership
214	School	Robinson, Lloyd, & Rowe	2008	14	—	14	0.39	—	28%	Principals on student achievement

Classroom compositional effects

Class size

No.	Domain	Author	Year	No. studies	Total no.	No. effects	Mean	se	CLE	Variable
215	School	Glass & Smith	1979	77	520,899	725	0.09	—	6%	Class size
216	School	McGiverin et al.	1999	10	—	24	0.34	—	24%	Class size
217	School	Goldstein, Yang, Omar, & Thompson	2000	9	29,440	36	0.20	—	14%	Class size

Open vs. traditional

No.	Domain	Author	Year	No. studies	Total no.	No. effects	Mean	se	CLE	Variable
218	School	Peterson	1980	45	—	45	0.12	—	8%	Traditional vs. open classrooms
219	School	Madamba	1980	72	—	72	-0.03	—	-2%	Traditional vs. open classrooms on reading
220	School	Hetzel, Rasher, Butcher, & Walberg	1980	45	—	45	-0.13	—	-9%	Traditional vs. open classrooms
221	School	Giaconia & Hedges	1982	153	—	171	0.06	0.032	4%	Traditional vs. open classrooms

Ability grouping

No.	Domain	Author	Year	No. studies	Total no.	No. effects	Mean	se	CLE	Variable
222	School	Kulik	1981	41	—	41	0.13	—	9%	Ability grouping on high school students
223	School	Kulik & Kulik	1982	52	—	51	0.10	0.045	7%	Ability grouping on high school students
224	School	Kulik & Kulik	1984	23	—	23	0.19	—	13%	Ability grouping in elementary grades
225	School	Bangert-Drowns, Kulik & Kulik	1985	85	—	85	0.15	—	11%	Inter-class ability grouping
226	School	Noland & Taylor	1986	50	—	720	-0.08	—	-6%	Ability grouping
227	School	Slavin	1987	14	—	17	0.00	—	0%	Ability grouping in elementary grades
228	School	Henderson	1989	6	—	6	0.23	—	16%	Ability grouping in elementary grades
229	School	Slavin	1990	29	—	29	-0.02	—	-1%	Ability grouping on high school students
230	School	Gutierrez & Slavin	1992	14	—	14	0.34	—	24%	Nongraded elementary schools
231	School	Kulik & Kulik	1992	56	—	51	0.03	—	2%	Ability grouping
232	School	Kim	1996	96	—	96	0.17	—	12%	Nongraded schools in Kentucky
233	School	Mosteller, Light, & Sachs	1996	10	—	10	0.00	—	0%	Ability grouping
234	School	Lou, Abrami, Spence, Poulsen, Chambers, & d'Apollonia	1996	12	—	12	0.12	—	8%	Ability grouping
235	School	Neber, Finsterwald & Urban	2001	12	—	214	0.33	—	23%	Homogeneous vs. heterogeneous on gifted

Multigrade/Age classes

No.	Domain	Author	Year	No. studies	Total no.	No. effects	Mean	se	CLE	Variable
236	School	Veenman	1995	11	—	11	-0.03	—	-2%	Multiage classes
237	School	Veenman	1996	56	—	34	-0.01	—	-1%	Multigrade classes

No.	Domain	Author	Year	No. studies	Total no.	No. effects	Mean	se	CLE	Variable
238	School	Kim	1996	27	—	27	0.17	—	12%	Nongraded vs. multigrade/multiage classes
Within class grouping										
239	School	Kulik	1985	78	—	78	0.15	—	11%	Inter-class ability grouping
240	School	Lou, Abrami, Spence, Poulsen, Chambers, & d'Apollonia	1996	51	16,073	103	0.17	—	12%	Within-class grouping
Small group learning										
241	School	Springer, Stanne & Donovan	1997	39	3,472	116	0.46	—	33%	Working in small groups in college
242	School	Springer, Stanne & Donovan	1999	39	—	39	0.51	—	36%	Working in small groups in science
Mainstreaming										
243	School	Carlberg & Kavale	1980	50	27,000	50	0.12	0.092	8%	Regular vs. special class placement
244	School	Baker	1994	13	2,532	129	0.08	—	6%	Regular vs. special class placement
245	School	Dixon & Marsh	1997	70	—	70	0.65	—	46%	Regular vs. special class placement
246	School	Baker, Wang, & Walberg	1994	6	—	6	0.20	—	14%	Regular vs. special class placement
247	School	Wang & Baker	1986	11	—	115	0.33	—	23%	Regular vs. special class placement
Retention										
248	School	Holmes	1983	7	—	527	-0.42	—	-30%	Retained vs. non-retained
249	School	Holmes & Matthews	1984	44	11,132	575	-0.37	—	-26%	Retention on all students on elementary students
250	School	Holmes	1986	17	—	217	-0.06	—	-4%	Retained vs. non-retained
251	School	Holmes	1989	63	—	861	-0.15	—	-11%	Retention on all students
252	School	Yoshida	1989	34	—	242	-0.38	—	-27%	Retention on elementary students
253	School	Draney & Wilson	1992	22	—	78	0.66	—	47%	Retained vs. non retained within same year
254	School	Jimerson	2001	20	2,806	175	-0.39	—	-28%	Retained vs. non-retained
School curricula for gifted students										
Ability grouping for gifted students										
255	School	Barget-Drowns, Kulik & Kulik	1985	25	—	25	0.25	—	18%	Classroom organization on gifted
256	School	Goldring	1986	23	—	146	0.35	0.059	25%	Ability grouping for gifted
257	School	Rogers	1991	13	—	13	0.43	—	30%	Grouping on gifted
258	School	Vaughn, Feldhusen, & Asher	1991	8	—	8	0.47	0.070	33%	Pull out programs for gifted
259	School	Kulik & Kulik	1992	56	—	10	0.02	—	1%	Classroom organization on gifted
Acceleration										
260	School	Kulik & Kulik	1984	26	—	13	0.88	0.183	62%	On achievement outcomes on gifted

Appendix A continues

Appendix A continued

No.	Domain	Author	Year	No. studies	Total no.	No. effects	Mean	se	CLE	Variable
261	School	Kulik	2004	11	4,340	11	0.87	—	62%	Acceleration with same age controls on gifted
Enrichment										
262	School	Wallace	1989	138	22,908	136	0.57	0.010	40%	Enrichment programs with gifted
263	School	Romney & Samuels	2001	40	13,428	47	0.35	0.025	24%	Feuerstein's instrumental enrichment with gifted
264	School	Shiell	2002	36	—	360	0.26	—	18%	Feuerstein's instrumental enrichment with gifted
Classroom influences										
Classroom management										
265	School	Marzano	2003	100	—	5	0.52	—	37%	Classroom management on achievement
Classroom cohesion										
266	School	Haertel, Walberg & Haertel	1980	12	17,805	403	0.17	0.016	12%	Classroom climate
267	School	Evans & Dion	1991	27	—	372	0.92	—	65%	Group cohesion
268	School	Mullen & Copper	1994	49	8,702	66	0.51	—	36%	Group cohesion
Classroom behavioral										
269	School	Bender & Smith	1990	25	—	124	1.101	0.13	78%	Classroom behavior of disabled and learning disabilities
270	School	DuPaul & Eckert	1997	63	—	637	0.58	0.450	41%	School programs for ADHD
271	School	Frazier, Youngstron, Glutting, & Watkins	2007	72	—	181	0.71	—	50%	Programs for ADHD
Decreasing disruptive behavior										
272	School	Skiba & Casey	1985	41	883	26	0.93	—	66%	Classroom disruptive behavior
273	School	Stage & Quiroz	1997	99	5,057	289	0.78	0.034	55%	Decreasing disruptive behavior
274	School	Reid, Gonzalez, Nordness, Trout, & Epstein	2004	25	2,486	101	-0.69	0.040	-49%	Emotional/behavioral disturbance
Peer influences										
275	School	Ide, Parkerson, Haertel, & Walberg	1980	12	—	122	0.53	—	37%	Peer influences on achievement
Teacher										
Teacher effects										
276	Teacher	Nye, Konstantopoulos, & Hedges	2004	18	—	18	0.32	0.020	23%	Overall teacher effects
Teacher training										
277	Teacher	Wu, Becker & Kennedy	2002	24	—	192	0.08	0.044	6%	Certified vs. alternative certified teachers
278	Teacher	Wu, Becker & Kennedy	2002	24	—	76	0.14	—	10%	Trad vs. emergency licensed teachers

No.	Domain	Author	Year	No. studies	Total no.	No. effects	Mean	se	CLE	Variable
279	Teacher	Sparks	2004	5	—	18	0.12	—	8%	Trad vs. emergency or probationary training
Micro teaching										
280	Teacher	Butcher	1981	47	—	47	0.55	—	39%	Teacher training on teacher skills
281	Teacher	Yeany & Padilla	1986	183	—	183	1.18	—	83%	Teacher training on teacher skills in science
282	Teacher	Bennett	1987	112	—	126	1.10	—	78%	Teacher training on teacher skills
283	Teacher	Metcalf	1995	60	—	83	0.70	—	49%	Lab experiences in teacher education on teacher skills
Teacher subject matter knowledge										
284	Teacher	Druva & Anderson	1983	65	—	360	0.06	—	4%	Teacher background in science
285	Teacher	Ahn & Choi	2004	27	—	64	0.12	0.016	8%	Teacher knowledge in mathematics
Quality of teaching										
286	Teacher	Cohen	1980	22	—	22	0.33	—	23%	Feedback from student ratings
287	Teacher	Cohen	1981	19	—	19	0.68	—	48%	Student rating of teacher
288	Teacher	Cohen	1981	41	—	68	0.48	—	34%	Student rating of teacher
289	Teacher	Abrami, Leventhal, & Perry	1982	12	—	12	0.29	—	20%	Expressiveness of teacher
290	Teacher	Cohen	1986	47	—	74	0.44	0.060	31%	Student rating of teacher
Teacher-student relationships										
291	Teacher	Cornelius-White	2007	229	355,325	1450	0.72	0.01	51%	Teacher-student relations on achievement
Professional development										
292	Teacher	Joslin	1980	137	47,000	902	0.81	—	57%	In-service teacher education
293	Teacher	Harrison	1980	47	—	47	0.80	—	56%	Staff development
294	Teacher	Wade	1985	91	—	715	0.37	—	26%	In-service teacher education on achievement
295	Teacher	Tinoca	2004	35	—	37	0.45	0.007	32%	PD in science
296	Teacher	Timperley, Wilson, Barrar, & Fung	2007	227	—	183	0.66	0.060	47%	PD on student outcomes
Expectations										
297	Teacher	Rosenthal & Rubin	1978	345	—	345	0.70	0.200	49%	Teacher expectations
298	Teacher	Smith	1980	46	—	149	0.82	—	58%	Teacher expectations
299	Teacher	Dusek & Joseph	1983	102	—	102	0.39	—	28%	Teacher expectations
300	Teacher	Raudenbush	1984	18	—	33	0.08	0.044	6%	Teacher expectations
301	Teacher	Harris & Rosenthal	1985	53	—	53	0.41	—	29%	Teacher expectations

Appendix A continues

Appendix A continued

No.	Domain	Author	Year	No. studies	Total no.	No. effects	Mean	se	CLE	Variable
302	Teacher	Ritts, Patterson, & Tubbs	1992	12	—	12	0.36	—	25%	Expectations of physical attractiveness and achievement
303	Teacher	Jackson, Hunter & Hodge	1995	59	—	51	0.47	0.042	33%	Physical attractiveness on achievement
304	Teacher	Tenebaum & Ruck	2007	39	—	39	0.23	0.040	16%	Teacher expectations

Not labeling students

305	Teacher	Fuchs, Fuchs, Mathes, Lipsey, & Roberts	2002	79	—	79	0.61	—	43%	Low achieving non-disabled students vs. learning disabled in reading

Teacher clarity

306	Teacher	Fendick	1990	na	—	na	0.75	—	53%	Teacher clarity on outcomes

Curricula Reading, writing, and the arts

Visual-perception programs

307	Curricula	Kavale	1980	31	4,400	101	0.70	0.102	49%	Auditory-visual integration
308	Curricula	Kavale	1981	106	—	723	0.767	—	54%	Auditory perception
309	Curricula	Kavale	1982	161	325,000	1571	0.81	0.008	57%	Visual perceptual skills in reading
310	Curricula	Kavale	1984	59	—	173	0.09	0.014	6%	Frostig developmental training in reading
311	Curricula	Kavale	1984	59	—	173	0.18	0.028	13%	Visual perceptual skills
312	Curricula	Kavale & Forness	2000	267	50,000	2294	0.76	0.012	54%	Auditory-visual processes

Vocabulary programs

313	Curricula	Kavale	1982	36	—	240	0.38	—	27%	Psycholinguistic training
314	Curricula	Stahl & Fairbanks	1986	41	—	41	0.97	0.127	69%	Vocabulary interventions
315	Curricula	Arnold, Myette, & Casto	1986	30	—	87	0.59	0.090	42%	Language intervention
316	Curricula	Nye, Foster, & Seaman	1987	61	—	299	1.04	0.107	74%	Language intervention
317	Curricula	Poirier	1989	61	—	61	0.5	—	35%	Language intervention
318	Curricula	Marmolejo	1990	33	—	33	0.69	—	49%	Vocabulary interventions
319	Curricula	Klesius & Searls	1990	39	—	39	0.50	—	35%	Vocabulary interventions

Phonics instruction

320	Curricula	Wagner	1988	16	—	1766	0.38	—	27%	Phonological processing abilities
321	Curricula	Fukkink & de Glopper	1998	12	—	21	0.43	0.120	30%	Deriving word meaning from context
322	Curricula	Metsala, Stanovich, & Brown	1998	17	1,116	38	0.58	0.060	41%	Spelling to sound regularities and reading
323	Curricula	Miller	1999	18	882	18	1.53	0.231	108%	Phonemic awareness programs
324	Curricula	Bus & van IJzendoorn	1999	70	5,843	1484	0.73	—	52%	Phonological awareness training

No.	Domain	Author	Year	No. studies	Total no.	No. effects	Mean	se	CLE	Variable
325	Curricula	Thomas	2000	8	715	10	1.02	—	72%	Phonemic awareness
326	Curricula	National Reading Panel	2000	52	—	96	0.53	—	37%	Phonemic awareness
327	Curricula	National Reading Panel	2000	38	—	66	0.44	—	31%	Phonics instruction
328	Curricula	National Reading Panel	2000	14	—	14	0.41	—	29%	Fluency
329	Curricula	Ehri, Nunes, Stahl, & Willows	2001	34	—	66	0.41	—	29%	Systematic phonics instruction
330	Curricula	Ehri, Nunes, Willows, Schuster, Yaghoub-Zadeh, & Shanahan	2001	52	—	72	0.53	—	37%	Phonemic awareness on reading
331	Curricula	Swanson, Trainin, Necoechea & Hammill	2003	35	3,568	2257	0.93	0.473	65%	Rapid naming, phonological awareness
332	Curricula	Camilli, Vargas, & Yirecko	2003	40	—	40	0.24	—	17%	Phonics instruction
333	Curricula	Torgerson, Brooks, & Hall	2006	19	—	20	0.27	—	19%	Phonics instruction
Sentence combining programs										
334	Curricula	Neville & Searls	1991	24	—	29	0.09	—	7%	Sentence combining on reading
335	Curricula	Fusaro	1993	11	—	11	0.20	0.087	14%	Effects of sentence combining
Repeated reading programs										
336	Curricula	Therrien	2004	33	—	28	0.65	0.080	46%	Repeated reading
337	Curricula	Chard, Vaughn, & Tyler	2002	21	—	128	0.68	—	48%	Repeated reading without a model
Comprehension programs										
338	Curricula	Pflaum, Walberg, Karegiances, & Rasher	1980	31	—	341	0.60	—	43%	Reading instruction
339	Curricula	Rowe	1985	137	—	1537	0.70	0.044	49%	Reading comprehension interventions
340	Curricula	Yang	1997	39	—	162	0.33	—	23%	Programs to enhance reading fluency
341	Curricula	O'Shaughnessy & Swanson	1998	41	1,783	161	0.61	0.069	43%	Normal vs. LD on memory processing of information
342	Curricula	Swanborn & de Glopper	1999	20	2,130	20	0.15	—	11%	Incidental word learning
343	Curricula	Swanson	1999	112	3,895	334	0.77	0.055	54%	Reading interventions
344	Curricula	Burger & Winner	2000	9	378	20	0.10	—	7%	Visual arts programs on reading
345	Curricula	Sencibaugh	2005	15	538	23	1.15	—	81%	Visual or auditory programs to improve comprehension
346	Curricula	Guthrie, McRae, & Klauda	2007	11	2,861	75	0.78	—	55%	Concept-oriented reading programs
Whole language										
347	Curricula	Stahl & Miller	1989	15	—	117	0.09	0.056	6%	Effects of whole language instruction

Appendix A continues

No.	Domain	Author	Year	No. studies	Total no.	No. effects	Mean	se	CLE	Variable
348	Curricula	Gee	1995	21	—	52	0.65	—	46%	Effects of whole language instruction
349	Curricula	Stahl, McKenna, & Pagnucco	1994	14	—	14	0.15	—	11%	Effects of whole language instruction
350	Curricula	Jeynes & Littell	2000	14	630	14	-0.65	—	-46%	Effects of whole language instruction
Exposure to reading										
351	Curricula	Bus, van IJzendoorn, & Pellegrini	1995	29	3,410	33	0.59	—	42%	Joint book reading
352	Curricula	Blok	1999	11	—	53	0.63	0.140	45%	Reading to young children
353	Curricula	Torgerson, King & Sowden	2002	8	—	8	0.19	—	13%	Volunteers helping to read
354	Curricula	Yoon	2002	7	3,183	7	0.12	0.040	8%	Sustained silent reading
355	Curricula	Lewis & Samuels	2003	49	112,000	182	0.10	—	7%	Time on reading
356	Curricula	Burger & Winner	2000	10	—	10	0.52	—	37%	Visual arts on reading readiness
Second/Third chance programs										
357	Curricula	Elbaum, Vaughn, Hughes & Moody	2000	16	—	16	0.66	—	47%	Reading recovery programs
358	Curricula	D'Agostino & Murphy	2004	36	5,685	1379	0.34	—	24%	Reading recovery programs
Writing programs										
359	Curricula	Hillocks	1984	60	11,705	73	0.28	0.020	20%	Teaching writing
360	Curricula	Atkinson	1993	20	—	55	0.40	0.063	28%	Writing projects
361	Curricula	Gersten & Baker	2001	13	—	13	0.81	0.031	57%	Expressive writing
362	Curricula	Bangert-Drowns, Hurley & Wilkinson	2004	46	5,416	46	0.26	0.058	18%	School-based writing to learn interventions
363	Curricula	Graham & Perin	2007	123	14,068	154	0.43	0.036	30%	Writing programs
Drama/Arts programs										
364	Curricula	Kardash & Wright	1987	16	—	36	0.67	0.090	47%	Creative dramatics
365	Curricula	Podlozny	2000	17	—	17	0.31	—	22%	Drama on reading
366	Curricula	Moga, Burger, Hetland, & Winner	2000	8	2,271	8	0.35	—	24%	Arts programs on creativity
367	Curricula	Winner & Cooper	2000	31	—	24	0.06	—	4%	Arts programs on achievement
368	Curricula	Keinanen, Hetland, & Winner	2000	527	69,564	527	0.43	—	30%	Dance on Reading
369	Curricula	Butzlaff	2000	30	5,734,878	30	0.35	—	24%	Music programs on reading
370	Curricula	Hetland	2000	15	1,170	15	0.80	—	56%	Music programs on spatial reasoning
371	Curricula	Hetland	2000	15	—	15	0.06	—	4%	Music programs on intelligence
372	Curricula	Vaughn	2000	20	—	20	0.30	—	21%	Music study/listening and math
373	Curricula	Hetland	2000b	36	—	36	0.23	—	16%	Listening to music

Math and sciences

Mathematics

No.	Domain	Author	Year	No. studies	Total no.	No. effects	Mean	se	CLE	Variable
374	Curricula	Athappilly	1978	134	—	810	0.24	0.030	17%	Modern vs. traditional math
375	Curricula	Parham	1983	64	—	171	0.53	0.099	37%	Manipulative materials
376	Curricula	Fuchs & Fuchs	1985	16	—	17	0.46	0.009	33%	Use of graphing paper
377	Curricula	Moin	1986	na	—	na	0.23	—	16%	Self-paced method of calculus instruction
378	Curricula	Friedman	1989	136	—	394	0.88	—	62%	Spatial effects in math
379	Curricula	LeNoir	1989	45	—	135	0.19	—	14%	Manipulative materials
380	Curricula	Sowell	1989	60	—	138	0.19	—	13%	Manipulative materials
381	Curricula	Fischer & Tarver	1997	7	277	22	1.01	—	71%	Videodisc math
382	Curricula	Lee	2000	61	5,172	97	0.60	0.100	42%	Math programs on LD students
383	Curricula	Baker, Gersten, & Lee	2002	15	1,271	39	0.51	—	36%	Feedback and peer tutoring with low achieving students
384	Curricula	Haas	2005	35	—	66	0.38	0.141	27%	Teaching methods in algebra
385	Curricula	Malofeeva	2005	29	1,845	29	0.47	0.047	33%	Math programs for K-2
386	Curricula	Hembree	1987	75	—	452	0.16	—	11%	Non-content variables

Use of calculators

No.	Domain	Author	Year	No. studies	Total no.	No. effects	Mean	se	CLE	Variable
387	Curricula	Hembree & Dessart	1986	79	—	524	0.14	—	10%	Use of calculators in pre-college students
388	Curricula	Smith	1996	24	—	54	0.25	—	17%	Use of calculators
389	Curricula	Ellington	2000	53	—	305	0.28	—	20%	Use of calculators in pre-college students
390	Curricula	Nikolaou	2001	24	—	103	0.49	0.092	35%	Use of calculators on problem solving
391	Curricula	Ellington	2006	42	—	97	0.19	—	13%	Use of Non-CAS graphing calculators

Science

No.	Domain	Author	Year	No. studies	Total no.	No. effects	Mean	se	CLE	Variable
392	Curricula	El-Nemr	1979	59	—	250	0.17	—	12%	Traditional vs. inquiry method for biology
393	Curricula	Bredderman	1980	50	—	17	0.12	—	8%	Textbooks vs. process curricula
394	Curricula	Weinstein, Boulanger, & Walberg	1982	33	19,149	33	0.31	—	22%	Science curriculum effects
395	Curricula	Bredderman	1983	57	13,000	400	0.35	—	25%	Activity-based methods
396	Curricula	Shymansky, Kyle, & Alport	1993	105	45,626	341	0.43	—	30%	New science curricula
397	Curricula	Wise & Okey	1983	160	—	400	0.34	—	24%	Science teaching strategies
398	Curricula	Shymansky	1984	47	6,035	43	0.64	—	45%	Biology science curricula
399	Curricula	Horak	1985	40	—	472	0.57	—	40%	Learning science from textual materials
400	Curricula	Guzzetti, Snyder, Glass, & Gamas	1993	23	—	35	0.29	—	21%	On misconceptions in reading

Appendix A continues

Appendix A continued

No.	Domain	Author	Year	No. studies	Total no.	No. effects	Mean	se	CLE	Variable
401	Curricula	Guzzetti, Snyder, Glass, & Gamas	1993	70	—	126	0.81	—	57%	Conceptual change in science
402	Curricula	Wise	1996	140	—	375	0.32	—	23%	Strategies for science teaching
403	Curricula	Rubin	1996	39	—	39	0.22	0.018	16%	Laboratory component in college science
404	Curricula	Schroeder, Scott, Tolson, Huang, & Lee	2007	61	159,695	61	0.67	—	47%	Teaching strategies in science

Other curricula programs
Values/Moral education programs

No.	Domain	Author	Year	No. studies	Total no.	No. effects	Mean	se	CLE	Variable
405	Curricula	Schlaefli, Rest, & Thoma	1985	55	—	68	0.28	—	20%	Effects on moral judgments
406	Curricula	Berg	2003	29	27,064	29	0.20	—	14%	Character education programs on knowledge

Perceptual-Motor programs

| 407 | Curricula | Kavale & Mattson | 1983 | 180 | 13,000 | 637 | 0.08 | 0.011 | 6% | PM programs on learning disabled |

Integrated curriculum programs

| 408 | Curricula | Hartzler | 2000 | 30 | — | 30 | 0.48 | 0.086 | 34% | Integrated curriculum programs |
| 409 | Curricula | Hurley | 2001 | 31 | 7,894 | 50 | 0.31 | 0.015 | 22% | Integrated science and math programs |

Tactile stimulation

| 410 | Curricula | Ottenbacher, Muller, Brandt, Heintzelman, Hojem, & Sharpe | 1987 | 19 | 505 | 103 | 0.58 | 0.145 | 41% | Tactile stimulation |

Social skills programs

411	Curricula	Denham & Almeida	1987	70	—	70	0.62	—	44%	Social problem solving programs
412	Curricula	Hanson	1988	63	—	586	0.65	0.034	46%	Social skill training
413	Curricula	Schneider	1992	79	—	12	0.19	—	13%	Enhancing peer relations
414	Curricula	Swanson & Malone	1992	39	3,944	366	0.72	0.043	51%	SS of learning disabled and non-disabled students
415	Curricula	Beelmann, Pfingsten, & Losel	1994	49	—	23	-0.04	—	-3%	Social competence training on achievement outcomes
416	Curricula	Forness & Kavale	1996	53	2,113	328	0.21	0.034	15%	SS with learning difficulties
417	Curricula	Kavale & Forness	1996	152	—	858	0.65	0.015	46%	SS of learning disabled and non-disabled students
418	Curricula	Quinn, Kavale, Mathur, Rutherford, & Forness	1999	35	1,123	35	0.20	0.03	2%	SS with emotional and behavioral disorders

Creativity programs

| 419 | Curricula | Rose & Lin | 1984 | 158 | — | 158 | 0.47 | 0.054 | 33% | Long term creativity programs |

No.	Domain	Author	Year	No. studies	Total no.	No. effects	Mean	se	CLE	Variable
420	Curricula	Cohn	1986	106	—	177	0.55	—	39%	Creativity training effectiveness
421	Curricula	Bangert-Drowns & Bankert	1990	20	—	20	0.37	—	26%	Explicit instruction of creativity
422	Curricula	Hollingsworth	1991	39	—	39	0.82	—	58%	Creativity programs
423	Curricula	Conard	1992	na	—	na	0.48	—	34%	Creative dramatics
424	Curricula	Scope	1998	30	—	40	0.90	0.188	64%	Instructional influences on creativity
425	Curricula	Scott, Leritz, & Mumford	2004	70	—	70	0.64	—	45%	Creativity programs
426	Curricula	Bertrand	2005	45	—	45	0.64	0.10	45%	Creativity programs
427	Curricula	Higgins, Hall, Baumfield, & Moseley	2005	19	—	19	0.62	—	44%	Thinking programs on achievement
428	Curricula	Huang	2005	51	—	62	0.89	0.098	63%	Creativity programs
429	Curricula	Berkowitz	2006	23	5,000	39	0.46	0.050	—	Various creative communication strategies
430	Curricula	Abrami, Bernard, Borokhovski, Surkes, Wade, & Zhang	2006	124	18,299	168	1.01	—	71%	Interventions to improve critical thinking skills

Outdoor programs

No.	Domain	Author	Year	No. studies	Total no.	No. effects	Mean	se	CLE	Variable
431	Curricula	Cason & Gillis	1994	43	11,238	10	0.61	0.051	43%	Outdoor education on high school achievement
432	Curricula	Hattie, Marsh, Neill, & Richards	1997	96	12,057	30	0.46	—	33%	Outward bound
433	Curricula	Laidlaw	2000	48	3,550	389	0.49	0.020	35%	Outdoor education on achievement

Play

No.	Domain	Author	Year	No. studies	Total no.	No. effects	Mean	se	CLE	Variable
434	Curricula	Spies	1987	24	2,491	24	0.26	—	19%	Impact of play on achievement
435	Curricula	Fisher	1992	46	2,565	46	0.74	—	52%	Impact of play on achievement

Bilingual programs

No.	Domain	Author	Year	No. studies	Total no.	No. effects	Mean	se	CLE	Variable
436	Curricula	Powers & Rossman	1984	16	1,257	16	0.12	—	8%	Bilingual programs
437	Curricula	Willig	1985	16	—	513	0.10	—	7%	Bilingual programs
438	Curricula	Oh	1987	54	6,207	115	1.21	0.140	86%	Bilingual programs for Asian students in NY
439	Curricula	Greene	1997	11	2,719	11	0.18	—	13%	Bilingual programs
440	Curricula	McField	2002	10	—	12	0.35	—	25%	Bilingual programs
441	Curricula	Rolstad, Mahoney, & Glass	2005	4	—	43	0.16	—	11%	Bilingual programs in Arizona
442	Curricula	Slavin & Cheung	2005	17	—	17	0.45	—	32%	Bilingual and English-only reading programs

Extra-curricular activities

No.	Domain	Author	Year	No. studies	Total no.	No. effects	Mean	se	CLE	Variable
443	Curricula	Scott-Little, Hamann, & Jurs	2002	6	—	—	0.18	—	5%	After-school care programs
444	Curricula	Lewis	2004	10	—	10	0.47	0.101	33%	General activities

Appendix A continues

Appendix A continued

No.	Domain	Author	Year	No. studies	Total no.	No. effects	Mean	se	CLE	Variable
445	Curricula	Lewis	2004	5	—	5	0.10	0.058	7%	Sports on achievement
446	Curricula	Lewis	2004	8	—	8	-0.01	0.058	5%	Work on achievement
447	Curricula	Durlak & Weisberg	2007	73	—	45	0.13	—	9%	After-school programs

Career interventions

448	Curricula	Baker & Popowicz	1983	18	—	118	0.50	0.050	35%	Evaluating career education on outcomes
449	Curricula	Oliver & Spokane	1988	58	—	58	0.48	—	34%	Career education interventions
450	Curricula	Evans & Burck	1992	67	159,243	67	0.17	—	12%	Career education interventions

Teaching   Strategies emphasizing learning intentions

Goals

451	Teaching	Chidester & Grigsby	1984	21	1,770	21	0.44	0.030	31%	Goal difficulty
452	Teaching	Fuchs & Fuchs	1985	18		96	0.64	—	45%	Long vs. & short term goals
453	Teaching	Tubbs	1986	87	—	147	0.58	0.030	41%	Goal difficulty, specificity and feedback
454	Teaching	Mento, Steel, & Karren	1987	70	7,407	118	0.58	0.018	41%	Goal difficulty
455	Teaching	Wood, Mento & Locke	1987	72	7,548	72	0.58	0.149	41%	Goal difficulty
456	Teaching	Wood, Mento & Locke	1987	53	6,635	53	0.43	0.063	30%	Goal specificity
457	Teaching	Wright	1990	70	7,161	70	0.55	0.018	39%	Goal difficulty
458	Teaching	Donovan & Radosevich	1998	21	2,360	21	0.36	—	25%	Goal commitment
459	Teaching	Klein, Wesson, Hollenbeck & Alge	1999	74		83	0.47	—		Goal commitment
460	Teaching	Burns	2004	55		45	0.82	0.089	58%	Degree of challenge
461	Teaching	Gollwitzer & Sheeran	2006	63	8,461	94	0.72	—	51%	Goal intentions on achievement

Behavioral objectives/advance organizers

462	Teaching	Kozlow	1978	77	—	91	0.89	0.017	63%	Advance organizers
463	Teaching	Luiten, Ames & Ackerman	1980	135	—	160	0.21	—	15%	Advance organizers
464	Teaching	Stone	1983	29	—	112	0.66	0.074	47%	Advance organizers
465	Teaching	Lott	1983	16	—	147	0.24	—	17%	Advance organizers in science
466	Teaching	Asencio	1984	111	—	111	0.12	—	8%	Behavioral objectives
467	Teaching	Klauer	1984	23	—	52	0.40	—	28%	Intentional learning
468	Teaching	Rolheiser-Bennett	1986	12	1,968	45	0.80	—	57%	Advance organizers
469	Teaching	Mahar	1992	50	—	50	0.44	—	31%	Advance organizers
470	Teaching	Catts	1992	14	—	80	-0.03	0.056	-2%	Incidental learning
471	Teaching	Catts	1992	90	—	1065	0.35	0.013	25%	Intentional learning
472	Teaching	Preiss & Gayle	2006	20	1,937	20	0.46	—	33%	Advance organizers

No.	Domain	Author	Year	No. studies	Total no.	No. effects	Mean	se	CLE	Variable
Concept mapping										
473	Teaching	Moore & Readence	1984	161	—	161	0.22	0.050	16%	Graphics organizers in mathematics
474	Teaching	Vásquez & Caraballo	1993	17	—	19	0.57	0.032	40%	Concept mapping in science
475	Teaching	Horton, McConney, Gallo, Woods, Senn, & Hamelin	1993	19	1,805	19	0.45	—	32%	Concept mapping in science
476	Teaching	Kang	2002	14	—	14	0.79	—	56%	Graphics organizers in reading with learning disabled
477	Teaching	Kim, Vaughn, Wanzek, & Wei	2004	21	848	52	0.81	0.081	57%	Graphics organizers in reading
478	Teaching	Nesbit & Adesope	2006	55	5,818	67	0.55	0.040	39%	Concept and knowledge maps
Learning hierarchies										
479	Teaching	Horon & Lynn	1980	24	—	24	0.19	—	13%	Learning hierarchies
Strategies emphasizing success criteria										
Mastery learning										
480	Teaching	Block & Burns	1976	45	—	45	0.83	—	59%	Mastery learning
481	Teaching	Willett, Yamashita & Anderson	1983	130	—	13	0.64	—	45%	Mastery teaching in science
482	Teaching	Guskey & Gates	1985	38	7,794	35	0.78	—	55%	Group-based mastery learning
483	Teaching	Hefner	1985	8	1,529	12	0.66	—	47%	Mastery learning/competency-based methods
484	Teaching	Kulik & Kulik	1986	49	—	49	0.54	0.055	38%	Mastery testing
485	Teaching	Slavin	1987	7	—	7	0.04	—	3%	Mastery learning
486	Teaching	Guskey & Pigott	1988	43	—	78	0.61	—	43%	Group-based mastery learning
487	Teaching	Hood	1990	23	—	23	0.56	—	40%	Mastery learning
488	Teaching	Kulik, Kulik, & Bangert-Drowns	1990	34	—	34	0.52	—	37%	Mastery learning
Keller personalized system of instruction										
489	Teaching	Kulik, Kulik, & Cohen	1979	61	—	75	0.49	—	35%	PSI and achievement
490	Teaching	Willett, Yamashita & Anderson	1983	130	—	15	0.60	—	42%	PSI in science
491	Teaching	Kulik, Kulik, & Bangert-Drowns	1988	72	—	72	0.49	—	35%	PSI in college students
Worked examples										
492	Teaching	Crissman	2006	62	3,324	151	0.57	0.042	40%	Worked examples on achievement
Strategies emphasizing feedback										
Feedback										
493	Teaching	Lysakowski & Walberg	1980	39	4,842	102	1.17	—	83%	Classroom reinforcement

Appendix A continued

No.	Domain	Author	Year	No. studies	Total no.	No. effects	Mean	se	CLE	Variable
494	Teaching	Wilkinson	1980	14	—	14	0.12	—	8%	Teacher praise
495	Teaching	Walberg	1982	19	—	19	0.81	—	57%	Cues and reinforcement
496	Teaching	Lysakowski & Walberg	1982	54	15,689	94	0.97	—	69%	Cues, participation, and corrective feedback
497	Teaching	Yeany & Miller	1983	49	—	49	0.52	—	37%	Diagnostic feedback in college science
498	Teaching	Schimmel	1983	15	—	15	0.47	0.034	33%	Feedback from computer instruction
499	Teaching	Getsie, Langer, & Glass	1985	89	—	89	0.14	—	10%	Rewards and punishment
500	Teaching	Skiba, Casey, & Center	1985	35	—	315	0.68	—	48%	Nonaversive procedures
501	Teaching	Menges & Brinko	1986	27	—	31	0.44	0.115	31%	Student evaluation as feedback
502	Teaching	Rummel & Feinberg	1988	45	—	45	0.60	—	42%	Extrinsic feedback rewards
503	Teaching	Kulik & Kulik	1988	53	—	53	0.49	—	35%	Timing of feedback
504	Teaching	Tenenbaum & Goldring	1989	15	522	15	0.72	—	51%	Cues and reinforcement
505	Teaching	L'Hommedieu, Menges, & Brinko	1990	28	1,698	28	0.34	—	24%	Feedback from college student ratings
506	Teaching	Bangert-Drowns, Kulik, Kulik, & Morgan	1991	40	—	58	0.26	0.060	18%	Feedback from tests
507	Teaching	Wiersma	1992	20	865	17	0.50	0.086	35%	Intrinsic vs. extrinsic rewards
508	Teaching	Travlos & Pratt	1995	17	—	17	0.71	0.010	50%	Knowledge of results
509	Teaching	Azevedo, R., & Bernard, R.M.	1995	22	—	22	0.80	—	57%	Computer-presented feedback
510	Teaching	Standley	1996	98	—	208	2.87	—	203%	Music as reinforcement
511	Teaching	Kluger & DeNisi	1996	470	12,652	470	0.38	—	27%	Feedback
512	Teaching	Neubert	1998	16	744	16	0.63	0.028	45%	Goals plus feedback
513	Teaching	Swanson & Lussier	2001	30	5,104	170	1.12	0.093	79%	Dynamic assessment (feedback)
514	Teaching	Baker & Dwyer	2005	11	1,341	122	0.93	—	66%	Field independent vs. field dependent
515	Teaching	Witt, Wheeless, & Allen	2006	81	24,474	81	1.15	—	82%	Immediacy of teacher feedback

Frequent/effects of testing

No.	Domain	Author	Year	No. studies	Total no.	No. effects	Mean	se	CLE	Variable
516	Teaching	Kulik, Kulik, & Bangert	1984	19	—	19	0.42	0.080	30%	Practice testing
517	Teaching	Fuchs & Fuchs	1986	22	1,489	34	0.28	—	20%	Examiner familiarity effects
518	Teaching	Bangert-Drowns, Kulik, & Kulik	1991	35	—	35	0.23	—	16%	Frequent testing
519	Teaching	Gocmen	2003	78	—	233	0.40	0.047	29%	Frequent testing
520	Teaching	Kim	2005	148	—	644	0.39	0.016	28%	Formative assessment
521	Teaching	Kim	2005	148	—	622	0.39	—	28%	Performance assessment on achievement
522	Teaching	Lee	2006	12	—	55	0.36	0.061	25%	Test driven external testing
523	Teaching	Hausknecht, Halpert, Di Paolo, & Gerrard	2007	107	134,436	107	0.26	0.016	18%	Practice and retesting effects

No.	Domain	Author	Year	No. studies	Total no.	No. effects	Mean	se	CLE	Variable
Teaching test taking										
524	Teaching	Messick & Jungeblut	1981	12	—	12	0.15	—	11%	Coaching for SAT
525	Teaching	Bangert-Drowns, Kulik & Kulik	1983	30	—	30	0.25	—	18%	Training in test taking skills
526	Teaching	DerSimonian & Laird	1983	36	15,772	36	0.07	—	5%	Coaching on the SAT-M/V
527	Teaching	Samson	1985	24	—	24	0.33	0.039	23%	Training in test taking skills
528	Teaching	Scruggs, White, & Bennion	1986	24	—	65	0.21	—	15%	Training in test taking skills
529	Teaching	Kalaian & Becker	1986	34	—	34	0.34	0.010	24%	Coaching for SAT
530	Teaching	Powers	1986	10	—	44	0.21	—	15%	Coaching for college admission
531	Teaching	Becker	1990	48	—	70	0.30	—	21%	Coaching for SAT
532	Teaching	Witt	1993	35	—	35	0.22	—	16%	Training in test taking skills
533	Teaching	Kulik, Bangert-Drowns, & Kulik	1984	14	—	14	0.15	—	11%	Coaching for SAT
Providing formative evaluation to teachers										
534	Teaching	Fuchs & Fuchs	1986	21	3,835	21	0.70	—	49%	Formative evaluation
535	Teaching	Burns & Symington	2002	9	—	57	1.10	0.079	78%	Use of pre-referral intervention teams
Questioning										
536	Teaching	Redfield & Rousseau	1981	14	—	14	0.73	—	52%	Teacher questioning
537	Teaching	Lyday	1983	65	—	65	0.57	—	40%	Adjunct questions
538	Teaching	Hamaker	1986	61	—	121	0.13	0.009	9%	Factual adjunct questions
539	Teaching	Samson, Strykowski, Weinstein, & Walberg	1987	14	—	14	0.26	0.086	18%	Teacher questioning
540	Teaching	Gliesmann, Pugh, Dowden, & Hutchins	1988	26	—	26	0.82	—	58%	Teacher questioning
541	Teaching	Gayle, Preiss, & Allen	2006	13	—	13	0.31	0.108	22%	Teacher questioning
542	Teaching	Randolph	2007	18	—	18	0.38	—	27%	Response cards to questioning
Teacher immediacy										
543	Teaching	Allen, Witt, & Wheeless	2006	16	5,437	16	0.16	—	8%	Immediacy on cognitive outcomes
Strategies emphasizing student perspectives in learning										
Time on task										
544	Teaching	Bloom	1976	11	—	28	0.75	—	53%	Time on task
545	Teaching	Fredrick	1980	35	—	35	0.34	—	24%	Time on task
546	Teaching	Catts	1992	18	—	37	0.19	0.101	13%	Time on task

Appendix A continues

Appendix A continued

No.	Domain	Author	Year	No. studies	Total no.	No. effects	Mean	se	CLE	Variable
547	Teaching	Shulruf, Keuskamp & Timperley	2006	36	—	36	0.24	—	17%	Taking more coursework
Spaced vs. mass practice										
548	Teaching	Lee & Genovese	1988	—	—	—	0.96	—	—	Spaced vs. massed practice
549	Teaching	Donovan & Radosevich	1999	63	—	112	0.46	—	—	Spaced vs. massed practice
Peer tutoring										
550	Teaching	Hartley	1977	29	—	50	0.63	0.089	44%	Effects on tutees in math
551	Teaching	Hartley	1977	29	—	18	0.58	0.201	41%	Effects on tutors in math
552	Teaching	Cohen, Kulik, & Kulik	1982	65	—	52	0.40	0.069	28%	Effects on tutees
553	Teaching	Cohen, Kulik, & Kulik	1982	65	—	33	0.33	0.090	23%	Effects on tutors
554	Teaching	Phillips	1983	302	—	302	0.98	—	69%	Tutorial training of conservation
555	Teaching	Cook, Scruggs, Mastropieri & Casto	1985	19	—	49	0.53	0.106	37%	Handicapped as tutors
556	Teaching	Cook, Scruggs, Mastropieri & Casto	1985	19	—	25	0.58	0.120	41%	Handicapped as tutees
557	Teaching	Mathes & Fuchs	1991	11	—	74	0.36	—	25%	Peer tutoring in reading
558	Teaching	Elbaum, Vaughn, Hughes & Moody	2000	32	1,248	216	0.41	—	29%	Peer tutoring in reading
559	Teaching	Elbaum, Vaughn, Hughes & Moody	2000	29	325	216	0.67	0.067	47%	One-one tutoring programs in reading
560	Teaching	Rohrbeck, Ginsburg-Block, Fantuzzo, & Miller	2003	90	—	90	0.59	0.095	42%	Peer assisted learning in elementary students
561	Teaching	Erion	2006	32	—	32	0.82	0.156	58%	Parent tutoring children
562	Teaching	Ginsburg-Block, Rohrbeck & Fantuzzo	2006	28	—	26	0.35	0.040	25%	Peer-assisted learning
563	Teaching	Kunsch, Jitendra, & Sood	2007	17	1,103	17	0.47	—	33%	Peer-mediated instruction in math with LD students
Mentoring										
564	Teaching	Eby, Allen, Evans, Ng, & DuBois	2008	31	10,250	31	0.16	0.04	11%	Mentoring on performance outcomes
565	Teaching	DuBois, Holloway, Valentine, & Cooper	2002	43	—	43	0.13	0.05	9%	Mentoring on academic outcomes
Strategies emphasizing student meta-cognitive/self-regulated learning										
Meta-cognition strategies										
566	Teaching	Haller, Child & Walberg	1988	20	1,553	20	0.71	0.181	50%	Meta-cognitive training programs in reading
567	Teaching	Chiu	1998	43	3,475	123	0.67	—	47%	Meta-cognitive interventions in reading
Study skills										
568	Teaching	Sanders	1979	28	6,140	28	0.37	—	26%	Reading-study programs

No.	Domain	Author	Year	No. studies	Total no.	No. effects	Mean	se	CLE	Variable
569	Teaching	Kulik, Kulik, & Shwalb	1983	57	—	57	0.27	0.042	19%	Study skills preparation programs
570	Teaching	Crismore	1985	100	—	100	1.04	—	74%	Summarizing strategies
571	Teaching	Henk & Stahl	1985	21	—	25	0.34	0.129	24%	Note taking
572	Teaching	Rolheiser-Bennett	1986	12	1,968	78	1.28	—	90%	Memory training
573	Teaching	Runyan	1987	32	3,698	51	0.64	—	45%	Mnemonic keyword recall program
574	Teaching	Mastropieri & Scruggs	1989	19	—	19	1.62	0.18	115%	Mnemonic keyword recall program
575	Teaching	Burley	1994	27	7,285	40	0.13	—	9%	College programs for underprepared
576	Teaching	Hattie, Biggs, & Purdie	1996	51	5,443	270	0.45	0.030	32%	Study skills
577	Teaching	Purdie & Hattie	1999	52	—	653	0.28	0.007	20%	Study skills
578	Teaching	Robbins, Lauver, Le, Davis, Langley, & Carlstrom	2004	109	476	279	0.41	0.240	29%	Study skills at college
	Self-verbalization/Self questioning									
579	Teaching	Lavery	2008	30	1,937	223	0.46	0.060	33%	Self-regulated learning
580	Teaching	Kobayashi	2005	57	—	131	0.22	—	16%	Effects of note taking
581	Teaching	Dignath, Buettner, & Langfeldt	2008	30	2,364	263	0.69	0.030	49%	Self-regulation strategies
	Self-verbalization/Self questioning									
582	Teaching	Rock	1985	47	1,398	684	0.51	0.060	36%	Special ed self-instructional training
583	Teaching	Duzinski	1987	45	—	377	0.84	—	59%	Self-verbalizing instruction training
584	Teaching	Huang	1991	21	1,700	89	0.58	—	41%	Student self-questioning
	Student control over learning									
585	Teaching	Niemiec, Sikorski, & Walberg	1996	24	—	24	-0.03	0.149	-2%	Student control over learning in CAI
586	Teaching	Patall, Cooper, & Robinson	2008	41	—	14	0.10	0.027	7%	Control over learning on subsequent control
	Aptitude-treatment interactions									
587	Teaching	Kavale & Forness	1987	39	—	318	0.28	—	19%	Modality testing and teaching
588	Teaching	Whitener	1989	22	1,434	22	0.11	0.070	8%	
	Matching style of teaching									
589	Teaching	Tamir	1985	54	—	13	0.02	—	1%	Cognitive preference
590	Teaching	Garlinger & Frank	1986	7	1,531	7	-0.03	—	-2%	Field independence/dependence on achievement
591	Teaching	Sullivan	1993	42	3,434	42	0.75	—	53%	Dunn and dunn learning styles matched to achievement
592	Teaching	Iliff	1994	101	—	486	0.33	0.026	23%	Kolb Learning Style matched to achievement
593	Teaching	Dunn, Griggs, Olson, Beasley, & Gorman	1995	36	3,181	65	0.76	—	53%	Interventions to match learning style on achievement

Appendix A continues

Appendix A continued

No.	Domain	Author	Year	No. studies	Total no.	No. effects	Mean	se	CLE	Variable
594	Teaching	Slemmer	2002	48	5,908	51	0.27	—	19%	Learning styles in hyper/technology environments
595	Teaching	Mangino	2004	47	8,661	386	0.54	0.006	38%	Dunn and dunn learning styles for adults
596	Teaching	Lovelace	2005	76	7,196	168	0.67	—	47%	Dunn and dunn learning styles matched to achievement

Individual instruction

597	Teaching	Hartley	1977	51	—	139	0.16	0.091	11%	Individualization in math
598	Teaching	Kulik & Kulik	1980	213	—	213	0.33	0.034	23%	Individualized college achievement
599	Teaching	Horak	1981	60	—	129	-0.07	—	-5%	Individualization in math
600	Teaching	Willett, Yamashita & Anderson	1983	130	—	131	0.17	—	12%	Individualized science curriculum
601	Teaching	Bangert, Kulik, & Kulik	1983	49	—	49	0.1	0.053	4%	Individualized in high schools
602	Teaching	Waxman, Wang, Anderson & Walberg	1985	38	7,200	309	0.45	—	32%	Adaptive methods (individual, continuous assessment, periodic evaluation)
603	Teaching	Atash & Dawson	1986	10	2,180	30	0.09	0.046	6%	Individualized science curriculum
604	Teaching	Dacanay & Cohen	1992	30	—	30	0.37	—	26%	Individual instruction in medical education
605	Teaching	Elbaum, Vaughn, Hughes & Moody	1999	19	—	116	0.43	—	30%	Special ed in reading

Implementations emphasizing teaching strategies

Teaching strategies

606	Teaching	Rosenbaum	1983	235	—	99	1.02	—	72%	Treatment programs for emotionally disturbed students
607	Teaching	O'Neal	1985	31	—	96	0.81	0.155	57%	With cerebral palsy students
608	Teaching	Baenninger & Newcombe	1989	26	—	26	0.51	—	36%	Spatial strategies on spatial outcomes
609	Teaching	Forness & Kavale	1993	268	8,000	819	0.71	0.122	50%	Teaching with low ability students
610	Teaching	Fan	1993	41	3,219	223	0.56	—	40%	Metacognitive training on reading comprehension
611	Teaching	Scheerens & Bosker	1997	228	—	545	0.20	0.030	14%	Various strategies on achievement
612	Teaching	White	1997	222	15,080	1796	0.39	0.046	28%	Cognitive learning strategies in reading with LD
613	Teaching	White	1997	72	8,527	831	0.20	0.039	14%	Cognitive learning strategies in math with LD
614	Teaching	Marzano	1998	4000	1,237,000	4000	0.65	0.014	46%	Classroom instructional techniques
615	Teaching	Swanson & Hoskyn	1998	180	38,716	1537	0.79	0.013	56%	Teaching with low ability students
616	Teaching	Xin & Jitendra	1999	14	—	653	0.89	—	63%	Word problem solving in reading
617	Teaching	Swanson	2000	180	180,827	1537	0.79	0.013	56%	Learning strategies for special ed students

No.	Domain	Author	Year	No. studies	Total no.	No. effects	Mean	se	CLE	Variable
618	Teaching	Swanson	2001	58	—	58	0.82	0.087	58%	Programs to enhance problem solving
619	Teaching	Seidel & Shavelson	2007	112	—	1352	0.07	—	5%	Teaching and learning processes
Reciprocal teaching										
620	Teaching	Rosenshine & Meister	1994	16	—	31	0.74	—	52%	Reciprocal teaching
621	Teaching	Galloway	2003	22	677	22	0.74	—	52%	Reciprocal teaching on reading comprehension
Direct instruction										
622	Teaching	White	1988	25	—	24	0.83	0.133	59%	DI in special education
623	Teaching	Adams & Engelmann	1996	37	—	372	0.75	—	53%	DI on reading
624	Teaching	Borman, Hewes, Overman, & Brown	2003	232	42,618	182	0.21	0.020	15%	DI from comprehensive schools reforms
625	Teaching	Haas	2005	10	—	19	0.55	0.135	39%	Teaching methods in algebra
Adjunct aids										
626	Teaching	Readence & Moore	1981	16	2,227	122	0.45	0.020	32%	Adjunct pictures in reading
627	Teaching	Levie & Lentz	1982	23	7,182	41	0.55	—	39%	Text illustrations
628	Teaching	Catts	1992	8	—	19	0.01	0.067	1%	Adjunct aids
629	Teaching	Hoeffler, Sumfleth, & Leutner	2006	26	—	76	0.46	—	33%	Instructional animation vs. static pictures
Inductive teaching										
630	Teaching	Lott	1983	24	—	24	0.06	—	4%	Inductive teaching in science
631	Teaching	Klauer & Phye	2008	73	3,595	79	0.59	0.035	42%	Inductive teaching
Inquiry based teaching										
632	Teaching	Sweitzer & Anderson	1983	68	—	19	0.44	0.154	31%	Inquiry teaching in science
633	Teaching	Shymansky, Hedges & Woodworth	1990	81	—	320	0.27	0.030	19%	Inquiry methods in science
634	Teaching	Bangert-Drowns	1992	21	—	21	0.37	—	26%	Inquiry teaching effects on critical thinking
635	Teaching	Smith	1996	35	7,437	60	0.17	—	12%	Inquiry method in science
Problem-solving teaching										
636	Teaching	Marcucci	1980	33	—	237	0.35	—	25%	Problem solving in math
637	Teaching	Curbelo	1984	68	10,629	343	0.54	0.037	38%	Problem solving on science and math
638	Teaching	Almeida & Denham	1984	18	2,398	18	0.72	0.136	51%	Interpersonal problem solving
639	Teaching	Mellinger	1991	25	—	35	1.13	0.060	80%	Increasing cognitive flexibility
640	Teaching	Hembree	1992	55	—	55	0.33	—	23%	Problem solving instructional methods

Appendix A continues

Appendix A continued

No.	Domain	Author	Year	No. studies	Total no.	No. effects	Mean	se	CLE	Variable
641	Teaching	Taconis, Ferguson-Hessler, & Broekkamp	2001	22	2,208	31	0.59	0.070	42%	Problem solving in science
Problem-based learning										
642	Teaching	Albanese & Mitchell	1993	11	2,208	66	0.27	0.043	19%	PBL in medicine
643	Teaching	Vernon & Blake	1993	8	—	28	-0.18	—	-13%	PBL in college level
644	Teaching	Dochy, Segers, Van den Bossche, & Gijbels	2003	43	21,365	35	0.12	—	8%	PBL on knowledge and skills
645	Teaching	Smith	2003	82	12,979	121	0.31	—	22%	PBL in medicine
646	Teaching	Newman	2004	12	—	12	-0.30	—	-21%	PBL in medicine
647	Teaching	Haas	2005	7	1,538	34	0.52	0.187	37%	Teaching methods in algebra
648	Teaching	Gijbels, Dochy, Van den Bossche, & Segers	2005	40	—	49	0.32	—	23%	PBL on assessment outcomes
649	Teaching	Walker & Leary	2008	82	—	201	0.13	0.025	9%	PBL across disciplines
Cooperative learning										
650	Teaching	Johnson, Maruyama, Johnson, Nelson, & Skon	1981	122	—	183	0.73	—	52%	Cooperative learning
651	Teaching	Rolheiser-Bennett	1986	23	4,002	78	0.48	—	34%	Cooperative learning
652	Teaching	Hall	1988	22	10,022	52	0.31	—	22%	Cooperative learning
653	Teaching	Stevens & Slavin	1990	4	—	4	0.48	—	34%	Cooperative learning
654	Teaching	Spuler	1993	19	6,137	19	0.54	—	38%	Cooperative learning in math
655	Teaching	Othman	1996	39	—	39	0.27	—	19%	Cooperative learning in math
656	Teaching	Howard	1996	13	—	42	0.37	—	26%	Scripted cooperative learning
657	Teaching	Bowen	2000	37	3,000	49	0.51	0.050	36%	Cooperative learning in high school chemistry
658	Teaching	Neber, Finsterwald & Urban	2001	12	—	314	0.13	—	9%	Cooperative learning with gifted
659	Teaching	McMaster & Fuchs	2002	15	864	49	0.30	0.070	21%	Cooperative learning
Cooperative vs. competitive learning										
660	Teaching	Johnson, Maruyama, Johnson, Nelson, & Skon	1981	122	—	9	0.56	—	40%	Cooperative with intergroup competition
661	Teaching	Johnson, Johnson, & Marayama	1983	98	—	83	0.82	0.093	58%	Cooperative vs. competition
662	Teaching	Johnson & Johnson	1987	453	—	36	0.59	0.165	42%	Cooperative vs. competition
663	Teaching	Hall	1988	18	—	83	0.28	—	20%	Cooperative vs. competition
664	Teaching	Qin, Johnson, & Johnson	1995	46	—	63	0.55	—	39%	Cooperative vs. competition

No.	Domain	Author	Year	No. studies	Total no.	No. effects	Mean	se	CLE	Variable
665	Teaching	Johnson, Johnson, & Stanne	2000	158	—	66	0.55	0.059	39%	Cooperative vs. competition
666	Teaching	Roseth, Johnson & Johnson	2008	129	17,000	593	0.46	0.130	33%	Cooperative vs. competition

Cooperative vs. individualistic learning

No.	Domain	Author	Year	No. studies	Total no.	No. effects	Mean	se	CLE	Variable
667	Teaching	Johnson & Johnson	1987	453	—	70	0.68	0.139	48%	Cooperative vs. individualistic
668	Teaching	Hall	1988	15	—	77	0.26	—	18%	Cooperative vs. individualistic
669	Teaching	Johnson, Johnson, & Stanne	2000	158	—	82	0.88	0.066	62%	Cooperative vs. individualistic
670	Teaching	Roseth, Fang, Johnson, & Johnson	2006	148	—	55	0.55	0.060	39%	Cooperative vs. individualistic in middle school

Competitive vs. individualistic learning

No.	Domain	Author	Year	No. studies	Total no.	No. effects	Mean	se	CLE	Variable
671	Teaching	Johnson, Maruyama, Johnson, Nelson, & Skon	1981	122	—	163	0.09	—	6%	Competitive learning
672	Teaching	Johnson, Johnson, & Marayama	1983	98	—	16	0.45	0.288	32%	Competitive vs. individualistic
673	Teaching	Johnson & Johnson	1987	453	—	12	0.36	0.271	25%	Competitive vs. individualistic
674	Teaching	Johnson, Johnson, & Stanne	2000	158	—	12	0.04	0.138	3%	Competitive vs. individualistic

Implementations that emphasize school-wide teaching strategies

Comprehensive teaching reforms

No.	Domain	Author	Year	No. studies	Total no.	No. effects	Mean	se	CLE	Variable
675	Teaching	Borman & D'Agostino	1996	17	41,706,196	657	0.12	—	8%	Evaluation of federal title I programs
676	Teaching	Friedrich	1997	33	—	50	0.38	—	27%	Alternative programs for at-risk youth
677	Teaching	Borman, Hewes, Overman, & Brown	2003	232	222,956	1111	0.15	—	11%	Comprehensive school reform

Interventions for learning disabled students

No.	Domain	Author	Year	No. studies	Total no.	No. effects	Mean	se	CLE	Variable
678	Teaching	Swanson, Carson, & Sachse-Lee	1996	78	—	324	0.85	0.065	60%	Programs for learning disabled students
679	Teaching	Swanson, Hoskyn, & Lee	1999	180	4,871	1537	0.56	0.017	40%	Between-group designs
680	Teaching	Swanson, Hoskyn, & Lee	1999	85	793	793	0.90	0.008	64%	Single-subject designs

Special college programs

No.	Domain	Author	Year	No. studies	Total no.	No. effects	Mean	se	CLE	Variable
681	Teaching	Kulik, Kulik, & Shwalb	1983	60	—	60	0.27	0.040	19%	College programs for high risk students
682	Teaching	Cohn	1985	48	—	48	0.20	—	14%	Innovative teaching vs. trad lectures in economics

Co-/Team teaching

No.	Domain	Author	Year	No. studies	Total no.	No. effects	Mean	se	CLE	Variable
683	Teaching	Murawski & Swanson	2001	6	1,617	6	0.31	0.057	22%	Co-teaching
684	Teaching	Willett, Yamashita & Anderson	1983	130	—	41	0.06	—	4%	Co-teaching in science

Appendix A continues

Implementations using technologies

Computer assisted instruction

No.	Domain	Author	Year	No. studies	Total no.	No. effects	Mean	se	CLE	Variable
685	Teaching	Hartley	1977	33	—	89	0.41	0.062	29%	CAI on achievement
686	Teaching	Aiello & Wolfe	1980	115	—	182	0.08	—	6%	CAI in high school science
687	Teaching	Kulik, Kulik & Cohen	1980	312	—	278	0.48	0.030	34%	CAI on college
688	Teaching	Burns & Bozeman	1981	40	—	40	0.40	—	28%	CAI in mathematics
689	Teaching	Leong	1981	22	—	106	0.08	—	6%	CAI in high school math
690	Teaching	Athappilly, Smidchens, & Kofel	1983	134	—	810	0.10	—	7%	CAI in Modern math vs. trad math
691	Teaching	Kulik, Kulik, & Bangert-Drowns	1985	51	—	51	0.32	—	23%	CAI on high school students
692	Teaching	Kulik, Bangert, & Williams	1983	97	—	97	0.36	0.035	25%	CAI with high school students
693	Teaching	Willett, Yamashita, & Anderson	1983	130	—	130	0.13	—	9%	CAI in science
694	Teaching	Kulik et al.	1984	25	—	25	0.48	0.063	34%	CAI with elementary school students
695	Teaching	Bangert-Drowns	1985	74	—	74	0.33	—	23%	CAI with pre-college students
696	Teaching	Bangert-Drowns, Kulik & Kulik	1985	42	—	42	0.26	0.063	18%	CAI in high schools
697	Teaching	Clark	1985	42	—	42	0.09	—	6%	CAI in schools
698	Teaching	Kulik, Kulik, & Bangert-Drowns	1985	32	—	32	0.47	0.055	33%	CAI with elementary school students
699	Teaching	Kulik & Kulik	1986	48	—	48	0.32	0.061	23%	CAI on college
700	Teaching	Kulik, Kulik, & Shwalb	1986	23	—	23	0.42	0.110	30%	CAI with adults
701	Teaching	Schmidt, Weinstein, Niemic, & Walberg	1986	18	—	48	0.67	0.048	47%	CAI with exceptional children
702	Teaching	Shwalb, Shwalb, & Azuma	1986	104	—	4	0.74	0.069	52%	CAI in Japan
703	Teaching	Gillingham & Guthrie	1987	13	—	13	1.05	—	74%	Computer-based instruction
704	Teaching	Kulik & Kulik	1987	199	—	199	0.31	—	22%	CAI on achievement
705	Teaching	Niemiec, Samson, Weinstein & Walberg	1987	48	—	224	0.32	—	23%	CAI with elementary school students
706	Teaching	Cunningham	1988	37	—	37	0.33	—	23%	Computer-generated graphics on achievement
707	Teaching	Roblyer, Castine & King	1988	85	—	85	0.26	—	18%	CAI on achievement
708	Teaching	Wise	1988	26	—	26	0.30	—	21%	CAI in science
709	Teaching	Kuchler	1988	65	—	65	0.44	0.068	31%	CAI to teach high school math
710	Teaching	McDermid	1989	15	—	15	0.57	—	40%	CAI on learning disabled and educably mentally retarded
711	Teaching	Bishop	1990	40	—	58	0.55	—	39%	Computers in elementary schools
712	Teaching	Wen-Cheng	1990	72	—	243	0.38	0.037	27%	CAI in elementary and high

No.	Domain	Author	Year	No. studies	Total no.	No. effects	Mean	se	CLE	Variable
713	Teaching	Gordon	1991	84	—	83	0.26	0.030	18%	Computer graphics and math and problem solving
714	Teaching	Jones	1991	40	—	58	0.31	—	22%	CAI on elementary school students
715	Teaching	Kulik & Kulik	1991	248	240	248	0.30	0.029	21%	CAI on achievement
716	Teaching	Liao & Bright	1991	65	—	432	0.41	0.020	29%	Computer programming on achievement
717	Teaching	Palmeter	1991	37	—	144	0.48	0.055	34%	CAI/Logo on higher cognitive processes
718	Teaching	Ryan	1991	40	—	58	0.31	—	22%	Microcomputer applications
719	Teaching	Schramm	1991	12	836	12	0.36	0.110	25%	Word processing on writing
720	Teaching	Cohen & Dacanay	1992	37	—	37	0.41	—	29%	Computer-based in health education
721	Teaching	Liao	1992	31	—	207	0.48	0.163	34%	CAI on achievement
722	Teaching	Bangert-Drowns	1993	32	—	32	0.39	—	28%	Word processing on writing
723	Teaching	Ouyang	1993	79	—	267	0.50	0.038	35%	CAI in elementary schools
724	Teaching	Chen	1994	76	—	98	0.47	0.071	33%	Computer-based in math
725	Teaching	Kulik & Kulik	1994	97	—	32	0.35	0.04	25%	CAI on achievement
726	Teaching	Kulik & Kulik	1994	97	—	97	0.32	—	23%	CAI in high schools
727	Teaching	Christmann	1995	35	3,476	35	0.23	—	16%	CAI in schools
728	Teaching	Fletcher-Flynn & Gravatt	1995	120	—	120	0.17	—	12%	CAI on achievement
729	Teaching	Hamilton	1995	41	—	253	0.66	0.033	46%	CAI in schools
730	Teaching	Ianno	1995		—		0.31	—	22%	CAI on reading of learning disabled
731	Teaching	Cassil	1996	21	—	349	0.29	—	21%	Mobile computers
732	Teaching	Chadwick	1997	41	8,170	41	0.51	—	36%	CAI in high school math
733	Teaching	Christmann, Badgett & Lucking	1997	27	—	27	0.21	—	15%	CAI in high schools
734	Teaching	King	1997	30	—	68	0.20	—	14%	CAI college math
735	Teaching	Christmann & Badgett	1999	11	5,020	11	0.28	—	20%	CAI in high schools
736	Teaching	Soe, Koki, & Chang	2000	17	—	33	0.27	0.022	19%	CAI in reading
737	Teaching	Woolf & Regian	2000	233	—	233	0.39	—	28%	CAI on achievement
738	Teaching	Lou, Abrami & d'Apollonia	2001	100	11,317	178	0.16	0.041	11%	CAI in small groups
739	Teaching	Lou, Abrami & d'Apollonia	2001	22	—	39	0.31	0.117	22%	CAI in small groups
740	Teaching	Yaakub & Finch	2001	21	2,969	28	0.35	—	25%	CAI-based technical education instruction
741	Teaching	Akiba	2002	21	—	21	0.37	—	26%	CAI on achievement
742	Teaching	Bayraktar	2002	42	—	108	0.27	—	19%	CAI in science education
743	Teaching	Blok, Oostdam, Otter, & Overmaat	2002	42	—	42	0.19	—	13%	CAI on beginning reading
744	Teaching	Roberts	2002	31	6,388	165	0.69	—	49%	CAI on achievement

Appendix A continues

Appendix A continued

No.	Domain	Author	Year	No. studies	Total no.	No. effects	Mean	se	CLE	Variable
745	Teaching	Torgerson & Elbourne	2002	7	—	7	0.37	—	26%	CAI on spelling
746	Teaching	Waxman, Connell, & Gray	2002	20	4,400	138	0.39	—	28%	Technology vs. traditional teaching on achievement
747	Teaching	Chambers	2002	57	64,766	125	0.51	—	36%	CAI in elementary and high school classrooms
748	Teaching	Chambers & Schreiber	2004	25	—	25	0.40	—	28%	CAI in elementary and high school classrooms
749	Teaching	Torgerson & Zhu	2003	212	—	43	0.26	0.094	18%	CAI on literacy
750	Teaching	Goldberg, Russell & Cook	2003	26	1,507	26	0.50	—	35%	Effects of CAI on writing
751	Teaching	Hsu	2003	25	—	31	0.43	—	30%	CAI in statistics
752	Teaching	Kroesbergen & Van Luit	2003	58	10,223	58	0.75	—	53%	CAI and math with special education
753	Teaching	Kulik	2003	12	—	12	0.88	—	62%	CAI on college
754	Teaching	Torgerson & Zhu	2003	17	—	17	0.36	—	25%	CAI and literacy outcomes
755	Teaching	Waxman, Lin, Michko	2003	29	7,728	167	0.54	0.061	38%	CAI on achievement
756	Teaching	Bernard, Abrami, Wade, Borokhovski, & Lou	2004	232	3,831,888	688	0.20	—	14%	CAI in distance education
757	Teaching	Lou	2004	71	—	399	0.15	—	11%	Small group vs. individual with CAI on tasks attempted
758	Teaching	Liao	2007	52	4,981	134	0.55	—	39%	CAI in Taiwan
759	Teaching	Pearson, Ferdig, Blomeyer, & Moran	2005	20	—	89	0.49	0.078	35%	Technology on reading
760	Teaching	Abrami, Bernard, Wade, Schmid, Borokhovski, Tamin, Surkes, Lowerison, Zhang, Nicolaidou, Newman, Wozney, & Peretiatkowics	2006	17	—	29	0.17	—	12%	e-learning in Canada
761	Teaching	Sandy-Hanson	2006	23	9,897	23	0.28	—	20%	CAI on achievement
762	Teaching	Shapiro, Kerssen-Griep, Gayle & Allen	2006	12	—	16	0.26	—	—	PowerPoint in the class
763	Teaching	Timmerman & Kruepke	2006	118	12,398	118	0.24	0.020	17%	CAI with college students
764	Teaching	Onuoha	2007	38	3,824	67	0.26	—	18%	Computer-based labs in science
765	Teaching	Rosen & Salomon	2007	32	—	32	0.46	—	33%	Constructivist technology intensive learning
Simulations										
766	Teaching	Dekkers & Donatti	1981	93	—	93	0.33	—	23%	Simulations and achievement
767	Teaching	Remmer & Jernstet	1982	21	—	21	0.20	—	14%	Computer simulations

No.	Domain	Author	Year	No. studies	Total no.	No. effects	Mean	se	CLE	Variable
768	Teaching	Szczurek	1982	58	—	58	0.33	—	23%	Simulation games
769	Teaching	VanSickle	1986	42	—	42	0.43	—	30%	Instructional simulation gaming
770	Teaching	Lee	1990	19	—	34	0.28	0.114	20%	Simulations on achievement
771	Teaching	McKenna	1991	26	—	118	0.38	0.070	27%	Simulations in economics
772	Teaching	Armstrong	1991	43	—	43	0.29	—	21%	Computers and simulations and games
773	Teaching	Lee	1999	19	—	19	0.40	—	28%	Computer simulations
774	Teaching	Lejeune	2002	40	6,416	54	0.34	—	24%	Computer simulated experiments in science
Web-based learning										
775	Teaching	Olson & Wisher	2002	15	—	15	0.24	0.150	17%	Web-based learning
776	Teaching	Sitzman, Kraiger, Stewart, & Wisher	2006	96	19,331	96	0.15	—	11%	Web-based and traditional classes
777	Teaching	Mukawa	2006	25	3,223	25	0.14	0.099	10%	Web-based learning principles
Interactive video										
778	Teaching	Clark & Angert	1980	23	4,800	1000	0.65	—	46%	
779	Teaching	Angert & Clark	1982	181	—	2607	0.51	—	36%	Media methods on achievement
780	Teaching	Shwalb, Shwalb, & Azuma	1986	104	—	33	0.49	0.055	35%	Technology in Japan
781	Teaching	Fletcher	1989	24	—	47	0.50	0.080	35%	Interactive video disk technology
782	Teaching	McNeil & Nelson	1991	63	—	100	0.53	0.097	37%	Multimedia technologies
783	Teaching	Liao	1999	46	—	143	0.41	0.073	29%	Hypermedia vs. traditional instruction
Audio/Visual methods										
784	Teaching	Kulik, Kulik & Cohen	1979	42	—	42	0.20	—	14%	Audio-based teaching
785	Teaching	Cohen, Ebeling, & Kulik	1981	65	—	65	0.15	—	11%	Visual-based instruction
786	Teaching	Willett, Yamashita & Anderson	1983	130	—	100	0.02	—	1%	Visual aids in science
787	Teaching	Shwalb, Shwalb, & Azuma	1986	104	—	6	0.09	0.110	6%	Audio-based teaching in Japan
788	Teaching	Blanchard, Stock & Marshall	1999	10	2,760	10	0.16	0.030	11%	Multi-medium using personal and video-game computers
789	Teaching	Baker & Dwyer	2000	8	—	8	0.71	—	50%	Use of visual aids in learning
Programmed instruction										
790	Teaching	Hartley	1977	40	—	81	0.11	0.111	8%	PI in mathematics
791	Teaching	Kulik, Cohen, & Ebeling	1980	57	—	57	0.24	—	17%	PI with college students
792	Teaching	Kulik, Kulik & Cohen	1980	56	—	56	0.24	—	17%	PI in college
793	Teaching	Kulik, Schwalb, & Kulik	1982	47	—	47	0.08	0.070	6%	PI in high schools

Appendix A continues

Appendix A continued

No.	Domain	Author	Year	No. studies	Total no.	No. effects	Mean	se	CLE	Variable
794	Teaching	Willett, Yamashita & Anderson	1983	130	—	52	0.17	—	12%	PI in science
795	Teaching	Shwalb, Shwalb, & Azuma	1986	104	—	39	0.43	0.028	30%	PI in Japan
796	Teaching	Boden, Archwamety, & MacFarland	2000	30	—	30	0.40	0.146	28%	PI in high schools

Implementations using out-of-school learning

Distance education

No.	Domain	Author	Year	No. studies	Total no.	No. effects	Mean	se	CLE	Variable
797	Teaching	Machtmes & Asher	2000	19	—	19	-0.01	—	-1%	Effectiveness of telecourses
798	Teaching	Cavanaugh	1999	19	—	19	0.13	—	9%	Interactive distance learning on achievement
799	Teaching	Cavanaugh	2001	19	929	19	0.15	0.106	10%	Interactive distance education
800	Teaching	Shachar & Neumann	2003	72	15,300	86	0.37	0.035	26%	Distance vs. traditional teaching
801	Teaching	Allen, Mabry, Mattrey, Bourhis, Titsworth, & Burrell	2004	25	71,731	39	0.10	—	7%	Distance vs. traditional classes
802	Teaching	Cavanaugh, Gillan, Kromrey, Hess, & Blomeyer	2004	14	7,561	116	-0.03	0.045	-2%	Distance in all classes
803	Teaching	Williams	2004	25	—	34	0.15	—	11%	Distance in allied health science programs
804	Teaching	Bernard, Abrami, Lou, Wozney, Borokhovski; Wallet, Wade, Fiset	2004	232	3,831,888	688	0.01	0.010	1%	Distance education
805	Teaching	Bernard, Lou, Abrami, Wozney, Borokhovski; Wallet, Wade, Fiset	2004	155	—	155	-0.02	0.015	-1%	Presence or not: asynchronous and asynchronous
806	Teaching	Zhao, Lei, Yan, Lai, & Tan	2005	51	11,477	98	0.10	—	7%	Distance vs. traditional classes
807	Teaching	Allen, Bourhis, Mabry, Burrell, & Timmerman	2006	54	74,275	54	0.09	—	7%	Distance vs. traditional teaching
808	Teaching	Lou, Bernard, & Abrami	2006	103	—	218	0.02	—	1%	Distance education in undergraduates
809	Teaching	Zhao, Lei, Yan, Lai, & Tan	2005	51	11,477	98	0.10	0.090	7%	Distance vs. traditional classes

Home-school programs

No.	Domain	Author	Year	No. studies	Total no.	No. effects	Mean	se	CLE	Variable
810	Teaching	Penuel, Kim, Michalchik, Lewis, Means, Murphy, Korbak, Whaley, & Allen	2002	14	—	14	0.16	—	11%	Laptop programs between school and home

Homework

No.	Domain	Author	Year	No. studies	Total no.	No. effects	Mean	se	CLE	Variable
811	Teaching	Paschal, Weinstein, & Walberg	1984	15	—	81	0.36	0.027	25%	Homework on learning
812	Teaching	Cooper	1989	20	2,154	20	0.21	—	15%	Homework on achievement
813	Teaching	DeBaz	1994	77	41,828	77	0.39	—	27%	Homework in science
814	Teaching	Cooper	1994	17	3,300	48	0.21	—	15%	Homework on learning
815	Teaching	Cooper, Robinson, & Patall	2006	32	58,000	69	0.28	—	20%	Homework from studies 1987-2004

Appendix B

The meta-analyses by rank order

Rank	Domain	Influence	d
1	Student	Self-report grades	1.44
2	Student	Piagetian programs	1.28
3	Teaching	Providing formative evaluation	0.90
4	Teacher	Micro teaching	0.88
5	School	Acceleration	0.88
6	School	Classroom behavioral	0.80
7	Teaching	Comprehensive interventions for learning disabled students	0.77
8	Teacher	Teacher clarity	0.75
9	Teaching	Reciprocal teaching	0.74
10	Teaching	Feedback	0.73
11	Teacher	Teacher-student relationships	0.72
12	Teaching	Spaced vs. mass practice	0.71
13	Teaching	Meta-cognitive strategies	0.69
14	Student	Prior achievement	0.67
15	Curricula	Vocabulary programs	0.67
16	Curricula	Repeated reading programs	0.67
17	Curricula	Creativity programs	0.65
18	Teaching	Self-verbalization/self-questioning	0.64
19	Teacher	Professional development	0.62
20	Teaching	Problem-solving teaching	0.61
21	Teacher	Not Labeling students	0.61
22	Curricula	Phonics instruction	0.60
23	Teaching	Teaching strategies	0.60
24	Teaching	Cooperative vs. individualistic learning	0.59
25	Teaching	Study skills	0.59
26	Teaching	Direct Instruction	0.59
27	Curricula	Tactile stimulation programs	0.58
28	Curricula	Comprehension programs	0.58
29	Teaching	Mastery learning	0.58
30	Teaching	Worked examples	0.57
31	Home	Home environment	0.57

Appendix B continues

Appendix B continued

Rank	Domain	Influence	d
32	Home	Socioeconomic status	0.57
33	Teaching	Concept mapping	0.57
34	Teaching	Goals	0.56
35	Curricula	Visual-perception programs	0.55
36	Teaching	Peer tutoring	0.55
37	Teaching	Cooperative vs. competitive learning	0.54
38	Student	Pre-term birth weight	0.54
39	School	Classroom cohesion	0.53
40	Teaching	Keller's PIS	0.53
41	School	Peer influences	0.53
42	School	Classroom management	0.52
43	Curricula	Outdoor/adventure Programs	0.52
44	Teaching	Interactive video methods	0.52
45	Home	Parental involvement	0.51
46	Curricula	Play programs	0.50
47	Curricula	Second/third chance programs	0.50
48	School	Small group learning	0.49
49	Student	Concentration/persistence/engagement	0.48
50	School	School effects	0.48
51	Student	Motivation	0.48
52	Student	Early intervention	0.47
53	Teaching	Questioning	0.46
54	Curricula	Mathematics	0.45
55	Student	Preschool programs	0.45
56	Teacher	Quality of Teaching	0.44
57	Curricula	Writing Programs	0.44
58	Teacher	Expectations	0.43
59	School	School size	0.43
60	Student	Self-concept	0.43
61	Teaching	Behavioral organizers/Adjunct questions	0.41
62	Teaching	Matching style of learning	0.41
63	Teaching	Cooperative learning	0.41
64	Curricula	Science	0.40
65	Curricula	Social skills programs	0.40
66	Student	Reducing anxiety	0.40
67	Curricula	Integrated Curriculum Programs	0.39
68	School	Enrichment	0.39
69	Curricula	Career Interventions	0.38
70	Teaching	Time on Task	0.38
71	Teaching	Computer assisted instruction	0.37
72	Teaching	Adjunct aids	0.37

Rank	Domain	Influence	*d*
73	Curricula	Bilingual programs	0.37
74	School	Principals/ school leaders	0.36
75	Student	Attitude to mathematics/science	0.36
76	Curricula	Exposure to reading	0.36
77	Curricula	Drama/Arts programs	0.35
78	Student	Creativity	0.35
79	Teaching	Frequent/effects of testing	0.34
80	School	Decreasing disruptive behavior	0.34
81	Student	Drugs	0.33
82	Teaching	Simulations	0.33
83	Teaching	Inductive teaching	0.33
84	Student	Positive view of own ethnicity	0.32
85	Teacher	Teacher effects	0.32
86	Teaching	Inquiry based teaching	0.31
87	School	Ability grouping for gifted Students	0.30
88	Teaching	Homework	0.29
89	Home	Home visiting	0.29
90	Student	Exercise/relaxation	0.28
91	School	Desegregation	0.28
92	School	Mainstreaming	0.28
93	Curricula	Use of calculators	0.27
94	Curricula	Values/moral education programs	0.24
95	Teaching	Programmed instruction	0.24
96	Teaching	Special college programs	0.24
97	Teaching	Competitive vs. individualistic learning	0.24
98	School	Summer school	0.23
99	School	Finances	0.23
100	Teaching	Individualized instruction	0.23
101	School	Religious Schools	0.23
102	Student	Lack of Illness	0.23
103	Teaching	Teaching test taking	0.22
104	Teaching	Visual/audio-visual methods	0.22
105	Teaching	Comprehensive teaching reforms	0.22
106	School	Class size	0.21
107	School	Charter Schools	0.20
108	Teaching	Aptitude/treatment interactions	0.19
109	Student	Personality	0.19
110	Teaching	Learning hierarchies	0.19
111	Teaching	Co-/ team teaching	0.19
112	Teaching	Web-based learning	0.18
113	Home	Family structure	0.17

Appendix B continues

Appendix B continued

Rank	Domain	Influence	d
114	Curricula	Extra-curricular programs	0.17
115	Teaching	Teacher immediacy	0.16
116	School	Within class grouping	0.16
117	Teaching	Home-school programs	0.16
118	Teaching	Problem-based learning	0.15
119	Curricula	Sentence combining programs	0.15
120	Teaching	Mentoring	0.15
121	School	Ability grouping	0.12
122	Student	Gender	0.12
123	Student	Diet	0.12
124	Teacher	Teacher training	0.11
125	Teacher	Teacher subject matter knowledge	0.09
126	Teaching	Distance Education	0.09
127	School	Out of school curricula experiences	0.09
128	Curricula	Perceptual-Motor programs	0.08
129	Curricula	Whole language	0.06
130	School	College halls of residence	0.05
131	School	Multi-grade/age classes	0.04
132	Teaching	Student control over learning	0.04
133	School	Open vs. traditional	0.01
134	School	Summer vacation	−0.09
135	Home	Welfare policies	−0.12
136	School	Retention	−0.16
137	Home	Television	−0.18
138	School	Mobility	−0.34

Bibliography

Abrami, P. C., Bernard, R. M., Borokhovski, E., Wade, A. C., Surkes, M. A., Tamim, R., et al. (2008, May). *Instructional interventions affecting critical thinking skills and dispositions: A stage one meta-analysis.* Paper presented at the eighth annual international Campbell Collaboration Colloquium, Vancouver, BC, Canada.

Abrami, P. C., Bernard, R. M., Wade, A. C., Schmid, R. F., Borokhovski, E., Tamim, R., et al. (2006). *A review of e-learning in Canada: A rough sketch of the evidence, gaps and promising directions.* Montreal, Quebec, Canada: Centre for the Study of Learning and Performance, Concordia University.

Abrami, P. C., Leventhal, L., & Perry, R. P. (1982). Educational seduction. *Review of Educational Research, 52*(3), 446–464.

Abt Associates. (1977). *Education as experimentation: A planned variation model: Vol. IV-B. Effects of Follow Through Models.* Cambridge, MA: Abt Associates.

Ackerman, P. L., & Goff, M. (1994). Typical intellectual engagement and personality: Reply to Rocklin (1994). *Journal of Educational Psychology, 86*(1), 150–153.

Adair, J. G., Sharpe, D., & Huynh, C. L. (1989). Hawthorne control procedures in educational experiments: A reconsideration of their use and effectiveness. *Review of Educational Research, 59*(2), 215.

Adams, G. L., & Engelmann, S. (1996). *Research on direct instruction: 20 years beyond DISTAR.* Seattle, WA: Educational Achievement Systems.

Aegisdottir, S., White, M. J., Spengler, P. M., Maugherman, A. S., Anderson, L. A., Cook, R. S., et al. (2006). The meta-analysis of clinical judgment project: Fifty-six years of accumulated research on clinical versus statistical prediction. *Counseling Psychologist, 34*(3), 341–382.

Ahn, S., & Choi, J. (2004, April). *Teachers' subject matter knowledge as a teacher qualification: A synthesis of the quantitative literature on students' mathematics achievement.* Paper presented at the American Educational Research Association, San Diego, CA.

Aiello, N. C., & Wolfle, L. M. (1980, April). *A meta-analysis of individualized instruction in science.* Paper presented at the Annual Meeting of the American Educational Research Association, Boston, MA.

Airasian, P. W. (1991). Perspectives on measurement instruction. *Educational Measurement: Issues and Practice, 10*(1), 13–16, 26.

Aitken, J. R. (1969). *A study of attitudes and attitudinal change of institutionalized delinquents through group guidance techniques.* Unpublished Ed.D., The University of Southern Mississippi, MS.

AJHR. (1939). *Appendices to the Journals of the House of Representatives, E1.* Wellington: New Zealand Government Printer.

Ajzen, I., & Madden, T. J. (1986). Prediction of goal-directed behavior: Attitudes, intentions, and perceived behavioral control. *Journal of Experimental Social Psychology, 22*(5), 453–474.

Akerhielm, K. (1995). Does class size matter? *Economics of Education Review, 14*(3), 229–241.

Akiba, M. (2002). Computer-assisted instruction. In Z. Barley, P. A. Lauer, S. A. Arens, H. A. Apthorp, K. S. Englert, D. Snow & M. Akiba (Eds.), *Helping At-Risk Students Meet Standards: A Synthesis of Evidence-Based Classroom Practices* (pp. 97–109). Aurora, CO: Mid-Continent Research for Education and Learning.

Albanese, M. A., & Mitchell, S. (1993). Problem-based learning: A review of literature on its outcomes and implementation issues. *Academic Medicine, 68*(1), 52–81.

Alessi, G. (1988). Diagnosis diagnosed: A systemic reaction. *Professional School Psychology, 3*, 145–151.

Alexander, K. L., Cook, M., & McDill, E. L. (1978). Curriculum tracking and educational stratification: Some further evidence. *American Sociological Review, 43*(1), 47–66.

Alexander, P. A. (2003). The development of expertise: The journey from acclimation to proficiency. *Educational Researcher, 32*(8), 10–14.

Allen, M. (1995, February). *Research productivity and positive teaching evaluations: Examining the relationship using meta-analysis.* Paper presented at the Annual Meeting of the Western States Communication Association.

Allen, M. (1996). Research productivity and positive teaching evaluations: Examining the relationship using meta-analysis. *Journal of the Association for Communication Administration, May*(2), 77–96.

Allen, M. (2006). Relationship of teaching evaluations to research productivity for college faculty. In B. M. Gayle, R. W. Preiss, N. Burrell & M. Allen (Eds.), *Classroom communication and instructional processes: Advances through meta-analysis.* Mahwah, NJ: Lawrence Erlbaum Associates.

Allen, M., Bourhis, J., Burrell, N., & Mabry, E. (2002). Comparing student satisfaction with distance education to traditional classrooms in higher education: A meta-analysis. *American Journal of Distance Education, 16*(2), 83–97.

Allen, M., Bourhis, J., Mabry, E., Burrell, N. A., & Timmerman, C. E. (2006). Comparing distance education to face-to-face methods of education. In B. M. Gayle, R. W. Preiss, N. Burrell & M. Allen (Eds.), *Classroom communication and instructional processes: Advances through meta-analysis* (pp. 229–244). Mahwah, NJ: Lawrence Erlbaum Associates.

Allen, M., Bradford, L., Grimes, D., Cooper, E., Howard, L., & Howard, U. (1999, November). *Racial group orientation and social outcomes: Summarizing relationships using meta-analysis.* Paper presented at the Annual meeting of the National Communication Association, Chicago.

Allen, M., Mabry, E., Mattrey, M., Bourhis, J., Titsworth, S., & Burrell, N. (2004). Evaluating the effectiveness of distance learning: A comparison using meta-analysis. *Journal of Communication, 54*(3), 402–420.

Allen, M., Witt, P. L., & Wheeless, L. R. (2006). The role of teacher immediacy as a motivational factor in student learning: Using meta-analysis to test a causal model. *Communication Education, 55*(1), 21–31.

Almeida, M. C., & Denham, S. A. (1984, April). *Interpersonal cognitive problem-solving: A meta-analysis.* Paper presented at the Annual Meeting of the Eastern Psychological Association, Baltimore.

Alton-Lee, A. (2003). *Quality teaching for diverse students in schooling: Best evidence synthesis iteration.* Wellington, New Zealand: Ministry of Education.

Amato, P. R. (2001). Children of divorce in the 1990s: An update of the Amato and Keith (1991) meta-analysis. *Journal of Family Psychology, 15*(3), 355–370.

Amato, P. R., & Gilbreth, J. G. (1999). Nonresident fathers and children's well-being: A meta-analysis. *Journal of Marriage and Family, 61*(3), 557–573.

Amato, P. R., & Keith, B. (1991). Parental divorce and the well-being of children: A meta-analysis. *Psychological Bulletin 110*(1), 26–46.

Ames, C. (1992). Classrooms: Goals, structures, and student motivation. *Journal of Educational Psychology, 84*(3), 261–271.

Amrein, A. L., & Berliner, D. C. (2002). High-stakes testing and student learning [Electronic Version]. *Education Policy Analysis Archives, 10.* Retrieved 28 April 2008 from http://epaa.asu.edu/epaa/v10n18/.

Anderman, L. H., & Anderman, E. M. (1999). Social predictors of changes in students' achievement goal orientations. *Contemporary Educational Psychology, 24*(1), 21–37.

Anderson, L. W., Krathwohl, D. R., & Bloom, B. S. (2001). *A taxonomy for learning, teaching, and assessing: A revision of Bloom's taxonomy of educational objectives* (Abridged ed.). New York: Longman.

Anderson, R. C., Hiebert, E. H., Scott, J. A., & Wilkinson, I. A. G. (1985). *Becoming a nation of readers: The report of the Commission on Reading.* Washington, DC: National Academy of Education, National Institute of Education, and Center for the Study of Reading.

Anderson, R. D., Kahl, S. R., Glass, G.V., & Smith, M. L. (1983). Science education: A meta-analysis of major questions. *Journal of Research in Science Teaching, 20*(5), 379–385.

Anderson, S. A. (1994). *Synthesis of research on mastery learning.* ERIC document 382 567.

Angert, J. F., & Clark, F. E. (1982, May). *Finding the rose among the thorns: Some thoughts on integrating media research.* Paper presented at the Annual Meeting of the Association for Educational Communications and Technology, Research and Theory Division, Dallas, TX.

Angrist, J. D., & Lavy, V. (1999). Using Maimonides' Rule to estimate the effect of class size on scholastic achievement. *Quarterly Journal of Economics, 114*(2), 533–575.

Applegate, B. (1986, November). *A meta-analysis of the effects of day care on development: preliminary findings.* Paper presented at the Annual Meeting of the Mid-South Educational Research Association, Memphis, TN.

Apter, M. J. (2001). *Motivational styles in everyday life: A guide to reversal theory* (1st ed.). Washington, DC: American Psychological Association.

Aristotle. (350BC/1908). *The Nicomachean ethics of Aristotle* (W. D. Ross, Trans.). Oxford, UK: Clarendon Press.

Armitage, C. J., & Conner, M. (2001). Efficacy of the theory of planned behaviour: A meta-analytic review. *British Journal of Social Psychology, 40,* 471–499.

Armor, D. J. (1983). *The evidence on desegregation and Black achievement.* Washington, DC: National Institute on Education.

Armstrong, D. G. (1977). Team teaching and academic achievement. *Review of Educational Research, 47*(1), 65–86.

Armstrong, P. S. (1991). *Computer-based simulations in learning environments: A meta-analysis of outcomes.* Unpublished Ph.D., Purdue University, IN.

Arnold, K. S., Myette, B. M., & Casto, G. (1986). Relationships of language intervention efficacy to certain subject characteristics in mentally retarded preschool children: A meta-analysis. *Education and Training of the Mentally Retarded, 21,* 108–116.

Asencio, C. E. (1984). *Effects of behavioral objectives on student achievement: A meta-analysis of findings.* Unpublished Ph.D., The Florida State University, FL.

Atash, M. N., & Dawson, G. O. (1986). Some effects of the ISCS program: A meta-analysis. *Journal of Research in Science Teaching, 23*(5), 377–385.

Athappilly, K., Smidchens, U., & Kofel, J. W. (1983). A computer-based meta-analysis of the effects of modern mathematics in comparison with traditional mathematics. *Educational Evaluation and Policy Analysis, 5*(4), 485–493.

Athappilly, K. (1978). *A meta-analysis of the effects of modern mathematics in comparison with traditional mathematics in the American educational system.* Unpublished Ed.D., Western Michigan University, MI.

Atkinson, D. L. (1993). *A meta-analysis of recent research in the teaching of writing: Workshops, computer applications, and inquiry.* Unpublished Ph.D., Purdue University, IN.

Au, W. (2007). High-stakes testing and curricular control: A qualitative metasynthesis. *Educational Researcher, 36*(5), 258–267.

Ausubel, D. P. (1968). *Educational psychology: A cognitive view.* New York: Holt, Rinehart, and Winston.

Azevedo, R., & Bernard, R. (1995). Assessing the effects of feedback in computer-assisted learning. *British Journal of Educational Technology, 26*(1), 57–58.

Baenninger, M., & Newcombe, N. (1989). The role of experience in spatial test performance: A meta-analysis. *Sex Roles, 20*(5–6), 327–344.

Baker, D. P., & Stevenson, D. L. (1986). Mothers' strategies for children's school achievement: Managing the transition to high school. *Sociology of Education, 59*(3), 156–166.

Baker, E. T. (1994). *Meta-analytic evidence for noninclusive educational practices: Does educational research support current practice for special needs students?* Unpublished Ph.D., Temple University, PA.

Baker, E. T., Wang, M. C., & Walberg, H. J. (1994). The effects of inclusion on learning. *Educational Leadership, 52*(4), 33–35.

Baker, R. M., & Dwyer, F. (2000). A meta-analytic assessment of the effect of visualized instruction. *International Journal of Instructional Media, 27*(4), 417–426.

Baker, R. M., & Dwyer, F. (2005). Effect of instructional strategies and individual differences: A meta-analytic assessment. *International Journal of Instructional Media, 32*(1), 69.

Baker, S., Gersten, R., & Lee, D. S. (2002). A synthesis of empirical research on teaching mathematics to low-achieving students. *Elementary School Journal, 103*(1), 51–73.

Baker, S. B., & Popowicz, C. L. (1983). Meta-analysis as a strategy for evaluating effects of career education interventions. *Vocational Guidance Quarterly, 31*(3), 178–186.

Bakermans-Kranenburg, M. J., van Ijzendoorn, M. H., & Bradley, R. H. (2005). Those who have, receive: The Matthew Effect in early childhood intervention in the home environment. *Review of Educational Research, 75*(1), 1–26.

Bandura, A., & Cervone, D. (1986). Differential engagement of self-reactive influences in cognitive motivation. *Organizational Behavior and Human Decision Processes, 38*(1), 92–113.

Bangert, R. L., Kulik, J. A., & Kulik, C. L. C. (1983). Individualized systems of instruction in secondary schools. *Review of Educational Research, 53*(2), 143–158.

Bangert-Drowns, R. L. (1985). Effectiveness of computer-based education in secondary schools. *Journal of Computer-Based Instruction, 12*(3), 59–68.

Bangert-Drowns, R. L. (1985, March-April). *Meta-analysis of findings on computer-based education with precollege students.* Paper presented at the Annual Meeting of the American Educational Research Association, Chicago.

Bangert-Drowns, R. L. (1991). Effects of frequent classroom testing. *Journal of Educational Research, 85*(2), 89–99.

Bangert-Drowns, R. L. (1992). *Meta-analysis of the effects of inquiry-based instruction on critical thinking.* Paper presented at the Annual meeting of the American Educational Research Association, San Francisco, CA.

Bangert-Drowns, R. L. (1993). The word processor as an instructional tool: A meta-analysis of word processing in writing instruction. *Review of Educational Research, 63*(1), 69–93.

Bangert-Drowns, R. L., & Bankert, E. (1990, April). *Meta-analysis of effects of explicit instruction for critical thinking.* Paper presented at the Annual Meeting of the American Educational Research Association Boston, MA.

Bangert-Drowns, R. L., Hurley, M. M., & Wilkinson, B. (2004). The effects of school-based writing-to-learn interventions on academic achievement: A meta-analysis. *Review of Educational Research, 74*(1), 29.

Bangert-Drowns, R. L., Kulik, C. L. C., Kulik, J. A., & Morgan, M. T. (1991). The instructional effect of feedback in test-like events. *Review of Educational Research, 61*(2), 213–238

Bangert-Drowns, R. L., Kulik, J. A., & Kulik, C. L. (1985). Effectiveness of computer-based education in secondary-schools. *Journal of Computer-Based Instruction, 12*(3), 59–68.

Bangert-Drowns, R. L., Kulik, J. A., & Kulik, C. L. C. (1983). Effects of coaching programs on achievement test performance. *Review of Educational Research, 53*(4), 571–585.

Bangert-Drowns, R. L., Kulik, J. A., & Kulik, C. L. C. (1991). Effects of frequent classroom testing. *Journal of Educational Research, 85*(2), 89.

Barab, S. A., & Roth, W.-M. (2006). Curriculum-based ecosystems: Supporting knowing from an ecological perspective. *Educational Researcher, 35*(5), 3–13.

Barley, Z., Lauer, P. A., Arens, S. A., Apthorp, H. A., Englert, K. S., Snow, D., et al. (2002). *Helping at-risk students meet standards: A synthesis of evidence-based classroom practices.* Aurora, CO: Mid-Continent Research for Education and Learning.

Barnette, J. J., Walsh, J. A., Orletsky, S. R., & Sattes, B. D. (1995). Staff development for improved classroom questioning and learning. *Research in the Schools, 2*(1), 1–10.

Barr, R., & Dreeben, R. (1983). *How schools work.* Chicago: University of Chicago Press.

Batten, M., & Girling-Butcher, S. (1981). *Perceptions of the quality of school life: A case study of schools and students* (No. ACER-RM-13). Hawthorn, Victoria, Australia: Australian Council for Educational Research.

Batts, J. W. (1988). *The effects of teacher consultation: A meta-analysis of controlled studies.* Unpublished Ph.D., University of Kentucky, KY.

Bayraktar, S. (2000). *A meta-analysis on the effectiveness of computer-assisted instruction in science education.* Unpublished Ph.D., Ohio University, OH.

Bayraktar, S. (2001–2002). A meta-analysis of the effectiveness of computer-assisted instruction in science education. *Journal of Research on Technology in Education, 34*(2), 173–188.

Bear, G. G., Minke, K. M., & Manning, M. A. (2002). Self-concept of students with learning disabilities: A meta-analysis. *School Psychology Review, 31*(3), 405–427.

Becker, B. J. (1989). Gender and science achievement: A reanalysis of studies from two meta-analyses. *Journal of Research in Science Teaching, 26*(2), 141–169.

Becker, B. J. (1990). Coaching for the scholastic aptitude test: Further synthesis and appraisal. *Review of Educational Research, 60*(3), 373–417.

Becker, B. J., & Chang, L. (1986, April). *Measurement of science achievement & its role in gender differences.* Paper presented at the Annual Meeting of the American Educational Research Association, San Francisco, CA.

Beckhard, R. (1967). The confrontation meeting. *Harvard Business Review, 45*(2), 149–155.

Beckhard, R. (1969). *Organization development: Strategies and models.* Reading, MA: Addison-Wesley.

Beelmann, A., Pfingsten, U., & Losel, F. (1994). Effects of training social competence in children: A meta-analysis of recent evaluation studies. *Journal of Clinical Child Psychology 23*(3), 260–271.

Bellini, S., & Akullian, J. (2007). A meta-analysis of video modeling and video self-modeling interventions for children and adolescents with autism spectrum disorders. (Brief article). *Exceptional Children, 73*(3), 264–287.

Bellini, S., Peters, J. K., Benner, L., & Hopf, A. (2007). A meta-analysis of school-based social skills interventions for children with autism spectrum disorders. *Remedial and Special Education, 28*(3), 153–162.

Ben-Ari, R., & Eliassy, L. (2003). The differential effects of the learning environment on student achievement motivation: A comparison between frontal and complex instruction strategies. *Social Behavior and Personality: An International Journal, 31*(2), 143.

Bender, W. N., & Smith, J. K. (1990). Classroom behavior of children and adolescents with learning disabilities: A meta-analysis. *Journal of Learning Disabilities 23*(5), 298–305.

Bendig, A. W. (1952). The use of student-rating scales in the evaluation of instructors in introductory psychology. *Journal of Educational Psychology, 43*(3), 167–175.

Bennett, B. B. (1987). *The effectiveness of staff development training practices: A meta-analysis.* Unpublished Ph.D., University of Oregon, Oregon, United States.

Benseman, J., Sutton, A., & Lander, J. (2005). *Working in the light of evidence, as well as aspiration: A literature review of the best available evidence about effective adult literacy, numeracy and language teaching.* Wellington: Ministry of Education and Auckland UniServices, Ltd.

Bereiter, C. (2002). *Education and mind in the knowledge age.* Mahwah, NJ: Lawrence Erlbaum Associates.

Berg, H. K. M. (2003). *Values-based character education: A meta-analysis of program effects on student knowledge, attitudes, and behaviors.* Unpublished M.A., California State University, Fresno, California, United States.

Bergstrom, B. A. (1992, April). *Ability measure equivalence of computer adaptive and pencil and paper tests: A research synthesis.* Paper presented at the Annual Meeting of the American Educational Research Association, San Francisco, CA.

Berkowitz, S. (2006). Developing critical thinking through forensics and communication education: Assessing the impact through meta-analysis. In B. M. Gayle (Ed.), *Classroom communication and instructional processes: Advances through meta-analysis* (pp. 43–59). Mahwah, NJ: Lawrence Erlbaum Associates.

Berliner, D. C. (1984). The half-full glass: A review of research on teaching. In P. L. Hosford (Ed.), *Using what we know about teaching* (pp. 51–84). Alexandria, VA: Association for Supervision and Curriculum Development.

Berliner, D. C. (1987). Ways of thinking about students and classrooms by more and less experienced teachers. In J. Calderhead (Ed.), *Exploring teachers' thinking* (pp. 60–83). London: Cassell Educational Limited.

Berliner, D. C. (1988). *The development of expertise in pedagogy*. Washington, DC: AACTE Publications.

Bernard, R. M., Abrami, P. C., Lou, Y., Borokhovski, E., Wade, A. C., Wozney, L., et al. (2004). How does distance education compare with classroom instruction? A meta-analysis of the empirical literature. *Review of Educational Research, 74*(3), 379–439.

Bernard, R. M., Abrami, P. C., Wade, A. C., Borokhovski, E., & Lou, Y. (2004, October). *The effects of synchronous and asynchronous distance education: A meta-analytical assessment of Simonson's "equivalency theory"*. Paper presented at the Association for Educational Communications and Technology, Chicago, IL.

Berndt, T. J. (2004). Children's friendships: Shifts over a half-century in perspectives on their development and their effects. *Merrill-Palmer Quarterly, 50*(3), 206–223.

Bertrand, J. R. (2005). *Can individual creativity be enhanced by training? A meta analysis*. Unpublished Ph.D., University of Southern California, CA.

Bhutta, A. T., Cleves, M. A., Casey, P. H., Cradock, M. M., & Anand, K. J. S. (2002). Cognitive and behavioral outcomes of school-aged children who were born preterm: A meta-analysis. *Journal of the American Medical Association, 288*(6), 728–737.

Biddle, B. J., & Berliner, D. C. (2002). *What research says about small classes and their effects*. Tempe, AZ: Education Policy Studies Lab, Arizona State University.

Biesta, G. (2007). Why "what works" won't work: Evidence-based practice and the democratic deficit in educational research. *Educational Theory, 57*(1), 1–22.

Biggs, J. B., & Collis, K. F. (1982). *Evaluating the quality of learning: The SOLO taxonomy (structure of the observed learning outcome)*. New York: Academic Press.

Bishop, L. K. (1990). *Meta-analysis of achievement effects of microcomputer applications in elementary schools*. Unpublished Ph.D.

Bishop, R. (2003). Changing power relations in education: Kaupapa Māori messages for "mainstream" education in Aotearoa/New Zealand. *Comparative Education, 39*(2), 221–238.

Bishop, R., Berryman, M., & Richardson, C. (2002). Te Toi Huarewa: Effective teaching and learning in total immersion Māori language educational settings. *Canadian Journal of Native Education, 26*(1), 44–61.

Black, M. M. (1991). Early intervention services for infants and toddlers: A focus on families. *Journal of Clinical Child Psychology, 20*(1), 51–57.

Black, P., & Wiliam, D. (1998). Assessment and classroom learning. *Assessment in Education: Principles, Policy and Practice, 5*(1), 7–74.

Black, T. L. (1996). *Home visiting for children with developmental delays: An empirical evaluation*. Unpublished M.S., Utah State University, UT.

Blanchard, J., Stock, W., & Marshall, J. (1999). Meta-analysis of research on a multimedia elementary school curriculum using personal and video-game computers. *Perceptual and Motor Skills, 88*(1), 329–336.

Blank, R. K. (1989, May). *Educational effects of magnet high schools*. Paper presented at the Conference on Choice and Control in American Education, Madison, WI.

Blank, R. K. (1990). Analyzing educational effects of magnet schools using local district data. *Sociological Practice Review, 1*(1), 40–51.

Blatchford, P. (2005). A multi-method approach to the study of school class size differences. *International Journal of Social Research Methodology, 8*, 195–205.

Blatchford, P., Goldstein, H., Martin, C., & Browne, W. (2002). A study of class size effects in English school reception year classes. *British Educational Research Journal, 28*(2), 169–185.

Blimling, G. S. (1999). A meta-analysis of the influence of college residence halls on academic performance. *Journal of College Student Development, 40*(5), 551–561.

Block, J. H., & Burns, R. B. (1976). Mastery learning. *Review of Research in Education, 4*, 3–49.

Blok, H. (1999). Reading to young children in educational settings: A meta-analysis of recent research. *Language Learning, 49*(2), 343–371.

Blok, H., Oostdam, R., Otter, M. E., & Overmaat, M. (2002). Computer-assisted instruction in support of beginning reading instruction: A review. *Review of Educational Research, 72*(1), 101–130.

Bloom, B. S. (1968). Mastery learning. *Evaluation Comment, 1*(2), 1–12.

Bloom, B. S. (1976). *Human characteristics and school learning.* New York: McGraw-Hill.

Bloom, B. S. (1984). The search for methods of group instruction as effective as one-to-one tutoring. *Educational Leadership, 41*(8), 4–17.

Blosser, P. E. (1985). *Meta-analysis research on science instruction.* Columbus, OH: ERIC Clearinghouse for Science, Mathematics, and Environmental Education.

Blosser, P. E. (1985). *Research related to instructional materials for science.* Columbus, OH: SMEAC Information Reference Center, The Ohio State University.

Blosser, P. E. (1986). What research says: Meta-analysis research on science instruction. *School Science and Mathematics, 86*(2), 166–170.

Boden, A., Archwamety, T., & McFarland, M. (2000, March–April). *Programmed instruction in secondary education: A meta-analysis of the impact of class size on its effectiveness.* Paper presented at the Annual Meeting of the National Association of School Psychologists, New Orleans, LA.

Bolhuis, S. (2003). Towards process-oriented teaching for self-directed lifelong learning: a multidimensional perspective. *Learning and Instruction, 13*(3), 327–347.

Borko, H., & Livingston, C. (1989). Cognition and improvisation: Differences in mathematics instruction by expert and novice teachers. *American Educational Research Journal, 26*(4), 473–498.

Borman, G. D., & D'Agostino, J. V. (1995). *Title I and student achievement: A meta-analysis of 30 years of test results.*

Borman, G. D., & D'Agostino, J. V. (1996). Title I and student achievement: A meta-analysis of federal evaluation results. *Educational Evaluation and Policy Analysis, 18*(4), 309–326.

Borman, G. D., Hewes, G. M., Overman, L. T., & Brown, S. (2003). Comprehensive school reform and achievement: A meta-analysis. *Review of Educational Research, 73*(2), 125–230.

Born, M. P., Bleichrodt, N., & Van Der Flier, H. (1987). Cross-cultural comparison of sex-related differences on intelligence tests: A meta-analysis. *Journal of Cross-Cultural Psychology, 18*(3), 283–314.

Bosker, R. J., & Witziers, B. (1995). *A meta-analytical approach regarding school effectiveness: The true size of school effects and the effect size of educational leadership.* Enschede, The Netherlands: Department of Education, The University of Twente.

Bosker, R. J., & Witziers, B. (1996). *The magnitude of school effects, or: Does it really matter which school a student attends?* Paper presented at the Annual Meeting of the American Educational Research Association, New York.

Boulanger, F. D. (1981). Instruction and science learning: A quantitative synthesis. *Journal of Research in Science Teaching, 18*(4), 311–327.

Bourhis, J., & Allen, M. (1992). Meta-analysis of the relationship between communication apprehension and cognitive performance. *Communication Education, 41*(1), 68–76.

Bowen, C. W. (2000). A quantitative literature review of cooperative learning effects on high school and college chemistry achievement. *Journal of Chemical Education, 77*(1), 116–119.

Boyd, R. L. (2007). *A meta-analysis of the relationship between extraversion and academic achievement.* Unpublished Ph.D., Hofstra University, New York.

Boyd, W. L. (1987). Balancing public and private schools: The Australian experience and American implications. *Educational Evaluation and Policy Analysis, 9*(3), 183–198.

Bracey, G. W. (1982). Computers in education: What the research shows. *ELECTRONIC Learning, 2*(3), 51–54.

Braddock, J. H., II. (1990). *Tracking: Implications for student race-ethnic subgroups* (No. 1). Baltimore, MD: Centre for Research on Effective Schooling for Disadvantaged Students, Johns Hopkins University.

Bradford, J. W. (1990). *A meta-analysis of selected research on student attitudes towards mathematics.* Unpublished Ph.D., The University of Iowa, Iowa City, IA.

Bradford, L., Cooper, E., Allen, M., Stanley, J., & Grimes, D. (2006). Race and the classroom: Interaction and image. In B. M. Gayle, R. W. Preiss, N. Burrell & M. Allen (Eds.), *Classroom communication and instructional processes: Advances through meta-analysis* (pp. 169–184). Mahwah, NJ: Lawrence Erlbaum Associates.

Bransford, J., Brown, A. L., Cocking, R. R., National Research Council (U.S.). Committee on Developments in the Science of Learning., and National Research Council (U.S.). Committee on Learning Research and Educational Practice. (2000). *How people learn: Brain, mind, experience, and school* (Expanded ed.). Washington, DC: National Academy Press.

Braun, H. (2004). Reconsidering the impact of high-stakes testing [Electronic Version]. *Education Policy Analysis Archives, 12*, 1–45. Retrieved 29 April 2008 from http://epaa.asu.edu/epaa/v12n1/.

Bray, M. (1999). *The shadow education system: Private tutoring and its implications for planners.* Paris: Unesco, International Institute for Educational Planning.

Bredderman, T. (1980). Process curricula in elementary school service. *Evaluation in Education, 4*, 43–44.

Bredderman, T. (1982). *The effects of activity-based elementary science programs on student outcomes and classroom practices: A meta analysis of controlled studies* (Research/Technical No. NSF-SED-82-001 SED-79-18717): New York State Univ. System, Albany.[BBB01014].

Bredderman, T. (1983). Effects of activity-based elementary science on student outcomes: A quantitative synthesis. *Review of Educational Research, 53*(4), 499–518.

Bredderman, T. (1985). Laboratory programs for elementary school science: A meta-analysis of effects on learning. *Science Education, 69*(4), 577–591.

Bretz, R. D. (1989). College grade point average as a predictor of adult success: A meta-analytic review and some additional evidence. *Public Personnel Management, 18*(1), 11.

Brewer, D. J., Krop, C., Gill, B. P., & Reichardt, R. (1999). Estimating the cost of national class size reductions under different policy alternatives. *Educational Evaluation and Policy Analysis, 21*(2), 179–192.

Bridgeland, J. M., DiIulio, J. J. J., & Morison, K. B. (2006). *The silent epidemic.* Washington, DC: Civic Enterprises.

Brock, P. (2004). *A passion for life.* Sydney, Australia: Australian Broadcasting Corporation.

Brookhart, S. M., & Freeman, D. J. (1992). Characteristics of entering teacher candidates. *Review of Educational Research, 62*(1), 37–60.

Brophy, J. E. (1983). Conceptualizing student motivation. *Educational Psychologist, 18*(3), 200–215.

Brown, G. T. L. (2002). *Teachers' conceptions of assessment.* Unpublished Ph.D., University of Auckland, Auckland, New Zealand.

Brown, G. T. L. (2004). Teachers' conceptions of assessment: implications for policy and professional development. *Assessment in Education: Principles, Policy and Practice, 11*(3), 301–318.

Brown, L. I. (2001). *A meta-analysis of research on the influence of leadership on student outcomes.* Unpublished Ph.D., Virginia Polytechnic Institute and State University, VA.

Brown, S. D., Tramayne, S., Hoxha, D., Telander, K., Fan, X., & Lent, R. W. (in press). Social cognitive predictors of college students' academic performance and persistence: A meta-analytic path analysis. *Journal of Vocational Behavior, 72(3)*, 298–308.

Brualdi, A. C. (1998). *Classroom questions. ERIC/AE Digest* (ERIC Publications ERIC Digests in Full Text No. EDO-TM-98-02 RR93002002). Washington, DC: ERIC Clearinghouse on Assessment and Evaluation.

Brunsma, D. L. (2004). *The school uniform movement and what it tells us about American education: A symbolic crusade.* Lanham, MD: Scarecrow Education.

Bryant, F. B. (1983, October). *Issues in omitting studies from research syntheses.* Paper presented at the 1983 Joint Meeting of the Evaluation Research Society and Evaluation Network, Chicago.

Bryk, A. S., Easton, J. Q., Kerbow, D., Rollow, S. G., & Sebring, P. A. (1993). *A view from the elementary schools: The state of reform in Chicago. A report of the Steering Committee, Consortium on Chicago School Research* (Reports – Evaluative). Chicago, IL: Consortium on Chicago School Research.

Bryk, A. S., & Schneider, B. L. (2002). *Trust in schools: A core resource for improvement*. New York: Russell Sage Foundation.

Buckingham, J. (2003). Class size and teacher quality. *Educational Research for Policy and Practice, 2*(1), 71–86.

Buckingham, J. (2003). Reforming school education: Class size and teacher quality. *Policy, 19*, 15–20.

Buckworth, J., & Dishman, R. K. (2002). *Exercise psychology*. Champaign, IL: Human Kinetics.

Buhs, E. S., & Ladd, G. W. (2001). Peer rejection as antecedent of young children's school adjustment: An examination of mediating processes. *Developmental Psychology, 37*(4), 550–560.

Buhs, E. S., Ladd, G. W., & Herald, S. L. (2006). Peer exclusion and victimization: Processes that mediate the relation between peer group rejection and children's classroom engagement and achievement? *Journal of Educational Psychology, 98*(1), 1–13.

Burger, K., & Winner, E. (2000). Instruction in visual art: Can it help children learn to read? *Journal of Aesthetic Education, 34*(3–4), 277–293.

Burkam, D. T., Ready, D. D., Lee, V. E., & LoGerfo, L. F. (2004). Social-class differences in summer learning between kindergarten and first grade: Model specification and estimation. *Sociology of Education, 77*(1), 1–31.

Burley, H. E. (1994, April). *A meta-analysis of the effects of developmental studies programs on college student achievement, attitude, and persistence.* Paper presented at the Annual Meeting of the American Educational Research Association, New Orleans, LA.

Burns, M. K. (2002). Comprehensive system of assessment to intervention using curriculum-based assessments. *Intervention in School and Clinic, 38*(1), 8–13.

Burns, M. K. (2004). Empirical analysis of drill ratio research: Refining the instructional level for drill tasks. *Remedial and Special Education, 25*(3), 167–173.

Burns, M. K., & Symington, T. (2002). A meta-analysis of prereferral intervention teams: Student and systemic outcomes. *Journal of School Psychology, 40*(5), 437–447

Burns, P. K., & Bozeman, W. C. (1981). Computer-assisted instruction and mathematics achievement: Is there a relationship? *Educational Technology, October*, 32–38.

Burns, R. B., & Mason, D. A. (1995). Organizational constraints on the formation of elementary school classes. *American Journal of Education, 103*(2), 185–212.

Bus, A. G., & van Ijzendoorn, M. H. (1999). Phonological awareness and early reading: A meta-analysis of experimental training studies. *Journal of Educational Psychology, 91*(3), 403–414.

Bus, A. G., van Ijzendoorn, M. H., & Pellegrini, A. D. (1995). Joint book reading makes for success in learning to read: A meta-analysis on intergenerational transmission of literacy. *Review of Educational Research, 65*(1), 1–21.

Busato, V. V., Prins, F. J., Elshout, J. J., & Hamaker, C. (1998). The relation between learning styles, the Big Five personality traits and achievement motivation in higher education. *Personality and Individual Differences, 26*(1), 129–140.

Butcher, P. M. (1981). *An experimental investigation of the effectiveness of a value claim strategy unit for use in teacher education.* Unpublished M.A., Macquarie University, Sydney.

Butzlaff, R. (2000). Can music be used to teach reading? *Journal of Aesthetic Education, 34*(3–4), 167–178.

Byrnes, D. A. (1989). Attitudes of students, parents, and educators toward repeating a grade. In L. A. Shepard & M. L. Smith (Eds.), *Flunking grades: Research and policies on retention* (pp. 108–131). London: Falmer Press.

Cahan, S., & Davis, D. (1987). A between-grade-levels approach to the investigation of the absolute effects of schooling on achievement. *American Educational Research Journal, 24*(1), 1–12.

Cahen, L. S., & Filby, N. N. (1979). The class size/achievement issue: New evidence and a research plan. *Phi Delta Kappan, 60*(7), 492–495, 538.

Camarena, M. (1990). Following the right track: A comparison of tracking practices in public and Catholic schools. In R. N. Page & L. Villi (Eds.), *Curriculum differentiation: Interpretive studies in US secondary schools* (pp. 159–182). Albany, NY: SUNY Press.

Cambourne, B. (2003). Taking a naturalistic viewpoint in early childhood literacy research. In N. Hall, J. Larson & J. Marsh (Eds.), *Handbook of Early Childhood Literacy* (pp. 411–423). London: Sage.

Cameron, J., & Pierce, W. D. (1994). Reinforcement, reward, and intrinsic motivation: A meta-analysis. *Review of Educational Research, 64*(3), 363–423.

Camilli, G., Vargas, S., & Yurecko, M. (2003). "Teaching children to read": The fragile link between science and federal education policy. *Education Policy Analysis Archives, 11*(15).

Cannon-Bowers, J.A., Rhodenizer, L., Salas, E., & Bowers, C.A. (1998). A framework for understanding pre-practice conditions and their impact on learning. *Personnel Psychology, 51*(2), 291–320.

Carlberg, C., & Kavale, K. A. (1980). The efficacy of special versus regular class placement for exceptional children: A meta-analysis. *Journal of Special Education, 14*(3), 295–309.

Carless, D. (2006). Differing perceptions in the feedback process. *Studies in Higher Education, 31*(2), 219–233.

Carlson, C. L., & Bunner, M. R. (1993). Effects of methylphenidate on the academic performance of children with attention-deficit. *School Psychology Review, 22*(2), 184–198.

Carnine, D. (2000). *Why education experts resist effective practices (and what it would take to make education more like medicine)*. Washington, DC: Thomas B. Fordham Foundation.

Carpenter, W. A. (2000). Ten years of silver bullets: Dissenting thoughts on education reform. *Phi Delta Kappan, 81*(5), 383–389.

Carroll, A., Hattie, J. A. C., Durkin, K., & Houghton, S. (2001). Goal-setting and reputation enhancement: Behavioral choices among delinquent, at-risk and not at-risk adolescents. *Legal and Criminological Psychology, 6*, 165–184.

Cason, D., & Gillis, H. L. L. (1994). A meta-analysis of outdoor adventure programming with adolescents. *Journal of Experiential Education, 17*(1), 40–47.

Caspe, M., Lopez, M. E., & Wolos, C. (2007). *Family involvement in early childhood education*. Cambridge, MA: Harvard Family Research Project, Harvard Graduate School of Education.

Caspe, M., Lopez, M. E., & Wolos, C. (2007). *Family involvement in elementary school children's education*. Cambridge, MA: Harvard Family Research Project, Harvard Graduate School of Education.

Caspe, M., Lopez, M. E., & Wolos, C. (2007). *Family involvement in middle and high school children's education*. Cambridge, MA: Harvard Family Research Project, Harvard Graduate School of Education.

Cassill, B. C. (1996). *Content analysis of student's perceptions of instructors*. Unpublished M.S., University of Tennessee at Chattanooga, Chattanooga, TN.

Casto, G., & Lewis, A. C. (1984). Parent involvement in infant and preschool programs. *Journal of the Division for Early Childhood, 9*(1), 49–56.

Casto, G., & Mastropieri, M. A. (1986). The efficacy of early intervention programs: A meta-analysis. *Exceptional Children, 52*(5), 417–424.

Casto, G., & White, K. R. (1985). The efficacy of early intervention programs with environmentally at-risk infants. *Journal of Children in Contemporary Society, 17*(1), 37–50.

Catts, R. (1992). *The integration of research findings: A review of meta-analysis methodology and an application to research on the effects of knowledge of objectives*. University of Sydney, Sydney, Australia.

Cavalluzzo, L. C. (2004). *Is National Board Certification an effective signal of teacher quality?* Alexandria, VA: CNA Corporation.

Cavanaugh, C., Gillan, K. J., Kromrey, J., Hess, M., & Blomeyer, R. (2004). *The effects of distance education on K-12 student outcomes: A meta-analysis*. Napler, IL: Learning Point Associates / North Central Regional Educational Laboratory.

Cavanaugh, C. S. (1999). *The effectiveness of interactive distance learning technologies on K-12 academic achievement*. Tampa, FL: University of South Florida.

Cavanaugh, C. S. (2001). The effectiveness of interactive distance education technologies in K-12 learning: A meta-analysis. *International Journal of Educational Telecommunications, 7*(1), 73–88.

Cepeda, N. J., Pashler, H., Vul, E., Wixted, J. T., & Rohrer, D. (2006). Distributed practice in verbal recall tasks: A review and quantitative synthesis. *Psychological Bulletin, 132*(3), 354–380.

Chadwick, D. K. H. (1997). *Computer-assisted instruction in secondary mathematics classrooms: A meta-analysis.* Unpublished Ed.D., Drake University, IA.

Chall, J. S. (1983). *Stages of reading development.* New York: McGraw-Hill.

Chall, J. S. (1996). *Stages of reading development* (2nd ed.). Fort Worth, TX: Harcourt Brace.

Chall, J. S. (2000). *The academic achievement challenge: What really works in the classroom?* New York: Guilford Press.

Chambers, E. A. (2002). *Efficacy of educational technology in elementary and secondary classrooms: A meta-analysis of the research literature from 1992–2002.* Unpublished Ph.D., Southern Illinois University at Carbondale, IL.

Chambers, E. A. (2004). An introduction to meta-analysis with articles from the Journal of Educational Research (1992–2002). *Journal of Educational Research, 98*(1), 35–44.

Chambers, E. A., & Schreiber, J. B. (2004). Girls' academic achievement: Varying associations of extracurricular activities. *Gender and Education, 16*(3), 327–346.

Chan, C. (2005, May). *Are small classes better? Or what makes a small class better?* Paper presented at the Conference on Learning Effectiveness and Class Size, University of Hong Kong, Hong Kong.

Chang, L., & Becker, B. J. (1987, April). *A comparison of three integrative review methods: Different methods, different findings?* Paper presented at the Annual Meeting of the American Educational Research Association, Washington, DC.

Chapman, J. W. (1988). Special education in the least restrictive environment: Mainstreaming or maindumping? *Journal of Intellectual and Developmental Disability, 14*(2), 123–134.

Chard, D. J., Vaughn, S., & Tyler, B.-J. (2002). A synthesis of research on effective interventions for building reading fluency with elementary students with learning disabilities. *Journal of Learning Disabilities, 35*(5), 386–406.

Charness, N., Tuffiash, M., Krampe, R., Reingold, E., & Vasyukova, E. (2005). The role of deliberate practice in chess expertise. *Applied Cognitive Psychology, 19*(2), 151–165.

Chen, T.-Y. (1994). *A meta-analysis of effectiveness of computer-based instruction in mathematics.* Unpublished Ph.D., The University of Oklahoma, OK.

Chi, M. T. H., Glaser, R., & Farr, M. J. (1988). *The nature of expertise.* Hillsdale, NJ: Lawrence Erlbaum Associates.

Chickering, A. W., & Ehrmann, S. C. (1996). Implementing the seven principles: Technology as lever. *AAHE Bulletin, October*, 3–6.

Chidester, T. R., & Grigsby, W. C. (1984). A meta-analysis of the goal setting-performance literature. *Academy of Management Proceedings*, 202–206.

Childs, T. S., & Shakeshaft, C. (1986). A meta-analysis of research on the relationship between educational expenditures and student achievement. *Journal of Education Finance, 12*, 249–263.

Childs, T. S., & Shakeshaft, C. (1987, April). *A meta-analysis of research on the relationship between educational expenditures and student achievement.* Paper presented at the Annual Meeting of the American Educational Research Association, Washington, DC.

Chin, J. M.-C. (2007). Meta-analysis of transformational school leadership effects on school outcomes in Taiwan and the USA. *Asia Pacific Education Review, 8*(2), 166–177.

Chiu, C. W. T. (1998, April). *Synthesizing metacognitive interventions: What training characteristics can improve reading performance?* Paper presented at the Annual Meeting of the American Educational Research Association San Diego, CA.

Christine, M. R.-D. (2006). Teacher expectations and student self-perceptions: Exploring relationships. *Psychology in the Schools, 43*(5), 537–552.

Christmann, E., & Badgett, J. (1997). Progressive comparison of the effects of computer-assisted instruction on the academic achievement of secondary students. *Journal of Research on Computing in Education, 29*(4), 325–237.

Christmann, E., Badgett, J., & Lucking, R. (1997). Microcomputer-based computer-assisted instruction within differing subject areas: A statistical deduction. *Journal of Educational Computing Research, 16*(3), 281–296.

Christmann, E., & Badgett, J. L. (1999). A meta-analytic comparison between the assigned academic achievement levels of students assessed with either traditional or alternative assessment techniques. *Louisiana Education Research Journal, 25*(1), 55–65.

Christmann, E., Lucking, R. A., & Badgett, J. L. (1997). The effectiveness of computer-assisted instruction on the academic achievement of secondary students: A meta-analytical comparison between urban, suburban, and rural educational settings. *Computers in the Schools, 13*(3–4), 31–40.

Christmann, E. P. (1995). *A meta-analysis of the effect of computer-assisted instruction on the academic achievement of students in grades 6 through 12: A comparison of urban, suburban, and rural educational settings.* Unpublished Ph.D., Old Dominion University, VA.

Christophel, D. M., & Gorham, J. (1995). A test-retest analysis of student motivation, teacher immediacy, and perceived sources of motivation and demotivation in college classes. *Communication Education, 44*(4), 292–306.

Clariana, R. B., & Koul, R. (2005). Multiple-try feedback and higher-order learning outcomes. *International Journal of Instructional Media, 32*(3), 239–245.

Clariana, R. B., & Koul, R. (2006). The effects of different forms of feedback on fuzzy and verbatim memory of science principles. *British Journal of Educational Psychology, 76*, 259–270.

Clark, F. E., & Angert, J. F. (1980, April). *A meta-analytic study of pictorial stimulus complexity.* Paper presented at the Annual Convention of the Association for Educational Communications and Technology, Denver, CO.

Clark, R. E. (1983). Reconsidering research on learning from media. *Review of Educational Research, 53*(4), 445–459.

Clark, R. E. (1985). Evidence for confounding in computer-based instruction studies: Analyzing the meta-analysis. *Educational Communication and Technology, 33*(4), 249–262.

Clark, R. E. (1989). When teaching kills learning: Research on mathemathantics. In H. N. Mandl, N. Bennett, E. de Corte & H. F. Freidrich (Eds.), *Learning and instruction: European research in an international* (Vol. 2, pp. 1–22). London: Pergamon.

Clarke, A. T. (2006). Coping with interpersonal stress and psychosocial health among children and adolescents: A meta-analysis. *Journal of Youth and Adolescence, 35*(1), 10–23.

Clarke, S. (2001). *Unlocking formative assessment: Practical strategies for enhancing pupils' learning in the primary classroom.* London: Hodder and Stoughton Educational.

Clarke, S., Timperley, H., & Hattie, J. A. C. (2003). *Unlocking formative assessment: Practical strategies for enhancing students' learning in the primary and intermediate classroom* (1st N.Z. ed.). Auckland, New Zealand: Hodder Moa Beckett.

Clinton, J. (1987). *A meta-analysis of the effectiveness of programs to enhance self-concept.* Unpublished M.Ed., University of Western Australia, Perth, Western Australia.

Clinton, J., Hattie, J. A. C., & Dixon, R. (2007). *Evaluation of the Flaxmere Project: When families learn the language of school.* Wellington, New Zealand: Ministry of Education, New Zealand.

Clotfelter, C. T., Ladd, H. F., & Vigdor, J. (2005). Who teaches whom? Race and the distribution of novice teachers. *Economics of Education Review, 24*(4), 377–392.

Clotfelter, C. T., Ladd, H. F., & Vigdor, J. L. (2007). *How and why do teacher credentials matter for student achievement?* Durham, NC: Duke University.

Cobb, C. W., & Douglas, P. H. (1928). A theory of production. *The American Economic Review, 18*(1), 139–165.

Cochran-Smith, M., & Zeichner, K. M. (2005). *Studying teacher education: The report of the AERA Panel on Research and Teacher Education.* Mahwah, NJ: Lawrence Erlbaum Associates.

Coffield, F., Moseley, D.V. M., Ecclestone, K., & Hall, E. (2004). *Learning styles and pedagogy: A systematic and critical review.* London: Learning and Skills Research Council.

Cohen, I. B. (1985). *Revolution in science.* Boston, MA: Harvard University Press.

Cohen, J. (1988). *Statistical power analysis for the behavioral sciences* (2nd ed.). Hillsdale, NJ: L. Erlbaum Associates.

Cohen, J. (1990). Things I have learned (so far). *American Psychologist, 45*(12), 1304–1312.

Cohen, J. (1992). Statistical power analysis. *Current Directions in Psychological Science, 1*(3), 98–101.

Cohen, P. A. (1980). Effectiveness of student-rating feedback for improving college instruction: A meta-analysis of findings. *Research in Higher Education, 13*(4), 321–341.

Cohen, P. A. (1981). Student ratings of instruction and student achievement: A meta-analysis of multisection validity studies. *Review of Educational Research, 51*(3), 281–309.

Cohen, P. A. (1984). College grades and adult achievement: A research synthesis. *Research in Higher Education, 20*(3), 281–293.

Cohen, P. A. (1984). An updated and expanded meta-analysis of multisection student rating validity studies. *Research in Higher Education, 20*(3), 281–293.

Cohen, P. A. (1986, April). *An updated and expanded meta-analysis of multisection student rating validity studies.* Paper presented at the Annual Meeting of the American Educational Research Association, San Francisco, CA.

Cohen, P. A., & Dacanay, L. S. (1992). Computer-based instruction and health professions education: A meta-analysis of outcomes. *Evaluation and the Health Professions, 15*(3), 259–281.

Cohen, P. A., & Dacanay, L. S. (1994). A meta-analysis of computer-based instruction in nursing education. *Computers in Nursing, 12*(2), 89–97.

Cohen, P. A., Ebeling, B. J., & Kulik, J. A. (1981). A meta-analysis of outcome studies of visual-based instruction. *Educational Communication and Technology: A Journal of Theory, Research, and Development, 29*(1), 26–36.

Cohen, P. A., Kulik, J. A., & Kulik, C. L. C. (1982). Educational outcomes of tutoring: A meta-analysis of findings. *Amferican Educational Research Journal, 19*(2), 237–248.

Cohn, C. L. (1985). *A meta-analysis of the effects of teaching innovations on achievement in college economics.* Unpublished D.A., Illinois State University, Illinois, United States.

Cohn, C. M. G. (1984). *Creativity training effectiveness: A research synthesis.* Unpublished Ph.D., Arizona State University, Arizona, United States.

Cohn, C. M. G. (1986, April). *A research synthesis of creativity training effectiveness: Methodological issues.* Paper presented at the Annual meeting of the American Educational Research Association, San Francisco, CA.

Cohn, L. D. (1991). Sex differences in the course of personality development: A meta-analysis. *Psychological Bulletin, 109*(2), 252–266.

Cole, N. S. (1982). The implications of coaching for ability testing. In A. K. Wigdor & W. R. Garner (Eds.), *Ability testing: Uses, consequences, and controversies part II: Documentation sections* (pp. 389–414). Washington, DC: National Academy Press.

Coleman, J. S. (1992). Some points on choice in education. *Sociology of Education, 65*(4), 260–262.

Coleman, J. S., National Center for Educational Statistics., and United States Office of Education. (1966). *Equality of educational opportunity.* Washington, DC: National Center for Educational Statistics.

Collins, R. C. (1984, April). *Head Start: A review of research with implications for practice in early childhood education.* Paper presented at the Annual Meeting of the American Educational Research Association, New Orleans, LA.

Collis, K. F., & Biggs, J. B. (1979). *Classroom examples of cognitive development phenomena: The SOLO taxonomy. Final report.* Woden, ACT: Educational Research and Development Committee.

Colliver, J. A. (2000). Effectiveness of problem-based learning curricula: Research and theory. *Academic Medicine, 75*(3), 259–266.

Colosimo, M. L. S. (1981). *The effect of practice or beginning teaching on the self concepts and attitudes of teachers: A quantitative synthesis.* Unpublished Ph.D., The University of Chicago, IL.

Colosimo, M. L. S. (1984). Attitude changes with initial teaching experience. *College Student Journal, 18*(2), 119–125.

Comfort, C. B. (2004). *Evaluating the effectiveness of parent training to improve outcomes for young children: A meta-analytic review of the published research.* Unpublished Ph.D., University of Calgary, Canada.

Conard, F. (1992). *The arts in education and a meta-analysis.* Unpublished Ph.D., Purdue University, IN.

Connell, N. (1996). *Getting off the list: School improvement in New York City.* New York: Education Priorities Panel.

Conrad, P. (2007). *The medicalization of society: On the transformation of human conditions into treatable disorders.* Baltimore, MA: Johns Hopkins University Press.

Cook, S. B., Scruggs, T. E., Mastropieri, M. A., & Casto, G. C. (1985). Handicapped students as tutors. *Journal of Special Education, 19*(4).

Cook, T. D. (1983). *What have Black children gained academically from school desegregation: Examination of the meta-analytic evidence.* Washington, DC: National Institute on Education.

Cook, T. D. (1984). *School desegregation and black achievement:* National Inst. of Education (ED), Washington, DC.[ED241 671].

Cook, T. D. (2000). *A critical appraisal of the case against using experiments to assess school (or community) effects.* Retrieved 6 May 2008, from http://media.hoover.org/documents/ednext20013unabridged_cook.pdf.

Cook, T. D. (2002). Randomized experiments in educational policy research: A critical examination of the reasons the educational evaluation community has offered for not doing them. *Educational Evaluation and Policy Analysis, 24*(3), 175–199.

Cook, T. D. (2003). Why have educational evaluators chosen not to do randomized experiments? *The ANNALS of the American Academy of Political and Social Science, 589*(1), 114–149.

Cook, T. D. (2004). *Beyond advocacy: Putting history and research into debates about the merits of social experiments (Social Policy Report, No. 12).* Ann Arbor, MI: Society for Research in Child Development.

Cook, T. D. (2004). Causal generalization: How Campbell and Cronbach influenced my theoretical thinking on this topic, including in Shadish, Cook, & Campbell. In M. Alkin (Ed.), *Evaluation roots: Tracing theorists' views and influences.* Thousand Oaks, CA: Sage.

Cooper, E., & Allen, M. (1997, November). *A meta-analytic examination of student race on classroom interaction.* Paper presented at the Annual Meeting of the National Communication Association, Chicago, IL.

Cooper, H. M. (1989). *Homework.* New York: Longman.

Cooper, H. M. (1989). Synthesis of research on homework. *Educational Leadership, 47*(3), 85–91.

Cooper, H. M. (1994). *The battle over homework.* Thousand Oaks, CA: Corwin Press.

Cooper, H. M. (2001). *Summer school: Research-based recommendations for policymakers. SERVE Policy Brief.* Greensboro, NC: SERVE: South Eastern Regional Vision for Education.

Cooper, H. M., Burger, J. M., & Good, T. L. (1980). Gender differences in learning control beliefs of young children. *Evaluation in Education, 4*, 73–75.

Cooper, H. M., Charlton, K., Valentine, J. C., Muhlenbruck, L., & Borman, G. D. (2000). Making the most of summer school: A meta-analytic and narrative review. *Monographs of the Society for Research in Child Development, 65*(1), 1–118.

Cooper, H. M., & Dorr, N. (1995). Race comparisons on need for achievement: A meta-analytic alternative to Graham's narrative review. *Review of Educational Research, 65*(4), 483–508.

Cooper, H. M., & Hedges, L. V. (1994). *The handbook of research synthesis.* New York: Russell Sage Foundation.

Cooper, H. M., Jackson, K., Nye, B., & Lindsay, J. J. (2001). A model of homework's influence on the performance evaluations of elementary school students. *The Journal of Experimental Education, 69*(2), 181–199.

Cooper, H. M., Lindsay, J. J., Nye, B., & Greathouse, S. (1998). Relationships among attitudes about homework, amount of homework assigned and completed, and student achievement. *Journal of Educational Psychology, 90*(1), 70–83.

Cooper, H. M., Nye, B., Charlton, K., Lindsay, J., & Greathouse, S. (1996). The effects of summer vacation on achievement test scores: A narrative and meta-analytic review. *Review of Educational Research, 66*(3), 227–268.

Cooper, H. M., Robinson, G. C., & Patall, E. A. (2006). Does homework improve academic achievement? A synthesis of research, 1987–2003. *Review of Educational Research, 76*(1), 1–62.

Cooper, H. M., & Valentine, J. C. (2001). Using research to answer practical questions about homework. *Educational Psychologist, 36*(3), 143–153.

Cooper, H. M., Valentine, J. C., Charlton, K., & Melson, A. (2003). The effects of modified school calendars on student achievement and on school and community attitudes. *Review of Educational Research, 73*(1), 1–52.

Cooper, J. M. (2006). *Classroom teaching skills* (8th ed.). Boston, MA: Houghton Mifflin Co.

Corbett, S. S., & Drewett, R. F. (2004). To what extent is failure to thrive in infancy associated with poorer cognitive development? A review and meta-analysis. *Journal of Child Psychology and Psychiatry, 45*(3), 641–654.

Cornelius-White, J. (in preparation). Who cares? Why teacher-student relationships matter.

Cornelius-White, J. (2007). Learner-centered teacher-student relationships are effective: A meta-analysis. *Review of Educational Research, 77*(1), 113–143.

Cortazzi, M., & Jin, L. (2001). Large classes in China: 'Good' teachers and interaction. In D. A. Watkins & J. B. Biggs (Eds.), *Teaching the Chinese learner: Psychological and pedagogical perspectives* (pp. 115–184). Hong Kong: CERC and ACER.

Cosden, M., Zimmer, J., & Tuss, P. (1993). The impact of age, sex, and ethnicity on kindergarten entry and retention decisions. *Educational Evaluation and Policy Analysis, 15*(2), 209–222.

Cotton, K. (1989). Classroom questioning [Electronic Version]. *School Improvement Research Series, Close Up 5*. Retrieved 4 February, 2007 from http://www.nwrel.org/scpd/sirs/3/cu5.html.

Cotton, S. E. (2000). *The training needs of vocational teachers for working with learners with special needs.* Unpublished Ph.D., Purdue University, Indiana, United States.

Cox, S. M., Davidson, W. S., & Bynum, T. S. (1995). A meta-analytic assessment of delinquency-related outcomes of alternative education programs. *Crime Delinquency, 41*(2), 219–234.

Craig, S. D., Sullins, J., Witherspoon, A., & Gholson, B. (2006). The deep-level-reasoning-question effect: The role of dialogue and deep-level-reasoning questions during vicarious learning. *Cognition and Instruction, 24*(4), 565–591.

Crain, R. L. (1983). *Dilemmas in meta-analysis: A reply to reanalyses of the desegregation-achievement synthesis.* Washington, DC: National Institute of Education.

Crain, R. L., & Mahard, R. E. (1982). *Desegregation plans that raise Black achievement: A review of the research.* Santa Monica, CA: Rand Corporation.

Crain, R. L., & Mahard, R. E. (1983). The effect of research methodology on desegregation-achievement studies: A meta-analysis. *American Journal of Sociology, 88*(5), 839–854.

Crawford, M. G. (2000). *High school teaching: The authoritative teacher relationship style.* Unpublished Ph.D., Vanderbilt University, Tennessee, United States.

Crenshaw, T. M. (1997). *Attention deficit hyperactivity disorder and the efficacy of stimulant medication: A meta-analysis.* Unpublished Ed.D., University of Virginia, VA.

Crimm, J. A. (1992). *Parent involvement and academic achievement: A meta-analysis.* Unpublished Ed.D., University of Georgia, GA.

Crismore, A. (Ed.). (1985). *Landscapes: A state-of-the-art assessment of reading comprehension research 1974–1984. Final Report* (Vol. 1). Bloomington, IN: Indiana University, Language Education Department.

Crissman, J. K. (2006). *The design and utilization of effective worked examples: A meta-analysis.* Unpublished Ph.D., The University of Nebraska, Lincoln, NE.

Cronbach, L. J. (1982). Prudent aspirations for social inquiry. In W. H. Kruskal (Ed.), *The social sciences: Their nature and uses* (pp. 61–81). Chicago, IL: The University of Chicago Press.

Cronbach, L. J., & Snow, R. E. (1977). *Aptitudes and instructional methods: a handbook for research on interactions.* New York: Irvington Publishers.

Crosby, E. G. (2004). *Meta-analysis of second generation early intervention efficacy research involving children with disabilities or delays.* Unpublished Ph.D., Pennsylvania State University, PA.

Csikszentmihalyi, M. (1997). *Creativity: Flow and the psychology of discovery and invention* (1st ed.). New York: HarperPerennial.

Csikszentmihalyi, M. (2000). *Beyond boredom and anxiety.* San Francisco: Jossey-Bass Publishers.

Csikszentmihalyi, M. (2002). *Flow: The classic work on how to achieve happiness.* London: Rider.

Cuban, L. (1984). *How teachers taught: Constancy and change in American classrooms, 1890–1980.* New York: Longman.

Cuban, L. (1984). Policy and research dilemmas in the teaching of reasoning: Unplanned designs. *Review of Educational Research, 54*(4), 655–681.

Cuban, L. (2001). *Oversold and underused: Computers in the classroom.* Cambridge, MA: Harvard University Press.

Cunningham, A. J. (1988). *The contribution of computer-generated instructional graphics on measured achievement gains: A meta-analysis.* Unpublished Ed.D., East Texas State University, TX.

Curbelo, J. (1984). *Effects of problem-solving instruction on science and mathematics student achievement: A meta-analysis of findings.* Unpublished Ph.D., The Florida State University, FL.

Dacanay, L. S., & Cohen, P. A. (1992). A meta-analysis of individualized instruction in dental education. *Journal of Dental Education, 56*(3), 183–189.

D'Agostino, J. V., & Murphy, J. A. (2004). A meta-analysis of Reading Recovery in United States schools. *Educational Evaluation and Policy Analysis, 26*(1), 23–28.

Daneman, M., & Merikle, P. M. (1996). Working memory and language comprehension: A meta-analysis. *Psychonomic Bulletin and Review, 3*(4), 422–433.

Daniels, H. (2001). *Vygotsky and pedagogy.* London: Routledge Falmer.

Darling-Hammond, L. (2006). Constructing 21st-century teacher education. *Journal of Teacher Education, 57*(3), 300–314.

Darling-Hammond, L. (2006). *Powerful teacher education: Lessons from exemplary programs.* San Francisco, CA: Jossey-Bass.

Darling-Hammond, L. (2006). Securing the right to learn: Policy and practice for powerful teaching and learning. *Educational Researcher, 35*(7), 13–24.

Datta, D. K., & Narayanan, V. K. (1989). A meta-analytic review of the concentration-performance relationship: Aggregating findings in strategic management. *Journal of Management, 15*(3), 469–483.

Dauber, S. L., Alexander, K. L., & Entwisle, D. R. (1993). Characteristics of retainees and early precursors of retention in grade: Who is held back? *Merrill-Palmer Quarterly, 39*(3), 326–343.

Dauber, S. L., Alexander, K. L., & Entwisle, D. R. (1996). Tracking and transitions through the middle grades: Channeling educational trajectories. *Sociology of Education, 69*(4), 290–307.

Davis-Kean, P. E., & Sandler, H. M. (2001). A meta-analysis of measures of self-esteem for young children: A framework for future measures. *Child Development, 72*(3), 887–906.

de Bruin, A. B. H., Rikers, R. M. J. P., & Schmidt, H. G. (2007). The effect of self-explanation and prediction on the development of principled understanding of chess in novices. *Contemporary Educational Psychology, 32*(2), 188–205.

DeBaz, T. P. (1994). *A meta-analysis of the relationship between students' characteristics and achievement and attitudes toward science.* Unpublished Ph.D., Ohio State University, OH.

Deci, E. L., Koestner, R., & Ryan, R. M. (1999). A meta-analytic review of experiments examining the effects of extrinsic rewards on intrinsic motivation. *Psychological Bulletin, 125*(6), 627–668.

Deci, E. L., & Ryan, R. M. (1985). *Intrinsic motivation and self-determination in human behavior.* New York: Plenum.

Dekkers, J., & Donatti, S. (1981). The integration of research studies on the use of simulation as an instructional strategy. *Journal of Educational Research, 74*(6), 424–427.

Deng, Z. (2007). Transforming the subject matter: Examining the intellectual roots of pedagogical content knowledge. *Curriculum Inquiry, 37*(3), 279–295.

Denham, S. A., & Almeida, M. C. (1987). Children's social problem-solving skills, behavioral adjustment, and interventions: A meta-analysis evaluating theory and practice. *Journal of Applied Developmental Psychology, 8*(4), 391–409.

DerSimonian, R., & Laird, N. M. (1983). Evaluating the effect of coaching on SAT scores: A meta-analysis. *Harvard Educational Review, 53*(1), 1–15

Dewey, J. (1938). *Logic: The theory of inquiry.* New York: Holt, Rinehart and Winston.

DeWitt-Brinks, D., & Rhodes, S. C. (1992, May). *Listening instruction: A qualitative meta-analysis of twenty-four selected studies.* Paper presented at the Annual Meeting of the International Communication Association, Miami, FL.

Diaz, P. E. (1992). Effects of transfer on academic performance of Community College students at the four-year institution. *Community/Junior College Quarterly of Research and Practice, 16*(3), 279–291.

Dickson, W. P. (1980). Referential communication performance. *Evaluation in Education, 4,* 84–85.

Dignath, C., Buettner, G., & Langfeldt, H. P. (2008). How can primary school students learn self-regulated learning strategies most effectively?: A meta-analysis on self-regulation training programmes. *Educational Research Review, In Press, Corrected Proof.*

Dignath, C., Büttner, G., & Langfeldt, H. P. (2007, August). *The efficacy of self-regulated learning interventions at primary and secondary school level: A meta-analysis.* Paper presented at the European Association on Learning and Instruction, Budapest, Hungary.

Dishman, R. K., & Buckworth, J. (1996). Increasing physical activity: A quantitative synthesis. *Medicine and Science in Sports and Exercise, 28*(6), 706–719.

Dixon, R. M., & Marsh, H. W. (1997, November). *The effect of different educational placements on the multidimensional self-concepts of students with mild disabilities: Preliminary results of a meta-analysis.* Paper presented at the Researching Education in New Times, Annual AARE Conference, Brisbane, Australia.

Dochy, F., Segers, M., Van den Bossche, P., & Gijbels, D. (2003). Effects of problem-based learning: A meta-analysis. *Learning and Instruction, 13*(5), 533–568.

Dolan, L. J. (1980). Home, school and pupil attitudes. *Evaluation in Education, 4,* 265–358.

Donovan, J. J., & Radosevich, D. J. (1998). The moderating role of goal commitment on the goal difficulty-performance relationship: A meta-analytic review and critical reanalysis. *Journal of Applied Psychology, 83*(2), 308–315.

Donovan, J. J., & Radosevich, D. J. (1999). A meta-analytic review of the distribution of practice effect: Now you see it, now you don't. *Journal of Applied Psychology, 84*(5), 795–805.

Dornbusch, S. M. (1994, February). *Off the track.* Paper presented at the Presidential Address to the Annual Meeting of the Society for Research on Adolescence, San Diego, CA.

Dörnyei, Z. (2001). *Teaching and researching motivation.* New York: Longman.

Doughty, S. S., Chase, P. N., & O'Shields, E. M. (2004). Effects of rate building on fluent performance: a review and commentary. *The Behavior Analyst, 27,* 7–23.

Draney, K., & Wilson, M. (1992, April). *The impact of design characteristics on study outcomes in retention research: A meta-analytic perspective.* Paper presented at the Annual Meeting of the American Educational Research Association, San Francisco, CA.

Dressman, M. (1999). On the use and misuse of research evidence: Decoding two states' reading initiatives. *Reading Research Quarterly, 34*(3), 258–285.

Druva, C. A., & Anderson, R. D. (1983). Science teacher characteristics by teacher behavior and by student outcome: A meta-analysis of research. *Journal of Research in Science Teaching, 20*(5), 467–479.

Druva-Roush, C. A., & Wu, Z. J. (1989, August). *Gender differences in visual spatial skills: A meta-analysis of doctoral theses.* Paper presented at the Annual Meeting of the American Psychological Association, New Orleans, LA.

DuBois, D. L., Holloway, B. E., Valentine, J. C., & Cooper, H. M. (2002). Effectiveness of mentoring programs for youth: A meta-analytic review. *American Journal of Community Psychology, 30*(2), 157–197.

Duncan, G. J., Dowsett, C. J., Claessens, A., Magnuson, K., Huston, A. C., Klebanov, P., et al. (2007). School readiness and later achievement. *Developmental Psychology, 43*(6), 1428–1446.

Dunn, R., Griggs, S. A., Olson, J., Beasley, M., & Gorman, B. S. (1995). A meta-analytic validation of the Dunn and Dunn model of learning-style preferences. *Journal of Educational Research, 88*(6), 353–362.

DuPaul, G. J., & Eckert, T. L. (1997). The effects of school-based interventions for attention deficit hyperactivity disorder: A meta-analysis. *School Psychology Review, 26*(1), 5–27.

Durlak, J. A., & Weissberg, R. P. (2007). *The impact of after-school programs that promote personal and social skills.* Chicago, IL: Collaborative for Academic, Social, and Emotional Learning.

Dusek, J. B., & Joseph, G. (1983). The bases of teacher expectancies: A meta-analysis. *Journal of Educational Psychology, 75*(3), 327–346.

Dusek, J. B., & Joseph, G. (1985). The bases of teacher expectancies. In J. B. Dusek (Ed.), *Teacher expectancies* (pp. 229–249). Hillsdale, NJ: Lawrence Erlbaum Associates.

Dustmann, C., Rajah, N., and van Soest, A. (2003). Class size, education, and wages. *The Economic Journal, 113*(485), F99–F120.

Duzinski, G. A. (1987). *The educational utility of cognitive behavior modification strategies with children: A quantitative synthesis.* Unpublished Ph.D., University of Illinois at Chicago, IL.

Dweck, C. (2006). *Mindset.* New York: Random House.

Eagly, A. H., & Johnson, B. T. (1990). Gender and leadership style: A meta-analysis. *Psychological Bulletin, 108*(2), 233–256.

Eagly, A. H., Karau, S. J., & Johnson, B. T. (1992). Gender and leadership style among school principals: A meta-analysis. *Educational Administration Quarterly, 28*(1), 76–102.

Earhart, J. A., Ramirez, L., Carlson, C., & Beretvas, S. N. (2006, August). *Meta-analysis of parent-component interventions targeting academic achievement.* Paper presented at the American Psychological Association 114th Annual Convention, New Orleans, LA.

Early Intervention Research Institute. (1983). *Final Report, 1982–83 Work Scope* (Reports – Evaluative). Logan, UT: Utah State University Exceptional Child Center.

Eaton, W. O., & Enns, L. R. (1986). Sex differences in human motor activity level. *Psychological Bulletin, 100*(1), 19–28.

Eby, L. T., Allen, T. D., Evans, S. C., Ng, T., & DuBois, D. L. (2008). Does mentoring matter? A multidisciplinary meta-analysis comparing mentored and non-mentored individuals. *Journal of Vocational Behavior, 72*(2), 254–267.

Ehrenberg, R. G., & Brewer, D. J. (1995). Did teachers' verbal ability and race matter in the 1960s? Coleman revisited. *Economics of Education Review, 14*(1), 1–21.

Ehri, L. C., Nunes, S. R., Stahl, S. A., & Willows, D. M. (2001). Systematic phonics instruction helps students learn to read: Evidence from the National Reading Panel's meta-analysis. *Review of Educational Research, 71*(3), 393–447.

Ehri, L. C., Nunes, S. R., Willows, D. M., Schuster, B. V., Yaghoub-Zadeh, Z., & Shanahan, T. (2001). Phonemic awareness instruction helps children learn to read: Evidence from the National Reading Panel's meta-analysis. *Reading Research Quarterly, 36*(3), 250–287.

Elbaum, B. (2002). The self-concept of students with learning disabilities: A meta-analysis of comparisons across different placements. *Learning Disabilities Research and Practice, 17*(4), 216–226.

Elbaum, B., & Vaughn, S. (2001). School-based interventions to enhance the self-concept of students with learning disabilities: A meta-analysis. *The Elementary School Journal, 101*(3), 303–329.

Elbaum, B., Vaughn, S., Hughes, M. T., & Moody, S. W. (1999). Grouping practices and reading outcomes for students with disabilities. *Exceptional Children, 65*(3), 399.

Elbaum, B., Vaughn, S., Hughes, M. T., & Moody, S. W. (2000). How effective are one-to-one tutoring programs in reading for elementary students at risk for reading failure? A meta-analysis of the intervention research. *Journal of Educational Psychology, 92*(4), 605–619.

Eliot, T. S. (1934). Choruses from "The Rock". London: Farber and Farber.

Ellington, A. J. (2000). *Effects of hand-held calculators on precollege students in mathematics classes: A meta-analysis.* Unpublished Ph.D., The University of Tennessee, TN.

Ellington, A. J. (2003). A meta-analysis of the effects of calculators on students' achievement and attitude levels in precollege mathematics classes. *Journal for Research in Mathematics Education, 34*(5), 433–463.

Ellington, A. J. (2006). The effects of non-CAS graphing calculators on student achievement and attitude levels in mathematics: A meta-analysis. *School Science and Mathematics, 106*(1), 16–26.

Elliott, E. S., & Dweck, C. S. (1988). Goals: An approach to motivation and achievement. *Journal of Personality and Social Psychology, 54*(1), 5–12.

Ellis, A. K., & Fouts, J. T. (1997). *Research on educational interventions.* Larchmont, NY: Eye on Education.

Ellis, T. I. (1984). *Class size*: ERIC Clearinghouse on Educational Management, Eugene, OR.[SJJ69850].

Ellis, T. I. (1985). Class size. *Research Roundup, 1*(2).

Elmore, R. F. (1996). Getting to scale with good educational practice. *Harvard Educational Review, 66*(1), 1–26.

El-Nemr, M. A. (1979). *Meta-analysis of the outcomes of teaching biology as inquiry.* Unpublished Ph.D., University of Colorado at Boulder, CO.

Else-Quest, N. M., Hyde, J. S., Goldsmith, H. H., & Hulle, C. A. V. (2006). Gender differences in temperament: A meta-analysis. *Psychological Bulletin, 132*(1), 33–72.

Elshout, J. J. (1987). Problem solving and education. In E. De Corte, H. Lodewijks, R. Parmentier & P. Span (Eds.), *Learning and instruction* (pp. 259–273). Pergamon Books: Oxford, UK.

Engelmann, S. (1991). Change schools through revolution, not evolution. *Journal of Behavioral Education, 1*(3), 295–304.

Ennemoser, M., & Schneider, W. (2007). Relations of television viewing and reading: Findings from a 4-year longitudinal study. *Journal of Educational Psychology, 99*(2), 349–368.

Epstein, J. L., & Mac Iver, D. J. (1990). *Education in the middle grades: Overview of national practices and trends.* (No. 45). Baltimore, MD: Center for Research on Elementary and Middle Schools, The Johns Hopkins University.

Ergene, T. (2003). Effective interventions on test anxiety reduction: A meta-analysis. *School Psychology International, 24*(3), 313–328.

Erion, J. (2006). Parent tutoring: A meta-analysis. *Education and Treatment of Children, 29*(1), 79–106.

Ernst, M. L. M. (2001). *Infant cognition and later intelligence.* Unpublished Ph.D., Loyola University of Chicago, IL.

Etnier, J. L., Nowell, P. M., Landers, D. M., & Sibley, B. A. (2006). A meta-regression to examine the relationship between aerobic fitness and cognitive performance. *Brain Research Reviews, 52*(1), 119–130.

Etnier, J. L., Salazar, W., Landers, D. M., Petruzzello, S. J., Han, M., & Nowell, P. (1997). The influence of physical fitness and exercise upon cognitive functioning: A meta-analysis. *Journal of Sport and Exercise Psychology, 19*(3), 249–277.

Etsey, Y. K., & Snetzler, S. (1998, April). *A meta-analysis of gender differences in student attitudes toward mathematics.* Paper presented at the Annual Meeting of the American Educational Research Association, San Diego, CA.

Evans, C. R., & Dion, K. L. (1991). Group cohesion and performance: A meta-analysis. *Small Group Research, 22*(2), 175–186.

Evans, J. H., Jr. (1986). *Effects of career education interventions on academic achievement: A meta-analysis.* Unpublished Ph.D., The Florida State University, FL.

Evans, J. H., Jr., & Burck, H. D. (1992). The effects of career education interventions on academic achievement: A meta-analysis. *Journal of Counseling and Development, 71*(1), 63–68.

Eysenck, H. J. (1984). Meta-Analysis: An abuse of research integration. *Journal of Special Education, 18*(1), 41–59.

Eysenck, H. J. (1995). Meta-analysis of best-evidence synthesis? *Journal of Evaluation in Clinical Practice, 1*(1), 29–36.

Fait, L. (1982). *Attitudes of parents and teachers concerning retention of elementary students in the State of Utah.* Unpublished Ed.D., Brigham Young University, UT.

Falbo, T., & Polit, D. F. (1986). Quantitative review of the only child literature: Research evidence and theory development. *Psychological Bulletin, 100*(2), 176–189.

Falchikov, N., & Boud, D. (1989). Student self-assessment in higher education: A meta-analysis. *Review of Educational Research, 59*(4), 395–430.

Falchikov, N., & Goldfinch, J. (2000). Student peer assessment in higher education: A meta-analysis comparing peer and teacher marks. *Review of Educational Research, 70*(3), 287–322.

Fan, W. (1993). *Metacognition and comprehension: A quantitative synthesis of metacognitive strategy instruction.* Unpublished Ed.D., University of Cincinnati, OH.

Fan, X., & Chen, M. (1999, April). *Parental involvement and students' academic achievement: A meta-analysis.* Paper presented at the Annual Meeting of the American Educational Research Association, Montreal, Quebec, Canada.

Fan, X., & Chen, M. (2001). Parental involvement and students' academic achievement: A meta-analysis. *Educational Psychology Review, 13*(1), 1–22.

Fanjiang, G., & Kleinman, R. E. (2007). Nutrition and performance in children. *Current Opinion in Clinical Nutrition and Metabolic Care, 10*(3), 342–347.

Feingold, A. (1994). Gender differences in variability in intellectual abilities: A cross-cultural perspective. *Sex Roles, 30*(1), 81–92.

Feingold, B. F., & Feingold, H. S. (1979). *The Feingold cookbook for hyperactive children, and others with problems associated with food additives and salicylates.* New York: Random House.

Feinstein, L. (2003). Inequality in the early cognitive development of British children in the 1970 cohort. *Economica, 70*(277), 73–97.

Feist, G. J. (1998). A meta-analysis of personality in scientific and artistic creativity. *Personality and Social Psychology Review, 2*(4), 290–309.

Feltz, D. L., & Landers, D. M. (1983). The effects of mental practice on motor skill learning and performance: A meta-analysis. *Journal of Sport Psychology, 5*, 25–57.

Fendick, F. (1990). *The correlation between teacher clarity of communication and student achievement gain: A meta-analysis.* Unpublished Ph.D., University of Florida, FL.

Fenstermacher, G. D., & Soltis, J. F. (2004). *Approaches to teaching* (4th ed.). New York: Teachers College Press.

Ferguson, R. F., & Ladd, H. F. (1996). How and why money matters: An analysis of Alabama schools. In H. F. Ladd (Ed.), *Holding schools accountable: Performance-based reform in education* (pp. 265–299). Washington, DC: Brookings Institution Press.

Fernanda, F., Karl, G. D. B., & Vittoria, F. (2002). Good-enough representations in language comprehension. *Current Directions in Psychological Science, 11*, 11–15.

Feuerstein, R. (1980). *Instrumental enrichment: An intervention program for cognitive modifiability.* Baltimore, MD: University Park Press.

Findley, M. J., & Cooper, H. M. (1983). Locus of control and academic achievement: A literature review. *Journal of Personality and Social Psychology, 44*(2), 419–427.

Finn, J. D. (1998). *Class size and students at risk. What is known? What is next? A Commissioned Paper.* Washington, DC: U.S. Department of Education, Office of Educational Research and Improvement, National Institute on the Education of At-Risk Students.

Finn, J. D. (2002). Class-size reduction in grades k–3. In A. Molnar (Ed.), *School reform proposals: The research evidence* (pp. 27–48). Greenwich, Conn.: Information Age Publishing.

Fischer, T. A., & Tarver, S. G. (1997). Meta-analysis of studies of mathematics curricula designed around big ideas. *Effective School Practices, 16*, 71–79.

Fisher, E. P. (1992). The impact of play on development: A meta-analysis. *Play and Culture, 5*(2), 159–181.

Fiske, E. B., & Ladd, H. F. (2000). *When schools compete: A cautionary tale.* Washington, DC: Brookings Institution Press.

Fitzgerald, D., Hattie, J. A. C., & Hughes, P. (1985). *Computer applications in Australian classrooms.* Canberra: Australian Department of Education.

Fitz-Gibbon, C., & Kochan, S. (2000). School effectiveness and education indicators. In C. Teddlie & D. Reynolds (Eds.), *The international handbook of school effectiveness research* (pp. 257–282). London: Falmer Press.

Fleming, M. L., & Malone, M. R. (1983). The relationship of student characteristics and student performance in science as viewed by meta-analysis research. *Journal of Research in Science Teaching, 20*(5), 481–495.

Fletcher, J. D. (1989). The effectiveness and cost of interactive videodisc instruction. *Machine-Mediated Learning, 3*(4), 361–385.

Fletcher-Flynn, C. M., & Gravatt, B. (1995). The efficacy of computer assisted instruction (CAI): A meta-analysis. *Journal of Educational Computing Research, 12*(3), 219–241.

Forestal, P. (1990). Talking: Toward classroom action. In M. Brubacher, R. Payne & K. Rickett (Eds.), *Perspectives on small group learning: Theory and practice* (pp. 159–173). Oakville, ON, Canada: Rubicon.

Forness, S. R., & Kavale, K. A. (1993). Strategies to improve basic learning and memory deficits in mental retardation: A meta-analysis of experimental studies. *Education and Training in Mental Retardation, 28*(2), 99–110.

Forness, S. R., & Kavale, K. A. (1996). Treating social skill deficits in children with learning disabilities: A meta-analysis of the research. *Learning Disability Quarterly, 19*(1), 2–13.

Forness, S. R., Kavale, K. A., Blum, I. M., & Lloyd, J. W. (1997). Mega-analysis of meta-analyses. *Teaching Exceptional Children, 29*(6), 4–9.

Forness, S. R., Kavale, K. A., & Crenshaw, T. M. (1999). Stimulant medication revisited: Effective treatment of children with ADHD. *Reclaiming Children and Youth: Journal of Emotional and Behavioral Problems, 7*(4), 230–233.

Foster, J. E. (1993). Retaining children in grade. *Childhood Education, 70*(1), 38–43.

Fowler, C. H., Konrad, M., Walker, A. R., Test, D. W., & Wood, W. M. (2007). Self-determination interventions' effects on the academic performance of students with developmental disabilities. *Education and Training in Developmental Disabilities, 42*(3), 270–285.

Fraser, B. J. (1989). Research syntheses on school and instructional effectiveness. *International Journal of Educational Research, 13*(7), 707–719.

Frazier, T. W., Demaree, H. A., & Youngstrom, E. A. (2004). Meta-analysis of intellectual and neuropsychological test performance in Attention-Deficit/Hyperactivity Disorder. *Neuropsychology, 18*(3), 543–555.

Frazier, T. W., Youngstrom, E. A., Glutting, J. J., & Watkins, M. W. (2007). ADHD and achievement: Meta-analysis of the child, adolescent, and adult literatures and a concomitant study with college students. *Journal of Learning Disabilities, 40*(1), 49–65.

Fredrick, W. C. (1980). Instructional time. *Evaluation in Education, 4,* 117–118.

Freeman, H. E. (1984). *A meta-analysis of gender differences in mathematics achievement.* Unpublished Ph.D., The University of Alabama, AL.

Friedman, L. (1989). Mathematics and the gender gap: A meta-analysis of recent studies on sex differences in mathematical tasks. *Review of Educational Research, 59*(2), 185–213.

Friedman, L. (1996). Meta-analysis and quantitative gender differences: Reconciliation. *Focus on Learning Problems in Mathematics, 18*(1–3), 123–128.

Friedrich, K. R. (1997). *Alternative education for at-risk youth: An analytical review of evaluation findings.* Unpublished Ph.D., Texas A&M University, College Station, TX.

Frieze, I., Whitley, B., Hanusa, B., & McHugh, M. (1982). Assessing the theoretical models for sex differences in causal attributions for success and failure. *Sex Roles, 8*(4), 333–343.

Froman, R. D. (1981, April). *Ability grouping: Why do we persist and should we?* Paper presented at the Annual Meeting of the American Educational Research Association, Los Angeles, CA.

Frost, L. A., Hyde, J. S., & Fennema, E. (1994). Gender, mathematics performance, and mathematics-related attitudes and affect: A meta-analytic synthesis. *International Journal of Educational Research, 21*, 373–385.

Fuchs, D., & Fuchs, L. S. (1985, March). *The importance of context in testing: A meta-analysis.* Paper presented at the Annual Meeting of the American Educational Research Association, Chicago, IL.

Fuchs, D., & Fuchs, L. S. (1986). Test procedure bias: A meta-analysis of examiner familiarity effects. *Review of Educational Research, 56*(2), 243–262.

Fuchs, D., & Fuchs, L. S. (1989). Effects of examiner familiarity on black, Caucasian, & Hispanic children: A meta-analysis. *Exceptional Children, 55*(4), 303–308.

Fuchs, D., Fuchs, L. S., Mathes, P. G., Lipsey, M. W., & Roberts, P. (2002). Is "learning disabilities" just a fancy term for low achievement? A meta-analysis of reading differences between low achievers with and without the label. In R. Bradley, L. Danielson & D. P. Hallahan (Eds.), *Identification of learning disabilities: Research to practice. The LEA series on special education and disability* (pp. 737–762). Mahwah, NJ: Lawrence Erlbaum Associates.

Fuchs, L. S., & Fuchs, D. (1985). *The effect of measuring student progress toward long vs. short-term goals: A meta-analysis.*

Fuchs, L. S., & Fuchs, D. (1985, March-April). *A quantitative synthesis of effects of formative evaluation on achievement.* Paper presented at the Annual Meeting of the American Educational Research Association, Chicago, IL.

Fuchs, L. S., & Fuchs, D. (1986). Curriculum-based assessment of progress toward long-term and short-term goals. *Journal of Special Education, 20*(1), 69–82.

Fuchs, L. S., & Fuchs, D. (1986, April). *Effects of alternative student performance graphing procedures on achievement.* Paper presented at the Annual Meeting of the American Educational Research Association, San Francisco, CA.

Fuchs, L. S., & Fuchs, D. (1986). Effects of long- and short-term goal assessment on student achievement (p. 32).

Fuchs, L. S., & Fuchs, D. (1986). Effects of systematic formative evaluation: A meta-analysis. *Exceptional Children, 53*(3), 199–208.

Fuchs, L. S., & Fuchs, D. (1987). The relation between methods of graphing student performance data and achievement: A meta-analysis. *Journal of Special Education Technology, 8*(3), 5–13.

Fukkink, R. G., & de Glopper, K. (1998). Effects of instruction in deriving word meaning from context: A meta-analysis. *Review of Educational Research, 68*(4), 450–469.

Fullan, M., Hill, P., & Crévola, C. (2006). *Breakthrough.* Thousand Oaks, CA: Corwin Press.

Fullan, M., & Stiegelbauer, S. (1991). *The new meaning of educational change* (2nd ed.). London: Cassell.

Fuller, B. (1987). What school factors raise achievement in the Third World? *Review of Educational Research, 57*(3), 255–292.

Fusaro, J. A. (1993). A meta-analysis of the effect of sentence-combining on reading comprehension. *Reading Improvement, 30*(4), 228–231.

Fusaro, J. A. (1997). The effect of full-day kindergarten on student achievement: A meta-analysis. *Child Study Journal, 27*(4), 269–277

Gadamer, H. G. (1993). *Truth and method* (2nd ed.). New York: Continuum.

Gage, N. L., & Berliner, D. C. (1998). *Educational psychology* (6th ed.). Boston: Houghton Mifflin.

Gale, P. S. (2004). A summative metaevaluation synthesis: State education agency evaluations of the comprehensive school reform program. *Dissertation Abstracts International Section A: Humanities and Social Sciences, 65*(6-A), pp.

Gall, M. D. (1970). The use of questions in teaching. *Review of Educational Research, 40*(5), 707–721.

Gall, M. D. (1984). Synthesis of research on teachers' questioning. *Educational Leadership, 42*(3), 40–47.

Galloway, A. M. (2003). *Improving reading comprehension through metacognitive strategy instruction: Evaluating the evidence for the effectiveness of the reciprocal teaching procedure.* Unpublished Ph.D., The University of Nebraska, Lincoln, NE.

Galton, M. J. (1995). *Crisis in the primary classroom.* London: D. Fulton Publishers.

Galton, M. J., & Willcocks, J. (1983). *Moving from the primary classroom.* London: Routledge and Kegan Paul.

Gamoran, A. (1993). Alternative uses of ability grouping in secondary schools: Can we bring high-quality instruction to low-ability classes? *American Journal of Education, 102*(1), 1–22.

Garland, H. (1985). A cognitive mediation theory of task goals and human performance. *Motivation and Emotion, 9*(4), 345–367.

Garlinger, D. K., & Frank, B. M. (1986). Teacher-student cognitive style and academic achievement: A review and mini-meta-analysis. *Journal of Classroom Interaction, 21*(2), 2–8.

Gasper, J. M. (1992). *Transformational leadership: An integrative review of the literature.* Unpublished Ed.D., Western Michigan University, MI.

Gaub, M., & Carlson, C. L. (1997). Gender differences in ADHD: A meta-analysis and critical review. *Journal of the American Academy of Child and Adolescent Psychiatry, 36*(8), 1036–1045.

Gayle, B. M., Preiss, R. W., & Allen, M. (2006). How effective are teacher-initiated classroom questions in enhancing student learning? In B. M. Gayle, R. W. Preiss, N. Burrell & M. Allen (Eds.), *Classroom communication and instructional processes: Advances through meta-analysis* (pp. 279–293). Mahwah, NJ: Lawrence Erlbaum Associates.

Gayle, B. M., Preiss, R. W., Burrell, N., & Allen, M. (Eds.). (2006). *Classroom communication and instructional processes: Advances through meta-analysis.* Mahwah, NJ: Lawrence Erlbaum Associates.

Gee, E. J. (1995, April). *The effects of a whole language approach to reading instruction on reading comprehension: A meta-analysis.* Paper presented at the Annual Meeting of the American Educational Research Association San Francisco, CA.

Gennetian, L. A., Duncan, G., Knox, V., Vargas, W., Clark-Kauffman, E., & London, A. S. (2004). How welfare policies affect adolescents' school outcomes: A synthesis of evidence from experimental studies. *Journal of Research on Adolescence, 14*(4), 399–423.

George, W. C., Cohn, S. J., & Stanley, J. C. (1979). *Educating the gifted: Acceleration and enrichment. Revised and expanded proceedings of the Ninth Annual Hyman Blumberg Symposium on Research in Early Childhood Education,* Baltimore, MD.

Gersten, R., & Baker, S. (1999, April). *Effective instruction for English-language learners: A multi-vocal approach toward research synthesis.* Paper presented at the Annual Meeting of the American Educational Research Association, Montreal, Quebec, Canada,.

Gersten, R., & Baker, S. (2001). Teaching expressive writing to students with learning disabilities: A meta-analysis. *The Elementary School Journal, 101*(3), 251–272.

Gersten, R., & Carnine, D. (1984). Direct instruction mathematics: A longitudinal evaluation of low-income elementary school students. *The Elementary School Journal, 84*(4), 395–407.

Gersten, R., & Keating, T. (1987). Long-term benefits from direct instruction. *Educational Leadership, 44*(6), 28.

Getsie, R. L., Langer, P., & Glass, G. V. (1985). Meta-analysis of the effects of type and combination of feedback on children's discrimination learning. *Review of Educational Research, 55*(1), 9–22.

Ghafoori, B. (2000). *Effectiveness of cognitive-behavioral therapy in reducing classroom disruptive behaviors: A meta-analysis.* Unpublished Ph.D., California School of Professional Psychology, Fresno, CA.

Giaconia, R. M., and Hedges, L. V. (1982). Identifying features of effective open education. *Review of Educational Research, 52*(4), 579–602.

Gickling, E. E. (1984, October). *Operationalizing academic learning time for low achieving and handicapped mainstreamed students.* Paper presented at the Annual Meeting of the Northern Rocky Mountain Educational Research Association, Jackson Hole, WY.

Gierl, M. J., Zheng, Y., & Cui, Y. (2008). Using the attribute hierarchy method to identify and interpret cognitive skills that produce group differences. *Journal of Educational Measurement, 45*(1), 65–89.

Gijbels, D. (2003). Effects of problem-based learning: A meta-analysis. *Learning and Instruction, 13*, 533–568.

Gijbels, D., Dochy, F., Van den Bossche, P., & Segers, M. (2005). Effects of problem-based learning: A meta-analysis from the angle of assessment. *Review of Educational Research, 75*(1), 27–61.

Gilliam, W. S., & Zigler. (2000). A critical meta-analysis of all evaluations of state-funded preschool from 1977 to 1998: Implications for policy, service delivery and program evaluation. *Early Childhood Research Quarterly, 15*(4), 441–473.

Gillibrand, E., Robinson, P., Brawn, R., & Osborne, A. (1999). Girls' participation in physics in single sex classes in mixed schools in relation to confidence and achievement. *International Journal of Science Education, 21*(4), 349–362.

Gilligan, C. (1982). *In a different voice: Psychological theory and women's development.* Cambridge, MA: Harvard University Press.

Gillingham, M. G., & Guthrie, J. T. (1987). Relationships between CBI and research on teaching. *Contemporary Educational Psychology, 12*(3), 189–199.

Gilner, M. W. (1988). *Research on family structure and school performance: A meta-analysis.* Unpublished Ph.D., St Louis University, MO.

Gilpin, A. R. (2008). Meta-analysis, and robustness: An empirical examination of Rosenthal and Rubin's effect size indicator. *Educational and Psychological Measurement, 68*(1), 42–57.

Ginns, P., Hollender, N., & Reimann, P. (2006, April 6). *Meta-analysis of the minimalist training model.* Paper presented at the Annual Meeting of the American Educational Research Association, San Francisco, CA.

Ginsburg-Block, M. D., Rohrbeck, C. A., & Fantuzzo, J. W. (2006). A meta-analytic review of social, self-concept, and behavioral outcomes of peer-assisted learning. *Journal of Educational Psychology, 98*(4), 732–749.

Gipps, C. V. (1994). *Beyond testing: Towards a theory of educational assessment.* London: Falmer Press.

Glass, G. V. (1970). Discussion. In M. C. Wittrock & D. E. Wiley (Eds.), *The evaluation of instruction: Issues and problems* (pp. 210–211). New York: Holt, Rinehart and Winston.

Glass, G. V. (1976). Primary, secondary, and meta-analysis of research. *Educational Researcher, 5*(10), 3–8.

Glass, G. V. (1977). Integrating findings: The meta-analysis of research. *Review of Research in Education, 5,* 351–379.

Glass, G. V. (1980). On criticism of our class size/student achievement research: No points conceded. *Phi Delta Kappan, 62*(4), 242–244.

Glass, G. V. (1982). Meta-analysis: An approach to the synthesis of research results. *Journal of Research in Science Teaching, 19*(2), 93–112.

Glass, G. V. (1982). *School class size: Research and policy.* Beverly Hills, CA: Sage.

Glass, G. V. (1987). What works: Politics and research. *Educational Researcher, 16*(3), 5–10.

Glass, G. V. (2000). Meta-analysis at 25 [Electronic Version]. Retrieved 13 November 2007 from http://glass.ed.asu.edu/gene/papers/meta25.html.

Glass, G. V., McGaw, B., & Smith, M. L. (1981). *Meta-analysis in social research.* Beverly Hills: Sage Publications.

Glass, G. V., & Smith, M. L. (1978). *Meta-analysis of research on the relationship of class-size and achievement. The class size and instruction project* (Research/Technical No. C8088). San Francisco, CA: Far West Lab. for Educational Research and Development.

Glass, G. V., & Smith, M. L. (1979). Meta-analysis of research on class size and achievement. *Educational Evaluation and Policy Analysis, 1*(1), 2–16.

Glazerman, S., Mayer, D., & Decker, P. (2006). Alternative routes to teaching: The impacts of Teach for America on student achievement and other outcomes. *Journal of Policy Analysis and Management, 25*(1), 75–96.

Gliessman, D. H., Pugh, R. C., Dowden, D. E., & Hutchins, T. F. (1988). Variables influencing the acquisition of a generic teaching skill. *Review of Educational Research, 58*(1), 25–46.

Gocmen, G. B. (2003). *Effectiveness of frequent testing over academic achievement: A meta-analysis study.* Unpublished Ph.D., Ohio University, Ohio, United States.

Goff, M., & Ackerman, P. L. (1992). Personality-intelligence relations: Assessment of typical intelligence engagement. *Journal of Educational Psychology, 84*(4), 537–552.

Goldberg, A., Russell, M., & Cook, A. (2003). The effect of computers on student writing: A meta-analysis of studies from 1992 to 2002 [Electronic Version]. *The Journal of Technology, Learning, and Assessment, 2.* Retrieved 16 April 2007 from http://www.jtla.org.

Goldberg, W. A., Prause, J., Lucas-Thompson, R., & Himsel, A. (2008). Maternal employment and children's achievement in context: A meta-analysis of four decades of research. *Psychological Bulletin, 134*(1), 77–108.

Goldhaber, D., & Anthony, E. (2004). *Can teacher quality be effectively assessed?* Seattle, WA: Center on Reinventing Public Education and the Urban Institute.

Goldin, G. A. (1992). Meta-analysis of problem-solving studies: A critical response. *Journal for Research in Mathematics Education, 23*(3), 274–283.

Goldring, E. B. (1990). Assessing the status of information on classroom organizational frameworks for gifted students. *Journal of Educational Research, 83*(6), 313–326.

Goldring, E. B., & Addi, A. (1989). Using meta-analysis to study policy issues: The ethnic composition of the classroom and achievement in Israel. *Studies In Educational Evaluation, 15*(2), 231–246.

Goldring, E. B., & Presbrey, L. S. (1986). Evaluating preschool programs: A meta-analytic approach. *Educational Evaluation and Policy Analysis, 8*(2), 179–188.

Goldstein, H., Yang, M., Omar, R., Turner, R., & Thompson, S. (2000). Meta-analysis using multilevel models with an application to the study of class size effects. *Journal of the Royal Statistical Society: Series C (Applied Statistics), 49*(3), 399–412.

Gollwitzer, P. M., & Sheeran, P. (2006). Implementation intentions and goal achievement: A meta-analysis of effects and processes. *Advances in Experimental Social Psychology, 38*, 69–119.

Gooding, R. Z., & Wagner, J. A., III. (1985). A meta-analytic review of the relationship between size and performance: The productivity and efficiency of organizations and their subunits. *Administrative Science Quarterly, 30*(4), 462–481.

Gordon, M. B. (1991). *A quantitative analysis of the relationship between computer graphics and mathematics achievement and problem-solving.* Unpublished Ed.D., University of Cincinnati, OH.

Gottfried, A. W. (1984). *Home environment and early cognitive development: Longitudinal research.* Orlando, FL: Academic Press.

Graham, S., & Perin, D. (2007). A meta-analysis of writing instruction for adolescent students. *Journal of Educational Psychology, 99*(3), 445–476.

Graham, S., & Perin, D. (2007). *Writing next: Effective strategies to improve writing of adolescents in middle and high schools – A report to Carnegie Corporation of New York.* Washington, DC: Alliance for Excellent Education.

Graue, M. E., Weinstein, T., & Walberg, H. J. (1983). School-based home instruction and learning: A quantitative synthesis. *Journal of Educational Research, 76*(6).

Gray, J. (1993). *Men are from Mars, women are from Venus: A practical guide for improving communication and getting what you want in your relationships.* London: Thorsons.

Greene, J. P. (1997). A meta-analysis of the Rossell and Baker review of bilingual education research. *Bilingual Research Journal, 21*(2–3), 103–122.

Greenwald, R., Hedges, L. V., & Laine, R. (1996). Interpreting research on school resources and student achievement: A rejoinder to Hanushek. *Review of Educational Research, 66*(3), 411–416.

Greenwald, R., Hedges, L. V., & Laine, R. D. (1996). The effect of school resources on student achievement. *Review of Educational Research, 66*(3), 361–396.

Greiff, A. H. (1997). *Utilization of computer-assistive technology for children with learning disabilities.* Unpublished M.S., Touro College, NY.

Greiner, J. M., & Karoly, P. (1976). Effects of self-control training on study activity and academic performance: An analysis of self-monitoring, self-reward, and systematic-planning components. *Journal of Counseling Psychology, 23*(6), 495–502.

Grigorenko, E. L. (2005). A conservative meta-analysis of linkage and linkage-association studies of developmental dyslexia. *Scientific Studies of Reading, 9*(3), 285–316.

Grissom, J. B., & Shepard, L. A. (1989). Repeating and dropping out of school. In L. A. Shepard & M. L. Smith (Eds.), *Flunking grades: Research and policies on retention* (pp. 34–63). London: Falmer Press.

Grodsky, E., & Gamoran, A. (2003). The relationship between professional development and professional community in American schools. *School Effectiveness and School Improvement, 14*(1), 1–29.

Groot, W., & Maassen van den Brink, H. (2000). Overeducation in the labor market: A meta-analysis. *Economics of Education Review, 19*(2), 149–158.

Guilford, J. P. (1954). *Psychometric methods* (2d ed.). New York: McGraw-Hill.

Guskey, T. R. (2007). Multiple sources of evidence: An analysis of stakeholders' perceptions of various indicators of student learning. *Educational Measurement: Issues and Practice, 26*(1), 19–27.

Guskey, T. R., & Gates, S. L. (1985, March-April). *A synthesis of research on group-based mastery learning programs.* Paper presented at the Annual Meeting of the American Educational Research Association, Chicago, IL.

Guskey, T. R., & Gates, S. L. (1986). Synthesis of research on the effects of mastery learning in elementary and secondary classrooms. *Educational Leadership, 43*(8), 73–80.

Guskey, T. R., & Pigott, T. D. (1988). Research on group-based mastery learning programs: A meta-analysis. *Journal of Educational Research, 81*(4), 197–216.

Guskin, S. L. (1984). Problems and promises of meta-analysis in special education. *Journal of Special Education, 18*(1), 73–80.

Guthrie, J. T., McRae, A., & Klauda, S. L. (2007). Contributions of concept-oriented reading instruction to knowledge about interventions for motivations in reading. *Educational Psychologist, 42*(4), 237–250.

Gutierrez, R., & Slavin, R. (1992). Achievement effects of the nongraded elementary school: A best evidence synthesis. *Review of Educational Research, 62*(4), 333–376.

Guzzetti, B. J., Snyder, T. E., Glass, G. V., & Gamas, W. S. (1993). Promoting conceptual change in science: A comparative meta-analysis of instructional interventions from reading education and science education. *Reading Research Quarterly, 28*(2), 116–159.

Guzzo, R. A., Jette, R. D., & Katzell, R. A. (1985). The effects of psychologically based intervention programs on worker productivity: A meta-analysis. *Personnel Psychology, 38*(2), 275–291.

Haas, M. (2005). Teaching methods for secondary algebra: A meta-analysis of findings. *NASSP Bulletin, 89*(642), 24–46.

Haertel, G. D., & Walberg, H. J. (1980). Investigating an educational productivity model. *Evaluation in Education, 4*, 103–104.

Haertel, G. D., Walberg, H. J., & Haertel, E. H. (1979, April). *Social-psychological environments and learning: A quantitative synthesis.* Paper presented at the Annual Meeting of the American Educational Research Association, San Francisco, CA.

Haertel, G. D., Walberg, H. J., & Haertel, E. H. (1980). Classroom socio-psychological environment. *Evaluation in Education, 4*, 113–114.

Haertel, G. D., Walberg, H. J., & Haertel, E. H. (1981). Socio-psychological environments and learning: A quantitative synthesis. *British Educational Research Journal, 7*(1), 27–36.

Hager, W., & Hasselhorn, M. (1998). The effectiveness of the cognitive training for children from a differential perspective: A meta-evaluation. *Learning and Instruction, 8*(5), 411–438.

Haig, B. D. (2005). An abductive theory of scientific method. *Psychological Methods, 10*(4), 371–388.

Haladyna, T., & Shaughnessy, J. (1982). Attitudes toward science: A quantitative synthesis. *Science Education, 66*(4), 547–563.

Hall, J. A. (1980). Gender difference in skill and sending and interpreting non-verbal emotional cues. *Evaluation in Education, 4*, 71–72.

Hall, L. E. (1988). *The effects of cooperative learning on achievement: A meta-analysis.* Unpublished Ed.D., University of Georgia, GA.

Haller, E. J., & Davis, S. A. (1980). Does socioeconomic status bias the assignment of elementary school students to reading groups? *American Educational Research Journal, 17*(4), 409–418.

Haller, E. P., Child, D. A., & Walberg, H. J. (1988). Can comprehension be taught? A quantitative synthesis of "metacognitive" studies. *Educational Researcher, 17*(9), 5–8.

Hallinger, P., & Murphy, J. F. (1986). The social context of effective schools. *American Journal of Education, 94*(3), 328–355.

Hamaker, C. (1986). The effects of adjunct questions on prose learning. *Review of Educational Research, 56*(2), 212–242.

Hamilton, W. A. (1995). *A meta-analysis of the comparative research on computer-assisted instruction and its effects on elementary and secondary mathematics achievement.* Unpublished Ed.D., Wayne State University, Michigan, United States.

Hamm, J. V., & Faircloth, B. S. (2005). The role of friendship in adolescents' sense of school belonging. *New Directions for Child and Adolescent Development, 2005*(107), 61–78.

Hampton, S. E., & Reiser, R. A. (2004). Effects of a theory-based feedback and consultation process on instruction and learning in college classrooms. *Research in Higher Education, 45*, 497–527.

Hansford, B. C., & Hattie, J. A. C. (1982). The relationship between self and achievement/performance measures. *Review of Educational Research, 52*(1), 123–142.

Hanson, R. E. (1988). *Social skill training: A critical meta-analytic review.* Unpublished Ph.D., Texas Woman's University, TX.

Hanushek, E. A. (1989). The impact of differential expenditures on school performance. *Educational Researcher, 18*(4), 45–62.

Hanushek, E. A. (1997). Outcomes, incentives, and beliefs: Reflections on analysis of the economics of schools. *Educational Evaluation and Policy Analysis, 19*(4), 301–308.

Hanushek, E. A. (1998). Conclusions and controversies about the effectiveness of school resources. *Federal Reserve Bank of New York Economic Policy Review, 4*(1), 11–27.

Hanushek, E. A. (2002). Teacher quality. In L. T. Izumi & W. M. Evers (Eds.), *Teacher quality* (pp. 1–12). Stanford, CA: Hoover Institution Press.

Hanushek, E. A. (2003). The failure of input-based schooling policies. *The Economic Journal, 113*(485), F64-F98.

Hanushek, E. A. (2005). *Economic outcomes and school quality.* Brussels, Belgium: International Academy of Education.

Harker, R. K., & Nash, R. (1996). Academic outcomes and school effectiveness: Type 'A' and type 'B' effects. *New Zealand Journal of Educational Studies, 32*, 143–170.

Harrell, A. (1983). *The effects of the Head Start Program on children's cognitive development. Preliminary report. Head Start evaluation, synthesis and utilization project.* Washington, DC: Superintendent of Documents, U.S. Government Printing Office.

Harris, M. J., & Rosenthal, R. (1985). Mediation of interpersonal expectancy effects: 31 meta-analyses. *Psychological Bulletin, 97*(3), 363–386.

Harris, M. J., & Rosenthal, R. (1986). Four factors in the mediation of teacher expectancy effects. In R. S. Feldman (Ed.), *The social psychology of education: Current research and theory* (pp. 91–114). Cambridge: Cambridge University Press.

Harris, T. L., & Hodges, R. E. (Eds.). (1995). *The literacy dictionary.* Newark, DE: International Reading Association.

Harrison, B. (1980). Training English teachers: "The dignity of thinking beings." *Use of English, 31*(3), 51–61.

Harrison, D. (1980). *Meta-analysis of selected studies of staff development.* Unpublished Ph.D., University of Florida, FL.

Hart, B., & Risley, T. R. (1995). *Meaningful differences in the everyday experience of young American children.* Baltimore: P.H. Brookes.

Hartley, S. S. (1977). *Meta-analysis of the effects of individually paced instruction in mathematics.* Unpublished Ph.D., University of Colorado at Boulder, CO.

Hartley, S. S. (1980). Instruction in mathematics. *Evaluation in Education, 4*, 56–57.

Hartzler, D. S. (2000). *A meta-analysis of studies conducted on integrated curriculum programs and their effects on student achievement.* Unpublished Ed.D., Indiana University, IN.

Hasselbring, T. S. (1986). Research on the effectiveness of computer-based instruction: A review. *International Review of Education, 32*(3), 313–324.

Hatano, G., & Inagaki, K. (1986). Two courses of expertise. In H. Stevenson, H. Azuma & K. Hakuta (Eds.), *Child development and education in Japan* (pp. 262–272). New York: W. H. Freeman.

Hattie, J. A. C. (1987). Identifying the salient facets of a model of student learning: A synthesis of meta-analyses. *International Journal of Educational Research, 11*(2), 187–212.

Hattie, J. A. C. (1992). Measuring the effects of schooling. *Australian Journal of Education, 36*(1), 5–13.

Hattie, J. A. C. (2002). Classroom composition and peer effects. *International Journal of Educational Research, 37*(5), 449–481.

Hattie, J. A. C. (2004, July). *The thread model of self-concept.* Paper presented at the Keynote Address to the International Self Conference, Max Plank Institute, Germany.

Hattie, J. A. C. (2005, August). *What is the nature of evidence that makes a difference to learning.* Paper presented at the ACER Annual Conference: Using data to support learning, Melbourne, Australia.

Hattie, J. A. C. (2006). The paradox of reducing class size and improved learning outcomes. *International Journal of Educational Research, 42*, 387–425.

Hattie, J. A. C. (2007). The status of reading in New Zealand schools: The upper primary plateau problem (PPP3). *Reading Forum, 22*(2), 25–39.

Hattie, J. A. C. (2008). Narrow the gap, fix the tail, or close the curves: The power of words. In C. Rubie & C. Rawlinson (Eds.), *Challenging thinking aobut teaching and learning*: Nova Science.

Hattie, J. A. C. (2008). Processes of integrating, developing, and processing self information. In H. W. Marsh, R. Craven & D. M. McInerney (Eds.), *Self-processes, learning, and enabling human potential: Dynamic new approaches* (Vol. 3). Greenwich, CN: Information Age Publishing.

Hattie, J. A. C., Biggs, J., & Purdie, N. (1996). Effects of learning skills interventions on student learning: A meta-analysis. *Review of Educational Research, 66*(2), 99–136.

Hattie, J. A. C., & Brown, G. T. L. (2004). *Cognitive processes in asTTle: The SOLO taxonomy. asTTle Technical Report* (No. 43). Auckland: University of Auckland and the Ministry of Education.

Hattie, J. A. C., Brown, G. T. L., & Keegan, P. J. (2003). A national teacher-managed, curriculum-based assessment system: Assessment Tools for Teaching and Learning (asTTle). *International Journal of Learning, 10*, 771–778.

Hattie, J. A. C., & Clinton, J. (2008). Identifying accomplished teachers: A validation study. In L. Ingvarson & J. A. C. Hattie (Eds.), *Assessing teachers for professional certification: The first decade of the National Board for Professional Teaching Standards* (pp. 313–344). Oxford, UK: Elsevier.

Hattie, J. A. C., Clinton, J. C., Baker, W. K., Jaeger, R. M., & Spence, K. (1998). *The cyber campus: The first year evaluation.* Raleigh, NC: National Institute for Statistical Sciences.

Hattie, J. A. C., Clinton, J. C., Nagle, B., Kelkor, V., Reid, W. K., Spence, K., et al. (1998). *Evaluating the Paideia Program in Guilford County Schools: First Year Report: 1997–98.* Greensboro, NC: Center for Educational Research and Evaluation, University of North Carolina, Greensboro.

Hattie, J. A. C., Clinton, J. C., Thompson, M., & Schmitt-Davis, H. (1996). *Identifying "highly accomplished" teachers. Report for the Technical Advisory Group.* Detroit, MI: National Board for Professional Teaching Standards.

Hattie, J. A. C., & Fitzgerald, D. (1987). Sex differences in attitudes, achievement and use of computers. *Australian Journal of Education, 31*(1), 3–26.

Hattie, J. A. C., & Hansford, B. C. (1980). *Evaluating the relationship between self and performance/achievement.* Paper presented at the Australian Association for Research in Education Annual Conference: Youth, schooling and unemployment, Sydney.

Hattie, J. A. C., & Hansford, B. C. (1982). Self measures and achievement: Comparing a traditional review of literature with meta-analysis. *Australian Journal of Education, 26*(1), 71–75.

Hattie, J. A. C., & Hansford, B. C. (1983). Reading performance and self-assessment: What is the relationship? *Reading Education, 8*, 17–23.

Hattie, J. A. C., & Jaeger, R. (1998). Assessment and classroom learning: A deductive approach. *Assessment in Education: Principles, Policy and Practice, 5*(1), 111–122.

Hattie, J. A. C., Mackay, A., Holt, A., Hurrell, P., Irving, E., & team. (2007). Generation II: e-asTTle V6. An internet computer application. Wellington, New Zealand: Ministry of Education.

Hattie, J. A. C., Mackay, A., Weston, B., Northover, A., & Simpson, R. (2007). *New York project evaluation report*. Auckland, New Zealand: Visible Learning Labs.

Hattie, J. A. C., Marsh, H. W., Neill, J. T., & Richards, G. E. (1997). Adventure education and outward bound: Out-of-class experiences that make a lasting difference. *Review of Educational Research, 67*(1), 43–87.

Hattie, J. A. C., & Purdie, N. (1998). The SOLO model: Addressing fundamental measurement issues. In B. C. Dart and G. M. Boulton-Lewis (Eds.), *Teaching and Learning in Higher Education* (pp. 145–176). Camberwell, Victoria, Australia: Australian Council of Educational Research.

Hattie, J. A. C., & Rogers, H. J. (1986). Factor models for assessing the relationship between creativity and intelligence. *Journal of Educational Psychology, 78*(6), 482–485.

Hattie, J. A. C., & Timperley, H. (2007). The power of feedback. *Review of Educational Research, 77*(1), 81–112.

Hausenblas, H. A., Carron, A. V., & Mack, D. E. (1997). Application to the theories of reasoned action and planned behavior to exercise behavior: A meta-analysis. *Journal of Sport and Exercise Psychology, 19*(1), 36–51.

Hausknecht, J. P., Halpert, J. A., Di Paolo, N. T., & Gerrard, M. O. M. (2007). Retesting in selection: A meta-analysis of coaching and practice effects for tests of cognitive ability. *Journal of Applied Psychology, 92*(2), 373–385.

Haynie, W. J. (2007). Effects of test taking on retention learning in technology education: A meta-analysis. *Journal of Technology Education, 18*(2), 24–36.

Hearold, S. L. (1979, April). *Meta-analysis of the effects of television on social behavior.* Paper presented at the Annual Meeting of the American Educational Research Association, San Francisco, CA.

Hearold, S. L. (1980). *Meta-analysis of the effects of television on social behavior.* University of Colorado, Boulder, CO, United States.

Hearold, S. L. (1980). Television and social behavior. *Evaluation in Education, 4*, 94–95.

Hedges, L. V., Laine, R. D., & Greenwald, R. (1994). An exchange: Part I: Does money matter? A meta-analysis of studies of the effects of differential school inputs on student outcomes. *Educational Researcher, 23*(3), 5–14.

Hedges, L. V., Laine, R. D., & Greenwald, R. (1994). Money does matter somewhere: A reply to Hanushek. *Educational Researcher, 23*(4), 9–10.

Hedges, L. V., & Olkin, I. (1985). *Statistical methods for meta-analysis.* Orlando: Academic Press.

Hedges, L. V., & Stock, W. (1983). The effects of class size: An examination of rival hypotheses. *American Educational Research Journal, 20*(1), 63–65.

Hefner, S. W. (1985). *The effects of a mastery learning/competency-based education instructional approach on facilitating students' retention of achievement in language arts and mathematics.* Unpublished Ed.D., University of South Carolina, SC.

Hembree, R. (1986). Research gives calculators a green light. *Arithmetic Teacher, 34*(1), 18–21.

Hembree, R. (1987). Effects of noncontent variables on mathematics test performance. *Journal for Research in Mathematics Education, 18*(3), 197–214.

Hembree, R. (1988). Correlates, causes, effects, and treatment of test anxiety. *Review of Educational Research, 58*(1), 47–77.

Hembree, R. (1990). Bibliography of research on problem solving in mathematics: Experiments and relational studies (p. 46).

Hembree, R. (1990). The nature, effects, and relief of mathematics anxiety. *Journal for Research in Mathematics Education, 21*(1), 33–46.

Hembree, R. (1992). Experiments and relational studies in problem solving: A meta-analysis. *Journal for Research in Mathematics Education, 23*(3), 242–273.

Hembree, R., & Dessart, D. J. (1986). Effects of hand-held calculators in precollege mathematics education: A meta-analysis. *Journal for Research in Mathematics Education, 17*(2), 83–99.

Henchey, N. (2001). *Schools that make a difference: Final Report. Twelve Canadian secondary schools in low-income settings.* Kelowna, BC, Canada: Society for the Advancement of Excellence in Education.

Henderson, L. (2007). Multi-level selective classes for gifted students. *International Education Journal, 8*(2), 60–67.

Henk, W. A., & Stahl, N. A. (1985, November). *A meta-analysis of the effect of notetaking on learning from lecture. College reading and learning assistance* Paper presented at the Annual Meeting of the National Reading Conference, St. Petersburg Beach, FL.

Herschbach, D. R. (1984). The questionable search for the content base of industrial arts. *Journal of Epsilon Pi Tau, 10*(1), 27–34.

Hess, F. (1979). *Class size revisited: Glass and Smith in perspective* (VIEWPOINTS (Opinion Papers, Position Papers, Essays, etc)): East Syracuse – Minoa Central Schools, East Syracuse, NY.[BBB11291].

Hetland, L. (2000). Learning to make music enhances spatial reasoning. *Journal of Aesthetic Education, 34*(3/4), 179–238.

Hetland, L. (2000). Listening to music enhances spatial-temporal reasoning: Evidence for the "Mozart Effect". *Journal of Aesthetic Education, 34*(3/4), 105–148.

Hetland, L. (2000). *The relationship between music and spatial processes: A meta-analysis.* Unpublished Ed.D., Harvard University, MA.

Hetzel, D. C., Rasher, S. P., Butcher, L., & Walberg, H. J. (1980, April). *A quantitative synthesis of the effects of open education.* Paper presented at the Annual Meeting of the American Educational Research Association, Boston, MA.

Heubusch, J. D., & Lloyd, J. W. (1998). Corrective feedback in oral reading. *Journal of Behavioral Education, 8*(1), 63–79.

Heyneman, S., Jamison, D., & Montenegro, X. (1983). Textbooks in the Philippines: Evaluation of the pedagogical impact of a nationwide investment. *Educational Evaluation and Policy Analysis, 6,* 139–150.

Heyneman, S. P., & Loxley, W. A. (1983). The effect of primary-school quality on academic achievement across twenty-nine high- and low-income countries. *The American Journal of Sociology, 88*(6), 1162–1194.

Hiebert, J., Gallimore, R., Garnier, H., Givvin, K. B., Hollingsworth, H., Jacobs, J., et al. (2003). Teaching Mathematics in Seven Countries: Results From the TIMSS 1999 Video Study (NCES 2003–013). *US Department of Education. Washington, DC: National Center for Education Statistics.*

Higgins, S., Hall, E., Baumfield, V., & Moseley, D. (2005). *A meta-analysis of the impact of the implementation of thinking skills approaches on pupils.* London: Social Science Research Unit, Institute of Education, University of London.

Hillocks, G., Jr. (1984). What works in teaching composition: A meta-analysis of experimental treatment studies. *American Journal of Education, 93*(1), 133–170.

Hines, H. E. (1989). *Gender-related differences in mathematics participation and achievement: A meta-analysis.* Unpublished Ed.D., University of Houston, Texas, United States.

Hoeffler, T. N., Sumfleth, E., & Leutner, D. (2006, April 5–6, 2006,). *The role of spatial ability when learning from an instructional animation or a series of static pictures.* Paper presented at the NYU Steinhardt Symposium on Technology and Learning, New York University, New York.

Höffler, T. N., & Leutner, D. (2007). Instructional animation versus static pictures: A meta-analysis. *Learning and Instruction, 17*(6), 722–738.

Holden, G. W., Moncher, M. S., Schinke, S. P., & Barker, K. M. (1990). Self-efficacy of children and adolescents: A meta-analysis. *Psychological Reports, 66*(3, Pt 1), 1044–1046.

Hollenbeck, J. R., & Brief, A. P. (1987). The effects of individual differences and goal origin on goal setting and performance. *Organizational Behavior and Human Decision Processes, 40*(3), 392–414.

Hollifield, J. (1987). Ability grouping in elementary schools. Urbana, IL: ERIC Clearinghouse on Elementary and Early Childhood Education.

Hollingsworth, M. A. (1991). *A meta-analysis of existing creativity training research: An evaluation of program effectiveness and possible confounding variables.* Unpublished M.A., Wake Forest University, Winston-Salem, NC.

Holly, J. G. (2002). *Facilitating optimal change: A meta-analysis of change theories and models.* Unpublished Ph.D., San Jose University, San Jose, CA.

Holmes, C. T. (1983). The fourth R: Retention. *Journal of Research and Development in Education, 17*(1), 1–6.

Holmes, C. T. (1986, April). *A synthesis of recent research on nonpromotion: A five year follow-up.* Paper presented at the Annual Meeting of the American Educational Research Association, San Francisco, CA.

Holmes, C. T. (1989). Grade level retention effects: A meta-analysis of research studies. In L. A. Shepard & M. L. Smith (Eds.), *Flunking grades: Research and policies on retention* (pp. 16–33). London: Falmer Press.

Holmes, C. T., & Matthews, K. M. (1984). The effects of nonpromotion on elementary and junior high school pupils: A meta-analysis. *Review of Educational Research, 54*(2), 225–236.

Holt, C., Denny, G., Capps, M., & De Vore, J. (2005). Teachers' ability to perceive student learning preferences: "I'm sorry, but I don't teach like that." *The Teachers College Record.* Date published: February 25, 2005 http://www.tcrecord.org ID Number: 11767, Date Accessed: 9/14/2008.

Hong, S., & Ho, H.-Z. (2005). Direct and indirect longitudinal effects of parental involvement on student achievement: Second-order latent growth modeling across ethnic groups. *Journal of Educational Psychology, 97*(1), 32–42.

Honig, A. S. (2007). Television and kids: Everything you need to know. *52*(12).

Hood, D. F. (1990). *Using meta-analysis for input evaluation.* Unpublished Ph.D., The Florida State University, FL.

Horak, V. M. (1981). A meta-analysis of research findings on individualized instruction in mathematics. *Journal of Educational Research, 74*(4).

Horak, W. J. (1985, April). *A meta-analysis of learning science concepts from textual materials.* Paper presented at the Annual Meeting of the National Association for Research in Science Teaching, French Lick Springs, IN.

Horn, W. F., & Packard, T. (1985). Early identification of learning problems: A meta-analysis. *Journal of Educational Psychology, 77*(5), 597–607.

Horon, P. F., & Lynn, D. D. (1980). Learning hierarchies research. *Evaluation in Education, 4*, 82–83.

Horton, P. B., McConney, A. A., Gallo, M., Woods, A. L., Senn, G. J., & Hamelin, D. (1993). An investigation of the effectiveness of concept mapping as an instructional tool. *Science Education, 77*(1), 95–111.

Hoskyn, M., & Swanson, H. L. (2000). Cognitive processing of low achievers and children with reading disabilities: A selective meta-analytic review of the published literature. *School Psychology Review, 29*(1), 102–119.

House, E. R. (1989). Policy implications of retention research. In L. A. Shepard & M. L. Smith (Eds.), *Flunking grades: Research and policies on retention* (pp. 202–213). London: Falmer Press.

House, E. R., Glass, G. V., McLean, L. D., & Walker, D. F. (1978). No simple answer: Critique of the Follow Through evaluation. *Harvard Educational Review, 28*, 128–160.

Housner, L. D., & Griffey, D. C. (1985). Teacher cognition: Differences in panning and interactive decision making between experienced and inexperienced teachers. *Research Quarterly for Exercise and Sport, 56*(1), 45–53.

Howard, B. C. (1996, February). *A meta-analysis of scripted cooperative learning.* Paper presented at the Annual Meeting of the Eastern Educational Research Association, Boston, MA.

Howe, K. R. (1994). Standards, assessment, and equality of educational opportunity. *Educational Researcher, 23*(8), 27–33.

Howley, C. B., & Bickel, R. (1999). *The Matthew Project: National report.* Columbus, OH: Ohio State University.

Hoxby, C. M. (2000). The effects of class size on student achievement: New evidence from population variation. *Quarterly Journal of Economics, 115*(4), 1239–1285.

Hsu, Y.-C. (2003). *The effectiveness of computer-assisted instruction in statistics education: A meta-analysis.* Unpublished Ph.D., The University of Arizona, AZ.

Huang, T.-Y. (2005). *Fostering creativity: A meta-analytic inquiry into the variability of effects.* Unpublished Ph.D., Texas A&M University, TX.

Huang, Z. (1991). *A meta-analysis of student self-questioning strategies.* Unpublished Ph.D., Hofstra University, NY.

Hunt, M. M. (1997). *How science takes stock: The story of meta-analysis.* New York: Russell Sage Foundation.

Hunter, J. E., & Schmidt, F. L. (1983). Quantifying the effects of psychological interventions on employee job performance and work-force productivity. *American Psychologist, 38*(4), 473–478.

Hunter, J. E., & Schmidt, F. L. (1990). *Methods of meta-analysis: Correcting error and bias in research findings.* Newbury Park, CA: Sage Publications.

Hurley, M. M. (2001). Reviewing integrated science and mathematics: The search for evidence and definitions from new perspectives. *School Science and Mathematics, 101*(5), 259.

Hutto, J. R. (1982). *The association of teacher manipulation of scientifically acquired learning styles information to the achievement and attitude of second and third grade remedial students.* Unpublished Ed.D., The University of Southern Mississippi, MS.

Hyde, J. S. (1981). How large are cognitive gender differences? *American Psychologist, 36*(8), 892–901.

Hyde, J. S. (1984). How large are gender differences in aggression? A developmental meta-analysis. *Developmental Psychology, 20*(4), 722–736.

Hyde, J. S. (1990). Meta-analysis and the psychology of gender differences. *Signs: Journal of Women in Culture and Society, 16*(1), 55.

Hyde, J. S. (2005). The gender similarities hypothesis. *American Psychologist, 60*(6), 581–592.

Hyde, J. S., Fennema, E., & Lamon, S. J. (1990). Gender differences in mathematics performance: A meta-analysis. *Psychological Bulletin, 107*(2), 139–155.

Hyde, J. S., Fennema, E., Ryan, M., Frost, L. A., & Hopp, C. (1990). Gender comparisons of mathematics attitudes and affect: A meta-analysis. *Psychology of Women Quarterly, 14*(3), 299–324.

Hyde, J. S., & Linn, M. C. (1988). Gender differences in verbal ability: A meta-analysis. *Psychological Bulletin, 104*(1), 53–69.

Hymel, G. M. (1990, April). *Harnessing the mastery learning literature: Past efforts, current status, and future directions.* Paper presented at the Annual Meeting of the American Educational Research Association, Boston, MA.

Ianno, A., Jr. (1995). *A meta-analysis of research on the effects of computer-assisted instruction on reading achievement of learning-disabled students.* Unpublished Ph.D., Southern Illinois University at Carbondale, IL.

Ide, J. C., Parkerson, J., Haertel, G. D., & Walberg, H. J. (1980). Peer influences. *Evaluation in Education, 4*, 111–112.

Ide, J. K., Parkerson, J., Haertel, G. D., & Walberg, H. J. (1981). Peer group influence on educational outcomes: A quantitative synthesis. *Journal of Educational Psychology, 73*(4), 472–484.

Iliff, C. H. (1994). *Kolb Learning Style Inventory: A meta-analysis.* Unpublished Ed.D., Boston University, MA.

Ingersoll, R. (2003). Is there a shortage among mathematics and science teachers? *Science Educator, 12*(1), 1–9.

Ingham, J. (1989). *An experimental investigation of the relationships among learning style, perceptual strength, instructional strategies, training achievement, and attitudes of corporate employees.* Unpublished Ed.D., St. John's University (New York), NY.

Ingham, J. M. (1991). Matching instruction with employee perceptual preference significantly increases training effectiveness. *Human Resource Development Quarterly, 2*(1), 53–64.

Inglis, J., & Lawson, J. S. (1987). Reanalysis of a meta-analysis of the validity of the Wechsler Scales in the diagnosis of learning disability. *Learning Disability Quarterly, 10*(3), 198–202.

Ingvarson, L., & Hattie, J. A. C. (Eds.). (2008). *Assessing teachers for professional certification: The first decade of the National Board for Professional Teaching Standards.* Oxford, UK: Elsevier.

Inhelder, B., & Piaget, J. (1964). *The early growth of logic in the child: Classification and seriation.* London: Routledge and Kegan Paul.

Innocenti, M. S., Huh, K., & Boyce, G. C. (1992). Families of children with disabilities: Normative data and other considerations on parenting stress. *Topics in Early Childhood Special Education, 12*(3), 403–427.

Innocenti, M. S., & White, K. R. (1993). Are more intensive early intervention programs more effective? A review of the literature. *Exceptionality, 4*(1), 31–50.

Irving, S. E. (2004). *The development and validation of a student evaluation instrument to identify highly accomplished mathematics teachers.* Unpublished Ph.D., The University of Auckland, Auckland, New Zealand.

Iverson, B. K., & Walberg, H. J. (1980). Home environment. *Evaluation in Education, 4*, 107–108.

Iverson, B. K., & Walberg, H. J. (1982). Home environment and school learning: A quantitative synthesis. *Journal of Experimental Education, 50*(3), 144–151.

Jackson, L. A., Hunter, J. E., & Hodge, C. N. (1995). Physical attractiveness and intellectual competence: A meta-analytic review. *Social Psychology Quarterly, 58*(2), 108–122.

Jaeger, R. M., & Hattie, J. A. C. (1995). Detracking America's schools: Should we really care? *Phi Delta Kappan, 77*(3), 218–219.

Jaeger, R. M., & Hattie, J. A. C. (1996). Artifact and artifice in education policy analysis: It's not all in the data. *School Administrator, 53*(5), 24–25, 28–29.

Jamison, D. T. (1982). Reduced class size and other alternatives for improving schools: An economist's view. In G. V. Glass, L. S. Cahen, M. L. Smith & N. N. Filby (Eds.), *School class size, research and policy* (pp. 116–129). Beverly Hills, CA: Sage.

Jeynes, W. H. (2002). A meta-analysis of the effects of attending religious schools and religiosity on Black and Hispanic academic achievement. *Education and Urban Society, 35*(1), 27–49.

Jeynes, W. H. (2003). A meta-analysis: The effects of parental involvement on minority children's academic achievement. *Education and Urban Society, 35*(2), 202–218.

Jeynes, W. H. (2004). A meta-analysis: Has the academic impact of religious schools changed over the last twenty years? *Journal of Empirical Theology, 17*(2), 197–216.

Jeynes, W. H. (2005). A meta-analysis of the relation of parental involvement to urban elementary school student academic achievement. *Urban Education, 40*(3), 237–269.

Jeynes, W. H. (2006). The impact of parental remarriage on children: A meta-analysis. *Marriage and Family Review, 40*(4), 75–102.

Jeynes, W. H. (2007). The relationship between parental involvement and urban secondary school student academic achievement: A meta-analysis. *Urban Education, 42*(1), 82–110.

Jeynes, W. H. (2008). A meta-analysis of the relationship between phonics instruction and minority elementary school student academic achievement. *Education and Urban Society, 40*(2), 151–166.

Jeynes, W. H., & Littell, S. W. (2000). A meta-analysis of studies examining the effect of whole language instruction on the literacy of low-SES students. *The Elementary School Journal, 101*(1), 21–33.

Jimerson, S. R. (2001). Meta-analysis of grade retention research: Implications for practice in the 21st century. *School Psychology Review, 30*(3), 420–437.

Johannessen, L. R. (1990, August). *Approaches to teaching writing that work.* Paper presented at the School District U-46 In-Service Program, Elgin, IL.

Johnson, B. T., & Eagly, A. H. (1989). Effects of involvement on persuasion: A meta-analysis. *Psychological Bulletin, 106*(2), 290–314.

Johnson, D. W., Jensen, B., Feeny, S., & Methakullawat, B. (2004, August). *Multivariate analysis of performance of Victorian schools.* Paper presented at the Making Schools Better Submit Conference, Melbourne, Australia.

Johnson, D. W., & Johnson, R. T. (1982, August). *Having your cake and eating it too: Maximizing achievement and cognitive-social development and socialization through cooperative learning.* Paper presented at the Annual Convention of the American Psychological Association, Washington, DC.

Johnson, D. W., & Johnson, R. T. (1987). Research shows the benefits of adult cooperation. *Educational Leadership, 45*(3), 27–30.

Johnson, D. W., & Johnson, R. T. (2001, April). *Teaching students to be peacemakers: A meta-analysis.* Paper presented at the Annual Meeting of the American Educational Research Association, Seattle, WA.

Johnson, D. W., & Johnson, R. T. (2002). Learning together and alone: Overview and meta-analysis. *Asia Pacific Journal of Education, 22*(1), 95–105.

Johnson, D. W., Johnson, R. T., & Maruyama, G. (1983). Interdependence and interpersonal attraction among heterogeneous and homogeneous individuals: A theoretical formulation and a meta-analysis of the research. *Review of Educational Research, 53*(1), 5–54.

Johnson, D. W., Johnson, R. T., & Stanne, M. B. (2000). Cooperative learning methods: A meta-analysis [Electronic Version]. Retrieved 6 May 2008 from http://www.co-operation.org/pages/cl-methods.html.

Johnson, D. W., Maruyama, G., Johnson, R. T., Nelson, D., & Skon, L. (1981). Effects of cooperative, competitive, and individualistic goal structures on achievement: A meta-analysis. *Psychological Bulletin, 89*(1), 47–62.

Johnson, E. G., & Zwick, R. (1990). *Focusing the new design: The NAEP 1988 Technical Report* (No. ISBN-0–88685–106–8). Princeton, NJ: National Assessment of Educational Progress (NAEP) and Educational Testing Service.

Johnson, E. S. (1984). Sex differences in problem solving. *Journal of Educational Psychology, 76*(6), 1359–1371.

Johnson, N. L. (1993). *Thinking is the key: Questioning makes the difference.* Cheltenham, Vic.: Hawker Brownlow Education.

Johnson, O. D., Jr. (2003). *Research syntheses in neighborhood studies: The influence of socioeconomic factors in the education of African-American and urban populations.* Unpublished Ph.D., University of Michigan, MI.

Johnson, R. T., Johnson, D. W., & Stanne, M. B. (1986). Comparison of computer-assisted cooperative, competitive, and individualistic learning. *American Educational Research Journal, 23*(3), 382–392.

Jones, A., & Jacka, S. (1995). Discourse of disadvantage: Girls' school achievement. *New Zealand Journal of Educational Studies, 30*(2), 165–175.

Jones, H. J. (1991). *The effects of the Writing to Read computer program on reading achievement and attitudes of second-grade children.* Unpublished Ph.D., Texas Woman's University, TX.

Jones, R. A. (1989). *The relationship of student achievement to mobility in the elementary school.* Unpublished Ph.D., Georgia State University, GA.

Jones, S. S. (2002). *The effect of all-day kindergarten on student cognitive growth: A meta-analysis.* Unpublished Ed.D., University of Kansas, KS.

Jordan, V. B., & Brownlee, L. (1981, April). *Meta-analysis of the relationship between Piagetian and school achievement tests.* Paper presented at the Annual Meeting of the American Educational Research Association, Los Angeles, CA.

Joslin, P. A. (1980). *Inservice teacher education: A meta-analysis of the research.* Unpublished Ed.D., University of Minnesota, MN.

Joyce, B., Showers, B., & Rolheiser-Bennett, C. (1987). Staff development and student learning: A synthesis of research on models of teaching. *Educational Leadership, 45*(2), 11–23.

Kaczala, C. (1991). *Grade retention: A longitudinal study of school correlates of rates of retention.* Cleveland, OH: Cleveland Public Schools.

Kahl, S. R., Fleming, M. L., & Malone, M. R. (1982, March). *Sex-related differences in pre-college science: Findings of the science meta-analysis project.* Paper presented at the Annual Meeting of the American Educational Research Association, New York.

Kalaian, S., & Becker, B. J. (1986, April). *Effects of coaching on Scholastic Aptitude Test (SAT) performance: A multivariate meta-analysis approach.* Paper presented at the Annual Meeting of the American Educational Research Association, San Francisco, CA.

Kalechstein, A. D., & Nowicki, S., Jr. (1997). A meta-analytic examination of the relationship between control expectancies and academic achievement: an 11-year follow-up to Findley and Cooper. *Genetic, Social, and General Psychology Monographs, 123*(1), 27–56.

Kang, O.-R. (2002). *A meta-analysis of graphic organizer interventions for students with learning disabilities.* Unpublished Ph.D., University of Oregon, OR.

Kardash, C. A. M., & Wright, L. (1987). Does creative drama benefit elementary school students: A meta-analysis. *Youth Theatre Journal, 1*(3), 11–18.

Karweit, N. (1984). Time-on-task reconsidered: Synthesis of research on time and learning. *Educational Leadership, 41*(8), 32–35.

Karweit, N. (1985). Should we lengthen the school term? *Educational Researcher, 14*(6), 9–15.

Kavale, K. A. (1980). Auditory-visual integration and its relationship to reading achievement: A meta-analysis. *Perceptual and Motor Skills, 51*(3), 947–955.

Kavale, K. A. (1980). Psycholinguistic training. *Evaluation in Education, 4,* 88–90.

Kavale, K. A. (1981). The relationship between auditory perceptual skills and reading ability: A meta-analysis. *Journal of Learning Disabilities, 14*(9), 539–546.

Kavale, K. A. (1982). The efficacy of stimulant drug treatment for hyperactivity: A meta-analysis. *Journal of Learning Disabilities, 15*(5).

Kavale, K. A. (1982). Meta-analysis of the relationship between visual perceptual skills and reading achievement. *Journal of Learning Disabilities, 15*(1), 42–51.

Kavale, K. A. (1982). Psycholinguistic training programs: Are there differential treatment effects? *International Journal of Disability, Development and Education, 29*(1), 21–30.

Kavale, K. A. (1984). A meta-analytic evaluation of the Frostig Test and training program. *International Journal of Disability, Development and Education, 31*(2), 134–141.

Kavale, K. A. (1995). Meta-analysis at 20: Retrospect and prospect. *Evaluation and the Health Professions, 18*(4), 349–369.

Kavale, K. A., & Carlberg, C. (1980). Regular versus special class placement for exceptional children. *Evaluation in Education, 4,* 91–93.

Kavale, K. A., & Dobbins, D. A. (1993). The equivocal nature of special education interventions. *Early Child Development and Care,* 23–37.

Kavale, K. A., Fuchs, D., & Scruggs, E. E. (1994). Setting the record straight on learning disability and low achievement: Implications for policymaking. *Learning Disabilities Research and Practice, 9*(2), 70–77.

Kavale, K. A., & Forness, S. R. (1983). Hyperactivity and diet treatment: A meta-analysis of the Feingold hypothesis. *Journal of Learning Disabilities, 16*(6), 324–330.

Kavale, K. A., & Forness, S. R. (1987). Substance over style: Assessing the efficacy of modality testing and teaching. *Exceptional Children, 54*(3), 228–239.

Kavale, K. A., & Forness, S. R. (1996). Social skill deficits and learning disabilities: A meta-analysis. *Journal of Learning Disabilities, 29*(3), 226.

Kavale, K. A., & Forness, S. R. (2000). Auditory and visual perception processes and reading ability: A quantitative reanalysis and historical reinterpretation. *Learning Disability Quarterly, 23*(4), 253–270.

Kavale, K. A., Hirshoren, A., & Forness, S. R. (1998). Meta-analytic validation of the Dunn and Dunn Model of learning-style preferences: A critique of what was Dunn. *Learning Disabilities Research and Practice, 13*(2), 75–80.

Kavale, K. A., & Mattson, P. D. (1983). "One jumped off the balance beam": Meta-analysis of perceptual motor training. *Journal of Learning Disabilities, 16*(3).

Kavale, K. A., & Mostert, M. P. (2004). Social skills interventions for individuals with learning disabilities. *Learning Disability Quarterly, 27*(1), 31–43.

Kavale, K. A., & Nye, C. (1984). The effectiveness of drug treatment for severe behavior disorders: A meta-analysis. *Behavioral Disorders, 9*(2), 117–130.

Kavale, K. A., & Nye, C. (1985). Parameters of learning disabilities in achievement, linguistic, neuropsychological, and social/behavioral domains. *Journal of Special Education, 19*(4), 443–458.

Kazdin, A. E., Bass, D., Ayers, W. A., & Rodgers, A. (1990). Empirical and clinical focus of child arnd adolescent psychotherapy research. *Journal of Consulting and Clinical Psychology, 58*(6), 729–740.

Keinanen, M., Hetland, L., & Winner, E. (2000). Teaching cognitive skill through dance: Evidence for near but not far transfer. *Journal of Aesthetic Education, 34*(3/4), 295–306.

Keller, F. S. (1968). "Good-bye, teacher …" *Journal of Applied Behavior Analysis 1*(1), 79–89.

Keller, F. S., & Sherman, J. G. (1974). *PSI, the Keller Plan Handbook: Essays on a personalized system of instruction.* Menlo Park, CA: Benjamin.

Kelley, P., & Camilli, G. (2007). *The impact of teacher education on outcomes in center-based early childhood education programs: A meta-analysis.* New Brunswick, NJ: National Institutue for Early Education Research, Rutgers, The State University of New Jersey.

Kember, D., & Wong, A. (2000). Implications for evaluation from a study of students' perceptions of good and poor teaching. *Higher Education, 40*(1), 69–97.

Kennedy, M. M. (1997). *Defining an ideal teacher education program.* Paper for the National Council for Accreditation of Teacher Education. Michigan State University.

Kennedy, M. M. (1999). Approximations to indicators of student outcomes. *Educational Evaluation and Policy Analysis, 21*(4), 345–363.

Kennedy, M. M. (1999). A test of some common contentions about educational research. *American Educational Research Journal, 36*(3), 511.

Kent, S. D. (1992). *The effects of acceleration on the social and emotional development of gifted elementary students: A meta-analysis.* Unpublished Ed.D., University of Georgia, GA.

Kim, A. H., Vaughn, S., Wanzek, J., & Wei, S. (2004). Graphic organizers and their effects on the reading comprehension of students with LD: A synthesis of research. *Journal of Learning Disabilities, 37*(2), 105–118.

Kim, J.-P. (1999, October). *Meta-analysis of equivalence of computerized and P&P tests on ability measures.* Paper presented at the Annual Meeting of the Mid-Western Educational Research Association, Chicago, IL.

Kim, J. P. (1996). *The impact of the nongraded program on students' affective domains and cognitive domains.* Unpublished Ed.D., University of Georgia, GA.

Kim, J. S. (2002). *A meta-analysis of academic summer programs.* Unpublished Ed.D., Harvard University, MA.

Kim, K. H. (2005). Can only intelligent people be creative? A meta-analysis. *Journal of Secondary Gifted Education, 16*(2–3), 57–66.

Kim, S.-E. (2005). *Effects of implementing performance assessments on student learning: Meta-analysis using HLM.* Unpublished Ph.D., The Pennsylvania State University, PA.

Kim, Y.-W., Innocenti, M., & Kim, J.-K. (1996, July). *When should we begin? A comprehensive review of age at start in early intervention.* Paper presented at the Annual World Congress of the International Association for the Scientific Study of Intellectual Disabilities, Helsinki, Finland.

King, H. J. (1997). *Effects of computer-enhanced instruction in college-level mathematics as determined by a meta-analysis.* Unpublished Ph.D., The University of Tennessee, TN.

Kintsch, W. (1988). The use of knowledge in discourse processing: A construction-integration model. *Psychological Review, 95*(2), 163–182.

Kirschner, P. A., Sweller, J., & Clark, R. E. (2006). Why minimal guidance during instruction does not work: An analysis of the failure of constructivist, discovery, problem-based, experiential, and inquiry-based teaching. *Educational Psychologist, 41*(2), 75–86.

Kisamore, J. L., & Brannick, M. T. (2008). An illustration of the consequences of meta-analysis model choice. *Organizational Research Methods, 11*(1), 35–53.

Klahr, D. (2000). *Exploring science: The cognition and development of discovery processes.* Cambridge, MA: MIT Press.

Klauer, K. J. (1981). Zielorientiertes lehren und lernen bei lehrtexten. Eine metaanalyse [Goal oriented teaching and learning in scholarly texts. A Meta-analysis]. *Unterrichtswissenschaft, 9,* 300–318.

Klauer, K. J. (1984). Intentional and incidental learning with instructional texts: A meta-analysis for 1970–1980. *American Educational Research Journal, 21*(2), 323–339.

Klauer, K. J., & Phye, G. D. (2008). Inductive reasoning: A training approach. *Review of Educational Research, 78*(1), 85–123.

Klein, H. J., Wesson, M. J., Hollenbeck, J. R., & Alge, B. J. (1999). Goal commitment and the goal-setting process: Conceptual clarification and empirical synthesis. *Journal of Applied Psychology, 84*(6), 885–896.

Klesius, J. P., & Searls, E. F. (1990). A meta-analysis of recent research in meaning vocabulary instruction. *Journal of Research and Development in Education, 23*(4), 226–235.

Kloss, R. J. (1988). Toward asking the right questions: The beautiful, the pretty, and the big messy ones. *Clearing House, 61*(6), 245–248.

Kluger, A. N., & DeNisi, A. (1996). The effects of feedback interventions on performance: A historical review, a meta-analysis, and a preliminary feedback intervention theory. *Psychological Bulletin, 119*(2), 254.

Kobayashi, K. (2005). What limits the encoding effect of note-taking? A meta-analytic examination. *Contemporary Educational Psychology, 30*(2), 242–262.

Kobayashi, K. (2006). Combined effects of note-taking: Reviewing on learning and the enhancement through Interventions: A meta-analytic review. *Educational Psychology, 26*(3), 459–477.

Kohn, A. (1997). How not to teach values: A critical look at character education. *Phi Delta Kappan, 78*(6), 428–439.

Koller, O., Baumert, J., & Schnabel, K. (2001). Does interest matter? The relationship between academic interest and achievement in mathematics. *Journal for Research in Mathematics Education, 32*(5), 448–470.

Konstantopoulos, S. (2005). *Trends of school effects on student achievement: Evidence from NLS:72, HSB:82, and NELS:92* (No. 1749). Bonn, Germany: Institute for the Study of Labor.

Koufogiannakis, D., & Wiebe, N. (2006). Effective methods for teaching information literacy skills to undergraduate students: A systematic review and meta-analysis. *Evidence Based Library and Information Practice, 1*(3), 3–43.

Kozlow, M. J. (1978). *A meta-analysis of selected advance organizer research reports from 1960–1977.* Unpublished Ph.D., The Ohio State University, OH.

Kozlow, M. J., & White, A. L. (1980). Advance organiser research. *Evaluation in Education, 4,* 47–48.

Kozol, J. (2005). *The shame of the nation: The restoration of apartheid schooling in America* (1st ed.). New York: Crown Publishers.

Krabbe, M. A. (1989, March). *A comparison of experienced and novice teachers routines and procedures during set and discussion instructional activity segments.* Paper presented at the Annual meeting of the American Educational Research Association, San Francisco, CA.

Kremer, B. K., Boulanger, F. D., Haertel, G. D., & Walberg, H. J. (1980). Science education research. *Evaluation in Education, 4,* 125–129.

Kroesbergen, E. H., & Van Luit, J. E. H. (2003). Mathematics interventions for children with special educational needs: A meta-analysis. *Remedial and Special Education, 24*(2), 97–114.

Krol, R. A. (1978). *A meta analysis of comparative research on the effects of desegregation on academic achievement.* Unpublished EdD, Western Michigan University, Kalamazoo, MI.

Krol, R. A. (1980). A meta analysis of the effects of desegregation on academic achievement. *The Urban Review, 12*(4), 211–224.

Kruse, A. M. (1987). *Sagde du konssegregering—med vilje? Paedagogik med rode stromper.* Kobenhavn: Danmarks Laererhojskole.

Kruse, A. M. (1989). Hvorfor pigeklasser? In A. Hilden & A.-M. Kruse (Eds.), *Pigernes skole* (pp. 249–263). Skive: Klim.

Kruse, A. M. (1990). Konsadskilt undervisning somkonsbevid st paedagogik. In H. Jacobsen & L. Hojgaard (Eds.), *Skolen er kon* (pp. 36–81). Viborg: Ligestillingsridet.

Kruse, A. M. (1992). "...We have learnt not just to sit back, twiddle our thumbs and let them take over." Single-sex settings and the development of a pedagogy for girls and a pedagogy for boys in Danish schools. *Gender and Education, 4*(1), 81–103.

Kruse, A. M. (1994). Hvordan er det med der forskelle pa piger og drenge? Interview med Harriet Bjerrum Nielsen. *Tidsskrift for borne and ungdomskultur, 34*, 51–65.

Kruse, A. M. (1996). Approaches to teaching girls and boys: Current debates, practices, and perspectives in Denmark. *Women's Studies International Forum, 19*(4), 429–445.

Kruse, A. M. (1996). Single-sex settings: Pedagogies for girls and boys in Danish schools. In P. F. Murphy & C. V. Gipps (Eds.), *Equity in the Classroom: Towards effective pedagogy for girls and boys* (pp. 173–191). London: Falmer.

Kuchler, J. M. (1998). *The effectiveness of using computers to teach secondary school (grades 6–12) mathematics: A meta-analysis.* Unpublished Ed.D., University of Massachusetts Lowell, MA.

Kulhavy, R. W. (1977). Feedback in written instruction. *Review of Educational Research, 47*(2), 211–232.

Kulik, C. L. C. (1985). Effectiveness of computer-based adult education. *Computers in Human Behavior, 1 (1),* 59–74

Kulik, C. L. C. (1985, August). *Effects of inter-class ability grouping on achievement and self-esteem.* Paper presented at the Annual Convention of the American Psychological Association, Los Angeles, CA.

Kulik, C. L. C. (1986, April). *Effects of testing for mastery on student learning.* Paper presented at the Annual Meeting of the American Educational Research Association, San Francisco, CA.

Kulik, C. L. C., & Kulik, J. A. (1982). Effects of ability grouping on secondary school students: A meta-analysis of evaluation findings. *American Educational Research Journal, 19*(3), 415–428.

Kulik, C. L. C., & Kulik, J. A. (1982). Research synthesis on ability grouping. *Educational Leadership, 39*(8), 619–621.

Kulik, C. L. C., & Kulik, J. A. (1984, August). *Effects of ability grouping on elementary school pupils: A meta-analysis.* Paper presented at the Annual Meeting of the American Psychological Association, Toronto, ON, Canada.

Kulik, C. L. C., & Kulik, J. A. (1986). Effectiveness of computer-based education in colleges. *AEDS Journal, 19*(2–3), 81–108.

Kulik, C. L. C., & Kulik, J. A. (1986). Mastery testing and student learning: A meta-analysis. *Journal of Educational Technology Systems, 15*(3), 325–345.

Kulik, C. L. C., & Kulik, J. A. (1991). Effectiveness of computer-based instruction: An updated analysis. *Computers in Human Behavior, 7*(1–2), 75–94.

Kulik, C. L. C., Kulik, J. A., & Bangert-Drowns, R. L. (1984, April). *Effects of computer-based education on elementary school pupils.* Paper presented at the Annual Meeting of the American Educational Research Association, New Orleans, LA.

Kulik, C. L. C., Kulik, J. A., & Bangert-Drowns, R. L. (1990). Effectiveness of mastery learning programs: A meta-analysis. *Review of Educational Research, 60*(2), 265–299.

Kulik, C. L. C., Kulik, J. A., & Cohen, P. A. (1980). Instructional technology and college teaching. *Teaching of Psychology, 7*(4), 199–205.

Kulik, C. L. C., Kulik, J. A., & Shwalb, B. J. (1983). College programs for high-risk and disadvantaged students: A meta-analysis of findings. *Review of Educational Research, 53*(3), 397–414.

Kulik, C. L. C., Kulik, J. A., & Shwalb, B. J. (1986). The effectiveness of computer-based adult education: A meta-analysis. *Journal of Educational Computing Research, 2*(2), 235–252.

Kulik, C. L. C., Shwalb, B. J., & Kulik, J. A. (1982). Programmed instruction in secondary education: A meta-analysis of evaluation findings. *Journal of Educational Research, 75*(3), 133–138.

Kulik, J. A. (1983). Synthesis of research on computer-based instruction. *Educational Leadership, 41*(1), 19–21.

Kulik, J. A. (1983). What can science educators teach chemists about teaching chemistry? A symposium: How can chemists use educational technology effectively? *Journal of Chemical Education, 60*(11), 957–959.

Kulik, J. A. (1984, April). *The fourth revolution in teaching: Meta-analyses.* Paper presented at the Annual Meeting of the American Educational Research Association, New Orleans, LA.

Kulik, J. A. (1994). Meta-analytical studies of findings on computer-based instruction. In E. L. Baker & H. F. O'Neil (Eds.), *Technology assessment in education and training* (pp. 9–33). Mahwah, NJ: Lawrence Erlbaum Associates.

Kulik, J. A. (2003). *Effects of using instructional technology in colleges and universities: What controlled evaluation studies say.* Arlington, VA: SRI International.

Kulik, J. A. (2004). Meta-analytic studies of acceleration. In N. Colangelo, S. G. Assouline & M. U. M. Gross (Eds.), *A nation deceived. How schools hold back America's brightest students* (Vol. 2, pp. 13–22). Iowa City, IA: The Connie Belin and Jacqueline N. Blank International Center for Gifted Education and Talent Development, College of Education, The University of Iowa.

Kulik, J. A., Bangert, R. L., & Williams, G. W. (1983). Effects of computer-based teaching on secondary school students. *Journal of Educational Psychology, 75*(1), 19–26.

Kulik, J. A., Bangert-Drowns, R. L., & Kulik, C.-L. C. (1984). Effectiveness of coaching for aptitude tests. *Psychological Bulletin, 95*(2), 179–188.

Kulik, J. A., Cohen, P. A., & Ebeling, B. J. (1980). Effectiveness of programmed instruction in higher education: A meta-analysis of findings. *Educational Evaluation and Policy Analysis, 2*(6), 51–64.

Kulik, J. A., & Kulik, C. L. C. (1980). Individualised college teaching. *Evaluation in Education, 4*, 64–67.

Kulik, J. A., & Kulik, C. L. C. (1984). Effects of accelerated instruction on students. *Review of Educational Research, 54*(3), 409–425

Kulik, J. A., & Kulik, C. L. C. (1984). Synthesis of research on effects of accelerated instruction. *Educational Leadership, 42*(2), 84–89.

Kulik, J. A., & Kulik, C. L. C. (1987, March). *Computer-based instruction: What 200 evaluations say.* Paper presented at the Annual Convention of the Association for Educational Communications and Technology, Atlanta, GA.

Kulik, J. A., & Kulik, C. L. C. (1987). Effects of ability grouping on student achievement. *Equity and Excellence in Education, 23*(1), 22–30.

Kulik, J. A., & Kulik, C. L. C. (1987). Review of recent research literature on computer-based instruction. *Contemporary Educational Psychology, 12*(3), 222–230.

Kulik, J. A., & Kulik, C. L. C. (1988). Timing of feedback and verbal learning. *Review of Educational Research, 58*(1), 79–97.

Kulik, J. A., & Kulik, C. L. C. (1989). The concept of meta-analysis. *International Journal of Educational Research, 13*(3), 227–340.

Kulik, J. A., & Kulik, C. L. C. (1992). Meta-analytic findings on grouping programs. *Gifted Child Quarterly, 36*(2), 73–77.

Kulik, J. A., Kulik, C. L. C., & Bangert, R. L. (1984). Effects of practice on aptitude and achievement test scores. *American Educational Research Journal, 21*(2), 435–447.

Kulik, J. A., Kulik, C. L. C., & Bangert-Drowns, R. L. (1985). Effectiveness of computer-based education in elementary schools. *Computers in Human Behavior, 1*(1), 59–74.

Kulik, J. A., Kulik, C. L. C., & Cohen, P. A. (1979). A meta-analysis of outcome studies of Keller's Personalized System of Instruction. *American Psychologist, 34*(4), 307–318.

Kulik, J. A., Kulik, C. L. C., & Cohen, P. A. (1979). Research on audio-tutorial instruction: A meta-analysis of comparative studies. *Research in Higher Education, 11*(4), 321–341.

Kulik, J. A., Kulik, C. L. C., & Cohen, P. A. (1980). Effectiveness of computer-based college teaching: A meta-analysis of findings. *Review of Educational Research, 50*(4), 525–544.

Kumar, D. D. (1991). A meta-analysis of the relationship between science instruction and student engagement. *Educational Review, 43*(1), 49–61.

Kuncel, N. R. (2003). *The prediction and structure of graduate student performance.* Unpublished Ph.D., University of Minnesota, MN.

Kuncel, N. R., Crede, M., & Thomas, L. L. (2005). The validity of self-reported grade point averages, class ranks, and test scores: A meta-analysis and review of the literature. *Review of Educational Research, 75*(1), 63–82.

Kuncel, N. R., Hezlett, S. A., & Ones, D. S. (2001). A comprehensive meta-analysis of the predictive validity of the graduate record examinations: Implications for graduate student selection and performance. *Psychological Bulletin, 127*(1), 162–181.

Kunsch, C. A., Jitendra, A. K., & Sood, S. (2007). The effects of peer-mediated instruction in mathematics for students with learning problems: A research synthesis. *Learning Disabilities Research and Practice, 22*(1), 1–12.

Kunz, J. (1995). The impact of divorce on children's intellectual functioning: A meta-analysis. *Family Perspective, 29*(1), 75–101.

Kunz, J. (2001). Parental divorce and children's interpersonal relationships: A meta-analysis. *Journal of Divorce and Remarriage, 34*(3/4), 19–47.

Kyle, W. C. J. (1982). *A meta-analysis of the effects on student performance of new curricular programs developed in science education since 1955.* Unpublished Ph.D., The University of Iowa, IA.

La Paro, K. M., & Pianta, R. C. (2000). Predicting children's competence in the early school years: A meta-analytic review. *Review of Educational Research, 70*(4), 443–484.

Ladd, G. W. (1990). Having friends, keeping friends, making friends, and being liked by peers in the classroom: Predictors of children's early school adjustment? *Child Development, 61*(4), 1081–1100.

Ladd, G. W., Kochenderfer, B. J., & Coleman, C. C. (1996). Friendship quality as a predictor of young children's early school adjustment. *Child Development, 67*(3), 1103–1118.

Ladd, G. W., Kochenderfer, B. J., & Coleman, C. C. (1997). Classroom peer acceptance, friendship, and victimization: Distinct relational systems that contribute uniquely to children's school adjustment? *Child Development, 68*(6), 1181–1197.

Laidlaw, J. S. (2000). *A meta-analysis of outdoor education programs.* Unpublished Ed.D., University of Northern Colorado, CO.

Lang, J., & Kersting, M. (2007). Regular feedback from student ratings of instruction: Do college teachers improve their ratings in the long run? *Instructional Science, 35*(3), 187–205.

Langenberg, N. L., Correro, G., Ferguson, G., Kamil, M. L., & Shaywitz, S. E. (2000). *Teaching children to read: An evidence-based assessment of the scientific research literature on reading and its implications for reading instruction.* Washington, DC: National Institute of Child Health and Development.

Langer, E. J. (1989). *Mindfulness.* New York: Da Capo Press.

Lapadat, J. C. (1991). Pragmatic language skills of students with language and/or learning disabilities: A quantitative synthesis. *Journal of Learning Disabilities, 24*(3), 147–158.

Lareau, A. (1987). Social class differences in family-school relationships: The importance of cultural capital. *Sociology of Education, 60*(2), 73–85.

Lashell, L. M. (1986). *An analysis of the effects of reading methods upon reading achievement and locus-of-control when individual reading style is matched for learning-disabled students.* Unpublished Ph.D., The Fielding Institute, CA.

Latham, G. P., & Locke, E. A. (2006). Enhancing the benefits and overcoming the pitfalls of goal setting. *Organizational Dynamics, 35*(4), 332–340.

Lauer, P. A., Akiba, M., Wilkerson, S. B., Apthorp, H. S., Snow, D., & Martin-Glenn, M. L. (2006). Out-of-school-time programs: A meta-analysis of effects for at-risk students. *Review of Educational Research, 76*(2), 275–313.

Lavery, L. (2008). *Self-regulated learning for academic success: An evaluation of instructional techniques.* Unpublished Ph.D., The University of Auckland, Auckland.

Law, J., Garrett, Z., & Nye, C. (2004). The efficacy of treatment for children with developmental speech and language delay/disorder: A meta-analysis. *Journal of Speech, Language, and Hearing Research, 47,* 924–943.

Lee, D.-S. (2000). *A meta-analysis of mathematics interventions reported for 1971–1998 on the mathematics achievement of students identified with learning disabilities and students identified as low achieving.* Unpublished Ph.D., University of Oregon, OR.

Lee Hearold, S. (1980). Television and social behaviour. *Evaluation in Education, 4,* 94–95.

Lee, J. (1999). Effectiveness of computer-based instructional simulation: A meta-analysis. *International Journal of Instructional Media, 26*(1), 71–85.

Lee, J. (2006, April). *Is test-driven external accountability effective? A meta-analysis of the evidence from cross-state causal-comparative and correlational studies.* Paper presented at the Annual meeting of American Educational Research Association, San Francisco, CA.

Lee, T. D., & Genovese, E. D. (1988). Distribution of practice in motor skill acquisition: Learning and performance effects reconsidered. *Research Quarterly for Exercise and Sport, 59*(4), 277–287.

Lee, V. E., & Smith, J. B. (1993). Effects of school restructuring on the achievement and engagement of middle-grade students. *Sociology of Education, 66*(3), 164–187.

Lee, V. E., & Smith, J. B. (1997). High school size: Which works best and for whom? *Educational Evaluation and Policy Analysis, 19*(3), 205–227.

Lee, W.-C. (1990). *The effectiveness of computer-assisted instruction and computer programming in elementary and secondary mathematics: A meta-analysis.* Unpublished Ed.D., University of Massachusetts Amherst, MA.

Leinhardt, G. (1983, March). *Routines in expert math teachers' thoughts and actions.* Paper presented at the Annual meeting of the American Educational Research Association, Montreal, Canada.

LeJeune, J.V. (2002). *A meta-analysis of outcomes from the use of computer-simulated experiments in science education.* Unpublished Ed.D., Texas A&M University, TX.

LeNoir, P. (1989). *The effects of manipulatives in mathematics instruction in grades K-college: A meta-analysis of thirty years of research.* Unpublished Ph.D., North Carolina State University, NC.

Leong, C.-L. (1981). *Meta-analysis of research on the adjunctive use of computers in secondary mathematics.* Unpublished Master's thesis, University of Toronto, Toronto, Canada.

Levie, W. H., & Lentz, R. (1982). Effects of text illustrations: A review of research. *Educational Communication and Technology: A Journal of Theory, Research, and Development, 30*(4), 195–232.

Levin, H. M. (1984). *Cost-effectiveness of four educational interventions*: Stanford Univ., CA. Inst. for Research on Educational Finance and Governance.[BBB16943].

Levin, H. M. (1988). *Accelerated schools for at-risk students. CPRE Research Report Series RR-010.* New Brunswick, NJ: Center for Policy Research in Education, Eagleton Institute of Politics, Rutgers, The State University of New Jersey.

Levin, H. M. (1988). Cost-effectiveness and educational policy. *Educational Evaluation and Policy Analysis, 10*(1), 51–69.

Levin, H. M., Glass, G. V., & Meister, G. R. (1987). Different approaches to improving performance at school. *Zeitschrift fur Internationale Erziehungs und Sozial Wissenschaftliche Forschung, 3,* 156–176.

Levin, H. M., Leitner, D., & Meister, G. R. (1986). *Cost-effectiveness of alternative approaches to computer-assisted instruction* (microform). Stanford, CA: Stanford University, Center for Educational Research.

Levin, H. M., & McEwan, P. J. (2001). *Cost-effectiveness analysis: Methods and applications* (2nd ed.). Thousand Oaks, CA: Sage Publications.

Levine, A. (2006). Educating school teachers [Electronic Version]. Retrieved 22 April 2008 from http://www.edschools.org/pdf/Educating_Teachers_Report.pdf.

Levy-Tossman, I., Kaplan, A., & Assor, A. (2007). Academic goal orientations, multiple goal profiles, and friendship intimacy among early adolescents. *Contemporary Educational Psychology, 32*(2), 231–252.

Lewis, C. P. (2004). *The relation between extracurricular activities with academic and social competencies in school-age children: A meta-analysis.* Unpublished Ph.D., Texas A&M University, TX.

Lewis, M., & Samuels, S. J. (2003). Read more–read better? A meta-analysis of the literature on the relationship between exposure to reading and reading achievement [Electronic Version]. Retrieved 12 March 2007 from http://www.tc.umn.edu/~samue001/publications.htm.

Lewis, R. J., & Vosburgh, W. T. (1988). Effectiveness of kindergarten intervention programs: A meta-analysis. *School Psychology International, 9*(4), 265–275.

Lewis, T. L. (1979). *The medusa and the snail: More notes of a biology watcher.* New York: Viking Press.

Ley, K., & Young, D. (2001). Instructional principles for self-regulation. *Educational Technology Research and Development, 49*(2), 93–103.

L'Hommedieu, R., Menges, R. J., & Brinko, K. T. (1990). Methodological explanations for the modest effects of feedback from student ratings. *Journal of Educational Psychology, 82*(2), 232–241.

Liao, Y. K. (1990). *Effects of computer-assisted instruction and computer programming on students' cognitive performance: A quantitative synthesis.* Unpublished Ed.D., University of Houston, TX.

Liao, Y. K. (1992). Effects of computer-assisted instruction on cognitive outcomes: A meta-analysis. *Journal of Research on Computing in Education, 24*(3), 367–380

Liao, Y. K. C. (1998). Effects of hypermedia versus traditional instruction on students' achievement: A meta-analysis. *Journal of Research on Computing in Education, 30*(4), 341–359.

Liao, Y. K. C. (1999). Effects of hypermedia on students' achievement: A meta-analysis. *Journal of Educational Multimedia and Hypermedia, 8*(3), 255–277.

Liao, Y. K. C. (2007). Effects of computer-assisted instruction on students' achievement in Taiwan: A meta-analysis. *Computers and Education, 48*(2), 216–233.

Liao, Y. K. C., & Bright, G. W. (1991). Effects of computer programming on cognitive outcomes: A meta-analysis. *Journal of Educational Computing Research, 7*(3), 251–268.

Lietz, P. (2006). A meta-analysis of gender differences in reading achievement at the secondary school level. *Studies In Educational Evaluation, 32*(4), 317–344.

Light, R. J., & Pillemer, D. B. (1984). *Summing up: The science of reviewing research.* Cambridge, MA: Harvard University Press.

Linn, M. C., & Hyde, J. S. (1989). Gender, mathematics, and science. *Educational Researcher, 18*(8), 17–27.

Linn, M. C., & Petersen, A. C. (1985). Emergence and characterization of sex differences in spatial ability: A meta-analysis. *Child Development, 56*(6), 1479–1498.

Lipsey, M. W., & Wilson, D. B. (1993). The efficacy of psychological, educational, and behavioral treatment: Confirmation from meta-analysis. *American Psychologist, 48*(12), 1181–1209.

Lipsey, M. W., & Wilson, D. B. (2001). *Practical meta-analysis.* Thousand Oaks, CA: Sage Publications.

Little, J. W. (2007). Teachers accounts of classroom experience as a resource for professional learning and instructional decision making. *Yearbook of the National Society for the Study of Education, 106*, 217–240.

Livingston, C., & Borko, H. (1990). High school mathematics review lessons: Expert-novice distinctions. *Journal for Research in Mathematics Education, 21*(5), 372–387.

Lloyd, J. W., Forness, S. R., & Kavale, K. A. (1998). Some methods are more effective than others. *Intervention in School and Clinic, 33*(4), 195–200.

Locke, E. A., Frederick, E., Lee, C., & Bobko, P. (1984). Effect of self-efficacy, goals, and task strategies on task performance. *Journal of Applied Psychology, 69*(2), 241–251.

Locke, E. A., & Latham, G. P. (1990). *A theory of goal setting and task performance.* Englewood Cliffs, NJ: Prentice Hall.

Long, M. H., & Sato, C. J. (1983). Classroom foreigner talk discourse: Forms and functions of teachers' questions. In H. Seliger & M. H. Long (Eds.), *Classroom oriented research in second language acquisition* (pp. 268–285). Rowley, MA: Newbury House.

Lorentz, J. L., & Coker, H. (1980). Teacher behaviour. *Evaluation in Education, 4*, 61–63.

Lortie, D. C. (2002). *Schoolteacher: A sociological study*. Chicago: University of Chicago Press.

Lott, G. W. (1983). The effect of inquiry teaching and advance organizers upon student outcomes in science education. *Journal of Research in Science Teaching, 20*(5), 437–451.

Lou, Y. (2004). Understanding process and affective factors in small group versus individual learning with technology. *Journal of Educational Computing Research, 31*(4), 337–369.

Lou, Y., Abrami, P. C., & d'Apollonia, S. (2001). Small group and individual learning with technology: A meta-analysis. *Review of Educational Research, 71*(3), 449–521.

Lou, Y., Abrami, P. C., Spence, J. C., Poulsen, C., Chambers, B., & d'Apollonia, S. (1996). Within-class grouping: A meta-analysis. *Review of Educational Research, 66*(4), 423–458.

Lou, Y., Bernard, R., & Abrami, P. (2006). Media and pedagogy in undergraduate distance education: A theory-based meta-analysis of empirical literature. *Educational Technology Research and Development, 54*(2), 141–176.

Lounsbury, J. H., & Clark, D. C. (1990). *Inside grade eight: From apathy to excitement*. Reston, VA: National Association of Secondary School Principals.

Lovelace, M. K. (2005). Meta-analysis of experimental research based on the Dunn and Dunn model. *Journal of Educational Research, 98*(3), 176–183.

Loveless, T. (1999). *The tracking wars: State reform meets school policy*. Washington, DC: Brookings Institution Press.

Lowe, J. (2001). Computer-based education: Is it a panacea? *Journal of Research on Technology in Education, 34*(2), 163–171.

Luecht, R. M. (2006, September). *Assessment engineering: An emerging discipline*. Paper presented at the Centre for Research in Applied Measurement and Evaluation, University of Alberta, Edmonton, AB, Canada.

Luecht, R. M., Gierl, M. J., Tan, X., & Huff, K. (2006, April). *Scalability and the development of useful diagnostic scales*. Paper presented at the Annual Meeting of the National Council on Measurement in Education, San Francisco, CA.

Luik, P. (2007). Characteristics of drills related to development of skills. *Journal of Computer Assisted Learning, 23*(1), 56–68.

Luiten, J., Ames, W., & Ackerman, G. (1980). A meta-analysis of the effects of advance organizers on learning and retention. *American Educational Research Journal, 17*(2), 211–218.

Lundeberg, M. A. (1987). Metacognitive aspects of reading comprehension: Studying understanding in legal case analysis. *Reading Research Quarterly, 22*(4), 407–432.

Lundeberg, M. A., & Fox, P. W. (1991). Do laboratory findings on test expectancy generalize to classroom outcomes? *Review of Educational Research, 61*(1), 94–106.

Luria, A. R. (1976). *Cognitive development: Its cultural and social foundations* (M. Lopez-Morillas & L. Solotaroff, Trans.). Cambridge, MA: Harvard University Press.

Lustick, D., & Sykes, G. (2006). National Board Certification as professional development: What are teachers learning? *Education Policy Analysis Archives, 14*(5), 1–43.

Lyday, N. L. (1983). *A meta-analysis of the adjunct question literature*. Unpublished Ph.D., The Pennsylvania State University, PA.

Lysakowski, R. S., & Walberg, H. J. (1980). Classroom reinforcement. *Evaluation in Education, 4*, 115–116.

Lysakowski, R. S., & Walberg, H. J. (1980, April). *Classroom reinforcement and learning: A quantitative synthesis*. Paper presented at the Annual Meeting of the American Educational Research Association, Boston, MA.

Lysakowski, R. S., & Walberg, H. J. (1982). Instructional effects of cues, participation, and corrective feedback: A quantitative synthesis. *American Educational Research Journal, 19*(4), 559–578.

Lytton, H., & Romney, D. M. (1991). Parents' differential socialization of boys and girls: A meta-analysis. *Psychological Bulletin, 109*(2), 267–296.

Lyubomirsky, S., King, L., & Diener, E. (2005). The benefits of frequent positive affect: Does happiness lead to success? *Psychological Bulletin, 131*(6), 803–855.

Ma, X. (1999). A meta-analysis of the relationship between anxiety toward mathematics and achievement in mathematics. *Journal for Research in Mathematics Education, 30*(5), 520–541.

Ma, X., & Kishor, N. (1997). Assessing the relationship between attitude toward mathematics and achievement in mathematics: A meta-analysis. *Journal for Research in Mathematics Education, 28*(1), 26–47.

Mabe, P. A., III, & West, S. G. (1982). Validity of self-evaluation of ability: A review and meta-analysis. *Journal of Applied Psychology, 67*(3), 280–296.

Machtmes, K., & Asher, J. W. (2000). A meta-analysis of the effectiveness of telecourses in distance education. *American Journal of Distance Education, 14*(1), 27–46.

Madamba, S. R. (1980). *Meta-analysis on the effects of open and traditional schooling on the teaching-learning of reading.* Unpublished Ph.D., University of California, Los Angeles, CA.

Maehr, M. L., & Steinkamp, M. (1983). *A synthesis of findings on sex differences in science education research. Final report* (Research/Technical No. NSF/SED-83001 NSF-SED-80–07857). Urbana, IL: Illinois University.

Mahar, C. L. (1992). *Thirty years after Ausubel: An updated meta-analysis of advance organizer research.* Unpublished Ph.D., University of Illinois at Urbana, Champaign, IL.

Malofeeva, E. V. (2005). *A meta-analysis of mathematics instruction with young children* Unpublished Ph.D., University of Notre Dame, Notre Dame, IN.

Malone, M. R. (1984, April). *Project MAFEX: Report on preservice field experiences in science education.* Paper presented at the Annual Meeting of the National Association for Research in Science Teaching, New Orleans, LA.

Mangino, C. (2004). *A meta-analysis of Dunn and Dunn model correlational research with adult populations.* Unpublished Ed.D., St. John's University (New York), NY.

Mantione, R. D., & Smead, S. (2003). *Weaving through words: Using the arts to teach reading comprehension strategies.* Newark, DE: International Reading Association.

Mantzicopoulos, P., & Morrison, D. (1992). Kindergarten retention: Academic and behavioral outcomes through the end of second grade. *American Educational Research Journal, 29*(1), 182–198.

Marcucci, R. G. (1980). *A meta-analysis of research on methods of teaching mathematical problem solving.* Unpublished Ph.D., The University of Iowa, IA.

Margo, A. M., & Thomas, E. S. (1989). Constructing more meaningful relationships: Mnemonic instruction for special populations. *Educational Psychology Review, 1*(2), 83–111.

Marmolejo, A. (1990). *The effects of vocabulary instruction with poor readers: A meta-analysis.* Unpublished Ed.D., Columbia University Teachers College, NY.

Marsh, H. (2007). Students' evaluations of university teaching: Dimensionality, reliability, validity, potential biases and usefulness. In R. P. Perry & J. C. Smart (Eds.), *The scholarship of teaching and learning in higher education: An evidence-based perspective* (pp. 319–383). Netherlands: Springer.

Marsh, H. W., & Rowe, K. J. (1996). The effects of single-sex and mixed-sex mathematics classes within a coeducational school: A reanalysis and comment. *Australian Journal of Education, 40*(2), 147–162.

Martin, A. D., Quinn, K. M., Ruger, T. W., & Kim, P. T. (2004). Competing approaches to predicting supreme court decision making. *Perspectives on Politics, 2*(4), 761–767.

Martin, A. J. (2006). Personal bests (PBs): A proposed multidimensional model and empirical analysis. *British Journal of Educational Psychology, 76*, 803–825.

Martin, D. M., Preiss, R. W., Gayle, B. M., & Allen, M. (2006). A meta-analytic assessment of the effect of humorous assessment lectures on learning. In B. M. Gayle, R. W. Preiss, N. Burrell & M. Allen (Eds.), *Classroom communication and instructional processes: Advances through meta-analysis* (pp. 295–313). Mahwah, NJ: Lawrence Erlbaum Associates.

Marzano, R. J. (1991). Creating an educational paradigm centered on learning through teacher-directed, naturalistic inquiry. In L. Idol & B. Fly (Eds.), *Educational values and cognitive instruction: Implications for reform* (pp. 411–441). Hillsdate, NJ: Lawrence Erlbaum Associates.

Marzano, R. J. (1991). *Cultivating thinking in English and the language arts* (No. ISBN-0–8141–0991–8). Urbana, IL: National Council of Teachers of English.

Marzano, R. J. (1991). Fostering thinking across the curriculum through knowledge restructuring. *Journal of Reading, 34*(7), 518–525.

Marzano, R. J. (1998). *A theory-based meta-analysis of research on instruction.* Aurora, CO: Mid-Continent Regional Educational Lab.

Marzano, R. J. (2000). *A new era of school reform: Going where the research takes us.* Aurora, CO: Mid-Continent Research for Education and Learning.

Marzano, R. J. (2003). *What works in schools: Translating research into action.* Alexandria, VA: Association for Supervision and Curriculum Development.

Marzano, R. J., Gaddy, B. B., & Dean, C. (2000). *What works in classroom instruction* (No. RJ96006101). Aurora, CO: Mid-Continent Research for Education and Learning.

Marzano, R. J., Marzano, J. S., & Pickering, D. (2003). *Classroom management that works: Research-based strategies for every teacher.* Alexandria, VA: Association for Supervision and Curriculum Development.

Marzano, R. J., Pickering, D. J., & Pollock, J. E. (2001). *Classroom instruction that works: Research-based strategies for increasing student achievement.* Aurora, CO: Mid-Continent Research for Education and Learning.

Masgoret, A. M., & Gardner, R. C. (2003). Attitudes, motivation, and second language learning: A meta-analysis of studies conducted by Gardner and Associates. *Language Learning, 53*(1), 123–163.

Mason, D. A., & Burns, R. B. (1995). Teachers' views of combination classes. *Journal of Educational Research, 89*(1), 36–45.

Mason, D. A., & Burns, R. B. (1996). "Simply no worse and simply no better" may simply be wrong: A critique of Veenman's conclusion about multigrade classes. *Review of Educational Research, 66*(3), 307–322.

Mason, D. A., & Doepner, R. W., III. (1998). Principals' views of combination classes, *Journal of Educational Research* (Vol. 91, pp. 160–172): Heldref Publications.

Mastropieri, M., & Scruggs, T. (1989). Constructing more meaningful relationships: Mnemonic instruction for special populations. *Educational Psychology Review, 1*(2), 83–111.

Mathes, P. G., & Fuchs, L. S. (1991). *The efficacy of peer tutoring in reading for students with disabilities: A best-evidence synthesis* (Information Analyses No. H023B0026). Nashville, TN: Vanderbilt University, Peabody College.

Mathes, P. G., & Fuchs, L. S. (1994). The efficacy of peer tutoring in reading for students with mild disabilities: A best-evidence. *School Psychology Review, 23*(1), 59.

Mayer, R. E. (1989). Systematic thinking fostered by illustrations in scientific text. *Journal of Educational Psychology, 81*(2), 240–246.

Mayer, R. E. (1999). Multimedia aids to problem-solving transfer – A dual coding approach. *International Journal of Educational Research, 31*, 611–623.

McCall, R. B., & Carriger, M. S. (1993). A meta-analysis of infant habituation and recognition memory performance as predictors of later IQ. *Child Development, 64*(1), 57–79.

McCrae, R. R., & Costa, P. T., Jr. (1997). Personality trait structure as a human universal. *American Psychologist, 52*(5), 509–516.

McDermid, R. D. (1989). *A quantitative analysis of the literature on computer-assisted instruction with the learning-disabled and educable mentally retarded.* Unpublished Ph.D., University of Kansas, KS.

McEvoy, T. J. (1982). *A meta-analysis of comparative research on the effect of desegregation on academic achievement and self-esteem of black students.* Unpublished EdD, Wayne State University, MI.

McField, G. P. (2002). *Does program quality matter? A meta-analysis of select bilingual education studies.* Unpublished Ph.D., University of Southern California, CA.

McGiverin, J., Gilman, D., & Tillitski, C. (1989). A meta-analysis of the relation between class size and achievement. *The Elementary School Journal, 90*(1), 47–56.

McGraw, K. O., & Wong, S. (1992). A common language effect size statistic. *Psychological Bulletin, 111*(2), 361–365.

McKenna, K. (1991). *The use and effectiveness of computer-based models of the economy in the teaching of macroeconomics.* Unpublished doctoral dissertation, University of Western Australia.

McKey, R. H., Condelli, L., Ganson, H., Barrett, B., McConkey, C., & Plantz, M. C. (1985). *The impact of Head Start on children, families, and their communities. Final Report of the Head Start Eealuation, synthesis and utilization project. Executive summary.* Washington, DC: CSR. Inc.

McLinden, D. J. (1988). Spatial task performance: A meta-analysis. *Journal of Visual Impairment and Blindness, 82*(6), 231–236.

McMaster, K. N., & Fuchs, D. (2002). Effects of cooperative learning on the academic achievement of students with learning disabilities: An update of Tateyama-Sniezek's review. *Learning Disabilities Research and Practice, 17*(2), 107–117.

McNeil, B. J., & Nelson, K. R. (1991). Meta-analysis of interactive video instruction: A 10 year review of achievement effects. *Journal of Computer-Based Instruction, 18*(1), 1–6.

Meehan, A. M. (1984). A meta-analysis of sex differences in formal operational thought. *Child Development, 55*(3), 1110–1124.

Meehl, P. E. (1954). *Clinical versus statistical prediction: A theoretical analysis and a review of the evidence.* Minneapolis, MN: University of Minnesota Press.

Mehana, M., & Reynolds, A. J. (2004). School mobility and achievement: A meta-analysis. *Children and Youth Services Review, 26*(1), 93–119.

Mehana, M. A. A. (1997). *A meta-analysis of school mobility effects on reading and math achievement in the elementary grades.* Unpublished PhD, The Pennsylvania State University, PA.

Meisels, S. J., & Liaw, F. R. (1993). Failure in grade: Do retained students catch up? *Journal of Educational Research, 87*(2), 69–77.

Mellinger, S. F. (1991). *The development of cognitive flexibility in problem-solving: Theory and application.* Unpublished Ph.D., The University of Alabama, AL.

Menges, R. J., & Brinko, K. T. (1986, April). *Effects of student evaluation feedback: A meta-analysis of higher education research.* Paper presented at the Annual Meeting of the American Educational Research Association, San Francisco, CA.

Mento, A. J., Steel, R. P., & Karren, R. J. (1987). A meta-analytic study of the effects of goal setting on task performance: 1966–1984. *Organizational Behavior and Human Decision Processes, 39*(1), 52–83.

Mentore, J. L. (1999). *The effectiveness of early intervention with young children "at risk": A decade in review.* Unpublished Ph.D., Fordham University, New York, United States.

Messick, S. (1990). *Validity of test interpretation and use.* Princeton, NJ: Educational Testing Service.

Messick, S., & Jungeblut, A. (1981). Time and method in coaching for the SAT. *Psychological Bulletin, 89*(2), 191–216.

Metcalf, K. K. (1995, April). *Laboratory experiences in teacher education: A meta-analytic review of research.* Paper presented at the Annual Meeting of the American Educational Research Association, San Francisco, CA.

Metsala, J. L., Stanovich, K. E., & Brown, G. D. A. (1998). Regularity effects and the phonological deficit model of reading disabilities: A meta-analytic review. *Journal of Educational Psychology, 90*(2), 279–293.

Meyer, G. J., Finn, S. E., Eyde, L. D., Kay, G. G., Moreland, K. L., Dies, R. R., et al. (2001). Psychological testing and psycohological assessment: A review of evidence and issues. *American Psychologist, 56*(2), 128–165.

Meyer, J. P., & Gellatly, I. R. (1988). Perceived performance norm as a mediator in the effect of assigned goal on personal goal and task performance. *Journal of Applied Psychology, 73*(3), 410–420.

Meyer, L. A. (1984). Long-term academic effects of the direct instruction project follow through. *The Elementary School Journal, 84*(4), 380–394.

Mikolashek, D. L. (2004). *A meta-analysis of empirical research studies on resilience among students at-risk for school failure.* Unpublished Ed.D., Florida International University, FL.

Miller, H. L., Jr. (1997). The New York City public schools integrated learning systems project: Evaluation and meta-evaluation. *International Journal of Educational Research, 27*(2), 91–183.

Miller, J. B. (1999). *The effects of training in phonemic awareness: A meta-analysis.* Unpublished Ed.D., University of Kansas, KS.

Miller, N., & Carlson, M. (1982). *School desegregation as a social reform: A meta-analysis of its effects on black academic achievement.* Washington, DC: National Institute of Education.

Miller, R. J., & Rowan, B. (2006). Effects of organic management on student achievement. *American Educational Research Journal, 43*(2), 219–253.

Milligan, K., Astington, J. W., & Dack, L. A. (2007). Language and theory of mind: Meta-analysis of the relation between language ability and false-belief understanding. *Child Development, 78*(2), 622–646.

Milligan, S., & Thomson, K. (1992). *Listening to girls: A report of the consultancy undertaken for the Australian Education Council Committee to Review the National Policy for the Education of Girls in Australian Schools.* Carlton, Victoria: Australian Education Council.

Milne, S., Sheeran, P., & Orbell, S. (2000). Prediction and intervention in health-related behavior: A meta-analytic review of protection motivation theory. *Journal of Applied Social Psychology, 30*(1), 106–143.

Minton, K. J. (2005). *Learning-related vision and academic success: A meta-analytical study.* Unpublished Ph.D., Union Institute and University, OH.

Miron, G., & Nelson, C. (2001). *Student academic achievement in charter schools: What we know and why we know so little* (Occasional Paper No. 41). New York: Columbia University, National Center for the Study of Privatization in Education.

Mislevy, R. J. (2007). Validity by design *Educational Researcher, 36*(8), 463–469.

Mitchell, M.L.W. (1987). *A comparison of the effectiveness of innovative instructional methods utilized in lower division mathematics as measured by student achievement: A meta-analysis of the findings.* Unpublished doctoral dissertation, University of Arizona.

Mitchell, D. E., & Beach, S. A. (1990). *How changing class size affects classrooms and students. Policy Briefs Number 12.* San Francisco, CA: Far West Laboratory for Educational Research and Development.

Moga, E., Burger, K., Hetland, L., & Winner, E. (2000). Does studying the arts engender creative thinking? Evidence for near but not far transfer. *Journal of Aesthetic Education, 34*(3/4), 91–104.

Mohr, K.A.J. (1998). Teacher talk: A summary analysis of effective teachers' discourse during primary literacy lessons *Journal of Classroom Interaction, 33*(2), 16–23.

Moin, A. K. (1986). *Relative effectiveness of various techniques of calculus instruction: A meta-analysis.* Unpublished Ph.D., Syracuse University, NY.

Molnar, A., Smith, P., Zahorik, J., Palmer, A., Halbach, A., & Ehrle, K. (1999). Evaluating the SAGE program: A pilot program in targeted pupil-teacher reduction in Wisconsin. *Educational Evaluation and Policy Analysis, 21*(2), 165–177.

Monk, D. H. (1994). Subject area preparation of secondary mathematics and science teachers and student achievement. *Economics of Education Review, 13*(2), 125–145.

Monk, D. H., Walberg, H. J., & Wang, M. C. (2001). *Improving educational productivity.* Greenwich, CT: Information Age Publishing.

Moon, C. E., Render, G. F., & Pendley, D.W. (1985, March-April). *Relaxation and educational outcomes: A meta-analysis.* Paper presented at the Annual Meeting of the American Educational Research Association, Chicago, IL.

Moore, D. W., & Readence, J. E. (1984). A quantitative and qualitative review of graphic organizer research. *Journal of Educational Research, 78*(1), 11–17.

Morris, C. H. (1995). *Meta-analysis of home visiting research with low-income families: Client, intervention, and outcome characteristics.* Unpublished M.S., Utah State University, UT.

Morris, D. R. (1993). Patterns of aggregate grade-retention rates. *American Educational Research Journal, 30*(3), 497–514.

Moseley, D., Baumfield, V., Higgins, S., Lin, M., Miller, J., Newton, D., et al. (2004). *Thinking skill frameworks for post-16 learners: An evaluation.* London: Learning and Skills Research Centre.

Mosteller, F., Light, R. J., & Sachs, J. A. (1996). Sustained inquiry in education: Lessons from skill grouping and class size. *Harvard Educational Review, 66*(4), 797.

Mottet, T. P. (1998, March). *Teaching from a distance: "Hello, is anyone out there?"* Paper presented at the Annual Ethnography in Research Forum, Philadelphia, PA.

Muhlenbruck, L., Cooper, H. M., Nye, B., & Lindsay, J. J. (1999). Homework and achievement: Explaining the different strengths of relation at the elementary and secondary school levels. *Social Psychology of Education, 3*(4), 295–317.

Muijs, D., & Reynolds, D. (2001). *Effective teaching: Evidence and practice.* London: Paul Chapman.

Mukawa, T. E. (2006). *Meta-analysis of the effectiveness of online instruction in higher education using Chickering and Gamson's seven principles for good practice.* Unpublished Ed.D., University of San Francisco, CA.

Mukawa, T. E. (2006). *Seven principles for good practice and effective online instruction in higher education.* Paper presented at the World Conference on E-Learning in Corporate, Government, Healthcare, and Higher Education 2006, Honolulu, HI.

Mukunda, K. V., & Hall, V. C. (1992). Does performance on memory for order correlate with performance on standardized measures of ability? A meta-analysis. *Intelligence, 16*(1), 81–97.

Mullen, B., & Copper, C. (1994). The relation between group cohesiveness and performance: An integration. *Psychological Bulletin, 115*(2), 210–227.

Mullen, B., Symons, C., Hu, L. T., & Salas, E. (1989). Group size, leadership behavior, and subordinate satisfaction. *Journal of General Psychology, 116*(2), 155–170.

Muller, J. C., Gullung, P., & Bocci, P. (1988). Concept de soi et performance scolaire: Une meta-analyse [Self-concept and academic performance: A meta-analysis]. *Orientation Scolaire et Professionnelle, 17,* 53–69.

Multon, K. D., Brown, S. D., & Lent, R. W. (1991). Relation of self-efficacy beliefs to academic outcomes: A meta-analytic investigation. *Journal of Counseling Psychology, 38*(1), 30–38.

Murawski, W. W., & Swanson, H. L. (2001). A meta-analysis of co-teaching research: Where are the data? *Rase: Remedial and Special Education, 22*(5), 258–267.

Murdock, T. A. (1987). It isn't just money: The effects of financial aid on student persistence. *Review of Higher Education, 11*(1), 75.

Murphy, P. K., & Alexander, P. A. (2006). *Understanding how students learn: A guide for instructional leaders.* Thousand Oaks, CA: Corwin Press.

Murphy, R., & Maree, D. J. F. (2006). Meta-analysis of dynamic assessment research in South Africa [Electronic Version]. *Journal of Cognitive Education and Psychology, 6,* 32–60. Retrieved 2 July 2007 from www.iacep.coged.org.

Murphy, R. T. (1991). *Educational effectiveness of Sesame Street: A review of the first twenty years of research, 1969–1989.* Princeton, NJ: Educational Testing Service.

Musselman, C. R., Wilson, A. K., & Lindsay, P. H. (1988). Effects of early intervention on hearing impaired children. *Exceptional Children, 55*(3), 222.

Naglieri, J. A., & Das, J. P. (1997). *Das-Naglieri cognitive assessment system.* Itasca, IL: Houghton Mifflin.

Naglieri, J. A., & Das, J. P. (1997). Intelligence revised: The planning, attention, simultaneous, successive (PASS) cognitive processing theory. In R. F. Dillon (Ed.), *Handbook on testing* (pp. 136–163). Westport, CT: Greenwood Press.

Nash, R., & Harker, R. K. (1997). *Progress at school: Final report to the Ministry of Education.* Palmerston North: Massey University, Educational Research and Development Centre.

National Centre for Educational Statistics. (1985). *High school and beyond: An analysis of course-taking patterns in secondary schools as related to student characteristics* (No. NCES-85–206). Washington, DC: US Government Printing Office.

National Council on the Accreditation of Teacher Education. (2000). NCATE 2000 unit standards [Electronic Version]. Retrieved June 19, 2000 from http://www.ncate.org/2000/200stds.pdf.

National Reading Panel. (2000). *Report of the National Reading Panel: Teaching children to read: An evidence-based assessment of the scientific research literature on reading and its implications for reading instruction: Reports of the subgroups.* Rockville, MD: NICHD Clearinghouse.

Neale, D. C. (1969). The role of attitudes in learning mathematics. *Arithmetic Teacher, 16*(8), 631–640.

Neber, H., Finsterwald, M., & Urban, N. (2001). Cooperative learning with gifted and high-achieving students: A review and meta-analyses of 12 studies. *High Ability Studies, 12*(2), 199–214.

Neill, J. T., & Richards, G. E. (1998). Does outdoor education really work? A summary of recent meta-analyses. *Australian Journal of Outdoor Education, 3*(2), 2–9.

Nelson, C. S. (1994). *A meta-analysis of parent education programs for children two to nine years.* Unpublished Psy.D., Adler School of Professional Psychology, IL.

Nelson, G., Westhues, A., & MacLeod, J. (2003). A meta-analysis of longitudinal research on preschool prevention programs for children. *Prevention and Treatment, 18*, 1–35.

Nesbit, J. C., & Adesope, O. O. (2006). Learning with concept and knowledge maps: A meta-analysis. *Review of Educational Research, 76*(3), 413–448.

Neubert, M. J. (1998). The value of feedback and goal setting over goal setting alone and potential moderators of this effect: A meta-analysis. *Human Performance, 11*(4), 321–335.

Neuman, G. A., Edwards, J. E., & Raju, N. S. (1989). Organizational development interventions: A meta-analysis of their effects on satisfaction and other attitudes. *Personnel Psychology, 42*(3), 461–489.

Neuman, S. B. (1986, July). *Television and reading: A research synthesis.* Paper presented at the International Television Studies Conference, London, England.

Neuman, S. B. (1988). The displacement effect: Assessing the relation between television viewing and reading performance. *Reading Research Quarterly, 23*(4), 414–440.

Neumann, A. (2006). Professing passion: Emotion in the scholarship of professors at research universities. *American Educational Research Journal, 43*(3), 381–424.

Neville, D. D., & Searls, E. F. (1991). A meta-analytic review of the effect of sentence-combining on reading comprehension. *Reading Research and Instruction, 31*(1), 63–76.

Newell, A. (1990). *Unified theories of cognition.* Cambridge, MA: Harvard University Press.

Newman, M. (2004). *Problem-based learning: An exploration of the method and evaluation of its effectiveness in a continuing nursing education programme.* London: Middlesex University.

Newman, M., Garrett, Z., Elbourne, D., Bradley, S., Noden, P., Taylor, J., et al. (2006). Does secondary school size make a difference?: A systematic review. *Educational Research Review, 1*(1), 41–60.

Niemiec, R. P. (1989). Comparing the cost-effectiveness of tutoring and computer-based instruction. *Journal of Educational Computing Research, 5*(4), 395–407.

Niemiec, R. P., Samson, G., Weinstein, T., & Walberg, H. J. (1987). The effects of computer-based instruction in elementary schools: A quantitative synthesis. *Journal of Research on Computing in Education, 20*(2), 85–103.

Niemiec, R. P., Sikorski, C., & Walberg, H. J. (1996). Learner-control effects: A review of reviews and a meta-analysis. *Journal of Educational Computing Research, 15*(2), 157–174.

Niemiec, R. P., & Walberg, H. J. (1985). Computers and achievement in the elementary schools. *Journal of Educational Computing Research, 1*(4), 435–440.

Niemiec, R. P., & Walberg, H. J. (1987). Comparative effects of computer-assisted instruction: A synthesis of reviews. *Journal of Educational Computing Research, 3*(1), 19–37.

Nikolaou, C. (2001). *Hand-held calculator use and achievement in mathematics: A meta-analysis.* Unpublished Ph.D., Georgia State University, GA.

Nishi, S. (1990). *Class size: The issue for policy makers in the State of Utah.* Salt Lake City, UT: Utah State Office of Education.

Nist, S. L., & Simpson, M. L. (1989). PLAE, a validated study strategy. *Journal of Reading, 33*(3), 182–186.

Noland, T. K., & Taylor, B. L. (1986, April). *The effects of ability grouping: A meta-analysis of research findings.* Paper presented at the Annual Meeting of the American Educational Research Association, San Francisco, CA.

Nordin, A. B. (1980). Improving learning: An experiment in rural primary schools in Malaysia. *Evaluation in Education, 4*, 143–263.

Novak, J. D. (1977). *A theory of education*. Ithaca, NY: Cornell University Press.

Novak, J. M., & Purkey, W. W. (2001). *Invitational education*. Bloomington, IN: Phi Delta Kappa Educational Foundation.

Novick, M. R., & Jackson, P. H. (1974). *Statistical methods for educational and psychological research*. New York: McGraw-Hill.

Nowicki, E. A. (2003). A meta-analysis of the social competence of children with learning disabilities compared to classmates of low and average to high achievement. *Learning Disability Quarterly, 26*(3), 171–188.

Ntoumanis, N., & Biddle, S. J. H. (1999). Affect and achievement goals in physical activity: a meta-analysis. *Scandinavian Journal of Medicine and Science in Sports, 9*(6), 315–332.

Nuthall, G. A. (1999). Introduction and background. *International Journal of Educational Research, 31*(3), 141–256.

Nuthall, G. A. (1999). Learning how to learn: The evolution of students' minds through the social processes and culture of the classroom. *International Journal of Educational Research, 31*(3), 141–256.

Nuthall, G. A. (2000). The role of memory in the acquisition and retention of knowledge in science and social studies units. *Cognition and Instruction, 18*(1), 83–139.

Nuthall, G. A. (2005). The cultural myths and realities of classroom teaching and learning: A personal journey. *Teachers College Record, 107*(5), 895–934.

Nuthall, G. A. (2007). *The hidden lives of learners*. Wellington, New Zealand: New Zealand Council for Educational Research.

Nye, B., Konstantopoulos, S., & Hedges, L. V. (2004). How large are teacher effects? *Educational Evaluation and Policy Analysis, 26*(3), 237–257.

Nye, C., Foster, S. H., & Seaman, D. (1987). Effectiveness of language intervention with the language/ learning disabled. *The Journal of speech and hearing disorders, 52*(4), 348–357.

O' Shaughnessy, T. E., & Swanson, H. L. (1998). Do immediate memory deficits in students with learning disabilities in reading reflect a developmental lag or deficit?: A selective meta-analysis of the literature. *Learning Disability Quarterly, 21*(2), 123–148.

Oakes, J. (1985). *Keeping track: How schools structure inequality*. New Haven: Yale University Press.

Oakes, J. (1987). *Tracking in secondary schools: A contextual perspective*. Santa Monica, CA: The Rand Corporation.

Oakes, J. (1992). Can tracking research inform practice? Technical, normative, and political considerations. *Educational Researcher, 21*(4), 12–21.

Oakes, J. (1993) Ability grouping, tracking and within-school segregation in the San Jose Unified School District. Report prepared in conjunction with *Vasquez v. San Jose Unified School District*, University of California, Los Angeles, School of Education. 633 C.F.R. (1993).

Oakes, J. (1995). Two cities' tracking and within-school segregation. *Teachers College Record, 96*(4), 681–690.

Oakes, J. (2005). *Keeping track: How schools structure inequality* (2nd ed.). New Haven, Conn.; London: Yale University Press.

Oakes, J., Gamoran, A., & Page, R. N. (1992). Curriculum differentiation: Opportunities, outcomes, and meanings. In P. W. Jackson (Ed.), *Handbook of research on curriculum: A project of the American Educational Research Association* (pp. 570–608). New York: Macmillan.

Oakes, J., & Guiton, G. (1995). Matchmaking: The dynamics of high school tracking decisions. *American Educational Research Journal, 32*(1), 3–33.

Oakes, J., Ormseth, T., Bell, R., & Camp, P. (1990). *Multiplying inequalities: The effects of race, social class, and tracking on opportunities to learn mathematics and science*. Santa Monica, CA: Rand.

Oakes, J., Quartz, K. H., Gong, J., Guiton, G., & Lipton, M. (1993). Creating middle schools: Technical, normative, and political considerations. *The Elementary School Journal, 93*(5), 461–480.

Oakes, J., & Wells, A. S. (1996). *Beyond the technicalities of school reform: Policy lessons from detracking schools*. Los Angeles, CA: UCLA Graduate School of Education and Information Studies.

Oakes, J., Wells, A. S., Jones, M., & Datnow, A. (1997). Detracking: The social construction of ability, cultural politics, and resistance to reform. *Teachers College Record, 98*(3), 482–510.

O'Connor, M. C., & Paunonen, S. V. (2007). Big Five personality predictors of post-secondary academic performance. *Personality and Individual Differences, 43*(5), 971–990.

Odden, A. (2007). *Redesigning school finance systems: Lessons from CPRE research. CPRE Policy Briefs. RB-50.* Philadelphia, PA: University of Pennsylvania, Consortium for Policy Research in Education.

Ogunyemi, O. A. (1983). *An analytic study of the efficacy of black-and-white pictorial instruction on achievement.*

Oh, S. S. (1987). *A comparative study of quantitative vs. qualitative synthesis of Title VII Bilingual Education Programs for Asian children in New York City.* Unpublished Ph.D., The Florida State University, FL.

Oliver, L. W., & Spokane, A. R. (1988). Career-intervention outcome: What contributes to client gain? *Journal of Counseling Psychology, 35*(4), 447–462.

Olson, D. R. (2003). *Psychological theory and educational reform: How school remakes mind and society.* Cambridge: Cambridge University Press.

Olson, T., & Wisher, R. A. (2002). The effectiveness of web-based instruction: An initial inquiry, *The International Review of Research in Open and Distance Learning [Online].*

O'Mara, A. J., Marsh, H. W., Craven, R. G., & Debus, R. L. (2006). Do self-concept interventions make a difference? A synergistic blend of construct validation and meta-analysis. *Educational Psychologist, 41*(3), 181–206.

O'Neal, M. R. (1985, November). *Cerebral palsy: The meta-analysis of selected interventions.* Paper presented at the Annual Conference of the Mid-South Educational Research Association, Biloxi, MS.

Onuoha, C. O. (2007). *Meta-analysis of the effectiveness of computer-based laboratory versus traditional hands-on laboratory in college and pre-college science instructions.* Unpublished Ph.D., Capella University, MN.

Oosterlaan, J., Logan, G. D., & Sergeant, J. A. (1998). Response inhibition in AD/HD, CD, Comorbid AD/HD+ CD, Anxious, and Control Children: A meta-analysis of studies with the stop task. *The Journal of Child Psychology and Psychiatry and Allied Disciplines, 39*(03), 411–425.

O'Shaughnessy, T. E., & Swanson, H. L. (1998). Do immediate memory deficits in students with learning disabilities in reading reflect a developmental lag or deficit?: A selective meta-analysis of the literature. *Learning Disability Quarterly, 21*(2), 123–148.

Ostendorf, V. A. (1997). Teaching by Television. *New Directions for Teaching and Learning, 1997*(71), 51–58.

Othman, N. (1996). *The effects of cooperative learning and traditional mathematics instruction in grades K-12: A meta-analysis of findings.* Unpublished Ed.D., West Virginia University, WV.

Ottenbacher, K., & Petersen, P. (1985). The efficacy of early intervention programs for children with organic impairment: A quantitative review. *Evaluation and Program Planning, 8*(2), 135–146.

Ottenbacher, K. J., & Cooper, H. M. (1983). Drug treatment of hyperactivity in children. *Developmental medicine and child neurology, 25*(3), 358–366.

Ottenbacher, K. J., Muller, L., Brandt, D., Heintzelman, A., Hojem, P., & Sharpe, P. (1987). The effectiveness of tactile stimulation as a form of early intervention: A quantitative evaluation. *Journal of developmental and behavioral pediatrics, 8*(2), 68–76.

Ouyang, R. (1993). *A meta-analysis: Effectiveness of computer-assisted instruction at the level of elementary education (K–6).* Unpublished Ed.D., Indiana University of Pennsylvania, PA.

Oyer, E. J. (1996). *Validity and impact of meta-analyses in early intervention research.* Unpublished Ph.D., Indiana University, IN.

Page, E. B., & Grandon, G. M. (1979). Family configuration and mental ability: Two theories contrasted with US data. *American Educational Research Journal, 16*(3), 257–272.

Page, E. B., & Grandon, G. M. (1981). Massive intervention and child intelligence the Milwaukee project in critical perspective. *Journal of Special Education, 15*(2), 239–256.

Page, R. N. (1991). *Lower-track classrooms: A curricular and cultural perspective.* New York: Teachers College Press.

Palmeter, F. R. D. (1991). *The effects of computer programming on children's higher-level cognitive processes: A review of the research on Logo.* Unpublished Ed.D., Rutgers The State University of New Jersey, New Brunswick, NJ.

Pang, S. (1998). *The relationship between giftedness and self-concept: A meta-analysis of gifted research.* Unpublished M.A., California State University, Long Beach, CA.

Pantili, L., Williams, J., & Fortune, J. (1991, April). *Principal assessment: Effective or not? A meta-analytic model.* Paper presented at the Annual Meeting of the American Educational Research Association, Chicago, IL.

Parham, J. L. (1983). *A meta-analysis of the use of manipulative materials and student achievement in elementary school mathematics.* Unpublished Ed.D., Auburn University, AL.

Parker, L. H. (1985). *A strategy for optimising the success of girls in mathematics: Report of a project of national significance.* Canberra, Australia: Commonwealth Schools Commission.

Parker, L. H., & Rennie, L. J. (1997). Teachers' perceptions of the implementation of single-sex classes in coeducational schools. *Australian Journal of Education, 41*(2), 119–133.

Paro, K. M. L., & Pianta, R. C. (2000). Predicting children's competence in the early school years: A meta-analytic review. *Review of Educational Research, 70*(4), 443–484.

Paschal, R. A., Weinstein, T., & Walberg, H. J. (1984). The effects of homework on learning: A quantitative synthesis. *Journal of Educational Research, 78*(2), 97–104.

Patall, E. A., Cooper, H. M., & Robinson, J. C. (2008). The effects of choice on intrinsic motivation and related outcomes: A meta-analysis of research findings. *Psychological Bulletin, 134*(2), 270–300.

Pearson, P. D., Ferdig, R. E., Blomeyer, J. R. L., & Moran, J. (2005). *The effects of technology on teading performance in the middle-school grades: A meta-analysis with recommendations for policy.* Naperville, IL: Learning Point Associates, North Central Regional Educational Laboratory (NCREL).

Peddie, R., Hattie, J. A. C., & Vaughan, K. (1999). *The use of exemplars in outcomes-based curricula: An international review of the literature. Report to the Ministry of Education.* Auckland: Auckland Uniservices Ltd.

Pegg, J. (2003). Assessment in mathematics: A developmental approach. In J. Royer (Ed.), *Mathematical cognition* (pp. 227–259). Greenwich, Conn: Information Age Publishing.

Pehkonen, E. (1992). *Problem fields in mathematics teaching, Part 3. Views of Finnish seventh-graders about mathematics teaching* (No. 108). Helsinki, Finland: University of Helsinki, Department of Teacher Education.

Péladeau, N., Forget, J., & Gagné, F. (2003). Effect of paced and unpaced practice on skill application and retention: How much is enough? *American Educational Research Journal, 40*(3), 769–801.

Penuel, W. R., Kim, D., Michalchik, V., Lewis, S., Means, B., Murphy, R., et al. (2002). *Using technology to enhance connections between home and school: A research synthesis. Prepared for the Planning and Evaluation Services, U.S. Department of Education.* Menlo Park, CA: SRI International.

Persell, C. H. (1979). *Education and inequality: The roots and results of stratification in America's schools.* New York: Free Press.

Peters, R. S. (1960). *The concept of motivation.* London: Routledge.

Peterson, P. L. (1980). Open versus traditional classrooms. *Evaluation in Education, 4,* 58–60.

Peterson, S. E., DeGracie, J. S., & Ayabe, C. R. (1987). A longitudinal study of the effects of retention/promotion on academic achievement. *American Educational Research Journal, 24*(1), 107–118.

Petty, G. (2006). *Evidence based teaching: A practical approach.* Cheltenham, UK: Nelson Thornes.

Pflaum, S. W. (1982). Synthesizing research in reading. *Reading Psychology, 3*(4), 325–337.

Pflaum, S. W., Walberg, H. J., Karegianes, M., & Rasher, S. P. (1980). Methods of teaching reading. *Evaluation in Education, 4,* 121–122.

Phillips, D. C. (1995). The good, the bad, and the ugly: The many faces of constructivism. *Educational Researcher, 24*(7), 5–12.

Phillips, G. W. (1983). *Learning the conservation concept: A meta-analysis.* Unpublished Ph.D., University of Kentucky, KY.

Phillips, N. B., Hamlett, C. L., Fuchs, L. S., & Fuchs, D. (1993). Combining classwide curriculum-based measurement and peer tutoring to help general educators provide adaptive education. *Learning Disabilities Research and Practice, 8*(3), 148–156.

Piaget, J. (1970). *Genetic epistemology.* New York,: Columbia University Press.

Piburn, M. D. (1993, April). *Evidence from meta-analysis for an expertise model of achievement in science.* Paper presented at the Annual Meeting of the National Association for Research in Science Teaching, Atlanta, GA.

Pintrich, P. R., Cross, D. R., Kozma, R. B., & McKeachie, W. J. (1986). Instructional psychology. *Annual Review of Psychology, 37*(1), 611–651.

Podlozny, A. (2000). Strengthening verbal skills through the use of classroom drama: A clear link. *Journal of Aesthetic Education, 34*(3/4), 239–275.

Poirier, B. M. (1989). *The effectiveness of language intervention with preschool handicapped children: An integrative review.* Unpublished Ph.D., Utah State University, UT.

Polit, D. F., & Falbo, T. (1987). Only children and personality development: A quantitative review. *Journal of Marriage and the Family, 49*(2), 309–325.

Pólya, G. (1945). *How to solve it: A new aspect of mathematical method.* Princeton, NJ: Princeton University Press.

Pong, S. l., Dronkers, J., & Hampden-Thompson, G. (2002). *Family policies and academic achievement by young children in single-parent families: an international comparison. Population research institute working paper* (Reports – Research No. PRI-WP-02–03 1-R24–HD41025). University Park, PA: Population Research Institute, The Pennsylvania State University.

Pong, S. l., Dronkers, J., & Hampden-Thompson, G. (2003). Family policies and children's school achievement in single- versus two-parent families. *Journal of Marriage and Family, 65*(3), 681–699.

Popham, W. J. (1969). Curriculum materials. *Review of Educational Research, 39*(3), 319–338.

Popham, W. J., Eisner, E., Sullivan, H., & Tyler, L. (1969). *Instructional objectives.* Washington, DC: American Educational Research Association.

Popper, K. R. (1963). *Conjectures and refutations. The growth of scientific knowledge.* London: Routledge.

Popper, K. R. (1968). *The logic of scientific discovery* (3rd ed.). London: Hutchinson.

Post, G. S. (1998). *An investigation into the application of accelerated learning theory as it relates to improving employee performance in the learning organization for the twenty-first century.* Unpublished Ed.D., Northern Illinois University, IL.

Powers, D. E. (1986). Relations of test item characteristics to test preparation/test practice effects: a quantitative summary. *Psychological Bulletin, 100*(1), 67–77.

Powers, D. E. (1993). Coaching for the SAT: A summary of the summaries and an update. *Educational Measurement: Issues and Practice, 12*(2), 24–30.

Powers, S., & Rossman, M. H. (1983, March). *Evidence of the impact of bilingual education: A meta-analysis.* Paper presented at the Annual Arizona Bilingual Education Conference, Tucson, AZ.

Powers, S., & Rossman, M. H. (1984). Evidence of the impact of bilingual education: A meta-analysis. *Journal of Instructional Psychology, 11*(2), 75–78.

Pratt, S., & George, R. (2005). Transferring friendship: Girls' and boys' friendships in the transition from primary to secondary school. *Children and Society, 19*(1), 16–26.

Preiss, R. W., & Gayle, B. M. (2006). A meta-analysis of the educational benefits of employing advanced organizers. In B. M. Gayle, R. W. Preiss, N. Burrell & M. Allen (Eds.), *Classroom communication and instructional processes: Advances through meta-analysis* (pp. 329–344). Mahwah, NJ: Lawrence Erlbaum Associates.

Pressey, S. L. (1949). *Educational acceleration: Appraisals and basic problems.* Columbus, OH: Ohio State University.

Pressley, M., & Afflerbach, P. (1995). *Verbal protocols of reading: The nature of constructively responsive reading.* Hillsdale, NJ: Lawrence Erlbaum Associates.

Pressley, M., Gaskins, I. W., Solic, K., & Collins, S. (2006). A portrait of Benchmark School: How a school produces high achievement in students who previously failed. *Journal of Educational Psychology, 98*(2), 282–306.

Pressley, M., Mohan, L., Raphael, L. M., & Fingeret, L. (2007). How does Bennett Woods Elementary School produce such high reading and writing achievement? *Journal of Educational Psychology, 99*(2), 221–240.

Prince, M. (2004). Does active learning work? A review of the research. *Journal of Engineering Education, 93*(3), 223–231.

Prins, F. J., Veenman, M. V. J., & Elshout, J. J. (2006). The impact of intellectual ability and metacognition on learning: New support for the threshold of problematicity theory. *Learning and Instruction, 16*(4), 374–387.

Prout, H. T., & DeMartino, R. A. (1986). A meta-analysis of school-based studies of psychotherapy. *Journal of School Psychology, 24*(3), 285–292.

Pugh, K. J., & Bergin, D. A. (2006). Motivational influences on transfer. *Educational Psychologist, 41*(3), 147–160.

Purdie, N. (2001). Self-regulation of learning in university contexts. *New Zealand Journal of Educational Studies, 36*(2), 259–270.

Purdie, N., & Hattie, J. A. C. (1999). The relationship between study skills and learning outcomes: A meta-analysis. *Australian Journal of Education, 43*(1), 72–86.

Purdie, N., & Hattie, J. A. C. (2002). Assessing students' conceptions of learning. *Australian Journal of Developmental and Educational Psychology, 2*, 17–32.

Purdie, N., Hattie, J. A. C., & Carroll, A. (2002). A review of the research on interventions for attention deficit hyperactivity disorder: What works best? *Review of Educational Research, 72*(1), 61–99.

Purkey, W. W. (1992). An introduction to invitational theory. *Journal of Invitational Theory and Practice, 1*(1), 5–15.

Qin, Z. (1992). *A meta-analysis of the effectiveness of achieving higher-order learning tasks in cooperative learning compared with competitive learning.* Unpublished Ph.D., University of Minnesota, MN.

Qin, Z., Johnson, D. W., & Johnson, R. T. (1995). Cooperative versus competitive efforts and problem solving. *Review of Educational Research, 65*(2), 129–143.

Qu, Y., & Becker, B. J. (2003, April). *Does traditional teacher certification imply quality? A meta-analysis.* Paper presented at the Annual Meeting of the American Educational Research Association, Chicago, IL.

Quinn, M. M., Kavale, K., A., Mathur, S. R., Rutherford, R. B. J., & Forness, S. R. (1999). A meta-analysis of social skill interventions for students with emotional or behavioral disorders. *Journal of Emotional and Behavioral Disorders, 7*(1), 54.

Randolph, J. J. (2005). A quantitative synthesis of response card research on student participation, academic achievement, classroom disruptive behavior, and student preference. 149–165.

Randolph, J. J. (2007). Meta-analysis of the research on response cards: Effects on test achievement, quiz achievement, participation, and off-task behavior. *Journal of Positive Behavior Interventions, 9*(2), 113–128.

Raudenbush, S. W. (1984). Magnitude of teacher expectancy effects on pupil IQ as a function of the credibility of expectancy induction: A synthesis of findings from 18 experiments. *Journal of Educational Psychology, 76*(1), 85–97.

Raymond, M. E., & Hanushek, E. A. (2003). High-stakes research: The campaign against accountability has brought forth a tide of negative anecdotes and deeply flawed research. Solid analysis reveals a brighter picture. *Education Next, 3*(3), 48–55.

Razel, M. (2001). The complex model of television viewing and educational achievement. *Journal of Educational Research, 94*(6), 371.

Readence, J. E., & Moore, D. W. (1981). A meta-analytic review of the effect of adjunct pictures on reading comprehension. *Psychology in the Schools, 18*(2), 218–224.

Ready, D. D., Lee, V. E., & Welner, K. G. (2004). Educational equity and school structure: School size, overcrowding, and schools-within-schools. *The Teachers College Record, 106*(10), 1989–2014.

Redfield, D. L., & Rousseau, E. W. (1981). A meta-analysis of experimental research on teacher questioning behavior. *Review of Educational Research, 51*(2), 237–245.

Reid, R., Gonzalez, J. E., Nordness, P. D., Trout, A., & Epstein, M. H. (2004). A meta-analysis of the academic status of students with emotional/behavioral disturbance. *The Journal of Special Education, 38*, 130–143.

Reid, R., Trout, A. L., & Schartz, M. (2005). Self-regulation interventions for children with attention deficit/hyperactivity disorder. *Exceptional Children, 71*(4), 361–377.

Reifman, A., Villa, L. C., Amans, J. A., Rethinam, V., & Telesca, T. Y. (2001). Children of divorce in the 1990s: A meta-analysis. *Journal of Divorce and Remarriage, 36*(1/2), 27–36.

Remmer, A. M., & Jernstedt, G. (1982). Comparative effectiveness of simulation games in secondary and college level instruction: A meta-analysis. *Psychological Reports, 51*(3, Pt 1), 742.

Reynolds, A. J., & Walberg, H. J. (Eds.). (1998). *Evaluation for educational productivity* (Vol. 7). Greenwich, CT: Elsevier Science/JAI Press.

Rice, J. K. (1999). The impact of class size on instructional strategies and the use of time in high school mathematics and science courses. *Educational Evaluation and Policy Analysis, 21*(2), 215–229.

Richmond, M. J., Jr. (1977). *Issues in year-round education*. North Quincy, Massachusetts: The Christopher Publishing House.

Ritts, V., Patterson, M. L., & Tubbs, M. E. (1992). Expectations, impressions, and judgments of physically attractive students: A review. *Review of Educational Research, 62*(4), 413–426.

Robbins, S. B., Lauver, K., Le, H., Davis, D., Langley, R., & Carlstrom, A. (2004). Do psychosocial and study skill factors predict college outcomes? A meta-analysis. *Psychological Bulletin, 130*(2), 261–288.

Roberts, B. W., Walton, K. E., & Viechtbauer, W. (2006). Patterns of mean-level change in personality traits across the life course: A meta-analysis of longitudinal studies. *Psychological Bulletin, 132*(1), 1–25.

Roberts, R. M. (2002). *The role of computers in school restructuring: A meta-analysis*. Unpublished M.A., California State University, Fresno, CA.

Roberts, T. (1998). *The power of Paideia schools: Defining lives through learning*. Alexandia, VA: ASCD Publications.

Roberts, T., & Billings, L. (1999). *The Paideia classroom: Teaching for understanding*. Larchmont, NY: Eye on Education.

Robinson, T. R., Smith, S. W., Miller, M. D., & Brownell, M. T. (1999). Cognitive behavior modification of hyperactivity-impulsivity and aggression: A meta-analysis of school-based studies. *Journal of Educational Psychology, 91*(2), 195–203.

Robinson, V. M. J., Lloyd, C., & Rowe, K. J. (2008). The impact of educational leadership on student outcomes: An analysis of the differential effects of leadership types. *Education Administration Quarterly, 44 (5)*.

Roblyer, M. D., Castine, W. H., & King, F. J. (1988). Assessing the impact of computer-based instruction: A review of recent research. *Computers in the Schools, 5*(3), 1–149.

Rock, S. L. (1985). *A meta-analysis of self-instructional training research*. Unpublished Ph.D., University of Illinois at Urbana-Champaign, IL.

Rodriguez, A. J. (1997). *Counting the runners who don't have shoes: Trends in student achievement in science by socioeconomic status and gender within ethnic groups. Research monograph*. Madison, WI: National Institute for Science Education.

Roessingh, H. (2004). Effective high school ESL programs: A synthesis and meta-analysis. *Canadian Modern Language Review/ La Revue canadienne des langues vivantes, 60*(5), 611–636.

Rogers, E. M. (1962). *Diffusion of innovations*. New York: Free Press of Glencoe.

Rogers, E. M. (2003). *Diffusion of innovations* (5th ed.). New York: Free Press.

Rogers, K. B. (1991). *The relationship of grouping practices to the education of the gifted and talented learner. Executive summary. Research-based decision making series*. Storrs, CT: University of Connecticut, National Research Center on the Gifted and Talented.

Rohrbeck, C. A., Ginsburg-Block, M. D., Fantuzzo, J. W., & Miller, T. R. (2003). Peer-assisted learning interventions with elementary school studies: A meta-analytic review. *Journal of Educational Psychology, 95*(2), 240–257.

Rolheiser-Bennett, N. C. (1986). *Four models of teaching: A meta-analysis of student outcomes.* Unpublished Ph.D., University of Oregon, OR.

Rolle, A. (2004). Out with the old–in with the new: Thoughts on the future of educational productivity research. *Peabody Journal of Education, 79*(3), 31–56.

Rolstad, K., Mahoney, K., & Glass, G. V. (2005). The big picture: A meta-analysis of program effectiveness research on English language learners. *Educational Policy, 19*(4), 572–594.

Romney, D. M., & Samuels, M. T. (2001). A meta-analytic evaluation of Feuerstein's Instrumental Enrichment program. *Educational and Child Psychology, 18*(4), 19–34.

Ropo, E. (1987, April). *Teachers' conceptions of teaching and teaching behavior: Some differences between expert and novice teachers.* Paper presented at the Annual meeting of the American Educational Research Association, Washington, DC.

Rose, L. H., & Lin, H. T. (1984). A meta-analysis of long-term creativity training programs. *Journal of Creative Behavior, 18*(1), 11–22.

Rosen, Y., & Salomon, G. (2007). The differential learning achievements of constructivist technology-intensive learning environments as compared with traditional ones: A meta-analysis. *Journal of Educational Computing Research, 36*(1), 1–14.

Rosenbaum, C. M. (1983). *A meta-analysis of the effectiveness of educational treatment programs for emotionally disturbed students.* Unpublished Ed. D., The College of William and Mary, VA.

Rosenbaum, J. E. (1980). Track misperceptions and frustrated college plans: An analysis of the effects of tracks and track perceptions in the National Longitudinal Survey. *Sociology of Education, 53*(2), 74–88.

Rosenshine, B. (2003). High-stakes testing: Another analysis [Electronic Version]. *Education Policy Analysis Archives, 11.* Retrieved 29 April 2008 from http://epaa.asu.edu/epaa/v11n24/.

Rosenshine, B., & Meister, C. (1994). Reciprocal teaching: A review of the research. *Review of Educational Research, 64*(4), 479–530.

Rosenthal, R. (1991). *Meta-analytic procedures for social research* (Rev. ed.). Newbury Park: Sage Publications.

Rosenthal, R. (1991). Teacher expectancy effects: A brief update 25 years after the Pygmalion experiment. *Journal of Research in Education, 1*(1), 3–12.

Rosenthal, R., & DiMatteo, M. R. (2001). Meta-analysis: Recent developments in quantitative methods for literature reviews. *Annual Review of Psychology, 52*(1), 59–82.

Rosenthal, R., & Jacobson, L. (1968). *Pygmalion in the classroom: Teacher expectation and pupils' intellectual development.* New York: Holt, Rinehart, and Winston.

Rosenthal, R., & Rubin, D. B. (1978). Interpersonal expectancy effects: The first 345 studies. *Behavioral and Brain Sciences, 1*(3), 377–415.

Rosenzweig, C. J. (2000). *A meta-analysis of parenting and school success: The role of parents in promoting students' academic performance.* Unpublished Ph.D., Hofstra University, NY.

Roseth, C. J., Fang, F., Johnson, D. W., & Johnson, R. T. (2006, April). *Effects of cooperative learning on middle school students: A meta-analysis.* Paper presented at the Annual Meeting of the American Educational Research Association, San Francisco, CA.

Roseth, C. J., Johnson, D. W., & Johnson, R. T. (2008). Promoting early adolescents' achievement and peer relationships: The effects of cooperative, competitive, and individualistic goal structures. *Psychological Bulletin, 134*(2), 223–246.

Ross, J. A. (1988). Controlling variables: A meta-analysis of training studies. *Review of Educational Research, 58*(4), 405–437.

Ross, S. (1998). Self-assessment in second language testing: a meta-analysis and analysis of experiential factors. *Language Testing, 15*(1), 1–20.

Roth, P. L., BeVier, C. A., Switzer, F. S., III, & Schippmann, J. S. (1996). Meta-analyzing the relationship between grades and job performance. *Journal of Applied Psychology, 81*(5), 548–556.

Rousseau, E. W., & Redfield, D. L. (1980). Teacher questioning. *Evaluation in Education, 4*, 51–52.

Rowan, K. S. (1988). *Learning styles and teacher inservice education.* Unpublished Ed.D., The University of Tennessee, TN.

Rowe, D. W. (1985). *The big picture: A quantitative meta-analysis of reading comprehension research.* Bloomington, IN: Indiana University, Language Education Department.

Rowe, K. J. (1988). Single-sex and mixed-sex classes: The effects of class type on student achievement, confidence and participation in mathematics. *Australian Journal of Education, 32*(2), 180–202.

Rowe, K. J. (2005). *Teaching reading: National inquiry into the teaching of literacy.* Canberra, Australia: Department of Education, Science and Training.

Rowe, K. J., & Rowe, K. S. (1993, November). *Assessing student behaviour: The utility and measurement properties of a simple parent and teacher-administered behavioural rating instrument for use in educational and epidemiological research.* Paper presented at the Annual Conference of the Australian Association for Research in Education, Fremantle, WA.

Rubie, C. (2003). *Expecting the best: Instructional practices, teacher beliefs, and student outcomes.* Unpublished PhD, University of Auckland, Auckland.

Rubie-Davies, C., Hattie, J. A. C., & Hamilton, R. (2006). Expecting the best for students: Teacher expectations and academic outcomes. *British Journal of Educational Psychology, 76*, 429–444.

Rubie-Davies, C. M. (2006). Teacher expectations and student self-perceptions: Exploring relationships. *Psychology in the Schools, 43*(5), 537–552.

Rubie-Davies, C. M. (2007). Classroom interactions: Exploring the practices of high- and low-expectation teachers. *British Journal of Educational Psychology, 77*, 289–306.

Rubin, S. F. (1996). *Evaluation and meta-analysis of selected research related to the laboratory component of beginning college level science instruction.* Unpublished Ed.D., Temple University, PA.

Rummel, A., & Feinberg, R. (1988). Cognitive evaluation theory: A meta-analytic review of the literature. *Social Behavior and Personality: An International Journal, 16*(2), 147–164.

Runyan, G. B. (1987). *Effects of the mnemonic-keyword method on recalling verbal information: A meta-analysis.* Unpublished Ph.D., The Florida State University, Florida, United States.

Rush, S. M. (1992). *Functional components of a local and a national profile of elementary school at-risk students as determined through meta-analysis and factor analysis.* Unpublished Ed.D., University of South Dakota, SD.

Russo, C. J., & Rogus, J. F. (1998). Catholic schools: Proud past, promising future. *School Business Affairs, 64*(6), 13–16.

Russo, R. (2007). *Bridge of sighs.* New York: Alfred A. Knopf.

Ryan, A. W. (1990). *Meta-analysis of achievement effects of microcomputer applications in elementary schools.* Unpublished Ph.D., New York University, NY.

Ryan, A. W. (1991). Meta-analysis of achievement effects of microcomputer applications in elementary schools. *Educational Administration Quarterly, 27*(2), 161–184.

Sabornie, E. J., Cullinan, D., Osborne, S. S., & Brock, L. B. (2005). Intellectual, academic, and behavioral functioning of students with high-incidence disabilities: A cross-categorical meta-analysis. *Exceptional Children, 72*(1), 47–63.

Sadler, D. R. (1989). Formative assessment and the design of instructional systems. *Instructional Science, 18*(2), 119–144.

Salomon, G., & Perkins, D. N. (1989). Rocky roads to transfer: Rethinking mechanism of a neglected phenomenon. *Educational Psychologist, 24*(2), 113–142.

Salzman, S. A. (1987, April). *Meta-analysis of studies investigating the effects of father absence on children's cognitive performance.* Paper presented at the Annual Meeting of the American Educational Research Association Washington, DC.

Salzman, S. A. (1988, April). *Father absence, socioeconomic status, and race: Relations to children's cognitive performance.* Paper presented at the Annual Meeting of the American Educational Research Association, New Orleans, LA.

Samson, G. E. (1985). Effects of training in test-taking skills on achievement test performance: A quantitative synthesis. *Journal of Educational Research, 78*(5), 261–266.

Samson, G. E. (1987). The effects of teacher questioning levels on student achievement: A quantitative synthesis. *Journal of Educational Research, 80*(5), 290–295.

Samson, G. E., Borger, J. B., Weinstein, T., & Walberg, H. J. (1984). Pre-teaching experiences and attitudes: A quantitative synthesis. *Journal of Research and Development in Education, 17*(4), 52–56.

Samson, G. E., Graue, M. E., Weinstein, T., & Walberg, H. J. (1984). Academic and occupational performance: A quantitative synthesis. *American Educational Research Journal, 21*(2), 311–321.

Samson, G. E., Strykowski, B., Weinstein, T., & Walberg, H. J. (1987). The effects of teacher questioning levels on student achievement: A quantitative synthesis. *Journal of Educational Research, 80*(5), 290–295.

Samuelstuen, M. S., & Bråten, I. (2007). Examining the validity of self-reports on scales measuring students' strategic processing. *British Journal of Educational Psychology, 77*(2), 351–378.

Sanders, V. A. H. (1979). *A meta-analysis: The relationship of program content and operation factors to measured effectiveness of college reading-study programs.* Unpublished Ed. D., University of the Pacific, CA.

Sanders, V. A. H. (1980, March). *College reading and study programs: Do they make any difference?* Paper presented at the Annual Meeting of the Western College Reading Association, San Francisco, CA.

Sanders, W. L. (2000). Value-added assessment from student achievement data: Opportunities and hurdles. *Journal of Personnel Evaluation in Education, 14*(4), 329–339.

Sanders, W. L., Ashton, J. J., & Wright, S. P. (2005). *Comparison of the effects of NBPTS certified teachers with other teachers on the rate of student academic progress. Final report.* Arlington, VA: National Board for Professional Teaching Standards.

Sanders, W. L., & Rivers, J. C. (1996). *Cumulative and residual effects of teachers on future student academic achievement*: University of Tennessee Value-Added Research and Assessment Center.

Sandy-Hanson, A. E. (2006). *A meta-analysis of the impact of computer technology versus traditional instruction on students in kindergarten through twelfth grade in the United States: A comparison of academic achievement, higher-order thinking skills, motivation, physical outcomes and social skills.* Unpublished Ph.D., Howard University, Washington, DC.

Schacter, J. (1999). *The impact of education technology on student achievement: What the most current research has to say*: Milken Exchange on Education Technology, Santa Monica, CA.[BBB35521].

Schagen, I., & Elliot, K. (2004). *But what does it mean? The use of effect sizes in educational research.* Slough, UK: NFER/Institute of Education.

Schatz, J. (2003). Academic achievement in children with sickle cell disease: A meta-analysis. Department of Psychology, University of South Carolina.

Schaubroeck, J., & Muralidhar, K. (1991). A meta-analysis of the relative effects of tabular and graphic display formats on decision-making performance. *Human Performance, 4*(2), 127–145.

Scheerens, J., & Bosker, R. J. (1997). *The foundations of educational effectiveness* (1st ed.). Oxford: Pergamon Press.

Scheerens, J., Vermeulen, C. J. A. J., & Pelgrum, W. J. (1989). Generalizibility of instructional and school effectiveness indicators across nations. *International Journal of Educational Research, 13*(7), 789–799.

Scherr, T. G. (2007). Educational experiences of children in foster care: Meta-analyses of special education, retention and discipline rates. *School Psychology International, 28*(4), 419–436.

Schiefele, U., Krapp, A., & Schreyer, I. (1993). Metaanalyse des Zusammenhangs von Interesse und schulischer Leistung [Meta-analysis of the relation between interest and academic achievement]. *Zeitschrift für Entwicklungspsychologie und Pädagogische Psychologie, 25*, 120–148.

Schiefele, U., Krapp, A., & Winteler, A. (1992). Interest as a predictor of academic achievement: A meta-analysis of research. In K. A. Renninger, S. Hidi & A. Krapp (Eds.), *The role of interest in learning and development* (pp. 183–212). Hillsdale, NJ: Lawrence Erlbaum Associates.

Schieffer, C., Marchand-Martella, N. E., Martella, R. C., Simonsen, F. L., & Waldron-Soler, K. M. (2002). An analysis of the Reading Mastery program: Effective components and research review. *Journal of Direct Instruction, 2*(2), 87–119

Schiller, D., Walberg, H. J., & Haertel, G. D. (1980). Quality of instruction. *Evaluation in Education, 4*, 119–120.

Schimmel, B. J. (1983, April). *A meta-analysis of feedback to learners in computerized and programmed instruction.* Paper presented at the Annual Meeting of the American Educational Research Association Montreal, Canada.

Schlaefli, A., Rest, J. R., & Thoma, S. J. (1985). Does moral education improve moral judgment? A meta-analysis of intervention studies using the defining issues test. *Review of Educational Research, 55*(3), 319–352.

Schmidt, M., Weinstein, T., Niemiec, R. P., & Walberg, H. J. (1986). Computer-assisted instruction with exceptional children. *Journal of Special Education, 19*(4), 493–501.

Schneider, B. H. (1992). Didactic methods for enhancing children's peer relations: A quantitative review. *Clinical Psychology Review, 12*(3), 363–382.

Scholl, B. J., & Leslie, A. M. (2001). Minds, modules, and meta-analysis. *Child Development, 72*, 696–701.

Schram, C. M. (1996). A meta-analysis of gender differences in applied statistics achievement. *Journal of Educational and Behavioral Statistics, 21*(1), 55–70.

Schramm, R. M. (1989). *The effects of using word processing equipment in writing instruction: A meta-analysis.* Unpublished Ed.D., Northern Illinois University, Illinois, United States.

Schramm, R. M. (1991). The effects of using word processing equipment in writing instruction. *Business Education Forum, 45*(5), 7–11.

Schroeder, C. M., Scott, T. P., Tolson, H., Huang, T. Y., & Lee, Y. H. (2007). A meta-analysis of national research: Effects of teaching strategies on student achievement in science in the United States. *Journal of Research in Science Teaching, 44*(10), 1436–1460.

Schuler, H., Funke, U., & Baron-Boldt, J. (1990). Predictive validity of school grades: A meta-analysis. *Applied Psychology: An International Review, 39*(1), 89–103.

Schulze, R. (2004). *Meta-analysis: A comparison of approaches.* Toronto: Hogrefe and Huber.

Schwienhorst, K. (2002). The state of VR: A meta-analysis of virtual reality tools in second language acquisition. *Computer Assisted Language Learning, 15*(3), 221–239.

Scope, E. E. (1998). *A meta-analysis of research on creativity: The effects of instructional variables.* Unpublished Ph.D., Fordham University, New York, United States.

Scott, G., Leritz, L. E., & Mumford, M. D. (2004). The effectiveness of creativity training: A quantitative review. *Creativity Research Journal, 16*(4), 361–388.

Scott, R. S. (1984). Meta-analysis: How useful in appraising desegregatory effects? *Psychological Reports, 55*(3), 739–743.

Scott, T. P., Tolson, H., Schroeder, C., Lee, Y.-H., Tse-Yang, H., Hu, X., et al. (2005). *Meta-analysis of national research regarding science teaching.* College Station, TX: Texas A&M University, Center for Mathematics and Science Education.

Scott-Little, C., Hamann, M. S., & Jurs, S. G. (2002). Evaluations of after-school programs: A meta-evaluation of methodologies and narrative synthesis of findings. *American Journal of Evaluation, 23*(4), 387–419.

Scriven, M. (1971). The logic of cause. *Theory and Decision, 2*(1), 49–66.

Scriven, M. (1975). Causation as explanation. *Nous, 9*(1), 3–16.

Scriven, M. (1987). Fallacies of statistical substitution. *Argumentation, 1*(3), 333–349.

Scriven, M. (2002). The limits of explication. *Argumentation, 16*(1), 47–57.

Scriven, M. (2005, December). *Can we infer causation from cross-sectional data?* Paper presented at the School Level Data Symposium, National Research Council, Washington DC.

Scriven, M. (2005). Causation. In S. Mathison (Ed.), *Encyclopedia of evaluation* (pp. 43–47). Thousand Oaks, CA: Sage.

Scruggs, T. E., & Mastropieri, M. A. (1996). Teacher perceptions of mainstreaming/inclusion, 1958–1995: A research synthesis. *Exceptional Children, 63*(1), 59–74.

Scruggs, T. E., White, K. R., & Bennion, C. (1986). Teaching test-taking skills to elementary-grade students: A meta-analysis. *Elementary School Journal, 87*(1), 69–82.

Seastrom, M. M., Gruber, K. J., Henke, R., McGrath, D. J., & Cohen, B. A. (2002). Qualifications of the public school teacher workforce: Prevalence of out-of-field teaching 1987–88 to 1999–2000. *Education Statistics Quarterly, 4*(3), 12–19.

Seastrom, M. M., Gruber, K. J., Henke, R., McGrath, D. J., & Cohen, B. A. (2002). *Qualifications of the public school teacher workforce: Prevalence of out-of-field teaching, 1987–88 to 1999–2000. Statistical analysis report.* Jessup, MD: ED Publications.

Seidel, T., & Shavelson, R. J. (2007). Teaching effectiveness research in the past decade: The role of theory and research design in disentangling meta-analysis results. *Review of Educational Research, 77*(4), 454–499.

Seipp, B. (1991). Anxiety and academic performance: A meta-analysis of findings. *Anxiety, Stress, and Coping, 4*(1), 27–41.

Selley, N. J. (1999). *The art of constructivist teaching in the primary school: A guide for students and teachers.* London: David Fulton.

Sencibaugh, J. M. (2005). *Meta-analysis of reading comprehension interventions for students with learning disabilities: Strategies and implications.* St Louis, MO: Harris-Stowe State Unversity,.

Sencibaugh, J. M. (2007). Meta-analysis of reading comprehension interventions for students with learning disabilities: strategies and implications. *Reading Improvement, 44*(1), 6–22.

Senechal, M. (2006). *The effect of family literacy interventions on children's acquisition of reading. From kindergarten to grade 3. A meta-analytic review.* Washington, DC National Institute for Literacy.

Severiens, S. E., & Ten Dam, G. T. N. (1994). Gender differences in learning styles: A narrative review and quantitative meta-analysis. *Higher Education, 27*(4), 487–501.

Shachar, M., & Neumann, Y. (2003). Differences between traditional and distance education academic performances: A meta-analytic approach [Electronic Version]. *The International Review of Research in Open and Distance Learning, 4*. Retrieved 29 June 2007 from http://www.irrodl.org/index.php/irrodl/article/view/153/704

Shah, A. K., & Oppenheimer, D. M. (2008). Heuristics made easy: An effort-reduction framework. *Psychological Bulletin, 134*(2), 207–222.

Shahid, J., & Thompson, D. (2001, April). *Teacher efficacy: A research synthesis.* Paper presented at the Annual Meeting of the American Educational Research Association, Seattle, WA.

Shakeshaft, C., & McNamara, J. F. (1980). Women in academic administration. *Evaluation in Education, 4*, 76–78.

Shanker, A. (1993). Public vs. private schools. National Forum. *Phi Kappa Phi Journal, 73*(4), 14–17.

Shanteau, J. (1992). Competence in experts: The role of task characteristics. *Organizational Behavior and Human Decision Processes, 53*, 252–266.

Shapiro, E. J., Kerssen-Griep, J., Gayle, B. M., & Allen, M. (2006). How powerful is PowerPoint? Analyzing the educational effects of desktop presentational programs in the classroom. In B. M. Gayle, R. W. Preiss, N. Burrell & M. Allen (Eds.), *Classroom communication and instructional processes: Advances through meta-analysis* (pp. 61–75). Mahwah, NJ: Lawrence Erlbaum Associates.

Sharpe, D., & Rossiter, L. (2002). Siblings of children with a chronic illness: A meta-analysis. *Journal of Pediatrric Psychology, 27*(8), 699–710.

Shaver, J. P., Curtis, C. K., Jesunathadas, J., & Strong, C. J. (1987, April). *The methodology and outcomes of research on modifying attitudes toward persons with disabilities: A comprehensive, systematic review.* Paper presented at the Annual Meeting of the American Educational Research Association, Washington, DC.

Shaver, J. P., Curtis, C. K., Jesunathadas, J., & Strong, C. J. (1987). *The modification of attitudes toward persons with handicaps: A comprehensive integrative review of research. Final report.* Logan, Utah: Bureau of Research Services, Utah State University.

Shaver, J. P., Curtis, C. K., Jesunathadas, J., & Strong, C. J. (1989). The modification of attitudes toward persons with disabilities: Is there a best way? *International Journal of Special Education, 4*(1), 33–57.

Sheeran, P. (2002). Intention-behavior relations: A conceptual and empirical review. *European Review of Social Psychology, 12*, 1–36.

Shepard, L. A. (1989). A review of research on kindergarten retention. In L. A. Shepard & M. L. Smith (Eds.), *Flunking grades: Research and policies on retention* (pp. 64–78). London: Falmer Press.

Shepard, L. A., & Smith, M. L. (Eds.). (1989). *Flunking grades: Research and policies on retention*. London: Falmer Press.

Shermer, M. (1997). *Why people believe weird things: Pseudoscience, superstition, and other confusions of our time*. New York: WH Freeman.

Shiell, J. L. (2002). *A meta-analysis of Feuerstein's Instrumental Enrichment*. Unpublished Ph.D., The University of British Columbia, Canada.

Shomoossi, N. (2004). The effect of teachers' questioning behavior on EFL classroom interaction: A classroom research study. *The Reading Matrix, 4*(2), 96–104.

Shrager, L., & Mayer, R. E. (1989). Note-taking fosters generative learning strategies in novices. *Journal of Educational Psychology, 81*(2), 263–264.

Shulman, L. S. (1987). Knowledge and teaching: Foundations of the new reform. *Harvard Educational Review, 57*(1), 1–22.

Shulruf, B., Keuskamp, D., & Timperley, H. (2006). *Coursetaking or subject choice?* (No. Technical Report #7). Auckland, New Zealand: Starpath: Project for Tertiary Participation and Support, The University of Auckland.

Shwalb, B. J., Shwalb, D. W., & Azuma, H. (1986). Educational technology in the Japanese schools – a meta-analysis of findings. *Educational Technology Research, 9*(1–2), 13–30.

Shymansky, J. A. (1983). The effects of new science curricula on student performance. *Journal of Research in Science Teaching, 20*(5), 387–404.

Shymansky, J. A. (1984). BSCS programs: Just how effective were they? *American Biology Teacher, 46*(1), 54–57.

Shymansky, J. A., Hedges, L. V., & Woodworth, G. (1990). A reassessment of the effects of inquiry-based science curricula of the 60's on student performance. *Journal of Research in Science Teaching, 27*(2), 127–144.

Shymansky, J. A., Kyle, W. C. J., & Alport, J. M. (1983). The effects of new science curricula on student performance. *Journal of Research in Science Teaching, 20*(5), 387–404.

Shymansky, J. A., & Others, A. (1987). A reassessment of the effects of 60's science curricula on student performance: Final report (p. 58).

Shymansky, J. A., Woodworth, G., Berg, C., & Hedges, L. V. (1986, March). *A study of uncertainties in the meta-analysis of research on the effectiveness of "new" science curricula. Preliminary report*. Paper presented at the Annual Meeting of the National Association for Research in Science Teaching, San Francisco, CA,.

Sibley, B. A., & Etnier, J. L. (2002). The effects of physical activity on cognition in children: a meta-analysis. *Medicine and Science in Sports and Exercise, 34*(5), S214.

Sibley, B. A., & Etnier, J. L. (2003). The relationship between physical activity and cognition in children: a meta-analysis. *Pediatric Exercise Science, 15*(3), 243–256.

Signorella, M. L., Frieze, I. H., & Hershey, S. W. (1996). Single-sex versus mixed-sex classes and gender schemata in children and adolescents. A longitudinal comparison. *Psychology of Women Quarterly, 20*(4), 599–607.

Silva, R. R., Munoz, D. M., & Alpert, M. (1996). Carbamazepine use in children and adolescents with features of attention-deficit hyperactivity disorder: a meta-analysis. *Journal of the American Academy of Child and Adolescent Psychiatry, 35*(3), 352–358.

Silver, H. C., & Greenhaiis, J. H. (1983). The impact of goal, task and personal characteristics on goal-setting behavior. *Eastern Academy of Management Proceedings*, 11–13.

Simmons, J. (1991). *Learning controversy: A situational perspective*.

Simpson, S. N. (1980). Comment on "Meta-Analysis of Research on Class Size and Achievement." *Educational Evaluation and Policy Analysis, 2*(3), 81–83.

Sindelar, P. T., & Wilson, R. J. (1984). The potential effects of meta-analysis on special education practice. *18*(1), 81–92.

Sipe, T. A., & Curlette, W. L. (1996, April). *A meta-meta-analysis: Methodological aspects of meta-analyses in educational achievement.* Paper presented at the Annual Meeting of the American Educational Research Association, New York.

Sipe, T. A., & Curlette, W. L. (1996). A meta-synthesis of factors related to educational achievement: A methodological approach to summarizing and synthesizing meta-analyses. *International Journal of Educational Research, 25*(7), 583–698.

Sirin, S. R. (2005). Socioeconomic status and academic achievement: A meta-analytic review of research. *Review of Educational Research, 75*(3), 417–453.

Sirotnik, K. A. (1983). What you see is what you get: Consistency, persistency, and mediocrity in classrooms. *Harvard Educational Review, 53*(1), 16–31.

Sirotnik, K. A. (1985). School effectiveness: A bandwagon in search of a tune. *Educational Administration Quarterly, 21*(2), 135–140.

Sitzmann, T., Kraiger, K., Stewart, D., & Wisher, R. (2006). The comparative effectiveness of web-based and classroom instruction: A meta-analysis. *Personnel Psychology, 59*(3), 623–664.

Sizemore, R. W. (1981). Do Black and White students look for the same characteristics in teachers? *Journal of Negro Education, 50*(1), 48–53.

Skiba, R. J., & Casey, A. (1985). Interventions for behaviorally disordered students: A quantitative review and methodological critique. *Behavioral Disorders, 10*(4), 239–252.

Skiba, R. J., Casey, A., & Center, B. A. (1985). Nonaversive procedures in the treatment of classroom behavior problems. *Journal of Special Education, 19*(4), 459–481.

Slavin, R. E. (1987). Ability grouping and student achievement in elementary schools: A best-evidence synthesis. *Review of Educational Research, 57*(3), 293–336.

Slavin, R. E. (1987). Mastery learning reconsidered. *Review of Educational Research, 57*(2), 175–213.

Slavin, R. E. (1989). Class size and student achievement: Small effects of small classes. *Educational Psychologist, 24*(1), 99–110.

Slavin, R. E. (1990). Achievement effects of ability grouping in secondary schools: A best-evidence synthesis. *Review of Educational Research, 60*(3), 471–499.

Slavin, R. E., & Cheung, A. (2005). A Synthesis of Research on Language of Reading Instruction for English Language Learners. *Review of Educational Research, 75*(2), 247–284.

Slavin, R. E., Cheung, A., Groff, C., & Lake, C. (in press). Effective reading programs for middle and high schools: A best-evidence synthesis. *Reading Research Quarterly.*

Slavin, R. E., & Stevens, R. J. (1991). Cooperative learning and mainstreaming. In J. W. Lloyd, N. Singh & A. Repp (Eds.), *The regular education initiative: Alternative perspectives on concepts, issues, and models* (pp. 177–192). Sycamore, IL: Sycamore.

Slee, R. (1998). High reliability organizations and liability students—The politics of recognition. In R. Slee, G. Weiner & S. Tomlinson (Eds.), *School effectiveness for whom? Challenges to the school effectiveness and school improvement movements* (pp. 101–114). London: Falmer Press.

Slemmer, D. L. (2002). *The effect of learning styles on student achievement in various hypertext, hypermedia, and technology-enhanced learning environments: A meta-analysis.* Unpublished Ed.D., Boise State University, ID.

Small, R. (2003). A fallacy in constructivist epistemology. *Journal of Philosophy of Education, 37*(3), 483–502.

Smith, B. A. (1996). *A meta-analysis of outcomes from the use of calculators in mathematics education.* Unpublished Ed.D., Texas A&M University, TX.

Smith, D. A. (1996). *A meta-analysis of student outcomes attributable to the teaching of science as inquiry as compared to traditional methodology.* Unpublished Ed.D., Temple University, Pennsylvania, United States.

Smith, M. L. (1980). Teacher expectations. *Evaluation in Education, 4*, 53–55.

Smith, M. L., & Glass, G. V. (1980). Meta-analysis of research on class size and its relationship to attitudes and instruction. *American Educational Research Journal, 17*(4), 419–433.

Smith, R. A. (2003). *Problem-based versus lecture-based medical teaching and learning: A meta-analysis of cognitive and noncognitive outcomes.* Unpublished Ph.D., University of Florida, FL.

Smith, T. W., Baker, W. K., Hattie, J. A. C., & Bond, L. (2008). A validity study of the certification system of the National Board For Professional Teaching Standards. In L. Ingvarson & J. A. C. Hattie (Eds.), *Assessing teachers for professional certification: The first decade of the National Board for Professional Teaching Standards* (pp. 345–378). Oxford, UK: Elsevier.

Snead, C. C., II. (2005). *A meta-analysis of attention deficit/hyperactivity disorder interventions: An empirical road to pragmatic solutions.* Unpublished Ed.D., Virginia Polytechnic Institute and State University, Virginia, United States.

Snook, I. (2003). *The ethical teacher.* Palmerston North, New Zealand: Dunmore Press.

Snow, C. E., Burns, M. S., & Griffin, P. (1998). *Preventing reading difficulties in young children.* Washington, DC: National Academy Press.

Snow, R. E. (1989). Aptitude–treatment interaction as a framework for research on individual differences in learning. In P. H. Ackerman, R. J. Sternberg & R. Glaser (Eds.), *Learning and individual differences: Advances in theory and research* (pp. 13–59.). New York: Freeman.

Snyder, S., & Sheehan, R. (1983). Integrating research in early childhood special education: The use of meta-analysis. *Diagnostique, 9*(1), 12–25.

Soe, K., Koki, S., & Chang, J. M. (2000). *Effect of computer-assisted instruction (CAI) on reading achievement: A meta-analysis.* Honolulu, HI: Pacific Resources for Education and Learning.

Sohn, D. (1982). Sex differences in achievement self-attributions: An effect size analysis. *Sex Roles, 8*(4), 345–357.

Song, E. Y., Pruitt, B. E., McNamara, J., & Colewell, B. (2000). A meta-analysis examining effects of school sexuality education programs on adolescents' sexual knowledge, 1960–1997. *Journal of School Health, 70*(10), 413–416.

Sowell, E. J. (1989). Effects of manipulative materials in mathematics instruction. *Journal for Research in Mathematics Education, 20*(5), 498–505.

Sparks, D. (2004). The looming danger of a two-tiered professional development system. *Phi Delta Kappan, 86*(4), 304–306.

Spielberger, C. D. (Ed.). (1972). *Anxiety: Current trends in theory and research* (Vol. 1). New York: Academic Press.

Spielberger, C. D., & Sarason, I. G. (Eds.). (1989). *Stress and anxiety* (Vol. 12). Washington: Hemisphere Publishing Corporation.

Spies, C. (1987). Play, problem solving, and creativity in young children, *Biennial Meeting of the Society for Research in Child Development* (p. 46). Baltimore, MD.

Spitz, H. H. (1999). Beleaguered Pygmalion: A history of the controversy over claims that teacher expectancy raises intelligence. *Intelligence, 27*(3), 199–234.

Springer, L., Stanne, M. E., & Donovan, S. S. (1997, November). *Effects of small-group learning on undergraduates in science, mathematics, engineering, and technology: A meta-analysis.* Paper presented at the Annual meeting of the Association for the Study of Higher Education, Albuquerque, NM.

Springer, L., Stanne, M. E., & Donovan, S. S. (1999). Effects of small-group learning on undergraduates in science, mathematics, engineering, and technology: A meta-analysis. *Review of Educational Research, 69*(1), 21–51.

Spuler, F. B. (1993). *A meta-analysis of the relative effectiveness of two cooperative learning models in increasing mathematics achievement.* Unpublished Ph.D., Old Dominion University, VA.

Stage, S. A., & Quiroz, D. R. (1997). A Meta-analysis of interventions to decrease disruptive classroom behavior in public education settings. *School Psychology Review, 26*(3), 333–368.

Stahl, S. A., & Fairbanks, M. M. (1986). The effects of vocabulary instruction: A model-based meta-analysis. *Review of Educational Research, 56*(1), 72–110.

Stahl, S. A., McKenna, M. C., & Pagnucco, J. R. (1994). The effects of whole-language instruction: An update and a reappraisal. *Educational Psychologist, 29*(4), 175–185.

Stahl, S. A., & Miller, P. D. (1989). Whole language and language experience approaches for beginning reading: A quantitative research synthesis. *Review of Educational Research, 59*(1), 87–116.

Stallings, J., Almy, M., Resnick, L. B., & Leinhardt, G. (1975). Implementation and child effects of teaching practices in Follow Through classrooms. *Monographs of the Society for Research in Child Development, 40*(7/8), 1–133.

Standley, J. M. (1996). A meta-analysis on the effects of music as reinforcement for education/therapy objectives. *Journal of Research in Music Education, 44*(2), 105–133.

Stebbins, L. B. (1976). *Education as experimentation: A planned variation model* (Vol. 3). Cambridge, MA: Abt Associates.

Stebbins, L. B., St. Pierre, R. G., Proper, E. C., Anderson, R. B., & Cerva, T. R. (1977). *Education as experimentation: A planned variation model.* (Vol. 4 A-D). Cambridge, MA: Abt Associates.

Steedman, J. (1983). *Examination results in mixed and single-sex schools: Findings from the National Child Development Study.* Manchester, UK: Equal Opportunities Commission.

Steinberg, L. D., Brown, B. B., & Dornbusch, S. M. (1997). *Beyond the classroom: Why school reform has failed and what parents need to do.* New York: Simon and Schuster.

Steinkamp, M. W. (1982, March). *Sex-related differences in attitude toward science: A quantitative synthesis of research.* Paper presented at the Annual Meeting of the American Educational Research Association, New York.

Steinkamp, M. W., & Maehr, M. L. (1983). Affect, ability, and science achievement: A quantitative synthesis of correlational research. *Review of Educational Research, 53*(3), 369–396.

Steinkamp, M. W., & Maehr, M. L. (1984). Gender differences in motivational orientations toward achievement in school science: A quantitative synthesis. *American Educational Research Journal, 21*(1), 39–59.

Stekelenburg, C. R. (1991). *The effects of public high school size on student achievement: A meta-analysis.* Unpublished EdD, University of Georgia, GA.

Stennett, R. G. (1985). *Computer assisted instruction: A review of the reviews* (No. 85–01): London Board of Education (Ontario). Educational Research Services. [BBB10459].

Stephan, W. G. (1983). *Blacks and "Brown": The effects of school desegregation on Black students.* Washington, DC: National Institute of Education.

Stephens, C. S. (2001). A meta-analysis of research on student team effectiveness: A proposed application of phased interventions. *Journal of Informatics Education Research, 8.*

Sternberg, R. J., & Horvath, J. A. (1995). A prototype view of expert teaching. *Educational Researcher, 24*(6), 9–17.

Stevens, R. J., & Slavin, R. E. (1990). When cooperative learning improves the achievement of students with mild disabilities: A response to Tateyama-Sniezek. *Exceptional Children, 57*(3), 276–280.

Stone, C. L. (1983). A meta-analysis of advance organizer studies. *Journal of Experimental Education, 51*(4), 194–199.

Strahan, D. B. (1989). How experienced and novice teachers frame their views of instruction: An analysis of semantic ordered trees. *Teaching and Teacher Education, 5*(1), 53–67.

Strenze, T. (2007). Intelligence and socioeconomic success: A meta-analytic review of longitudinal research. *Intelligence, 35*(5), 401–426.

Strom, R. E., & Boster, F. J. (2007). Dropping out of high school: A meta-analysis assessing the effect of messages in the home and in school. *Communication Education, 56*(4), 433–452.

Strong, W. B., Malina, R. M., Blimkie, C. J. R., Daniels, S. R., Dishman, R. K., Gutin, B., et al. (2005). Evidence based physical activity for school-age youth. *The Journal of Pediatrics, 146*(6), 732–737.

Strube, M. J. (1981). Meta-analysis and cross-cultural comparison: Sex differences in child competitiveness. *Journal of Cross-Cultural Psychology, 12*(1), 3–20.

Stuebing, K. K., Fletcher, J., M., LeDoux, J., M., Lyon, G. R., Shaywitz, S. E., & Shaywitz, B. A. (2002). Validity of IQ-discrepancy classifications of reading disabilities: A meta-analysis. *American Educational Research Journal, 39*(2), 469–518.

Stuebing, K. K., Barth, A. E., Cirino, P. T., Francis, D. J., & Fletcher, J. M. (2008). Response to recent reanalyses of the National Reading Panel Report: Effects of systematic phonics instruction are practically significant. *Journal of Educational Psychology, 100*(1), 123–134.

Stumpf, H., & Klieme, E. (1989). Sex-related differences in spatial ability: More evidence for convergence. *Perceptual and Motor Skills, 69*(3, Pt 1), 915–921.

Subotnik, R. F., & Walberg, H. J. (2006). *The scientific basis of educational productivity.* Greenwich, CN: Information Age Publishing.

Sullivan, M. H. (1993). *A meta-analysis of experimental research studies based on the Dunn and Dunn Learning Style Model and its relationship to academic achievement and performance.* St John's University, NY.

Swanborn, M. S. L., & de Glopper, K. (1999). Incidental word learning while reading: A meta-analysis. *Review of Educational Research, 69*(3), 261–285.

Swanborn, M. S. L., & de Glopper, K. (2002). Impact of reading purpose on incidental word learning from context. *Language Learning, 52*(1), 95–117.

Swanson, H. L. (1999). Reading research for students with LD: A meta-analysis of intervention outcomes. *Journal of Learning Disabilities, 32*(6), 504–532.

Swanson, H. L. (2000). What instruction works for students with learning disabilities? Summarizing the results of a meta-analysis of intervention studies. In R. M. Gersten, E. P. Schiller & S. Vaughn (Eds.), *Contemporary special education research: syntheses of the knowledge base on critical instructional issues* (pp. 1–30). Mahwah, NJ: Lawrence Erlbaum Associates.

Swanson, H. L. (2001). Research on interventions for adolescents with learning disabilities: A meta-analysis of outcomes related to higher-order processing. *The Elementary School Journal, 101*(3), 331–348.

Swanson, H. L. (2001). Searching for the best model for instructing students with learning disabilities. *Focus on Exceptional Children, 34*(2), 1–15.

Swanson, H. L., Carson, C., & Sachse-Lee, C. M. (1996). A selective synthesis of intervention research for students with learning disabilities. *School Psychology Review, 25*(3), 370–391.

Swanson, H. L., & Hoskyn, M. (1998). Experimental intervention research on students with learning disabilities: A meta-analysis of treatment outcomes. *Review of Educational Research, 68*(3), 277–321.

Swanson, H. L., & Hoskyn, M. (2001). Instructing adolescents with learning disabilities: A component and composite analysis. *Learning Disabilities: Research and Practice, 16*(2), 109–119.

Swanson, H. L., Hoskyn, M., & Lee, C. (1999). *Interventions for students with learning disabilities: A meta-analysis of treatment outcomes.* New York: Guilford Press.

Swanson, H. L., & Jerman, O. (2006). Math disabilities: A selective meta-analysis of the literature. *Review of Educational Research, 76*(2), 249–274.

Swanson, H. L., & Lussier, C. M. (2001). A selective synthesis of the experimental literature on dynamic assessment. *Review of Educational Research, 71*(2), 321–363.

Swanson, H. L., & Malone, S. (1992). Social skills and learning disabilities: A meta-analysis of the literature. *School Psychology Review, 21*(3), 427–442.

Swanson, H. L., O'Connor, J. E., & Cooney, J. B. (1990). An information processing analysis of expert and novice teachers' problem solving. *American Educational Research Journal, 27*(3), 533–556.

Swanson, H. L., Trainin, G., Necoechea, D. M., & Hammill, D. D. (2003). Rapid naming, phonological awareness, and reading: A meta-analysis of the correlation evidence. *Review of Educational Research, 73*(4), 407.

Swanson, J. M., McBurnett, K., Wigal, T., Pfiffner, L. J., & et al. (1993). Effect of stimulant medication on children with attention deficit disorder: A "review of reviews". *Exceptional Children, 60*(2), 154–162.

Sweet, M. A., & Appelbaum, M. I. (2004). Is home visiting an effective strategy? A meta-analytic review of home visiting programs for families with young children. *Child Development, 75*(5), 1435–1456.

Sweitzer, G. L., & Anderson, R. D. (1983). A meta-analysis of research on science teacher education practices associated with inquiry strategy. *Journal of Research in Science Teaching, 20*(5), 453–466.

Sweller, J. (2006). Discussion of 'Emerging topics in cognitive load research: Using learner and information characteristics in the design of powerful learning environments'. *Applied Cognitive Psychology, 20*(3), 353–357.

Sweller, J. (2008). Cognitive load theory and the use of educational technology. *Educational Technology, 48*(1), 32–34.

Szczurek, M. (1982). *Meta-analysis of simulation games effectiveness for cognitive learning.* Unpublished Ed.D., Indiana University, IN.

Taconis, R., Ferguson-Hessler, M. G. M., & Broekkamp, H. (2001). Teaching science problem solving: An overview of experimental work. *Journal of Research in Science Teaching, 38*(4), 442–468.

Tagomori, H. T., & Bishop, L. A. (1995). Student evaluation of teaching: Flaws in the instruments. *Thought and Action, 11*(1), 63–78.

Tamir, P. (1985). Meta-analysis of cognitive preferences and learning. *Journal of Research in Science Teaching, 22*(1), 1–17.

Taylor, L. A., III. (1984). *Strategic alternative and goal level effects on decision quality and goal commitment.* Unpublished D.B.A., Indiana University, Graduate School of Business, IN.

te Nijenhuis, J., Resing, W., Tolboom, E., & Bleichrodt, N. (2004). Short-term memory as an additional predictor of school achievement for immigrant children? *Intelligence, 32*(2), 203–213.

Teddlie, C., Reynolds, D., & Sammons, P. (2000). The methodology and scientific properties of school effectiveness research. In C. Teddlie & D. Reynolds (Eds.), *The international handbook of school effectiveness research* (pp. 55–133). London: Falmer Press.

Teddlie, C., & Springfield, S. (1993). Schools make a difference: Lessons learned from a 10 year study of school effects. New York: Teachers College Press.

Tellez, K., & Waxman, H. (2004). *Quality teachers for English language learners: A research synthesis.* Philadelphia, PA: Mid Atlantic Lab for Student Success.

Tenenbaum, G., & Goldring, E. (1989). A meta-analysis of the effect of enhanced instruction: Cues, participation, reinforcement and feedback, and correctives on motor skill learning. *Journal of Research and Development in Education, 22*(3), 53–64.

Tenenbaum, H. R., & Ruck, M. D. (2007). Are teachers' expectations different for racial minority than for European American students? A meta-analysis. *Journal of Educational Psychology, 99*(2), 253–273.

Tettegah, S., & Anderson, C. J. (2007). Pre-service teachers' empathy and cognitions: Statistical analysis of text data by graphical models. *Contemporary Educational Psychology, 32*(1), 48–82.

Therrien, W. J. (2004). Fluency and comprehension gains as a result of repeated reading: A meta-analysis. *Remedial and Special Education, 25*(4), 252–260.

Thomas, A. M. (2000). *The effects of phonemic awareness instruction on reading achievement of kindergarten students: A meta-analysis.* Unpublished Ed.D., University of Sarasota, FL.

Thomas, J. R., & French, K. E. (1985). Gender differences across age in motor performance a meta-analysis. *Psychological Bulletin, 98*(2), 260–282.

Thomas, L. (1979). *The medusa and the snail: More notes of a biology watcher.* New York: Viking Press.

Thorne, S., Jensen, L., Kearney, M. H., Noblit, G., & Sandelowski, M. (2004). Qualitative metasynthesis: Reflections on methodological orientation and ideological agenda. *Qualitative Health Research, 14*(10), 1342–1365.

Thum, Y. M. (2002). *Measuring student and school progress with the California API. CSE Technical Report.* Los Angeles, CA: Center for the Study of Evaluation, National Center for Research on Evaluation, Standards, and Student Testing, California University.

Thurber, S., & Walker, C. E. (1983). Medication and hyperactivity: A meta-analysis. *Journal of General Psychology, 108*(1), 79–86.

Timmerman, C. E., & Kruepke, K. A. (2006). Computer-assisted instruction, media richness, and college student performance. *Communication Education, 55*(1), 73–104.

Timmerman, L. M. (2006). Family care versus day care: Effects on children. In B. M. Gayle, R. W. Preiss, N. Burrell & M. Allen (Eds.), *Classroom communication and instructional processes: Advances through meta-analysis* (pp. 245–260). Mahwah, NJ: Lawrence Erlbaum Associates.

Timperley, H., Wilson, A., Barrar, H., & Fung, I. Y. Y. (2007). Teacher professional learning and development: Best evidence synthesis iteration In. Wellington, New Zealand: Ministry of Education.

Tinoca, L. F. (2004). *From professional development for science teachers to student learning in science.* Unpublished Ph.D., The University of Texas at Austin, TX.

Tohidi, N. E. (1982). *Sex differences in cognitive performance on Piaget-like tasks: A meta-analysis of findings.* Unpublished Ph.D., University of Illinois at Urbana-Champaign, IL.

Tohidi, N. E., Steinkamp, M. W., & Maehr, M. L. (1986). *Gender differences in performance on tests of cognitive functioning: A meta-analysis of research findings.* Washington, DC: National Science Foundation.

Tomchin, E. M., & Impara, J. C. (1992). Unraveling teachers' beliefs about grade retention. *American Educational Research Journal, 29*(1), 199–223.

Torgerson, C. J., Brooks, G., & Hall, J. (2006). *A systematic review of the research literature on the use of phonics in the teaching of reading and spelling.* London: Department for Education and Skills.

Torgerson, C. J., Brooks, G., Porthouse, J., Burton, M., Robinson, A., Wright, K., et al. (2004). *Adult literacy and numeracy interventions and outcomes: A review of controlled trials.* London: National Research and Development Centre for Adult Literacy and Numeracy.

Torgerson, C. J., & Elbourne, D. (2002). A systematic review and meta-analysis of the effectiveness of information and communication technology (ICT) on the teaching of spelling. *Journal of Research in Reading, 25*(2), 129–143.

Torgerson, C. J., King, S. E., & Sowden, A. J. (2002). Do volunteers in schools help children learn to read? A systematic review of randomized controlled trials. *Educational Studies, 28*(4), 433–444.

Torgerson, C. J., Porthouse, J., & Brooks, G. (2005). A systematic review and meta-analysis of controlled trials evaluating interventions in adult literacy and numeracy. *Journal of Research in Reading, 28*(2), 87–107.

Torgerson, C. J., & Zhu, D. (2003). *A systematic review and meta-analysis of the effectiveness of ICT on literacy learning in English, 5–16.* London: EPPI-Centre, Social Science Research Unit, Institute of Education, University of London.

Torrance, H., & Pryor, J. (1998). *Investigating formative assessment: Teaching, learning and assessment in the classroom.* Buckingham: Open University Press.

Trachtenburg, P., & Ferruggia, A. (1989). Big books from little voices: Reaching high risk beginning readers. *The Reading Teacher, 42*(4), 284–289.

Trapmann, S., Hell, B., Weigand, S., & Schuler, H. (2007). Die Validität von Schulnoten zur Vorhersage des Studienerfolgs – eine Metaanalyse [The validity of school grades for academic achievement–a meta-analysis]. *Zeitschrift für Pädagogische Psychologie, 21*(1), 11–27.

Trautwein, U., Köller, O., Schmitz, B., & Baumert, J. (2002). Do homework assignments enhance achievement? A multilevel analysis in 7th-grade mathematics. *Contemporary Educational Psychology, 27*(1), 26–50.

Travlos, A. K., & Pratt, J. (1995). Temporal locus of knowledge of results: A meta-analytic review. *Perceptual and Motor Skills, 80*(1), 3–14.

Trussell-Cullen, A. (1994). *Whatever happened to times tables? Every parent's guide to New Zealand education.* Auckland, New Zealand: Reed Books.

Tubbs, M. E. (1986). Goal setting: A meta-analytic examination of the empirical evidence. *Journal of Applied Psychology, 71*(3), 474–483.

Tudor, M. T. (1992). Expert and novice differences in strategies to problem solve an environmental issue. *Contemporary Educational Psychology, 17*(4), 329–339.

Tunmer, W. E., & Nesdale, A. R. (1985). Phonemic segmentation skill and beginning reading. *Journal of Educational Psychology, 77*(4), 417–427.

Twenge, J. M., Zhang, L., & Im, C. (2004). It's beyond my control: A cross-temporal meta-analysis of increasing externality in locus of control, 1960–2002. *Personality and Social Psychology Review, 8*(3), 308–319.

Tyack, D. B., & Cuban, L. (1995). *Tinkering toward utopia: A century of public school reform.* Cambridge, Mass.: Harvard University Press.

Uguroglu, M. E., & Walberg, H. J. (1979). Motivation and achievement: A quantitative synthesis. *American Educational Research Journal, 16*(4), 375–389.

Uguroglu, M. E., & Walberg, H. J. (1980). Motivation. *Evaluation in Education, 4,* 105–106.

Uhry, J. K., & Shepherd, M. J. (1993). Segmentation/spelling instruction as part of a first-grade reading program: Effects on several measures of reading. *Reading Research Quarterly, 28*(3), 219–233.

Underhill, C. M. (2006). The effectiveness of mentoring programs in corporate settings: A meta-analytical review of the literature. *Journal of Vocational Behavior, 68*(2), 292–307.

Urquiola, M. S. (2000). *Essays on educational financing and effectiveness in the United States and Bolivia.* Unpublished Ph.D., University of California, Berkeley, CA.

Useem, E. L. (1991). Student selection into course sequences in mathematics: The impact of parental involvement and school policies. *Journal of Research on Adolescence, 1*(3), 231–250.

Useem, E. L. (1992). Middle schools and math groups: Parents' involvement in children's placement. *Sociology of Education, 65*(4), 263–279.

Valentine, J. C. (2001). *The relation between self-concept and achievement: A meta-analytic review.* Unpublished Ph.D., University of Missouri, Columbia, MO.

Valentine, J. C., DuBois, D. L., & Cooper, H. M. (2004). The relation between self-beliefs and academic achievement: A meta-analytic review. *Educational Psychologist, 39*(2), 111–133.

van der Mars, H., Vogler, E. W., Darst, P. W., & Cusimano, B. (1995). *Novice and expert physical education teachers: They may think and decide differently … but do they behave differently?* Washington, DC: Department of Education.

van Gog, T., Ericsson, K. A., Rikers, R., M. J. P., & Paas, F. (2005). Instructional design for advanced learners: Establishing connections between the theoretical frameworks of cognitive load and deliberate practice. *Educational Technology, Research and Development, 53*(3), 73–81.

van Ijzendoorn, M. H., & Bus, A. G. (1994). Meta-analytic confirmation of the nonword reading deficit in developmental dyslexia. *Reading Research Quarterly, 29*(3), 266–275.

van Ijzendoorn, M. H., & Juffer, F. (2005). Adoption is a successful natural intervention enhancing adopted children's IQ and school performance. *Current Directions in Psychological Science, 14*(6), 326–330.

van Ijzendoorn, M. H., Juffer, F., & Poelhuis, C. W. K. (2005). Adoption and cognitive development: A meta-analytic comparison of adopted and nonadopted children's IQ and school performance. *Psychological Bulletin, 131*(2), 301–316.

van Lier, L. (1988). *The classroom and the language learner: Ethnography and second Language classroom research.* London: Longman.

van Lier, L. (1998). The relationship between consciousness, interaction, and language learning. *Language Awareness, 7*(2/3), 128–143.

Vandell, D. L., Reisner, E. R., & Pierce, K. M. (2007). *Outcomes linked to high-quality afterschool programs: Longitudinal findings from the study of promising afterschool programs.* University of California, Irvine; University of Wisconsin – Madison; and Policy Studies Associates, Inc.

Vandevoort, L. G., Amrein-Beardsley, A., & Berliner, D. C. (2004). National Board Certified Teachers and their students' achievement. *Education Policy Analysis Archives, 12*(46), 1–117.

Vanfossen, B. E., Jones, J. D., & Spade, J. Z. (1987). Curriculum tracking and status maintenance. *Sociology of Education, 60*(2), 104–122.

VanSickle, R. L. (1986). A quantitative review of research on instructional simulation gaming: A twenty-year perspective. *Theory and Research in Social Education, 14*(3), 245–264.

Varble, M. E., & Gilman, D. A. (1988). *A study of the relationship between class size and achievement.* Bloomington, IN: Indiana State University.

Vásquez, O.V., & Caraballo, J. N. (1993, August). *Meta-analysis of the effectiveness of concept mapping as a learning strategy in science education.* Paper presented at the Third International Seminar on the Misconceptions and Educational Strategies in Science and Mathematics Education, Ithaca, NY.

Vaughn, K. (2000). Music and mathematics: Modest support for the oft-claimed relationship. *Journal of Aesthetic Education, 34*(3–4), 149–166.

Vaughn, K., & Winner, E. (2000). SAT scores of students who study the arts: What we can and cannot conclude about the association. *Journal of Aesthetic Education, 34*(3/4), 77–89.

Vaughn, S., Gersten, R., & Chard, D. J. (2000). The underlying message in LD intervention research: Findings from research syntheses. *Exceptional Children, 67*(1), 99–116.

Vaughn, S., Kim, A.-H., Sloan, C.V. M., Hughes, M.T., Elbaum, B., & Sridhar, D. (2003). Social skills interventions for young children with disabilities: A synthesis of group design studies. *Remedial and Special Education, 24*(1), 2.

Vaughn, V. (1990). *Meta-analysis of pull-out programs in gifted education.* Paper presented at the Annual Convention of the National Association for Gifted Children, Little Rock, AR.

Vaughn, V. L., Feldhusen, J. F., & Asher, J.W. (1991). Meta-analyses and review of research on pull-out programs in gifted education. *Gifted Child Quarterly, 35*(2), 92–98.

Veenman, M.V. J., & Elshout, J. J. (1995). Differential effects of instructional support on learning in simulation environments. *Instructional Science, 22*(5), 363–383.

Veenman, M.V. J., Prins, F. J., & Elshout, J. J. (2002). Initial inductive learning in a complex computer simulated environment: The role of metacognitive skills and intellectual ability. *Computers in Human Behavior, 18*(3), 327–341.

Veenman, M. V. J., & Verheij, J. (2001). Technical students' metacognitive skills: Relating general vs. specific metacognitive skills to study success. *Learning and Individual Differences, 13*(3), 259–272.

Veenman, S. (1995). Cognitive and noncognitive effects of multigrade and multi-age classes: A best-evidence synthesis. *Review of Educational Research, 65*(4), 319.

Veenman, S. (1996). Effects of multigrade and multi-age classes reconsidered. *Review of Educational Research, 66*(3), 323–340.

Veenman, S. (1997). Combination classrooms revisited. *Educational Research and Evaluation, 3*(3), 262–276.

Vernon, D. T., & Blake, R. L. (1993). Does problem-based learning work? A meta-analysis of evaluative research. *Academic Medicine, 68*(7), 550–563.

Violato, C., & Russell, C. (2000). A meta-analysis of published research on the psychological effects of nonmaternal care on child development: Social policy implications. University of Calgary.

Vogel, J. J., Vogel, D. S., Cannon-Bowers, J., Bowers, C. A., Muse, K., & Wright, M. (2006). Computer gaming and interactive simulations for learning: A meta-analysis. *Journal of Educational Computing Research, 34*(3), 229–243.

von Glasersfeld, E. (1995). *Radical constructivism: A way of knowing and learning.* London: Falmer Press.

Vosniadou, S. (2001). *How children learn:* The International Academy of Education and the International Bureau of Education.

Waddington, T. S. H. (1995, April). *Why mastery matters.* Paper presented at the Annual Meeting of the American Educational Research Association, San Francisco, CA.

Wade, R. K. (1985). What makes a difference in inservice teacher education? A meta-analysis of research. *Educational Leadership, 42*(4), 48–54.

Wade, S. E., & Moje, E. B. (2000). The role of text in classroom learning. In M. L. Kamil, P. B. Mosenthal, P. D. Pearson & R. Barr (Eds.), *Handbook of reading research* (Vol. 3, pp. 609–627). Mahwah, NJ: Lawrence Erlbaum Associates.

Wagemaker, H. (1993). *Achievement in reading literacy: New Zealand's performance in a national and international context.*

Wagner, R. K. (1988). Causal relations between the development of phonological processing abilities and the acquisition of reading skills: A meta-analysis. *Merrill-Palmer Quarterly, 34*(3), 261–279.

Waight, C. L., Willging, P. A., & Wentling, T. L. (2002). *Recurrent themes in e-learning: A meta-analysis of major e-learning reports.* Campaign, IL: National Centre for Supercomputing Applications: Knowledge and Systems Group

Walberg, H. J. (1980). *A meta-analysis of productive factors in science learning grades 6 through 12. Final Technical Report* (Research/Technical No. NSF-SED78–17374). Chicago, IL: College of Education, Illinois University.

Walberg, H. J. (1982). *Desegregation and educational productivity. Final report.* Washington, DC: National Institute on Education.

Walberg, H. J. (1984). Improving the productivity of America's schools. *Educational Leadership, 41*(8), 19–27.

Walberg, H. J. (1985). Research synthesis in special education introduction and overview. *Journal of Special Education, 19*(4).

Walberg, H. J. (1986). Syntheses of research on teaching. In M. C. Wittrock (Ed.), *Handbook of research on teaching* (3rd ed., pp. 241–229). New York: Macmillan.

Walberg, H. J. (2006). Improving educational productivity: An assessment of extant research. In R. F. Subotnik & H. J. Walberg (Eds.), *The scientific basis of educational productivity* (pp. 103–160). Charlotte, NC: Information Age Publishing.

Walberg, H. J., Niemiec, R. P., & Frederick, W. C. (1994). Productive curriculum time. *Peabody Journal of Education, 69*(3), 86–100.

Walberg, H. J., & Walberg, H. J., III. (1994). Losing local control. *Educational Researcher, 23*(5), 19–26.

Walker, A. E., & Leary, H. (2008). A problem based learning meta analysis: Differences across problem types, implementation types, disciplines, and assessment levels. *Interdisciplinary Journal of Problem Based Learning.*

Walker, D., Greenwood, C., Hart, B., & Carta, J. (1994). Prediction of school outcomes based on early language production and socioeconomic factors. *Child Development, 65*(2), 606–621.

Walker, J. T. (2001). *The effect of a problem-based learning curriculum on students' perceptions about self-directed learning.* Unpublished Ph.D., The University of Mississippi, MS.

Wallace, T. A. (1989). *The effects of enrichment on gifted students: A quantitative synthesis.* Unpublished Ph.D., University of Illinois at Chicago, IL.

Walsh, K. (2006). Teacher education: Coming up empty. *Fwd, 3*(1), 1–6.

Wang, M. C., & Baker, E. T. (1986). Mainstreaming programs: Design features and effects. *Journal of Special Education, 19*(4), 503–521.

Wang, M. C., Haertel, G. D., & Walberg, H. J. (1993). Toward a knowledge base for school learning. *Review of Educational Research, 63*(3), 249–294.

Wang, S., Jiao, H., Young, M. J., Brooks, T., & Olson, J. (2008). Comparability of computer-based and paper-and-pencil testing in K-12 reading assessments: A meta-analysis of testing mode effects. *Educational and Psychological Measurement, 68*(1), 5–24.

Ward, S. A. (1980). Studies of knowledge synthesis. *Evaluation in Education, 4*, 130–142.

Waters, T., Marzano, R. J., & McNulty, B. (2003). *Balanced leadership: What 30 years of research tells us about the effect of leadership on student achievement. A working paper.* Mid-Continent Regional Educational Lab., Aurora, CO.[BBB23081].

Waters, T. J., & Marzano, R. J. (2006). *School district leadership that works: The effect of superintendent leadership on student achievement.* Denver, CO: Mid-continent Research for Education and Learning.

Watkins, D. (2001). Correlates of approaches to learning: A cross-cultural meta-analysis. In R. J. Sternberg & L.-F. Zhang (Eds.), *Perspectives on thinking, learning, and cognitive styles* (pp. 165–196). Mahwah, NJ: Lawrence Erlbaum Associates.

Waxman, H. C., Lin, M. F., & Michko, G. M. (2003). *A meta-analysis of the effectiveness of teaching and learning with technology on student outcomes.* Naperville, Illinois: Learning Point Associates.

Waxman, H. C., & Tellez, K. (2002). *Research synthesis on effective teaching practices for English language learners* (Information Analyses No. LSS-Pub-Ser-2002–3). Philadelphia, PA: Mid-Atlantic Lab for Student Success.

Waxman, H. C., & Walberg, H. J. (1980). Teacher effectiveness. *Evaluation in Education, 4*, 123–124.

Waxman, H. C., Wang, M. C., Anderson, K. A., & Walberg, H. J. (1985). Adaptive education and student outcomes: A quantitative synthesis. *Journal of Educational Research, 78*(4).

Waxman, H. C., Wang, M. C., Anderson, K. A., & Walberg, H. J. (1985). Synthesis of research on the effects of adaptive education. *Educational Leadership, 43*(1), 26–29.

Webb, T. L., & Sheeran, P. (2006). Does changing behavioral intentions engender behavior change? A meta-analysis of the experimental evidence. *Psychological Bulletin, 132*(2), 249–268.

Weinburgh, M. (1995). Gender differences in student attitudes toward science: A meta-analysis of the literature from 1970 to 1991. *Journal of Research in Science Teaching, 32*(4), 387–398.

Weinstein, R. S. (2002). *Reaching higher: The power of expectations in schooling.* Cambridge, MA: Harvard University Press.

Weinstein, T., Boulanger, F. D., & Walberg, H. J. (1982). Science curriculum effects in high school: A quantitative synthesis. *Journal of Research in Science Teaching, 19*(6), 511–522.

Weiss, B., Weisz, J. R., & Bromfield, R. (1986). Performance of retarded and nonretarded persons on information-processing tasks: Further tests of the similar structure hypothesis. *Psychological Bulletin, 100*(2), 157–175.

Weisz, J. R., Weiss, B., Alicke, M. D., & Klotz, M. L. (1987). Effectiveness of psychotherapy with children and adolescents: A meta-analysis for clinicians. *Journal of Consulting and Clinical Psychology, 55*(4), 542–549.

Wells, A. S., & Oakes, J. (1996). Potential pitfalls of systemic reform: Early lessons from research on detracking. *Sociology of Education, 69*, 135–143.

Westerman, D. A. (1991). Expert and novice teacher decision making. *Journal of Teacher Education, 42*(4), 292–305.

Wheelock, A. (1992). *Crossing the tracks: How "untracking" can save America's schools.* New York: New Press.

White, K. R. (1980). Socio-economic status and academic achievement. *Evaluation in Education, 4*, 79–81.

White, K. R. (1982). The relation between socioeconomic status and academic achievement. *Psychological Bulletin, 91*(3), 461–481.

White, K. R. (1986). Efficacy of early intervention. *Journal of Special Education, 19*(4), 401–416.

White, K. R., Bush, D. W., & Casto, G. C. (1985). Learning from reviews of early intervention. *Journal of Special Education, 19*(4), 417–428.

White, K. R., & Casto, G. (1985). An integrative review of early intervention efficacy studies with at-risk children: Implications for the handicapped. *Analysis and Intervention in Developmental Disabilities, 5*(1–2), 7–31.

White, K. R., Taylor, M. J., & Moss, V. D. (1992). Does research support claims about the benefits of involving parents in early intervention programs? *Review of Educational Research, 62*(1), 91–125.

White, M. R. (1997). *The effects of cognitive learning strategies interventions with learning disabled students, in the topical areas of reading and mathematics.* Unpublished Ph.D., The University of Iowa, IA.

White, W. A. T. (1988). A meta-analysis of the effects of direct instruction in special education. *Education and Treatment of Children, 11*(4), 364–374.

Whitehead, A. N. (1943). *Essays in science and philosophy.* New York: Philosphical Library.

Whitener, E. M. (1989). A meta-analytic review of the effect of learning on the interaction between prior achievement and instructional support. *Review of Educational Research, 59*(1), 65–86.

Whitley, B. E. (1997). Gender differences in computer-related attitudes and behavior: A meta-analysis. *Computers in Human Behavior, 13*(1), 1–22.

Whitley, B. E., Jr., & Frieze, I. H. (1985). Children's casual attributions for success and failure in achievement settings: A meta-analysis. *Journal of Educational Psychology, 77*(5), 608–616.

Whitley, B. E., Jr., Nelson, A. B., & Jones, C. J. (1999). Gender differences in cheating attitudes and classroom cheating behavior: A meta-analysis. *Sex Roles, 41*(9/10), 657–680

Wickline, V. B. (2003, August). *Ethnic differences in the self-ssteem/academic achievement relationship: A meta-analysis.* Paper presented at the Annual Conference of the American Psychological Association, Toronto, ON, Canada.

Wideen, M., Mayer-Smith, J., & Moon, B. (1998). A critical analysis of the research on learning to teach: Making the case for an ecological perspective on inquiry. *Review of Educational Research, 68*(2), 130–178.

Wiersma, U. J. (1992). The effects of extrinsic rewards in intrinsic motivation: A meta-analysis. *Journal of Occupational and Organizational Psychology, 65*(2), 101–114.

Wierzbicki, M. (1993). Psychological adjustment of adoptees: A meta-analysis. *Journal of Clinical Child and Adolescent Psychology, 22*(4), 447–454.

Wiggins, G. P., & McTighe, J. (2005). *Understanding by design* (Expanded 2nd ed.). Alexandia, VA: Association for Supervision and Curriculum Development.

Wilen, W. W. (1991). *Questioning skills for teachers. What research says to the teacher* (2nd ed.). Washington, DC: National Education Association.

Wilkinson, I. A. G., & Fung, I. Y. Y. (2002). Small-group composition and peer effects. *International Journal of Educational Research, 37*(5), 425–447.

Wilkinson, I. A. G., Parr, J. M., Fung, I. Y. Y., Hattie, J. A. C., & Townsend, M. A. R. (2002). Discussion: Modeling and maximizing peer effects in school. *International Journal of Educational Research, 37*(5), 521–535.

Wilkinson, S. S. (1980). *The relationship of teacher praise and student achievement: A meta-analysis of selected research.* Unpublished Ed.D., University of Florida, FL.

Willett, J. B., Yamashita, J. J. M., & Anderson, R. D. (1983). A meta-analysis of instructional systems applied in science teaching. *Journal of Research in Science Teaching, 20*(5), 405–417.

Williams, P. A., Haertel, E. H., Haertel, G. D., & Walberg, H. J. (1982). The impact of leisure-time television on school learning: A research synthesis. *American Educational Research Journal, 19*(1), 19–50.

Williams, S. L. (2004). *A meta-analysis of the effectiveness of distance education in allied health science programs.* Unpublished Ph.D., University of Cincinnati, OH.

Willig, A. C. (1985). A meta-analysis of selected studies on the effectiveness of bilingual education. *Review of Educational Research, 55*(3), 269–317.

Willis, S., & Kenway, J. (1986). On overcoming sexism in schooling: to marginalize or mainstream. *Australian Journal of Education, 30*(2), 132–149.

Willms, J. D. (2000). Monitoring school performance for "standards-based reform". *Evaluation and Research in Education, 14,* 237–253.

Willson, V. L. (1983). A meta-analysis of the relationship between science achievement and science attitude: Kindergarten through college. *Journal of Research in Science Teaching, 20*(9), 839–850.

Willson, V. L. (1984). Adding results to a meta-analysis: Theory and example. *Journal of Research in Science Teaching, 21*(6), 649–658.

Winne, P. H., & Butler, D. L. (1994). Student cognition in learning from teaching. In T. Husen & T. Postlethwaite (Eds.), *International encyclopedia of education* (2nd ed., pp. 5738–5745). Oxford, England: Pergamon.

Winner, E., & Cooper, M. (2000). Mute those claims: No evidence (yet) for a causal link between arts study and academic achievement. *Journal of Aesthetic Education, 34*(3/4), 11–75.

Winner, E., & Hetland, L. (2000). The arts in education: Evaluating the evidence for a causal link. *Journal of Aesthetic Education, 34*(3/4), 3–10.

Wise, K. C. (1988). The effects of using computing technologies in science instruction: A synthesis of classroom research. In J. D. Ellis (Ed.), *1988 AETS Yearbook* (pp. 105–118). Colorado Springs, CO: Office of Educational Research and Improvement, U. S. Department of Education.

Wise, K. C. (1996). Strategies for teaching science: What works? *Clearing House, 69*(6), 337–338.

Wise, K. C., & Okey, J. R. (1983). A meta-analysis of the effects of various science teaching strategies on achievement. *Journal of Research in Science Teaching, 20*(5), 419–435.

Wiseman, A. W. (2002, February). *Principals' instructional management activity and student achievement: A meta-analysis.* Paper presented at the Annual Meeting of the Southwestern Educational Research Association, Austin, TX.

Witt, E. A. (1993, April). *Meta-analysis and the effects of coaching for aptitude tests.* Paper presented at the Annual Meeting of the American Educational Research Association, Atlanta, GA.

Witt, P. L., Wheeless, L. R., & Allen, M. (2004). A meta-analytical review of the relationship between teacher immediacy and student learning. *Communication Monographs, 71*(2), 184–207.

Witt, P. L., Wheeless, L. R., & Allen, M. (2006). A relationship between teacher immediacy and student learning: A meta-analysis. In B. M. Gayle, R. W. Preiss, N. Burrell & M. Allen (Eds.), *Classroom communication and instructional processes: Advances through meta-analysis* (pp. 149–168). Mahwah, NJ: Lawrence Erlbaum Associates.

Witter, R. A., Okun, M. A., Stock, W. A., & Haring, M. J. (1984). Education and subjective well-being: A meta-analysis. *Educational Evaluation and Policy Analysis, 6*(2), 165–173.

Wittgenstein, L. (1958). *Philosophical investigations* (G. E. M. Anscombe, Trans. 2nd ed.). Oxford: Blackwell.

Witziers, B., Bosker, R. J., & Kruger, M. L. (2003). Educational leadership and student achievement: The elusive search for an association. *Educational Administration Quarterly, 39*(3), 398–425.

Wixson, K. K., Peters, C. W., Weber, E. M., & Roeber, E. D. (1987). New directions in statewide reading assessment. *Reading Teacher, 40*(8), 749–754.

Wofford, J. C., Goodwin, V. L., & Premack, S. (1992). Meta-analysis of the antecedents of personal goal level and of the antecedents and consequences of goal commitment. *Journal of Management, 18*(3), 595–615.

Wood, R. E., & Locke, E. A. (1987). The relation of self-efficacy and grade goals to academic performance. *Educational and Psychological Measurement, 47*(4), 1013–1024.

Wood, R. E., Mento, A. J., & Locke, E. A. (1987). Task complexity as a moderator of goal effects: A meta-analysis. *Journal of Applied Psychology, 72*(3), 416–425.

Wood, W. (1987). Meta-analytic review of sex differences in group performance. *Psychological Bulletin, 102*(1), 53–71.

Woolf, B. P., & Regian, J. W. (2000). Knowledge-based training systems and the engineering of instruction. In S. Tobias & J. D. Fletcher (Eds.), *Training and retraining: A handbook for business, industry, government, and the military* (pp. 339–356). New York: Macmillan Reference.

Woolfolk Hoy, A. (1998). *Educational psychology* (7th ed.). Boston: Allyn & Bacon.

Worthington, J. (1991, May). *Reading groups: Problems, solutions.* Paper presented at the Annual Meeting of the International Reading Association, Las Vegas, NV.

Wortman, P. M. (1983). *School desegregation and Black achievement: An integrative review.* Washington, DC: National Institute on Education.

Wortman, P. M., & Bryant, F. B. (1985). School desegregation and Black achievement: An integrative review. *Sociological Methods Research, 13*(3), 289–324.

Wortman, P. M., & Napoli, A. R. (1996). A meta-analysis of the impact of academic and social integration of persistence of community college students. *Journal of Applied Research in the Community College, 4*(1), 5–21.

Wright, P. M. (1990). Operationalization of goal difficulty as a moderator of the goal difficulty-performance relationship. *Journal of Applied Psychology, 75*(3), 227–234.

Xin, Y. P., Grasso, E., Dipipi-Hoy, C. M., & Jitendra, A. (2005). The effects of purchasing skill instruction for individuals with developmental disabilities: A meta-analysis. *Exceptional Children, 71*(4), 379–400.

Xin, Y. P., & Jitendra, A. K. (1999). The effects of instruction in solving mathematical word problems for students with learning problems: A meta-analysis. *Journal of Special Education, 32*(4), 207.

Yaakub, M. N., & Finch, C. R. (2001). Effectiveness of computer-assisted instruction in technical education: A meta-analysis. *Workforce Education Forum, 28*(2), 1–15.

Yair, G. (2000). Educational battlefields in America: The tug-of-war over students' engagement with instruction. *Sociology of Education, 73*(4), 247–269.

Yang, W.-L. (1997, March). *Validity issues in cross-national relational analyses: A meta-analytic approach to perceived gender differences on mathematics learning.* Paper presented at the Annual Meeting of the American Educational Research Association, Chicago, IL.

Yates, G. C. R. (2008). Roadblocks to scientific thinking in educational decision making. *Australiasian Journal of Special Education, 32*(1), 125–137.

Yaworski, J. (2000). Using computer-based technology to support the college reading classroom. *Journal of College Reading and Learning, 31*(1), 19–41.

Yeany, R. H., & Miller, P. A. (1983). Effects of diagnostic/remedial instruction on science learning: A meta-analysis. *Journal of Research in Science Teaching, 20*(1), 19–26.

Yeany, R. H., & Padilla, M. J. (1986). Training science teachers to utilize better teaching strategies: A research synthesis. *Journal of Research in Science Teaching, 23*(2), 85–95.

Yekovich, F. R., Thompson, M. A., & Walker, C. H. (1991). Generation and verification of inferences by experts and trained nonexperts. *American Educational Research Journal, 28*(1), 189–209.

Yoshida, S. A. (1989). *A meta-analysis of the effects of grade retention on the achievement of elementary school children.* Unpublished Ph.D., Fordham University, NY.

Yoon, J.-C. (2002). Three decades of sustained silent reading: a meta-analytic review of the effects of SSR on attitude toward reading. *Reading Improvement, 39*(4), 186–195.

Zhao, Y., Lei, J., Yan, B., Lai, C., & Tan, H. S. (2005). What makes the difference? A practical analysis of research on the effectiveness of distance education. *Teachers College Record, 107*(8), 1836–1884.

Zippert, C. P. (1985). *The effectiveness of adjusting teaching strategies to assessed learning styles of adult students.* Unpublished Ph.D., The University of Alabama, AL.

Index

eBooks – at www.eBookstore.tandf.co.uk

A library at your fingertips!

eBooks are electronic versions of printed books. You can store them on your PC/laptop or browse them online.

They have advantages for anyone needing rapid access to a wide variety of published, copyright information.

eBooks can help your research by enabling you to bookmark chapters, annotate text and use instant searches to find specific words or phrases. Several eBook files would fit on even a small laptop or PDA.

NEW: Save money by eSubscribing: cheap, online access to any eBook for as long as you need it.

Annual subscription packages

We now offer special low-cost bulk subscriptions to packages of eBooks in certain subject areas. These are available to libraries or to individuals.

For more information please contact webmaster.ebooks@tandf.co.uk

We're continually developing the eBook concept, so keep up to date by visiting the website.

www.eBookstore.tandf.co.uk